For:

Charles Nnolim
Bernth Lindfors
Abiola Irele
Dan Izevbaye

For indelible footprints in Achebe scholarship.

Table of Contents

Part Five: Critical Perspectives on *Anthills of the Savannah*

Part Six: Critical Perspectives on *Beware, Soul Brother*

Preface

THE 24th ANNUAL CONFERENCE of the African Literature Association (U.S.A.) held in Austin, Texas (March 25–29, 1998) was the key catalyst in the inspiration for the production and publication of two seminal volumes of critical essays on Chinua Achebe, Africa's master storyteller and pioneer literary philosopher of the 20th Century. The volumes: *OMENKA: The Master Artist* and *ISINKA: The Artistic Purpose* seek to establish the impact of Chinua Achebe on the development of both African creative writing, and the criticism of African Literature in the 20th Century.

Some weeks before the conference, Bernth Lindfors, the co-convener and a good friend of mine, had contacted me and requested that I introduce the Keynote Speaker, Chinua Achebe in "the most befitting manner of the Igbo tradition." This got me thinking about the traditional Igbo society about which Achebe himself had emphatically declared that age was revered but achievements were respected. Chinua Achebe had both age and solid achievements. He had taken the highest title in his hometown, Ogidi, and achieved universal fame in World Literature. I thought also about orators in the traditional Igbo society, about whom Achebe too, had stated that verbal dexterity was enriched by the use of proverbs, which for them had become "the palm oil with which words are eaten." In the traditional Igbo society, if a famous and great man were to be presented to an audience, a skilled orator would begin with special praise names reminding the gathering that the pre-eminent person before them had gone to battle and brought home human heads; he had crossed seven rivers and climbed seven mountains and returned home safely; he had gone to the land of the spirits and wrestled the hydra-headed spirit to the ground and returned to the human world unscathed. Chinua Achebe is the great man whose fame has spread all over the globe like the impestuous harmattan fire. Armed with all these facts and fore-knowledge, I proceeded to prepare a nine-page introduction for the occasion. A few days later, the advance copy which I had sent to Bernth Lindfors was returned with a cherry note:

Dear Ernest,

Here's my hatchet job on your introduction. I was trying to reduce it to 2½ pages (about 5 minutes reading time) and almost succeeded but there was too much good material in it. But do keep it brief.

Best wishes,
Bernth

The introduction, when it was presented on March 27, 1998 before a crowded auditorium at the University of Texas, Austin, was precise. It portrayed Chinua Achebe as a Nigerian-born novelist, who at the young age of twenty-eight, and only five years after obtaining a Bachelors degree in Arts (English, History, & Religion) at Nigeria's premier university (Ibadan), had produced a first novel (1958) which was to change the course of World Literature in English, and define for future generations of mankind, the African novel – its character, its function, its tongue, and its unique features. That introduction is reproduced here as still appropriate for introducing Chinua Achebe to the wider literary world of the 21st Century.

> The Igbo people have a cryptic way of articulating the dilemma of a person who has been given a "burden", though pleasant, much above his status. He is like a child of humble circumstances who suddenly sits face to face with an enormous plate of food, the like of which he had never before encountered in his life. No matter how hungry or tempted he might be, he does not pounce on the food immediately. He tries to find out from the host, who else would be sharing the food with him. "Nobody", the host would reply with an understanding twinkle of the eye, "it's all yours." The subsequent reaction of the child comes with a mixture of joy and fear. I am this evening facing a prodigious mound of pounded yam, the like of which I have never before encountered.
>
> In the Igbo pantheon, there is a hierarchy of deities with varying degrees of aura and reverence. It is said that, during a ritual performance, there are deities who can be carried with just a few fingers, some within one palm, some with one full hand; but there are deities who require two or more hands to carry. In our act of worship tonight we are invoking the deity of deities who requires not two hands, not four hands but indeed eight hands and more, to carry.
>
> My job has been made relatively easier by the fact that every member of the African Literature Association sitting here tonight, can legitimately claim and assert to be a friend of our speaker, Chinua Achebe. Now, you do not introduce a friend to his friends. You only present him, reminding his friends of a few things which might have transpired since the last get-together. It is a great honor for me to be asked to present Chinua Achebe to his friends.
>
> In 1978, when the then University of Ife became the first Nigerian University to award you an honorary doctorate degree, the university orator, Professor Wole Soyinka, praised you for "making the life of your fellow men (and women) better through literature," for which we salute you. In 1985, when the university of Nigeria, Nsukka, appointed you Professor Emeritus, you were described as

a man whose humility, transparent honesty, inner peace, and yet keen sense of humor have fascinated colleagues and friends; a man whose pen has edified and inspired peoples the world over by producing clear and eloquent ideas which have endeared you to millions of readers; a man who has always performed the noble role of a teacher, a seeker of truth, whose exemplary leadership the community has fully recognized and appreciated," for which we are proud of you.

You have through your works touched and changed many lives. You have been a caring frontiersman and a generous brother's keeper both in Africa and the African diaspora. Nuruddin Farah says that he and many of his contemporaries "owe a great deal to you, many having learnt the craft from you," as "Africa's best novelist and craftsman, and one of the world's greatest, living or dead." Mariama Ba told you in 1980, before her tragic death in 1981, that she "started writing after reading *Things Fall Apart*." Toni Morrison has thanked you for "doors which you figuratively opened for her." To Jerome Brooks you are the "necessary angel who restored for us (Africans in the diaspora) something that slavery took from us." James Baldwin held you in such high esteem that at his death his family presented to you his most priceless possession as a writer, his briefcase, believing that "he would have wanted you to have it."

Distinguished ladies and gentlemen, I find nothing more appropriate to present our noble speaker to you tonight, than the words of Professor Ola Rotimi, Orator of the University of Port Harcourt, Nigeria in February 1991, when the University bestowed on Chinua Achebe an honorary doctorate degree.

Chinua, son of Achebe, let me from this point on, address you in the style of traditional African Oratory... Speaker in proverbs, we salute you. Exponent of the values of Africa's cultural heritage, I say, it is you we greet. You who ventured into the forest of world literature and came back a hero.

> If danger aims its arrow at you again,
> The arrows will never fly.
> If they do fly,
> They will not hit you.
> If they do hit you,
> They will not wound you.
> If they do wound you,
> You will not weaken.
> If you do weaken,
> You will not fall down.
> If you do fall down,
> You will not faint.
> If you do faint,
> You will not... die!

Distinguished guests, please welcome the immortal *Akwa Akwuru I of African Literature, the Ugo N'abo of Ogidi*, "the man of letters, the man of ideas, the man of words,' Professor Chinua Achebe.

Hours after that introduction, I was approached by Mr Kassahun Checole, President/Publisher of Africa World Press, with a request to edit essays on Chinua Achebe for their *Emerging Perspectives on African Writers Series*. By the existing format of the series, a writer is chosen and a volume of critical essays devoted to all aspects of his or her writing. But in the case of Achebe, the publisher requested two volumes, and left the nature, organization, and contents entirely to me. After consultations with some colleagues, I decided to focus the first volume on Achebe's creative works and the second on his non-fictional writings which buttress his concept and philosophy of art and the artist in the African situation. Professors Emmanuel N. Obiechina and Clement A. Okafor lent their expertise in Igbo thought and wisdom in the wording of the titles of the two volumes.

There are altogether sixty-seven essays in the two volumes, contributed by scholars from various parts of the world, with an impressive number coming from scholars based on the African continent. A considerable number of publishable papers were unfortunately, because of space constraints, left out. Even after the volumes had gone to press, scholars from all over the world were still making inquiries about submitting their papers. Chinua Achebe seems never to have a shortage of readers of his creative works as he never seems to lack erudite commentators on his literary and theoretical ideas. These readers, teachers, and research scholars speak eloquently about Chinua Achebe's unprecedented impact on the World Literature in English, and the art of the novel in global second language situations since the second half of the 20th Century. In his fictional explorations of the colonial encounters with indigenous non-European races, and in his indigenization of the English Language to suit local sensibilities, Chinua Achebe seems to have no rival in contemporary World Literature. The contributors to these two volumes have provided ample evidence to support these declarations.

It is, therefore, strange and baffling to literary scholars around the globe that Chinua Achebe has to date not been honored with a Nobel Prize for Literature. We have in him more than any other writer in the second half of the 20th Century, an artist who has influenced for the better, the course of World Literature in English not only for his generation, but for eternity; a writer who, through his works, has touched and changed many lives; an African novelist who has "provided a renewed sense of African heritage, history, and tradition." The two volumes, *OMENKA* and *ISINKA* establish Chinua Achebe's legacy as a creative and philosophical genius whose pen has touched and changed a large portion of humanity regardless of race, color, tongue, or creed. The literary world continues watching!

Ernest N. Emenyonu
Chair, Department of Africana Studies
University of Michigan-Flint
Flint, Michigan, June 2003

Acknowledgements

The editor and publishers of this book of essays are very grateful to the following individuals and institutions for their permissions to reprint formerly published materials or materials to which they hold or administer copyrights:

Charles Nnolim for his essay "Technique and Meaning in *Arrow of God*."
Emmanuel Obiechina for his essay "The Human Dimensions of History in Chinua Achebe's *Arrow of God*."
Bernth Lindfors for his essay: "Achebe's African Parable."
Ousseynou B. Traore, Editor of *The Literary Griot* for Chris Walsh's essay: "A Balance of Stories or Pay-back: Chinua Achebe, Joyce Cary and the Literature of Africa", published in Volume 13 Numbers 1& 2, Spring/Fall 2001.
Charles Henry Rowell, Editor of *Callaloo* for Ernest N. Emenyonu's essay "Selection and Validation of Oral Materials For Children's Literature: Artistic Resources in Chinua Achebe's Fiction for Children", published in Volume 25, Number 2, Spring 2002.
Front and back cover photo: Patricia T. Emenyonu.
The editor acknowledges and thanks Dr. Sally Harris, Director, Office Research, University of Michigan-Flint, for financial assistance and technical support which facilitated the final product of the manuscript.

Introduction

Ernest N. Emenyonu

CHINUA ACHEBE, A LITERARY icon of the 20th Century is widely regarded as Africa's best novelist to date, and one of the world's greatest in modern times. His narrative style and techniques have given rise to what has been characterized as the African art of the novel. It consists of ingenious indigenization and skillful manipulation of the English language to enable it convey essential and intricate traditional African speech patterns and sensibilities. It also portrays an assertive African cultural voice telling the African story, the African way.

OMENKA celebrates this modern African literary tradition which owes its origin to Achebe's landmark classic novel, *Things Fall Apart* (1958), which in over 55 languages and more than 8 million copies in sales, is the most widely read African novel, inside and outside the African continent. Some critical anthologies have been published on Achebe's fiction at various stages of his writing, but OMENKA is the first work of criticism in the 21st Century which covers all of Chinua Achebe's fictional writings up to the end of the 20th Century. It has 37 essays by eminent scholars from Africa, Europe, Canada, and the United States. The essays provide global perspectives of Chinua Achebe as an artist with a proper sense of history, an imaginative writer with an invoilable sense of cultural mission and political commitment; Achebe, the "careful and fastidious artist full of control of his art," a versatile creative writer whose spectacular craftsmanship manifests itself no matter the form and the genre he chooses for the exploration of the human condition in Africa.

The book has eight parts. Part I consists of essays which discuss authoritatively, various aspects of *Things Fall Apart* from innovative stylistics to intriguing feminism in the African context; and from cross-cultural dimensions to Igbo cosmology. Part II has essays that focus on *No Longer at Ease*, highlighting with intense particularity the artistic and situational significance of this least studied of Achebe's novels. Part III contains essays on *Arrow of God* ranging from, discourse on the duality of the Chief Priest, Ezulu's personality, to the tragic muse and cultural hero in the novel. Part IV has essays which examine the various facets of *A Man of the People*, from political symbolism to Igbo (African) leadership ideals. Part V has essays, which argue from intriguingly contrasting perspectives, 'the woman question' and the phenomenon of military dictatorship in *Anthills of the Savannah*. Part VI consists of eloquent essays on Achebe's responses to the Nigerian civil war in *Girls at War and Other Stories*, and *Beware Soul Brother and Other Poems*. Part VII is devoted to the symbolism in Achebe's short stories using "*The Mad Man*" for precise illustration. The book ends with Part VIII which has essays that focus on the versatile thematic dimensions and artistic dexterity in Achebe's four books for young readers.

There are a number of interesting revelations about Achebe scholarship evident in the essays. The essays seem to reflect consciously or unconsciously the ranking of Achebe's creative works in the minds of literary scholars. Those works which have been most frequently used in classrooms world-wide, have attracted the highest number of critical responses. Accordingly the distribution of the 37 essays in OMENKA is as follows: *Things Fall Apart* (10), *No Longer at Ease* (4), *Arrow of God* (6), *A Man of the People* (4), *Anthills of the Savannah* (6), while Achebe's poetry, short stories, and children's books account for seven essays. Thus, *Things Fall Apart*, the most widely read African novel inside and outside the African continent, is invariably also the most critically discussed of Achebe's creative works. The least discussed is *No Longer at Ease* and this is rather unfortunate because it is a very important novel which has a remarkable place in Achebe's canon. It appears as if by coming next in the order of publication to the best selling *Things Fall Apart*, the historical significance of *No Longer at Ease* has been totally eclipsed and overshadowed by its predecessor. Yet if *Things Fall Apart* had been published the way it was originally written by the author, *No Longer at Ease*, instead of being a separate novel, would have been part of the total artistry that has given *Things Fall Apart* a universal appeal. This is because the story of *No Longer at Ease* was part of the original story of *Things Fall Apart*, but was later carved out siamese-like, as a separate novel at the point of publication. Accordingly, soon after *Things Fall Apart*, *No Longer at Ease* was published because the material was there and waiting. Sandwiched, therefore, between *Things Fall Apart* (1958) spanning the pre-colonial and early colonial periods, and *Arrow of God* (1964) spanning the same period, *No Longer at Ease* (1960) spanning the era just before political independence, seems to be out of sequence with the historical events which validate Achebe's vision of history. Scholars, therefore, tend to find all the evidence to authenticate the colonial experience in *Things Fall Apart* and *Arrow of God*. By this approach literary scholars have created a gap not only in Achebe scholarship but more significantly, a gap in the study of a critical period in African Literature. The foregoing serves as a caution to scholars of African Literature who perfunctorily, have begun to see Achebe's first three novels as a trilogy. They are not!

The authors of the four essays on *No Longer at Ease* in this volume, have written compellingly to underscore the textual richness and arresting creative devices and strategies which the novel possesses. Very few African novels have portrayed with comparable passion and integrity, the theme of individual disorientation at the historic moment of transition from colonial rule to self government; the brief interim period when the emerging African elite existed side by side in the civil service with the last crop of European colonial officers from whom they were soon to take over. Needless to say that there was no love-lost between the two. The colonial officers in spite of the imminent wind of change staring them in the face, still conceived of themselves no less colonial overlords as the dogmatic masters of the eras of Captain Winterbottom or his arrogant and egocentric peers in Joyce Cary's *Mister Johnson*. *No Longer at Ease* far more than *A Man of the People* explains and portrays the backgrounds of the predicament of post-independence leadership in Africa. It shows more than any other novel in Nigeria, the incompetence, inertia, and absolute irresponsibility in the emerging Nigerian elite which doomed the independence era ever before it came into being and devalued the much anticipated fruits of independence. It also clearly represents a foreboding and premonition that in the circumstances, made an alternative government, especially the military, a matter of time. *No Longer at Ease* is one novel that requires and deserves more intensive classroom attention by teachers, and a lot more critical discourse by scholars and critics than it has got so far.

Achebe's novels are thematically structured to follow the sequence of African historical development from pre-colonial to post-colonial. His imaginary characters act true to their settings, times, and environments. Achebe's accurate portrayals of the political and social characteristics of each period, is proof of his unassailable integrity as a writer. He is without doubt, Africa's master storyteller of the 20th Century. He gave modern African writers a theme (message) and a pen (style) with which to convey the message. He positioned himself at the forefront of the struggle for Africa's literary independence after centuries of colonial occupation. He has left legacies for his contemporaries and generations after. Today we can confidently talk about colonial and post-colonial African writings because both exist and we have things that clearly distinguish one from the other. One is foreign, uninformed, and derogatory in outlook and motive. The other is indigenous, well informed, and dignified even when probing internal flaws, weaknesses, and failures. The former is defamatory and condescending in tone with the sole purpose to denigrate and emasculate its African characters. The latter is relentlessly assertive, unabashedly militant in tone and at will, and socially poignant with the sole purpose to awaken and rehabilitate the African soul and mind. In their chosen fronts,

20th century African writers have been resoundingly successful. So successful that in the last two decades of the century, they brought home to Africa three Nobel Prizes for Literature, the modern version of Okonkwo's human heads which bore testimonies of triumph and decisive victorious battles in *Things Fall Apart*.

One wished that one could say the same for African politicians who engaged in the struggle for political independence at the same time that Achebe was writing *Things Fall Apart*. It is very clear today that where African writers have succeeded, African politicians have woefully failed. Where African writers have brought home glories and laurels, African politicians have brought bowed and bloodied heads. Where African writers have ushered in an era of post-colonial literature in word and deed, African politicians have introduced neo-colonialism. So Africa has to contend with decolonized, post-colonial, post-independence literature in the midst of neo-colonial, subdued, and subverted political environment. Contemporary African politics has in effect become contemporary African literature's albatross. African politics needs an urgent liberation and deliverance to enable 21st Century African Literature flourish and blossom to its fullest potentials. African politics and African literature are, therefore, inextricably intertwined in some sort of way.

Chinua Achebe has challenged African writers to do fresh unrelenting battle with the decolonization of the African mind without which political independence will be worthless in Africa. In an interview with Kalu Ogbaa (1980), Achebe had this to say:

> We are talking about modernization, industrialization, and so on, but we do not realize that we cannot even industrialize unless we have tackled the mind, the imagination, and thus the attitude of the people to themselves, to their society, to work, and so on. How do you do these things if you cannot get to their (people's) minds, to their imagination? So literature is not a luxury for us. It is a life and death affair because we are fashioning a new man. The Nigerian (African) is a new man. How do we get to his mind? Is it by preaching to him once in a while-by the leaders? No, I think it is something we must put into his consciousness. That is what he reads, what he believes, and what he loves. We must dramatize his predicament so that he can see the choices and choose right (Bernth Lindfors ED., *Conversations with Chinua Achebe*. University Press of Mississippi, 1997: 75).

Towards the end of the editing of OMENKA, I thought it would be of interest to the literary world to seek Achebe's views on some major issues which were of concern to him as an African writer half a century ago, and find out whether there have been shifts in his positions in those areas. I posed two questions for him on his vision of African Literature in the 21st Century, and his message for young African writers in the 21st Century. The two questions and his responses are reproduced in full below.

What is your vision of African literature in the 21st Century?

Achievements since mid-20th Century can be categorized as setting the appropriate stage and nurturing the ground for the future. What now lies ahead is to establish the balance of stories between Africa and the West. The lack of balance is the burden that Africa has carried in the last 500 years since the continent encountered Europe. Europe created stories of Africa to make it possible for Europeans to enslave Africans and colonize them thereafter. What African writers of the 20th Century have done, has been to challenge these stories and show how their ancestors dreamed their world. We are still at the beginning of that task which has been appropriately defined. The 21st Century will move it forward and reduce the gap. We are one foot in the door. My hope is that the 21st Century will bring us fully into the arena of world literature and that we will witness the real flourishing of African literature.

What is your message for young African writers in the new millennium?

They should keep at it (writing). If you feel you have a story to tell, go ahead and tell it in writing. Everyone has a story to tell but those who feel strongly about it, should go ahead and tell their stories. But remember it is not easy. It is not as glamorous as it may seem on the surface. It requires a lot of hard work, and sacrifice of time and energy. But if you feel the urge, keep on working on it. You don't need anybody to tell you how to go about it. Write, edit, and shape it and take full responsibility for the way it is. And when you have written your story there will not be any need to chase it to explain what it is and why. Once the story is out of your hands, leave it to find its way. Don't be too much concerned about current fashions of either the work or the conduct of the writer. Don't be distracted by issues of how an artist looks or the latest topics to write on. Don't be concerned with all that. Just go the way the spirit moves you. But this is not saying that there is no value in reading what others have written. Read widely to find out what is missing in the gallery of the world's (African) stories and make a contribution towards filling that gap.

Omenka (Igbo term for "the Master artist"), comes at a most appropriate moment to offer a defining approach to the fiction of Chinua Achebe in the new millennium. Individually and collectively, the thirty-seven essays establish the multiple facets of Chinua Achebe's Legacy to African Creative writing in the 20th Century.

Invocation

Anecdote on Chinua Achebe's Works

When things fall apart
People will no longer be at ease.
The arrow of god will
Hit a man of the people,
The sacrificial egg.
Chike dived deep into the rippling river,
The insider, to see how the Leopard got his claws.

Morning yet on creation day
Has created Okike, creation itself,
African commentary, and Uwa ndi Igbo
Ensuring that we don't let Okigbo die...
Since the flute and the drum vibrate
And girls are now at war
Soul brother is warned to beware
of the trouble with Nigeria
of hopes and impediments
Because military dictatorship thrives
In anthills of the savannah.

Innocent Chimela K. Enyinnaya

Part One:

Critical Perspectives on *Things Fall Apart*

Chapter 1

Worldliness, Territoriality, and Narrative: *Things Fall Apart* and the Rhetoric of Nationalism

Francis Ngaboh-Smart

NEARLY FIFTY YEARS AGO Achebe published his groundbreaking novel, *Things Fall Apart*. African and post-colonial studies have since emerged as major fields of inquiry and scores of new African novels have appeared on the world scene, but *Things Fall Apart* continues to hold a prominent place in academic departments devoted to the study of African literature. This does not mean that Achebe is the first African novelist, a designation he has called blasphemous, since even in Nigeria Amos Tutola and Cyprian Ekwensi had published prose fiction before *Things Fall Apart*. When his *Things Fall Apart* was published, though, it suddenly became a source of Black Nationalist pride in that it "provided a new way of reorganizing African cultures" as well as showed the "limitless possibilities of inventing a new national community" (*Gikandi* 3). It also started a model of writing for a whole generation of Africans that Kofi Awoonor has called "clash of cultures novelists" (279–280). In its nationalist impulse of re-inscribing Africans into the cultural space disrupted by colonialism, *Things Fall Apart* will indeed remain the quintessential African narrative. Any discussion of nationalist reconstruction of identity should thus take *Things Fall Apart* as its point of departure since it deals with issues that were endemic to nationalist rhetoric: modes of creating historical knowledge, the struggle for cultural positions, the dialectic of self and culture, among others. These are issues Achebe's subsequent novels and those of many other African writers will only more or less reorganize.

That *Things Fall Apart* is a nationalist work is obvious from its date of publication, 1958, the tail end of the decade of intensive nationalist movements for independence. 1958 not only precedes the two turbulent years leading to Nigeria's independence, but also marks the height of the nationalist ferment in Africa as a whole: Ghana had received its independence in 1957 and many African countries will soon receive theirs in the 1960s, a decade referred to as Africa's decade of freedom. These political events are important precisely because they seem to have affected Achebe's mode of narration, which he assumes to be a contract between a writer and a national community. In other words, his narratives, he insisted in a 1962 interview with Lewis Nkosi, are designed "to have an influence…in the schools… [on] the next generation" (6). It is the assumption that writing can somehow mold minds or that "questions of national identity are closely related to narrative strategies" (*Gikandi* 2), that situates Achebe's writing at the center of race, politics, and the discourse on nationhood.

Our concern should therefore be with how Achebe perceives history or the past in relation to the future, since such a relation invariably governs his perspective on identity and nationhood. Does his view of history approximate to what Nietzsche calls "monumental history," for example? That is, is he a writer that "preserves and reveres" the past, and sees historical events as "effects in themselves." Or, is he a "superior man" with a "critical" consciousness who writes history from the perspective of the present and knows that "when the past speaks it always speaks as an oracle [and] only if you are an architect of the future and know the present will you understand it?" (94).

Either perspective is bound to affect a writer's configuration of identity and his or her characters' mode of encoding social values. At the cost of some simplification, a monumental attitude to the past is likely to posit a unified self whereas a critical attitude radicalizes the self's domination by Umuofia's cultural codes. The latter has however, always been underscored, probably because critics see the preponderance of sociological and anthropological details in *Things Fall Apart* as an indication of Achebe's desire to posit a past totality. Such a reading runs the risk of ignoring the political or nationalist resonance of the work.

This is to say that Achebe's subtle narrative engages in a double reading of history or culture, monumental and critical, which are the two levels at which the novel frames identity. The monumental level, which one can also call the manifest level, is the level at which the novel presents identity as always already mediated by the world in which the self is situated. The critical level, also the latent level, is the level at which self-fashioning in the novel becomes a perpetual dialectic of embodiment and disruption, identification and hate, and it is the level at which Achebe's so-called objectivity can be located.

At the first level, then, the omniscient narrator projects events as "effects in themselves," and narrative becomes a gesture that must search for and affirm origins.

Viewed from this perspective, *Things Fall Apart* is an example of the postcoloniality of "normativity... in which the writer or critic speaks to, or for, or in the name of the post-independence nation state, the regional or continental community, the pan-ethnic, racial or cultural agglomeration of homelands and diasporas" (Biodun Jeyifo 52). The truth of Jeyifo's argument is obvious not just in the pervasive cultural backcloth in which Achebe weaves his narrative but also in most of the events of the novel, starting with the first episode.

The story opens with a wrestling match through which Okonkwo, the hero, enhances the reputation of his village by defeating his legendary opponent. "Okonkwo," we are told, "was well known throughout the nine villages and even beyond... As a young man of eighteen he had brought honour to his village by throwing Amalinze the cat... The great wrestler who for seven years was unbeaten, from Umuofia to Mbaino... It was this man that Okonkwo threw in a fight which the old man agreed was one of the fiercest since the founder of their town engaged a spirit of the wild for seven days and seven nights" (3).

Ousseynou B. Traoré and Simon Gikandi have made perceptive comments on the place of this episode in Achebe's narrative ideology. Traoré sees the event as a "foundation myth [which] provides a positive epic hero model for Okonkwo and [that]... the founder's deed marks the birth of the new community of Umuofia, while Okonkwo's reenactment of this feat at the New Yam festival coincides with his self-extension and the creation of his new identity" (69–70). Gikandi also argues that the event "is a temporal marker, a reminder of a distant time in which Umuofia was founded; it is the evocation of a historicity and...a mode of cultural production." "Achebe," Gikandi continues, "evokes this temporal situation not merely to show that the Umuofians are a people with a history, but also to address one of the central problematics in the Igbo epistemology-the question of origins and foundations" (29).

Indeed both arguments somewhat capture Achebe's politics of writing, since the wrestling is designed to show the Africans' capacity of engendering their own history in a world that would rather deny them such an accomplishment. Achebe's desire of reorganizing and historicizing a people's past somehow shows that his own exposure to and understanding of Western discourses must have nurtured in him what Peter Brooks would call a post romantic "anxiety...[whereby] the plotting of the individual or social or institutional life story takes on a new urgency as a means of organizing and explaining the world" (6). And, inasmuch as the post-romantic imagination is essentially a modernist imagination, Achebe's narrative is implicated in, predated by, and an elaboration of a wider modernist project that seeks to create significant cosmologies and to inscribe the self within the reinvented order. The entire story, not just the first episode, thus becomes Achebe's way of tracing a coherent story about how Africans got to their present position, although it is in creating such a genealogy that we also see the dilemma of the nationalist or post-colonial writer. That is, the post-colonial writer must use narrative to engender both race and self, but his or her plotting of race is essentially part of a modernist ethos, an ethos he or she must repudiate as well as appropriate. In either case Achebe or the post-colonial writer may well "recover forms already established or at least influenced or infiltrated by the culture of empire" (*Said* 210).

That narrative can reconstitute a coherent story about origins is central to Achebe's recuperation of identity in *Things Fall Apart*, although he does so in the shadow of post-romantic or modernist thought. His belief in origins is thus a belief he shares with that icon of modernism, Freud, who also assumes that somewhere there is a "racial master plot" that memory can recuperate. In discussing primal fantasy and the individual life narrative, Freud saw both as heavily shadowed by a "phylogenetic" story. He cautioned that both "scenes" can "sometimes [be] indisputably false and sometimes equally certainly correct, and in most cases compounded of truth and falsehood" (456, 457), but he still insisted that "in them, the individual reaches beyond his own experience...filling in the gaps in the individual truth with prehistoric truth" (461).

Thus, if Okonkwo's wrestling feat is a reenactment of "the founder's deed," a "reminder of a distant past that is supposed to address...the question of origins and foundations," it is so because Achebe's narrative ideology assumes that the artist can recreate the "prehistoric truth" of a community. As Achebe himself says, "*Things Fall Apart* [is] an act of atonement with [his] past, the ritual return and homage of a prodigal son" (38). But is Achebe's "ritual return" an ironic admission that narrative is "born of and treats of admitted doubt...of the impossibility of its own place," as Gikandi's appropriation of deCerteau's reading of history would seem to suggest? (*Gikandi* 320).

Certainly not, since such a reading does not sufficiently respond to *Things Fall Apart as* a cultural text, especially at the manifest level. After all, Achebe during this period of anti-colonial revolt was certain that it was possible and necessary to insert the self into a historical order for long degraded but nonetheless capably organizes, explains, and justifies individual existence like any other cultural regime. In short, Achebe must have believed that the "primeval" plot and the plot of individual existence are mutually intelligible, or that the self is a repetition of a cultural plot that is already replete with significance. Read in this way, *Things Fall Apart* may not be "superfluous", always the debtor of a death, indebted in respect to the disappearance of a genealogical and territorial 'substance" (320). Rather, it displays, in Freudian terms, that "mysterious power" which the artist alone possesses of making "it possible for other people once more to derive consolation and alleviation from their own sources of pleasure in their unconscious which have become inaccessible to them" (468). The text then becomes the space in which, as Achebe once said, the artist's "aims and the deepest aspirations of his (or her) society meet" (44).

So, once we see the opening scene in the light of its play with origins or culture, it is not also difficult to see the novel's plot as a comprehensive organization of the codes that regulate self-actualization in Igbo culture. Thus where Western representations and representatives from Lugard to Joyce to Joyce Cary have cast the West as the transcendent horizon or the point of reference, Achebe contests the inevitability of such representations by circulating counter-codes: religious, social, administrative, and juridical, through which the novel is ideologically invested as a "normative" on self-formation.

In *Things Fall Apart* the codes that regulate the relationship between self and society are numerous, of course, but they are all interconnected. The most important is the religious code and its proliferating network of referents, stretching from *Chukwu*, the supreme deity, to the individual's personal spirit, *chi*. Between these two axes, the rhythm of work (brushing, planting, and harvesting) and the scope for self-elaboration are defined in spiritual terms. Umuofia's external relations and its military adventures are, for example, heavily mediated by religion. "In fairness to Umuofia," we are told, "it never went to war unless its case was clear and accepted as such by its...Oracle of the Hills and the Caves" (9).

Planting and harvesting, the seasonal or temporal markers of life in this essentially agricultural community, are also defined by the limits imposed by religion. Tradition, which seems to have acquired the orthodoxy of religion, decrees that before planting the clan observes a week of peace "to honour [the] great goddess of the earth" (22). Also, the transition from one season to the other, the calendrical time in which the self marks the processes of its unfolding, starts with a feast in honor of the ancestor and the earth goddess: The Feast of the New Yam. "Men and women, young and old," says the narrator, "looked forward to the New Yam Festival because it began the season of plenty-the New Year" (26). It is no coincidence that wrestling, a sport that according to Foucault construes self-elaboration as "a field of action" (1986), is the culmination of the festivities. Society, it seems, must stage the self as a panegyric to the earth.

Moreover, social, administrative, or internal control mechanisms function within a framework that is heavily grounded in religion. That is, although social units such as the age group and the family do seem to have some control on self-definition, where such controls are not irrelevant, they are peripheral compared with those imposed by religion-mediated mechanisms. At the apex of the administrative hierarchy, for example, is the "council of elders or *ndichie*." They must owe their position of prominence in the hierarchy of power to their proximity to the noumenal realm. That is, as old people they will soon take their place among the ancestors from where they are supposed to bridge the gap between the community and the spirit world and thus become forces for propitiation and shrines. Furthermore, the ultimate juridical force in the land, the *egwugwu*, is an incarnation of the founding fathers of the clan: "each of the nine *egwugwu* represented a village of the clan... The nine villages of Umuofia had grown out of the nine sons of the first father of the clan" (63). These mutually reinforcing systemic controls, strengthened by a spiritual conscience, mediate almost every social intercourse and inscribe a passion for order within the citizens of Umuofia. The impression that Achebe succeeds in creating, according to Eustace Palmer, "is a society that announces its internal sufficiency" and that is aware of itself as an entity opposed to other worlds. In other words, the implications of this closure for practices of the self or identity are obvious, for when a text presents culture as its point of departure, as is the case in most nationalist narratives, analysis must equally concern itself with the "search for [the] normative language... the moral consciousness of society in its point of tangency with the individual" (Brooks 91). This is where a sustained analysis of the protagonist becomes unavoidable because if as nationalist rhetoric assumes narrative cannot be separated from social institutions or human populations, then it is Okonkwo that best articulates such an assumption.

To show that the novel is concerned with the existence of the African, we must however examine Okonkwo within the context of totality. Achebe has been emphatic about "presenting a total world and a total being" (12, 81). In this regard, Achebe's notion of totality may well coincide with Lukács' famous distinction between pre-modern and modern modes of consciousness. For Lukács Homeric Greece or the "integrated 'you,' can disturb its homogeneity" (32). On the contrary, the modern world has destroyed the "extensive totality" so humanity is plagued by a "transcendental homelessness," and "the immanence of meaning in life has become a problem" (41, 56). Bakhtin has also written about the place of the self in the epic which implicitly builds on the contrast between the modern and pre-modern inherent in the concept of totality, and since Achebe's imagination is predominantly epic rather than novelistic, Bakhtin's concept may also be similar to Achebe's. Bakhtin tells us,

> The individual in the high-distanced genre... is a fully finished and completed being. This has been accomplished on a lofty heroic level, but what is complete is also something hopelessly ready-made; he is all there, from beginning to end he coincides with himself, he is absolutely equal to himself. He is, furthermore, completely externalized. There is not the slightest gap between his authentic essence and its external manifestation. All his potential, all his possibilities are realized utterly in his external social position, in the whole of his fate and even external appearance; outside of his predetermined fate and predetermined posi-

> tion there is nothing... He is entirely externalized in most elementary, almost literal sense (34).

Achebe may not be talking about totality in the sense in which it is used by Lukács and Bakhtin, but writing at the dawn of Nigerian independence, he must have felt the need to remind his world about its past, which is what epic valorization is supposed to accomplish. After all, "the space between the hero of the epic and the singer and listener is filled with the national tradition" (Bakhtin 15). Okonkwo's style of embodying the norms of his society is thus designed to show how to live the national community, namely, by ensuring that one's "potential" and "possibilities" are "hopelessly" "predetermined" by one's nation.

As it turns out, from the time he re-engenders the Igbo community through his victory in the wrestling match, Okonkwo's activities seem to revolve around nurturing and sustaining the community in that he is preoccupied with modes of how to be in Igbo culture. For example, Umuofia is a patriarchal, aggressively competitive and power conscious culture, and Okonkwo embraces this value with almost unflinching rigor. Born to an "improvident" father, "Okonkwo did not have the start in life which many young men had. He neither inherited a barn nor a title, nor even a young wife" (13). But realizing that his society defines the self primarily in material terms, Okonkwo zestfully immerses himself in work. He acquires all the status symbols of his clan: "He had won fame as the greatest wrestler in the nine villages. He was a wealthy farmer and had two barns full of yams, and had just married his third wife" (6).

For its survival, probably, the clan emphasizes physical strength and dexterity in warfare. Okonkwo proves indomitable in this domain, too. He has brought "home a human head," a booty from Umuofia's last war; and he has earned enough respect to be able to mediate between his clan and its neighbors. That is why the clan entrusted Ikemefuna into Okonkwo's care. Like most Umuofians, Okonkwo takes exaggerated care to build shrines for "the wooden symbols of his personal god and of his ancestral spirits." In short, every step that Okonkwo takes is almost calculated to align his will with the will of his society.

Okonkwo is thus at the center of the novel, a symbolic node for the norms of the clan. His basic impulses are also the impulses of his society. Eustace Palmer, for example, has gone as far as to posit a correlation between Okonkwo's character and his environment based on a deterministic conception of character, especially Hardy's Wessex novels where Health becomes a "character in its own right," limiting, controlling and, at times, directing human destiny. Palmer writes:

> Okonkwo is what his society has made him, for his most conspicuous qualities are responses to the demands of his society. If he is plagued by fear of failure

> and of weakness it is because his society puts such a premium on success; if he is obsessed with status it is because his society is preoccupied with rank and prestige; if he is always itching to demonstrate his prowess in war it is because his society reveres bravery and courage and measures a man's success by the number of human heads a man has won; if he is contemptuous of weaker men it is because his society has conditioned him into despising cowards. Okonkwo is the personification of his society's values (53).

Palmer's reading is very insightful, and, as we shall later demonstrate, there is a sense in which the environment in this novel can be construed as an ubiquitous grammar that holds out the only possibility for self-representation. Indeed, contrary to what some critics have said, we shall argue that Achebe makes Okonkwo and his society isomorphous even down to Okonkwo's suicide, although the society views suicide as a sacrilege. In short, Okonkwo is the externalization of even what is a potential in Umuofia society. Some of the demands of the society, like the injunction to kill Ikemefuna, would have, by all accounts, required a more circumspect action, but Okonkwo participates in the killing precipitously because the oracle calls for it. Thus, he is like a Racinian hero, Barthes would say, who may be aware that "the world is a... diffuse sanction... fear of which does not exclude its use" (35). So, the earth, to Okonkwo, is the mother and "a child's fingers are not scalded by a piece of hot yam which its mother puts into its palm" (47).

Of course, Okonkwo does at times violate the codes of this society. He confounds the community by beating Ojiugo during the week of peace, he almost kills his wife Ekwefi during the New Yam Festival, he participates in the killing of his surrogate son, Ikemefuna, against all plausible advice, and he accidentally kills a kinsman. Although psychoanalytic concepts such as "displacement" and "blockage" could and are being evoked to account for the infractions, it is still difficult to account for the exaggerated attempts Okonkwo makes to be reabsorbed into the culture. For example, fined with a "she-goat, one hen, a length of cloth and a hundred cowries" for breaking the week of peace, Okonkwo adds "a pot of palm-wine to show his remorse." Exiled for a crime he inadvertently commits, he accepts the tribe's verdict with calm resignation. In exile, he pursues goals for his re-acceptance by the clan, and he refuses to return to Umuofia by even one day "earlier" for fear of taking "something from the full penalty of seven years."

Okonkwo's behavior does indeed scandalize his community from time to time, but the same attributes that define and situate him within his culture simultaneously define his society. In fact, it is Okonkwo's public actions, what Bakhtin would call his "external manifestation...[where] everything in him is exposed and loudly expressed...[as] his view of himself coincides completely with others' view of him" (34), that endear him to a lot of people. It is in his public domain that he demonstrates his unquestionable loyalty to the structuring codes of his society. It is in his public voice that he longs to see the values of his culture bequeathed to posterity in an undiluted form. And it is through his worshipful regard for the public domain that we are called upon to share in the force and pathos of what he thinks would be the consequence of Nwoye's capitulation to the new forces: "annihilation" (108).

Using Okonkwo's incarnation of public values as our point of reference, then, we may argue that it is the insistent social practices, the guarantee of status held out by success and reputation, the fear of shame, and many other culturally mediated values that define the self in Umuofia. Hence the narrating voice is at times dismayed by the culture's prodigious effort at normalizing the self since Umuofia does not seem to have other avenues for self-definition. Okonkwo and perhaps most other Umuofians thus experience the "imposition of an imaginary order of exclusion [through which] culture [is] invoked as a stable entity within which there are characteristic representations that [should be]...accommodated" by the self (Stephen Greenblatt 121). For a majority of people, in other words, Umuofia's values, which they must compulsively encode, operate almost by unconscious means.

The preponderance of cultural norms and their impact on the self thus turn *Things Fall Apart* into what Peter Brooks would call a novel of "worldliness." That is, narrative "exploitation of the drama inherent in man's social existence, the encounter of the personal style within the framework and code provided by society" (4). Brooks insists that "worldliness can arise only when society becomes an object of conscious cultivation, when it asserts outward closure and inward publicity...and becomes a positive entity attended to and cultivated for its own sake" (5). "Worldliness" is Brook's model for dealing with a corpus of writing that attempted to capture the truths about self-fashioning in a turbulent and transitory moment in French culture, when the self began to oscillate between the pre-assumed codes of pre-Napoleonic France and the almost horizontal world created in the wake of the revolution. This is the world of Julien Sorel. Similarly, Achebe's narrative can be located at the point of transition from a primary culture to capitalist colonialism and even independence, which makes discussing the work from the perspective of "worldliness" theoretically fruitful. After all, Okonkwo's articulation of public values would support Brooks' argument that where "worldliness" assumes dominance, "the individual's imagination of society makes him a voluntary, artistic self creation called upon to play a self-representation...before the eyes of others who are constantly trying to master his role" (287).

"Worldliness" in *Thing Fall Apart* could achieve a special resonance if we extended the concept to include a "territorial" mode of self-representation. "Territoriality," as theorized by Gilles Deleuze and Felix Guattari, deals with, among other things, how social formations function in relation to the human agents and the productive forces that are found in a given environment. In their attempt to critique capitalist society, they present three social regimes, pre-state, state, and post-state, but it is the pre-state regime and its corresponding mode of subject formation that is especially relevant to *Things Fall Apart*.

Deleuze and Guattari argue that the fundamental component of a pre-state culture or "socious" is the "abstract machine of society" (Massumi 75), the earth, not as a geological entity but as a social machine, that undertakes "a variety of interventions" (141). That is, the earth, as the "divine precondition," predetermines modes of production, distribution, and subject position because "the full body of the goddess earth gathers to itself the cultivable species, the agricultural implements, and the human population" (142).

How is the self-created related to its territorial regime? Deleuze and Guattari tell us that this is "a socious of inscription where the essential thing is to mark and be marked" through the "collective investment of organs" (142). "The essence of the recording socious," they continue, "resides in tattooing, excising, carving, and initiation" (144), but what appears as cruelty is actually a way of creating memory for humanity. In other words, all human organs or emanations from human organs, including voice, hand, and eye, are "collectively invested" in the process of self-fashioning. Rather than the pre-eminence of a single organ, then, we have "a voice that intones, a sign marked in bare flesh, an eye that extracts enjoyment from pain" (189). It is the multiple investment in all organs that constitutes "a territory of resonance and retention" or that creates identity in a territorial culture. Such a culture is akin to traditional societies of the type we see in Umuofia. In Umuofia, as we have seen, identity is not entirely dependent on but connected to the voice, as opposed to a capitalist society or what Deleuze and Guattari call a "despotic regime," where identity relies on the voice and only the voice (188). Thus, quite apart from its application in other domains, the territorial model remarkably captures the signifying practices of Umuofia culture. That is, as a "worldly" or "territorial" semiotic, Umuofia society still has "a greater affinity with desiring machines," or its inhabitants have not yet been afflicted with alienation (184), and they could thus be seen as emanations of the earth. In short, Okonkwo's Umuofia makes identity dependent on territory or the earth, an earth that erases process inasmuch as it presents itself as a "limitative body," meaning a force with a whole "set of [codes]...for its inhabitants, the better to exploit their habit-forming potential" (Massumi 76).

For example, *Things Fall Apart* makes a disproportionate amount of references to earth and activities that are either played out on or conditioned by the earth. All major festivals and all productive activities are structured around the earth, which is what enhances the prestige of "Ani, the earth goddess and the source of all fertility": She "played a greater part in the life of the people than any other deity. She was the ultimate judge of morality and conduct. And what was more she was in close communion with the departed fathers of the clan whose bodies had been committed to earth" (26).

We thus see a triangulation of earth, ancestors, and the individual in which the earth is accorded the greatest visibility. When, for example, a man wants knowledge of his ancestors he "crawls" into the bowels of the earth, into the shrine of the Oracle of the Hills and Caves. Also, in Umuofia's highest court, the ultimate judgment is given by "the spirit of the ancestors just emerged from the earth" (62). Further, the earth is the precondition for communication; Unoka's most telling points are often rendered through his drawings on the earth. And there are moments when it seems that Umuofians are engaged in a desperate search to make their bodies into mini-theaters to reflect the tone of the earth. "Okonkwo's wives," we are told, "had scrubbed the walls and the huts with real earth until they reflected light. They had then set about painting themselves with camwood and drawing beautiful black patterns on their stomachs and on their backs" (27). Hence, the periodic need for cleansing the earth to ensure its perpetual replenishment and dynamism. For example, after Okonkwo desecrates the land by killing a kinsman, the earth was purified by "men...dressed in garbs of war. They set fire to [Okonkwo's] houses, demolished his red walls, killed his animals and destroyed his barn....They had no hatred in their hearts against Okonkwo....They were merely cleansing the land which Okonkwo had polluted with the blood of a clansman" (87). Also, when the earth asserts itself such as in the uncontrollable deluge in the middle of the rainy season, or when it heats up to a point where even resourceful farmers such as Okonkwo can only agonize over the loss of their crops, humanity is humbled, humiliated, and dwarfed. Or, one is supposed to learn that "the personal dynamism required to counter the forces of [the earth] would be far too great for the human frame" (24). Thus, "worldliness" or "territoriality" is Achebe's way of positioning the self as bounded, closed, and in "reciprocal sympathy" with the unmediated codes of society that the earth obviously symbolizes. Through such codes, Brooks would say, *Things Fall Apart* attempts "to show that the individual [is] a significant repetition of a story already endowed with meaning" (280).

Such a perspective on identity also seems to govern Achebe's understanding of the operation of language in *Things Fall Apart*, about which Gikandi tells us that "signs, the grammar of the Igbo world," are "naturalized" to the point where they function to "signify a cosmology." Gikandi also believes that there is "a natural order of things and a natural order of knowledge," and a "logocentric linkage between language and being becomes in effect a precondition for an empirical cultural order." "There is," according to Gikandi, "a predetermined order of knowledge" because hermeneutic activities are "a formality"; after all, we have an "ideal" order in which "being, language, and nature" are linked (32, 33).

Gikandi's analysis of language and being is persuasive and his argument may not be significantly different from the point we have made thus far about identity and modes of territorial representation. The difference perhaps is that Gikandi uses The Derrudeab concept of "logocentrism" to criticize, and rightly so, the West's usurpation of the Igbo voice, a synonym for African presence or identity. "Achebe," Gikandi writes, "seems to be making a case for the absolute and inescapable linkage between being and voice. After all, the most obvious sign of the destruction of Igbo culture and its authority is the repression of Igbo voices at the end of the novel when colonialism imposes its grammatology and henceforth represents the African as a subject with neither a voice nor a logos" (33).

Of course the politics of voice is inescapable in *Things Fall Apart*, but the problem with an inordinate emphasis on voice is the assumption that voice is the only mode of self-representation in Umuofia or Igbo culture. In a territorial regime such as Umuofia, voice is part of a whole network of signifying mechanisms, including the eye and the hand. In the important first paragraph, where Okonkwo re-stages the founding of Umuofia, there is, for example, a visual emphasis that is almost tantamount to what Martin Jay would call an "ontology of sight" (143), although sound also plays a part. Also, when Unoka marks the walls with chalk, or when Obierika's wives draw patterns on their bodies, drawings that Gikandi rightly perceive as constitutive of "a cultural order and its spirit of things," voice is not the main determinant of presence but rather the "graphim' perpetuated by the hand. So, as important as voice is to Achebe's cultural politics, when its role is overemphasized it can easily obscure the active nature of the process of self-formation peculiar to Umuofia culture. In other words, the signifying practices of Achebe's Umuofia rely on a process in which the sign "is not aligned on the voice and not subordinate to it, but [only] connected to it" (188).

Having situated the narrative within the space opened up by "worldliness" and "territoriality," we are thus in a better position to understand the trajectory of Okonkwo's life, the character that best incarnates and dramatizes the codes of the society. Okonkwo is banished from Umuofia for seven years for accidentally killing a kinsman. During his absence in Mbanta, the forces of Christianity and Western administration invade and gain ascendance, resulting in a restructuring of the priorities of Okonkwo's Umuofia. A school, an administrative center, and a commercial store are now part of the Umuofia cultural landscape. Okonkwo is one of the few who are opposed to the white presence, since for most others, "The white man had indeed brought a lunatic religion, but he had also built a trading store and for the first time... much money flowed into Umuofia" (126).

These changes hardly touch Okonkwo; he starts planning for reintegration into the culture in terms of how the old social codes define one's position in Umuofia. Although he obviously knows that the marks that used to give accent to his identity are somewhat being reorganized, he still consoles himself that the "losses [are] not irreparable. "He is determined that his return "should be marked by his people": "He would build a bigger barn than he had before and he would build huts for two new wives...[and] show his wealth by initiating his sons into the *ozo* society. Only the really great men in the clan were able to do this. Okonkwo saw clearly the high esteem in which he would be held" (121). This is the Okonkwo we meet in the final pages of the novel, whose internalization of "the obligatory language" of his culture is so complete that it" forecloses [his mind to] the play of other cultural signs" and who is prepared to defend the codes of his culture to death.

For example, the oracle makes the gloomy prediction that "Christianity will spread destruction" in Igboland: this is a sacrilege to Okonkwo: "God will not permit it." During his exile the clan has recognized the need for exercising moderation; it has seen the complexity of the new situation and is slowly coming to the conclusion that "if Umuofia failed to send her children to school strangers would come from other places to rule them." The tribe is adjusting to change, but Okonkwo is shocked by the changes: "What has happened to our people? Why have they lost the power to fight" (159)? He feels that fighting is the answer.

After his return, the clan burn down the white man's church; Okonkwo and other elders are arrested and imprisoned. In the meeting after their release from prison, the debate centers on the type of latitude the clan can give to the new force. This is a reasonable attitude, one would believe, in the circumstances. Okonkwo is shocked and says in resentment, "I shall leave them and plan my own revenge" (180). While he is thinking about tribal inertia, a court messenger arrives. Unable to contain his anger, apprehensive of Umuofia's unwillingness to act, Okonkwo brutally beheads the messenger, and in turn commits suicide. He thus fails to side with the clan. Unfortunately, suicide is "an offense against the earth": "It is an abomination for a man to take his own life...and a man who commits it will not be buried by his clansmen. His body is evil, and only strangers may touch it" (147). The possibility this ending opens up for conflicting interpretations is immense.

Interpretations have ranged from psychological readings of Okonkwo's character to extremely problematic socio-cultural ones. The interpretations include Donald Cook's point that Okonkwo's death is a "gesture of stubborn defiant opposition to the arrogant presumption of white rule and the calculated degradation of a great tradition" (72). There is also John Povey's argument that "in demanding the old cohesion of the past now, he [Okonkwo] is splitting that remnant of necessary cohesion that remains" (110). One cannot also ignore Oyekan Owomoyela whose conflicting statements, if anything, reveal the complexity of Okonkwo's suicide. Approaching the tragedy with great confidence, Owomoyela tells us that "the destruction of Okonkwo is a personal, not a communal tragedy because the community survives and will in time be rid of the white strangers. What tragedy there is, limited to the ending of a monolithic order bound to the whims of sometimes capricious gods"

(88). This is almost irreconcilable with Owomoyela's previous statement: "Because the African is expected to be motivated communally, therefore, interest in individual motivations is out of place because it would assume an individualism that is actually nonexistent except as an aberration" (82).

Notwithstanding the conflicting interpretations, if as we have thus far assumed that there is a manifest level, a level at which the narrative is steeped in the ideology of origin and identity and at which Achebe perceives Okonkwo as a cultural hero, then the novel can be construed as an epic. That is, it can be invested with social meaning. And once we accept Okonkwo as an epic hero, his suicide or tragedy can be interpreted along a communal axis. Okonkwo's death in other words becomes a psychosocial drama that stages the dilemma of the community, and which forces the community to hold a dialogue with itself. After all, as Peter Brooks would say, "Tragedy is like a mass participation: 'a mimesis of sacrifice'-in which the audience are communicants," and what it "does is to redeem the hero in the mind of the reader" (213). Further, if one agrees with Aristotle who sees the end of a tragedy or the moment of "recognition" as the crucial moment, one can, with Brooks, underscore the fact that since "the moment of recognition is always too late for the tragic hero, the real importance of the hero's sacrifice is the enlightenment it brings for the audience...The moment of the plot's consummation [is thus] the moment of meaning" (213).

In short, the ideological force of *Things Fall Apart* emerges precisely because of Okonkwo's suicide or because of the "consummation of the plot" he so thoroughly animates. For, it is not until after Okonkwo's death (or after the District Commissioner decides to frame the suicide and the lives of the people of the lower Niger within a colonial narrative) that Achebe takes us to the source of his own narrative. The District Commissioner, we learn, cannot afford to be frivolous with space, and with so many things to write about, his *Pacification of the Primitive Tribes of the Lower Niger* would include "not a whole chapter but a reasonable paragraph" about Okonkwo and his people (147–8). The arrogance of the commissioner would thus indicate that Okonkwo's tragedy or Achebe's entire story began as a response to and is about representation, framing, and modes of narrative transference in colonial and post-colonial cultures. This in turn reminds one of Greenblatt's sobering meditations on the "war of representation" in colonial encounters:

> When I contemplate this torrent of words and images, I feel overwhelmed – a lifetime would not suffice to grasp what was disseminated throughout Europe in the first few generations alone. And there are, of course, even vaster silences – the silences of the unlettered and those who, though literate, did not have occasion, license, or motive to leave a record of their thoughts. The responses of the natives to the fatal advent of the Europeans survive only in the most fragmentary and problematical form; much of what I would like to

> learn is forever lost, and much of what is lost exists only through the mediation of those Europeans who for one reason or another – missionary, commercial, literary, historical, or philosophical – saw fit to register the voices of the native. The natives themselves seem most silent at those rare moments in which they are made to speak. (145–6)

Seeing Okonkwo's death as a symbol for the silencing of a culture even as that culture is, paradoxically, disseminated by the Western technology of representation, is to understand the novel as Achebe's call to every Nigerian, indeed, every African, to become a "communicant" in a "mass sacrifice." The sacrifice is the silence imposed by colonialism but which should also be a source of determination and a moment of value for the new nation.

Like other nationalist works, then, *Things Fall Apart* is a reconfiguration of the Western episteme, especially in its impulse to reread and rewrite documents in which colonial empires elaborated themselves. It is in this regard that one can call Okonkwo's death an "expressive death...a death overloaded with historical, affective content" (*Barthes* 186–87), while at the same time admitting that the narrative is beyond the shaping will of an individual: Okonkwo. To say this is to accept Achebe's ideological commitment to the postcoloniality of assertive identity, as well as to insert *Things Fall Apart* into the identity discourse of cultural nationalism. In ideological orientation, in other words, it is difficult to divorce *Things Fall Apart* from the basic tenets of negritude, from Cabral's return to the sources, or from the anticolonial texts of the late 50s and early 60s through which,

> The African scholar succeeded the anthropologist, the "native" theologian replace the missionary, [the African novelist replaced the novelist of empire], and the politician took the place of the colonial commissioner. All of them find reasons for their vocations in the dialectic of the same and the other.... They tend to rationalize their missions in terms of an encounter between a narcissistic relation to the self and the dual relation with the other (*Mudimbe* 180–81).

And the manifest concern of *Things Fall Apart*, as thus far discussed, would remain important for all colonized people in the battle against foreign categorizations.

However, a latent level has also been discerned in *Things Fall Apart*. This is the level at which the textuality of the novel is often underscored and presumed to posit a hybridized postcoloniality, what Jeyifo would call an "interstitial...mode of self-fashioning...which is neither First world nor Third world, neither securely and smugly metropolitan, nor assertively and combatively Third worldist." "Of course, the novel does lend itself to such a deconstructive reading, as indeed any text is likely to do when read in certain ways. Considering the historical and ideological moment in which the novel is composed, though, any undue emphasis on the novel's putative textuality will probably be inaccurate. If we treat ambivalence at all, it is not to underscore the polyphony of the text in any deconstructive sense, but to show how ambiguity or textuality functions as a narrative strategy for anticipating a ruptured identity in the post-Okonkwo world. We shall then situate the rupture in source not primarily emanating from within the text.

A deconstructive reading of *Things Fall Apart* begins when the main character Okonkwo is made to carry an undue psychological weight. And almost every major study of *Things Fall Apart* emphasizes Okonkwo's psychological dysfunction. According to Gikandi, for instance, Okonkwo's dislike of his improvident father leads to a "repression" of those principles that his father stands for: feminine principle, resulting in a "displacement," a condition in which "affect is transferred from an unacceptable object to an acceptable one." Okonkwo's "blockage" of the "originary desires" means that he "lives against his true nature, and has created a personal ideology of self which, nevertheless, undermines the selfhood it is supposed to sustain" (39, 43).

Gikandi's analysis is insightful and one would argue that the text itself solicits such an interpretation, but such a reading has its limits. The point at issue is not that privatization of the self does not exist in a territorial culture, since Oedipus is a shadow that haunts all cultural formations. But in a territorial society of the type we find in Umuofia, although desire may show instances of "blockage" or coding in some individuals, the "blockage" is easily absorbed by "the interior of the socious" (165). So the magnitude of privatization emphasized by Gikandi is unimaginable in a pre-state society. This is because organs are still actively invested, the capitalist regime that reduces everything to familial production has still not arrived, and the process of endowing objects with lack may be negligible, if non-existent. It is, therefore, unlikely that Umuofia society, or for that matter any traditional society, can easily create the lack that is necessary for oedipalization or "blockage."

What is probably responsible for such readings is the effect of the Lacanian project, which has made oedipalism a tremendously mobile regime (52). That is, the tendency among critics to privatize Okonkwo may be due to a retrospective re-reading of traditional societies from the perspective of contemporary notions of culture. It is in this regard that Achebe the artist seems to be far ahead of his critics. For what he dangles before the unwary critic is the existence of an oedipal potential in Okonkwo and his society; but his ideological position demands he move the narrative from its familial site. In short, Okonkwo's simultaneous embodiment and disruption of his society's values can be explained in other ways.

First, one can argue that it is the result of the incapacity of the society to inscribe itself fully in the consciousness of individuals. Second, but paradoxically, that social formations are never completely closed. This is a point Bourdieu makes in his reading of culture. Bourdieu argues that as semiotic configurations, cultural formations are constantly constituting conditions for their own interrogation, since sign fields are never pure limits and a sign constitutes itself in competition with other signs ("supplement") that may be equally valid. These are "supplements" that always haunt the coherence of the cultural symbolic so much so that even for self-fashioning, when society sees its role as that of projecting codes for practices on or by individuals, society can only inscribe itself on individuals through force. That is, society can only impose itself and its codes on the self through acts of usurpation, force, and symbolic violence, but even such forceful actions are never total in their effect on the individual (64). Achebe may be aware of such a fundamental operation of culture: culture as the site of a mixed semiotic. But since most critics ignore this elementary mode of cultural processing they invariably engage in a deep psychological reading of Okonkwo's character.

Our awareness of the unstable nature of social formations should also help us account for Achebe's mimetic adequacy or objectivity that, through the use oral devices and the character, Obierika, generates much of the ambiguity that has been discerned at the latent level. The objectivity is, for example, evident in the novel's emphasis on the dynamism of society, which Okonkwo would want to deny. Ogbuefi Ezeudu tells us that the punishment for breaking the week of peace is milder than before. The clan, too, we are told, is like a lizard that replaces its tail with a new one when the old one falls off, hence a man's place is not always there waiting for him. Uchendu talks about the "good days when a man has friends in distant clans."

Similarly, there is a parallel, micro-social world, the repressed conscience of the dominant epistemology, constituted by what is fashionably called "the feminine principle" in Achebean criticism. This is what the reference to the women that are always hovering on the "margins" of some of the momentous gatherings of the clan is about. Also, women are never allowed to grow yam, the "king of crops," and even in fictional activities they can only tell stories of love, not of bloodshed. But despite the suppression of this vibrant feminine culture, one of the hermeneutic forces in the clan, the Oracle of Hills and Caves, is controlled by a woman, Chielo and the source of Umuofia's respectability, its "potent war-medicine," has a woman as "the active principle." The medicine itself is called *agadi-nwayi*, or "old woman." These, together with the *Osu*, are gaps or parallel cultures or competing experiential realities within the same society that pose the threat of vampirizing the dominant culture.

More than objectivity, however, the parallel cultures should really be perceived as the novel's way of acknowledging the complexity of social formations. That is, Achebe's objectivity, apart from being the product of his awareness of a mixed semiotic, probably has a lot to do with the fact that the narrative is composed in the shadow of his own liberal education. This forces him to reject a system's closure and its claim to absolute authority. So, Achebe does admire the totality of the past; he even cultivates it, savoring the assurance a regime of codes and symbols affords the self. But he can already imagine a process of transformation in which a line of self-articulation seems to be opening up that would be opposed to the territoriality of traditional culture. It is at such a juncture that he locates Obierika, where his impeccable mastery of the Western narrative tradition coalesces with his oral narrative grammar.

After the oracle demands that Ikemefuna die, Obierika, as a transgressive voice, feels that it is not always necessary to blindly act as the "messenger" of the "Earth," which is what he blames his friend, Okonkwo, for. He tells Okonkwo: "if the oracle said that my son should be killed I would neither dispute it nor be the one to do it" (47). Also, after the destruction of Okonkwo's compound for a crime he accidentally commits, Obierika again questions the sense of "the will of the goddess" to himself: "why should a man suffer so grievously for an offense he had committed inadvertently? But although he thought so grievously for a long time he found no answer. He was merely led into greater complexities. He remembered his wife's twin children, whom he had thrown away. What crime had they committed" (87)? Although for most people Obierika is nothing other than the ironic conscience of the narrative, or the means of commenting on the failures of the Igbo society, there are indications that his transgressive location within the text could be explained in the predictive sense I seem to be emphasizing. In other words, the presence of such a trangressive voice alerts us to the inaccuracy of a simple formalistic assessment: the objective point of view.

Such a reading assumes that the parallel epistemologies the narrative so laboriously marks are seeking reconciliation. But the position of Obierika in the narrative however opens up the novel to Achebe's understanding of the process of cultural operation: the difficulty of constituting a unique subjectivity by encoding an ideal order when all cultural regimes are always already threatened by a severe tension. Obierika is thus the site at which we perceive the harassment of the manifest cultural text.

Similarly, like Obierika's positioning within the narrative, the embedding of oral materials in the text (folktales and proverbs) should not be seen as simply a way of naturalizing the novel within an African environment. This is not the way intercalated narratives always function, since textual embedding alerts us to the possibility of a hybrid construction: "a narrative matrix that connects different voices and different acts of writing" (*Duyfhuizen* 123). Rightly enough, Duyghuizen believes that such embedded narratives" explore the mysteries of identity...in the midst of a historical fragmentation of the word and world" (131). In terms of identity the result is a "multivoiced discourse" that in Bakhtinian grammar can never be site of mastery, authorial or "characterological." Rather, it is a zone of "tension," "the author utilizes now one language, now another, in order to avoid giving himself up wholly to either of them" (314). So as we try to wrestle with the multiple signals that the novel emits, the ambiguous position Obierika occupies, the oral-written interface, we should begin to think beyond a mere formal concern with objectivity, or even the naturalization of one aesthetic register by another. We have to accept that the narrative is prolonging the discourse on the self, transferring the issue of identity onto a new terrain. The new terrain would be that on which the self will confront the problematic of nationhood, as the reorganization of society undermines once again the stability and unity the colonial state hastily constructed and imposed on an otherwise diverse population and their conflicting cultural texts. That is, the novel already seems to be talking about the future of independent Nigeria in ways similar to how, according to Soyinka, art in Yoruba ethos brings the "present...the ancestral, [and] the unborn within the affectiveness of life" (20). In short, for colonized people history can probably only make sense when presented in a pendular mode, which is to say that narrating the past in a postcolonial context implies a desire to have or talk about the past, the present, and the future at once. That *Things Fall Apart* is such a pendular narrative shows Achebe's mastery of reality.

Works Cited

Achebe, Chinua, *Hopes and Impediments*. New York: Doubleday, 1989.

———. *Things Fall Apart*. Portsmouth: Heinemann, 1986.

Awoonor, Kofi. The Breast of the Earth: A Survey of the City History, Culture, and Literature of Africa South of the Sahara. Garden: Anchor/Doubleday, 1975.

Barthes, Roland. A Barthes Reader. Ed. Susan Sontag. New York: Hill and Wang, 1982.

———. The Pleasure of the Text. Trans. Richard Miller. New York:
Hill and Wang, 1975.

———. S/Z. Trans. Richard Miller. New York: Hill and Wang, 1974.

———. On Racine. Trans. Richard Howard. New York: Hill and Wang, 1964.

Brooks, Peter. *Reading for the Plot*. New York: Alfred A. Knopf, 1984.

Cabral, Amilcar. *National Liberation and Culture*. Trans. Maureen Webster. Syracuse: Syracuse University, 1970.

Deleuze, Gilles, and Félix Guattari. *A Thousand Plateaus*. Trans. & For. Brian Massumi. Minneapolis: University of Minnesota Press, 1987.

———. *Kafka: Toward a Minor Literature*. Trans. Sana Polan. For.
Re'da Bensmaia. Minneapolis: University of Minnesota Press, 1986.

———. *Anti-Oedipus*. Trans. Robert Hurley, Mark Seem, and Helen R. Lane. Minneapolis: University Press, 1992.

Duyfhuizen, Bernard. *Narratives of Transmission*. Rutherford, N.J.: fairleigh Dichenson University Press, 1992.

Foucault, Michel. "Technologies of the Self." *Technologies of the Self*. Eds.
H. Gutman et al. Amherst, University of Massachusetts Press, 1988: 16–49.

Freud, Sigmund. *Introductory Lectures on Psychoanalysis*. Trans. James Strachey.New York: W.W. Norton & Company, Inc. 1966.

Gikandi, Simon. *Reading Chinua Achebe*. Pourthsmouth: Heinemann, 1991.

Greenblatt, Stephen. *Marvelous Possessions*. Chicago: The University of Chicago Press, 1988.

Jeyifo, Biodun. "For Chinua Achebe: The Resilience and Predicament of Obierika." *Chinua Achebe: A Celebration*. Eds. Kristen Holst Peterson and Anna Rutherfor. Sydney: Dangaroo Press, 1991: 51–70.

———. "The Reinvention of Theatrical Tradition: Critical discourses on Interculturalism in African Theatre." *The Dramatic Touch of Difference: Theatre, Own and Foreign*. Eds.

Fischer-Lichte, Erika, Josephine Riley, and Michael Gissenwehrer. Tubingen: Gunter Narr Verlag, 1990: 239–252.

———. *The Truthful Lie: Essays in the Sociology of African Drama*. London: New Beacon Books, 1985.

Lukács, Georg. *The Historical Novel*. Trans Hannah and Stanley Mitchell. Lincoln: University of Nebraska Press, 1983.

———. *The Theory of the Novel*. Trans. Anna Bostock. Cambridge: Massachusetts, University Press, 1971.

Massumi, Brian. *A User's Guide to Capitalism and Schizophrenia*. Cambridge: The MIT Press, 1992.

Mudimbe, V.Y. *The Invention of Africa: Gnosis, Philosophy, and the Order of Knowledge*. Bloomington: Indiana University Press, 1988.

Nietzsche, Friedrich. *Untimely Meditations*. Trans. R.J. Hollingdale. Cambridge: Cambridge University Press, 1986.

Owomoyela, Oyekan. *African Literatures: An Introduction*. Waltham: Crossroads Press, 1979.

Palmer, Eustace. *The Growth of the African Novel*. London: Heineman, 1979.

———. *An Introduction to the African Novel*. New York: Africana Publishing Corporation, 1972.

Soyinka, Wole. *Art, Dialogue, and Outrage*. New York: Pantheon Books, 1994.

Tiffin, Helen. "Post-Colonial Literatures and Counter-Discourse." *Kunapipi* 9, no. 3, 1987: 17–34.

Traoré, B. Ousseynou. "Matrical Approach to *Things Fall Apart*: A Poetics of Epic and Mythic Paradigms." *Approaches to Teaching Achebe's Things Fall Apart*. Ed. Bernth Lindfors. New York: Modern Language Association of America, 1991: 64–73.

White, Hayden. *Metahistory*. Baltimore: The Johns Hopkins University Press, 1990.

———. *The Content of the Form*. Baltimore: The John Hopkins University Press, 1987.

Chapter 2

Beyond the Igbo Cosmos: Achebe's *Things Fall Apart* as a Cross-Cultural Novel

Francis Ibe Mogu

MUCH, VERY MUCH HAS been written about Chinua Achebe's premier novel, *Things Fall Apart* (1958). The work which was intended to counter the depiction of black Africa in Joyce Cary's *Mister Johnson* and other related texts written by European colonial and Eurocentric authors, has now defied the expectations of even the most adept optimists in terms of its cultural and economic imports. *Things Fall Apart* is not only consistently popular among Igbo students and scholars, it is very popular with other Nigerian and African people and aptly mirrors cultural aspects shared by the Igbo and other Africans. It is now the given; the novel to read, as a pointer to other works in the African literary canon.

As a Nigerian from a minority ethnic group (in this case, the Ejaghams of Ogoja in Cross River State), a reading of *Things Fall Apart* drew immediate parallels and revealed the multiple similarities between the Igbo people and the Ejaghams of Ogoja.

The aspects of the novel that touch cords which bind our people and which elicited by instant response range from the organization of the Igbo society, the various festivals and religious worship, the folklore (especially proverbs) the dances and masquerades, the marital rites, the belief in ancestral spirits, among other things. Achebe should be praised for his ability to mirror within the narrow confines of *Things Fall Apart*, the salient cultural attributes of not only the Igbo people in Nigeria but also those of other ethnic groups within and outside Nigeria.

Among the Igbo (as among neighboring ethnic groups such as the Bakor – Ejaghams of Ogoja), a lot of the cultural attributes so ably reflected by Achebe though applicable, have undergone changes and modifications. Western Christianity, intellectualism and economics have in no small measure, interfered with the traditional African setting visible especially at the outset of *Things Fall Apart*. This assessment is equally applicable to *Arrow of God*, his other masterpiece. However, since culture is dynamic, there would still have been changes in aspects of the culture reflected in the novel, with or without interference from Christianity or the West.

Things Fall Apart reveals that the Igbo community is ordered around a hierarchy of male elders, who serve as collective leaders in both the secular and spiritual realms. These elders (*Ndichie*) consist of respected men and achievers in the land. They are very conspicuous and rare, the ancestral spirits succeed in commanding respect and fear from members of the community. In an incident which warrants the intervention of the *egwugu* (ancestral spirits), the Umuofia community (which is central in this novel) assembles on the village *ilo* – the Village Square or playground, to hear their verdict in a case involving two families over a marital rift:

> An iron gong sounded, setting up a wave of expectation in the crowd. Everyone looked in the direction of the egwugwu house. Gome, gome, gome, gome went the gong, and a powerful flute blew a high-pitch blast. Then came the voice of the egwugwu, guttural and awesome. The wave stuck the women and children and there was a backward stampede. But it was momentary. They were already far enough where they stood and there was room for running away if any of the egwugwu should go towards them.
>
> ....No woman ever asked questions about the most powerful and the most secret cult in the clan (Achebe: 1958 (1976 Reset): 62–63).

The verdict of the ancestral spirits is final and binding on the squabbling parties or disputing factions. What is immediately glaring upon a reading of the proceedings in the case, is the relegation of the female folk to the background in the scheme of things. The essentially male – prone or patriarchal society depicted by Achebe is what contemporary feminists oppose. The situation above is largely similar to what prevailed in the past among the Ejagham people. Rather than centralizing power in an individual in the community (such as the king, Chief, etc), a council of elders vested with the responsibility to preside over and direct affairs affecting the community was constituted. Of course, this was based on certain criteria which became, with time, part of the community's statues. As among the Igbo, the influence of European colonialism introduced a new element into the ordering of affairs in the Ejagham set-up. So that, nowadays we have in addition to the council of elders, token chiefs (figure Heads) who, superficially are in charge of their communities and whose loyalties to their people remain questionable. In the strictly traditional past however, as Achebe reflects in *Things Fall Apart*, the elders presided ever the community effectively and power was not vested in an individual.

The Nkum clan in Ogoja (which is part of the Bakor – Ejagham ethnic group) consists of seven villages, some of which are bigger than others. These villages (Ukpe, Ukpagada, Mbagide, Alladim, Igodor, Ikandangha and Ibil) in the past had a similar pattern of administration by council of elders who played both secular and spiritual roles.

Specifically, in Kkum (as in all other Ejagham speaking areas) masquerades play a prominent role by fostering cohesion and space in the community. When the environment is perceived to be infested with evil (nocturnal practices such as witchcraft), an alarm is raised by the council of elders or other concerned members of the community. Thereafter, the elders meet and map out strategies to curb the perceived menace in order to restore trust and tranquility. Although masquerades serve to purify or cleanse the society at specific periods (such as the period preceding the New Yam Festival), they also manifest themselves in moments of calamity or perceived threats or danger to the existence of the community or of its individuals. They are essentially viewed as spiritual essences largely representing departed ancestors who intervene benevolently in the community because they are perceived to be custodians of such societies and are therefore keenly interested in whatever happens to their people. These masquerades are of two kinds: the '*Atam*' are the more revered of the two and are seen as ancestral spirits that purify and cleanse the community especially before (or after) an evil visits the land, while the 'Irom' are largely, dancing masquerades that entertain at functions such as funerals or other community functions and festivals. They too are highly revered, but the '*Atam*' is accorded greater reverence.

The villages in the clan were closely knit and each village had its own elders overseeing its affairs and reporting directly to the central council of elders. Ibil was the administrative headquarters, while Ukpe was spiritually very significant. Today however, in the Nkum clan, you have clan and village heads who interfere with the work of the council of elders. Also, with the advent of Christianity and Western education, these elders have largely been relegated to their religious duties. Traditional African modes of worship have largely been overtaken by Western Christianity with churches playing an increasingly dominant role in the affairs of the community.

As in *Things Fall Apart*, festivals and ceremonies which serve to reaffirm commonalities among Ejagham people such as the New Yam Festival (in Ogoja, yam is also a king of all crops and the festival is second only to Christmas in the modern sense, although in the past it was viewed as the most important event in the land) and initiation to various esteemed positions in the society, prevail to date. The age grade system, the naming of days of the week to coincide with market days in the villages within the clan, etc compare favorably with what obtains in *Things Fall Apart*. Today however, the western week has effectively replaced the traditional one which was anchored on market days in the clan.

Charles Nnolim has argued in his *Approaches to the African Novel: Essays in Analysis* (1992) that Achebe manifests a "technique in the use of the folk tradition" to drive home his message and that he does this by employing "the least complicated element: the simple folk tale":

> In *Things Fall Apart* a memorable folk tale is told Ezinma by her mother, Ekwefi. It is the story of the birds and the tortoise who accompanied the former to a great feast in the sky, this story is sandwiched between chapter 10, where it is revealed that Okonkwo has attained the second highest position of importance in Umuofia as a masked Egwugwu during the case between Uzowulu and Mgbafor, and chapter 13, where Okonkwo was forced into exile for the inadvertent murder of Ezeudu's son (18).

Nnolim further reasons that, "The simple tale of Tortoise and the birds is a paradigm for the entire novel. It is the story of the sudden rise and fall of the Tortoise, Just as *Things Fall Apart* is the story of the rise and fall of Okonkwo" (18). The folk tradition (which embraces folk tales, proverbs and parables), though anchored in the rural past, serves to advise, fore-warn against or pre-empt ugly situations and, it is only the discerning that can read and interpret the writing on the wall. Okonkwo was sufficiently counseled and warned to desist from 'destroying himself' by not taking part in killing Ikemefuna – the ransom lad from Mbaino. He however went against the advice and suffered as a result. He was banished from Umuofia (his father land) for seven years. Thus his pride precipitates his disaster: pride, the sourer of disobedience, regularly leads to a fall or demise. Such tales serve to warn other people of the danger inherent in excessive pride (what one may term 'being full of oneself' to the point that one ignores other people's counseling in the vain belief that one has ample answers to all problems within the vicinity). Traditional folktales like this are common and appear to reinforce or draw from the Christian biblical account of the creation and the fall – both of Lucifer and man, owing to pride and subsequent disobedience.

Among the Ejagham and as among the Igbo, another folk tradition that continues to blossom in spite of the rapidly changing values such as westernization and Christianization of the local communities, is the New Yam Festival. The Bakor – Ejagham people observe the event in mid-September every year. Although the festival reaches its peak on September 15 annually, celebrations marking the harvest of the 'new' yam begin at least a week prior to that date and continue effectively for the next few days after that date. During the New Yam festival (and since yam is the king of all crops), the *Atam* masquerade ensures that the society is purified and cleansed of all evil spirits. Subsequently, there are dances all through the fiesta characterized by the active presence of the *Irom* masquerades which consist mainly of star dancers in the community. Unlike the 'Irom', the 'Atam' consists of only revered and accomplished elders. In *Things Fall Apart,* Achebe elaborately dwells on the New Yam Festival in Umuofia as a way to amplify its significance as an avenue for the reaffirmation of the values that held these people together as a closely-knit community. The festival accomplished this through bringing people together. This occasion actually marked the beginning of a new year for the Igbo people as it did for the Ejagham and other ancillary ethnic groups:

> The feast of the new yam was approaching and Umuofia was in a festival mood. It was an occasion for giving thanks to Ani, the earth goddess and the source of all fertility....
>
> The feast of the New Yam was held every year before the harvest began, to honour the earth goddess and the ancestral spirits of the clan. New Yams could not be eaten until some had first been offered to these powers. Men and Women, young and old, looked forward to the New Yam Festival because it began the season of plenty – the New Year. (Achebe: 1958 (1976 Reset): 26).

While effectively countering the white colonial portrayal of Africa, *Things Fall Apart* also presents itself as a useful source material for both the Igbo and non-Igbo ethnic groups. For, especially minority groups which are ancillary to the Igbo, the novel has the potential to propel scholars to embark on similar imaginative and artistic recreations of their societies prior to the interference by white European colonizers in the affairs of sub-Saharan Africa. Achebe argues that,

> *Things Fall Apart,* was... a deliberate (and successful) effort to recreate a per-Westernized African reality, using authentic Igbo characters, situations, values and religious concepts, and bending the English language to express Igbo proverbs and idioms. (Chinweizu, et al 1980: 288–289).

The European colonial enterprise in Nigeria and the rest of Africa was decidedly geared towards the total eradication of the African cultural heritage and its replacement with the Western (eurocentric) culture. The absence of authentic historical, literary and sociological materials to counter the colonizer's assessment and subsequent categorization of issues relating to Africa would have made it more difficult to convince the rest of the world that ours was not a dark and primitive continent as alleged by the Europeans. Indeed, Africa, was not the jungle, 'upon which the white Man acting on God's behalf sought to civilize,' (Achebe 1975) as *Things Fall Apart* and other creative Afrocentric works vividly show. Instead, through this novel, the author asserts strongly that the coming of the white man to Africa caused much dislocation to our people and values. Aigboje Higo draws this conclusion in his introduction to the novel:

> *Thins Fall Apart*, then, is about a clan which once thought like one, spoke like one, shared a common awareness and acted like one. The white man came and his coming broke this unity. In the process many heads rolled; new words, new usages and new applications gained entrance into men's heads and hearts and the old society gradually gave away. The process continues even today. (Achebe: 1958 (1976 Reset): v).

The trend of dislocation referred to above is as pronounced among the Igbo as it is among the non-Igbo, especially the minority ethnic groups in Nigeria. For instance, the languages, dialects and thought-processes of members of these groups are permeated with English vocabulary through and through either in the standard usage or in the pidgin rendition. The interesting and refreshing point in this regard about texts by Afro-centric writers such as Achebe (*Things Fall Apart, Arrow of God*) and Ngugi (*Weep Not Child, The River Between and Petals of Blood*) is that aspects of the indigenous language, or culture which have no English equivalent are left intact and, later, these find their way into mainstream usage as words or terminology in the English language. For example, 'Iroko Tree' (Achebe: 1958 (1976 Reset): 31). In other words, *Things Fall Apart* and other related texts have contributed immensely to the enrichment of the English language: Surely, nowadays English is no longer a western only affair.

Also, one would be right by simply stating that this novel which dwells on the Igbo past, is not rendered in the Igbo language (even though it transliterates and views phenomena from the angle of the Igbo people as much as possible), is cross-cultural since it is rendered primarily in English – a foreign language!

It is clear therefore that Achebe's premier novel acts as a bridge; a link between the Igbo cultural heritage and other cultures both within and outside Nigeria – especially Sub-Saharan Africa.

Other aspects of the African cultural heritage which Achebe dwells at length on in the novel include the traditional marital system which allows a man to marry as many wives as he can afford and the funeral rites accorded the dead, especially elders. Both the marital and funeral rites cut across most African ethnic groups. Differences – where these exist, are only in the details. The reverence and emphasis accorded these rites in the African traditional set-up (sub-Saharan Africa especially) are great. In *Things Fall Apart*, it is revealed that the protagonist, Okonkwo has three wives, all of who prepare and serve him meals, tend his farms, bear and fend for his children. (Achebe: 1958 (1976 Reset): 10, 36–32).

Regarding, marital rites, the novel recounts a life-like, occurrence in which the various stages are spelt out and implemented in a relaxed and friendly manner. There is a gathering of members of both the suitor's and bride's families in the bride's father's compound and, amidst good natured conversation, wining and dining, the bride price is determined amicably to the mutual acceptance and pleasure of both families. Friends of the two families are also present, so that at the end of the ceremony it becomes clear that marriage among the Igbo people is not just between the bride and the bridegroom, instead, the entire communities are involved. The bond that is therefore cemented with the marriage lasts beyond the ceremony and breeds enduring goodwill between the relevant communities. The bond is summarized in the statement made during the haggling by the bride's family:

> 'We had not thought to go below thirty. But as the dog said, "If I fall down for you and you fall down for me, it is a play". Marriage should be a play and not a fight; so we are falling down again. (Achebe: 1958 (1976 Reset): 51).

And so, the two families enter into an enduring marital bond which follows strict Igbo traditional conventions. This type of marriage is still common among many ethnic groups in West Africa.

The full details of the marital ceremony and the pomp and pageantry involved are provided in Chapter Twelve (77–83). The intricacies make it abundantly clear that marriage is not a brief, one day affair, but an enduring ritual which binds people, families and communities, while turning strangers into not only friends, but kinsmen and kinswomen.

The death of the Umuofia elder, Ezeudu (Chapter Thirteen) reveals to readers of *Things Fall Apart*, the intricacies involved in the interment of distinguished Igbo elders:

> Ezeudu was a great man and so all the clan was at his funeral. The ancient drums of death beat, guns and cannon were fired, and men dashed about in frenzy, cutting down every tree or animal they saw, jumping over walls and dancing on the roof. It was a warrior's funeral, and from morning till night warriors came and went in their age groups. They all wore smoked raffia skirts and their bodies were painted with chalk and charcoal. Now and again an ancestral spirit or *Egwugwu* appeared from the underworld, speaking in a tremulous, unearthly voice and completely covered in raffia. (Achebe: 1958 (1976 Reset): 84–85).

Like other ethnic groups in sub-Saharan-Africa, the belief in reincarnation, the ancestral spirits and life as a continuous process (even after death) prevails. The author states clearly that:

> The land of the living was not far removed from the domain of the ancestors. There was coming and going between them, especially at festivals and also when an old man died, because an old man was very close to the ancestors. A man's life from birth to death was a series of transition rites which brought him nearer and nearer to his ancestors. (Achebe: 1958 (1976 Reset): 86).

Indeed, this belief summarizes the African cosmology especially with regard to religion. And, in any case, every aspect of the African worldview tends to embrace aspects of religious worship and veneration. Every activity seems to be carried out with the prevailing realization that the spiritual realm is actively present and determines the course of events. Without the tacit approval of the ancestral/spirit world of the departed ancestors and the gods, nothing gets done in the human realm. Ezeudu's funeral therefore vividly mirrors the general order of such ceremonies in most Saharan African societies. The parallel is so great with the Ejagham funeral rites that one wonders after a reading of Achebe's text if, after all, the Ejagham and other neighboring ethnic groups are really different from the Igbo and whether they have a common origin or ancestry. The parallel is further strengthened with the eulogy to the late elder, Ezeulu, which is made by a revered ancestral spirit who is "one handed" and "came, carrying a basket full of water." Such eulogies are completely similar to what obtains among ethnic groups that are ancillary to Igbo:

> 'Ezeudu!' he called in his guttural voice. 'If you had been poor in your last life, I would have asked you to be rich when you come again. But you were rich. If you had been a coward, I would have asked you to bring courage. But you wee a fearless warrior. If you had died young, I would have asked you to get life. But you lived long. So I shall ask you to come again the way you came before. If your death was the death of nature, go in peace. But if a man caused it, do not allow him a moment's rest'. (Achebe: 1958 (1976 Reset): 86).

Generally therefore, *Things Fall Apart* is an African novel because it aptly mirrors African sensibilities, culture and world view, while specifically relying on Igbo cosmology to attain its objectives. It does this by exploring core aspects of the Igbo tradition and customs at the threshold of the European colonization or intervention in the internal affairs of the Igbo. The experiences and response of the Igbo bear very close resemblance to those of other traditional societies in Africa, especially in the Southern part of Nigeria. The Ejagham of Eastern Nigeria are mentioned in passing to provide one such instance. A more detailed analysis showing the vast similarities between the two cultural groups would have necessitated an anthropological or sociological study which the literary import of this exercise does not make room for.

Works Cited

Primary

Achebe, Chinua. *Things Fall Apart.* London: Heinemann Educational Books Ltd., 1958 (1976 Reset).

Secondary

Achebe, Chinua. *Arrow of God.* New York: Doubleday and company, 1969.

———. *Morning Yet on Creation Day.* London: Heinemann, 1975.

Beier, Ulli. *Python: Igbo Poetry.* Port Moresby: Papua Pocket Poets, 1967.

Bill, Ashcroft, and others. *The Empire Writes Book: Theory and Practice in Post Colonial Literarure.* London: Routledge, 1989.

Chinweizu. The West and the Rest of the Us. New York, Random House, 1975.

Chinweizu & others. Toward The *Decolonization of African Literature, Vol.* 1: African Fiction and Poetry and their critics. Enugu: Fourth Dimension Publishers, 1980.

Diop, Cheikh Anta. *The African Origin of Civilization.* Westport, Ct.: Lawerence Hill & Company, 1974.

———. *The Cultural Unity of Black Africa.* Chicago: Third World Press, 1978.

Echeruo, Michael. *Mortality.* London: Longmans, 1968.

Finnegan, Ruth. *Oral Literature in Africa.* Nairobi: Oxford University Press, 1970.

Jahn, Jahnheinz. *A History of Neo African Literature.* London: Oxford University Press, 1968.

King, Bruce, *Introuduction to Nigerian Literature.* New York: Africana Publishers Corporation, 1972.

Nnolim, Charles E. "Achebe's *Things Fall Apart*: An Igbo National Epic." Black Academy Review 2, 1 & 2: 55–60, 1971.

———. Saros International Publishers, 1992. *Approaches to the African Novel: Essay in Analysis.* London:

Nwoga, Donatus Ibe, ed. *Literature and Modern West African Culture.* Benin City: Ethiope Publishing Company, 1978.

Palmer, Eustace. *An Introuduction to the African Novel.* New York: Africana Publishing Co., 1972.

Povey, John. "The Novels of Chinua Achebe," *Introduction to Nigerian Literature*, ed. Bruce King, 97–112. New York: Africana Publishing Co., 1972.

Roscoe, Adrian A. *Mother is Gold: A study in West African Literature*. Cambridge University Press, 1971.

Chapter 3

Search for Lost Identity in Achebe's *Things Fall Apart*

Ifeoma Onyemelukwe

Introduction

EVEN WITH A CURSORY reading of *Things Fall Apart*, (TFA), it does not fail to strike the reader that Okonkwo, the central character of this anti-colonial novel published in 1958 as Achebe's literary debut yet remaining to date a masterpiece and finest of all his novels (significantly *No Longer at Ease*, *Arrow of God*, *A Man of the People* and *Anthills of the Savannah*, and one of the finest novels from Anglophone and Francophone Africa), dies in the frantic search for his lost identity. Our interest in this work lies in tracing Okonkwo's identity crisis/formation, loss of this hard earned identity and ruthless determination to recover it.

The Concept of Identity

Chambers 21st Century Dictionary defines identity as the state or quality of being a specified person or thing; who or what a person or thing is. In other words, it is the sense of knowing who the individual is. In the words of Rapport (1972: 308) "it is the awareness of the self as distinct from the other, of a continuing experiencing even though changing 'I'...."

Personality psychologists (Sigmund Freud, Erikson) have shown that as the individual develops or passes through the various stages of psychosexual/psychosocial development, the process of identity formation goes on but is most prominent during the period of adolescence. Simply put, this refers to the individual's struggles to define himself, to discover himself, to understand himself, to know himself. The person tries to grapple with such questions as: Who am I? What am I? How do people see me? How do I see myself? What do I want to become? How can I connect myself to explorations with the opportunities and demands of society? The way parents see him or want him to be may differ from the way peers see him or want him to be. Crises set in. These are known as identity crises.

It has been shown that identity crises are most severe in adolescent period otherwise known as the period of "storm and stress" (Hall, 1904), a time of confusion and despair, conflict with parents, anxiety about scholastic achievement and pressures for peer recognition. (McFarlane, 1964). The adolescent period is also characterized with the resolution of identity crises, with subsequent emergence of the person's personal identity. (Erikson, 1968; Achor and Onyemelukwe, 1992).

Identity crisis, as aptly observed by Achor and Onyemelukwe, has implication for the personality the individual turns out to be as a young adult and also for coping with problems of adolescents and youth in the micro-society (family) as well as the macro-society. The ideas the individual has about himself, his family, friends and society in adolescence tend to influence his self-concept and shape his identity. A time comes when he decides amidst the various perceptions of him that "This is what I want to be." His identity crisis is resolved and he comes up with his own identity. In other words his identity is formed.

Proper management of the adolescent helps to resolve his identity crisis fairly well. If poorly resolved, the individual may develop a low self-concept and low self-esteem. Proper management of the adolescent augurs well for healthy adjustment of the individual in society. If not properly managed, the individual may end up as a maladjusted person; a delinquent or even a social misfit. Medza and Zambo in Mongo Beti's *Mission Terminée* who end up in "*une vie d' errance*" (a life of wandering), Toundi in Oyono's *Une vie de boy* who flees home, are they not maladjusted individuals? What of Samba Diallo of Cheik Hamido Kane's *L' aventure ambiguä*, Ahouna of Olympe Bhêly-Quénum's *Un piège sans fin*, Magamou Seck of Malick Fall's *La plaie*, lyoni in François Evembé's *Sur la terre en passant*? What of Obi Okonkwo in Achebe's *No Longer at Ease*, Okolo in Gabriel Okara's *The Voice* and Clarence in Camara Laye's *Radiance of the King*? Are all these protagonists not maladjusted individuals who, conditioned by internal values, have become introverted? Are these not examples of the man of the two worlds bogey that characterizes several African literary works? These are individuals caught between two worlds, two civilizations (Western and traditional African), two value systems. Failing to comprehend the 'absurd' world around them, they become interiorized and are plunged into a perpetual search; a search for authentic values in an inauthentic and depraved world, which Anozie calls "la quête longue et labyrinthique".

The critic, Njoku (1994: 177) while analyzing the growth of the female characters in Zaynab Alkali's novels Libira or Li for short, and Faku in *The Stillborn*, Nana Ai, Laila and Hajjo in *The Virtuous Woman*, the two novels set in muslim patriarchal society, observes that the muslim society in Northern Nigeria tries to stifle the growth of personal identity in the female by a process of socialization which restricts personal awareness and freedom.

She notes that the growth of Nigerian womanhood is hampered because the development of personal identity which is central in the development of adult personality is repressed by the culture and tradition. Some African cultures are generally repressive and adversely affect identity formation of both males and females. However, the females are more affected as Njoku illustrates in her analysis of female characters in Alkali's novels.

The pertinent question is: Does the Igbo culture help in shaping Okonkwo's identity and personality? This brings us to the next part of this essay.

Okonkwo's Identity Crisis / Formation

> Okonkwo was well known throughout the nine villages and even beyond. His fame rested on *solid personal achievements*. As a young man of eighteen he had brought honour to his village by throwing the cat. Amalinze was the great wrestler who for seven years was unbeaten ... He was called the Cat ... It was this man that Okonkwo threw in a fight which ... was one of the fiercest ... (Achebe, 1958: 3) (emphasis added).

This passage draws the reader's attention to the character, Okonkwo, who has succeeded in having his identity formed. Who is Okonkwo? or What is Okonkwo? Okonkwo, as can be deduced from the cited passage, is the man who was able to resolve his identity crisis in late adolescence. At age 18 he had developed self-confidence, a high self-concept, self-esteem and had high achievement motivation as typical of the average Igbo man. The consequence of this is his reverberating achievement and celebrity. "Okonkwo was well known throughout the nine villages and even beyond." The narrator adds: "His fame had grown like a bush-fire in the harmattan." This figure of speech shows the great wrestler, warrior and farmer to have attained a pedestal where he is enjoying more and more successes.

It should be noted that the Okonkwo being x-rayed in this passage has grown. He is about thirty-eight years old; and grows even the more in the novel. He is now a mature adult member of a male hegemonious society which upholds cultural practices that predispose the woman to subjugation and oppression and stifle her development and progress in society somewhat like Alkali's mimetic world in *The Stillborn* and *The Virtuous Woman*. He is married to three wives and has many children; polygamy and large unit being also indices of greatness in this culture. *Things Fall Apart* depicts very successful Okonkwo as showing no empathy or sympathy to less fortunate men like his father, Unoka. Such individuals, to his mind, are simply *agbala* (Igbo word for woman) or she-men.

It is not surprising that Okonkwo stands out in the novel as a macho man with a great deal of self-esteem and self-confidence.

The cap fits Okonkwo in many instances in the given description. True, TFA portrays him as one who is neither patient nor tolerant. As the narrator puts it:

> He (Okonkwo) had no patience with unsuccessful men. He had had no patience with his father (3).

Okonkwo's example tallies with what Mbefo (1996) had observed about the Igbo man:

> The Igbo man does not expect to be second or third. Only the first is enough to support his ego....
>
> The Igbo selfhood is geared towards being the master of his chosen activity or profession. This manifests in the quest for mastery of one's trade, occupation or talent. Thus a hunter is called '*dinta*' i.e. master of hunting, wine tapper '*diochi*' meaning master of tapping; '*dimgba*' meaning master of wrestling and '*dike*' a strong fellow (Mbefo, 1996).

Okonkwo is shown in TFA to be an excellent warrior, wrestler and farmer. Where others may have failed, he succeeds. Take, for example, he throws Amalinze, the *Cat* who nobody could defeat in a fight for seven good years. Further, he excels as a farmer starting with share-cropping, a thing many youths of his time cannot cope with. The third person narrator of TFA has rightly noted that he, Okonkwo "was clearly cut out for great things" (6).

Essentially, Okonkwo worked hard to attain that great height in society. "His fame rested on solid personal achievements" (3). It was at the age of eighteen that he threw Amalinze, The Cat. In the words of the narrator:

> He (Okonkwo) was still young but he had won fame as the *greatest wrestler* in the nine villages. He was *a wealthy farmer* and had two barns full of yams and *had just married his third wife*. To crown it all, he had taken two titles and had shown *incredible prowess in two inter-tribal wars* (6); (emphasis mine).

This passage, without doubt, arms the reader with a catalogue of Okonkwo's marks of greatness. The passage, further, throws into relief the fact that he started climbing the ladder of greatness even as a teenager. That, of course, was incumbent on his successful resolution of his identity crisis and subsequent formation of his identity.

That Okonkwo had serious identity crisis is patent in TFA; what with a father who is slothful, frivolous, given to drinking and merriment, improvident and poor. This lily-livered father who can hardly provide for his family fills Okonkwo with disdain.

Crises and conflict set in. Okonkwo's identity crisis emanates probably from internal contradictions. What he would want to be is at variance with what his father is. The narrator tells us that "even as a little boy" Okonkwo "had resented his father's failure and weakness" and had suffered from people making a mockery of his father, who owes shamelessly and dies without taking even a title. In Igbo culture a man without title is regarded as a woman and treated so. One can imagine Okonkwo's inferiority complex as a child and the shame he had had to put up with. Cognizant of the fact that unlike most of his peers he inherited nothing from his "loafer" of a father he realizes that he has got to work extra hard to make it in life. And he desires to be a success not a failure like his father. Okonkwo ends up being the polar opposite of his father, Unoka. The choice is his. He rejects the father's image and settles for who he wants to be: The exact opposite of Unoka. He becomes intrinsically motivated, his resentment for his *agbala* of a father being the propelling force. Diligent, determined, dedicated with a sense of direction, Okonkwo becomes famous through 'solid personal achievements.' Okonkwo finally resolves his identity crisis fairly well, evolves his personal identity and emerges as one of the most outstanding achievers of his time in Umuofia and its environs.

That notwithstanding, the author of *TFA* draws the reader's attention to the adverse impact of identity crisis on Okonkwo's personality development. Okonkwo is transformed into a monomaniac of male dominance. He develops a split personality: the fearless warrior who has brought home human skull, is dominated by fear, "fear of failure and of weakness," (9), fear of taking after his father. This psychological phobia leads him to hate everything that his father, Unoka had loved" (10), such as gentleness and idleness. If Okonkwo treats his wives and children tyrannically like Medza's father in Beti's *Mission Terminée*, it is linked to this psychological phobia. The same explanation goes for his inclination to wife-battery and other excesses of his in the novel, like killing Ikemefuna who called him "father" or firing a shot at Ekwefi, his beloved second wife. Palmer (54) puts it succinctly: "this fear which dominates all his actions contributes to his subsequent catastrophe."

It would seem that Chinua Achebe, apart from his anti-colonial combat which constitutes the central theme of the novel, launches a subtle attack on unhealthy child raising practices: extreme authoritarianism and extreme permissiveness. His message in *TFA*, among others, appears to be that excessively harsh parents (like Okonkwo) just like excessively permissive or weak parents (like Unoka) cause problems for their children with resolution of identity crisis. Such children may end up maladjusted in one way or the other. This is the lot of Okonkwo's first son. Nwoye who flees home like Medza in Beti's *Mission Terminée* and Toundi in Oyono's *Une vie de boy*. Medza's father is dubbed "papa omnipotent" ("omnipotent father") (Beti, 1957: 94), "un tyran au foyer" ("a tyrant in the home") (Beti, 1957: 230). Okonkwo, for his part, "ruled his household with a heavy hand." (9).

Okonkwo's monomania of male dominance which bears from his deep-rooted resentment for his effeminate father lends him easily to wife subjugation and wife-battery, these reprehensible practices which Achebe holds up in derision. By juxtaposing Okonkwo's relationship with his wives, characterized by male chauvinism and female subjugation with Ndulu-Ozoemena husband-wife rapport characterized by mutual love and respect, Achebe appears to use the technique of contrast to expose and denounce wife-battery, wife ill treatment, female subjugation and oppression. It does not fail to strike us that Achebe deliberately blows out of proportion Okonkwo's show of masculinity to better ridicule this cultural trait that tends to relegate the woman to inferior position where she can only play the second fiddle.

It is necessary to examine at this juncture some factors that enabled Okonkwo to resolve his identity crisis. These are:

Recognition of Personal Identity and Social Mobility / Achievement

In Okonkwo's society, a man was judged according to his worth and not according to the worth of his father." (*TFA* 6) This comment by the narrator shows that Okonkwo's people, by their culture, recognize personal identity and personal achievement. In other words, what matters to the community is who you are not who your father is; what you are not what your father is. It is a society that makes allowance for social mobility unlike the caste system. Thus, even if an individual is born of wretched parents, he may through dint of hard work become one of the rich, famous and respected people in the land. This is true of Igbo culture. The realization of this truth is probably one of the factors that ginger Okonkwo to decide positively to succeed where the father had failed. Okonkwo rises sharply from "great poverty and misfortune to be one of the lords of the clan". Achebe buttresses the fact of personal achievement being revered in Igbo culture with the use of an apt proverb as typical of his style in *TFA* and other works. Thus, with reference to Okonkwo, the narrator says that "if a child washed his hands he could eat with kings"; Okonkwo had clearly washed his hands and so he ate with kings and elders (6).

Recognition of Patriotism / Heroism by the Community

Patriotism which means the love of one's country or community demands the exhibition of acts of heroism or outstanding acts or fits for the progress of the society. Okonkwo's is a community that recognizes and rewards acts of patriotism/heroism. Thus the community plays a vital role in the life of the Igbo person. According to Onyenemegan (1985) an Igbo man views his belonging to a community with a spirit of cooperation and responsibility. For Mbiti (1969) an Igbo man is more likely to say: "I am because we are and since we are, therefore I am." Knowing fully well that in displaying valour for his community, an individual gets recognition from the community, Okonkwo is motivated to perform exploits for the good of the community to which he belongs. Thus at 18 years, he is able to do his community proud by throwing the Cat. In Umuofia's latest war he was the first to bring home a human head. The great warrior, relevant for social security of the whole community, had helped his community to win two inter-tribal wars, and had brought home 5 human heads, the highest record in his society. It is not surprising that even as a young man Okonkwo "was already one of the greatest men of his time" (6). Achebe once again uses an apt proverb to communicate this truth:

> When a man says yes his *chi* says yes also. Okonkwo said yes very strongly; so his chi agreed. And not only his *chi* but his clan too… (19).

Thus as the individual renders useful service to the community, the community, in turn, helps to build up the individual through recognition of his positive contributions to the community. The awareness of this cultural trend seems to have helped Okonkwo to resolve his identity crisis and come up with his personal identity which in turn fuels his outstanding achievements in life.

Okonkwo and Loss of His Identity

> His (Okonkwo's) life had been ruled by a great passion to become one of the lords of the clan. That had been his life-spring. And he had all but achieved it. Then everything had been broken. He had been cast out of his clan like a fish on a dry sandy beach, panting. Clearly his personal god or *chi* was not made for great things. A man could not rise beyond the destiny of his *chi*.... Here was a man whose chi said nay despite his affirmation (92).

The last sentence is quite paradoxical. The same Okonkwo portrayed in the first part of the novel as saying "yes and his personal god agreeing is now portrayed as saying "yes and his *chi* saying 'no'. The Igbo proverb "*Onye kwe chi ya ekwe*" (When a man says 'yes' his *chi* says 'yes' also) is thus depicted with a measure of relativity. In other words, it holds true sometimes while at other times it does not. The second part of *TFA* describes Okonkwo's tragedy and great fall from grace to grass. During Ezeudu's funeral, Okonkwo inadvertently kills a clansman, one of Ezeudu's sons. This fratricide because it is accidental, is treated as a female crime (that is, female *ochu*) and attracts for the culprit compulsory banishment for seven years as well as destruction of his house and all his property by way of cleansing or purging the land which has been polluted with the blood of a clansman. Okonkwo, thus goes on self-exile to Mbanta, his mother's village with his wives and children; taking along some of his valuable belongings. At dawn, his compound is besieged by a large crowd of men from Ezeudu's quarters who set his house on fire, destroy his red walls, kill his animals and erase his barn. How are the mighty fallen! Overnight, great Okonkwo, the great warrior, the great farmer, the great wrestler, one of the most outstanding achievers of his time, most respected and revered, loses all he has laboured to achieve just in the twinkle of an eye. His hope of remaining "one of the lords of the clan," is shattered.

His flight to Mbanta implies starting life afresh, from the scratch. It means loss of self-esteem, peace, happiness. His ego is obviously punctured. His fame transforms into shame. His identity crumbles. Crises and conflict set in again. Okonkwo's tragic fall seems to attract the author's sympathy as expressed through the mouth of Okonkwo's intimate friend, Obierika, who though he joins in exacting punishment on Okonkwo, mourns the latter's calamity. He ruminates:

> Why should a man suffer so grievously for an offence he had committed inadvertently? (87)

This question only leads Obierika into a state of autocriticism: "What crime did his wife's twin children whom he had killed, commit?" he soberly reflects. Apparently, Achebe is using Obierika to condemn some of the horrible Igbo cultural practices like killing of twins and excessively harsh punishment meted out to one guilty of manslaughter. In civilized communities as it is in even present day Igbo society, manslaughter can only fetch the offender some years of imprisonment. It does not warrant the crude law of utter demolition of the man's property.

Disgraced, depersonalized, Okonkwo is thrust into a state of despair, melancholy and depression as quickly observed by his maternal uncle, Uchendu (92). Uchendu's good counsel to him may well have given him new strength, courage and determination to start all over again. As the narrator notes:

> Okonkwo... knew that he had lost his place among the nine masked spirits (Egwugwu cult) who administered justice in the clan. He had lost the chance to lead his warlike clan against the new religion.... Which had gained ground. He had lost the years in which he might have taken the highest title in the clan. But some of these losses are not irreparable. He was determined that his return would be marked by his people. He would return with a flourish, and regain the seven wasted years (121).

Therefore, Okonkwo goes determinedly in search of his lost identity.

Okonkwo in Search of His Lost Identity

The last third of *Things Fall Apart* offers the reader a glimpse of the frantic efforts made by Okonkwo to regain his lost identity. He is determined to return to Umuofia in a big way and restore all that is lost in a tremendous way. The narrator states that, "even in his first year in exile he had begun to plan for his return." His restoration plan includes: rebuilding his compound on a more magnificent scale, building a bigger barn, marrying two more wives and building huts for them, initiating his sons into the *Ozo* society, a thing done only by men who are really great in the clan; and taking the highest title in the land following his eventual position as the highly esteemed.

To concretize his dream plan, Okonkwo implores his two big daughters, Ezinma and Obiageli not to marry in Mbanta but to wait and marry from among the prosperous men of Umuofia on return home. This advice draws less from his interest in his daughters' welfare than from his materialistic calculation to recover his social prestige,self-esteem and identity especially as he hopes too to increase substantially his string of wives. Evidently, the Igbo man marries from among the daughters of the land for social and political influence, for procurement of alliances, to secure his social position/security; to boost his social prestige.

Balandier (120–121) has rightly observed that for the traditional Bantu of which the Igbo man is one, the possession of multiple wives is the major symbol of affluence and the daughters are necessary for the procurement of social alliances.

In spite of these laudable plans, Okonkwo's return to Umuofia is not memorable. Umuofia does not "appear to have taken any special notice of the warrior's return" (129). This is partly because the clan had undergone profound changes during his period of exile. Moreover, with colonial incursion, missionary activities (establishment of schools and churches and the missionary's proselytism of the natives of Umuofia and its environs), the town of Umuofia is turned into what Okonkwo perceives as "female town". He mourns also for the warlike Umuofia men who have become, to his mind, soft as women. Umuofia, which prior to colonial presence is described as the town of warlike men, now ranks, in Okonkwo's eye, with Abame and Aninta (where titled men climb trees and pound *foofoo* for their wives) and Mbanta, as women's towns. Okonkwo, the central character of *TFA*, who is manhood personified, cannot stand this drastic change.

Okonkwo incites his clansmen to collective revolt and violence involving the destruction of the church short of killing Rev. James Smith, the missionary who believes in clear-cut positions unlike his predecessor, Mr. Brown, whose policy was that of accommodation and compromise with the natives. At the end of the collective action Okonkwo and five others are arrested and hurled into detention where they are beaten and molested, starved, but released on payment of a fine of 250 bags of cowries. This is another thwarted attempt to regain his lost identity.

Okonkwo spoils for vengeance; for a war to fight the whiteman and his cohorts. He has reminiscences of his past military conquests in those inter-tribal wars. But can he or his clan contend with the colonizers' naked power? Okika has hardly started his oration, a sensitization campaign to call Umuofians to action to stop colonial incursion, when the gathering was ordered by the head messenger to bring the meeting to a stop. Four other messengers came along with him. Okonkwo cuts off the head messenger's head. There is chaos, and the crowd, with minimal cohesion, disintegrates leaving Okonkwo isolated. "Why did he do it?" he heard voices asking. Okonkwo thus defeated, hangs himself behind his compound. What a tragic end! The tragic hero's drama is embedded in the incisive remark of Obierika to the District Commissioner:

> That man (Okonkwo) was one of the greatest men in Umuofia. You drove him to kill himself; and now he will be buried like a dog (147).

True, Okonkwo will be buried like a dog because for *Ndigbo*, suicide is an abomination and one who commits suicide is not fit to be buried by his clansmen but only by strangers.

Is Obierika correct to impute Okonkwo's tragic end to the colonizers? Is his comment endorsed by Achebe? It would seem that the author of TFA shares Obierika's view, judging from the determinant "unnecessarily" that follows the messenger's 'Shut up!' The author-narrator implies that it was pointless trying to silence Obierika given perhaps, that his comment, an oblique attack on the ills of colonialism, makes a lot of sense. Achebe, in this sense, sympathizes with Okonkwo. Does this mean that Achebe is against change in society? Is he conservative? Probably not. As a creative artist, he seems to depict the social reality of the time: collapse of an old order as a result of an invasion by a dominating alien system. There is no denying the fact that Achebe is condemning the negative effects of colonialism, for example, compounding the hero's psychological phobia, fear of failure and weakness, of not being in control of the situation, of having his clansmen turned into a bunch of women, of losing the position where he is seen to dominate all others. It is this accelerated fear that drives him to kill the Head Court Messenger and commit suicide. Achebe, the starry-eyed critic condemns in TFA his people's obnoxious cultural practices which militate against development and progress of man in society, for example, killing of twins, superstitious beliefs, wife-battery, male dominance, women subjugation and oppression. This shows Achebe as a progressive and a reformer.

We feel that Okonkwo is partially responsible for his tragic end. Certain psychological character traits of his, impulsiveness, extreme extroversion, lead him to some of his excesses apart from the fear of being perceived as weak. Furthermore, Okonkwo's tragic fall from grace to grass finds partial explanation in his ruthless resistance to change; an act that is clearly dissonant with the natural inclination of *Ndi Igbo*.

Njaka (1974) notes that the evidences of Igbo receptivity to change abound in Igbo folk stories, plays, novels, proverbs and dances. The convenient marriage of the Igbo traditional culture to change has been said to be a source of strength to *Ndigbo* because they are ready for change and maneuverability. *Ndigbo* are essentially tolerant and accommodating. These attributes make them easily receptive to change (e. g. their polyglotism), which is one of their methods of regional and global integration.

Finally, it is noteworthy that Okonkwo's tragic end emanates, to a certain extent, from his unwavering determination to regain his self-esteem and identity, this identity which has suffered reverses because of the Igbo philosophy and polity of male hegemony that follows the hierarchical order: Family, Umunna (commune), class, village, community. The Igbo polity is quite democratic but suffocating. Unlike what obtains in civilized individualistic societies, the Igbo man feels he exists because he belongs to the family, the *umunna*, the clan, etc. In other words, he thinks always in terms of collective anonymity, group identity with its rigid purifying or cleansing system when *ani* (the land) for example is desecrated in one way or another. Does Okonkwo really have to lose his hard earned identity to an inadvertent fratricide? This is only an equivalent of manslaughter. In civilized communities this will only fetch the individual some fine or a short-term imprisonment. Wali (32) while finding explanation to the loneliness and frustration of the central characters in Laye's *The Radiance of the King*, Achebe's *No Longer at Ease* and Okara's *The Voice* (Clarence, Obi Okonkwo, and Okolo respectively) makes this assertion:

> In a real sense, the chief obstruction to the three characters is the community with its tyranny and incomprehensibility; the community where the individual does not exist in his own right but is compelled to lose his identity for the sake of social cohesion.

Although Okonkwo in TFA differs remarkably from the three characters referred to in this affirmation, in the sense that the former is extroverted and is a character that is fully developed, that lives before us as opposed to the later ones who are introverted or what Anozie calls intro-active heroes, Wali's comment applies to him. The same Okonkwo who is compelled to lose his identity in the interest of social cohesion fails to elicit the cooperation of his clansmen when he tries to restore his identity and group identity by cutting colonial authorities to size, which he considers a heroic act. Sadly enough, Okonkwo's move meets with a shattered hope of group solidarity and social cohesion which he enjoyed at the point he was resolving his identity crisis what with those inter-tribal wars/inter-clanic wrestling contests which created opportunities for individual and collective exploits/achievements/successes. This is so because at the point in question, things have greatly fallen apart at both individual and collective levels.

Okonkwo's Doomed Illusion: Implication for *Ndigbo*

The unraveling of the plot of TFA appears to be pessimistic. Since Okonkwo, the symbol *par excellence* of the Igbo man dies in an attempt to recover his lost identity, does it imply that the attempt by *Ndigbo* to recover their lost identity is more or less suicidal? The Igbo man lost his hard earned identity at the end of the Nigerian Civil War (1970), a war that lasted for 3 years (1967–1970) and decimated badly the population of *Ndigbo*. Completely disarmed, dislocated, destabilized, depersonalized, dehumanized, shunned, abandoned, relegated, excluded, frozen out like banished Okonkwo after committing a fractricide, the Igbo man starts life afresh, from the scratch at the end of the war when every adult Igbo person, no matter how fat his monetary asset is made to receive only £20 (Twenty pounds sterling) in exchange. He has ever since then been making frantic efforts to restore his lost identity and esteem. As Achebe (157) opines:

> The worst thing that can happen to any people is the loss of their dignity and self-respect.

He adds that:

> The writer's duty is to help them regain it by showing them in human terms what happened to them, what they lost... the novelist's duty is... To explore in depth the human condition.

In so doing, Achebe is, characteristically, playing out the role of the African writer, which to his mind is that of a teacher.

It is important to remark that Okonkwo's tragedy somewhat transcends that of *Ndigbo* to represent also that of colonized Africans and even subjugated Blacks elsewhere. Achebe appears to say in TFA that many African peoples had lost their dignity in the colonial era just like Okonkwo and they must try to regain it. Specifically, *Ndigbo* lost their identity, and are desperately searching for it to regain it. Thus, the crucial issue in TFA is not just as Achebe (158) puts it "a spiritual search for one's roots," but a frantic search to regain one's lost identity. The latter, of course, subsumes the former.

Works Cited

Achebe, Chinua. *Things Fall Apart*. London: Heinemann. Transl. *Lemonde s' effondre*. 1958.

Achebe, Chinua. "The Role of the Writer in a new Nation," *Nigeria Magazine*, No. 81, June, 1964.

Cf. i. Achebe, Chinua, "The Novelist as Teacher," in Press, John (Ed.) *Commonwealth Literature*. London: Heinemann, 1965.

ii. Asein, Samuel. "Literature as History: Crisis, Violence and Strategies for Commitment in Nigerian Writing," in Nwoga, Donatus (Ed.) *Literature and modern West African Culture*. Benin: Ethiope Publishing Co, 1978.

Achor, P.E. and Onyemelukwe, I.M. "Coping with Adolescent Problems in our changing Society" A paper presented at the 8th National Conference of the National Association of Educational Psychologists at Alvan Ikoku College of Education, Owerri, 25th–28th March, 1992.

Anozie, Sunday. *Sociologie du Roman Africain*. Paris: Aubier-Montaigne, 1970.

Balandier, George. *Sociologie actuelle de l'Afrique noire: dynamique sociale en Afrique Centrale. Paris: Presses universitaire de France,* 1955.

Beti, Mongo. *Mission Terminée*. Paris: Eds. Buchet/chastel, 1957.

Erikson, E.H. *Identity: Youth and Crisis.* New York: Macmillan Publishing. Coy, 1968.

Hall, G.S. *Adolescence*. New York: Appleton, 1904.

Mbefo, L.N. *Coping with Nigeria's twofold Heritage*. Onitsha: Spiritan Publication, 1996.

McFarlane, J.W. "Perspectives on Personality Consistency and Exchange from Guidance Study." *Vita Human*, 7, 1964: 115–126.

Njaka, E.N. *Igbo Political Culture*. Evanston: North Western Univ. Press, 1974.

Njoku, Teresa. "Personal Identity and the Growth of the Nigerian Woman in Zaynab Alkali's *The Stillborn* and *The Virtuous Woman*," in Chukwuma, Helen (Ed.) *Feminism in African Literature*. Enugu: New Generation Ventures Ltd, 1994.

Onyenemegan, J.O. *Pastoral Care of the Sick in Igbo Community in Nigeria*. Unpublished Doctoral Thesis, Rome, 1985.

Palmer, Eustace. *An Introduction to the African Novel*. London: Heinemann, 1972.

Rapport, Leon. *Personality Development: The Chronology of* Experience. Glenview, Illinois: Scott Foresman & Co, 1972.

Wali, Obiajunwa. "The Individual and the Novel in Africa," *Transition* No. 18, 1965.

Chapter 4

Masculinity, Power and Language in Chinua Achebe's *Things Fall Apart*:

Ada Uzoamaka Azodo

> To recognize diversity in masculinities is not enough. We must also recognize the relations between the different kinds of masculinity: relations of alliance, dominance and subordination. These relationships are constructed through practices that exclude and include, that intimidate, exploit, and so on. There is gender politics within masculinity" (R.W. Cornell. *Masculinities*. Oxford: Polity Press, 1995, 32).

In issues of gender and language, discussions usually center around theories of dominance and difference, masculinity and language, power and identity, notions of competition and cooperation, and the fluidity of masculine subjectivity. It is from these points of view that Johnson and Meinhoff, have attempted to theorize masculinity and language (1997). According to the two scholars, most of feminist criticism and critical theory, and studies in women's subjectivity and identity, engage in stereotyping of women and in lumping all men into a male-as-one, whereas they should be problematizing masculinity. Men are seen as the norm, at once the neutral and in the center. What is hardly ever taken note of is the variety of male identities, notwithstanding the reality that power is usually cited as the most important factor used by men to construct their own identities as the "ungendered representatives of humanity" (1997, 12). Johnson and Meinhoff have also raised the need to discuss masculinity in feminist studies, seen that "excessive preoccupation with male/female difference always has its root in essentialist notions of gender." Before Johnson and Meinhoff, Toril Moi and Chris Weedo had also indicated the same (12–15).

Comparing male and female speech patterns, Anthony Easthope states that male speech is seen as assertive whereas women's speech is seen as hesitant and indirect. We argue that it is merely trivializing issues if gender studies should always be reduced to comparing and contrasting masculinity and femininity. Gender differences, like class differences, are socially constructed and endowed with different values and qualities. Men are as prone to differences as women. Since much of gender is about power relations, there is need to challenge openly and problematize the status quo, rather than condone inequality by legitimizing the norm. Our goal, therefore, is primarily to embrace the anti-essentialist approach to masculinity by deconstructing the notion of uni-masculinity. We intend to show that male power, prestige and dominance differ according to a man's temperament, personality and uniqueness for, according to Jack Saltlel: "the starting point for understanding masculinity lies, not in its contrast with femininity, but in the asymmetric dominance and prestige which accrue to males in ... society" (1995, 119). Secondly, we intend to demonstrate how men use language, ranking in social structures, and hegemonic gatherings to entrench men as the powers of the day in their communities. According to the concept of hegemony expounded by the Italian Marxist philosopher Antonio Gramsci, a precursor of Althusser's theories on ideology, men in power do not always use direct coercion to rule. Men can use indirect coercion to exercise leadership in their groups. In Althusser's Ideological State Apparatuses, people become inadvertently conspirators in their own subordination and exploitation. Gramsci, for his part, has stressed the role of culture in contributing to how people view themselves in their communities. Even commonplace activities such as leisure, contribute to the people's sense of self and world view, unwittingly reinforcing and perpetuating the status quo. Being thus immersed in ideology in their day to day lives, people imbibe cultural practices as normal and natural (Webster, 1996, 63–64). Finally, because the construction of identity is a creative enterprise, rather than something that just happens, we mean to see how group ideology and male language forge different identities. The pertinent questions to ask are: How do men construct their identities through language? What are the different kinds of power? How do they work with men when they gather or meet in palaver groups to discuss issues?[1]

We shall adopt the investigative method for the study of four selected dialogues in Chinua Achebe's *Things Fall Apart*, in order to gain insights into how male hegemonic cults achieve, construct and prolong patriarchal traditions that ensure male superiority. In the Umuofia community of *Things Fall Apart*, Igbo men are constrained to achieve and flaunt it, in order to be seen and respected. To be able to draw upon divergent types of power, men apply different resources during discussions, including the use of irony, riddles, proverbs, sarcasm, jokes, oratory, voice and status, to mention only these few. The Umuofia community of *Things Fall Apart* being a close-knit one, each man is known along with his foibles, weaknesses and strengths, all of these attributes and qualities force the kind of personality and/or power he can muster at any gathering. When he speaks, such a man by his gestures, stance, posture and gaze is forced to live up to community expectations without appearing strange or incoherent to himself or his community.

The plan of this paper imposes the following three imperatives: theoretical exploration of the ideological framework of the study; practical discussion of particular ideologies of masculinity and power in *Things Fall Apart*; and finally, a discussion of the ideology of power among a selected number of men in the village of Umuofia. We shall conclude by pulling together salient aspects of our arguments to illustrate how men construct different types of identities and power.

* * *

Theoretically, at the forefront of studies in masculinity should be a consideration of men's speaking patterns, not only to show how they use language in oral and written texts, but also how males, *ad infinitum*, construct their subjectivity through hegemonic discourses. According to the French theorist, Michel Foucault, in *The Subject and Power* (1982), power is essentially an action which modifies another action immediately or mediately, indirectly or directly, in an unreal or real manner. People show their power when they deem it necessary to counter an action with another action. For power to be effective, it must be appropriate to the situation and the subjects so acted upon must sense it and accept it as such. To this end, illusions can have the same effect as actions which motivate the subject to counter a situation with other actions, when such a subject deems it necessary to do so to avoid some serious consequences. To the observer, certain actions might appear illogical and irrational, but that is only because the reasons behind the actions are not known or are not clear to the observer. A few examples might suffice to illustrate this point. Power show, to avoid emotion of fear or lack of self-esteem, might appear incomprehensible to the observer. Actions, to avoid being seen as weak or ineffective, could also appear illogical to the Other, though rational and logical to the subject. In the final analysis, it is the values of the community as well as their perception of power which are valid in determining what constitute serious consequences when certain actions are not taken in the presence of other actions or appear illogical to the one who has not the where-with-all to make a full and informed judgment. Therefore, our present study necessarily has to delve into the values and ideologies of the Umuofia community in *Things Fall Apart*, just as should any analysis of issues of power and masculinity.

Practically speaking, people in powerful positions act many roles at different times. This is the reason why successful politicians seem to do well, for they know how to play different roles at different times, as the occasion demands. Such power is usually constructed through the medium of language because only particular ways of speaking are appropriate to particular roles, situations and circumstances, A personality might be dominated by one role, but more often than not, such a personality is made of other aspects of roles which come together on occasion to define such a personality. To determine these roles and demonstrations of power, we seek to understand how a masculine and/or powerful discourse is affected by formal or informal community structures.

In the manner that Scott Fabius Kiesling has done it (Johnson and Meinhoff, 1997, 67–79), we have identified seven processes in *Things Fall Apart* from which individual men construct their identities: physical (coercive and ability); economic; knowledge; structural; nurturing; demeanor, and ideological. The agents of the British colonial administration show *coercive physical power* when they punish and beat up the indigenous population of Umuofia at the slightest provocation or transgression of their stringent rules. Okonkwo, the protagonist of the novel, shows coercive power when he beats up his wives. On the other hand, Okonkwo shows *ability physical power*, which is a combination of skill and ability power, when he beats the community expert wrestler, Amalinze, otherwise known as the Cat, who had not been beaten for seven years. In the sports calendar of Umuofia, seven years is equivalent to a life time. With that singular feat, Okonkwo's "fame had grown like bush-fire in the harmattan" (1959: 1). He won the heart of the village beauty, Ekwefi, who would later become his second wife and the mother of his precocious daughter Ezinma. Even "the old agreed it (the fight) was one of the fiercest since the founder of their town engaged a spirit of the wild for seven days and seven nights (1). Again we see the symbolism of the number seven as equivalent to the Jewish "forty days and forty nights," which Jesus Christ spent in the wilderness being tempted by the devil. Later, we learn that the extremely male Okonkwo "ruled his household with a heavy hand" (13). Needless to add that it is the values and ideologies of the community which have given birth to the stuff of which Okonkwo is made. We also note that another wrestler Okafor, "quick as the lightning of Amadiora" threw his opponent, Ikezue, again demonstrating *ability physical power* which prompted his supporters to carry him shoulder high, bursting into this antiphonal song, constructed on the spur of the moment, and accompanied with the clapping of hands:

> Who will wrestle for our village?
> Okafor will wrestle for our village.
> Has he thrown a hundred men?
> He has thrown four hundred men?
> Has he thrown a hundred Cats?
> He has thrown four hundred Cats.

Wrestling, in the view of this community, although a source of entertainment, is a masculine competitive sport. Women are excluded from it, though they may attend as spectators and fans.

Economic power is seen in Okonkwo's enterprising spirit. He borrows a hundred seed yams, toils hard on his farm and realizes a bountiful harvest. He doubles his barn, accumulates his own seed yams and is able to return what he had borrowed as capital (18–25) Even in the year of the horrible harvest when there was not enough rain for the crops, thanks to the climatic inconsistencies of the moving Intertropical Convergence Zone,[2] Okonkwo survives by sheer will power in the face of great odds. Soon, he is able to marry three wives, a sign of affluence in his community. He supports his family and controls his women as he is expected to do, his achievements having gone into his head to a lesser or greater extent. Later he takes titles, aiming for the fourth and the ultimate, the *Ozo* title. Title taking is an expensive undertaking which is possible only with men of a certain ease of living. That Okonkwo was finally unable to attain his ambition, due to his encounters with the British administration, was a mortal blow.

Power from *knowledge* is the process of acquiring knowledge in order to perform some specific functions. For example, even lazy Unoka, Okonkwo's father, though he did not take any title, for indeed in the eyes of the community he was nothing more than an *agbala* (a woman), was an accomplished flutist who thrilled gatherings and functioned as emissary in gay and sorrowful community gatherings (6–7).

Structural power is seen in the power accorded an individual in the hierarchy of the village system. Ogbuefi Ezeudu, the oldest man in Umuofia "who had been a great and fearless warrior in his time, ... was now accorded great respect in all the clan" (57). It was on that authority and power that he advised Okonkwo, out of sight and earshot of all and sundry, not to be involved in the murder of the unfortunate youth, Ikemefuna, billed to be sacrificed to the Earth goddess, Ani, as atonement for the murder of a daughter of a contiguous clan:

> That boy calls you father. Do not bear a hand in his death....
>
> Yes, Umuofia has decided to kill him. The Oracle of the Hills and the Caves has pronounced it. They will take him outside Umuofia as is the custom, and kill him there. But I want you to have nothing to do with it. He calls you father" (57).

When Ogbuefi Ezeudu chooses to say to Okonkwo, "I *want* you to" (my emphasis) rather than "I *would like you* to" (again, my emphasis), he demonstrates his authority and power as an elder who has seen many moons and has become very wise. Words proffered from such a man should never have been disregarded by Okonkwo. And Okonkwo paid dearly for his transgression with his exile and dispossession by the community. Okonkwo's fate took a downward turn from this point on in the plot of the novel. He goes from isolation and exile to suicide and interment in the evil forest reserved only for the dregs and other never-do-wells of the village community. That his cadaver was refused an abode with Mother Earth is the highest insult that he could have been given in death. He was left to rot on the surface of the earth under the elements or to be devoured by preying beasts of the wild.

Nurturing power is of two types – feeding and teaching – and is seen as the power that an individual wields over another or a group in the process of rendering help. Such a power is demonstrated by male heads of households who could hold up family cooking as women of the household and their children waited for the common husband and father to dole out rations of yam, the king and male crop. According to Achebe's narrator during the New Yam Festival (37–45):

> Early that morning, as Okonkwo offered a sacrifice of new yam and palm oil to his ancestors he asked them to protect him, his children and their mothers in the new year (39).

A little further, Achebe explains thus the significance of the New Yam Festival, the mark of a new beginning in Igbo mythology, during which each male leader of a household officiated practically as a priest:

The New Yam Festival was thus an occasion for joy throughout Umuofia. And *every man whose arm was strong*, as the Ibo [sic] people say, was expected to invite large numbers of guests from far and wide. Okonkwo always asked his wives' relations, and since he now had three wives his guests would make a fairly big crowd (37) (my emphasis).

In another sense, a great nurturer was he who like Achebe's proverbial Igbo strong man, "set before his guests a mound of foo-foo so high that those who sat on one side could not see what was happening on the other (37). Without taking into account the obvious hyperbole or overstatement inherent in the citation, it is evident that a provider could have an enormous power on the people who look up to him.

Nurturing power in form of teaching is seen in Uchendu, Okonkwo's aged maternal uncle who, during Okonkwo's exile, tried to alleviate his depression and despair by recalling the connotation of the name, Nneka, as maternal home of refuge. This is perhaps one singular point in the novel when a man actually lauded the female element in Igbo cosmology, destroying once and for all the myth that all men hold all women in total disregard:

> It's true that a child belongs to its father. But when a father beats his child, it seeks sympathy in its mother's hut. A man belongs to his fatherland when things are good and life is sweet. But when there is sorrow and bitterness he finds refuge in his motherland.

> Your mother is there to protect you. She is buried there. And that is why we say that mother is supreme .... If you think you are the greatest sufferer in the world ask my daughter, Akueni, how many twins she has borne and thrown away. Have you not heard the song they sing when a woman dies?
>
> For whom is it well, for whom is it well?
> There is no one for whom it is well.
> I have no more to say to you (135).

Demeanor power is the power of solidarity by which one is seen as a good person with whom people would like to be associated. Such a person is a good friend with high moral values, even in the face of adversity. A classical example is Obierika whose name actually signifies his atrributes, that of "a man with a very large heart". He is one who can always be depended upon. The day that Okonkwo's compound was sacked, following a community decree at the heels of the manslaughter of a citizen at the funeral of the old man Ezeudu, it was Obierika who alone, single-handedly, even though he participated in the macabre cleansing of the land, "with no hatred in his heart for Okonkwo (125), had followed him into exile, bringing him money he had collected from the sale of his yams which he, Obierika, had saved before a mighty conflagration engulfed Okonkwo's compound, razing it to the ground. Obierika's commitment to a man he regards as a friend even though he sanctioned his punishment for his misdeeds is very touching:

> That is money from your yams .... I sold the big ones as soon as you left. Later on I sold some of the seed yams and gave out others to share croppers. I shall do that every year until you return. But I thought you would need the money now and so I brought it. Who knows what may happen tomorrow? Perhaps green men will come to our clan and shoot us (142).

It might be problematic to see *demeanor* as power, because the subject acts from emotion of love, fraternity, friendship or other, which in general are viewed as weak emotions. Yet, because Okonkwo feels happy, respectful and grateful, it can be said that Obierika exerted a *demeanor power* over Okonkwo. It is Obierika's kindness in this instance which constitutes his power over Okonkwo who, by his nature, is not known to brook any nonsense or allow himself to be put in a weak and disadvantageous position by anyone. Even Okonkwo was overwhelmed with emotion, and as he put it, even killing one of his (Okonkwo's) sons for Obierika would not have compensated adequately for the latter's kindness and generosity (142).

Lastly, the most important of powers, as we have inferred above is *ideological power*. In the words of Kiesling, it is "the power whereby ways of thinking about the world are naturalized into a community's behavior" (Johnson and Meinhoff 1997: 68). The ideological process defines and ratifies certain traits as powerful and determines which of the other processes are available, that is identifies the role in the community. Put simply and differently, the ideological process determines what is or is not powerful in all the other six processes.

Suffice it to say that even though we have separated all the seven power processes for the practical ease and purpose of analysis and explication, all are intertwined, as Foucault would say, in "a net-like organization ..., something which circulates, or rather something which only functions in the form of a chain" (1980: 98). Umuofia community's dominant ideology thus appears to be that of extreme masculine competition and systematic hierarchy, where the world is really male. Even a pubescent male adolescent appears more important than a woman old enough to be his mother. This ideology affects men's demeanor, title-taking culture, occupations (such as hunting and farming), pastime and recreational activities (such as games, palm-wine drinking, goat-meat pepper soup eating, and wrestling), roles of the male household head (who invariably officiates also as priest in the family shrine and is the chief nurturer of the family). The list could go on and on. In this community, "Age was respected... but achievement was revered. As the elders said, if a child washes his hands he could eat with kings" (12). A man has made it when he wields physical, economic, knowledge, structural, nurturing and demeanor processes of power. It is for this reason that the eventual fall of Okonkwo makes *Things Fall Apart* a classical Igbo tragedy, approaching the dimensions of classical Greek tragedy, such as *Oedipus Rex*.

The local show of power in Umuofia then is a miniature of power processes in world communities. This singular comparison makes Achebe's *Things Fall Apart* still one of the most important African literary texts in the new millennium. From our angle of vision, power is constructed, defined and ratified by Umuofia community's parameters of values, constraining them to fit themselves into not only sex roles, but indeed also into gender roles at any given time. It is either you are male or you become a female even when you have the male sex but are unable to attain the expectations of the community. Unoka, in the eyes of Umuofia, was a woman, *agbala*. (13). This notoriety would eternally plague his son, Okonkwo, driving him to vaunt his exploits by running other less achieving men down (28), and imbuing himself with such an extreme and destructive paranoia of failure, which would later become his Achille's Heel, his dark shadow, his sore-spot and the primary cause for his down-fall:

> With a father like Unoka, Okonkwo did not have the start in life which many young men had. He neither inherited a barn nor a title, nor even a young wife. But in spite of these disadvantages, he had begun even in his father's lifetime to lay the foundations of a prosperous future. It was slow and painful. But he threw himself into it like one possessed. And indeed he was possessed by the fear of his father's contemptible life and shameful death (21).

But what roles and/or identities do men fall into as they create power in encounters with other men? How do we compare Umuofia with contemporary society? We turn to ideology of power among a selected number of male characters in *Things Fall Apart* as we attempt to respond to these questions.

How does a man, following his initial socialization into the community at puberty, gain status and, in the several roles available to him, project the kind of identity expected of him?

As a full-fledged adult member of the community, a man is expected to build and own his own hut, marry a wife and have children, preferably male children. He is expected to work hard daily on his farm, without feeling fatigue or if he does, not show it. He should have several rows of yam in his barn (86). He should be seen to provide adequately for his family. Any deviation from the norm earned such a man an inability to become titled. He would not become an ancestor on his death for none of the living would like to put him up as a mentor and guide for the next generation to come. So difficult and expensive was title-taking that "only one or two in any generation ever achieved the fourth and highest" (123), the *Ozo* title. The wise old man, Ezeudu, managed to take only three of the four titles. Holders of *Ozo* title are forbidden to climb the palm tree, though they may tap it standing on the ground (169). The men institute measures geared towards conferring prestige, esteem and dignity to the title, which is signified by a thin thread worn around the ankle. At death, the high-ranking persons are "buried after dark with only a glowing brand to light the sacred ceremony." (123) Men take care of themselves in death in this way, seeing to it that death does not expose the corpse of a male to ridicule.

Moreover, real men are prosperous. This is visible in their households with a large compound secured by a high brick wall. The head of the household, the man, is everything for his family. His hut or his *obi*, as it is known in Umuofia, sits prominently close to the gate of the compound, a vantage point from which he investigates all the goings-in and comings-out of his compound. Long stalls of yam bespeak his affluence (25), even as animals (goats for the man and chickens for the woman) and coco yam of his wives attest further to his economic vigor. The man has a personal shrine where he worships his personal deity, his *Chi* (14). His relationship with his wives and children is that of fear of his wrath. Hence Okonkwo's frequent outbursts of anger are likened to the claps of thunder. A "real" man shuns the company of women. A man romantically involved with his wife is seen as weak and not at all the stuff of which real men are made (68).

The legislative arm of the village system of government is exclusively in the hands of men. Elders of the community, who are invariably titled men, make up the group, "the most powerful and most secret cult in the clan" (88). They deliver justice according to the dictates of tradition, social harmony and peace expectations of the community. It is for this reason that the *Egwugwu*, the community of masked spirits, is treated with utmost sanctity, that is as the spirits of the ancestors, when they sit in judgment over the living. They are held to be sacrosanct and women and children view them from the fringes, from the periphery, while the center is reserved and occupied by the men. Four selected dialogues involving some of the more notable characters in the novel would help us understand better the dynamics of power in the community of Umuofia.

Power Ideology 1: Unoka and Okoye:

Background information on Unoka as a youth and an old man reveals that, in contrast to his son, Okonkwo, even as a youth, Unoka was "lazy and imprudent and was quite incapable of thinking about tomorrow" (8). He spent the meager money he had drinking palm-wine and making merry. He was, therefore, a debtor who was despised by his community. His demeanor reflects his good-for-nothing life, for he wore a "haggard and mournful look," except when he was playing his flute (8). He was thus a "failure" as a grown-up. He was "poor and his wife and children had barely enough to eat." He was a "loafer" and a "coward".

The encounter between wily Unoka and dignified Okoye, who "had a large barn full of yams and had three wives" and was about to take the "idemili title," the third highest title in the land, sways the reader inadvertently to Okoye's side (10). Human beings are such that with conditioning they imbibe the values of the community and culture they live in. A well-entrenched and established citizen is certainly more beneficial to a community than a loafer and a drunkard. However, by the end of their encounter, Unoka had succeeded in turning the table against Okoye, making him out as silly and ineffective at best, at worst a Shylock, the proverbial oppressor, who has come to demand his "pound of flesh:"

> As soon as Unoka understood what his friend was driving at, he burst out laughing. He laughed loud and long and his voice rang out clear as the ogene, and tears stood in his eyes. His visitor was amazed, and sat speechless. At the end, Unoka was able to give an answer between fresh outbursts of mirth.
>
> "Look at that wall," he said .... "Look at those lines of chalk" .... Unoka had a sense of the dramatic and so he allowed a pause, in which he took a pinch of snuff and sneezed noisily, and then he continued: "Each group there represents a debt to someone, and each stroke is one hundred cowries. You see, I owe that man a thousand cowries, but he has not come to wake me up in the morning for it. I shall pay you, but not today. Our elders say that the sun will shine on those who stand before it shines on those who kneel under them. I shall pay my big debts first." And he took another pinch of snuff, as if that was paying the big debts first. Okoye rolled his goatskin and departed (11).

Unoka outwitted Okoye by exercising physical ability power through the length and timber of his outbursts of laughter, the ring of his voice, his dramatic presentation of the case and above all the clinching of the whole episode with a very apt proverb. It is important to recall that among the Igbo, proverbs are "the palm-oil with which words are eaten" (13).

Power Ideology 2: Mr. Smith and the Elders of Umuofia:

Compared to his predecessor, Mr. Brown, the new white, British administrator, Mr. Smith, is not liked, because he treats Africans and their gods with contempt. Some overzealous converts to the new Christian religion unmask the *egwugwu* in protest against African religion. When the group of six men destroy the new Christian church building in retaliation, they are invited into the presence of the District Commissioner, ostensibly for dialogue. But, the cunning administrator tactically "disarms" the community leaders before they have a chance to unsheathe their machetes, that is assuming they are even in the disposition to wage a battle against the administrator. Here is the process of his display of power. First of all, the Commissioner gets the group of six men to trust him and so put down their guard by coming in alone and sitting down. Secondly, he invites their spokesperson to tell him the group's version of what had happened between the villagers and the agents of the British colonial administration. As Ogbuefi Ekuweme the leader of the group rises to his feet to give his deposition, the Commissioner interrupts him, thus stressing that he, the Commissioner, is the power broker. He gives power of speech and takes it back at will. It turns out he wants to bring in his men at that point, again ostensibly to be privy to the dialogue, so that there would be no further mistakes. How would the group of six men have known that his real intention was to have them bound up and that he had no need to hear their side of the case? All become clear to them when they are surrounded and hand-cuffed. To hand-cuff a man is to impose one's ultimate physical power on his person. He loses all ability to use his limbs. Even running any great distance in hand-cuffs is a near impossibility. Then the administrator moves methodically to the next stage. Having emasculated the men, he is no longer pleading, or feigning to plead. He is again the agent of the Queen of England whose Britannica rules the waves:

> We shall not do you any harm ..., if only you agree to cooperate with us. We have brought a peaceful administration to you and your people so that you may be happy. If any man ill-treats you we shall come to your rescue. But we will not allow you to ill-treat others. We have a court of law where we judge cases and administer justice just as it is done in our own country under a great queen. I have brought you here because you joined together to molest others, to burn people's houses and their place of worship. That must not happen in the dominion of the queen, the most powerful ruler in the world. I have decided

> that you will pay a fine of two hundred bags of cowries. You will be released as soon as you agree to this and undertake to collect that fine from your people. What do you say to that?
>
> The six men remained sullen and silent and the Commissioner left them for a while (178).

The District Commissioner finishes his address by imposing a fine on the six men, which he expects them to collect from their people by themselves or face worse treatments. The six are undoubtedly dumb-founded at the realization, in the end, of how a single man has been able to overpower a group. His African agents, the court messengers, follow-up on their master's footsteps, confirming Grimsci and Althusser's ideologies on how members of a group embrace the tactics of the oppressor and inadvertently foster his aggression even against themselves as a distinct group. They shaved the men's hair, beat them and taunted them: "Who is the chief among you? ... We see that every pauper wears the anklet of title in Umuofia. Does it cost as much as ten cowries?" (178). The group's only recourse was silence and hunger strike. Even when they are left alone by the Commissioner's men "they found no words to speak to one another" (179), until they were tired and had to give in to save themselves further torture. When the ordeal of the six finally filtered down to their subjects, "Umuofia was like a startled animal with ears erect, sniffing the silent, ominous air and not knowing which way to run" (180). It is significant that even the community's reaction was only defensive, not aggressive. They were minded only to see "which way to run." By subduing the leaders of the group, the Commissioner has subdued the entire community of Umuofia.

The Commissioner was able to exercise power and control by using a varied strategy in dealing with his victims. He exercised coercive power and ability to use it indirectly by getting his agents to do his dirty job. He had knowledge of the gullibility of the populace and used it to his advantage. Structurally speaking, he is the "white man," the servant of the Queen of England, the Lord administrator of her overseas dominion of Africa. His predecessors sacked the whole town of Abame for killing a single white man, the narrator of *Things Fall Apart* tells us. So, even before the community had to deal with the District Commissioner, this community was already in awe of his powers. He had economic power, for his administration had made it possible for the local people to earn money for the first time in their lives from the sale of palm fruits and palm-oil. From this angle of vision, he was an employer who could hire and fire. He was therefore a nurturer. He tells the men he "shall" protect them against their oppressors." The peculiar use of "shall" is very poignant when compared to his assertion later that he "will" not tolerate any dissidence. Ideologically, the six men were already defeated before the Commissioner came into their presence after a long delay.

Power Ideology 3: Okika, the Orator

Following the detention of the group of six, Okika, one of them, seethes with anger. This opportunistic emotion transforms his words into a veritable fire of words, as he breathes fire and promises death to the perpetrators of the heinous misdeed. Okika, unlike Egonwanne, the oldest man of the village who would have toed the path of compromise, wanted to match power with power, might with might. Onyeka, who had a "booming voice" was asked to clear the stage for him, for even though he was a great orator, he was not blessed with a booming voice. Okika's speech is a veritable classic of rhetoric, and we see the need to cite it in its entirety, so that the stages of his power of language on the people may become clear:

> You all know why we are here, when we ought to be building our barns or mending our huts, when we should be putting our compounds in order. My father used to say to me: "Whenever you see a toad jumping in broad daylight, then know that something is after its life." When I saw you all pouring into this meeting from all the quarters of our clan so early in the morning, I knew that something was after our life." He paused for a brief moment and then began again:
>
> All our gods are weeping. Idemili is weeping, Ogwugwu is weeping, Agbala is weeping, and all the others. Our dead fathers are weeping because of the shameful sacrilege they are suffering and the abomination we have all seen with our eyes." He stopped again to steady his trembling voice.
>
> This is a great gathering. No clan can boast of greater numbers or greater valor. But are we all here? I ask you: Are all the sons of Umuofia with us here?" A deep murmur swept through the crowd. They are not, ... They have broken the clan and gone their several ways. We who are here this morning have remained true to our fathers, but our brothers have deserted us and joined a stranger to soil their fatherland. If we fight the stranger we shall hit our brothers and perhaps shed the blood of a clansman. But we must do it. Our fathers never dreamed of such a thing, they never killed their brothers. But a white man never came to them. So we must do what our fathers would have done. Eneke the bird was asked why he was always on the wing and he replied: "Men have learned to shoot without missing their mark and I have learned to fly without perching on a twig." We must root out this evil. And if our brothers take the side of evil we must root them out too. And we must do it now. We must bale this water now that it is only ankle-deep..." (186–187).

Having sensitized the gathering to the emergent nature of the situation, Okika does not waste time but goes on, employing run-on phrases. Then the first pause. He allows the people to internalize what he just told them. When he begins to speak again, he bemoans the sacrilegious nature of the offense, adding that in the face of adversity, the community has not seen it fit to stand together. The inference is that a house divided unto itself cannot stand. He intones that the forefathers whose presence is eternally with the living would not have condoned such an act.

As worthy descendants of the ancestors, they should do what their forebears would have done. It is significant that most Igbo proverbs begin with "As our fathers say. "At this stage, Okika begins to lay the ground rules for action. It is almost as if he was saying, "But we must do it," "So we must do what our fathers would have done," "We must root them out too."

Okika has a lot of ability power, power of demeanor and knowledge. He knows how to pick the right words and work effectively on the psychology of his audience. When five court messengers of the British administration showed up to interrupt the gathering, charging that, "The white man whose power you know too well has ordered this meeting to stop," Okonkwo was ready for action, to counter indirect coercive power with direct coercive power:

> In a flash Okonkwo drew his machete. The messenger crouched to avoid the bow. It was useless, Okonkwo's machete descended twice and the man's head lay beside his uniformed body (188).

Power Ideology 4: Obierika and the District Commissioner

The four escaping agents of the British Commissioner, report to their master the murder of one of them by Okonkwo. Enraged, the Commissioner comes down from Government Hill to seek redress:

> 'Which among you is called Okonkwo?' he asked through his interpreter.
> 'He is not here,' replied Obierika.
> 'Where is he?'
> 'He is not here!'

The Commissioner becomes visibly angry. In spite of the apparent dichotomy in the degree of social power, in the end, we can say that it is a perfect power match. First of all, Obierika refuses, right from the start, to volunteer more information than is necessary to respond to the Commissioner's question without appearing to be disrespectful. This tactic is not lost on the Commissioner who begins to be irritated: "Where is he?" he asks in reply to Obierika's non-committal first response: "He is not here." Following the repeat of this same statement, the Commissioner loses total control of his temper. He warns that there will be adverse consequences to disobedience of his orders. At that point, Obierika recognizes the danger in prolonging his register. He thus changes his strategy, although still determined to match power with power. "We can take you where he is, and perhaps your men will help us." (189) The British commissioner finds Obierika's circumlocution very annoying. Beaten in his own game, he leads a band of men into the bush where he finds Okonkwo hanging on his suicide rope. It is a total defeat for the Commissioner who would never get to arrest his victim and punish him at will. Obierika feels triumphant for he recognizes that Okonkwo, his friend, has escaped the commissioner's wrath through suicide. He robs salt into injury when he asks the commissioner and his men, lumping them together as strangers to the land and instruments of the oppression of the people, to help them take down the dead body:

> Perhaps your men can help us bring him down and bury him. We have sent for strangers from another village to do it for us, but they may be a long time coming (190).

By casting the commissioner and his men as the Other, Obierika has de-centered power, moving it to the margin. He has successfully negotiated ideological power, turning it on its head. With great ability, knowledge and demeanor, Obierika has reversed the roles of the master and the subaltern, putting the subaltern, albeit temporarily, over the master.

* * *

We have tried to depart from the norm of discussing masculinity in opposition to femininity, but rather see men's shows of power, privilege and force in its variety, through language in force, language fore-grounded, back-grounded, presupposed or absent in Chinua Achebe's *Things Fall Apart*. Through the study of four pieces of communication between a man and a group, an African and a European, and two men, one on one, we have been able to identify a variety of masculinity and powers of men through language. First, a man or a group of men can be cowered when that man or the group of men feels less powerful than the opponent, the Other. On an individual basis, a man can achieve superiority with silence, by merely refusing to respond when he thinks it is below his dignity to respond to the Other he considers inferior to him. On a group basis, we find that even a whole community can be routed by a powerful man, due to his position in the group and because of the perception of this group of his power. Second, a good speaker can sway or "conquer" a whole community by his sheer artistry in the manipulation of language. Third, two men can do a war of words with no one having a clear upper-hand in the dialogue, due to the tenacity of purpose of both interlocutors. Anyone desirous of being taken seriously can gain insights from this study and also learn to avoid being made out as a victim. Chinua Achebe's *Things Fall Apart* has lent itself to the exploration of how in a traditional and patriarchal community, African men manifest a variety of identity and subjectivity. Perhaps, it is about time gender studies shifted from sheer comparison of femininity and masculinity alone to studies about how masculinity is initiated and fostered in society.

Notes

1 It is important to note that in African palaver groups, men discuss important issues facing the people before making far-reaching decisions. It is typically, formally and informally the structure around which the village government thrived. A corollary could be women's groups on the farm or cooking or fetching water or firewood, or even the *Umuada* group. With male informal groups, such as the age-grade, the sole criterion for entry seems to be age within two to four years of one another. For more formal groups, like the *egwugwu*, the *ndichie* or the council of elders, entrance into the group is more selective and restricted. First of all, a member has to be titled and be one of the most highly regarded in the ward or canton or clan. Each member has to be initiated into the cult of the spirits and will remain a member, an elder of some sort, so long as he has not done anything to tarnish his name. He must always be above board and be a mentor and an example to the young ones and future generations born and yet unborn.

April A. Gordon & Donald L. Gordon. *Understanding Contemporary Africa* (second edition. Boulder and London: Lynne Rienner Publishers, 1996, 8–9.

2 "The ITCZ (Intertropical Convergence zone) represents a meteorological phenomenon whereby large scale airflows from generally opposite directions converge or meet, creating a relatively constant updraft of displaced air. The vertical movement is supplemented by buoyant heated air from the sun-soaked, warm surface conditions of the tropical regions. The rising air cools off rapidly, causing atmospheric water vapor (if presented to condense into droplets first, then precipitation. At least this is the ideal chain of events, and the ITCZ is the primary rainmaking mechanism not only in Africa but throughout the tropical world. Rainfall often occurs as daily thunderstorms and can be torrential during the rainy season ... Sometimes the ITCZ 'misbehaves' and does not shift when it's normally expected to or move where it usually should, bringing stress to the life that depends on it."

Works Cited

Achebe, Chinua. *Things Fall Apart.* New York: Fawcett Crest, 1959.

Cahn, Victor L. *Gender and Power in the Plays of Harold Pinter.* New York: Saint Martin's Press, 1993.

Cornell, R.W. *Gender and Power.* Stanford: Stanford University Press, 1987.

———. *Masculinities.* Oxford: Polity Press, 1995, 37.

Easthope, Anthony. *What a Man's Gotta Do: The Masculine Myth in Popular Culture.* Boston: Unwin Hyman Press, 1986.

Foucault, Michel. *The Subject and Power.* In. *Critical Inquiry 8.* 777–795.

Gordon, April A. & Donald L. Gordon *Understanding Contemporary Africa* (second edition). Boulder and London: Lynne Rienner Publishers, 1996.

Johnson, Sally and Ulrike Hanna Meinhoff. *Language and Masculinity.* Cambridge, Mass.: Blackwell Publishers, 1997.

Kiesling, Scott Fabius. "Power and Language of Men." In: Sally Johnson and Ulrike Hanna Meinhoff. *Language and Masculinity.* Cambridge, Mass.: Blackwell Publishers, 1997.

Kaye/Kantrowitz, Melanie. *The Issue is Power: Essays on Women, Jews, Violence and Resistance.* San Franciso: Aunt Lute Books, 1992.

Lang, Hermann. *Language and the Unconscious: Jacques Lacan's Hermeneutics of Psychoanalysis* (translated from the German by Thomas Brockelman). New Jersey: Humanities Press, 1997.

Obelitala, Alphonse. *L'initiation en Afrique noire et en Grece: Confrontation de quelques rites de passage.* Brazzaville: P. Kivaiva Verlag, 1982.

Poole, Adrian. *Tragedy: Shakespeare and the Greek Example.* New York: Basil Blackwell, Inc., 1987.

Pucci, Pietro. Ed. *Language and the Tragic Hero: Essays on Greek Tragedy in the Honour of Gordon M. Kirkwood.* Atlanta: Scholars Press, 1988.

Saltlel, Jack. "Men, inexpressiveness, and Power." In: B. Thorne, C. Kramarae and N. Henley. Eds. *Language, Gender and Society.* Cambridge, MA: Newbury House, 1995. 119–124.

Segal. Erich. Ed. *Greek Tragedy: Modern Essays in Criticism.* Cambridge and London and Mexico City: Harper and Row Publishers, 1983.

Thorne, B.C. Kramarae, and N. Henley. Eds. *Language, Gender and Society.* Cambridge, MA: Newbury House, 1995.

Webster, Roger. *Studying Literary Theory: An Introduction* (second edition). London/New York/Sydney/Auckland: Arnold Publishers, 1990.

Weigman, Robyn and Elena Glasberg. *Literature and Gender: Thinking Critically Through Fiction, Poetry, and Drama.* Longman: New York/Sydney/Amsterdam, 1999.

Chapter 5

The Child-Victim in Chinua Achebe's *Things Fall Apart*

Julie Agbasiere

THE IMPORTANCE OF THE child in the traditional African society cannot be over-emphasized. Construed as the link between the past, for he is the re-incarnation of dead ancestors, and the future, by virtue of his own children, the child becomes the synthesis of the present, the past and the future of the society. He is the pivot of the life cycle both of the community in general and the family in particular. Sule considers him as "an important link in the chain for perpetuation of the society" (72). Because of his strategic importance, parents and the society make it their responsibility to protect, nurture and bring up the child to be a responsible and useful member of the society. For, as Gye-Wado emphasizes, "The future human resources and leadership of any society is inextricably linked to the manner and ways in which its children are nurtured and developed" (52).

Important as the child is in the traditional African society, it is observed that he lives in a harsh environment where his very existence is at times threatened. The child finds himself a victim of societal beliefs and prejudices, of inter-communal clashes and wars, of parental excesses and repression, and of infant mortality. This is the issue we wish to examine in Chinua Achebe's *Things Fall Apart*, a novel set in the traditional past.

The Child: Victim of Societal Prejudices and Practices

In the traditional African society, bearing children is the *raison d'etre* of contracting marriages and every family aspires to have many children, especially boys. In marriage negotiations and betrothal, a prayer for fecundity is always said for the bride-to-be.

The desire for children is not only manifested in parental good wishes. The women themselves undergo rituals believed to be capable of inducing pregnancy. In Umuofia, it is believed that the spirits of good children waiting to be born live in a big ancient and sacred silk-cotton tree located in the village square. So, women who desire children go to sit under its shadow so as to be blessed with children.

It is an irony in Umuofia that this society that places high premium on children is disposed to rejecting them because of certain beliefs and taboos. Multiple birth is considered an abomination and twins are believed to be sinister and a threat to communal survival, hence the practice of getting rid of them. They are put in an earthen pot and left in the evil forest to die. This practice denies the child the right to live. The cries of twins in the forest are an accusation on the conscience of the society, and an assault on the sensibilities of members of the community. They exude an eerie feeling on passers-by, as Nwoye experiences when he is returning from the farm with members of his family.

> A sudden hush had fallen on the women, who had been talking, and they had quickened their steps. . . . A vague chill had descended on him and his head had seemed to swell, like a solitary walker at night who passes an evil spirit on the way. Then something had given way inside him (43).

As twins are a communal taboo, the individual feels incapacitated to do something about it, especially the mother for whom it is a heart-breaking loss. However, the coming of Christianity offers a desired solace. As it champions the right of the babies to life, prospective mothers of twins flee their matrimonial homes and seek refuge in the church. This is the case of Nneka, Amadi's wife, in Achebe's *Things Fall Apart*, who has had sets of twins in four consecutive pregnancies and births. This time around, heavy with child, she joins the Christians because she is afraid of giving birth to twins and the community throwing them away.[1]

The Child: Victim of Inter-communal Clashes

Generally, the adverse impact of any social upheaval or calamity is mostly on women and children. When communities go to war or try to avert one, children become victims of such moves. The conflict that brings Umuofia and Mbaino at daggers drawn is caused by the murder of Ogbuefi Udo's wife, a daughter of Umuofia, in Mbaino. Umuofia feels aggrieved and insulted and is ready to go to war. It has the duty of protecting its image and its members. Gye-Wado reiterates that "The community as a whole was expected to protect every member of the community and any harm or danger to one was considered harm or danger to the whole community" (54). However, Umuofia gives its offending neighbor a choice between going to war or paying a compensation which consists of handing over a virgin and a young lad to Umuofia. Mbaino, afraid of the martial might of Umuofia, opts to pay compensation and hands over a young girl and Ikemefuna to Okonkwo, the leader of the delegation. Evidently, it is the child who is at the receiving end of these diplomatic moves.

In settling their differences, the adults make children suffer. Umuofia asks as compensation children who are both innocent and ignorant of the offense committed by their parents. It is visiting the sins of the fathers on their sons. As it seeks to save its neck, Mbaino sacrifices Ikemefuna and the young girl. They are uprooted from their community and homes to an alien community where their security and safety are not guaranteed. Ikemefuna feels completely lost. He is afraid and does not understand what is happening to him:

> How could he know that his father had taken a hand in killing a daughter of Umuofia? All he knew was that a few men had arrived at their house, conversing with his father in low tones, and at the end he had been taken out and handed over to a stranger. His mother had wept bitterly, but he had been too surprised to weep (11).

It is then left to Umuofia to decide the fate of the two children. In giving the young girl to Ogbuefi Udo to replace the murdered wife, the community deprives her of the happiness that goes with marriage ceremonies and the role her parents should have played. She is taken to Ogbuefi Udo as a sacrificial lamb. Martial justice as this may be regarded, is nevertheless a grave injustice to the young girl.

The action meted out to Ikemefuna is all the more brutal as the boy is not allowed to live, and at a time when he has been fully integrated in the community. He has become a member of Okonkwo's household, provides a good and purposeful companionship to Nwoye and makes himself accepted and liked by all. He takes Okonkwo as father and the latter has become fond of Ikemefuna, treating him as a son and allowing him to carry his stool and goat-skin bag when he goes to important village meetings or communal ancestral feasts. The gods decree his death. But the will of the gods, supreme as it may be, does not go down well with some people in the community. That is why Ogbuefi Ezeudu warns Okonkwo not to take part in killing Ikemefuna: it also explains why Okonkwo finds it difficult to convince Obierika that he, Okonkwo, is justified in killing the lad. Okonkwo has killed a son.

The sad story of Ikemefuna is a pointer to the helplessness of the child in an adult world. It portrays the supremacy of the gods and of the collectivity over the individual. The parents of Ikemefuna and the young girl failed to protect them from the decisions of their community, and Okonkwo cannot defend the boy against the decree of the Oracle.

The Child: Victim of Parental Excesses and Repression

As the child grows up, he is expected to imbibe the values and norms of behavior of the society. He is taught to do things correctly and any misbehavior is corrected. As Okonkwo states, "such correction may involve physical chastisement or other punitive measures" (21). In the traditional milieu, the child learns the hard way on account of certain beliefs that regulate the handling of a child's education. Eya enumerates them, some of which are: "A child is spoilt and will be of no good if he is not flogged"; "Physical punishment is best in dealing with the difficult child"; "A child who is made to suffer grows in wisdom" (74). With such underlying principles, the parents dish out large doses of beatings to their children in order to turn them into successful and respectable members of the society. This is the plight of Nwoye, the eldest son of Okonkwo.

As his first son, Okonkwo expects Nwoye to be his worthy successor and heir to his family. He would like Nwoye to maintain his prestige and high position in the community by the time he ceases to exist. He would like him to follow Okonkwo's footsteps and become an achiever and an illustrious son right from his tender age. If Nwoye had started early in life to show signs of greatness such as prowess in wrestling and excessive love for hard work, Okonkwo would have been pleased and content. But at the age of twelve years, Nwoye is causing his father great concern because he appears lazy and Okonkwo does not want him to be lazy and a failure in life. Okonkwo's attitude is borne out of the fact that his father, Unoka, was a total failure. He was a lazy man who lived in abject poverty, was heavily in debt and died of an abominable disease. Okonkwo is ashamed of him and does not want himself or any other person in his lineage, especially Nwoye, to follow his footsteps. Throughout his life, Okonkwo is haunted by "The fear of his father's contemptible life and shameful death" (13).

The problem for which Nwoye is causing his father great anxiety is laziness. The idea of laziness conjures up Unoka's worthless life and Okonkwo's resentment to it. So Okonkwo "sought to correct him by constant nagging and beating" (10), for this is the only way Okonkwo believes that the problem can be solved. Besides, Okonkwo has a fiery temper and beats his wives on the least provocation even when custom forbids him to do so. He instills fear in his household, roaring at them all the time. So, by his ambitions and temperament, Okonkwo is disposed to batter Nwoye.

Okonkwo's approach is preventive for it is not categorically stated that Nwoye is lazy as seen in the underlined statement in *Things Fall Apart*:

> Okonkwo's first son, Nwoye, was then twelve years old but was already causing his father great anxiety for his incipient laziness. *At any rate that was how it looked to his father* (10); (emphasis added).

Okonkwo appears to be expecting too much from the boy and he knows it. For when he rebukes Nwoye as well as Ikemefuna for not cutting seed yams properly, it is said:

> Inwardly Okonkwo knew that the boys were still too young to understand fully the difficult art of preparing seed-yams. But he thought that one could not begin too early (24).

So he intentionally seeks to mold the boy right from a tender age.

In trying to mold Nwoye to fit his model, Okonkwo pursues two objectives: first, to prevent Nwoye from behaving like his own father, Unoka; and second, to make the boy lay the foundation of greatness. He reiterates his motives almost every time he seeks to correct his son. When he screams at Nwoye for not cutting seed-yams properly, it is because "Okonkwo wanted his son to be a great farmer and a great man" (24). And he goes on to say:

> I will not have a son who cannot hold up his head in the gathering of the clan. I would sooner strangle him with my own hands (24).

When Nwoye grumbles about women (his father's wives) and their problems, Okonkwo is happy because he wants the boy to "grow into a tough young man capable of ruling his father's household when he was dead and gone to join the ancestors" (37). So, Okonkwo is consumed by the desire to see Nwoye become a great man and in so doing he continues to beat the boy mercilessly. He nearly strangles Nwoye the day he learns that the boy has joined the Christians.

Okonkwo is impatient and as such does not give Nwoye the time to assimilate his teachings, and mature. He is disappointed and on the brink of despair as he tells Obierika, "I have done my best to make Nwoye grow into a man, but there is too much of his mother in him" (46). He does not accept Obierika's opinion that the boy is yet very young and that Okonkwo is worrying himself for nothing.

Okonkwo's correctional measures create problems for Nwoye. The constant beatings result in his "developing into a sad-faced youth" (10). Nwoye learns to pretend, to avoid being beaten. Although he prefers animal stories told by his mother, he listens to his father's war stories:

> And so he feigned that he no longer cared for women's stories. And when he did this, he knew that his father was pleased and no longer rebuked him (38).

The problem with Nwoye's upbringing is that he has a soft human touch and is sensitive, facts which Okonkwo does not appreciate. In fact Okonkwo tries to eradicate these feelings which he considers effeminate. That is why he beats Nwoye mercilessly whenever he cries. But that does not prevent Nwoye from being deeply moved by human suffering such as the crying of twins abandoned in the forest and the killing of Ikemefuna. In each case "something seemed to give way inside him, like the snapping of a tightened bow" (43).

Nwoye eventually revolts against his father's harsh treatment. The coming of the missionaries to the land marks a turning point in his development. The new religion somehow resolves his conflicts and gives him some peace of mind. He is captivated not by the logic of its teachings but by the singing:

> The hymn about brothers who sat in the darkness and in fear seemed to answer a vague and persistent question that haunted his young soul – the question of the twins crying in the bush and the question of Ikemefuna who was killed (104).

Nwoye joins the Christians in Mbanta and becomes a changed person. When next his father beats and nearly strangles him, he simply walks out on him and goes forever. Liberated from his father's stranglehold, Nwoye becomes an individual, a person capable of taking decisions. He tells Kiaga, the local head of the congregation, of his wish to move to Umuofia, a bigger station. There he takes a new identity and is henceforth called Isaac. Thereafter, he is sent to Umuru to train as a teacher.

Nwoye's story demonstrates that constant verbal assaults and battering of the child produce negative effects. The child is fearful and becomes defiant. Ultimately, he revolts and then starts the quest for his identity. Nwoye rejects his father and all that he stands for. He takes his life in his hands. Odejide rightly asserts that "an adequate dose of suffering or deprivation is good for children since it has a maturational and even emancipatory quality" (156). However, in the case of Nwoye, this maturation is attained through revolt.

The Child: Victim of Infant Mortality

The child in Umuofia is also a victim of premature death usually before the age of five. Such a child is called "Ogbanje",[2] that is "one of those wicked children who when they died, entered their mothers' wombs to be born again" (54). Once a woman begets such a child, the chances are that subsequent births will produce "Ogbanje" children. Ekwefi is such an unfortunate mother. Okonkwo's second wife, Ekwefi has known such hardships and heartbreaks that make her despair:

> Ekwefi had suffered a good deal in her life. She had borne ten children and nine of them had died in infancy, usually before the age of three. As she buried one child after another her sorrow gave way to despair and then to grim resignation. The birth of her children, which should be a woman's crowning glory, became for Ekwefi mere physical agony devoid of promise (54).

All efforts to stop the re-birth of such a child prove abortive. The birth of Ezinma, Ekwefi's tenth child, is therefore, greeted with apprehension and resignation. Frail and sickly, Ezinma survives the first five years of existence, thereby giving her mother the impression that she may have come to stay. This brings back to Ekwefi maternal love and the determination to nurse her child to health. It then becomes necessary to break the bond that unites her with the other dead siblings, according to the people's belief, by digging out her "iyi uwa," abode of her pact with the supernatural beings [3]. Ezinma's "iyi uwa," a well-polished pebble wrapped in rags, is dug out and this gives Ekwefi the hope that her daughter will survive. Ezinma remains a source of anxiety to her parents. Both of them give her immediate and maximum attention whenever she falls sick. They are ready to defend her in all circumstances, even against the gods.

Ezinma strikes a balance in reciprocating her parents' love. She is close to her mother and father. She is chatty and gives Ekwefi effective companionship. In fact she takes liberties with her, calling her, unlike all other children, by her first name. An intimacy is developed between the two, leading to harmless conspiracies such as Ekwefi giving Ezinma eggs in their bedroom, for children are not allowed to eat eggs in the community. The relationship that crystallizes is not that of mother and child but rather that of companionship between adults and equals. Similarly, she has a deep understanding with her father. She is quick in understanding his every mood and keeps him good company. When Okonkwo is depressed after killing Ikemefuna, it is on Ezinma's persuasion and insistence that he manages to take some food. It becomes obvious that "of all his children, she alone understood his every mood. A bond of sympathy had grown between them as the years had passed" (122). As she grows up, beautiful and full of life, Ezinma tolerates only her father each time she suffers from depression.

Ezinma is loved and pampered without being spoilt. She is not subjected to Okonkwo's nagging and beating, unlike Nwoye who is often beaten. She grows up without suffering from personality conflict. She is a source of pride and joy to her family. She is intelligent and perspicacious, and reacts the way a man would do in Umuofia. When Okonkwo is detained at Umuru with other elders, Ezinma cuts short her visit to her future husband's place and rushes home. Her first action is not to cry but to go to Obierika to make sure that something is being done for the release of her father. Little wonder Okonkwo continues wishing that she were a boy!

Ezinma's story shows that it is not only the child who is a victim of infant mortality. Where the child dies, the family is moved to despair, and where he lives, he becomes a source of anxiety to his parents. As a surviving child, Ezinma is loved beyond measure and is spared the harsh treatment reserved for children in the traditional society.

Conclusion

Our study so far has shown that the child is an endangered species in the traditional African society. So many forces threaten his survival. The society is a major threat, for the child is either smarting under hostile beliefs and practices of the adult world or he is groaning under the iron grip of parental discipline. He is also victim to mysterious premature death. The child who escapes death enjoys the love and solicitude of his parents. The adult world in which the child lives is harsh and violent. However, the plight of the child in Umuofia is similar to what obtains elsewhere. Oguike finds that "The Francophone literary history of the African child is one of survival through physical and mental suffering and torment" (124). Nevertheless, the coming of Christianity provides an instrument for combating taboos that are injurious to the survival of the child such as the issue of twins. The child has to survive for his destiny is intricately linked with that of the society.

Notes

1. The rejection of twins was a common practice in some areas of Igboland from the eighteenth through the early nineteenth centuries. Attitudes started changing with the coming of Christianity. Reminiscence of the past persists with the institution of Motherless Babies Homes, which in areas concerned give sanctuary to abandoned babies including twins. This finds an echo in fictional works, which reflect the bridging of old and new attitudes. In Flora Nwapa's *One is Enough*, Rev. Fr. Izu McLaid, a rescued twin, fathers Amaka's set of twins who are joyfully accepted and celebrated even in Amaka's village.

2. The "Ogbanje" syndrome is one of those legacies from the African traditional past. As a myth, it seeks to explain the phenomenon of premature death in children. Acholonu postulates that the "Ogbanje" is characterized by fatality, the certitude that the child must die as decreed by fate and his restless spirit will be repeatedly reincarnated" (104). An Ogbanje who escapes death as a child meets it in early adulthood. Achebe describes such an adult "Ogbanje" as "one of those mysterious elusive and often highly talented beings who hurry to leave the world and to come again" (Acholonu 105). The concept of "Ogbanje" cuts across cultures. In the Yoruba worldview, the myth reoccurs as "Abiku". It is illustrated by Soyinka's poem "Abiku". Osundare explains that "In a society plagued by phenomenal infant mortality, the Abiku myth becomes a way of coping with the painful reality of premature death; sacrifices must be made, libation poured, to appease the Abiku child-god and stem its evil course" (93). Modern thought tends to ascribe this phenomenon to sickle cell anemia disease, which spells doom and premature death especially to children.

3. This is the Ogbanje's most prized secret which he is most reluctant to divulge. It takes a lot of persuasion, not threats, to get the Ogbanje child to show the spot where he hid the "iyi-uwa," usually under the earth.

Works Cited

Achebe, Chinua. *Things Fall Apart.* London, Ibadan: Heinemann, 1958.

Achebe, Chinua and Dubem Okafor (eds). *Don't Let Him Die.* Cited by Catherine Acholonu, "Ogbanje: A Motif and a Theme in the Poetry of Christopher Okigbo". *Oral and Written Poetry in African Literature Today.* 16 (1988): 103–111.

Acholonu, Catherine. "Ogbanje: A Motif and a Theme in the Poetry of Christopher Okigbo." *Op. Cit.* 103–111

Eya, Regina. "Mass Education: A Condition for Child Abuse Legislation in Nigeria". Cited by Peter Ebigbo. "The Problems of Child Abuse and Neglect in Nigeria and Strategies for Overcoming Them". *The Nigerian Child: Now and in the Future.* L.S. Aminu and Bayo Olikoshi (eds). Lagos: The Federal Ministry of Health and Human Services, and UNICEF, 1990. 74–102.

Gye-Wado, Onje. "Human Rights, the Rights of the Child and the African Charter on Human and People's Rights". *The Nigerian Child: Now and in the Future.* 52–62.

Nwapa, Flora. *One is Enough.* Enugu: Tana Press, 1981.

Odejide, Abiola. "The Abused Child Motif in Nigerian Children's Realistic Fiction." *Children and Literature in Africa.* Eds. Chidi Ikonne, Emelia Oko, Peter Onwudinjo. Ibadan: Heinemann, 1992

Oguike, Uche A. "Children in Francophone West African Novels: The Power of Childhood." *Children and Literature in Africa.* 108–126.

Okonkwo, C.O. "The Child and Criminal Responsibility: The Nigerian Perspective". *The Nigerian Child Now and in the Future.* 16–28.

Osundare, Niyi. "The Poem as a Mytho – Linguistic Event. A Study of Soyinka's Abiku." *Oral and Written Poetry in African Literature Today.* 91–102.

Sule, Bello "The Concept and Treatment of the Child in Nigerian Culture: A Brief Commentary." *The Nigerian Child Now and in the Future.* 71–73.

Chapter 6

Things Do Not Fall Apart

Joseph Obi

Introduction

THINGS FALL APART (TFA) enjoys a solid reputation as one of the world's classic tales. According to Griswold, "it is by far the best known, most read, and most cited Nigerian novel, both in Nigeria and abroad" (716). As a contestation of the "crypto-fascist theories of primitivism" (Zabus, 1997: 463) underlying some of the constructions of Africa in colonialist discourse, TFA stands as a powerful narrative of liberation. This, however, is not a paper about TFA's nationalist thrust (an issue that has received copious attention), rather, our concern is with the construction of the subaltern's universe in the novel. Specifically, I argue that it is a world characterized by difference and flexibility. I believe that this polyvocality is consistent with the optic of the Igbo that Achebe works through. Furthermore, the commonfolk of TFA are invested with agency as they make conscious choices on how to deal with the intrusions into their world. Both these issues have implications for how we perceive social formations on the continent and how we probe culture as students of Africa. Indeed, this paper is an attempt to identify important lessons to be gleaned from Achebe's classic.

Polyvalent Umuofia:

One of the great strengths of *Things Fall Apart* lies in its depiction of ambivalence as an existential condition. The text manifests the Igbo distrust of absolutes. Given the many contradictions in Umuofian society and its environs, it would be simplistic to see them as some idealized gemeinschaft. Consider the following antimonies:

Unoka is denigrated for his laziness but recognized for his artristic pursuits, "manliness" is counterbalanced by a feminine principle, the missionary effort is disruptive, yet resonates with certain members of society, Okonkwo and Obierika disagree on the former's involvement in killing Ikemefuna, indeed colonialism simultaneously closes and opens possibilities for the villagers. This fictive beginning-of-century Igbo world is polyvalent – a characteristic of profound significance in end-of-century Africa. We shall return to this point presently. For now, let us explore the construction of Okonkwo within Umuofia as an exemplification of a kind of ambivalence.

As a hero, Okonkwo represents, and eventually contradicts the values of his society. His rigidity and monological outlook on life ultimately bring him down. While most of his kinsfolk confront the incipient globalizing front (of Christianity and colonialism) in creative, nuanced, pragmatic, and interest-begotten ways, Okonkwo reaches blindly for secure ontological niches. The object of his desire however, turns out to be more imagined than real for dynamism, malleability, and ambivalence are elements of that culture. Simon Gikandi (1991: 42) correctly observes that, "He (Okonkwo) is too faithful to the collective mythology, and his interpretation of linguistic and ideological codes is too literal." Along the same lines, Achebe has since claimed that his sympathies were not entirely with Okonkwo, for in refusing to accept change, he was bound to be swept aside (see Egejuru, 1978: 207). Thus while Okonkwo was destroyed, Umuofia's culture was merely disturbed – the commonfolk, informed by autochthonous notions of cultural flexibility on the one hand, and perhaps, an appreciation of realpolitik on the other, cleverly adapt to the changed circumstances since life must go on. This emphasis on adaptation is best illustrated by the Igbo proverb (often quoted by Achebe), "Wherever something stands something else will stand beside it." (Achebe, 1975: 161). Clearly *Things Fall Apart* is not fixated by the past. There are those critics who put emphasize the "crumbling society" as the theme of the novel (Larson, 1968; Waghmare, 1985, Griswold, 1992). We argue beyond this – Achebe reveals an awareness of new inexorable forces of history coming into being in a society that is ever dynamic. We know that Umuofia will continue, its people will adapt in the face of varying new orders in the March of history. In the end, Okonkwo is quixotic compared to his kinsfolk who have begun to sample the new trade arrangements brought in by the colonial system. According to Achebe:

> Like the adaptable bird in our proverb, we must learn to fly without perching or perish from man's new-learnt marksmanship. So there is the need for a culture to be alive and active and ready to adjust, ready to take challenges. A culture that fails to take challenges will die. But if we are ready to take challenges, to make concessions that are necessary without accepting anything that undermines our fundamental belief in the dignity of man, I think we would be doing what is expected of us (1981: 4).

The relevance of the ambivalent condition depicted in TFA cannot be overestimated in contemporary Africa. The twentieth century witnessed the intensification of worldwide social densities and evidence of a world society, and Achebe's tale underscores the importance of calibrating our narratives in ways that are small enough to capture the modulations of the social formations we examine.

In other words, we will be well served by avoiding the seductions of an "illusion of unanimity" (Appiah, 1992).

On a related note, TFA demonstrates the capacity of culture to reinvent itself – albeit on core of relatively constant moorings. The text highlighted – forty years ago – the importance of interrogating "essential" identities in the run of history. Today's cultural globalization trends have made available multiple identities especially with the time and space compression wrought by new information technologies. Africans, as well as everyone else, live amidst a swirl of deterritorialized signifiers that mark their worlds profoundly.

Readers as Heroes

Things Fall Apart anticipated the dynamics that was to become central in African cultural studies in the latter half of the twentieth century, namely the processes by which extraneous cultural elements are received. As is understood in the anthropology of mass communications, media do not affect all receivers equally or in the same way (i.e. the "magic bullet" theory). Audiences are discriminating active decoders. As Andrew Lyons (1990: 433) notes, "It is... interesting to learn how a set of symbolic messages encoded by Americans in Place A is going to be decoded by Nigerians in Place B." Obviously, at some points there would be a convergence of meanings and at other time, "aberrant" decoding. Receivers of cultural texts (as our Umuofians) bring their own templates to the task of reading the grammar of culture – theirs and others'. Indeed, the village folk are constructivist in their encounter with the colonial and missionary enterprise. Ezeudu, Obierika, Nwoye, and numerous others all move from side to side as they watch the new masquerade – accepting its offerings here, rejecting there, in varying degrees, for various reasons.

The immediately preceding point is critical for the literary enterprise in Africa. Our logical phenomenal instincts tell us that every time a text is read, it is rewritten according to the reader's interpretative scheme (Eco, 1979). TFA invites us to explore how Africans rewrite the texts of their new hybridized locales. Scholars have paid scanty attention to how Africans themselves read *Things Fall Apart* and the rest of the continent's written literature. Let us dwell on the latter for a moment. There is a dearth of scholarly research on who reads what, why, when, where, and how in Africa. In line with our creativist paradigm, it behooves us to build a sturdy body of knowledge on the aesthetics of cultural consumption in Africa. What "horizons of expectations" (Jauss, 1982) do readers bring to comprehending a text? Africans will need to know how and why groups tend to make meaning in certain ways. What are the collectively constructed aesthetic criteria in operation at any given time? It is indeed time to configure the reader as hero.

The importance of the aesthetics of reception is borne out by Chris Dunton's (1994) revealing study of reading (of various texts) among the people of Moniya in the Western part of Nigeria. They display considerable variety and autonomy in confronting texts. One calls the format of Soyinka's *The Trials of Brother Jero* "silly". Another only reads religious literature because secular texts were "polluting". Yet another contends that books are full of other people's problems which do not concern him. Perhaps the most interesting is one (by a tailor) that maintains that "all I need to read is my tape measure".

Comments such as the above indicate that we cannot assume an inter subjective coupling between the didactic author and the responsive reader. On a continent where literature is routinely written to awaken and transform consciousness into an active force, this is critical. Beyond literature, the lesson for studying culture in Africa is that there is an urgent need for the results of scholarship whose paradigms are interpretive, ethnographic, and documentary (the latter in the phenomenological sense), for "globalization" is experienced differently. As mentioned above, Achebe's village folk are not passive. They respond to missionary and colonial activities on the basis of their definition of the situation. There is no basis to say that those who "accommodate" change are less Umuofian than Okonkwo. Achebe himself has no problems "writing back" to the "center" in a language (English) and form (the novel) that have roots outside Africa. Has it not been argued that, in this sense, globalization (especially in the context of asymmetrical power relations) does lead to the valorization of particular identities? (Appadurai, 1990; Pieterse, 1995).

One point that the history of "encountering" has made manifest is that not all extraneous elements are absorbed or adjusted to. In Okonkwo we see how globalizing trends may lead to the valorization of local identity. While it may be fairly easy to theorize the rejection of some extraneous cultural traits in Africa, more work needs to be done by way of identifying those (translocal?) affinities that allow for the absorption of others. Onyemaechi Udumukwu (1991) argues that Umuofia already has fault lines and paradigms that presumably, predispose some of its members to embrace the new elements. In an interview with Bill Moyers, Achebe remarks that there are similarities between Christianity and Igbo religious beliefs (Moyers Interview, 1988). Both of these points may well explain the ease with which Okonkwo's son, Nwoye and Umuofia's marginalized slide into the Christian camp. Along these lines, we suggest investigations into the dynamics of similar cultural processes in postcolonial Africa. What, for instance is behind the enormous success of say reggae or (American) country music in Nigeria?

Conclusion

All told, Africa is Umuofia in all its complexity and fluidity. The continent is part of the crisscrossing currents of cultural globalization. As we leave behind a century that was marked by the greatest time and space compression known in mankind's history, *Things Fall Apart* will remain an important portrait of human agency and complexity in the early stages of Africa's continuing encounter with the West. The twenty-first century promises to be an interesting one for African cultural studies since culture – that great centrifuge – will continue to spin with all the collisions, fusions, and repulsions entailed in the process. I will give Achebe the last word:

> The Igbo culture was not destroyed by Europe. It was disturbed very seriously, but that is nothing new in the world. Cultures are constantly influenced, challenged, pushed about by other cultures that may have some kind of advantage of force, persuasion, wealth or whatever.... A culture which is healthy will survive. It will not survive in the form in which it was met by the invading culture, but it will modify itself and move on. And this is the great thing about culture, if it is alive. The people who own it will ensure that they make adjustments (Interview with Ogbaa, 1981: 3).

Work Cited

Achebe, Chinua. (1975) *Morning Yet on Creation Day*. New York: Anchor/Doubleday.

———. Interviewed by Bill Moyers (1988) *A World of Ideas with Bill Moyers*, New York: Public Affairs Television Inc.

———. (1981) Interviewed by Kalu Ogbaa. *Research in African Literatures*, 12, 1: 1–13.

Afigbo, A.E. (1981) *Ropes of Sand: Studies in Igbo Culture and History*. Ibadan: Univ. Press.

Appadurai, A. (1991) "Disjuncture and Difference in the Global Political Economy," in M. Featherstone (ed). *Global Culture: Nationalism, Modernization, and Modernity*. London: Sage, 295–310.

Appiah, Anthony (1992) "Inventing an African Practice in Philosophy: Epistemological Issues," in V.Y. Mudimbe (ed.) *The Surreptitious Speech: Presence Africaine and the Politics of Otherness*. Chicago: Univ. of Chicago, 227–237.

Dunton, Chris (1994) "What a Silly Way to Write a Book." Paper delivered at the African Literature Conference, Accra, Ghana, March.

Eco, Umberto (1979) *The Role of the Reader: Explorations in the Semiotics of Texts*. Bloomington: Indiana Univ. Press.

Egejuru, Phanuel (1978) *Black Writers White Audience*. Hicksville, NY: Exposition.

Gikandi, Simon (1991) *Reading Chinua Achebe*. London: J. Currey.

Griswold, Wendy (1992) "The Writing on the Mud Wall: Nigerian Novels and the Imaginary Village," *American Sociological Review*, 57, Dec.:709–724.

———. (1993) "Recent Moves in the Sociology of Literature," *Annual Review of Sociology*, 19:455–467.

Jauss, H.R. (1982) *Towards an Aesthetic of Reception*. (Trans. By Timothy Bahti) Minneapolis: Univ. of Minn. Press.

Larson, Charles (1968) *The Emergence of African Literature*. London: Macmillan.

Lee, Raymond (1994) "Modernization, Postmodernism and the Third World," *Current Sociology* 42, 2: 1–63.

Lyons, Andrew (1990) "The Television and the Shrine: Towards a Theoretical Model for The Study of Mass Communication in Nigeria," *Visual Anthropology*, 3:429–456.

Lyons, Harriet (1990) "Television in Contemporary Urban Life: Benin City, Nigeria" *Visual Anthropology*, 3:411–428.

Pieterse, Jan N. (1995) "Globalization as Hybridization," in Mike Featherstone, Scott Lash, and Roland Robertson (eds.) *Global Modernities*. London: Sage.

Udumukwu, Onyemaechi (1991) "The Antimony of Anticolonial Discourse: A Revisionist Marxist Study of Achebe's *Things Fall Apart*," *Neohelicon* 18, 2:317–336.
Waghmare, J.M. (1985) "Chinua Achebe's Vision of a Crumbling Past," in G.S. Amur, V.R.N. Prasad, B.V. Nemade, and N.K. Nihalami (eds.) *Indian Readings in Commonwealth Literature*. New Delhi: Sterling, 117–123.
Zabus, Chantal (1997) "Postmodernism in African Literature in English," in Hans Bertens and Douwe Fokkema. *International Postmodernism*. Amsterdam: John Benjamins, 463–467.

Chapter 7

Igbo Cosmology and the Parameters of Individual Accomplishment in *Things Fall Apart*

Clement Okafor

SINCE THE PUBLICATION OF Chinua Achebe's *Things Fall Apart* in 1958, the novel has developed into a truly remarkable literary phenomenon; it is not only the most widely read book in Africa except for the Bible, but also is now part of the global literary canon. Furthermore, *Things Fall Apart* has sold more than eight million copies and has been translated into fifty-five languages of the world.

As the literary world enjoys almost fifty years of the publication of this classic, it is more important now than ever before that we establish an appropriate epistemological framework that can profitably inform our critical discussions of *Things Fall Apart.*

Since literature is contextual, the interrogation of the setting of a literary opus creates opportunities for a deep and rewarding interpretation of the work under consideration. *Things Fall Apart* is set in Igboland in the second half of the Nineteenth Century, the time when Britain was in the process of colonizing not only Igboland but also the other African territories allotted to her at the Berlin Conference of 1884/85. An exploration of traditional Igbo cosmology is, therefore, a valuable strategy for establishing the desired epistemological framework in which to place our further discourse on the novel.

Throughout this paper, the term "cosmology" is used to convey the sense of a society's perception of the world in which it lives. Such a concept usually explores the complex interlocking relationships between human beings and the pantheon of forces that function within their society's universe.

First, a word about the Igbo. The Igbo inhabit the territory of Southeastern Nigeria, and their homeland is located on both banks of *Orimili* (the great river) the River Niger, from which Nigeria derives her name. According to Basden, "the Ibo nation ranks as one of the largest in the whole of Africa" (xi). Igbo people now number about twenty-five million, a population larger than those of Norway, Sweden, and Denmark combined.

Igbo society is historically egalitarian and democratic in the sense that the people have never had rulers with anything approaching autocratic powers. According to Green, the Igbo "have no hierarchy of powers rising from a broad democratic basis through ascending levels to one central peak", rather, "Ibo democracy unlike English, works through a number of juxtaposed groups and a system of balances rather than on a unitary hierarchical principle" (145). This egalitarian principle is expressed in the famous statement: *Igbo enwe eze* (The Igbo do not have kings).

The town, which is the basic unity of Igbo traditional political organization, is made up of various villages that together comprise about twenty to thirty thousand people. Although these towns are "not united by central government authority, nor arranged in any political hierarchy, they are none the less interlinked horizontally each with its neighbors by the social bonds of inter-marriage" that is based on the principle of exogamy; thus although the towns are politically independent, they are socially linked by a web of relationships centered around exogamous marriages, which means that everybody has links not only with his own hometown but also, as Green affirms, "with the birthplace of his mother, with that of his wife, and the various places into which his sisters have married" (151), not to mention the towns into which his brothers have married. Every town has a market, which is held every four or eight days and is a socially unifying force; among the Igbo the market is also a place where people socialize.

As Simon Ottenberg has observed in his study, the democratic nature of Igbo society – with its encouragement of healthy individual and group rivalry coupled with the premium it places on individual, personal accomplishment – has enabled its people to adapt rapidly to the modern, western way of life. In Igbo cosmology, there is Chukwu or *ama ama amasi amasi* (the one who can never be fully understood). Below him is a pantheon of deities whose domain may be limited to specific aspects of life on earth. Examples of these are Amadiora, the god of thunder, Ufiojioku, the god of the harvest, and Anyanwu, the sun god. Principal among these deities is Ani, the Earth goddess, who is the arbiter of ethical conduct. The major deities have special shrines and priests dedicated to their worship and it is the duty of human beings to strive at all times to live righteously by conducting their lives in accordance with the ethics of the community and by avoiding societal taboos. If for any reason human beings transgress these rules, they are expected to atone for their offenses by performing prescribed ritual acts of expiation.

When those who live well die, they become ancestors in *ani muo* (land of the dead) provided their living relatives have performed the appropriate funeral rites; it is these rites that initiate the dead into the company of the powerful ancestors. Such ancestors take an active interest in the welfare of the living members of their family, who pour libations to them and make offerings to their memory on certain occasions.

Igbo cosomology admits of the existence of evil spirits, *umunadi*, who are believed to live in the liminal, uninhabited spaces beyond the village settlements and also in the bad bush. It also admits of the existence of *ogbanje,* the spirits of children who reincarnate and are born to die, often in infancy, only to be born again by the same or another unfortunate mother.

Duality or the phenomenology of pairing is another very important aspect of Igbo cosmology. In Igbo thought, nothing can exist by itself, since wherever something exists, something else exists beside it. As the proverb says: *Ife kwulu, ife akwudebe ya* (When one thing stands, something else stands beside it.) Thus, there can be no unpaired manifestation of any force or being. Arising from this phenomenon is the Igbo concern for the maintenance of balance in one's life. Because Igbo cosmology envisages the simultaneous functioning of numerous and sometimes, antagonistic forces, one is counseled to tread one's way cautiously so as not to offend any of the contending spirits. Extremism of any kind is thus perceived to be dangerous, as is encapsulated in the following proverb: *ife belu n'oke ka dibia n'agwo* (The healer can cure only something within bounds.)

Reincarnation is a cardinal principle in Igbo cosmology. Ancestors who are well cared for by their living offspring may take on new human bodies and be born as loving children to their former sons and daughters. However, reincarnation is not limited to the ancestors. As has been mentioned earlier, the spirits of some children are also believed to reincarnate only to die young.

Central to Igbo cosmology is one's choice of a destiny. This choice is made freely before the moment of incarnation and is witnessed and sealed by one's chi or personal guiding spirit. The choice the individual makes usually compensates for the circumstances of his or her previous life. Thus, somebody who is killed by his jealous neighbors on account of his excessive wealth in one life may elect to be poor in his next incarnation. However, once the choice has been made and the child is born, his destiny is guarded throughout his life by his chi and cannot be changed. More importantly, once the child is born, he suffers total amnesia with respect to his chosen destiny.

As the child grows, he is socialized into the strong ethos of hard work for which the Igbo people are known, while the egalitarian organization of society encourages him to believe that there is no limit to what he can achieve in life. It is the same ethos of hard work and high self-esteem that Olaudah Equiano refers to in the following description of his Igbo people more that two centuries ago:

> Agriculture is our chief employment; and every one, even the children and women are engaged in it. Thus we are all habituated to labour from earliest years. Every one contributes something to the common stock; and as we are unacquainted with idleness we have no beggars (145).

The amnesia at birth ensures that the pre-incarnation choice (as to whether the individual will be a success or a failure) does not deter the person from striving to achieve the best possible life, since only his chi knows what destiny he has chosen. Regardless of what one's conscious desires may be, the prior choice made functions as the subconscious drive that predisposes the individual to acting in such a way as to fulfill the individual's destiny. This situation does not make the people fatalistic, however, because in the first place, no one remembers what manner of life he or she has chosen. In the second place, the Igbo also firmly believe that human agency is critical to the actualization of one's destiny and that hard work results in a better life. It is only after a person has been dogged by misfortune, despite his or her best effort, that he begins to suspect that he may not be destined for good things after all. Still, the final judgment is withheld until after the death of the individual. It is only after someone's death that the living can then assess his destiny fully. This practice is encapsulated in the proverb: *Chi ejilu ada akalu abosi* (One must not condemn the day until it is over.)

The foregoing is a brief overview of the Igbo cosmology that was in place at the onset of British colonization of Igboland, the historical setting of *Things Fall Apart*. It remains for us to show how this paradigm is reflected in the novel itself.

Things Fall Apart is like an expansive narrative that uses its larger form to frame numerous smaller thematic strands. The main story of the novel is about Okonkwo, the protagonist, who is introduced in the first word of the text. At that point, Okonkwo is already famous on account of his personal accomplishments, especially for his earlier spectacular wrestling victory that is likened to that of the legendary founder of his hometown, who is reputed to have wrestled a spirit of the wilderness for seven days and seven nights. Okonkwo's victory over Amalinze, the Cat, who has held the wrestling championship title for seven years, shows his affinity to his town's founding father. Thus, even at eighteen he has shown that he is a worthy son of Umuofia and appears to be marked out for great achievements.

Sadly, Okonkwo's psyche is so traumatized by his father's penury and the poverty of his early childhood that his psyche remains mortally wounded throughout his life, although his hard work enables him to improve his material welfare; hence, he does not see the full range of dual possibilities inherent in every situation.

Because he loathes his father, he instinctively hates everything that reminds him of Unoka. Because Unoka is weak, Okonkwo strives at all times to exhibit heroic courage, which pushes him to commit excesses like killing Ikemefuna that drive a wedge between him and his son, Nwoye. From the perspective of Igbo cosmology, Okonkwo's inability to recognize the duality and complexity of life situations is a major handicap, since it reveals a fundamental lack of balance in his life.

Okonkwo's problems also emanate from his inability to practice another Igbo ideal, balance in one's assessment of situations, since he usually takes extremist positions in life. For instance, he cannot understand how a strong man like Ogbuefi Ndulue can do nothing without consulting his wife first. Again, to Okonkwo, the new colonial dispensation is an unmitigated evil that should be expunged from his home and he does not realize that many of his people viewed it differently:

> There were many men and women in Umuofia who did not feel as strongly as Okonkwo about the new dispensation. The white man had indeed brought a lunatic religion, but he had also brought a trading store and for the first time palm oil and kernel became things of great price and much money flowed into Umuofia. And even in the matter of religion there was a growing feeling that there might be something in it after all, something vaguely akin to method in the overwhelming madness (2583).

This difference in perception of the problem explains why Umuofia does not join Okonkwo in a battle to drive out the new colonial administration and the Christian missionaries. So in the end, Okonkwo's tragic demise arises from his lack of full understanding of his people and their culture.

However, *Things Fall Apart* is not only the story of the protagonist, Okonkwo; it is also the story of an African community, Umuofia. Contrary to the Hegelian ethnocentric theory of history, which posits that Africa has neither a history nor a future, the Igbo society that Achebe portrays in this novel is keenly aware of its history and the legendary feats of its founding father. It is a society in which someone at the beginning of his career can go to an elder and obtain without any collateral the resources with which to establish himself in life. Above all, it is a society that judges a man not by the size of his inheritance, but rather by his own personal accomplishments. Moreover, in Umuofia, the African community portrayed in the novel, there is marital amity and social problems are resolved on the basis of the consensus emanating from open public debate in a manner that protects not only the rights of the individuals concerned but also the corporate interests of the community.

What informs Achebe's portrait of Umuofia is not mawkish sentimentality, since he shows that the community has its share of internal contradictions, as is true of all human societies. These internal contradictions in all societies explain why new laws are being made to deal with new contradictions as well as to revisit old ones. What is remarkable in the African society portrayed in the novel is that it has achieved a great degree of stability by maintaining a balance between its centrifugal and centripetal forces. Indeed, what informs the novelist's portrait of the society is his conviction, which he has expressed on several occasions, that the African needs to tell his own side of the colonial story himself:

> At the University I read some appalling novels about Africa (including Joyce Cary's much praised *Mr. Johnson*) and decided that the story we had to tell could not be told for us by anyone else, no matter how gifted or well-intentioned ("Named for Victoria" 123).

Like the traditional epics that use the major narratives to frame the many minor ones, *Things Fall Apart* frames numerous minor stories within the major narratives about Okonkwo and his community. One of these minor narratives in the novel is the interrogation of the relationships between fathers and their sons. Igbo society is largely patriarchal and patrilineal; hence, families here depend on the male offspring for succession and the perpetuation of their names. This places a burden on the relationships between fathers and their sons, particularly their first sons. In the novel, Unoka is the founder of his lineage, but he is not successful in agriculture, the principal occupation of his people. His forte is music making and the happiest time of the year for him are those two or three moons after the harvest when the community relaxes from the rigors of farming and entertains itself with music and dance. Regrettably, he is so improvident that he owes his neighbors a lot of money. However, he has a tremendous sense of humor and drama, which he exhibits when one of his creditors, Okoye, asks him to pay him back the money he owes him:

> As soon as Unoka understood what his friend was driving at, he burst out laughing. He laughed loud and long and his voice rang out clear as the ogene, and tears stood in his *eyes*. His visitor was amazed, and sat speechless. At the end, Unoka was able to give an answer between fresh outbursts of mirth. "Look at that wall," he said pointing at the far wall of his hut, which was rubbed with red earth so it shone. "Look at those lines of chalk;" and Okoye saw groups of short perpendicular lines. There were five groups and the smallest group had ten lines. Unoka had a sense of the dramatic; and so he allowed a pause, in which he took a pinch of snuff and sneezed noisily and then continued: "Each group there represents a debt to someone and each stroke is one hundred cowries. You see, I owe that man a thousand cowries. But he has not come to wake me up in the morning for it. I shall pay you, but not today. Our elders say that the sun will shine on those who stand before it shines on those who kneel under them. I shall pay my big debts first." And he took another pinch of snuff, as if that was paying the big debts first. Okoye rolled his goatskin and departed (2506).

Furthermore, Unoka is undoubtedly a coward, and his people regard him as a failure. He is a burden on his son and the other members of his family; hence, Okonkwo is thoroughly ashamed of him.

Ironically, the dysfunctional relationship Okonkwo has with his father is duplicated in the one he has with his own son, Nwoye. Being an Igbo man, Okonkwo must have dreaded (even without admitting it to himself) the uncanny resemblance between Nwoye's temperament and that of Unoka. He must have feared that Nwoye may well be a reincarnation of his father. This may explain why Okonkwo tries to root out in his young son any personality trait he despised in his father. Hence, he encourages Nwoye to come to his dwelling place in order to imbibe the martial traditions of his people. However, the son prefers listening to the folktales, which the father despises as being fit for the ears of women only.

Because Nwoye has come to look up to Ikemefuna as if he were an elder brother, he is devastated by the ritual murder of this role model. This further aggravates the friction between father and son. In addition, there is something in Nwoye, which cannot find fulfillment within the martial ethos of his society. It is indeed this search for something, which his community cannot satisfy, that leads Nwoye into an exploration of the new religion. Unfortunately, Okonkwo's handling of the news that his son has been seen in the company of the missionaries severs the already weak link between the two and emboldens the son to reject his father completely.

Another minor narrative in *Things Fall Apart* is the portrait of the relationships between fathers and their daughters. Igbo society is mainly patrilineal and succession is through the male offspring, who also perpetuates the family name. The society's concern for the survival of the lineage is expressed in such names like Amaechina (may the compound not perish/disappear) or Obiechina (may the household not perish). As is often the case with such patriarchal societies, they treasure their sons more highly than their daughters. Perhaps, because these families expect more from boys than from girls, they exert greater pressure on the boys to succeed than on the girls.

The irony in *Things Fall Apart is* that the boy, Nwoye, runs away from his father, while his sister, Ezinma, dotes on Okonkwo. It is, thus, not surprising that there is a special bond between father and his daughter and that Okonkwo wishes that Ezinma were a boy, as may be seen in the following dialogue between them:

> "You have not eaten for two days," said his daughter Ezinma when she brought the food to him. "So you must finish this."
>
> She sat down and stretched her legs in front of her. Okonkwo ate the food absent-mindedly. "She should have been a boy," he thought as he looked at his ten-year old daughter. He passed her a piece of fish.

> "Go and bring me some cold water," he said. Ezinma rushed out of the hut, chewing the fish, and soon returned with a bowl of cool water from the earthen pot in her mother's hut....
>
> "She should have been a boy," Okonkwo said to himself again" (2532).

Indeed, the bond between Okonkwo and Ezinma is so strong that later when they are in exile a mere word from Okonkwo, expressing his desire that she should hold off getting married until their return to Umuofia makes Ezinma dismiss all good suitors from Mbanta, their place of exile. Thus, it is not unlikely that Okonkwo must have been frustrated that everything he has struggled to accomplish in life will be inherited by his sons, who may not be as deserving as this daughter.

The portrait of the relationships between husbands and their wives is yet another significant narrative framed in *Things Fall Apart.* In Umuofia marriage is more than an affair between two individuals; it is a union of two family groups, who have a mutual interest in preserving that liaison. Marriages here are contracted after elaborate negotiations and public ceremonies, as is exemplified in the *uri* ceremony of Akueke, Obierika's daughter. On this occasion, Obierika's family entertains almost the entire village.

Like marriages all over the world, however, some of the marriages contracted in Umuofia later become dysfunctional, despite the best effort of the two families involved. Some are so bad that they are referred to the community elders for arbitration in the public square, as is the case with the dispute between Uzowulu and his wife. However, even Okonkwo, who abuses his wives, has a very endearing relationship with one of them, Ekwefi – his childhood sweetheart. She has been married before to someone else because Okonkwo was then too poor to finance the required ceremonies. That marriage notwithstanding, Ekwefi one day walks out on her husband and into Okonkwo's home. Thereafter, she becomes his wife. Not surprisingly, the special relationship that exists between Okonkwo and Ekwefi is transferred to their daughter, Ezinma.

Even truly romantic love affairs do exist among some married couples in this society, as is exemplified by the marital bliss of Ogbuefi Ndulue and his wife Ozoemena. So strong is their love for one another that the husband never does anything without consulting his wife first. Indeed, so well known is their love for one another that their community has composed a song about them. The husband and wife are so inseparable, even in their old age, that when Ozoemena learns of the death of her husband, she immediately loses all interest in life. She walks to her house, lies down and passes away that very day.

Another minor narrative that is framed in *Things Fall Apart is* the portrait of the relationships between leadership and followership. In the novel, the highest leadership positions are those of the nine *egwugwu,* who represent the nine villages of the town. Symbolizing the ancestors of the community, these elders arbitrate public disputes and their authority is never challenged, as may be seen in the following formulaic dialogue between Evil Forest, their spokesman, and Uzowulu:

> "Uzowulu's body, I salute you," he said. Spirits always address humans as "bodies." Uzowulu bent down and touched the earth with his right hand as a sign of submission."Our father, my hand has touched the ground," he said. "Uzowulu's body, do you know me?" asked the spirit. "How can I know you, father? You are beyond our knowledge" (2545).

In such situations, the *egwugwu* first allow the contending parties to present their cases and thereafter pronounce a verdict that is not only fair to the parties, but helps to preserve the solidarity of the community.

In *Things Fall Apart,* matters of public concern are generally discussed at town meetings that are open to every male adult. Although, the views of titled men carry infinitely more weight at such public gatherings, yet, everyone who so desires can express his opinion. Eventually a consensus emerges through a reconciliation of the competing viewpoints; whereupon, the consensus becomes the view of the entire community and is, thereafter, expected to be implemented without dissent. This is the case when Ogbuefi Udo's wife is killed in Mbaino. The consensus is that Umuofia should give Mbaino an ultimatum to choose either to pay the agreed upon compensation or to go to war. On another occasion when the peace of the community is threatened by the excesses of the fanatical Christians, a meeting is called and there is a consensus as to how the society should respond. Here again, the community acts as one and speaks with one unmistakable voice. One may rightly deduce then that this is the ideal Igbo political process. It follows, therefore, that good leaders among the Igbo must have consensus building skills. Viewed from this perspective, Okonkwo's leadership skills fail when he is unable to build a consensus as to how Umuofia should respond to the District Commissioner's imprisonment of the community's elders.

Thus far we have shown that in *Things Fall Apart,* there are many minor narratives that are framed by two major ones: the first portrays an individual's single-minded struggle to rise from the humble circumstances of birth to a position of prominence in his community; the second is the narrative of a community that has evolved a civilization through the years as it struggles to adapt to colonial conquest and domination. These two narratives, however, merge into one, since that individual eventually becomes one of the six leaders imprisoned by the District Commissioner.

It now remains for us to show that the universe of *Things Fall Apart is* a reflection of the Igbo cosmology described above. A close examination of the cosmos of *Things Fall Apart* shows that the world portrayed in the novel parallels very closely the universe of Igbo cosmology. For example, in both the Igbo paradigm and *Things Fall Apart,* the town is the unit of political organization. In *Things Fall Apart,* towns like Umuofia, Mbaino, Mbanta, Abame, etc. are also units of political organization since the people see themselves as citizens of these communities. Ordinarily, these autonomous communities live peacefully with one another, except when cordial relations are disturbed by the hostile actions of a neighboring town, as in the murder of an Umuofia woman by a citizen of Mbaino. Even in this case, the prompt payment of a ransom restores the good relations that had been consolidated over the generations through numerous exogamous inter-town marriages. Furthermore, councils of elders rule these towns, as is the case in the real Igbo society.

In addition, the events in the lives of the characters in the novel resemble those of the people one encounters in the Igbo cosmos. For instance, the Igbo concept of reincarnation is reflected in Ezinma's life, since she is *ogbanje* – one of those children who are born to die in infancy and re-enter their mothers' wombs to be born again and again. This explains the intervention of the medicine man who locates Ezinma's *iyi uwa* in his effort to enable her to break the cycle and live.

Furthermore, the marriages in *Things Fall Apart* are negotiated and celebrated in true Igbo manner. Again, the punishment for Okonkwo's involuntary homicide in the novel is a replica of the Igbo response to such a crime. The corpse of someone who takes his or her own life is an abomination and a source of pollution not only to the earth but also to anyone who comes in contact with it. Indeed, the Igbo consider those who take their lives as being so despicable that they are not mourned and, as in Okonkwo's case, only strangers can handle their bodies. Above all, the pervasive role ascribed to Okonkwo's *chi* is a replica of the dominant role that is ascribed to that guardian spirit in Igbo cosmology. These examples demonstrate incontrovertibly that the universe portrayed in *Things Fall Apart* closely reflects the cosmos delineated above.

If, according to the Igbo paradigm, nobody can accomplish anything without the support of his *chi,* to what extent is Okonkwo then responsible for his tragic end? As Achebe himself explains, although no one can achieve anything without the assistance of his *chi,* the Igbo believe that human agency is essential to the realization of one's destiny. Again, in Igbo cosmology, amnesia at birth ensures that each person is unaware of the choice previously made and leads his life in accordance with the Igbo ethos encapsulated in the following proverb: *Onye kwe chi ya ekwe* (When somebody says yes, his *chi* says yes also).

A review of the career of the protagonist shows that he has a very high self-esteem. On account of his individual accomplishments, Okonkwo sees himself as the legendary lizard which jumped down from the high iroko tree and was able to escape from the seven agile men who were waiting to catch it. Indeed, Okonkwo seems to exemplify the Igbo ethos of hard work; by his hard work he has raised himself from the penury of his childhood to the highest leadership position in his society. He has said yes and it seems that his *chi* also supports his efforts, at least initially. Sadly, his traumatic childhood, however, seems to have permanently wounded his psyche and endowed him with a one-dimensional perception of reality that makes him take the personal decisions that precipitate his calamitous end. The Igbo belief that a person cannot achieve anything without the consent of his *chi* must not mislead one to conclude that Okonkwo is merely a pawn in the hands of his guiding spirit. On the contrary, Okonkwo's personality flaws precipitate his catastrophic demise and nullify his individual accomplishments.

By situating *Things Fall Apart* in its cultural milieu, the exposition above has attempted to create for the ever-growing readership of the masterpiece an appropriate epistemological framework that should inform future discourse on its merits and meanings.

Works Cited

Achebe, Chinua. *Things Fall Apart. World Masterpieces.* Ed. Maynard Mack. New York: Norton, 1995. 2498–2597.

Achebe, Chinua. *Morning Yet on Creation Day.* New York: Anchor/Double Day, 1975.

Basden, G.T. *The Niger Ibos.* London: Seely Associates, 1938.

Equiano, Olaudah. *Narrative of the Life of Olaudah Equiano. African American Literature.* Ed. Henry Louis Gates and Nellie Y. McKay. New York: Norton, 1977.

Green, Margaret M. *Ibo Village Affairs.* London: Frank Cass, 1964.

Ottenberg, Simon. "Ibo Receptivity to Change." *Continuity and Change in African Culture.* Ed. William Bascom and Melville Herskovits. Chicago: University of Chicago Press, 1970. 130–143.

Webster's Third New International Dictionary. Springfield, MA: Merriam Webster, 1993.

Chapter 8

Dialogue and Power in Achebe's *Things Fall Apart*

Ifeoma Okoye

THE STUDY REPORTED IN this paper uses a model of conversational analysis to investigate Achebe's use of dialogue, which is fictional conversation, in portraying his theme of power and weakness in *Things Fall Apart*. Conversations, according to discourse analysts, are in some situations power struggles between participants. In such situations participants adopt various strategies to make sure that conversational outcomes match their conversational goals, an achievement that indicates some sort of supremacy. The strategies that conversationalists use in this direction include the use of moves, turns, and some types of speech acts. The results of the study indicate that Achebe successfully uses these strategies to underscore his theme of power and weakness in *Things Fall Apart* and also to delineate Okonkwo's character.

Fictional dialogue (or conversation) has certain important functions. It is used by writers, among other things, to advance plot, delineate character and underscore themes. The purpose of this paper is to investigate whether Achebe in *Things Fall Apart* uses dialogue as a literary artifice to underscore his theme of power and weakness and to delineate his characters. Using a model of conversational analysis, I intend to search for undercurrents of power struggles in pieces of dialogue between Okonkwo and the other characters in the novel. This is in line with the proposition made by some discourse analysts that conversations, in some situations, are power struggles between participants who adopt certain conversational strategies to achieve their goals. I hope that such an analysis will increase the understanding and interpretation of the novel.

Natural conversation, as to be expected, differs in some ways from fictional dialogue. For instance, natural conversation is spontaneous. It also contains more false starts, hesitations, repetitions and blurred utterances than fictional conversation which is often pruned, edited and directed towards what is essential for the forward movement of the story and the delineation of character. All the same, as Toolan (1989: 195) rightly points out, 'certain structural and functional principles govern fictional dialogue as they do natural dialogue.' Following this argument, it is not out of place to use the same tools in analyzing both natural and fictional conversation.

This article is in four parts. The first part briefly discusses conversational analysis and some of its features. The second part presents an outline of the analytical model used in the analysis of the dialogue between Okonkwo and the other characters in *Things Fall Apart*, while the third part presents the results of the analysis. The last part of the article discusses what Achebe's artistic use of dialogue reveals about Okonkwo's character and about the theme of power in the novel.

Conversational Analysis

Conversational analysis is the analysis of naturally occurring conversation. The aim of this type of analysis is to identify the structure and linguistic characteristics of conversation and also to investigate how conversation is used in ordinary life. Conversational analysis, according to Carter and Simpson (1989: 280), 'stresses speaker's own interpretations of the structure of interaction'. It also emphasizes 'the close observation of the behavior of participants in talk and on patterns which recur over a wide range of natural data' (McCarthy 1991: 6).

Conversational analysts have studied a wide range of topics related to conversation. Some of these topics are, according to McCarthy (1991: 24), 'how pairs of utterances relate to one another..., how turn-taking is managed, how conversation openings and closings are effected, how topics enter and disappear from conversation, and how speakers engage in strategic acts of politeness, face preservation and so on.' A full discussion of these topics and others not listed is beyond the scope of this paper. Consequently, only features of conversation that are directly related to the analysis carried out in this article will be briefly discussed.

Some Features of Conversation

Conversation has certain features that distinguish it from other forms of language use. These features occur mostly because conversation takes place between people who are present at the same time and place. The features of conversation which are relevant to and which will be discussed in this paper are *utterance, turn, adjacency pair, speech act, move, exchange* and *transaction.*

a. Utterance

An utterance can be defined in terms of syntax and of semantics. It is a stretch of talk that is an independent clause or an elliptical clause. Expressions like *yes, really,* and tags like *Are you?* are also utterances. An utterance expresses a proposition. However, some conversation analysts posit that expressions like *yah, erm, ugh,* which have no propositional content and which are used to cover confusion or embarrassment are also utterances.

b. Turn

The turn is the basic analytical unit in conversational analysis. It is defined by Gramley and Patzold (1992: 229) as 'consisting of all the speaker's utterances up to the point when another person takes over the role of speaker.' Participants in a conversation know when to speak and when to listen and not to speak. They follow some rules without which conversation will break down as participants interrupt one another or talk simultaneously. An example of turn from *Things Fall Apart* is given below. The example contains two turns, one by Ezinwa and another by Okonkwo:

Example 1

'Obiageli broke her pot today,' Ezinma said.
'Yes, she has told me about it,' Okonkwo said between mouthfuls (32).

c. Adjacency Pair

An adjacency pair is a sequence of two related utterances produced by two different speakers with the second utterance always a response to the first. It consists of two utterances successively produced by different speakers in a fixed order. Examples of adjacency pair include a question followed by an answer, a greeting followed by a greeting, and a complaint followed by an apology, a denial or a justification.

An adjacency pair has two parts: the first pair part and the second pair part. In a question and answer sequence, the question is the first pair part while the answer is the second pair part. Sometimes, however, the two parts do not follow on immediately because other conversational matters are inserted.

Participants in a conversation usually know what is often expected (preferred second) after an adjacency pair and what is not (dispreferred second). For example, speakers prefer their questions to be followed by answers, their requests by grants, and their invitations, by acceptances. As Coulthard (1985: 70) puts it, 'The first pair part provides specifically for the second and therefore the absence of the second is noticeable and noticed.' For instance, when a speaker receives no reply to his or her question, or when his or her greeting is not returned, he or she infers that something is wrong. Below is an example of an adjacency pair with a dispreferred second pair part from *Things Fall Apart.* One of Okonkwo's wives wants to know how long Ikemefuna is going to stay with them.

Example 2

'Is he staying long with us?' she asked.

> 'Do what you are told, woman,' Okonkwo thundered and stammered. 'When did you become one of the ndichie of Umuofia?' (10)

From our knowledge of adjacency pairs, we expect Okonkwo to provide an answer to his wife's question but what we get, surprisingly, is a directive and another question.

d. Speech Acts

The term speech act, according to Carter and Simpson (1989: 290), 'refers to what is done when something is said (e.g. requesting, stating, declaring, warning, threatening, etc.).' It is the expression of the function an utterance has in discourse. The term was coined by the linguist philosopher Austin (1962) and developed by another philosopher Searl (1969).

In speech act theory, utterances have two kinds of meaning: the propositional meaning (or locutionary force) and the illocutionary meaning (illocutionary force). The propositional meaning is the 'basic literal meaning of the utterance that is conveyed by the particular words and structures which the utterance contained' (Richards, Platt and Webber: 1985: 265), For example, the utterance, "Go", has the propositional meaning of an imperative. The illocutionary meaning, on the other hand, is the effect the utterance has on the hearer. For instance, depending on the context of situation, "Go" may perform the illocutionary force of ordering or advising someone to go, or granting someone the permission to go.

A speech act that is performed indirectly is called an indirect speech act. It is expressed through the performance of another speech act. It often shows a discrepancy between grammatical form and communicative function. In such a situation the declarative, interrogative, and imperative moods do not (exclusively) realise statements, questions, and orders. The utterance, *Have you a pen?* may not be a question but an indirect way of requesting for a pen (request). Indirect speech acts are often polite ways of performing some kinds of speech acts like requests and refusals.

e. Move

The move is roughly the same as a speaker's turn and is the minimal interactive unit in discourse. It has an internal structure of its own and consists of one or more acts. Moves, in Toolan's (1989: 198) words, 'are the primary level for the propulsion of talk, and mark the transition points at which subsequent speakers are chiefly drawn to respond.' In the example below, which is taken from *Things Fall Apart,* there are two moves, an opening move and an answering move. Okonkwo makes the opening move.

> Example 3
>
> 'Where is Ojiugo?' he asked his second wife.
> 'She has gone to plait her hair' (21).

f. Exchange

Exchange is defined by Stubbs (1983: 104) as 'the minimal interactive unit'. In the simplest example, an exchange consists of two moves only: a speaker initiates a conversation (Initiate) and the hearer reacts positively to this move (Respond). Below is an example of an Initiation and Response (IR) from *Things Fall Apart:*

Example 4

'You must take him to salute our father,' said one of the cousins.
'Yes,' replied Okonkwo, 'we are going directly...' (96).

g. Transaction

A transaction is made up of one or more exchanges, all of which relate to the same general topic. For example, in *Things Fall Apart,* all the exchanges by Okonkwo and his senior wife as he introduces Ikemefuna to her make up one transaction. (10–11).

A Framework for the Analysis

I now wish to draw upon some important features of conversation that have been found by conversational analysts to portray some power relationship between participants. In this section I am going to discuss these features and try to define them operationally.

a. Directive

A directive is a speech act whose function is to request a non-linguistic response. It can be realized by interrogatives, imperatives, and declaratives as the examples below illustrate:

Example 5

a. Will you stop interrupting? (a directive realized by interrogative)
b. Go away. (a directive realized by an imperative)
c. You must see me tomorrow. (a directive realized by a declarative)

Below are some examples of directives from *Things Fall Apart:*

Example 6

a. Do what you are told, woman (10).
b. Take away your kola nut... (21).
c. Do not bear a hand in his death (40).
d. Leave that boy at once (107).

Conversational analysts assert that power may be exercised through the use of directives in conversations. For instance, Coulthard (1985: 183) after a conversational analysis of Pinter's play *The Dumb Waiter,* concludes that Ben, a character in the play, 'is dominating because he performs the acts that dominating participants perform: he issues more than sixty directives, receives four (and ignores three of them). Similarly, Short (1989: 155) in his analysis of Shaw's *Major Barbara* seems to support Coulthard when he states that Lady Britomart's frequent use of command (directive) demonstrates her complete dominance of her son.

In the same vein, directives in Igbo culture are most likely to be given to the less powerful by the more powerful. One cannot imagine a child in Igboland saying to his father, *'Come here'* or a slave giving a directive to a freeborn.

b. Turn-taking

A very important feature of turn taking, especially for the analysis reported in this article, is that turns to speak are valued and speakers compete for them. People who are shy, inarticulate, timid, self-effacing and diffident might find it difficult to select themselves to speak, to take their turns when they are nominated by a speaker, or to break into a conversation so as to be heard.

Some features of turn taking have been identified as power indicators. For example, Short (1989: 155) states that 'factors which indicate dominant relation in conversation (or fictional/dramatic dialogue) 'are who speaks first, and hence initiates the exchange, and who speaks the most.'

c. Moves

Another feature of conversation that has been identified as power indicator is the move. Two types of moves have been found to be connected with power. One is the opening move. According to Short (1989: 155), initiating the exchange, that is, making an opening move, indicates dominance. Explaining this assertion, Coulthard (1985: 83) states that the person who makes the opening move usually decides the topic, and deciding the topic of conversation and controlling the topic indicate dominance.

The second type of move that is connected with power is the challenging move. The use of challenging move indicates dominance because it is often powerful people who challenge the weak or who interrupt the weak, and the challenging move is a type of interruptive language.

Opening moves and challenging moves are defined by Burton (1980) as follows:

> *opening moves:* essentially topic-carrying items which are recognizably 'new' in terms of the immediately preceding talk;
> *challenging moves:* function to hold up the progress of topic or the introduction of a topic in some way.

The Analysis

Using the features of conversation that indicate power and dominance, I constructed an analytical framework. In each transaction I worked out the following:

a) the number of directives issued by each participant;
b) the participant who makes the opening move;
c) the participant(s) who make(s) challenging moves;
d) the number of turns taken by each participant and
e) The participant who makes the largest number of turns in a transaction. I analyzed only pieces of dialogue in which Okonkwo is a participant.

Results of the Analysis

Altogether there are twenty-nine transactions in which Okonkwo takes part: seven with his wives, three with his children, six with the elders, twelve with Obierika (and others) and one with the interpreter. In these twenty-nine transactions Okonkwo makes fifteen opening moves altogether. He initiates all transactions with his wives, all but one with his children, and five out of the nine transactions he has with his bosom friend, Obierika. Okonkwo does not initiate any of the transactions he has with his elders: Ogbuefi Ezeudu, Ezeani the Priest of Earth, Ogbuefi Ezenwa and Uchendu.

The same pattern occurs in turn taking. Okonkwo has more turns in his transactions with his wives and children: seventeen out of twenty-seven and seven out of eleven respectively. He shares the turns equally with Obierika and has only eight turns out of twenty-eight turns in transactions with his elders.

Altogether, twenty-two directives occur in pieces of dialogue between Okonkwo and the other participants. Of this number fourteen are from Okonkwo, three from Ezeani, the Priest of the Earth Goddess, two from Uchendu, Okonkwo's uncle, one from Ogbuefi Ezeudu, and one from Ezinma and one from Okonkwo's cousin. Okonkwo gives three directives to his senior wife, five to Ekwefi, his other wife, three to his wives in general, and three to Ezinma, his daughter. Okonkwo does not give any directives to Ezeani, Ogbuefi Ezeudu and Uchendu. On the other hand, he receives three from Ezeani, and two from Ezeudu. He also receives one from Ezinma, one from Obierika. Examples of directives in the novel are:

> Take away your Kola nut (21) (Ezeani to Okonkwo).
> Sit like a woman (32) (Okonkwo to his daughter).
> Do not bear a hand in his death (40) (Ezeudu to Okonkwo).
> Go home and sleep (76) (Okonkwo to Ekwefi his wife).

Interpretation of Results

From these results what can we infer about Okonkwo's character and about power relations between him and the other characters in the novel? What do these findings say about the theme of power and weakness in *Things Fall Apart*?

The results uncover some interesting things about Okonkwo's power or strength. The first is that he is powerless in the presence of the elders and priests: Ogbuefi Ezeudu, Ogbuefi Ezeani, Ezenwa and Uchendu. He stands in awe in front of these people. They give him directives, which he carries out without argument and they receive no directives from him. They frighten him so much that he is afraid to take his conversational turns in transactions with them. Sometimes when he summons up courage to speak to them, he is cowed. Two examples will suffice to illustrate these points: the interaction between Okonkwo and Ezeani, the Priest of the Earth Goddess and the one between Okonkwo and his uncle Uchendu:

> (a). Interaction between Okonkwo and Ezeani:
> His tone now changed from anger to command. 'You will bring to the shrine of Ani tomorrow one she goat, one hen, a length of cloth and a hundred cowries.' He rose and left the hut. Okonkwo did as the priest said (22).
> (b). Interaction between Okonkwo and Uchendu:
> 'Leave that boy at once!' said a voice in outer compound. It was Okonkwo's uncle Uchendu. 'Are you mad?' Okonkwo did not answer. But he left hold of Nwoye, who walked away and never returned (107).

In each of these instances Okoknwo forfeits his turn to speak and obeys the directives immediately.

Another important point to note is that Okonkwo's power seems to be limited to his household – his wives and children. He gives them directives and receives none from them except one from Ezinma, his favorite daughter. He frightens his wives into forfeiting their conversational turns or bombards them with questions. Below are some examples:

> 'Are you all deaf and dumb?' (27)

This is a directive to all his wives. It is an indirect speech act meaning that they should speak up.

> 'Get me a pot'
> 'Are you deaf?'
> 'Bring a low stool for Ezinwa and a thick mat' (53).

All these directives are given to Ekwefi his wife. The significance of Okonkwo's directives to his wives is underscored by authorial description of Okonkwo's relationship with his family:

> Okonkwo ruled his household with a heavy hand. His wives, especially the youngest, lived in perpetual fear of his fiery temper (9).

A third point that can be inferred from the results of the analysis is that Okonkwo does not display his power when he is dealing with those that are dear to him. He allows his favorite daughter to give him a directive without rebuking her:

> 'You have not eaten for two days,' said his daughter Ezinma when she brought the food to him, 'so you must finish this.' She sat down and stretched her legs in front of her. Okonkwo ate the food absent-mindedly (44).

In the extract quoted above, Ezinma, besides giving the directive, '*You must finish this,*' to her father, makes the opening move – a move that indicates, like giving a directive, that she is not dominated by her father. Unfortunately, this is not the case between Okonkwo and his wives. None of them makes an opening move in all their transactions with him. This state of affairs might mean that Okonkwo's wives are below his favorite daughter in the rungs of power in the family.

A second favorite of Okonkwo who is not dominated by him is Obierika. In all his interactions with Obierika, Okonkwo gives him no directives. In the eleven interactions between the two, Okonkwo makes five opening moves while Obierika makes six. All these go to show that the two friends treat each other as equals.

One of Okonkwo's ambitions is to be seen as a powerful man. He tries, though unsuccessfully to a certain extent, to accomplish his goal through conversational and other strategies.

Works Cited

Austin, J.L. (1962). *How To Do Things With Words.* Oxford: Oxford University Press.

Carter, Ronald and Simpson, Paul. (eds) (1989). *Language, Discourse and Literature: An Introductory Reader in Discourse Stylistics.* London: Unwin Hyman.

Coulthard, Malcolm. (1985). *An Introduction to Discourse Analysis.* London: Longman.

Gramley, Stephen and Patzold, Kurt-Michael. (1992). *A Survey of Modern English.* London: Routledge.

McCarthy, Michael. (1991). *Discourse Analysis for Language Teachers.* Cambridge: Cambridge University Press.

Richards, Jack, John Platt and Heidi Weber. (1985). *A Dictionary of Linguistics.* London: Longman.

Sinclair, J. Coulthard, R.M. (1975). *Towards An Analysis of Discourse.* Oxford: Oxford University Press

Short, Mich. (1989). "Discourse Analysis and the Analysis of Drama." In Ronald Carter and Paul Simpson (eds) *Language, Discourse and Literature. An Introductory Reader in Discourse Stylistics.* London: Unwin Hyman.

Stubbs, M. (1983). *Discourse Analysis.* Blackwell: Oxford.

Toolan, Michael. (1989). "Analysing Conversation in Fiction: An Example from Joyce's Portrait." In Ronald Carter and Paul Simpson (eds).

Chapter 9

A Balance of Stories or Pay-back: Chinua Achebe, Joyce Cary, and the Literature of Africa

Chris Walsh

IN HIS NEW BOOK of essays, *Home and Exile,* Chinua Achebe recalls the big blue mail trucks brought by British colonials, trucks that barreled perilously down the narrow village roads. *Ogbu-akwu-okwu,* the village children called them – "Killer who doesn't pay back" (77). Paying back was crucial in Achebe's native Igbo culture as he depicted it in his landmark novel, *Things Fall Apart.* The hero, Okonkwo, having accidentally shot and killed a boy, knows that he must leave his clan for seven years. A friend wonders at the fairness of such punishment:

> Why should a man suffer so grievously for an offense he had committed inadvertently? But although he thought for a long time he found no answer. He was merely led into greater complexities. He remembered his wife's twin children, whom he had thrown away. What crime had they committed? The Earth had decreed that they were an offense on the land and must be destroyed. And if the clan did not exact punishment for an offense against the great goddess, her wrath was loosed on all the land and not just on the offender. As the elders said, if one finger brought oil it soiled the others (125).

Without glossing over the brutality of Igbo culture, Achebe shows in its mode of justice clear accountability – a transparent, if hardly a logical, connection between cause and consequence. Obviously not so, in the eyes of the village children, for *Ogbu-akwu-okwu.*

To this day, foreigners driving in Africa are often advised – usually by other foreigners – not to stop if they are involved in an accident. Better to keep driving than face instant extra-legal justice. One is tempted to see in this advice a reflection of western attitudes toward Africa. We have run it over, it is wounded, ravaged, diseased, and all things considered it is best to keep on truckin'. Achebe does not use such a gross metaphor. He does see though, in the writing of just about every western observer of Africa up until independence, a malicious, patronizing and self-serving account – "hundreds of years of sustained denigration" that Africans have "been subjected to in order to make our colonization [and enslavement] possible and excusable" (33).

> This tradition of derogation must be countered, Achebe writes, though he acknowledges the difficulties of such a project, calling, as it must do, on every faculty of mind and spirit; drawing, as it must, from every resource of memory and imagination and from a familiarity with our history, our arts and culture; but also from an unflinching consciousness of the flaws that blemished our inheritance – such an enterprise could not be expected to be easy. And it has not been (79–80).

Achebe knows; he writes with the well-earned authority of a veteran of the battle – a battle far from over, and far from lost. He is refreshingly sanguine about the potential and proven ability of Africans to reclaim their narratives, to tell their own stories in their own ways. The territory of the imagination, though easy to invade, seems impossible quite to subdue.

Yet in *Home and Exile*, Achebe tendentiously dismisses works that deserve more considered attention and in so doing, he undermines the very project he has worked so hard and so successfully to advance. His critique of Joseph Conrad is by now perhaps well known, but he returns to it here and fails to make his case any more convincing. He quotes Marlow's statement about the Congolese in *Heart of Darkness* – "Well, you know, that was the worst of it – this suspicion of their not being inhuman" – and proceeds to give a close misreading of it:

> Note first the narrator's suspicion; just suspicion, nothing more. And, note also that even the faint glimmer of apparent charitableness around this speculation is not, as you might have thought, a good thing, but actually the worst of it! And note finally the coup de grace of double negation, like a pair of prison guards restraining that problematic being on each side (46–47).

Ignored is the irony (probable on Marlow's part, certain on Conrad's) indicated by the hesitation of "Well, you know," by the monstrous understatement of "suspicion," and by the confusing negations which are not jailers constraining us to a single unproblematic reading, but rather flags waving for our second thoughts. Never minded is the context in which Marlow tells his tale, that he begins by directing his auditors' (and the reader's) gaze to the Thames that flows beneath them, saying,

"And this also... has been one of the dark places of the earth" (19). The sly ambiguity of the imperfect past tense should discourage the reader from jumping to conclusions – "has been" might still be. But Achebe is in too much of a hurry to condemn pausing for such nuance.

Conrad, however, probably does not need defending; he can take care of himself. More troublesome is Achebe's thoroughgoing attack on a novel and novelist less likely to be recognized for their considerable merits, *Mister Johnson* by Joyce Cary. This is a shame for the book and its writer, but perhaps more importantly it is a shame for current and future writing about Africa. Achebe's attack stifles rather than liberates the imaginative investigation, revelation and reclamation of Africa as a literary subject.

Legend has it that it was Cary's book that provoked Achebe to become a writer – a legend elaborated upon in *Home and Exile*. The novel was assigned by one of Achebe's European professors at the University of Ibadan, presumably in an effort to make the curriculum more relevant to Nigerian students. To the astonishment of the professor, all the students hated the book, especially its main character. There was consensus "exasperation at this bumbling idiot... whom Joyce Cary and our teacher were so assiduously passing off as a poet when he was nothing but an embarrassing nitwit!" (23). Nonetheless, Achebe was grateful to have read the novel. It "open[ed] my eyes to the fact that my home was under attack," he writes, "and that my home was not merely a house or a town but, more importantly, an awakening story in whose ambience my own existence had first begun to assemble its fragments into a coherence and meaning...." This "awakening story," the one Achebe has since spent his life writing, is emphatically "not," he says, "the same story Joyce Cary intended me to have" (38). *Mister Johnson* delivered a bracing slap to the young Achebe, shocking him into an awareness of the tradition of derogatory "African literature," of which it was only the latest and most prominent example.

It is hard to refute the bad impression a given book makes on a given reader, and it is hard to regret such an impression if it stimulates the production of a body of fiction such as Achebe's. But *Mister Johnson is* in fact one of the pioneers, in the most positive sense, of the project Achebe so stirringly promotes. The novel enriches our understanding of the African colonial experience as lived by both colonists and colonized, showing in its comedy the rich human potential of the continent and in its tragedy the manifold ways in which this potential is mocked and smothered. It also, as a foundational text, enriches our understanding of the literature that has followed it, including not least – indeed, including especially – *Things Fall Apart*.

Achebe's Okonkwo is a fiercesome defender of tradition, unbending to the tragic end to the new white "civilization." Cary's Mister Johnson is a clerk in colonial Nigeria who could not be more enthusiastic in his embrace of the new civilization – he too to the tragic end. Origins help explain these characters' different responses to colonization. While Okonkwo, driven in his quest for pride of place among his people by the shame of his failure of a father, is a storied man, celebrated as a wrestler and warrior, the background of Mister Johnson is nearly blank. In the town of Fada, where the novel is set, he is a stranger to both the local Africans and British colonials. All we know is his last name and that he "is a temporary clerk, still on probation... only seventeen and completely alone" (17). Johnson could be one of the strangers in the new Native Court that helps *Things Fall Apart* in Achebe's novel. "Most of these strangers came from the distant town of Umuru on the bank of the Great River where the white man first went." Okonkwo hates them. While he was in exile, they convinced many of the adults of his home village that "leaders of the land in the future would be men and women who had learned to read and write" and so children should be sent to the white man's school (181).

Johnson has apparently been at the white man's school all his short life, and has drunk deeply of the spirit, if he has not learned the exact letter, of its lessons. "England is my country," he sings:

> Oh, England my home all on de big water.
> Dat King of England is my King,
> De bes' man in de worl', his heart is too big.
> Oh, England my home all on de big water (35).

Thus praising England and King, Johnson dances "with peculiar looseness as if all his joints are turned to macaroni" into a celebration of self, into the King praising *him,* and thence into an ecstatic colonial vision of mutual glorification:

> Hi, you general dar, bring me de cole beer,
>
> I, Mister Johnson, from Fada, I belong for King's service, Hi, you judge dar, in yo crinkly wig, Roll me out dat bed, hang me up dat royal net.... Hi, you coachy man with you peaky hat, Bring me dat gold pot for I make my night water. I, Mister Johnson from Fada, I big man for Fada,.... De King, he say....
>
> I know dat Johnson from Fada, he my faithful clerk from Fada, He drunk for me, he drunk for love of his royal King, He drunk becas he come here, he doanno how to be so happy, He got no practice in dem great big happiness.... (36–37).

It is easy to see why Johnson strikes Achebe as an "embarrassing nitwit." His love of Western civilization is hardly requited. He is beaten, accused (justly) of embezzlement and incompetence, fired, reduced to rags, rehabilitated, arrested, finally executed. What sort of fool would suffer this all as Johnson does – so gladly and gratefully?

> It is Johnson's blessing and curse to have an exuberant, unflagging imaginion.
>
> To him Africa is simply perpetual experience, exciting, amusing, alarming or delightful, which he soaks into himself through all five senses at once, and

> produces again in the form of reflections, comments, songs, jokes, all in the pure Johnsonian form. Like a horse or a rose tree, he can turn the simplest and crudest form of fodder into beauty and power of his own quality (112).

Or, to name the obvious literary progenitor, like Don Quixote. But the object of Quixote's obsession is more forgiving than that of Johnson's. Knight-errancy is already something of the past by the time Quixote gets to it, and has nothing to lose from an imaginative embrace. "Civilization" as it comes to Africa is of the present and future; it cannot afford to tolerate aberrations like Johnson. V.S. Pritchett asserts that "'civilization' has got angry with [Johnson] [b]ecause it doesn't understand his kind of imagination" (*xv*). It is possible to be more exact. In Cary's depiction, "civilization" is an inexorable force, but it requires and rewards not exuberant engagement, as Johnson renders unto it, but winking allegiance, half-measures and half-hearts. "[A]bove all," says one of the colonial administrators, "not too much zeal" (269). Achebe sees this too. The most successful missionary in *Things Fall Apart* "preached against... excess of zeal. Everything was possible, he told his energetic flock, but everything was not expedient" (178).

It is precisely Johnson's zeal that makes him a tragic character. Tragic and, yes, embarrassing, too – not just for Achebe and his fellow Nigerian students, but for every reader caught up in and (inevitably) compromised by "civilization." Okonkwo will have nothing of compromise or accommodation. "Let us not reason like cowards," he says, and he vows to fight alone, if need be, against the white man (158). His belligerence, his contrary zeal, is of course as intolerable as Johnson's enthusiasm. The fates of these men are as similar as their characters are different; both are doomed from the start.

If Johnson is a worthy descendant of Quixote, he is also a worthy ancestor of, for example, the narrator of Ken Saro-Wiwa's *Sozaboy: A Novel in Rotten English.* Young Mene becomes Sozaboy – a soldier-boy – for some of the same reasons Johnson becomes a clerk – out of vanity, to get a girl, to become important.

> In the town I was telling everybody, prouding that I am now going to soza tomorrow. That I will fight the enemy to nonsense. That I will bring plenty things back to Dukana afterwards. And whenever I talk, the people are looking at me like I am wonderful porson and saying "Sozaboy" (68).

The trials of war correct Sozaboy's vainglory, while Johnson takes his civilized delusions to the grave; but then the blandishments of civilization are more seductive and sustaining than the brutality of war (though civilization has its brutality, and war its blandishments).

In Wole Soyinka's play, *The Lion and the Jewel,* the notion of "civilization" gets liberated (at least partially) from England, but the ardor of Lakunle, the schoolteacher in the play, matches Johnson's. Lakunle disparages "savage custom" (8) and without irony heralds "progress":

> We'll burn the forest, cut the trees
> Then plant a modern park for lovers
> We'll print newspapers every day
> With pictures of seductive girls.
> The world will judge our progress by
> The girls that win beauty contests.
> While Lagos builds new factories daily
> We only play "ayo" and gossip.
> Where is our school of ballroom dancing?
> Who here can throw a cocktail party?
> We must be modern with the rest
> Or live forgotten by the world
> We must reject the palm wine habit
> And take to tea, with milk and sugar (34).

We appear to have stumbled upon a stock character in African literature – a dandy of sorts, on the make towards what he sees as the future, and, unlike the understandably reactionary Okonkwo, enjoying what cannot be helped. Surely on a continent as large and various as Africa, a character like Mr. Johnson (or Sozaboy, or Lakunle) *could* happen; surely this is better measure of realism and authenticity, of worthiness for inclusion in the "awakening story" than whether certain readers find him a "bumbling idiot." An author who depicts such a character does not thereby tout the West or fault Africa. He recognizes a phenomenon, a persona that sometimes manifests itself in the colonial setting, with all its imbalance, corruption and perversion.

Cary's British colonials do not know what to make of Johnson, and so they make very little of him indeed. The suggestively named Rudbeck, an Assistant District Officer, is incapable of ideas himself but a predecessor has impressed upon him the importance of transportation infrastructure. He becomes obsessed with building a connection to trading routes in the North: the road is on his back. It is Johnson, however, who makes the connection possible, coaxing villagers to work on the road by making a party and a contest of the project. Rudbeck acknowledges his ingenuity in this, telling a superior that Johnson is "the man with the ideas." But he cannot believe himself. He is "surprised by his own remark. He gazes at Johnson thoughtfully as if to get a new conception of him. Then he gives a snort of laughter, which means that the accepted idea will have to do for the present... "(189). He must be, as Achebe has him, a nitwit; but Cary has, subtly but amply, given the lie to this "accepted idea."

Rudbeck's wife updates Dicken's Mrs. Jellyby, whose "telescopic philanthropy" entailed charity to all creatures on God's earth, just so long as they were far, far away-somewhere like Africa. The world is a smaller place in the twentieth century, and Celia Rudbeck has come to Africa, insisting on being the good "government wife," insisting that Johnson take her to see the people her husband has come to save and enlighten (112). From England Mrs. Jellyby "could see nothing nearer than Africa," but Mrs. Rudbeck from up close can take in only a prefabricated picture of the continent. Her eyes "see only native huts, African bush; not human dwellings, Johnson's home, living trees" (117). To her Johnson is, affectionately she thinks, "Wog" – a term that reflects the extent of her vision and imagination, so woefully limited compared to the man she derogates.

Sergeant Gollup is a storekeeper, a former British Army man whom the people of Fada find likably gruff, brute though he is. He beats his girlfriend – "on week days... he uses only his feet or fists" but on Sundays, when he gets especially drunk, "he will sometimes thrash [her] with a stick, flog her, or even batter her with a chair until she lies on the floor covered with blood" (156) – and he beats Johnson too. When Johnson hits back, Gollup is full of respect for him (though he still fires him): "I say, you're too good for a nig, Johnson – ah, it's a pity – you ought to been one of the higher races, wot got the intelligence too" (172). One fears that Achebe would miss the irony of such a statement made in such a way, coming from such a person – and with the n-word the book disappears off the few syllabi on which it might have remained.

Like Conrad, Cary shows that it is possible to be both a perpetrator and victim of colonialism. The British colonials he portrays are more helpless and ignorant than those they subject; they just have some power. Significant power, certainly, power of life and death, it turns out, but no control, nor even any understanding, of the forces that are shaping the destiny of Africa, and their own destiny. The road embodies these forces. When a lorry comes "pounding out of the shadows," its impatient driver oblivious to the men still laboring to finish their work, the road "open[s] itself" (208). It brings equally (or perhaps not quite equally) trade and crime, enlightenment and repression, hospitals and disease. (It will, one can assume, eventually also bring a postal system too, and those trucks that do not pay back.) The road demonstrates a self-determining will unique in the novel and, after it completes itself, it speaks to Rudbeck with unrivalled impudence and authority:

> I am the revolution. I am giving you plenty of trouble already, you governors, and I am going to give you plenty more. I destroy and I make new. What are you going to do about it? I am your idea. You made me, so I suppose you know (215).

But Rudbeck does not know; none of the colonials has any idea what is happening.

All they have is a purblind faith in Mother England – a faith fully blind in Johnson, because so fully imagined. For this, he must be sacrificed.

In *Things Fall Apart,* Achebe captures the savagery and the insidiousness of colonialism's carrot-and-stick advance. When the first white man came to a nearby village on a bicycle, "the clan killed [him] and tied the iron horse to their sacred tree because it looked as though it would run away to call the man's friends" (138). Soon thereafter, whites orchestrate a massacre of market-goers. When a white missionary then comes to Umuofia, Okonkwo's home village, he promises iron horses to the villagers themselves. Missionaries bring not only bicycles and "a lunatic religion, but... also a trading store and for the first time palm-oil and kernel became things of great price, and much money flowed into Umuofia" (178). Soon the missionaries convert many people from Okonkwo's clan, including even his own son. They also divert Okonkwo's clansmen from his return from exile, so preoccupied are they by the "new religion and government and the trading stores" (182). His hatred and resentment could not be deeper.

In contrast to the people of Umuofia, the people of Fada have had much experience of colonials and so possess "an intelligent or intuitive penetration into the white man's mind.... They know him and his thoughts far better, probably, than his own family relations at home. They give more concentration to the study of them, and they have less distractions" (82). The always eloquent Benjamin, the post office clerk, sees early on the danger of Sergeant Gollup: "it is all simply stupid and senseless if a savage man like that can spoil your health," he tells Johnson (169). Later he warns Johnson against the robbery of Gollup that is his final undoing. He distinguishes the proposed theft from other crimes – "To steal money like that... it's a bad kind of robbery" – and criticizes it on moral and religious grounds: "But Johnson, if all people did so... there would be nothing but bad trouble everywhere. There would be no civilization possible.... I fear you will be sorry, Johnson. It is always dangerous for a Christian to do serious crimes" (247–250).

Fadans also offer comic commentary on white ways. When Johnson plays the romantic suitor, elaborately praising his wife-to-be, Bamu, she asks, "Why does he go on like that?" (24). At their wedding she maintains her dignity by refusing to participate in the Christian charade of repeating the wedding vow: "Don't be silly – I know how to get married" (41). This is the voice of common sense, secure in its cultural heritage, uncorrupted by power or wealth, undisturbed by travel. Its stubborn close-mindedness is part of its dignity.

Cary presents a full complement of self-regarding, ambitious, cruel, and petty natives too. The picture as a whole that emerges, white and black, is of the usual individual human folly exacerbated by the more general and novel folly of the colonial encounter.

Achebe would obviously not agree with this characterization. It is finally not

Johnson, "infuriating" though he is, that troubles him most, but a "certain undertow of uncharitableness just below the surface on which [Cary's] narrative moves and from where, at the slightest chance, a contagion of distaste, hatred and mockery breaks through to poison his tale" (24). He quotes Cary's description of Fada as damning evidence of this lack of charity:

> Fada is the ordinary native town of the Western Sudan. It has no beauty, convenience or health. It is a dwelling place at one stage from the rabbit warren or the badger burrow; and not so cleanly kept as the latter. It is a pioneer settlement five or six hundred years old, built on its own rubbish heaps, without charm even of antiquity. Its squalor and its stinks are all new. Its oldest compounds, except the Emir's mud box, is not twenty years old. The sun and the rain destroy all its antiquity, even of smell.
>
> But neither has it the freshness of the new. All its mud walls are eaten as if by smallpox; half of the mats in any compound are always rotten. Poverty and ignorance, the absolute government of jealous savages, conservative as only the savage can be, have kept it at the first frontier of civilization. Its people would not know the change if time jumped back fifty thousand years. They live like mice or rats in a palace floor; all the magnificence and variety of the arts, the ideas, the learning and the battles of civilization go on over their heads and they do not even imagine them (121).

Good old misanthropy should not be mistaken for racism; also, subjected to a simultaneously negligent and oppressive occupation, to alien arms and germs, and in the wake of the slave trade, in a harsh climate with depleted soils, a village might subsist in the state Cary describes. But his stridency here is difficult to defend, particularly in the paragraph's last sentence. In the event of their characterizations, Cary does not reduce any Fadan to a rodent on a palace floor, but he largely fails to show the "beauty... the arts, the ideas," the mores, the standards and cosmology which endure all but the most abject poverty. For a proper appreciation, celebratory but not uncritical, of the human culture of the so-called "primitive" African society, we must turn to, for instance, Achebe.

Cary for his part does include sympathetic, almost romanticized versions of village life. When Johnson makes his pitch to men to help build the road,

> The village assembly listens in silence. The harvest for the year is over, it is holiday time; the days grow hotter. The women are brewing the New Year's beer. Every week there is a hunt; the grass is set on fire to drive the deer, the men lie in wait for them and afterwards there is a feast of meat. There are songs and dances, drumming all night. The whole village gets drunk. It is the happy time, the good time of the year when, after months of hard work, a man can live, day and night, in friendship and the joy of his heart (196–7).

Naturally, Achebe might object, with some reason, to the simplistic noble savagery of this scene. But this sort of game – "Look, the author says something nice here!" "No, he doesn't!" – has no place in the criticism or the appreciation of literature. A novelist does not know charity, justice or injustice except as these are determined by the story he tells. The bleak description of Fada undergirds the character study that is at the heart of *Mister Johnson.* Balzac in *Pere Goriot* compares the squalid neighborhood where Rastignac lives in a boarding house to the Catacombs. "It's a good comparison!" the narrator insists. "Who's to say what's more horrible to see [there], the dried hearts or the empty heads?" (29). Of course these are living people he describes; but the hyperbole helps us understand the desire that drives Rastignac throughout the *Comedie Humaine* – the desire to overcome, once and for all. At the grave of Old Goriot he famously shakes his fist at Paris and says, "It's between you and me now," and the reader understands and believes. Johnson's plight is not unlike Rastignac's. He is a "temporary clerk, still on probation"-and he does not make it through probation. Thanks to his striking Gollup and other misadventures, we find him halfway through the novel, "dressed in a filthy pair of drawers and the brim of a soft felt hat. He is accompanied by a young woman, also in rags, with a baby on her back" (185–186). The uncharitable undertow has got him, and his wife and child. The reader (this reader) sees not a nitwit but a young man whose innate, powerful imagination has been deranged by desperation. The "pure Johnsonian" goes crazy, is made grotesque by circumstance.

Achebe also quotes Cary's ghoulish depiction of "the demonic appearance of naked dancers, grinning, shrieking, scowling, or with faces which seemed entirely dislocated, senseless, and unhuman, like twisted bags of lard, or burst bladders" (138; quoted 24). Such language dehumanizes, to be sure, but then part of the function and fun of dance can be to make monkeys, or whatever, of the dancer. One is tempted to suggest that Achebe attend a rave in London, and see how humanely he can describe the X-dosed children of bankers and barristers spasming to the monotonous techno-beat.

To this Achebe would say that he should not, that, as he says in *Home and Exile,* there are plenty of novelists who write about the West, and "too few" about Nigeria (97). In this new book, in the course of explicating that which is implicit in *Things Fall Apart,* he shows how instructive, even corrective, the Nigerian point of view can be.

To the Igbo, the British empire, with its multifarious systems (political, economic, judicial, postal) threatened anarchy of a particularly menacing kind – centralized anarchy. In Igbo culture each person worships his or her own "personal god" or *chi,* whose will is at times indistinguishable from the worshipper's. "The Ibo people have a proverb," Achebe writes in *Things Fall Apart,* "that when a man says yes his *chi* says yes also" (27). Such a deity constitutes as strong a sanction of individuality as any Rousseau or Emerson has ever offered. The threat of anarchy inherent in this sanction is checked (but hardly nullified) by the worship of higher gods and by Igbo reluctance to "foist" one's beliefs on others (one reason: if you impose your god on another, then that god is no longer all yours). This reluctance was obviously not shared by evangelical religions (such as Christianity or Islam) or colonial conquerors, to whom the decentralized Igbo organization looked itself anarchic (not to mention vulnerable). Colonists could not imagine civilization without statism.

Achebe does not say that Igbo culture has all the answers, of course, but in *Home and Exile* he makes it apparent that he thinks things have not fallen so far apart that they are irretrievable; some of these things are even worth retrieving. Achebe argues that the West's presumptive model of "universal civilization" may not be the best one, and it should not be the only one. To use an evolutionary (and not a revolutionary) metaphor, there are Igbo genes that might prove especially resistant to consuming globalization, a globalization which, for all its talk of diversity, can be as oppressive as colonialism ever was.

To achieve a "balance of stories" Achebe extols the cultivation of homegrown "authenticity" (79; 43). This impulse is understandable, given the centuries of "sustained denigration," of the deprivation and imposition of narrative, and fostering native talent is never a bad idea. But to discredit any particular kind of story – the uncharitable kind, for instance – from any particular kind of source – foreign sources, for instance – has a depressing effect on the literary enterprise as a whole, whose motive force is the uncharted and unchartered imagination. A balance of stories is precisely what *Mister Johnson* and *Things Fall Apart* provide, to their very last words.

Upon killing a messenger of the British court, Okonkwo quickly sees that his people will not go to war to finish what he started, and he hangs himself. *Things Fall Apart* concludes with the British District Commissioner walking away from the scene of the hanging, mulling over a paragraph, which might digest the story of Okonkwo, the story Achebe has written a novel to tell. The Commissioner "had already chosen the title of the book [in which the paragraph would figure], after much thought: *The Pacification of the Primitive Tribes of the Lower Niger*" (209). A more bitterly fitting ending to an illustration of the phenomenon Achebe laments in *Home and Exile* – "the colonization of one people's story by another" – is hard to imagine.

Cary has imagined just such an ending. After Johnson kills Gollup in a bungled robbery, Rudbeck, now a full District Officer, is required by law to sentence him to death by hanging. Johnson's last request is that he be shot instead, by Rudbeck himself. "The very idea startles Rudbeck so much" – recall that he is not a man of ideas – "that he does not contemplate it at all" (277). In the end though,

Rudbeck does shoot Johnson. The novel concludes with him telling his wife about the execution, about his brave departure from official regulations. "[G]rowing ever more free in the inspiration which seems already his own idea," he says to Mrs. Rudbeck, "I couldn't let anyone else do it, could I?" (294). Pompous though he is, Achebe's Commissioner does not claim credit for Okonkwo's final choice, his mode of dying; the pathetic Rudbeck does exactly that.

To blithely condemn and dismiss *Mister Johnson* as Achebe has done is the wrong kind of payback. A certain amount of rivalry seems inevitable between writers who choose the same milieu, but the parallels between *Mister Johnson* and *Things Fall Apart* are just that – parallels, not identities, not redundancies. Together, they give contour and depth to our perspective on the vital matter at hand.

Works Cited

Achebe, Chinua. *Home and Exile.* Cambridge, MA: Harvard University Press, 2000.*Hopes and Impediments: Selected Essays* (London: Heinemann, 1988). *Things Fall Apart.* Random House: New York, 1994 (orig. 1959).

Balzac, Honore de. *Pere Goriot. Comedie Humaine.*

Cary, Joyce. *Mister Johnson.* Alexandria, Virginia: Time Reading Program, 1981 (orig. 1939).

Conrad, Joseph. *Heart of Darkness. A Case Study in Contemporary Criticism.* Bedford: Boston, 1989.

Ngugi wa Thiong'o. *Decolonizing the Mind: The Politics of Language in African Literature.* Heinemann: Portsmouth, N.H., 1986.

Pritchett, V.S. Introduction to *Mister Johnson. By* Joyce Cary. xi-xv.

Reader, John. *Africa: A Biography of the Continent.* Vintage: New York, 1997.

Soyinka, Wole. *Collected Plays 2.* (*The Lion and the Jewel.* 1–58). Oxford: Oxford University Press, 1974 (orig. 1963).

Chapter 10

"A Mouth with Which to Tell the Story" Silence, Violence, and Speech in Chinua Achebe's *Things Fall Apart*

Joseph R. Slaughter

"We are not so black (in the Niger) as they have painted us," writes George Goldie, head of the British owned Royal Niger Company, in a letter dated November 13, 1887 (quoted in Flint, 105). Goldie's missive to John Holt, an economic arch-rival and a man with competing trade interests through the Liverpool based African Association, helps to close the deal for a unification of trading partners that has been the subject of semi-secret negotiations during the last few months of 1887. Taking exception to recent reports issuing from the African Association and delivered to the British Foreign Office, Goldie's letter proposes to end the bad press through an amalgamation of the various trading companies. Goldie imagines that the elimination of market competition for the resources of the Niger and the Niger Delta would benefit the companies in a number of ways: 1) with the end of provincial economic interest, the profits of the trading concerns in relation to the untapped potential of the area would increase; 2) the potentially damaging reports of the Royal Niger Company's exploitative forms of production and its unfair trading practices might be quieted; and 3) the amalgamation would postpone, if not completely stave off, discovery of the Company's failure to comply with its Royal Charter by not having established an effective system of governance and administrative infrastructure on the Niger, which risked royal displeasure and the revocation of the Company's charter.

In his letter, Goldie addresses the subject of the Liverpool reports by explicitly challenging the representation of their substance: 'They say that we have been aggressive and pushing! I do not admit 'aggression'" (105). The ambiguity of the significance of the "aggression" – whether it refers domestically to the charges of monopolizing tendencies or to some more humanitarian notion of unfair labor practices – whether it refers to the charges of monopolizing tendencies or to some more humanitarian notion of unfair labor practices retains its rhetorical tangle throughout his sardonic exposition: "But, if true [that we have been aggressive], so much the better for them when they become our partners, our Co-Directors, and our co-rulers.

> They will re-christen 'aggression'; they will call it 'laudable energy,' and they will emulate us in its display" (105).

In his letter to the African Association, Goldie's "wit" in describing his enterprise's commercial demeanor as "not so black" suggests, beyond its obvious racist implications, that the representations of his actions are at least as important to his project as the actual "nature" of his dealings. The rest of his response proceeds to foreground clearly a seemingly pedestrian point, that a colonial/imperial dressing up of the public language can mask an identified malignancy. The capitalized stress on the commercial promotion of his future partners to "Co-Directors," while the imperial "co-rulers" remains uncapitalized, typographically suggests that the appeal of corporate amalgamation lies in its economic rather than its bureaucratic and "civilizing" aspects. This sort of rhetorical sleight of hand is, of course, not peculiar to Goldie and his prospective partners.

Tzvetan Todorov identifies this same syncretic move as part and parcel of Spain's earlier conquest of the "Indies," and thus as a paradigm for subsequent European incursions into other parts of the world. Todorov's comments on the Valladolid controversy of 1571 that precipitated the drawing up of royal ordinances directing the mode of Spanish conquest in 1573 – namely, that "Discoveries are not to be called conquests," and that "preachers should ask for their [the natives'] children under the pretext of teaching them and keeping them as hostages" such that "by these and other means are the Indians to be pacified and indoctrinated" – underscore the regal directness of the text: "it is not conquests that are to be banished, but the word *conquest;* "pacification" is nothing but another word to designate the same things, but let us not suppose that this linguistic concern is a futile one. Subsequently, one is to act *under cover* of commerce, by *manifesting* love, and without *showing* greed" (his italics, 174). Todorov's argument suggests that framing differently the language of conquest affects not only a rhetorical cover for a "potentially" immoral project, but that a shift in representational perspective will also produce an imperial approach with a manifestly different appearance.

The rhetoric of the Spanish royal ordinances again finds its purpose in George

Goldie's original petition on behalf of the National African Company, which was granted its Royal Charter on July 10, 1886. The language of the petition is repeated as preambular material to the actual charter: "whereas the Petition further states that the condition of the natives inhabiting the aforesaid territories would be materially improved, and the development of such territories and those contiguous thereto, and the civilization of their peoples would be greatly advanced..." (reprinted in Flint, 331). The material improvement and the advancement of "civilization" alluded to in the opening sections of the charter falls out of the actual articulations of rights and responsibilities royally granted to the Company in the subsequent text. However, the rhetorical pretext of economic improvement and humanitarian advancement continues to occupy a privileged place in the communications between England and the territories as the interests move from commercial to imperial. Thus, in a letter from the British Foreign Office to Major C.M. Macdonald dated April 18, 1891, the British Secretary describes the goals of the administration in the southern Oil Rivers Protectorate: "I am to observe that your object should be, by developing legitimate trade, by promoting civilization, by inducing the natives to relinquish inhuman and barbarous customs, and by gradually abolishing slavery, to pave the way for placing the territories over which Her Majesty's protection is and may be extended directly under British rule" (reprinted in Newbury, 263). It is this language – of economics, pacification, and civilization – that Achebe ironizes in 1958 at the close of *Things Fall Apart* where, after the hero Okonkwo has hung himself in despair, the British colonial officer's interior monologue occupies the novel's final words:

> In the many years in which he had toiled to bring civilization to the different parts of Africa he had learnt a number of things. One of them was that a District Commissioner must never attend to such undignified details as cutting down a hanged man from the tree. Such attention would give the natives a poor opinion of him. In the book, which he planned to write, he would stress that point. As he walked back to the court he thought about that book. Every day brought him some new material. The story of this man who had killed a messenger and hanged himself would make interesting reading. One could almost write a whole chapter on him. Perhaps not a whole chapter but a reasonable paragraph, at any rate. There was so much else to include, and one must be firm in cutting out details. He had already chosen the title of the book, after much thought: *The Pacification of the Primitive Tribes of the Lower Niger* (147–48).

The closing scene of the novel allegorizes the production of colonial and commercial knowledge that I will examine in greater detail throughout this essay. In the District Commissioner's writings the life of the hero, whose trials, troubles, and joys have mattered for the last 147 pages, will, at best, become for colonial officers and armchair imperial fanatics a short exemplum in the Blue Books of British history.

Most of the writing about the Niger territories in the late 19th and early 20th centuries was produced by the colonial powers. Dan Izevbaye explains that "The colonial administrations accumulated such a mass of information in their intelligence reports and other field studies of the different ethnic groups that many of these documents continue to serve scholars as important historical sources" (46). One might question the simultaneous over- and under-valuing of the term *important,* given that administrative reports were, perhaps, the major British import and that they were very often confidential. Izevbaye concludes that "while these sources seemed adequate to the British administration, they did not appear to have helped the colonial administrators to a sympathetic understanding of certain 'native institutions'" (46).

As part of the corpus of private and personal correspondence that led to the protectionist amalgamation of trading interests on the Niger and in the southern oil states, Goldie's letter to Hunt candidly recasts charges of violating native institutions that had been leveled against his own company by imputing them to the threat of a British government takeover of all concerned territories. Thus, Goldie attempts to unify his competition against the unprofitable and "impracticable" possibility of a nationalized English colonialism by appealing to a sense of progress and economic pragmatism that will not want to lose precious resources to a "fictitious and premature development" (Flint 105). The threat that official imperialism seems to pose to the commercial interests of private enterprise suggests that, at least in the case of Nigeria, evolutionary and developmental rhetoric may ambiguously underpin both economic and "civilizing" endeavors.

To this point I have tabled some of the concepts that will reappear throughout this essay: notions of language (and particularly writing) as a tool in the representation and function of colonial/imperial projects, ideas of fiction and development, and in particular a relationship that recognizes the rhetoric of development, or at least "premature development," as fictitious. These, perhaps, parallel, though I want to be suggestive rather than strict about this, the postcolonial "silence, violence, and speech" in the title of this essay. As a way to link (and unlink) these tenuous relationships, I will finish setting the table by turning to comments Achebe makes in his essays that fit more comfortably with literary notions of fiction and development. In "Colonialist Criticism," Achebe directly addresses what he calls "big-brother arrogance" in much Western literary scholarship on Africa. "The latter-day colonialist critic," Achebe argues, "sees the African writer as a somewhat unfinished European who with patient guidance will grow up one day and write like every other European, but meanwhile must be humble, must learn all he can and while at it give due credit to his teachers in the form of either direct praise or, even better since praise sometimes goes bad and becomes embarrassing, manifest self-contempt" (*Hopes* 69). It is perhaps enough here to suggest the pervasiveness of these ideas by reminding the reader of an oftquoted statement, and one that Achebe himself refers to, by which the missionary and humanitarian Albert Schweizer explained his medical work in Africa: "The African is indeed my brother, but my junior brother" (69). The apparently alluring notion of evolutionary cultural and social development, the relationship of a younger brother to an elder, is here identified by Achebe as one which has migrated into the language and theories of literary criticism. That is, the same organic theories of development that underpinned a European colonialism make an appearance in the literary critical language that still tends to locate the African novel at a stage of "immaturity" in relation to writing in the "West."

What follows in this essay is an examination not of a detailed relationship between any particular genre of colonial writing and the production of colonial knowledge but rather a broader attempt to contextualize *Things Fall Apart* in a field of colonial discourse. I claim, in some sense, that reaction to the novel, and the various generic labels it has elicited from western critics, can best be explained by recognizing its implicit relationships to the range of writing that meant to represent the Niger region and the experiences of its inhabitants. The examples of the various types of writing produced during the commercial and colonial periods of Nigeria's history are meant, then, to be illustrative, perhaps even paradigmatic, but by no means exhaustive of the full complex of writings. Ultimately, I am arguing that when *Things Fall Apart* is read in relation to these various modes of colonial writing, the novelistic techniques and themes can be recognized as at once allegorized and explicit responses, even antidotes, to the imperial forms of textual knowing. Grouping the wide range of writings that I will look at in one essay might seem careless (and certainly each of the modes deserves its own treatment), but as David Spun explains in his book on colonialist journalism, "Colonial discourse is not a matter of a given ideological position, but rather a series of rhetorical principles that remain constant in their application to the colonial situation regardless of the particular ideology which the writer espouses" (39). This essay examines two of the rhetorical principles that seem to remain constant in writings from and about turn-of-the-century "Nigeria."

"Nearer to his Ancestors": Organic Development and Knowledge

"Go-di-di-go-go-di-go," announce the drums that inform the people of Umuofia of the death of a great man, setting the scene of the funeral in chapter thirteen of Achebe's novel. Textually the funeral provides the occasion for Okonkwo to commit his accidental killing of the dead man's son and precipitates his removal from the village. But in a sort of reversal of a European teleological notion of individual development, the third person narrator takes the occasion of the ceremony to comment on the human life cycle: "A man's life from birth to death was a series of transition rites which brought him nearer and nearer to his ancestors" (85). What should be stressed in this description is not so much a notion that aging brings the individual closer to death and therefore closer to the dead but rather that through each transitional "rite" the individual concentrates his/her relationship among ancestors. This conception of development contrasts that invoked by colonial rhetoric in the eighteenth and nineteenth centuries.

In his essay "On Liberty" from 1859, J.S. Mill explains that "Very few facts are able to tell their own story, without comments to bring out their meaning" (21). One of those "facts" that turns out to require comment is his statement in the same work that "Despotism is a legitimate mode of government" (11). Just before entering into the central argument of "On Liberty," Mill pauses to consider the applicability of his analysis:

> It is, perhaps, hardly necessary to say that this doctrine is meant to apply only to human beings in the maturity of their faculties. We are not speaking of children, or of young persons below the age, which the law may fix as that of manhood or womanhood. Those who are still in a state to require being taken care of by others must be protected against their own actions as well as against external injury. For the same reason, we may leave-out of consideration those backward states of society in which the race itself may be considered as in its nonage. The early difficulties in the way of spontaneous progress are so great, that there is seldom any choice or means for overcoming them; and a ruler full of the spirit of improvement is warranted in the use of any expedients that will attain an end, perhaps otherwise unattainable. Despotism is a legitimate mode of government *in dealing with barbarians*, provided the end be their improvement, and the means justified by actually effecting that end. Liberty, as a principle, has no application to any state of things anterior to the time when mankind have become capable of being improved by free and equal discussion (11) (italics mine).

Mill's reservations about the applicability of his thought on liberty reflect an evolutionary notion of development, for individuals as for nations and peoples that had gained currency in the eighteenth and nineteenth centuries. His argument provides the theoretical/philosophical warrant that backs the imperial justifications for colonialism.

Perhaps the most influential elaboration of an organic, if fostered, theory of development appears in Rousseau's 1762 treatise on natural education, *The Emile.* Rousseau's suggestion that the French peasantry have little need of the kind of education he propounds because they already exist in some proto-natural relationship to development that has been socialized out of their urban compatriots, explains his choice of hypothetical pupil. "Let us choose our scholar among the rich," writes Rousseau, explaining that "we shall at least have made another man; the poor may come to manhood without our help. For the same reason I should not be sorry if Emile came of a good family" (22–3). Too, Rousseau ponders the impact of geography and climate on development and education, arguing that "if I want my pupil to be a citizen of the world I will choose him in the temperate zone, in France for example" (22). Unlike his disposition towards a romanticized version of the poor and the peasantry of France, Rousseau's thoughts on the role of climate offer a geographical explanation for his theory of racial inferiority: "a negro cannot live in Tornea nor a Samoyed in Benin. It seems also as if the brain were less perfectly organised in the two extremes. Neither the negroes nor the Laps are as wise as Europeans" (22). For Rousseau's tutor the non-European is not only less wise than the European, but the brain is less well organized. Perhaps Rousseau only means that the brains of non-Europeans organize information differently, but given an organic/evolutionary model of development, those differences in organization (if they can be located along a vector of "civilization") would suggest a sort of "primitiveness."

For Rousseau, as for Mill a century later, the acquisition of language represents an important stage in the progressive development of the individual and of civilization. Emile is, Rousseau says, born "twice over; born into existence, and born into life; born a human being, and born a man" (206). The emergence from a second birth corresponds to puberty in Rousseau, but it is also the moment after which the pupil "speaks himself" (207). Mill's evolutionary conceptions of human development and civilization mean that his principles of liberty are only applicable when "mankind has become capable of being improved by free and equal discussion" (11). And, in fact, his statement invokes the classical definition of barbarian as one who misuses, or is without, language. Thus, the development of, and the dealing with, "barbarians" could never, in an etymological sense, entail free speech and discussion. For both Mill and Rousseau language is conceived of as a means and an end in the movement towards liberty and maturity. As a means, language organizes knowledge in ways that are beneficial to the development of individuals. As an end, the existence of language and the possibility of discourse become evidence of development and civilization.

The appeal and influence of these evolutionary models in the nineteenth century can be seen not only in colonial administrators' writings, but also in the work of Africans living in Europe. In 1868 James Africanus Beale Horton, a Sierra Leonean of Igbo descent trained as a medical doctor in England, published a book called *West African Countries and Peoples* in which he states that "it will be my province to prove the capability of the African for possessing a real political government and national independence" (3). Horton's polemic, however, seems to subscribe to the European rhetoric of development when he adds that "a more stable and efficient Government might yet be formed in Western Africa, under the supervision of a civilized nation" (3). The rest of the book proceeds to argue that the West Africans are capable of being "civilized." While the book employs British colonial rhetoric – for example, in his section on the Igbo he recontextualizes a stereotype that "The Egboes are considered the most imitative and emulative of people in the whole of Western Africa; place them where you will, or introduce to them any manners and customs, you will find that they very easily adapt themselves to them" (157) – it does so in a fashion that, sometimes too subtly for today's reader, makes a case for the dignity and identity of the African. So, despite the fact that Horton makes a frank appeal for colonialism based on an evolutionary conception of cultures, he also explicitly recognizes dangers inherent in that call. Though Horton writes that "Nothing tends more to the civilization of a barbarous country than the immigration of civilized individuals into it.... It is impossible for a nation to civilize itself; civilization must come from abroad" (175), he tempers his position by warning against a commercialized colonialism and its merchant abuses: "It must be remembered that the English are considered the mildest of all civilized nations in their dealing with savage nations; but if among them we find men capable of such barbarity [a trader's inexplicable stripping and flogging of a native], what civilization must they expect from other nations, and how many centuries will it require for their civilization by merchants?" (176–7). Of course, the history of British colonialism in Nigeria eventually proved accurate Horton's assessment of the dangers of a commercialized colonialism.

In *The Order of Things,* Foucault locates a shift in modes of knowledge at the end of the eighteenth century that, in its most general formulation, structures the ways in which knowledge is collected, ordered, and disseminated. Foucault identifies *taxinomia* as the paradigm of ordering in the seventeenth and eighteenth centuries and genesis as the principle subsequently. Thus he argues that "*taxinomia* establishes the table of visible differences; genesis presupposes a progressive series; the first treats of signs in their spatial simultaneity, as a syntax; the second divides them up into an analogon of time, as a chronology" (74). Foucault's explanation of "genesis" as an ordering principle corresponds to the ideas that underpin European notions of evolutionary development, and thus might make sense of a colonialist rhetoric that argues for the savageness of the Niger natives. However, much of the writing produced under colonial regimes collects and organizes information in a taxonomic or tabular form.

Edward Said's examination of the work of early orientalists describes the product of their studies in terms that resonate with Foucault's. Said characterizes the scholarship that introduced the modern language of Orientalism in the anthropology of Silvestre de Sacy as "essentially compilatory" and in the philology of Ernest Renan as harboring "the most esoteric notions of temporality, origins, development, relationship, and human worth" (134). The two strains of knowledge ordering that Foucault identifies in his work seem to coexist and to account for the beginnings of modern Orientalism in Said's analysis. In fact, the coexistence of these two models of thought continues to support each other through the stages of British colonialism. That is, while Foucault may be correct when he identifies a general epistemological shift in European thought, the majority of colonial/commercial writing about the Niger remains committed to representing its information, or "findings," in taxonomic and tabular form. The potential paradox of this fact can be explained by recognizing the founding paradox of much European colonialism. If Foucault is right, then perhaps the reliance on tabular/taxonomic ordering in colonial writings can be accounted for by the genetic principle itself. From a colonialist perspective, the evolutionary primitive mode of ordering represented by the table might seem to suit the study of a people who the genetic theory of civilization has designated savage.

These two modes of ordering will, in the British colonial context of Nigeria, reinforce two seemingly contrary textual principles of accounting and recounting, or, in the more literary models, invoicing and voicing. Showing that one form or the other of these textual principles has a greater affinity for a commercial or an imperial colonialism would require a more thorough examination of the available writings than I undertake here. However, for convenience sake and the organization of this essay, I associate more examples of writing informed by a narrative principle of voicing with the imperial as opposed to the commercial periods of colonialism. At any account, the intimacy between the commercial enterprises and the British government makes the discrimination of distinct colonial forms difficult, if not impossible.

Returning to *Things Fall Apart,* the notion of development in the novel is also intimately linked to the acquisition and use of language, but stress is placed on the role of language in creating a social and cultural space to accommodate the announcement of the individual. It is, for instance, only when Okonkwo's daughter, Ezinma, can speak for herself, can tell the village where her *iyi-uwa* is buried that she takes her place among the living as a person, but also as a viable social being capable of narrating her own existence: "*No ogbanje* would yield her secrets easily, and most of them never did because they died too young – before they could be asked questions" (57). A child suspected to be an *ogbanje* – a child who dies, is reborn, and dies again to plague repeatedly its parents – can only demonstrate its humanity, and, therefore, its intention to remain among the living, at the point when it comes into speech as a social function. Other parts of the novel concern the troubled relationship between Okonkwo and his eldest son, Nwoye. Okonkwo has been sorely disappointed in his son until the arrival of Ikemefuna, a boy ransomed to the people of Umuofia as settlement for the killing of one of its daughters by another village. After spending three years in Okonkwo's family, Ikemefuna seems to have had, at least in Okonkwo's mind, a good influence on Nwoye. The narrator explains that "Okonkwo was inwardly pleased at his son's development.... He wanted Nwoye to grow into a tough young man capable of ruling his father's household.... And so he was always happy when he heard him grumbling about women. That showed that in time he would be able to control his women-folk" (37). Okonkwo is, of course, deluded by Nwoye's feigning annoyance at women, but in that delusion he proceeds to encourage Nwoye's maturation.

In the novel's terms, Nwoye's development is represented by physical displacement, from the "childishness" of his mother's hut to the "manliness" of his father's *obi.* Part of the displacement and development of Nwoye's personality and masculinity entails a narrative shift as well, and Okonkwo introduces him to "stories of the land – masculine stories of violence and bloodshed.... stories about tribal wars or how he had stalked his victim, over-powered him and obtained his first human head" (37). The associative gendering of stories in the novel creates a competition between genres of speech and storytelling, and the trouble between Okonkwo and Nwoye is only aggravated by the fact that although "Nwoye knew that it was right to be masculine and to be violent," somehow "he still preferred the stories that his mother used to tell ... stories of the tortoise and his wily ways, and of the bird *eneke-nti-oba* who challenged the whole world to a wrestling contest and was finally thrown by the cat" (37–8). The distinctiveness of story forms in the novel suggests the existence of alternative relationships to knowledge and modes of organizing that knowledge. From a European perspective, "feminine" stories take on the role of myths and "masculine" stories that of history. The "mother" stories also tend to be metaphoric while the "father" stories arrange the world metonymically; that is, Okonkwo's stories create a sort of history through inventory (of heads, yams, and titles) while the women's stories allegorize the role of speech and stories themselves in relation to both the teller and the listener. The contest between these two genres, and the mediating appeal of the "poetry of the new religion," provides the motivational force that eventually drives Nwoye out of the village and into the Christian mission, the story of which is narrated not by Okonkwo but by Nwoye's mother (104).

For the current purposes of this discussion, the importance of these stories is not their content but the fact that the novel depicts the movement from one form of narrative to another as part of the process of development in Umuofia. The novel, in fact, suggests that individual development in Igbo society entails, or at least is emblematized by, a coming into, and a facility with, language and stories. The narrator's observation that "Among the Ibo the art of conversation is regarded very highly, and proverbs are the palm-oil with which words are eaten" delimits an end of social and cultural development that values language and a narrative order of knowing (5).

Goldie's Game: Recording Secrets in the Colonial Archive

In a July 2, 1894 letter formalizing an employment offer with the Royal Niger Company, Sir George Goldie writes to then Captain Frederick Lugard officially reminding him of the agreement they had previously entered into orally. Goldie writes that "The Company" has been engaged in "opening up tropical Africa," an endeavor "practicable," he argues, only on the condition that, "in view of the difficulties resulting from the climate, the difficulty of access to inner Africa, the barbarism of the populations and other abnormal causes, abnormal energy, persistence, patience, and above all, *discipline* should be displayed by all the officials of The Company" (Perham and Bull 52). The condition of discipline, or at least its display, on the part of officials is stressed repeatedly as a way to avoid the "two greatest dangers at home": "the apathy of public opinion ... about western Africa" and "the excitability of public opinion, for short periods, when led astray on some popular hobby, by one sided or exaggerated reports" (53). Discipline, for Goldie, becomes a way to maintain the company's monopoly in the project of "opening up" tropical Africa, and the precise meaning of corporate discipline is elaborated in the final portions of his letter:

> Every official of The Company, whether a member of the Council or a judge or an Executive officer or a soldier is very properly bound not to publish, nor to communicate to anyone likely to publish, anything connected with The Company as a Government or as a commercial society, or the Company's Territories or regions visited when in The Company's service, without the previous assent of the Governing Body of The Company.
>
> You will understand that in the difficult and complicated game which The Company is playing, every move of which has to be calculated with the greatest care, it would be intolerable that any individual should be allowed to be the judge of what he might (directly or indirectly) publish or communicate to other persons than the Council of The Company (53).

The discipline that Goldie seeks imposes a gag order meant to keep secret any information or knowledge gathered by the Company's employees. The rules of Goldie's game, although not completely in place until the signing of the *General Act of the Conference of Berlin* in 1885, are dictated by international law and agreements made by the European powers for the scrambling of Africa. The movements of the pieces, however, are only generally suggested in the articles of the Company's charter. The rules declare that "The trade of all nations shall enjoy complete freedom" and that "All the Powers exercising sovereign rights or influence in the aforesaid territories bind themselves to watch over the preservation of the native tribes, and to care for the improvement of the conditions of their moral and material well-being, and to help in suppressing slavery" (*General Act*). While the Berlin Act grants trade its freedom, no nation or individual with imperial/economic interests in Africa construed the document to suggest that information about trade obtained the same right. Thus, alluding to a sort of practical statute of limitations on the utility of information about the Niger, Goldie writes to Lugard that "There will be no difficulty about your publishing books or delivering addresses after your return, *provided that all proofs are subject to the revision of the Council*" (his stress, *Perham and Bull* 53).

In a personal statement appended to the official letter from the Company, Goldie explains that "it must not be imagined that The Company has any desire to hide its actions under a bushel, but it claims and insists on its right to state its own case" (54). Further, Goldie honors Lugard's sense of discipline with the personal assurance that "I have no reason to doubt that whatever you might write would pass the necessary revision in this office with but little alteration; but it is only fair to say that there are a great number of matters on which it would be decidedly inadvisable that anything should as yet be published" (54). Lugard affixes his signature and remits the proper portions of the letter to the Company, zealously pledging himself "to observe the conditions required of me, not only during my term of service with The Company, but for five years after its conclusion" (55).

The prohibition against publication and the disposition of secrecy serve a pragmatic function in light of the stories that were making the rounds among Liverpool merchants of atrocities committed by King Leopold's interests in the Belgian Congo (Pakenham 586). It seems a safe conclusion to assume that the information gathered under the objectives Goldie details are at least some of what Lugard was to keep secret. Thus, beyond Lugard's attempts to conclude diplomatically land right treaties with the natives, he is to gather survey data, to "collect general information of every kind ... but especially to make inquires as to the existence of gold," "to obtain from natives ... the greatest possible number of lists of itineraries," and "to note specially prevalence of Gum trees, Shea Butter trees, and rubber vines" (Perham and Bull 59). What is not suggested in Goldie's guidelines is a need to conceal relations and confrontations with the natives. A certain tendency in colonialist discourse would have made such a warning unnecessary, although Margery Perham and Mary Bull do discuss the issue of Africans in the notes on their editorial policy that preface the publication of Lugard's diaries: "Africans do not play a large part in Lugard's account, and it has not been possible to find biographical details for any of the men mentioned" (42).

The exigencies of secrecy obviously affect the manner in which information is conveyed from the colonial territories to England, but they also affect and order the ways in which individuals working for the Company relate to each other and the language in which they write their own private stories. Lugard's diaries were not published until the 1950s, and, as the introduction to them makes explicit, they were intended to be secret and to serve, in part at least, as a daily record from which he could prepare the company's reports (12). The diaries read much like other travel writings by Europeans in Africa.

Mary Louise Pratt's extensive reading of the features found in the writing of Europeans in Africa provides a thorough account of the narrative structure of those texts, and, rather than retread her ground, a quick summary of her conclusions should suffice to describe generally Lugard's diaries. A particularly poignant evaluation of John Barrow's *Account of Travels into the Interior of Southern Africa in the Years 1797 and 1798* leads Pratt to identify some of the conventional features of this explorer/travel writing: "In the main, what is narrated proves to be a descriptive sequence of sights/sites, with the travelers present chiefly as a kind of collective moving eye which registers these sights. Their presence as agents scarcely registers at all" (142). Stressing the "objective," self-effacing tendencies in another passage from Barrow's writings, Pratt shows how "the travelers' struggle to cross the river is not narrated but expressed in a much more mediated fashion, as an enumeration of the traits of the river that produced the difficulty" (142). Beyond the elision of a perceptive subject in these passages, what stands out as peculiarly distinctive about the "African landscape," and the African peoples as they are encountered, is a narrative "othering" that makes the individual, or the discrete episode, stand for an eternalized and static "history" or "truth." Thus, as Pratt explains, the 'He' that pronominalizes a particular African "is *a sui generis* configuration, often only a list of features set in a temporal order different from that of the perceiving and speaking subject" (140). This conventionalizing of description is, of course, not limited to travel and explorer writing. Rather, the invoicing and atomizing mode of much colonialist writing effaces and circumscribes the presence and voicings of individuals, both the "natives" and the "explorers," involved in actual encounters and struggles.

The features of travel narratives that Pratt identifies secret the same information that the corporate account books and reports elide, namely the existence of a native people that stands behind the text's metonymic constructive principles. In fact, the objectives that Goldie set before Lugard requested lists and taxonomies as the medium of representing to the Company both his experiences and the resource potential of the Niger. Lugard's diaries similarly take an inventory of events, places, and people encountered on his forays rather than emplotting his experience in a particular setting with individual characters.

The tendency of colonial/commercial discourse to secrecy may be best illustrated by the fate of reports that were prepared in contravention to the normal constructive principle.

In the late 1880s Major C.M. Macdonald was asked by the British Foreign Office to prepare two studies on the effectiveness and impact in the region of Goldie's Niger Company. The Foreign Office kept both reports confidential, allowing them to be seen limitedly for the first time in 1952. Macdonald found that the Company had dealt unfairly with the natives, had responded to discontent with violent reprisals from its private armed forces, and that it had failed to establish the administrative infrastructure that the charter required. Macdonald also discovered that at least some of the treaties made with local leaders had been concluded under false pretenses, hearing from one of the Company's native translators that "I made him [the 'King'] understand that he ceded his country to the Company. I made him understand that he gave his country to the Company for trading purposes ... but I was not aware that 'ceding' meant giving over the rights of government and I dare not have made that suggestion to him" (quoted in Flint 139).

Rather than recount the findings of the reports, I want to stress the manner in which they were prepared and written. John Flint, who has studied the original confidential papers in the Foreign Office, explains that colonial reports of this type were generally prepared under the prescriptive guiding principle of "Imperial interests." Major Macdonald, however, seems to have "assumed ... that his task was to find out the wishes of the Africans, and implement them. For him 'Imperial interests' were the interests of the Africans" (130). Thus, Macdonald conducted a "rudimentary kind of plebiscite" as he traveled around the Oil Rivers region, gathering as many different opinions and stories as he could elicit from the people: locals, administrators, and traders alike (130). The final reports, of course, could not possibly find accommodation in a colonial discourse that demanded secrecy and inventory, or perhaps secrecy through inventory, and were, therefore, relegated to the vaults in the British offices. The imposition of secrecy contractually agreed to by Lugard and imposed upon Macdonald is a clear example of the ways in which colonial discourse polices its practitioners. Literary texts tend not to be quite so crude in their configurations, examinations, and constructions of silence.

"Where one's mouth was": Secrets and Lies and Other Oversights of Empire

"The night," writes Achebe at the beginning of Chapter Eleven of *Things Fall Apart*, "was impenetrably dark" (67). The narrative voice that opens this episode of the novel sets the environment in which the night's events take place with a Conradian epithet that at once borrows from and revises Marlow's own narrative practices in *Heart of Darkness.*

However, unlike Marlow's sweeping assignment of "impenetrable darkness" to an inhuman African nature and condition, Achebe's narrator humorously and matter-of-factly unpacks the impenetrability of that circadian darkness: "The moon had been rising later and later every night until now it was seen only at dawn. And whenever the moon forsook evening and rose at cock-crow the nights were as black as coal" (67). In Conrad, the "impenetrable darkness" has a metaphysical, if "inscrutable," cause and, therefore, meaning. Conradian darkness, in part, prompts a ruminative Marlow to entertain a "suspicion" of remote kinship with the Africans he cannot perceive, but, like other forms of colonial account keeping, it also relegates Africa and Africans to the metaphorically "dark" eras and spaces of European thought. An often-quoted example from Marlow's narrative equates impenetrability not only with prehistory and emptiness but also with silence: "Going up that river was like traveling back to the earliest beginnings of the world, when vegetation rioted on the earth and the big trees were kings. An empty stream, a great silence, an impenetrable forest" (66). The silence of impenetrability variously possesses Marlow and Kurtz and is possessed by them. However, the story Marlow tells sets up the antagonism between a voicing narrative – the kind which Kurtz cannot tell as a result of the reduction of his capacities to a state of pure, disembodied voice – and an imperial invoicing project – figured as a keeping and itemizing of accounts most explicitly represented by the station clerk and his clinical, antiseptic ledgers and lists. The contest for imperial control of the story line, of representation, and thus the contest over how to understand Kurtz in relation to the company's project, and Marlow's relation of the story, becomes an implicitly thematic conflict for the characters in the novel itself. Marlow, lying on the deck of the steamship while it is under repair, overhears the manager and his nephew discussing the necessity for the upcoming journey to the inner station. Responding to a description of the complications Kurtz causes the station manager, the uncle consoles him by explaining that "The climate may do away with this difficulty for you" (63). The conversation proceeds, illustrating the constructive and representative competition between voicing and invoicing:

> "He [Kurtz] sent his assistant down the river with a note to me in these terms: 'Clear this poor devil out of the country, and don't bother sending more of that sort. I had rather be alone than have the kind of men you can dispose of with me.' It was more than a year ago. Can you imagine such impudence!" "Anything since then?" asked the other hoarsely. "Ivory," jerked the nephew; "lots of it – prime sort – lots most annoying, from him." "And with that?" questioned the heavy rumble. "Invoice," was the reply fired out, so to speak. Then silence (63).

Voicing in *Heart of Darkness is* not an uncomplicated affirmation of narrative capacity, just as invoicing is clearly not an inherently contemptible mode of discursive accounting. But Marlow's narrative is structured around the principles of invoicing and secrecy, and although he claims to detest lying, he misrepresents Kurtz's pamphlet on the civilization of the "savages" by excising the offending postscriptum in which Kurtz scrawled the infamous words "Exterminate the brutes."

Philosophically, and even theologically, Conrad uses the Jansenist trope of "impenetrable darkness" to signify the inscrutable beginnings of man. That is, Africa stands in the European imagination on the timeline of organic development as that place from which human beings emerged, and thus as a place that is ultimately unknowable. This, of course, is another way of deploying the evolutionary model of development so that Africa becomes the physical location for the staging of a

European confrontation with its pre-existence. What the editors of Lugard's journals said about the role of Africans in his writings could equally be said of *Heart of Darkness,* that "they do not play a large part." The secrecy that enshrouds the figure of the African may, in fact, be dictated by the same commercial interests that quieted Lugard. Early in his narrative, after he has signed the company contract, Marlow says that "I undertook amongst other things not to disclose any trade secrets," and he affirmatively submits, "Well, I am not going to" (36). Later in the novel, after determining that the native heads displayed on spikes outside of Kurtz's hut are not "ornamental but symbolic," Marlow reiterates his commitment to secrecy: "I am not disclosing any trade secrets" (96–7). As a reader, one must wonder what precisely are the secrets Marlow keeps, but as a critic it seems compelling to ask how a principle of narrative secrecy inflects the text. These questions cannot likely be answered by looking at Conrad's text in isolation, and I believe that Achebe suggests a response in his novel.

The passage that opened this section of the essay in which Achebe debunks the impenetrability of darkness by explaining certain facts about the moon and the night continues by exploring the importance of speech and the shapes of stories that are shared in the darkness of an African night. However, rather than inf(l)ecting the narrative with secrecy, the narrator domesticates the darkness, ironizing Marlow's fixation by explaining that inside one of Okonkwo's wife's huts "A palm-oil lamp gave out a yellowish light. Without it, it would have been impossible to eat; one could not have known where one's mouth was in the darkness of that night" (67). In a direct affront to the European imagination of "impenetrable darkness," the characters in the novel are capable not only of finding their mouths for eating, but also for speaking.

This introduction to darkness establishes the scene of speech in which the most elaborate of the narrative interventions continues the polyphony of voices in the novel. Ekwefi, Okonkwo's youngest wife, and her daughter Ezinma, his favorite child, exchange stories through acts of narration that are more than mere ways to pass the time, more than idle and simple lessons in the guise of parable. Rather, the sharing of stories is itself figured as a process of development in which the daughter practices her storytelling skills as part of her matrimonial heritage. Barbara Harlow has commented on this scene and noted that an examination of the role of women in *Things Fall Apart* "would identify women as the main storytellers... a function that, on the one hand, affirms African women as the bearers and nurturers of African traditions but that, on the other hand, subjects that charge to a new interpretation when these very traditions are rewritten and given a vital assignment within the strategies of national liberation" (79 n.1). Harlow reads the mothertale of the Tortoise and the Birds as an anti-colonialist allegory, one which demonstrates the need for the natives of the nation (the birds) to use both force and rhetoric to overthrow a colonialist power (the tortoise). The story Ekwefi tells to her daughter through the impenetrable darkness can also, however, be read as a warning passed from mother to daughter against Okonkwo's fathertales. Ekwefi's story recounts how all the birds had been invited to a feast in the sky. The wily Tortoise soon discovered their plans and, despite their initial protestations, convinced the birds to provide him with feathers so he could accompany them to the feast. As they were all flying to the party, the birds elected Tortoise to be their spokesman. He explained it was customary that they all take new names for the event. After the birds had chosen their names, Tortoise declared that "He was to be called *All of you*" (68). When the people of the sky offered their food to all of you, Tortoise convinced the birds that it was the people's custom to feed the spokesman first. Soon there was nothing left; the birds took back their feathers and abandoned Tortoise with no way to return home. Parrot, however, agreed to deliver a message to his wife. When Parrot reached Tortoise's house, he told his wife to place all of the hard objects they owned out in front of the house. Tortoise, unable to see clearly because of the height, jumped and broke his shell on the "hoes, matchets, spears, guns and even his cannon" (70). A medicine man repaired his shell, but, according to Ezinma's story, it has not been smooth since.

While this story would likely be read from an ethnological perspective as a pseudoscientific, mythical explanation of how tortoise broke his shell, Harlow has persuasively argued that the story also illustrates an anti-colonial imperative of using the tools of both rhetoric and weaponry to unburden a colonized country (75). While I find Harlow's explication of the story provocative and convincing, I think the one-to-one mapping of the story onto a strict anti-colonialist allegory risks diminishing other insinuative aspects of the tale. The story not only illuminates generally the colonial situation, but it also provides a particular warning against the dangers of a metonymic system of political and civic representation in Igbo society. That is, the story contains significant warnings about both external and internal threats from an ambitious and universalizing individualism.

Perhaps the most illustrative example of the internal metonymic usurpation of the people's voice is reflected in the language of the Royal Niger Company's treaties. In his essays, Achebe explains that there are two general strains of myths in his home village of Ogidi that explain the absence of kings in his society (*Hopes* 163–4). And yet, the British required sovereigns to authorize the legitimacy of the treaties they concluded with the people of southeastern Nigeria. Thus, they sometimes rhetorically created kings and kingships where none had existed before. The language of the *Agreement between Onitsha and the National African Company* from 20 August *1884* and the subsequent revisions of that Agreement in the *Onitsha Protectorate Treaty* of 9 October 1884 exemplify this point. The first agreement states that "We, the undersigned King and Chiefs of Onitsha, after many years of experience, fully recognize the benefit accorded to our country and people by their intercourse with the National African Company (Limited), and in recognition of this we now cede the whole of our territory to the National African Company (limited) and their administrators for ever" (reprinted in Newbury 107). The second agreement, concluded by the British government when questions arose about the legitimacy of private enterprise treaties under international law, reads "The King, Queen, and chiefs of Onitsha hereby engage to assist the British Consular or other officers in the execution of such duties as may be assigned to them, and further, to act upon their advice in matters relating to the administration of justice, the development of the resources of the country, the interests of commerce, or in any other matter in relation to peace, order, and good government, and the general progress of civilization" (109).

In a further tortoisy move, H.P. Anderson circulates a confidential memorandum in the British Foreign Office that asks for guidance in interpreting the treaties for the upcoming Berlin Conference. "We should have to refer in Conference to our Treaties," he worries. "The first question to be decided ... is what interpretation we put on those Treaties.... They do not, like the French Treaties, mention the word 'suzerainete', but they are believed to be much on the same lines of the German Treaties. The Germans, as we know, interpret these as conferring an exclusive German Protectorate; *what view should we say* that we take of ours?" (my emphasis 186). The concern over a unified interpretative stance in relation to the treaties stresses the rhetorical use of the "agreements." In a preface to a governmental collection of British West African documents, the authors explain that none of the treaties were considered to have the force of law; rather, "The obligations they impose are of a moral, not a legal order; and if the Crown disregards them there is no redress" (Wight 8). Thus, the documentary elevation of a native individual to the status of king, to a metonymically usurped form of tortoise's "all of you," does not establish a speaking subject among the Igbo, but rather rhetorically sanctions a voice that guarantees the transfer of that capacity to the British.

The tale of the Tortoise and the Birds, however, cannot be limited to an allegorized version of these historical events. At a more general level, the breaking of Tortoise's shell foreshadows Okonkwo's self-destruction and reconfirms the danger of a metonymic, atomizing practice of representation. Both Tortoise and Okonkwo have committed the same rhetorical/narrative crime. There is some textual justification for Okonkwo's sense that he has somehow earned the right to act unilaterally on behalf of the people of Umuofia. The novel opens with a mythologizing of Okonkwo:

> His fame rested on solid personal achievements. As a young man of eighteen he had brought honor to his village by throwing Amalinze the Cat. Amalinze

> was the great wrestler who for seven years was unbeaten, from Umuofia to Mbaino. He was called the Cat because his back would never touch the earth. It was this man that Okonkwo threw in a fight which the old men agreed was one of the fiercest since the founder of their town engaged a spirit of the wild for seven days and seven nights. The drums beat and the flutes sang and the spectators held their breath. Amalinze was a wily craftsman, but Okonkwo was as slippery as a fish in water. Every nerve and every muscle stood out on their arms, on their backs and their thighs, and one almost heard them stretching to breaking point. In the end Okonkwo threw the Cat (3).

But, in an often-overlooked passage, Okonkwo is replaced in the symbolic order of things by a newcomer twenty years after his own match. Umuofia enshrines the young wrestler in Okonkwo's place, in the words of the new village song: "Who will wrestle for our village? Okafo will wrestle for our village.... Has he thrown a hundred Cats? He has thrown four hundred Cats. Then send him word to fight for us" (36). In the village of Umuofia, Okonkwo's role as a fighter, as a doer, has waned; what is left to him as expression of his influence is that which is left to all of the village elders, language and speech, demonstrations that are difficult for a stammering man. Okonkwo's undoing at the end of the novel results from his inability to speak persuasively and from his rash preference for decisive action over the culturally sanctioned discursive form of mediation.

The allegory of the Tortoise and the Birds underscores the need for balance in responding to an immediate threat. The fact that the story can be interpreted as both a lesson in colonial resistance and a warning against the sort of isolated hotheaded response of the individual dramatically illustrates the subtlety of the African *griot.* Examining a Hausa tale, Achebe emphasizes the inherent subversive power in its structure, a power which will surface, he says, in "a revolutionary time, and when it comes you don't need another story. It is the same story that will stand ready to be used; and this to me is the excellence of the griot in creating laughter and hiding what you might call the glint of steel." (Rowell 90) Not only is the tale of the Tortoise and the Birds narratively associated with the women of Okonkwo's household, but the role specifically gendered in the story as feminine is that of the wife who literally employs all the "glints of steel" hidden in her house and who is directly responsible for the destruction of Tortoise's shell. Okonkwo, not recognizing the rhetorical threat of Ekwefi's steel, dismisses the story as foolishness.

"We can eat the chick": Textual Institutions of Colonialism in Nigeria

"The village was astir," observes the narrator, reporting on the communal effects of the imprisonment of Umuofia's leaders, insinuatively adding, "in a silent, suppressed way" (140). After Okonkwo and his family return to Umuofia from his motherland Mbanta, silence obtains greater import in the narrative description of life among Okonkwo's people. During Okonkwo's absence, not only had the missions established their presence, but the colonial administration had "built a court where the District Commissioner judged cases in ignorance" (123). *Things Fall Apart* represents the threat of both institutions in terms of generic inclusion and exclusion. That is, the intrusions of the church and the state radically transform the life of the natives not only by challenging the social, cultural, and political institutions of Umuofia but also by restructuring the kinds of speech and language in which life is conducted. The threat represented by the "new religion," in the form of the stories and songs that seduced Okonkwo's son Nwoye to convert, has its parallels in the juridical/administrative genres of testimony and palaver. While the narrator increasingly stresses the imposition of silence in Umuofia, the plot foregrounds the encounters between Igbo individuals and the colonial institutions. Silence, then, becomes the paradigmatic medium of negotiation, resistance, and resignation.

Before the silence imposed by colonial administration infects the relationships between the characters in the novel, Obierika, Okonkwo's levelheaded neighbor, delivers the news of the destruction of Abame to Okonkwo's clan in his motherland. Robert M. Wren has examined the historical and documentary sources for Achebe's fictionalization of the British raid on the Aro Igbo in relation to *Things Fall Apart.* Rather than reiterate the historical evidence and precedents for the relation, I want to look at the illustrative story Okonkwo's uncle Uchendu tells the younger men from Umuofia. Uchendu inquires of Obierika the details of the encounter between the white man and his Igbo killers that precipitated the massacre of Abame: "What did the white man say before they killed him?" (98). "He said nothing" is the initial reply; "He said something, only they did not understand him" is the revised response (98). Uchendu continues to listen and then delivers his tale and judgment:

"Never kill a man who says nothing. Those men of Abame were fools. What did they know about the man?" He ground his teeth again and told a story to illustrate his point. "Mother Kite once sent her daughter to bring food. She went, and brought back a duckling. "You have done very well," said Mother Kite to her daughter, "but tell me, what did the mother of this duckling say when you swooped and carried its child away?" "It said nothing," replied the young kite. "It just walked away." "You must return the duckling," said Mother Kite. "There is something ominous behind the silence." And so Daughter Kite returned the duckling and took a chick instead. "What did the mother of this chick do?" asked the old kite. "It cried and raved and cursed me," said the young kite. "Then we can eat the chick," said the mother. "There is nothing to fear from someone who shouts." Those men of Abame were fools (98–99).

Okonkwo, not understanding the allegorical nature of this story, preferring as he does metonymic narratives, concurs with Uchendu's assessment that the men of Abame were indeed fools. His concurrence, however, demonstrates his misapprehension of the story: "They had been warned that danger was ahead. They should have armed themselves with their guns and their matchets even when they went to market" (99). Uchendu's story establishes a contest of genres, a clash of speech functions. The fact that Achebe locates this all-female-cast story, told by a brother of Okonkwo's mother, in his motherland after he has committed a "female" crime of inadvertently killing a clansman, all but overstates Okonkwo's ignorance in not learning "feminine" rhetoric. After listening to Uchendu's explanation about the virtues of having both a fatherland and a motherland, Okonkwo names his first born Nneka ("Mother is Supreme"). Yet, as the narrator tells us, "two years later when a son was born he called him Nwofia – 'Begotten in the Wilderness'" (115). Okonkwo's belief in the protective powers of Mother follows the rigid distinction he maintains between mother-tales and father-tales. "Mother is Supreme" is a suitable name only for a daughter; a son must learn to negotiate physical danger from the start. Biodun Jeyifo attributes the maintenance of this dichotomy to psychology: "Okonkwo both loathes the memory of his father and represses the lore of his mother; in the process he distorts both the 'masculine' and the 'feminine,' by keeping them rigidly apart and by the ferocity of his war on the 'feminine' " (851).

Beyond the gendering of story types, of speech functions, Uchendu's story turns the discourse of European colonialism on its head. The colonial infrastructure demands from its subject's language of self-contempt, self-incrimination, and/or self-abnegation that seems to insist upon the importance of the native speaking but instead perverts that speech to relegate the native to silence. Uchendu's story reinvests silence with a kinetic potential, hidden as a glint of static steel that can never be accounted for by the oppressors. Achebe's text investigates this rhetorical paradox in the meetings that most immediately lead to Okonkwo's suicide. The District Commissioner responds to the moment when Umuofia speaks with the force of a singular voice, in the form of the *egwugwu* Ajofia, by inviting the leaders of Umuofia to the table.

But the pretense of palaver is violently perverted when the District Commissioner actually enters the conversation. "Ogbuefi Ekwueme rose to his feet and began to tell the story," explains the narrator, describing the scene at the courthouse (137). The District Commissioner interrupts, saying that he would like others to hear the story; "They sat together with the men of Umuofia, and Ogbuefi Ekwueme began again to tell the story of how Enoch murdered an *egwugwu*" (137). The pretended dialogue ends with the abduction of the tribal leaders, ending days later only with the "judicial" ransom by the village. The narrator describes the experience as silencing; "Even when the men were left alone they found no words to speak to one another" (138). The silence, as described in the early part of this section, is, however, one with kinetic force and potential. And after the man's release, Okonkwo's sense of impotence overboils at the moment he produces his matchet, usurping the decision making powers from the rest of the village with his murder of a colonial messenger. Neither the silence nor the violence serves to repair wholly the social, cultural, and political wounds that colonialism has visited on Umuofia. But, Okonkwo's personal fate is exacerbated by colonialism and missionary adventurism. The text suggests that his inability to accommodate and adapt to the social and cultural structures of Umuofia made him not long for its world.

The colonial record was, of course, no better than commercial enterprises at depicting or admitting the existence of the peoples of Southeastern Nigeria. The categories of description changed, but the itemizing discourse remained. The "history of record," as distilled and refined in the British colonial account books, commonly known as the Blue Books, categorized and atomized the shape of the new nation in terms established by the colonizers. The article from the early constitutions that mandated the form and substance of the Blue Books provides the categories under which information about Nigeria was to be organized: "The Governor shall punctually forward to Us from year to year, through one of Our Principal Secretaries of State, the annual book of returns for the Colony, commonly called the Blue Book, relating to the Revenue and Expenditure, Defence, Public Works, Legislation, Civil Establishments, Pensions, Population, Schools, Course of Exchange, Imports and Exports, Agriculture, Produce, Manufactures, and other matters in the said Blue Book more particularly specified, with reference to the state and condition of the Colony" (Wight 184). These categories of knowledge, meant to describe the "state and condition" of the colony, circumscribe the bureaucratic language available to the colonial officer for representing the order of the nation.

These Blue Books were to be read in the Colonial office in England and presented to Parliament. They often did not see publication until a couple of years after the period over which they report. In their general shape, any single Blue Book is as revealing as any other. In the 1951 report, for instance, the book opens with a typical account of "important" events from the previous year: "In annual reports of this kind it is sometimes not easy to pick out this or that event or series of events as the most important of the year" (3). Before moving on to report on the mandated categories of Commerce, Production, Art, Literature and Sport, the book rehearses the history of Nigeria and its people as it has come to be indexed in the colonial accounts. "Nigeria has been described as 'an arbitrary block of Africa'. Its ancient history is largely lost in the mists of legend and little accurate data are now available," the history begins (92). The rehearsal of the history functions simultaneously to "educate" the metropolitan reader in England and, in Prosperonian fashion, to "remind" the native of, or the lack of, her own history. Speaking directly to the subject of the Igbo, the Blue Book reports that "The tribes of what is now southeastern Nigeria have little or no known early history prior to British occupation, with the exception of certain of the coastal peoples, who were long known as keen and enterprising traders" (94). Praising the natives' capacity for institutional service, the report explains that "Since the establishment of the Protectorate, however, the rapid spread of education has brought great changes and both the Ibos and the less numerous Ibibios now exercise a most important influence on the social, economic and political life of Nigeria" (94).

The distilling and reaffirmation of colonial history continues year after year in the Blue Books, reducing last year's events to the minor context in the larger history elaborated by the reports, a process of revision and excision that the District Commissioner undertakes mentally at the end of *Things Fall Apart*. This textual process parallels the physical imperial one and is itself characterized in the reports: "Neither the acquisition by the British crown of the colony of Lagos nor the establishment of a Protectorate over large areas of the interior was the result of deliberate long-range planning by the governments of the day" (94). The non-deliberative aspects of this process are retroactively described in terms of a courtship where "the events covering the whole period from the early discovery of Nigeria to the present day may roughly be set out under three heads, the period of exploration, that of penetration and finally that of consolidation of the ground won" (94). The consolidation of the colony, and thus of history itself, is textually represented by the marginalization of all resistance to the imperial process, locating the one defiant act about which the Blue Book reports after the official history: "In all this period there was only one major threat to law and order in the territory. This was the women's rising which occurred in the Owerri and Calabar Provinces in 1929 and largely resulted in the destruction of the local system of government which had been set up and in the establishment of Native Administrations based closely on the indigenous customs of the people" (100).

The Blue Book categories prescribe a certain kind of narrative description of individuals and events. That is, the colonial records do not merely provide a commercial/political accounting of Nigeria; they also establish the categories by which individual character and plot are to be constructed, measured, and evaluated. The employment of this atomizing discourse to describe the people of Nigeria is mostly clearly evident in P. Amaury Talbot's 1923 census, in which he undertook not only to count the colonial assets but to schematize the cultural, social, political, legal, and religious aspects of those "holdings." Talbot interprets his mandate in the Foreword to his four volume report: "The chief work has been an attempt to classify the tribes and sub-tribes and to define their boundaries" (vi). The use to which the work should be put is prescribed as "a brief description of the Southern Provinces with a few notes on their history-in the hope that they may be of interest to the people of this country and of some use to new administrators, who have had no opportunity of gaining knowledge on the subject" (vi). Talbot expresses regret about what he sees as a lack of scientific taxonomy in his work, placing the blame for that lack on the difficulties and delays presented by the very environment and people about which the study reports: "Unfortunately the provisional classification adopted has had to depend almost entirely on the basis of language, since ... the results of an anthropometrical survey of several thousand natives will arrive too late for use in the present volumes" (vi).

Despite his misgivings that the census is organized around linguistic, as opposed to corporeal affinities, Talbot provides an elaborate classification of the populations of Nigeria. For colonial administrative use, he supplies intricate tabular data that presume to arrange the collection of human details that describe a native's individual circumstance. One of his poster-sized renderings tabulates the cultural and judicial response of the native Nigerians to "manslaughter." I have excerpted below a number of his entries that demonstrate the range of possible reactions to the accidental killing of another human being that he identifies as Igbo justice.

TribeSub-TribeCases judged by Manslaughter Igbo Abam Chiefs, sub-chiefs, and elders Carries out burial and undergoes all expenses. Igbo (Onitsha) Chiefs, sub-chiefs, and elders Pay burial expenses or hand over daughter; in default, his family did so. Igbo Awtanzu (Awtanchara) Chiefs, sub-chiefs, and elders Runs away for three years. Igbo Awtanzu (Awtanzu) Chiefs, sub-chiefs, and elders-Nothing done if escapes for three years; if caught substitution by daughter or son. Igbo Ezza "Titled man" and some sensible elders. Fined 2 cows, 1 goat and cloth given to parents, and fowl and goat sacrificed to Ala. Igbo Ngwa (Oloko) Chiefs, sub-chiefs and sensible old men. Hanged. Igbo Oru (Oru) Serious cases by Eze, sub-chiefs and Ndi-nze. Minor cases by "quarter" chiefs. If through negligence treated as murder. In other cases, has to pay funeral expenses. Igbo Ore (Olo) Chiefs, sub-chiefs, and elders has to run away for three years; on return, offers sacrifice. Compiled from P. Amaury Talbot's The Peoples of Southern Nigeria, 1923. Table 19. p. 677.

I have chosen the example of manslaughter because the crimes, procedures, and punishments Talbot describes would appear to apply to the plot of *Things Fall Apart.* Okonkwo's "female crime" of accidentally killing a fellow clansman would seem to fall under Talbot's British label of manslaughter, yet the resulting punishment described in Achebe's novel appears, as one might expect, no where in Talbot's schema. Talbot's 1923 census delimits, at least practically if not actually, the range of possible "cultural" practices that a young colonial officer might encounter in the "bush." Thus, from the perspective of a District Commissioner, Talbot's tables stultify the "full" range of plot, character, and setting over which he is to take control. I am not arguing about the obvious inaccuracies and incompleteness of Talbot's rubrics; rather, I want to be clear that the colonial administration must treat this tabulation as the complete representation of a finite number of responses to manslaughter. This tendency of the accountant's report to finitude stabilizes, stills, and makes. manageable the story lines of the natives. Yet, it is from within the space of that "silence" that the stories of resistance and contest are created. From Uchendu's point of view, the relegation of the natives to silence superficially confirms the dismissiveness of British administrative discourse and the prejudicial rationalizations for the introduction of a culture of bureaucratic speech while it establishes a discursive negation from within which a culture can continue and threaten the very structure itself.

Although Talbot's census and the colonial Blue Books do not represent the full range of official accounting of the colonial/administrative experience, they do represent the general modes of ordering knowledge about the colony and its peoples. The narrative depiction of Umuofia in *Things Fall Apart* represents, in the context of the other writings on Igbo life, a re-inscription into the record of the complexities, contradictions, and range of the Igbo world. The novelized treatment of Okonkwo allegorizes, in some way, the competition over discursive representation. As narrative, it directly challenges the itemizing and atomizing tendencies of European scientific and colonial language that presumed to represent, at least for bureaucratic and imperial purposes, the data of empire. But while this colonial discourse presumes to speak about the "state and condition" of the colonies, it simultaneously monopolizes the generic conventions for representation, naturalizing itself as the only significant form of information necessary for ordering and knowing the colonial world. Achebe's novel debunks this naturalization by exploring the generic encounter not only between the European and the African but also by examining a similar contradiction internal to Umuofia society. Ultimately, Okonkwo's inability to negotiate the native genres of story telling – gendered as masculine and feminine – illustrates the larger failure of colonial discourse that silences him for his own silencing attempts.

Achebe's novel suggests that a complex reorganization of rhetoric and generic convention are necessary for the survival of Umuofia. Ultimately, Okonkwo's suicide attests to his own inability to negotiate the new exigencies of narration that the colonial administration presents but also to his intransigence in the face of domestic cultural pressures that pre-exist the coming of the white man to Umuofia. That is, Okonkwo's own overvaluation of, and dependence on stories that itemize – stories of the land and of his first human head – exemplifies the inadequacy and misrepresentational aspects of a tabular, metonymic, mode of narration. A "masculine" order of things is thus revealed to be structured around as much a principle of secrecy and exclusion as the contractual orders that Lugard so readily agreed to observe. Okonkwo's own predilections for the tabular forms of story telling, and ordering things, place him in opposition to the more dynamically speech-oriented forms of knowing promoted within the Igbo society of the novel.

"Africans come out": Challenges to Silence, Violence, and Speech

In 1967, Sir Rex Niven, ex-Administrator for the Northern provinces, writes of southern Nigeria that "Historically the area is disappointing" (54). "No one," he says, "has left us any reliable account of the coastal peoples; to them the local population were mere 'natives' who could be amusing, irritating or exasperating, according to their moods; the idea that they, their customs and their beliefs could be interesting would have been laughable" (54). Not withstanding the terribly ambiguous relationships between Niven's pronouns and his antecedents, his comments accurately describe a general lack of written records about the Igbo and other southern peoples. Niven's remedy for that lack, however, is questionable: "There are some personal narratives, but the Africans come out of them as comic, ridiculous or brutal; there was no serious attempt to describe their way of life or their religions or even their superstitions, still less to trace their origins" (54). On whose part, the question might be asked, and Niven responds: "It was not – perhaps surprisingly – until the administration got into its stride that a real attempt was made to enquire into these important matters" (54–5). Niven's deprecatory remarks about personal narratives and his laudatory evaluation of colonial scholarship quite succinctly describe an administrative attitude towards language. Since Niven never names the "personal narratives" to which he refers, we are left to judge his apparent disdain for them based on the words he uses to characterize the narrative construction, and his warnings about the narratives are clear enough: "Africans come out of them." Whether as comic and ridiculous, in Niven's estimation, or as dignified, social, and complex in Equiano's or Horton's writing, the threat to a colonialist discourse of consumption and atomization on the Niger is precisely the emergence of Africans.

Achebe remarked in a recent interview that his desire to write responded to the wisdom of a proverb he values: "Until the lions have their own historians, the history of the hunt will always glorify the hunter.... Once I realized that, I had to be a writer. I had to be that historian" (*Art of Fiction*). The need for "that historian" is suggested by the discursive principles of secrecy and inventory in colonial writing that seem to naturalize the underlying evolutionary notions of development that locate Igbo society in a pre-European, read "primitive," stage. Thus, it is difficult to determine precisely whether the mode of ordering knowledge about colonial Nigeria is produced by a belief that the colonizers are confronting and encountering the "barbarous," that is without language, or whether the mode of ordering itself imposes silence and secrecy.

Colonialist discourse in southern Nigeria, both through its conformity to the representational exigencies of secrecy and in the mode of its ordering, configures the native as speechless, and, having justified that relegation of the people to a prelinguistic existence with an organic model of civilization, it proceeds to malign their capacity for action. That is, as Mill argues, the nineteenth century British notion of liberty and society is predicated on the idea that action can only legitimately be taken when the individual is capable of freely discussing the motives, a capacity rhetorically, generically, and politically disallowed Africans. The yoking of silence to violence, and the liberating potential of speech has been patently enshrined as the justification for international law in general (a full investigation is needed into the role of speech and violence as justificatory terms for the humanist rhetoric of ending slavery that underpinned the Conference of Berlin) and international human rights law in particular in the *1948 Universal Declaration of Human Rights,* where the freedom of speech is posited as the antidote to violence (preamble of UDHR). Achebe argues that "Nobody is, of course, going to be so naive as to claim for language the power to dispose of all, or even most, violence" (Hopes 128). *Things Fall Apart,* by allegorizing many of the modes of colonial discourse that claimed to represent a Nigerian reality, suggests that some mediating principle between speech and violence, some principle outside of an organic mode of knowing and an itemizing form of collection, needs to exist if humans are to exist. For Achebe that mode is narrative, as he explains in his aptly titled essay "What has Literature Got to Do with It?"; "The universal creative rondo revolves on people and stories. *People create stories create people;* or rather, *stories create people create stories"* (Hopes 162).

Things Fall Apart is, in part, a corrective to discourses structured by secrets and silence. It is not that *Things Fall Apart* fills out that which cannot be told in the colonial discourses, but rather that it explodes the very category of not telling. It rejects the capitalist, imperialist imperative of corporate and narrative secrecy (a rejection that is, of course, as important for Nigeria in the time it was written as in the time it is set and in the present circumstance), threatening the idea of narrative as secrecy. In his *1959* (one year after Achebe published his novel) statement to the Second Congress of Black Artists and Writers in Rome, Frantz Fanon argued that "We must rid ourselves of the habit, now that we are in the thick of the fight, of minimizing the action of our fathers or of feigning incomprehension when considering their silence and passivity" (206–7). Fanon's comments are intended to enlist the African intellectuals in the popular struggles against colonialism and for independence, but his remarks also suggest that a normative notion of silence (and therefore violence and speech) will not accurately describe the resistant history of the colonial peoples and ancestral participation in that resistance. Achebe's novel thematizes the impositions of silence and the equally important representations of silence, suggesting that no easy equation between silence and passivity is possible.

Works Cited

Achebe, Chinua. "The Art of Fiction: An Interview with Chinua Achebe." Online. 16 April 1995.

———. *Things Fall Apart.* (1958) London: Heinemann, 1986.

———. *Hopes and Impediments.* New York: Doubleday, 1989.

Cohen, Sir Andrew. *British Policy in Changing Africa.* Evanston: Northwestern UP, 1959.

Conrad, Joseph. *Heart of Darkness.* (1902) New York: Penguin Books, 1989.

Fanon, Frantz. *The Wretched of the Earth.* Trans. Constance Farrington. New York: Grove Weidenfeld, 1963.

Flint, John E. *Sir George Goldie and the Making of Nigeria.* London: Oxford UP, 1960.

Foucault, Michel. *The Order of Things: An Archeology of the Human Sciences.* (1966) New York: Vintage, 1994.

Harlow, Barbara. "The Tortoise and the Birds': Strategies of Resistance in *Things Fall Apart. Approaches to Teaching Achebe's Things Fall Apart.* Ed. Bernth Lindfors. New York: Modern Language Association, 1991.

Horton, James Africanus. *West African Countries and Peoples.* (1868) Edinburgh: Edinburgh UP, 1969.

Isichei, Elizabeth. *The Ibo People and the Europeans.* New York: St. Martin's Press, 1973.

Izevbaye, Dan. "The Igbo as Exceptional Colonial Subjects: Fictionalizing an Abnormal Historical Situation." *Approaches to Teaching Achebe's Things Fall Apart.* Ed. Bernth Lindfors. New York: Modern Language Association, 1991.

Jeyifo, Biodun. "Okonkwo and His Mother: *Things Fall Apart* and Issues of Gender in the Constitution of African Postcolonial Discourse." *Callaloo 16.4:* 847–58.

Kirk-Greene, A.H.M. (ed.). *Lugard and the Amalgamation of Nigeria: A Documentary Record.* London: Frank Cass and Co., 1968.

Lubiano, Wahneema. "Narrative, Metacommentary, and Politics in a 'Simple Story.'" *Approaches to Teaching Achebe's Things Fall Apart.* Ed. Bernth Lindfors. New York: Modern Language Association, 1991.

Mill, John Stuart. *On Liberty.* Ed. David Spitz. New York: W.W. Norton, 1975.

Newbury, C.W. (ed.). *British Policy Towards West Africa.* Oxford: Clarendon Press, 1971.

Niven, Sir Rex. *Nigeria.* New York: Praeger, 1967.

Obiechina, Emmanuel. "Following the Author in *Things Fall Apart.*" *Approaches to Teaching Achebe's Things Fall Apart.* Ed. Bernth Lindfors. New York: Modern Language Association, 1991.

Pakenham, Thomas. *The Scramble for Africa: White Man's Conquest of the DarkContinent from 1876 to 1912*. London: Weidenfeld & Nicolson, 1991.
Perham, Margery and Mary Bull (eds). *The Diaries of Lord Lugard*. Four Volumes. Evanston: Northwestern UP, 1963.
Pratt, Mary Louise. "Scratches on the Face of the Country; or, What Mr. Barrow Saw in the Land of the Bushmen." in *"Race," Writing, and Differance*. Ed. Henry Louis Gates, Jr. Chicago: Chicago UP, 1986.
Rousseau, Jean-Jacques. *Smile*. (1762) trans. Barbara Foxley. Rutland, Vermont: Everyman, 1997.
Rowell, Charles H. "An Interview with Chinua Achebe." *Callaloo* (Winter: 1990) 86101.
Said, Edward W. *Orientalism*. New York: Vintage, 1979.
Schipper, Mineke. *Beyond the Boundaries: African Literature and Literary Theory*. London: W.H. Allen and Co., 1989.
Soyinka, Wole. *Myth, Literature, and the African World*. Cambridge: Cambridge UP, 1978.
Spurr, David. *The Rhetoric of Empire: Colonial Discourse in Journalism, Travel Writing, and Imperial Administration*. Durham: Duke UP, 1993.
Talbot, P. Amaury. *The Peoples of Southern Nigeria*. (1926). Four Volumes. London: Frank Cass and Co., 1969.
Todorov, Tzvetan. *The Conquest of America: The Question of the Other*. trans. Richard Howard. New York: Harper Colophon, 1985.
Wight, Martin. *British Colonial Constitutions*. Oxford: Clarendon, 1952.
Wren, Robert M. *Achebe's World: The Historical and Cultural Context of the Novels*. Washington D.C.: Three Continents Press, 1980.

Part Two:

Critical Perspectives on No Longer At Ease

Chapter 11

Obi Okonkwo's "Bowl of Wormwood" a Reading of Chinua Achebe's *No Longer at Ease* (1960)

Augustine C. Okere

THIS PAPER EXAMINES ACHEBE'S portrayal of Obi Okonkwo in *No longer at Ease* in the light of the negative opinion of him by many critics. The issue is whether, given Obi's situation and his reactions to his external circumstances, it can be said that Achebe intends that his readers see Obi as a tragic hero.

While there is a consensus of opinion among many critics that *No Longer at Ease* has a tragic denouement, only a few reluctantly accord Obi the status of a tragic hero. Many say that there is nothing heroic about him.

Philip Rogers, in a brilliant essay that explores Achebe's literary references and allusions in the novel, calls Obi "the anti-hero of Achebe's *No Longer at Ease*."

He refers to him as *a man of nothing but words whose downfall is precipitated by his inability to act* (165).

Quoting Achebe's description of Obi's state at the time of his last bribe and subsequent arrest, Rogers says, "Paralyzed by his thoughts, he destroys himself through inaction" (165). Rogers debunks the opinion of some critics who, according to him, believe that Obi's definition of tragedy in the novel is Achebe's and therefore hold that Obi's story in *No Longer at Ease* is Achebe's illustration of that definition (182).

In his analysis of Achebe's literary references and allusions in *No Longer at Ease* and what he calls Obi's "literary sensibility" Rogers links Obi with some of the so-called anti-heroes of modern English literature: T.S. Eliot's Prufrock, ("The Love Song of J. Alfred Prufrock"), W.H. Auden's Icarus ("Musée Des Beaux Arts"),

Evelyn Waugh's Tony Last (*A Handful of Dust*), Graham Greene's Scobie (*The Heart of the Matter*) and Josef Conrad's Mr. Kurtz (*Heart of Darkness*) (165).

There is no doubt that Achebe was aware of the thematic implications of the references and allusions he was making in *No Longer at Ease.* At the time he studied English at the University College Ibadan, twentieth century authors like Yeats, Eliot, Auden, Housman, Dylan Thomas, Greene, Conrad and Pound were household names among the Honours undergraduates.

What he seems to be doing in some of the allusions and references is to remind the reader that Obi Okonkwo is just one more of the wrecks of the twentieth century civilization. Like Prufrock's predicament, Obi's tragedy is the tragedy of modern man in a world of inverted and confused values. Unlike Prufrock, Obi does not seek escape in trivialities although Rogers thinks that he does. In Obi's case, as in the case of the Magi, the confusion brings unease because of the struggle between living up to the ideals he has imbibed during his sojourn in England and meeting the demands of the pragmatic world of Lagos City.

In addition, contrary to what Rogers says, Obi in *No Longer at Ease* (*NLAE*) does not define tragedy. He is quoting "an old man" in his "village, a Christian convert who suffered one calamity after another" (39). This gives the definition the status of the wisdom of the ancients, which, among the Igbos is used to lend authenticity to a saying or an argument. According to Obi, the old man said that:

> life is like a bowl of wormwood which one sips a little at a time world without end (39).

Obi's exegesis, as Rogers puts it, is intended to explain the old man's lore to the European Chairman of the interview board whose idea of tragedy is certainly Aristotelian. Obi is trying to show him that the Igbo conception of tragedy is not the same as the conventional, West European definition. The chairman's comment, "That is most interesting," shows that Obi has said something worth thinking about. Scobie, in Graham Greene's *The Heart of the Matter*, commits suicide just as Ogbuefi Okonkwo does in *Things Fall Apart*. Both Scobie and Okonkwo conform to the conventional definition of a tragic hero. By saying that Obi's definition denies his grandfather the status of a tragic hero, Rogers shows that he belongs with the chairman. He needs therefore to look more closely at Obi's exegesis in the context of Igbo culture to which Obi belongs. In Igbo ontology, death is a release from suffering brought about by poverty, illness and the like. Therefore, worse than death, what is tragic to the Igboman is interminable suffering. This is what Obi intends to convey when he says:

> Real tragedy is never resolved. It goes on hopelessly forever. Conventional tragedy is too easy. The hero dies and we feel a purging of emotions. A real tragedy

> takes place in a corner, in an untidy spot, to quote Auden. The rest of the world is unaware of it. Like that man in *A Handful of Dust* who reads Dickens to Mr. Todd. There is no release for him. When the story ends he is still reading. There is no purging of emotions because we are not there (39).

Rogers says, quite correctly, that the central concern of "Musée Des Beaux Arts," the Auden poem quoted, is:

> the human response to the suffering of others (171).

He is also correct when he says that:

> in Auden's view of the Breughel painting the world is not *unaware* of Icarus tragedy but simply *indifferent* (171) (my emphasis).

In the world of *No Longer at Ease,* the distinction between *unaware* and *indifferent* would be rather too subtle to account for the difference Rogers is pointing out. To the Igbo psyche, *indifference* would pre-suppose *unawareness* as is evident in the Igbo dictum *"onye aghala nwanneya"* (one should not abandon one's sibling), that is, when the latter is in distress. What Rogers says of the concern of various people about Obi's several predicaments strengthens this point. The aspect of Obi's predicament of which the people of Umuofia are aware is his arrest and subsequent conviction. Nobody in Umuofia is aware of Obi's real tragedy, the spiritual dilemma of his idealism in tragic confrontation with his external circumstances. Many critics are also unaware of this dimension, or else deliberately ignore it, with serious interpretive consequences.

In relating Obi to Tony Last of Evelyn Waugh's *A Handful of Dust* Rogers hits the nail on the head. Obi's tragedy is the destruction of the idealist in him by forces in the wasteland of modern civilization. There is a popular slogan regularly displayed on local television screens, which says, "the tragedy of a man is what dies in him while he lives."

Shatto Arthur Gakwandi (28) also denies Obi the capacity to act. According to him Obi cannot be seen as a tragic hero because he "gives in too easily...does not show much ability to face up to the reality of his situation." (28) Although he agrees that Obi "is torn between two alternative ways of life", he says, "his dilemma does not move us deeply because the author fails to convey any deep human anguish or struggle" (35).

Abiola Irele argues in the same vein. Not only does he deny the heroism of Obi; he berates Achebe's treatment of the theme. According to him, Obi "is not the stuff of which a tragic hero is made" and "the theme is not given an adequately tragic treatment" John Povey's assessment of Obi is ambivalent. After summarizing the plot of *No Longer at Ease* as concerning

> ... the fall of Obi Okonkwo from the eager promise of the first Government job that crowns an excellent academic career to the penalty of jail for the taking of bribes
>
> The issues may be scarcely heroic enough in any way to constitute a tragedy and yet the events happen with the same inescapable inevitability that brings a tragic hero to his down fall (104).

On the other hand, Echeruo who seems to appreciate better what Achebe is doing in *No longer at Ease,* says that the novel has the same kind of tragic denouement as *Things Fall Apart.* He observes further that the (tragic) conflict is shown through the spiritual agony within the hero..." (153). Following from Echeruo's assessment, Obi should be categorized with such prisoners of irresolution as Shakespeare's Hamlet. It will be recalled that in *Hamlet* the weakness of the hero is his inability to act spontaneously and avenge his father's murder. Othello's tragedy does not reside in his killing of Desdemona and committing suicide afterwards, or in his earlier achievements in battle but in the mental agony he goes through as he worries about his wife's supposed infidelity as well as in his inability to see through Iago's treachery.

The inconsistency in the assessment of Obi shows most compellingly in the conflicting assessment of him in two essays by a single critic. In his *Introduction to West African Literature* (1967), Oladele Taiwo says:

> The hero of this novel (*No Longer at Ease*) is not an unusual type. We all know dozens of people like him. He is not as unforgettable as his grandfather, the warrior Okonkwo, the hero of *Things Fall Apart.* But this novel is about the new Nigerian middle-class and like most middle-class groups the Nigerian middle-class has not produced particularly colourful or memorable characters.[14]

This assessment obviously recognizes the nature of tragedy and of tragic heroism in the modern world. Nine years later, in his *Culture and the Nigerian Novel* (1976), he says, apparently echoing Irele:

> He (Obi) is certainly not the stuff of which a hero is made. Tragedy in *No Longer at Ease* does not result from any heroism displayed by Obi ...he is altogether unheroic in his approach to his problems... but from the confrontation between the old and new values (124).

What emerges from all these inconsistencies and ambivalence is the need to take a closer look at what Achebe is doing in *No Longer at Ease.*

In his essay "The Novelist as Teacher" Achebe states clearly his commitment, as a novelist, to his people. Part of this commitment is "to help my society regain belief in itself and put away the complexes of the years of denigration and self abasement"...to teach them that the harmattan is as fit a subject to write on as winter (45). Achebe refers to the imperfections of the past but he does not shy away from those imperfections, nor does he deny the imperfections of the present. Writing about them is a way of showing his people, as he says, "where the rain started to beat them." He quotes the Ghanaian professor of philosophy who says:

> Just as African scientists undertake to solve some of the scientific problems of Africa, African historians go into the history of Africa, African political scientists concern themselves with the politics of Africa; why should African literary creators be exempted from the services that they themselves recognize as genuine? (45).

No Longer at Ease can thus be said to be an *exposé* of the Nigerian situation at the time as well as an attempt by the author to project the African (Igbo) dimension to tragedy.

Things Fall Apart portrays events in Igboland between 1875 and 1904 while *No Longer at Ease* is set in the fifties. Achebe links the two novels through the characters Okonkwo and Obi. Obi of *No Longer at Ease* is the grandson of Okonkwo the hero of *Things Fall Apart*. Just as *Things Fall Apart* marks the end of the epoch of the traditional order in Igbo history and the advent of a new order of the white man's civilization so does *No Longer at Ease* mark the end of another epoch, the epoch of colonial rule in Nigeria, and the beginning of self rule by Nigerians. Both transitions are marked by uncertainties, conflicts and fears. Thus, both Ogbuefi Okonkwo of *Things Fall Apart* and Obiajulu Okonkwo of *No Longer at Ease* find themselves in conflict situations that destroy them.

That Achebe intends his readers to see both men as being the same stock at different stages of Igbo civilization is certain. One of the characters in *No Longer at Ease*, Ogbuefi Odogwu, says of Obi:

> Remark him ... he is Ogbuefi Okonkwo come back.
> He is Okonkwo *kwom kwem* exact, perfect (53).

Later in the novel, as he eulogizes the Umuofia clan, he says:

> Iguedo breeds great men ...when I was young
> I knew of them – Okonkwo, Ezendu Obierika,
> *Okolo, Nwosu* ... (54) (my emphasis).

Obi is conceived of as a modern version of these great men. This is the point of the Rev. Mr. Ikedi's speech at the send-off party arranged for Obi by the people of Umuofia:

> In times past ... Umuofia would have required of you to fight in her wars and bring home human heads ...Today we send you to bring knowledge (10).

Obi is therefore seen by Umuofia as a hero of the new dispensation, a great man of the new Iguedo.

Contrary to this overt and unqualified identification between grandfather and grandson as well as with the great men of a past generation, Rogers insists that Obi is like his grandfather only in their "willful, self destructive individualism." As he puts it,

> This single likeness is strikingly ironic because in all other aspects of their characters the grandfather and Grandson differ absolutely.... A man of violent action, he (Okonkwo) was unable to express himself in words.... and whenever he was angry and could not get his words out quickly enough, he would use his fists .... Obi in contrast is nothing but a man of words (165).

This comment misses much of what Achebe says of Obi in the novel. It should be noted that Obi, like his grandfather, finds it difficult to bring out his words quickly enough whenever he is angry. It is equally noteworthy that it is at such times that he is violent, albeit to the degree that his situation and environment permit. His rage when the President of Umuofia Progressive Union, Lagos Branch introduces the issue of his association with Clara is just one example. Achebe says that "at such times words always deserted him (NLAE, 83). Also, when Clara tells him that she is an *osu* Obi remains silent for a time and when he finds words, he shouts "as if by shouting it he could wipe away *those seconds of silence, when everything had seemed to stop, waiting in vain to speak*" (71) (my emphasis).

Implied in these comments is the suggestion that the moments of loss of speech are common with Obi, as with his grandfather, and that they correspond with moments of emotional stress for both characters. The question to ask at this point is whether Obi, as he is portrayed in *No Longer at Ease*, has a place in the conventional notion of a tragic hero.

In historical terms, Obi belongs to the class of well educated Nigerians of the early fifties, the class who were expected to take over the civil service at independence when the colonial officers occupying those positions would leave. Achebe himself belongs to this class. He studied at the University College Ibadan when, as Echeruo points out, "the University of Ibadan became the most important concentration of the best minds of the time reacting strongly and fervently against colonialism" (159). That was the period also when intelligent and promising youth were sponsored for higher education by their communities through various forms of scholarship.

In *No Longer at Ease,* we are told that Obi was an undisputed choice in Umuofia for such a community scholarship. We are told also that he was the first and only son of Umuofia to study in England.

From what is said of him at his send-off party to, and at his reception from England, it is obvious that the people of Umuofia see Obi as an important person. There is no doubt also that Obi has the same perception of himself and of his role among his people. Even the judge who convicts him refers to his "brilliant promise." Because of his achievement as the first and only Umuofia son to get a top-government job, the people of Umuofia expect him to influence, positively, the fortunes of their members working and living in Lagos. It should be assumed, therefore, that his imprisonment has an adverse effect on Umuofia generally. Apart from losing the money he is given as a loan for his study abroad, they also lose the only foothold they have in government.

From the point of view of his position in Umuofia Obi shares in the conventional notion of the Aristotlean tragic hero, and the notions of spiritual conflict and tragic flaw. Achebe goes further to expand the boundaries of tragedy and of a tragic hero, as they are perceived in West European literature.

From the time of Aristotle, the concept of tragedy and what it takes to be a tragic hero has been re-defined from age to age according to the significance held by the age in question. Greek tragedy aroused the emotions of fear and pity because the audience identified itself with the plight of the hero who was usually a person of renown. The twentieth century tragic hero has no such constituency as he can come from any stratum of society. He is often portrayed as "a victim of social, hereditary and environmental forces (Holman 531). It is possible that in the portrayal of Obi, Achebe was thinking of the kind of tragedy that treats man in terms of his godlike potential; of his transcendental ideals; of the part of himself that is in rebellion against not only the implacable universe but the frailty of his own flesh and will (Holman 533).

If this assumption is right, both Taiwo and Gakwandi seem, therefore, to miss the point Achebe is making about Obi. Taiwo says:

> It is true that Obi often shows a keen moral awareness and usually arrives at a correct intellectual assessment of a given situation, but as soon becomes evident, he never has enough courage to follow up his conviction with appropriate action... A consistent display of self-will would no doubt have made him unpopular with the U.P.U. but might have saved his relationship with Clara (126).

Gakwandi, who is more critical of Obi's performance, says:

> Obi does not recognize the contradictions of his life-style until he goes through painful experiences that bring him into conflict with his fiancée, his family, his tribe and the law as well as his own ideals .... We find it difficult to give him our full sympathy and the author himself seems to invite pity at best.... The betrayal of his original principles remains unmitigated by any dignity or irony or motive (28–29).

Taiwo's "keen moral awareness" cancels out Gakwandi's "lack of recognition of the contradictions..." leaving as justifiable criticism Obi's inability to act and lack of dignity. Both also fail to recognize the implacable social and environmental forces, which consistently negate Obi's attempts at the exercise of his self-will; the attempts to practise the ideals he believes in. These forces are apparent in two crucial aspects of his story, namely, his failure to marry Clara and his corrupting his office through bribe taking and seducing of the female candidate for scholarship.

Achebe's portrayal of the Obi-Clara affair shows Obi to be a sincere and determined lover while Clara, knowing that she is an *osu,* forbidden by custom to marry a non-*osu* is, except for occasional flashes of infatuation, diffident, hedgy and uncommitted. Achebe says of Obi that before he met Clara "on board the cargo-boat, *Sasa* he had thought of love as another grossly over-rated European invention.... But "with Clara it was different from the first" (70). Critics have given wrong signals on the issue of Obi's momentary silence after Clara declares that they cannot marry because she is an *osu.* Obi's reaction requires some scrutiny. It is a reaction that signals the normal shock that follows a sudden negative revelation of the kind made by Clara. Every Igbo man or woman in Obi's position would experience the same kind of torpor, especially as it is unusual for an *osu* to make such a declaration so boldly. Achebe's description of the events of the moment brings out Obi's feeling clearly. It is a moment when, as he says, "everything seemed to stop" (71). Obi's shout: "Nonsense" is partly an expression of disbelief and partly of rage. It comes only after his recovery from the torpor. What he tells his friend, Joseph, later that evening is a decision: "I am going to marry the girl. I wasn't actually seeking your approval" (72). Achebe's comment on this is very illuminating:

> Obi felt better and more confident in his *decision* now that there was an opponent, the first of hundreds to come no doubt. Perhaps it was not a decision really; for him there could be only one choice. It was scandalous that in the middle of the twentieth century a man could be barred from marrying a girl simply because her great-great-great-grandfather had been dedicated to serve a god, thereby setting himself apart and turning his descendants into a forbidden caste to the end of time. Quite unbelievable (72).

Obi's "decision" or "choice" appears final. He declares that not even his mother (who is known to have the closest ties with him) could stop him (72). He underscores his determination by going to Kingsway Stores the following day and buying "a twenty-pound engagement ring" for Clara. In a later argument on the matter with Joseph he says: "A pioneer is one who shows the way. That is what I am doing." (75). He does not say it is what he is going to do but what he is doing. This means that he sees himself as already marrying Clara. When the issue is brought up at the meeting of the U.P.U. Lagos Branch, we are told that "Obi leapt up to his feet trembling with rage (83). This is rage from the heart and a re-affirmation of his stand on the Clara issue. When he is requested to sit down and hear the President out, he retorts, shouting:

> Sit down my foot...This is preposterous I could take you to court for that ... for that... for that (83).

He refuses to listen any more to the President and warns:

> don't you dare interfere in my affairs again. And if this is what you meet about ... you may cut off my two legs if you ever find them here again (83).

We are told that Obi storms out of the meeting ordering his driver to drive off in-spite of the pleading of many members of the union, including Joseph, his closest friend.

Later, also, in his celebrated debate with his father over the Clara affair, Obi's point remains the same. He tells his father:

> What made the osu different from other men and women was ignorance of their forefathers (134).
>
> He reminds him that they "who have seen the light of the gospel should not remain in that ignorance" (134).

In spite of his very tender feelings towards his mother and her insistence that she would kill herself if Obi dares marry Clara while she is alive, Obi remains undaunted. In narrating the story to Clara, Obi "had done his best to make the whole thing sound unimportant." The objection by his father and mother is just a temporary set-back and no more. Everything would work out nicely in the end. All we need to do is to lie quiet for a while" (142).

That this last sentence has been quoted as an illustration of Obi's feebleness shows how prone some critics are to misunderstanding Achebe's intentions in *No Longer at Ease.* The sentence derives from a well-known Igbo aphorism in which the bed-bug tells its children to endure patiently the hot water poured on them as what is hot will eventually get cold. Anybody who is familiar with the Igbo society, where the *osu* caste system still operates, would know that situations like the one Obi and Clara are facing always cool off with time and the lovers get married, albeit, estranged for a while from the relations of the non-*osu* partner.

Clara, on the other hand, is diffident and pessimistic as the event on the eve of Obi's journey to Umuofia demonstrates. After arranging Obi's luggage, Clara suddenly begins to weep. She tells Obi that she has something to tell him. Although her disclosure is reported, its tone has a finality that does not admit of any discussion:

> Clara said she was very sorry to let him down at this eleventh hour. But she was sure it would be in everybody's best interest if they broke of their engagement (123).

Although Clara sounds more realistic and pre-emptive, it cannot be said that she is doing what Obi wants to do but cannot get himself to do it. Achebe comments that "Obi was deeply stung, but said nothing for a long time." (83) When he finds words to answer Clara, he merely says "Bunk."

That Clara is hasty in returning the engagement ring is also part of the *osu* psychology. Given Obi's other problems and worries at the time of the incident and the deepening tragic hubris occasioned by them, one can hardly say that Obi's subsequent actions are not trance-like. This does not imply, as Gakwandi holds, that Obi "is never in the mood for consecutive thinking" (29). Even if he were prepared to take "a firm stand against an irrational custom" (128) as Taiwo urges, he is dealing with another human individual whose own determination must also be taken into consideration. It is Obi's idealistic self-will versus Clara's pragmatic self-will.

When they get to the doctor for the abortion, it is Clara who says unequivocally: "I don't want to marry him" (145). Obi's anxieties before she is admitted show a deep concern for a lover. At the time the doctor drives off with Clara, Obi, we are told, "wanted to rush out of his car and shout, 'stop, let's go and get married now,' but 'he couldn't and didn't.' The doctor's car drove away." Achebe then comments:

> It couldn't have been more than a minute, or at most two. Obi's mind was made up. He reversed his car and chased after the doctor's to stop them. But they were no longer in sight … (149).

Obi's desperate attempts to stop Clara from committing the abortion speak eloquently of his sincerity. Despite all that, however, Clara refuses to see him not only while in hospital but thereafter, as she leaves Lagos immediately on her discharge from hospital.

More than Obi's failure to marry Clara, the circumstances of his "bribes" constitute the basis for much of the assessment of him by critics. Robert Wren claims that "Achebe's novel is built around 'kola', a bribery" (47). While this claim can be faulted on the ground that bribery is not the central theme of the novel, what is true is that Obi's imprisonment for bribery is the greatest irony of the novel. Obi's anti-bribery crusade started while he was a student in England. There, he had written a paper on the evil of corruption in Nigeria and came up with the theory that "the public service of Nigeria would remain corrupt until the old Africans at the top were replaced by young men from the universities" (38). In his debate on bribery with his friend, Christopher, he restates his stand, pointing out that, having no intellectual foundations" the old people in the service "worked steadily to the top through bribery – an ordeal by bribery." For such people, "bribe is natural. He gave it and expects it." Then he goes on to say:

> Our people say that if you pay homage to the man on top, others will pay homage to you when it is your turn to be on top. Well, that is what the old men say (21).

For the young men, according to Obi, "bribery is no problem."

> They come straight to the top without bribing any one. It is not that they are necessarily better than others, it's simply that they can afford to be virtuous. But even that virtue can become a habit.
>
> He considers the "Lands Officer jailed last year ...an exception" (21).

Achebe expects his readers to scrutinize the irony of Obi's eventual conviction for a crime he has been most vocal in its condemnation. In convicting Obi, Mr. Justice William Galloway, Judge of the High Court of Lagos and the Southern Cameroons, says that he "cannot comprehend how a young man of [Obi's] education and brilliant promise could have done this" (2). As Achebe says:

> Everybody wondered why...The British Council man, even the men of Umuofia did not know. And we must presume that, in spite of his certitude Mr. Green did not know either (170).

The crux of the novel is why Obi commits the crime.

Mr. Green asserts that Obi commits the crime because, as he puts it:

> The African is corrupt through and through [having] been sapped mentally and physically [by] the worst climate in the world and every imaginable disease (3).

Mr. Green's opinion is the kind of pseudo-scientific conclusions typical of the early colonial officers. It is comparable to the assumption of the Colonial Officer in *Things Fall Apart* who sees in the story of Okonkwo material for a chapter in his book on *The Pacification of the Primitive Tribes of the Lower Niger.* It is an aspect of the European fallacy about Africa and Africans, which constitutes Achebe's target for criticism. Povey debunks this fallacy and maintains that although Green thinks that his theory "is confirmed by Obi's crime, it is not true or there would be no struggle at all... simply a story of villainy and its punishment" (105). Another fallacy is advanced, unfortunately, by Gakwandi, an African, who claims that Obi "takes bribes merely to keep up appearances as a member of the affluent elite who are busy maintaining their cars and paying back loans for their education" (28). Like Mr. Green's assertion, this is too superficial a reading to represent the real issues involved in Obi's predicament.

Oladele Taiwo is closer to the truth. According to him:

> Obi's isolation results from the conflicting and simultaneous demands made on him by various groups including the U.P.U. in financial terms these demands are high and exert a real pressure on his slender resources (125–126).

It will be recalled that Obi had said that the young people of his dream for the Nigerian civil service could *afford* to be virtuous. In other words, he realizes that virtue in their case derives from self-sufficiency. One can therefore assert that he would never have succumbed to taking bribes if he did not find himself in a financial straight-jacket. Obi has debts to pay back to Umuofia Progressive Union, to Clara, to Hon. Sam Okoli as well as paying back the Bank overdraft.

These are, for him, moral obligations; Clara's in particular, considering what has happened between them. More than the debts, the Igbo family set-up imposes on him the equally moral responsibility of paying school fees for his younger brother and paying his mother's hospital and funeral bills; all these in addition to the normal routine bills such as the insurance premium, his income tax, electricity and other house-keeping bills.

By making all these come up at the same time, Achebe wants to make it clear that Obi is a victim of these pressures. They constitute a shattering test of his idealistic self-will. Rogers says that Obi "accepts the bribe only because he can find no reason to refuse it" (72). The reasons he has "not to refuse it" are indeed palpable, as has been mentioned already. Achebe's paragraph beginning "It was again the season for scholarships..." in fact argues for Obi (183). It suggests that he had withstood the temptations of the first season (of Mr. Mark and his sister). And this was because he did not have the problems that now beset him.

Achebe's comment on Obi's theory of corruption in the public service of Nigeria shows clearly that Obi is a determined moral crusader:

> Unlike most theories formed by students in London, this one survived the first impact of homecoming. in fact within a month of his return Obi came across two classic examples of his old African (38).

His rebuff of the Customs Officer, and Mr. Mark speak boldly of his determination.

Even as he takes the bribes, Obi is not delineated as one desperate for bribe. His lack-lustre disposition when the first person comes is informative. When the man tells him:

> I don't want to waste your time ...My son is going to England in September. I want him to get scholarship. If you can do it for me here is fifty pounds... Obi told him it was not possible.
>
> In the first place, I don't give scholarships. All I do is go through the applications and recommend those who satisfy the requirements to the scholarship Board... (167, 168).

We are told that "the man rose to his feet, placed the wad of notes on the occasional table before Obi," saying, "*This is small kola...*" Achebe comments that

> The wad of notes lay where he had placed it for the rest of the day and all night Obi placed a newspaper over it and secured the door. "This is terrible!" he mut-

> tered. "Terrible!" he said aloud. He woke up with a start in the middle of the night and he did not go back to sleep again for a long time afterwards (167).

There is, in Obi's utterance and the fact of his sleeplessness, a strong indication of an oppressed mind. He is torn between his ideals and his needs. At the time of the last, fated bribe, Obi shows the same degree of reluctance and helplessness. Achebe says that:

> As the man left, Obi realized that he could stand it no more. People say that one gets used to these things but he had not found it like that at all. Every incident had been a hundred times worse than the one before it. The money lay on the table. he would have preferred not to look in its direction, but he seemed to have no choice. He just sat looking at it, paralyzed by his thoughts. (168)

The truth, indeed, is that Obi has no choice. In his position, a "more positive effort" as Gakwandi suggests, is impossible. The assault on his ideal by the topsy-turvy world of Lagos city proves more devastating than the pressures inflicted by his family and other commitments.

How, for example, could he justifiably continue to keep Clara's money after social pressures have thwarted their plans to marry?

Having been liberated from his idealism by the fact of his mother's death, Obi has learnt that he has "to stand on the earth and go with her at her pace" (167). That earth is Obi's homeland where a member of the Civil Service Interview Board reminds him that people go into the civil service to take bribes; where it is popularly believed that one might have more trouble refusing bribes than by taking it; where even messengers allege that the white officers in their departments take more bribes than the blacks; where his friend, Christopher, calls him "the biggest ass in Nigeria" because he refused to take "advantage of a girl straight from school who wants to go to university."

A close reading of *No Longer at Ease* shows that there is at least a mental struggle up to the time of Obi's fall. His tragic flaw is his inability to sustain his ideal to the last. This places him on the scroll of tragic heroes in the conventional Aristotelian sense. It is best, however, to see him as one dogged by an implacable destiny, thus putting him in the same mould as Thomas Hardy's Micheal Henchard. Obi's story is, as Arthur Rovenscroft points out, the story of a man "caught between the irreconcilable values of different ways of life" (20). Echeruo agrees when he says, "Obi's tragedy is that of a man caught between the ideal in which he believes and a reality which impels him to compromise that ideal" (154).

However, Achebe is doing more than mere categorization. Obi lives on in his defeat, disgrace and shame to sip "his bowl of wormwood" until the end of Time. In his portrayal of Obi, Achebe has extended the frontiers of the conventional, West European notion of a tragic hero.

Works Cited

Achebe, Chinua. *No Longer At Ease.* London: Heinemann, 1960. Subsequent references are from this edition and enclosed in parentheses in the text.

———. "The Novelist as Teacher." In *Morning Yet On Creation Day: Essays.* London: Heinemann, 1977.

Echeruo, Michael J.C. "Chinua Achebe." *A Celebration of Black and African Writing.* In Ed. Bruce King and Kolawole Ogungbesan. Oxford: Oxford University Press, 1975.

Gakwandi, Shatto Arthur. "Illusions of Progress: Achebe's *No Longer At Ease.*" In *The Novel in Contemporary Experience in Africa.* London/Nairobi: Heinemann. 1977: 27–36.

Holman, Hugh. *A Handbook to Literature.* 3rd Ed. The Odyssey Press, 1978.

Irele, Abiola. "The Tragic Conflict in the Novels of Chinua Achebe." In *Critical Perspectives on Chinua Achebe.* Ed. Catherine Innes and Bernth Lindfors. Washington, D.C.: Three Continents Press, 1978.

Povey, John. "The Novels of Chinua Achebe." In *Introduction to Nigerian Literature.* Ed. Bruce King. Lagos: Evans Brothers Ltd., 1971.

Ravenscroft, Arthur. *Chinua Achebe.* London: Longman, 1969.

Rogers, Philips. "No Longer At Ease: Chinua Achebe's Heart of Whiteness." Research in African Literatures. Vol. 14, No. 2. Summer 1983: 165–183.

Taiwo, Oladele. *An Introduction to West African Literature.* London: Thomas Nelson, 1967.

Wren, Robert. *Achebe's World: The Historical and Cultural Context of the Novels of Chinua Achebe.* London: Longman, 1980.

Chapter 12

Achebe the Traditionalist: A Critical Analysis of *No Longer at Ease*

Blessing Diala

CHINUA ACHEBE WAS RAISED in his village, Ogidi, in the Eastern part of Nigeria. Much of Achebe's ideas in his writings is evidently informed by the rich traditional heritage of his Ogidi home. In *No Longer at Ease*, Achebe brings up a number of conflicts between traditional and modern values. This conflict revolves around the protagonist Obi Okonkwo, who is the grandson of Okonkwo in *Things Fall Apart*. In reading *Things Fall Apart*, it is evident that the changes brought in Umuofia by the Missionaries have ironically affected the people negatively. This is portrayed in the protagonist in *No Longer at Ease*. In *Things Fall Apart*, Okonkwo commits suicide because he does not want to see the culture and values he believes in destroyed by the Missionaries. Obi's father, Nwoye, who later changes his name to Isaac embraces the Christian religion and runs away with the Missionaries because he was afraid of Okonkwo's high-handedness and rigidity. Obi, the protagonist of *No Longer at Ease*, therefore, becomes a Christian by virtue of his father's belief.

The novel, *No Longer at Ease,* opens with a flashback on the trial of Obi Okonkwo for accepting bribe as a civil servant. Obi is expected to live above board with his British education but he brings shame and humiliation to himself, his parents and the people of Umuofia because of what he did. Obi is sent abroad on a scholarship by his people (Umuofia Progressive Union) to study Law. He disappoints them by getting a degree in English. On his return, he is filled with idealism and determination to rid his country of corruption and help create a better nation. Obi further disappoints his people during his reception by not dressing in suit and by speaking simple English when he is addressing the audience. The people expected to hear jaw-breaking words from him just like the Secretary of the union in his welcome address. According to Achebe, the Secretary "wrote the kind of English they admired if not understood; the kind that filled the mouth like the proverbial dried meat".

Another disappointment from Obi is his relationship with Clara, a girl he met on-board the ship on his way from London. Clara is an *osu*, an outcast in Igbo tradition and should not be married to a free born. Obi gets a job as a secretary in the scholarship division of the Ministry of Education. He resists several attempts to take bribes from people who want to get scholarship to study abroad. His friends Christopher and Joseph, his parents and his people in Lagos, vehemently oppose his relationship with Clara. His people are ready to forgive his shortcomings, but not his relationship with Clara. The President of Umuofia Progressive Union raises the issue in one of their meetings when Obi requests them to give him four months grace before he starts paying back his scholarship loan of five hundred pounds. The President interjects "… I have heard that you are moving around with a girl of doubtful ancestry and even thinking of marrying her…" (94). Obi gets angry and storms out of the meeting with a resolve to start paying back immediately the loan he took from the Union. Even Joseph his close friend can not stop him from leaving.

Obi encounters a number of problems. He has to pay back his scholarship loan and also pay his brother's school fees and his expired car insurance; thus he can no longer make ends meet. To meet his financial demands, he cuts down on his life style and succumbs to accepting bribe. His parents' disapproval of Clara makes him postpone his marriage to her. Clara has to get an abortion and never returns to Obi again.

Obi's dealings with his people and his parents explain the clash between traditional and modern values. While his people are looking for a son, well dressed in suit, he comes to his reception in a simple shirt and trouser. He goes against tradition by having an affair with Clara. It is not that Obi is not aware of the tradition, he thinks that with his education, he feels that his private affair should not be interfered with. Thus he tries to use religion to justify his relationship with Clara when he says to his father "the bible says that in Christ there are no bond or free…" Our fathers in their darkness and ignorance called an innocent man *osu*, a thing given to idols and thereafter he became an outcast, and his children's children forever. But have we not seen the light of the gospel?" (151).

Obi uses the very words his father would have used in the bid to convince him but his father observes that "*Osu* is like leprosy in the minds of our people. I beg of you my son, not to bring the mark of shame and leprosy into your family. If you do, your children and your children's children unto the third and fourth generations will curse your memory. It is not for myself I speak, my days are few. You will bring sorrow on your head and on the heads of your children. Who will marry your daughters? Whose daughters will your sons marry? Think of that, my son. We are Christians, but we cannot marry our daughters" (152) Obi loves his mother and looks forward to her support. His mother who has been sick for a long time says: "I have nothing to tell you in this matter except one thing. If you want to marry this girl, you must wait until I am no more. If God hears my prayers you will not wait long ... But if you do the thing while I am still alive, you will have my blood on your head, because I shall kill myself (154). At this point, according to Killam (1982: 40) "Obi's moral resolution capable of resisting the pressures to which he is subjected in his professional life, cannot withstand more powerful conviction of his mother... shortly after this his mother dies and paradoxically his European morality with her."

These conversations between Obi and his parents reveal the extent of the seriousness of this tradition in Igbo land. Achebe uses authorial intuition to expose the discrimination against the *Osu* and wonders why with civilization, education and religion, the *Osu* caste system is still prevalent in the Igbo culture.

Style and Technique

Achebe uses a number of techniques in this novel to bring his point home. We see the use of irony, humor, proverbs, and transliteration to mention a few. It is an irony that Nwoye renamed Isaac, rejected his father's ways because of their inflexibility and brutality, epitomized in the death of Ikemefuna and replaced them with the notion of Christian beliefs only to revert years later to the same old beliefs he had jettisoned to embrace Christianity. Obi points out to his father the inconsistency between Christian beliefs and the *Osu* held by his father. Isaac observes "I know Josiah Okeke very well... we are Christians but we cannot marry our own daughters" (121). It is also ironical that Obi's western education and the moral standards he derives from it render him incapable of standing against the traditional and conservative beliefs of his parents and their generation (but existing effectively in modern Nigeria). Obi can therefore be seen as a tragic figure and a victim of the same historical circumstance, which overwhelmed his grand father, the fact of colonialism. The adamant attitude in Okonkwo's traditional beliefs is transferred to Nwoye's beliefs in the Christian religion. This stubborn attitude and rigidity seen in Obi's reflection of tradition for modernity. Nothing could change his mind except his financial predicament. We notice that Nwoye, Obi's father, did not attend his father's funeral because of his Christian beliefs. In the same way Obi could not attend his mother's funeral because he could not afford the money, instead he sent the little money he had home for the funeral. Umuofia people see this as absurd considering the fact that his father had done the same thing years ago. According to Umuofia people, "blood never lies". One of them who comes to condole Obi over his mother's death says "a man may go to England, become a lawyer or a doctor, but it does not change his blood" (182). It is satirical that Obi turned down Mr. Mark's request (99) and threatened to hand over a customs officer clearing his goods from the ship to the police (35) without knowing that someday he would condescend to accepting bribes himself.

The use of satire is seen in Mr. Steven Udom's disappointment when he does not see the usual crowd waiting for Mr. Sasa. As soon as he sights Lagos, "he had returned to his cabin to emerge half an hour later in a black suit, bowler hat and rolled umbrella, even though it was a hot October day" (34). Proverbs are used in this novel, but not as much as in *Things Fall Apart*. The people of Umuofia in Lagos rallied around Obi in his time of trouble saying that "a kinsman in trouble had to be saved, not blamed, anger against a brother was felt in the flesh not in the bone" (6). In blaming Obi, the people of Umuofia had said "if you want to eat a toad, you should look for a fat and juicy one (4). This shows that they are disappointed that Obi accepts bribe, but they are more disappointed at the meager sum that put him into trouble. When Obi's relationship with Clara is being discussed, one of the men from Umuofia says, "if one finger brings oil, it soils the others" (86). In other words, if Obi marries Clara, his is bringing a bad name to himself and his family.

Achebe uses transliteration in *No Longer at Ease* to get his message across to his readers. For example, "I have always said that your head is not correct".... "You may laugh if laughter catches you... it does not catch me" (17). Another example, "it was said that he fought during the Kaiser's war and that it had gone to his head" (73). We notice the use of Pidgin to differentiate the levels of education of the characters. The Minister's steward asks Obi and Clara, "wetin master and madam go drink?" Obi replies in the way the steward will understand, "make you no worry, Samson, just tell Minister say we call" (107). There is also the use of traditional artifacts such as goatskins used to spread on the floor, breaking of kolanuts, incantations, folktales and myth. For example, "there were not enough chairs for all of them to sit on, so that many sat on their goatskins spread on the floor. It did not make much difference whether one sat on a chair or on the floor because even those who sat on the chairs spread their goatskins on them first (58).

During an incantation, the oldest man in the meeting says, "he that brings kolanut brings life. We do not seek to hurt any man, but if any man seeks to hurt us may he break his neck.... We are strangers in this land, if good comes to it, may we have our share... but if bad comes, let it go to the owners of the land who know what gods should be appeased.... Many towns have four or five, even ten of their sons in European posts in this city. Umuofia has only one, and now our enemies say that even that one is too many for us. But our ancestors will not agree to such a thing. Amen. An only palm fruit does not get lost in the fire" (7). Achebe uses a lot of humor in this novel. During Obi's send off party, Mr. Ikedi tells a story of how wedding feasts had been steadily declining in towns since the invention of invitation cards. Many people whistled in disbelief when he told them that a man could not go to his neighbors unless he was given one of these papers on which they wrote RSVP, meaning rice and stew very plenty (11–12). The passengers in the bus Obi was travelling with to his village sang this song that shows some humor (50):

> An in-law went to see his in-law O yiemu-o;
> His in-law sees him and kills him – O yiemu-o;
> Bring a canoe; bring a paddle – O yiemu-o;
> The paddle speaks English – O yiemu-o.

Conclusion

Obi Okonkwo is as stubborn as his father and his grand father. Like his father and grandfather he did whatever he set out to do. For example, he insists on marrying Clara even though it was a taboo for a freeborn to marry an *Osu*. Obi's return from overseas turns out to be an embarrassment to his people because of his nonconformity and lack of respect for their tradition. Furthermore, he finds it difficult to alleviate his parents' financial difficulty. He could not help any body from his town to secure a job. He chooses to ostracize himself by insisting on marrying Clara even when he knows it is a taboo. Obi tries to defend himself by quoting the Bible that is very flexible and can serve any purpose one wants it to serve. However, his total disregard of the tradition and culture of his people was his undoing ultimately. Obi's insistence on marrying Clara broke his mother's heart and hastened her death.

In my opinion, Obi should give the traditional society what belongs to them while living the life of a modem man. He should have swallowed his pride, listened to the voice of reason, and agreed with the terms of the repayment of his loan to U.P.U. to make life easier for him and others who would have benefited from their community loan's program.

Works Cited

Achebe, Chinua. *No Longer at Ease*. London: Heinemann Books Ltd., 1960 Quotations are from the Anchor Doubleday edition.

Achebe, Chinua. *Things Fall Apart.* London: Heinemann Books Ltd., 1958.

Killam, G.D. *The Novels of Chinua Achebe*. London: Heinemann, 1982.

Palmer, Eustace. *An Introduction To the African Novel.* London: Heinemann Books Ltd., 1972.

Chapter 13

What's in a Name: Irony as a Narrative Strategy in Chinua Achebe's *No Longer at Ease*

Clement A. Okafor

NO LONGER AT EASE portrays the inherent contradictions of the dual heritage of the modern African who has to mediate in his daily life the unrelenting tensions between the Western universe of his formal education and the African cosmos of his social life. In this novel, Obi's work environment is controlled by the British colonial officers who judge his actions entirely from the Western perspective. His social life, however, is governed by African concepts of caste avoidance and one's duties within the extended family. Neither the colonial administrators nor his kinsmen fully understand his predicament. As a result, he inhabits a world of psychic loneliness and isolation. Furthermore, he cannot benefit from the experience of his predecessors; never before has any of his people been faced with such a dilemma. Thus, his life is like a journey through an uncharted territory. The choices he makes are as dangerous as those of a farmer who has to plough a farm strewn with landmines but without the benefit of markers. Not surprisingly, Obi is devastated in the end, as he traverses the treacherous terrain of his dual heritage. Herein lies the dilemma of the cultural pioneer. How far can such a pioneer venture into the potentially perilous cultural twilight zone without endangering himself in the process?

In summing up the case against Obi, Judge Galloway highlights the contrast between Obi's bright prospects in the colonial Nigerian civil service and the catastrophic demise he brought upon himself. The irony emphasized by the Judge is, however, only a layer in the series of ironies or paradoxes upon which *No Longer at Ease* is constructed.

The dominant layer of irony in the novel is that of the name of the protagonist, Obi, whose fill name is "Obiajulu – the mind at last is at rest." (6). Like the Jews, the Igbo people of Nigeria-among whom the novel is set, name each child on the eighth day of the birth of the baby. On such an occasion, a father gives his child a name that is usually a statement about the family's circumstances. Again, in Igboland as in most traditional, patrilineal societies, families are anxious to have male offspring who will perpetuate their names. Thus, Isaac Okonkwo, Obi's father, is anxious about the future of his lineage, especially after the birth of his fourth female child. This anxiety seems to be assuaged when a baby boy, Obi, is born as his fifth child; whereupon, the happy father names him Obiajulu to show that his mind is at rest, now that he has a potential heir. The irony is that Obi brings neither rest nor peace to his parents or to the others he encounters throughout his life. Obi's first act of rebellion is the letter he writes to Hitler while Obi is merely a child in primary school and at a time when all the other children in the school are collecting palm kernels to contribute to the British war effort. Next, Umuofia Progressive Union sends him to Britain to study Law so that he may defend them in their land disputes with their neighbors. However, Obi changes his course and studies English instead. Worse still, when he returns to Nigeria, he outrages not only members of the Union but especially his own parents by wanting to marry a girl belonging to an untouchable caste. In the end, his imprisonment on a bribery charge brings nothing but shame and disgrace to the community that has sacrificed so much to install him into the higher echelons of respectable society.

The corruption of the moral values of the protagonist is yet another layer of irony that is portrayed in *No Longer at Ease*. According to Obi's earlier theory, corruption persists in the Nigerian civil service because old but uneducated men are at the helm of affairs. The scourge will disappear, he argues, when such old men are replaced by young university graduates. Referring to the new breed, he says:

> To most of them bribery is no problem. They come straight to the top without bribing anyone. It's not that they're necessarily better than others, it's simply that they can afford to be virtuous. But even that kind of virtue can become a habit (21).

In keeping with Obi's high ideals, he wards off Mr. Mark, who offers him a bribe. As the protagonist gloats over his victory, he convinces himself that all it takes to avoid bribery is to say no: "It was easy to keep one's hands clean. It required no more than the ability to say: 'I'm sorry Mr. So-and-So, but I cannot continue this discussion. Good morning'" (88). However, that is before his financial problems begin to mount. Soon after this incident, his mother is hospitalized and he has to pay her hospital bill. In addition to the monthly installmental repayment of his university loan, he has to pay his enormous electricity bill as well as his annual car license fee. Besides, he has to pay the school fees for his younger brother and somehow pay his annual car insurance premium. Furthermore, he has to finance Clara's abortion and repay the big loan she gave him earlier. Regrettably, these expenses prove to be too much for his salary, and he begins to supplement his earnings with bribes from scholarship candidates and their family members. Unfortunately, before long he is arrested and jailed.

Although Obi may not be aware of it, his career is an exact mirror image of the profile of the young Turks he would like to inherit the Nigerian civil service: Obi is young, a university graduate, and has got to the top without having to offer bribes to any one. According to his earlier theory on bribery, someone with these attributes would not accept bribes. Obi's initial moral distaste for corruption is exemplified by his refusal to bribe the Customs clerk at the Lagos wharf, and his willingness to be delayed by that official until everyone else in the boat has been processed. Again, during Obi's journey home, he scares the traffic policeman from accepting the bribe that is being offered to him. The irony here is that Obi's intervention makes the same officer extort five times the initial sum later. It is, therefore, doubly ironic that this anticorruption crusader himself should in the end be imprisoned on a corruption charge.

Obi's initial decision to marry Clara even after he has found out that she is *osu*, a member of an untouchable caste, presents yet another layer of irony in *No Longer at Ease.* At first, he is very sure of himself:

> Obi felt better and more confident in his decision now that there was an opponent, the first of hundreds to come no doubt. Perhaps it was not a decision really; for him there could be only one choice. It was scandalous that in the middle of the twentieth century a man could be barred from marrying a girl simply because her great-great-great-great grandfather had been dedicated to serve a god, thereby setting him apart and turning his descendants into a forbidden caste to the end of Time. Quite unbelievable. And here was an educated man telling Obi he did not understand. Not even my mother can stop me,' he said as he lay down beside Joseph (72).

The very next day he buys Clara an engagement ring as a sign of his defiance of his people's tradition and later storms out of a meeting of the Umuofia Progressive Union because the President mentions the relationship. Because of Obi's special relationship with his mother, he pretends that he can persuade her to support his plan to defy the marriage traditions of his people: "I can handle them," said Obi, "especially my mother" (75). The irony is that in the end it is the mother, rather than his father, who is implacably opposed to the proposal. To emphasize her opposition, she threatens to commit suicide, should Obi ignore her strong views on the matter. Surprisingly, the father does not put up a spirited battle. On the contrary, Obi's father is convinced that the impending contagion that his son is about to introduce to his household is a consequence of his own father's earlier curse on him when he joined the ranks of the foreign missionaries. As the old man sees it, Obi is not responsible for the contagion. Rather, the father's earlier transgression is being visited upon his son; in which case, Obi's actions are the consequence of the curse of the ancestors. According to the father:

> I was no more than a boy when I left my father's house and went with the missionaries. He placed a curse on me. I was not there, but my brothers told me it was true. When a man curses his own child it is a terrible thing. And I was his first son. Obi had never heard about the curse. In broad daylight and in happier circumstances he would not have attached any importance to it. But that night he felt strangely moved with pity for his lather (138).

It is immensely ironic that Obi's previously defiant posture collapses after this encounter with his parents. Consequently, he swallows his pride and readily finances Clara's abortion to bring closure to this phase of his life.

Umuofia Progressive Union's investment in Obi's education portrays another layer of irony in *No Longer at Ease*: the irony of education. The Union's decision to establish a loan scholarship scheme is informed by its desire to have a townsman among the ranks of the national elite. They award the scholarship to Obi on account of his impressive educational credentials:

> The selection of the first candidate had not presented any difficulty to the Union. Obi was an obvious choice. At tie age of twelve or thirteen he had passed his Standard Six examination at tie top of the whole province.
>
> Then he had won a scholarship to one of the best secondary schools in Eastern Nigeria. At the end of five years he passed the Cambridge School Certificate with distinction in all subjects. He was in fact a village celebrity, and his name was regularly invoked at the mission school where he had been a pupil (7–8).

The high expectation of the Union is reflected in the send-off party organized in Obi's honor in Umuofia. According to Reverend Ikedi Chairman of the occasion, Obi's imminent depa rture for England is the fulfillment of the biblical prophecy of light coming to a people who live in darkness. The accompanying feast is Obi's father's way of expressing his delight with his family's good fortune. Furthermore, the elaborate welcome party that the Union organizes in Lagos on Obi's return from England expresses tie members' delight with their investment in Obi's university education. Their welcome address speaks of the great honor he has brought to their ancient town and the women's song lionizes his achievements. These sentiments are affirmed in the festivity with which the entire town welcomes back heroic graduate son:

> Bands of music-makers went out two miles on the Umuofia-Onitsha road to await Obi's arrival. There were at least five different groups, if one excludes the brass band of the CMS School Umuofia. It looked as if the entire village was celebrating a feast. Those who were not waiting along the road, elderly people especially, were already arriving in large numbers at Mr. Okonkwo's compound (48).
>
> In their conversations at the reception, the villagers liken Obi to the legendary hero who returns victorious to the land of the living from his awesome wrestling match in the land of die spirits. The elders present refer to him as the embodiment of their valiant ancestors: "He is the grandson of Ogbuefi Okonkwo who faced the white man single-handed and died in the fight" (53).

These events clearly show that Obi is held in high esteem and is regarded by his people as an excellent role-model for aspiring youngsters. Even so, there is ironic tension between the appearance and the reality; this light coming to a people who live in darkness victorious hero returning triumphantly from his exploits in the land of the spirits soon destroys through his own deliberate actions the enormous goodwill that he has built up among his people. By so doing, he transforms himself from being the paradigm of success to being the epitome of failure. Yet, even in his moment of failure, Obi continues to symbolize the dilemma of the cultural pioneer who is destroyed in his effort to synthesize his sometimes antagonistic dual heritage. A major factor that contributes to Obi's downfall is his desire to marry his sweetheart who belongs to an untouchable caste – an action that is permissible in Western societies but is forbidden by the traditions of his people. Obi's persistence in this romance alienates him from the Union and makes it necessary for him to begin to pay back the scholarship loan immediately. This, in turn, helps to create the unbearable financial pressure that breaks him eventually. However, another major contributing factor to his catastrophic demise is his commitment to his extended family; he supplements his income with bribes in order to provide for the needs of his parents and younger brother.

Thus, *No Longer at Ease* portrays the dilemma of a cultural pioneer who attempts to mediate in his daily life the conflicting imperatives of the Western universe of his formal education and work environment on the one hand and the African cosmos of his social life on the other. The novel highlights the psychic loneliness of the pioneer-hero and raises the fundamental issue of how much such trailblazers can venture into the potentially dangerous uncharted territory without being devastated in the process.

The discussion above shows that *No Longer at Ease* is built on several layers of irony or dichotomy between the initial expectation and the paradox of the eventual outcome. These layers of paradox are the ironies of corruption, defiance, and education. Uniting them all is the irony of the name of the protagonist. So what is in a name? The answer is *a great deal.* In *No Longer at Ease,* Chinua Achebe has used the ironic name of the protagonist as an effective narrative strategy for successfully prosecuting his artistic endeavor.

Works Cited

Achebe, Chinua. *No Longer at Ease*. New York: Astor-Honor, 1961. All Subsequent citations are taken from this edition.

Chapter 14

Verbal Abundance: The Contexts of Igbo Speech Acts in *No Longer at Ease*

Chiji Akoma.

COMPARED TO THE CRITICAL attention given to its forerunner, *Things Fall Apart, No Longer at Ease* seems to have suffered the fate of a child born after an enterprising and famous sibling: few essays have been written on it; it does not boast of translations into other languages; and its hero, Obi Okonkwo, fails to enjoy even the faintest echoes of the fame of his grandfather, Okonkwo, of *Things Fall Apart.* Could it be that our fascination with Okonkwo is because he appeals to our sense of the heroic age, the age when valor could be quantified by counting the number of human heads harvested in internecine wars? In contrast to Okonkwo's world, Obi's is tepid, marked by its stark ordinariness. There are no physical wars to be fought, no white District Commissioner and his minions to contend with. No matter how vicious the skirmishes between Mr. Green and Obi, or the drawn out philosophical conflict between Obi and his kinsmen, they cannot draw blood as Okonkwo's act literally does when he confronts the messenger at the fateful village meeting. In short, *No Longer at Ease* appears to have set itself up to be thrown to the ground by its ebullient older sibling.

Maybe the picture is not so grim. While the volume of critical attention given to *No Longer at Ease is* sparse, it is not insignificant in quality, though some of the positions stated in such efforts are contestable. Simon Gikandi has, for example, addressed the unfairness of comparing the novel with Achebe's earlier work. He notes how the conflict between colonial and African cultures are clearly delineated, and how this conflict is at the heart of *Things Fall Apart.* In the second novel, however,

Gikandi notes, "where the terms which defined the African experience in the colonial context have been destabilised by nationalism, mere oppositions are not enough to produce meanings; narration seems to take place in a hiatus" (82). Representation in *No Longer at Ease,* Gikandi argues, is undertaken in an "improvisational" mode, and the novel has a "contemporary and experimental nature" (79). The distinction Gikandi makes about the thematic focus in each of the two novels are valid, but when he states that *No Longer at Ease* "does not arouse any passion for meaning, [and that] the tone adopted by the narrator ... is one of boredom or cynicism," I would suggest that such conclusions misrepresent the narrative dynamic in the novel (91). Part of this essay's agenda will be to offer a more meaningful appraisal of the rhetorical strategies of narration in the novel.

The process of such an appraisal necessarily demands that *No Longer at Ease* be placed within an Igbo narrative and cultural context. Though the Nigerian nationalist agenda informs the political context of the novel, there is no doubt that the conflicts which confront Obi Okonkwo are deeply embedded in the cultural attitude of his Umuofia clan. The novel's narrator is equally aware of the significance of this attitude in resolving the problems faced by his protagonist. Thus, David Carroll misses the point when he expresses disappointment that the work, "in a limiting sense, [is] a West African novel" and that it does not address a "universal theme" (85). It is baffling how the novel's successful representation of a slice of humanity becomes a reason for approbation, apart from the suspicious accusation of lacking a "universal" appeal.[1] What is not clear is whether Carroll has given adequate recognition to the necessity for the novel's cultural specificity. At the same time, Kole Omotoso's advice that critics of Nigerian writing and writers "must understand the multi-lingual, multi-ethnic and multi-cultural background from which they spring" is worth heeding (109).

The conflicts which arise and how they are (not) resolved are based on the cultural and artistic philosophy of a particular milieu. Consider the discussion between Obi and the British Chairman of the Commission at Obi's job interview when they delve into the nature of tragedy in Graham Greene's work. Probed to explain himself after making a statement that seems to go contrary to his interviewer's notion of the form, Obi draws his definition from the apt metaphor supplied by an elderly kinsman who is, ironically, a Christian convert: "He [old man] said life was like a bowl of wormwood which one sips a little at a time world without end. He understood the nature of tragedy" (45). The Chairman describes Obi's argument as "most interesting," but that is where Achebe allows the English Honors graduate that Obi is to articulate a different aesthetic which the old Umuofian Christian convert knows so well. For, though Obi and his white interview share some common literary texts, their appreciation of the works are based on different values.

Another issue which has been raised in some studies on Achebe's second novel is the place of proverbs. Of course, the subject is not limited to scholarship on *No Longer at Ease;* it is a staple discourse in Achebe criticism and for good reason. No other Nigerian novelist has invested so much of his or her narrative scheme in the grammar and meaning of the proverb like Achebe has done. In *Things Fall Apart,* the narrator intones, "Among the Ibo the art of conversation is regarded very highly, and proverbs are the palm-oil with which words are eaten" (4). The aspect of this often quoted statement dealing with the high esteem the Igbo place a good conversation is clear enough;[2] what has not been clearly understood is, interestingly, the symbolic relationship between the palm oil and the word. In other words, is the proverb an absolute necessity for the performance of a conversation or it is a complement – the palm oil which makes for a tasty meal but which a dish could still do without?

Among the critical responses to Achebe's earlier narratives, the tendency is to see proverbs as thematic markers, the road map for understanding the positions in the novels. Perhaps the most noted essay in this category is Bernth Lindfors's essay, "The Palm-oil with which Achebe's Words are Eaten." Lindfors identifies some proverbs that recur in each of the three novels examined, arguing that the proverbs' value is not aesthetic. Instead, "Achebe's proverbs," he states, "can serve as keys to an understanding of his novels because he uses them not merely to add touches of local but to sound and reiterate themes, to sharpen characterization, to clarify conflict, and to focus on the values of the society he is portraying" (50). Lindfors's utilitarian view of the Igbo proverb is demonstrated by the painstaking efforts he makes in his essay to extract and itemize every proverbial statement in the novels without a compensatory effort to situate them in the context of their narrative performance. It is as if whenever a proverb appears in a narrative, it must be for this one functional purpose. But as Achebe himself has tried to explain in various interviews, a proverb is "also a very elegant and artistic performance in itself.... proverbs are both utilitarian and little vignettes of art" (*Conversations* 67).[3]

It is tempting to see meaning in Achebe's novels mainly through the proverb, but as Achebe's statement makes clear, there is a performative value to proverbs in Igbo speech forms. In dialogues or in narrations, the proverb is part of the performative repertoire of the speaker. Oftentimes, the performer of the proverb is interested in the sheer exhibition of his or her verbal dexterity; to speak in proverbs (sometimes perceived as an equivalent of speaking in riddles) is a symbol of rootedness, of being conversant with the idioms of the language.[4] There is no doubt that the speaker is interested in making a dazzling impression on the audience. Igbo speech and narrative traditions celebrate the spoken word, the ability of the speaker or narrator to excel the audience or interlocutor through the process of what may be described as "verbal abundance." In oral narration, this verbal abundance is shown in the narrator's constant effort to maintain control of the performance and the attention of the audience through anecdotes, songs, and proverbs. What one may consider the "story" in the performance is only a part of the creative process. There is a story behind a proverb; there are anecdotes to be dramatized for full comedic effects, and a member of the audience might interject into the narration in a way that might affect the story profoundly. In this performance environment, to solely follow the thematic trajectory of proverbs is to miss the other aspects of the creative process.

In *No Longer at Ease,* Achebe strives to recreate the storytelling process. The novel presents situations which draw their significance from their relationship to this process. The performance of proverbs and anecdotes, and the presence of the sensational in this novel are rooted in this Igbo narrative process. Evidently, there are limitations to the representation of the process. For one, the written medium imposes a radically different format for the recreation. However, Achebe confronts the difference by clearly setting off the contexts of Igbo language usage. In those contexts of code-switching into Igbo, there is a heightening of speech as a performance event which, despite the written medium, is adequate to recreate a portion of the traditional narrative form.

There is a remarkable irony in the way the function and process of storytelling in Achebe's first novel changes in the second. To instill courage and masculinity into his two male wards, Ikemefuna and Nwoye, Okonkwo regales them with "masculine stories of violence and bloodshed" (*Things Fall Apart* 46). Okonkwo, described as a man of few words who chooses to despise the artistic talents of his father Unoka, still exploits the virtues of this cultural activity that privileges the elaborate and specialized use of words. To Okonkwo's disappointment, the boys show preference for the "feminine" tales Nwoye's mother and Ekwefi perform in their hut. This is important, for it is the nature of the women's stories that tugs at the heart of the young Nwoye, and eventually leads to his conversion to Christianity (*Things Fall Apart* 46, 128). For good or bad reasons, Okonkwo loses his son to a more subtle power of storytelling, a power he too had tried to exploit.

Nwoye, now known by his Christian name Isaac, bans his storytelling wife Hannah from telling stories to her children (66). The irony is that Isaac forbids the domestic tradition which nurtured and led him to his emotional and spiritual freedom from his overbearing father. By prohibiting his family from telling or listening to stories, Isaac Okonkwo sets out to cut his family off from the life line of his people's social and cultural well being. As colonial as the education in the village school is, the curriculum makes room for "Oral," a class period when each pupil is required to perform a folk story. Obi recalls his failure at his first call to perform this "basic" task among his peers and the derision he receives from them. He cannot succeed in the formal and colonial educational system until he masters the art of oral storytelling: he does not merely tell a story his mother teaches him;

rather, he "added a little touch to the end which made everyone laugh" (68). Obi must learn to tell the tale, and tell it to win the approval of his peers. The "Oral" which Obi must excel in while undergoing colonial education is the kind of media interplay prevalent in the novel. Obi and the other characters may be responding to a world that has been remade in the image of the colonizer, but Achebe depicts the characters as responding through an Igbo verbal tradition. The European novelistic practice exists with the Igbo narrative. When Gikandi sees the proverb as "no longer the paramount trope in Igbo culture" (89) based on his reading of Obi and his kinsmen living in Lagos, the kind of subtle interplay Achebe works with is not accounted for. A similar opinion is expressed by Gareth Griffiths who sees in *No Longer at Ease,* "the growing inadequacy of the proverbial language to function effectively in a world whose demands are phrased in directly opposed terms" (98). What Griffiths suggests is that the proverb belongs to a by-gone age, and cannot fit into the modern sensibility in which *No Longer at Ease is* composed.

On the contrary, the novel reveals an astute commingling of the traditional oral (proverbial) rhetoric and the modern. At the Umuofia Progressive Union's welcoming party for Obi on his return from England, we observe the nature of this inter-relationship. The Secretary of the Union presents a welcome speech which includes the passage, The importance of having one of our sons in the vanguard of this march of progress is nothing short of axiomatic. Our people have a saying "Ours is ours, but mine is mine." Every town and village struggles at this momentous epoch in our political evolution [i.e., political independence] to possess that of which it can say: "This is mine." We are happy that today we have such an invaluable possession in the person of our illustrious son and guest of honor (36).

While the concern in the Secretary's speech addresses the current move toward independence, it nonetheless sees this historical moment in the light of proverbial truth. Obi Okonkwo's place in the movement, and indeed the philosophy behind the formation of the UPU in far away Lagos, is embodied in an Igbo proverb but expressed in a flourish of English.

More importantly, the Secretary's speech illustrates the verbal abundance ever present in the traditional Igbo narrative and speech. Surely the Secretary knows that the party has been convened in honor of Obi. Yet, the welcome speech is an occasion to show his verbal ability, an ability made even more forceful through the medium of English. His performance is roundly applauded, and as the narrator notes, his audience agrees that he "wrote the kind of English they admired if not understood: the kind that filled the mouth, like the proverbial dry meat" (37).

Obi does not follow the grandiloquent example of the Secretary, thereby disappointing his kinsmen who expect a graduate of English to speechify with an even more highfalutin choice of words than their less educated Secretary. "He spoke 'is' and 'was,'" the narrator wryly observes (37). However, this is not an indication of his incompetence in both the English language and his mother tongue. Perhaps, on this occasion, Obi chooses to yield the verbal arena to the Secretary who has more to prove, since Obi is self-assured and "certified." He is aware of the high premium his people place on verbal performance, and how audience esteem is related to rhetorical exuberance. In another meeting of the UPU, Obi exploits this cultural convention as he makes a proverb laden speech in which he asks for a deferment of his loan repayment to the Union. Even though the narrator states that it is a "prepared speech," the verbal tradition he is drawing from is obvious:

> Obi rose to his feet and thanked them for having such a useful meeting, for did not the Psalmist say that it is good for brethren to meet together in harmony? "Our fathers also have a saying about the danger of living apart. They say it is the curse of the snake. If all snakes lived together in one place, who would approach them? But they live every one unto himself and so fall easy prey to man" (92–93).

Obi expands the proverb on the snake's curse to impress upon his audience his native ecological knowledge, and the biblical reference shows his awareness of how Christian values, even if nominally invoked for their rhetorical weight, have become a complementary aspect of Umuofia's verbal repertoire. A tactful performer, "Obi knew he was making a good impression. His listeners nodded their heads and made suitable rejoinders" (93). He understands the aesthetic preferences of his kinsmen, and Achebe is careful not to simply report this speech. The compositional process is highlighted: "He [Obi] tried to improvise a joke about beer and palm-wine, but it did not come off, and he hurried to the next point" (93). The narrator is interested in showing the process of selection, the performer's immediate "reading" of his audience to determine his choice of words. This is not to be overlooked is the context of Obi's performance. To despite his relatively high paying job, he knows that a secure deferment of the loan payment "'is' and 'was'" speech would not impress his kinsmen.

Sometimes, though, audience response to verbal abundance is expressed in gestures. For example, at Obi's farewell party, Mary, an ardent Christian believer and Hannah's friend, is asked to say grace. Ordinarily a solemn act, Mary turns the moment into a speech ceremony: "She went on and on reeling off proverb after proverb and painting picture after picture. Finally, she got round to the subject of the gathering .... When she was done, people blinked and rubbed their eyes to get used to the evening light once more" (10). Mary's ardent faith is the channel through which she delivers a fervent prayer that reveals her verbal ability more than her belief in the potency of her supplication. It is an elaborate and extended performance, and the time lapse is represented by blinking eyes.

At yet another meeting of the UPU, a humorous but significant compositional information is provided by the narrator. Some members of the group are expressing their horror that Obi was absent at his mother's funeral. In the random flow of opinions at the gathering, an elderly Umuofian successfully commands the attention of the group by offering the dramatic explanation that Obi's abominable action runs in the family.[5] "There was some excitement at this [the revelation]," the narrator reports. As another elderly man, equally informed about this aspect of the Okonkwo family history, ventures to contribute to the unfolding story, the first teller asserts his "ownership" over the tale. Writes the knowing narrator, "'I say that his father did the same thing,' said the first man very quickly, lest the story be taken from his mouth" (182). It is part of the novel's faithfulness to the oral antecedent that the narrator presents the above dialogue in its performance context.

The old man who resists being upstaged by a kinsman among members of an attentive audience exploits his audience's thirst for the fantastic tale. It is a performance strategy certain to generate positive audience response. Obi deploys the same formula when his father's guests desire to know how far England is from Umuofia "*from the mouth* of their young kinsman" (58) (emphasis added). Obi responds to an obvious invitation to dramatize, to supply them with a piece of information whose veracity is not as important as the telling. Obi immediately takes the pose of the bard, and the ordinary steam boat journey which had been read earlier, assumes a legendary character:

> It is not something that can be told.... It took the white man's ship sixteen days – four market weeks – to do the journey.... Sometimes for a whole market week there is no land to be seen .... No land in front, behind, to the right, and to the left. Only water (58).

Each bit of information Obi presents in exaggerated manner generates an equally exaggerated confirmation by his audience. It is a mutually understood and culturally approved process of exchanging fantastic tales and creating a sense of wonder. Even the village war veteran bully whose stories about Lagos Obi recalls on his return to the sprawling city, spins his (the bully's) own yarn to create that effect: "'There is no darkness there,' he told his admirers, 'because at night the electric shines like the sun, and people are always walking about, that is, those who want to walk. If you don't want to walk you only have to wave your hand and a pleasure car stops for you.' His audience made sounds of wonderment" (15).

Except for Obi's rehearsed speech and the UPU Secretary's prepared welcome address, one notices how the other examples of performance cited above are impromptu. They do not constitute the plot of the novel; instead, they could be considered "asides." Yet these occasions of performance, brief as they are, are at the core of the novel's integrity as an Igbo narrative; they show Achebe imitating the fluid context of oral performance. R.N. Egudu makes a corresponding observation in his analysis of anecdotes in Achebe's novels. Egudu's essay which deals with Achebe's indebtedness to the Igbo narrative tradition, points out that anecdotes and proverbs are related to storytelling. He rightly describes anecdotes as "the means by which a story is told," (52) as they "rid the art of narration of any kind of boredom" (49). Perhaps they exist more to demonstrate that verbal abundance I mentioned than to eliminate boredom. The anecdote is the storyteller's means of impressing his or her audience with the stock of stories in his or her repertoire. The same principle applies to the contexts of performance in *No Longer at Ease*. We are reminded of the oral roots of Achebe's narration at the moments the narrator represents these brief performance acts.

On the issue of the roots of Achebe's narrative, Ernest Emenyonu's assertion that such a discussion is "partly an examination of Chinua Achebe's debt to Pita Nwana's *Omenuko,*" a classic Igbo language novel, needs to be placed in context (155). Nwana's novel, published 25 years before *Things Fall Apart,* remains a popular text among Igbo readers because of its rich and learned diction and its unambiguous didacticism.[6] The story of Omenuko, an enterprising merchant who, on a fateful stormy night, loses all his goods and without much consideration, sells his apprentices to recoup his losses is sensational enough. Omenuko is an intriguing character; his life-long struggle is to redress the terrible deed (later he pays the ransom on the children and returns them to their families). He is constantly vindicated at the end of each confrontation with his enemies, and he has an ambiguous principle on the acquisition of wealth and influence. Above all, Omenuko is an Igbo alter ego: he represents free enterprise, possesses a migratory spirit, and a dogged determination to thrive in foreign lands. Also, that Omenuko initially flees his homeland to avoid punishment and finds no respite abroad, despite his successes, clearly espouses the Igbo high regard for community.

As a literary work, *Omenuko is* written in a lineal plot, characteristic of an oral tale. Though largely narrated in the third person singular, there are occasional intrusions of an "I" or "we"; at such times, there appears to be a restatement of the narrator's status as a member of Omenuko's community and an assumtion that the reader is one as well. But it is Nwana's use of the proverb that demands greater examination. In *Omenuko,* proverbs appear either in the direct speech of characters or in the narrator's words; sometimes though, the distinction is not easily identifiable. Just as the occasional "I" interventions help to indigenize the narrator, the use of proverbs by both the characters and the narrator suggests the commonality of that verbal tool. There is one such concurrence which deserves a closer examination. Having fully replenished his wealth, Omenuko searches for and finds out that the kinsmen he had sold away are still alive. He sends his brother Okorafo to buy back the three apprentices from the traders to whom he had sold them. The first two merchants Okorafo meets agree to accept the monetary ransom he offers.

The traders then accompany Omenuko's brother to the home of the third trader, Okpara. As Okorafo announces his mission, Okpara requests to confer with his associates to determine how much to demand as compensation. From there, the narrative proceeds,

> Ha wee laghachi n'izu ha. Ha wee si Okorafo, "Anyi agbaala izu laghachikwa. Okpara kwere ekwe. o sikwa ebe o bu na anyi na gi ahutala anya na the di na ya bu e mee nwa ka e mere ibe ya, obi adi ya mma."...Ha wee sirita onwe ha na ha ga-ahapu ya bu okwu, ka o diwa echi n'ihi na nkwu foro to a, chaa to a, abughi the oma (49).
>
> (Then they returned from their deliberations. They said to Okorafo, "We have concluded our deliberations and have come back. Okpara has agreed. He also says that since we [two] have already met with you, what is there is that when a child is treated favorably as his peer, he is satisfied."...They all agreed to let the matter rest for the day and to continue their negotiation the next day, for the palm tree which fruits and ripens on the same day is not a good thing.)

In the interval of a few sentences, two sayings occur, and they offer an interesting glimpse into the performance of proverbs in Igbo social discourse. In the first instance, Okpara's colleagues present his position to Omenuko's agent through a proverb. Despite the quotation marks attributing the saying to them, it is not clear whether the proverb is Okpara's exact words or a proverbial summation of his stand by the speakers. In the second proverb, the same complexity exists. Is it a reported speech or is it simply the narrator's display of verbal abundance to impress his fellow Igbo speakers that the men's decision to defer their negotiations to the next day is based on their awareness of this proverb? Nwana can afford this type of narrative ambiguity, if it is one, because his Igbo readers are able to infer that no matter who the speaker is, the proverbs are operating within the wider aesthetic principles of Igbo rhetoric. It is this general application of proverbs – the "palm-oil" value – that Achebe's and Nwana's novels share in common.

However, the dramatic power of Achebe's performance, both in the area of proverbs and narration, separates his novels from *Omenuko.* Despite the sensational note which sets off Nwana's story, the narrative mood is subdued and moves with the spare plot of an oral performance, albeit without the evocative presence of the spoken word. There are no anecdotes, no revealing and elaborate dialogues, and Omenuko's character suffers from extreme moralizing. The result is that much of the informal and light mood which goes with the performance of the proverb and such other extremely condensed narratives (even in serious contexts), is hard to find in *Omenuko. No longer at Ease,* on the other hand, capitalizes on the dramatic and the sensational. At the beginning of the novel, a sensational "case that had been the talk of Lagos for a number of weeks" is about to be resolved. Some civil servants are so keen on witnessing the sentencing that they "paid as much as ten shillings and six pence to obtain a doctor's certificate of illness for the day" (2). Only at the end does the narrator tell us the reason for the uproar: a promising civil servant has been caught accepting a paltry bribe. Before then, he "sweetens" the tale and entertains his audience with various situations that celebrate the vigorous speech acts of his characters.

The moral vision in *No Longer at Ease is* ambiguous. Obi's kinsmen do not condemn him for accepting a bribe; instead, they are scandalized by the paltry sum, twenty pounds, which incriminates him. In another incident, Hannah, Obi's mother, refuses to endorse Obi's choice of a marriage partner based on an oppressive cultural prejudice despite her many years as a Christian convert. Nevertheless, the novel succeeds in managing the contradictions through the compositeness of proverbial truth: the contending positions and actions by the major characters find their "justification" in the elegant ring of their rhetorical choices. It seems, therefore, that the novel invests in the amplification of the contexts of verbal performance more than it seeks to depict the evolving social and political world of pre-independent Nigeria. Achebe may be writing a novel which continues his historicization of modern Nigerian reality, but he shows greater interest in representing the process of Igbo storytelling and speech events. As an Igbo writer, he uses the unfolding story of the rising Nigerian nation to demonstrate the continued viability of Igbo speech and narrative traditions.

So what shall we say about *No Longer at Ease* and its famous sibling? It may never catch up with the fame of the elder, but on this it can be sure: the novel has not failed to represent, with equal vitality, the verbal abundance first captured in *Things Fall Apart* and which continues to inform Achebe's creative imagination.

Notes

1. See Achebe's "Colonialist Criticism" where he discusses the problem of judging African literature based on their unAfrican "universality." Refer especially to pp. 74–79.

2. Camara Laye, the Guinean Negritude novelist, makes a similar statement when he states, "one of the fundamental aspects of the African soul: the word, the love of palaver and dialogue, the rhythm of talk, that love of speech that can keep the old men a whole month under the palaver tree settling some dispute – that is what really characterizes the African peoples" (26).

3. See also Achebe's interview with Charles H. Rowell, p. 180.

4. There is an equal burden on the audience to quickly make meaning out of the performer's proverb without the performer's assistance. The Igbo saying, "when a proverb is told to one and then explained, the bride price paid on one's mother was a waste," heightens this burden on the listener and absolves the speaker of the responsibility to justify his or her deployment of this verbal resource.

5. In his study of Achebe's Igbo narrative roots, Ernest Emenyonu argues that in No Longer at Ease Achebe "portrays the world of his hero with too many exaggerations and sensationalism." By this mode, Emenyonu further argues that the novelist "veers closely towards the tradition of Onitsha Market Literature in its sensational attempt to elicit feelings of wonderment and horror" (161, 162). It should be noted that the Onitsha Market writers, who were mostly Igbo speaking, were attempting to use the resources of the English language to represent the ebullient Igbo speech and narrative traditions in their literary works. What Emenyonu identifies as the narrative tense of the novel, I see as the specific devise the old man uses to grab the attention of his fellow UPU members. See Emmanuel Obiechina's An African Popular Literature for an excellent study of the Onitsha Market literary era.

6. Over thirty years after the publication of Omenuko, Ben Ezuma, an Onitsha Market writer, would publish The Flight of Omenuko: A Play in Verse in which Omenuko, the protagonist of Nwana's novel, is given an opportunity to explain why he sold his kinsmen. In the play, the reason is for "immediate cashing gain," and his hope that he would redeem his kinsmen later "when Fortune smiled once again" (26). Nwana does not provide this reason explicitly.

Works Cited

Achebe, Chinua. Interview with Kalu Ogbaa. Lindfors, *Conversations* 64–75. *No Longer at Ease*. 1960. New York: Anchor/Doubleday, 1994. *Things Fall Apart*. With Introduction by Kwame Anthony Appiah. 1958. New York: Alfred A. Knopf/Everyman's Library, 1992. Interview with Charles H. Rowell. *Callaloo* 13 (1990): 165–84.

"Colonialist Criticism." *Hopes and Impediments: Selected Essays*. New York: Anchor/Doubleday, 1989 Carroll, David. *Chinua Achebe: Novelist, Poet, Critic*. London, UK: Macmillan, 1990.

Egudu, R.N. "Achebe and the Igbo Narrative Tradition." *Research in African Literatures* 12.1 (1981): 43–54. Emenyonu, Ernest. *The Rise of the Igbo Novel*. Ibadan, Nigeria: Oxford UP, 1978.

Ezuma, Ben. *The Flight of Omenuko: A Play in Verse*. Onitsha, Nigeria: Etudo Limited, 1965.

Gikandi, Simon. *Reading Chinua Achebe: Language and Ideology in Fiction*. Portsmouth: Heinemann, 1991.

Griffiths, Gareth. "Language and Action in the Novels of Chinua Achebe." *African Literature Today* 5 (1971): 88105.

Laye, Camara. *The Guardian of the Word: Kouma Lafolo Kouma*. Trans. James Kirkup. Glasgow, UK: Fontana/Collins, 1980.

Lindfors, Bernth, ed. *Conversations with Chinua Achebe*. Jackson: UP of Mississippi, 1997.

———. "The Palm-oil with which Achebe's Words are Eaten." Critical Perspectives on Chinua Achebe. Eds. C.L. Innes and Lindfors, 1978.

Nwana, Pita. *Omenuko*. 1933. Official orthography edition, transliterated by J.O. Iroaganachi. Enugu, Nigeria:Longman, 1963.

Obiechina, Emmanuel. *An African Popular Literature: A Study of Onitsha Market Pamphlets*. Cambridge, UK: Cambridge UP, 1973.

Omotoso, Kole. *Achebe or Soyinka? A Study in Contrasts*. London: Hans Zell, 1996.

Part Three:

Critical Perspectives on Arrow of God

Chapter 15

The Priest/Artist Tradition in Achebe's *Arrow of God*

Anthonia C. Kalu

In his efforts to validate the African literary artist's vision, Chinua Achebe has frequently spoken out against art for art's sake. He asserts in *Morning Yet on Creation Day* that:

> ... art is, and was always, in the service of man. Our ancestors created their myths and legends and told their stories for a human purpose (including no doubt, the excitation of wonder and pure delight); they made their sculptures in wood and terra cotta, stone and bronze to serve the needs of their times. Their artists lived and moved and had their beings in society and created their works for the good of that society (29).

In this functional view of art, Achebe appears to agree with Ernst Fischer (1963) that the arts express a higher purpose in man's existence. Achebe considers himself and other African artists, within this framework, Achebe recognizes that all African artists (including himself), teachers and recorders of African history and culture need "to look back and try to find out where we went wrong, where the rain began to beat us" (70). He uses the Igbo society to demonstrate that the arts contribute to man's sensitivity about a "fullness of life of which individuality with all its limitations cheats him" (Fischer 8). Achebe argues in his works that the Igbo art tradition is based on Igbo thought which contemplates an inscrutable order that humanity constantly attempts to reorder and control. In his works, Achebe identifies certain major characters and situations in Igbo life, using these as the people do in their oral art tradition to portray their perception of the harmonizing principles in their lives.

Achebe's interpretation of Igbo thought through art reveals a relationship between political and religious institutions. It is in these relationships that the Igbo artist and art traditions are most important. In recreating and revealing these connections, Achebe assumes the venerable role of the Igbo priest and artist.

Achebe's initial exploration of this relationship is in *Things Fall Apart* where Chielo, the priestess is portrayed in her performance of her duties to *Agbala*. However, this presentation of Chielo does not allow analysis adequate to the purposes of this work. His demonstration of this link is most fully realized in *Arrow of God* in which he uses Ezeulu, the priest of *Ulu*, to explore these institutions in an Igbo community. Ezeulu's priestly functions, and his involvement, through *Ulu*, in making and implementing plans for the security of Umuaro, are combined with his attitude toward life and understanding of Igbo thought to give an insight into the Igbo society. In the performance of his duties to *Ulu* and Umuaro, he shows a desire to preserve both for posterity. *Ulu*, created by the people in a time of stress, is Umuaro's god of protection and symbolizes the Igbo's emphasis on the group. Ezeulu's desire to preserve this concept becomes the core of Achebe's portrayal of duality in Igbo thought. The depiction of this concept in *Arrow of God* revolves around Ezeulu and his responsibilities as the priest of Ulu, facilitating Achebe's exploration of Igbo traditions and art. In his work, Achebe participates in group preservation in a way that is normally the responsibility of only priestly elders. The difference is the location of emphasis. In his direct involvement with the traditional society, Ezeulu tries to bring everything together under religion, while Achebe explains the society, including Ezeulu, through art. Achebe's exploration of the many facets of Igbo life in *Arrow of God* simultaneously delineates the complementary discourses that inform their significance within Igbo thought.

The locus of his presentation of the priest/artist tradition, will be used here to show how Igbo traditional religion, politics, philosophy, and art were combined to give meaning to the abstract notion of duality, a concept central to most of Achebe's work and most deliberately explored in *Arrow of God*.

Community Sanction

The traditional Igbo priest bridges the real and supernatural worlds, striving to maintain harmony between them. He is able to do this because he has a special relationship with the people and is perceived by them as having special powers. The priest and his functions must be sanctioned by the community. The man who becomes a priest has to demonstrate that he is in harmony with his environment. He must exhibit an understanding of Igbo thought. The priest of *Ala*, the earth goddess, for instance, must manifest *Agwu*, divination force, in his life. In an article in which the *Ala* priesthood is discussed, M.S.O. Olisa says:

> One of the initial signs that a man is "called" to assume Ala Priesthood is the manifestation of "*Agwu*" in his life, a mild display by him of mental abnormality in which he sees visions and has supernatural communications with all sorts of spiritual forces. After undergoing this experience the Igbo often initiate and confer on him the title of Ezeani (20).

Community sanction of such manifestations involves the people in the relationship that this individual now has with the supernatural world. When Boi Adagbom, a chief priest in Ika, was asked about his calling to the priesthood, he replied, "... If you were chosen, you would just know. Certain violent changes occur in you and you would 'answer the spirit's voice'"(Isichei 20) The changes enable the individual to act as a link between the two worlds. He is then able to perform rituals and sacrifices to the god who has called him. He becomes an instrument of mediation between the community and its god. Like Wole Soyinka's singer of Yoruba tragic music, he becomes:

> ... a mouthpiece of the chthonic forces of the matrix and his somnambulist "improvisations"a simultaneity of musical and poetic forms – which are not representations of the ancestor, recognitions of the living or unborn, but of the no man's land of transition between and around these temporal definitions of experience (148).

At moments when he communes with the gods, during sacrifices and divinations, he becomes like spirits, unknown. Then he dresses and acts the part, becoming the concrete interpretation and evidence of the people's relationship with the gods and each other. He interprets and balances and briefly becomes the major, visible part of the abstract principle governing these relationships. At all other times, he is an ordinary man, though this does not detract from his importance in the community. As a result of his special powers, the priest plays an important role in the making and execution of laws, becoming the direct connection between the gods and the people through the elders. He guides the elders in their efforts to communicate with the gods in the maintenance of a harmonious society. Additionally, the rest of the community uses him to seek the god's will through sacrifices and divinations. This is not to say that Igbo society is theocratic, however, "... gods and the supernatural do play dominant roles in its political life" (Olisa 22).

Role of Traditional Institutions and Rituals

In traditional society, the functions and attributes of the priest are taken for granted because of the assumption of shared beliefs and experiences. This is most evident in the art tradition. In Igbo oral narrative performance, for instance, the performer does not need to explain any images from the people's traditions when they occur in the story. The narratives become coded carriers of such information. In the contemporary and literate society, writers of Igbo fiction make assumptions similar to those that govern oral narrative performance traditions. Some of these assumptions are based on Igbo aesthetics, others are part of the norms and values of Igbo life. Consequently, the intersection of orality and literacy in Igbo life remains a location for interrogation of the conflict between Igbo and Western thought. Frequently, Igbo writers during the early part of the colonial period rejected or ignored the significance of Igbo thought in their works. For instance, J.U.T. Nzeako and Leopold BellGam, in writing about some aspects of Igbo traditions, reflect a Westernized and Christian point of view, portraying traditional customs as backward and pagan. In *Omenuko* and *Elelea Na Ihe O Mere*, the functions of traditional priests are portrayed but unexplained. Achebe, in his first novel, *Things Fall Apart*, also presupposes the reader's familiarity with such information. He only briefly mentions the priestess Chielo's authority in relation to the Oracle of the Hills and Caves. Her brief appearance during Ezinma's illness provides scant insight regarding the existence and significance of the Oracle or its role in the lives of the people of Umuofia. When Ikemefuna's death is announced, one learns from Ezeudu that:

> Yes, Umuofia has decided to kill him. The Oracle of the Hills and Caves has pronounced it. They will take him outside Umuofia as is the custom and kill him there ... (40).

The reader has to know more about Igbo traditional religion, religious beliefs and political systems to fully understand Chielo, her *Agbala* and Ezeudu's announcement.

It is in *Arrow of God* that Achebe offers interpretations and explanations for the existence of such institutions, merging their complexities in Ezeulu. In his office as the priest of Ulu, he is portrayed as halfman, halfspirit. Achebe invests him with special powers, rights and privileges which give him a strong voice among the elders of Umuaro. His thoughts and actions strongly affect the rest of the community. In fact, his special powers are influential on the members of his household. As a result, the actions taken by the latter are important to the people. This is the case when Oduche is sent to the new church and when he tries to suffocate the sacred python. Both incidents become major issues for discussion and action in the community because of Ezeulu's status. In *Arrow of God* Achebe interprets most aspects of Igbo traditional priesthood through Ezeulu. He discusses the rivalry between Ezeulu's sons over succession to the priesthood, and also Ezeulu's eldest son's apprehension about becoming a priest at his father's death. However, it is Nwafo, Ezeulu's youngest son, whom Achebe uses to show how one may be called to the priesthood. Nwafo's closeness to Ezeulu and his interest in the rituals mark him as a possible choice, among Ezeulu's sons, as successor to his father:

> His youngest son Nwafo now came into the *Obi*, saluted Ezeulu by name and took his favorite position on the mudbed at the far end, close to the shorter

> threshold. Although he was still only a child it looked as though the deity had already marked him out as his future Chief Priest. Even before he had learnt to speak more than a few words he had been strongly drawn to the god's ritual (4).

Nwafo is strongly attracted to the service of the god, *Ulu*. When Ezeulu is detained at Okperi, it is Nwafo who wonders what should be done about announcing the new moon:

> However as dusk came down Nwafo took his position where his father always sat. He did not wait very long before he saw the young thin moon. It looked very thin and reluctant. Nwafo reached for the *ogene* and made to beat it but fear stopped his hand (187).

Although he takes "his position where his father always sat," he is old enough to know that his father's successor has to be appointed by *Ulu* and endorsed by the people of Umuaro.

During the festival of the First Pumpkin Leaves, Ezeulu reenacts the first coming of *Ulu*, showing how the people's support made it possible for him to lead them through his priestly office:

> 'At that time,' he said, 'when lizards were still in ones and twos, the whole people assembled and chose me to carry their new deity'. I said to them:
>
> 'Who am I to carry this fire on my bare head? A man who knows that his anus is small does not swallow an *Udala* seed.'
>
> 'They said to me:
>
> 'Fear not. The man who sends a child to catch a shrew will also give him water to wash his hand.'
>
> 'I said: 'So be it' (81).

As Ezeulu continues with the retelling of the legend of the first coming of *Ulu*, the duties that go with his priesthood become apparent. He is expected not only to stand between the people and the things that threaten them, but also to eliminate the sources of these threats. He derives strength and confidence from the knowledge that the people support him at all times. Also, Ezeulu's role as buffer between his people and their god is comparable to that of the priests/medicine men in *Omenuko* and *Elelea na Ihe O Mere* who cleanse the land and the people of abominations. However, Ezeulu's office differs from theirs in that he is also involved in decisionmaking in Umuaro. The nature of *Ulu* makes it necessary for him to be concerned with Umuaro's safety and to play an important philosophical role in the sociopolitical welfare of the people.

Ezeulu demonstrates his awareness of the possible results of the changing times when he tries to secure Umuaro's future by sending Oduche to the new religion. Conscious of the Igbo's concern for the preservation of the community, he sees the need to be in control of the present as well as anticipate events of the future. In the past, this consciousness in the people's world view led to the amalgamation of the villages that make up Umuaro. Ezeulu therefore makes Oduche his ambassador to the new religion, Christianity: "I want one of my sons to join these people and be my eye there. If there is nothing in it you will come back. But if there is something there you will bring home my share" (51). Linfors agrees with Ugoye, Oduche's mother, in her assertion that Oduche was sacrificed to the white man's religion (58). This is true only to the extent that Oduche is the first person from his family to get involved with the new religion. From Ezeulu's point of view, as the keeper of the people's god of protection, he is using Oduche to maintain a balance in their lives. Achebe points this out in Ezeulu's reply to Ugoye:

> ... Do you not know that in a great man's household there must be people who follow all kinds of strange ways? There must be good people and bad people, honest workers and thieves, peacemakers and destroyers; that is the mark of a great *Obi*. In such a place, whatever music you beat on your drum there is somebody who can dance to it" (51).

It may be true that historically such a decision may not have been made by a man of Ezeulu's social status, but the point here is that this type of thinking made it possible for the Igbo to tolerate their own people who joined the new group. Since they could neither chase away nor kill the strangers without harming or even losing their own people, the best approach was to fit the phenomenon into a known and existing world view. Achebe points this out several times in *Arrow of God*. When Obika is whipped by Mr. Wright, for instance, instead of confronting Mr. Wright or doing anything else that might make him angrier, the young men quickly reactivate an already existing quarrel, and Achebe comments: "It was much easier to deal with an old quarrel than with a new and unprecedented incident" (94). The meeting ends with Nweke Ukpaka's speech, which begins, "What a man does not know is greater than he ..." (94). Nweke Ukpaka advises his agemates to let Unachukwu the carpenter who interprets for Mr. Wright stay during their deliberations because he is their only link with the white man. Unachukwu is allowed to stay for the same reason that Ezeulu sends Oduche to the new church both are a way of controlling, from a distance, an unprecedented threat to their wellbeing.

Transitions and the New Dispensation

Ezeulu's use of Oduche as his "eye" in the new culture parallels the people's authorization of his own priestly responsibilities to Ulu. He can be seen as the people's "eye" in the supernatural world of spirits and gods which is beyond their human vision. The most obvious physical demonstration of this is evidenced in Ezeulu's function as watchman for the new moon. Apart from this visible calendarkeeping function of his watch, there is also the symbolic but un-emphasized function of the priest as the person who keeps the people alert to changes in nature. He keeps an eye on nature, and as a result the people are kept aware of the passing of the seasons. This duty is so ritualized that even his house is built in a special way, emphasizing his distinctness in this regard:

> His *obi* was built differently from other men's huts. There was the usual long threshold in front but also a shorter one on the right as you entered. The eaves on this additional entrance were cut back so that sitting on the floor, Ezeulu could watch that part of the sky where the moon had its door (1).

Achebe here describes a physical relationship based on an abstract principle: Ezeulu, the priest, watches for the moon through the cutting in the eaves of his house. In Ezeulu's words to Oduche when the latter is sent to join the new religion, the priest is the "eye" of Umuaro. The cutting in the eaves of his house constitutes another eye, linking Ezeulu to the universe which is symbolized in the moon. The people see the approach of the seasons through the moon. This arrangement constitutes one aspect of Ezeulu's bridging function between the people and their world. He becomes one of the tools which Umuaro uses in its attempt to live harmoniously with nature. It is an important manifestation of his priestly responsibility.

Ezeulu, more than anybody else, realizes the symbolic nature of this arrangement and of his duties to Umuaro through *Ulu*. However, he becomes politically involved in Umuaro's affairs beyond the requirements of his priestly office. He wants *Ulu* to become a nature god like *Idemili* or *Udo*, with his priest in complete command of choosing and naming the days of all Umuaro's feasts.

Achebe uses Ezeulu's interests in politics to explore the priest's human attributes, the other aspect of his duality. He pushes Ezeulu into a position where even though Ezeulu recognizes his duties to the people, he is forced to choose between them and their god. He chooses to listen to the voice of *Ulu*, knowing that the people are no longer behind him. Caught between the gods and men, he lets his human side assert itself, and forgets that the gods came into being to serve men. He disregards his favorite proverb: "When an adult is in the house, the shegoat is not left to bear its young from the tether." Ezeulu, the adult in the Umuaro household, allows his people to suffer, and like the man who brings home antinfested faggots, he should have expected the visit of lizards.

However, Achebe strikes a balance between Ezeulu, the priest, and Ezeulu, the man. The priest in Ezeulu remains conscious of his duties toward *Ulu* and Umuaro's safety. He sees clearly the limits of the authority of his office. As the priest of *Ulu*, conscious of the people's voice supporting him, he warns against the dangers of fighting a "war of blame" against Okperi. His vision in this regard remains clear in spite of opposition from Nwaka and his group.

Duality, Politics, and Igbo Art

Essentially, Achebe expresses at the peak of the performance of Ezeulu's priestly duties the latter's duality and that of the people's world view. This is portrayed during the festival of the First Pumpkin Leaves. Ezeulu, in his full regalia as *Ulu*'s priest, comes into the village square:

> He wore smoked raffia which descended from his waist to the knee. The left half of his body from forehead to toe was painted with white chalk. Around his head was a leather band from which an eagle feather pointed backwards. On his right hand he carried *Nne ofo*, the mother of all staff of authority in Umuaro ... (80).

The figure of the priest embodies in artistic form the people's perception of their world. His painted body symbolizes his ability to bridge the gap between reality and the supernatural, reaffirming for them the harmonious existence of the two. It is also a concrete, visible way of bringing together the people's view of duality as it makes that which is intangible visible. In Ezeulu's hand is the staff of authority which orders their lives, and on his head is the eagle feather, a symbol of affluence (Nwoya 26). Artistically, this image brings together the apparently unrelated institutions of politics and religion. The harmonious merging results in plenitude, a mark of social and economic stability. It is significant that this symbol is manifested during the Festival of the First Pumpkin Leaves, the first foodrelated item to be harvested in the year. The harmonious society works together to produce life-giving food. The abundant green leaves, carried by the women, symbolize life and good health. Continuity of the group is reaffirmed and assured.

Another important aspect of this image involves Ezeulu as a work of art. In full priestly regalia, he visually refers to such ritual art objects as the *ofo*, the ancestral staff of authority and justice, and the *okposi*, carved representations of renowned departed ancestors. Like Ezeulu in priestly regalia, these are fashioned by the people to aid them in their communication with their gods and ancestors. As the priest moves in the circle made by the people, the women throw pumpkin leaves at him. He becomes the scapegoat which must carry away and bury their sins of the past year. The only difference between him and other ritual art objects is that he is living.

Consequently, he becomes both intermediary and representation; a combination of reality and art. However, as with other ritual situations, the emphasis is on the priest as representation rather than on the priest as an individual, reflecting the people's concern for the expression of community will over that of the individual.

This concern in Igbo thought led to their intolerance of recalcitrant individuals, priests or even gods. Achebe refers to this aspect of Igbo thought when he portrays Ezeulu's attempts to attach too much importance to himself and his god. This individualistic tendency in Ezeulu allows Achebe's in-depth exploration of dualism within the society's systems and in the person of the priest in *Arrow of God.*

Achebe: The Artist/Priest

Achebe's use of Ezeulu to illustrate salient aspects of Igbo thought parallels the traditional narrators' use of characters who are not allowed to win in confrontations between themselves and either their **chi** or the community. Such characters are usually portrayed as achievers who are discouraged from indulging in excesses but are encouraged to work towards the good of their families and communities. Its importance in Igbo thought is evidenced by its continued expression even in works like Leopold BellGam's *Ije Odumodu Jere* which is not primarily concerned with the celebration of Igbo world view or art tradition. Achebe's *Arrow of God* is possibly his most deliberate attempt at the celebration of Igbo traditions. Most Igbo authors working within the novel or short story forms portray characters which, because of shared beliefs and experiences, become re-affirmations of aspects of Igbo thought. Oral traditional genres range from the oral tale to the reenactment of myth during festivals in which many different art forms are employed. Contemporary and written Igbo literature uses most of the oral narrative techniques but has yet to achieve the unity of festival drama. Achebe tries to achieve this unity through explanations of the people's world view, descriptive images of customs and traditions, transliteration of the Igbo language into English, and a combination of Igbo oral narrative techniques with those of the Western novel.

In *Arrow of God*, for instance, Chinua Achebe demonstrates the various uses of the proverbs in Igbo language and culture. The proverb serves as a point of reference and linguistic signpost among the Igbo people. In the novel, it performs the artistic objective of unifying the story line. Proverbs are repositories of the wisdom of the ancestors. Like any other aspect of Igbo thought, proverbs are open to manipulation. As Achebe demonstrates, one can explicate issues using them, or they can become a starting point, a premise to an argument. Since their meanings are dynamic, they can work backwards or forwards, for or against a given argument. Hence, the assumption among the Igbo of the effectiveness of proverbs in rhetoric. In *Arrow of God* Achebe uses the proverb, "When an adult is in the house the shegoat is not left to suffer the pain of parturition on its tether" (20), for instance, to show Ezeulu as committed to protecting the people's interest in the Okperi land case, but Ezeulu also gets angry enough to hurt them when they refuse to act like adults during his confrontation with the British. The alternate interpretation makes him out as the goat; thus, he reacts by inverting the situation (with *Ulu*'s help?) and making the elders suffer. This proverb works in an oblique way with the other frequently quoted proverb in the novel: "a man who brings home antinfested faggots should expect the visit of lizards" (148). When Ezeulu and the elders refuse to act like knowledgeable adults, that is, like wise statesmen whose titles bequeath elegance in manner, the best behavior and the responsibility to rational action, they become subject to the balancing natural principles of which they are supposed to be guardians.

In none of the known works of fiction by writers of Igbo origin have the Igbo art tradition and world view been as exhaustively treated as in Achebe's *Arrow of God.* The portrayal of Ezeulu shows Achebe's understanding of Igbo society and thought, paralleling him to the traditional elders of the land. His interpretations of Igbo life places him among the artists and philosophers of Igbo tradition. Achebe has claimed to be an ancestor worshipper (Ekwensi 286), and insists that the African novelist is a teacher ("The Uses of African American Literature" 10). He contends in *Morning Yet On Creation Day* that:

> The writer cannot expect to be excused from the task of reeducation and regeneration that must be done. In fact he should march right in front. For he is after all as Ezekiel Mphahlele says in his *African Image* – the sensitive point of his community (72).

This assertion makes his role similar to Ezeulu's, the priest of Umuaro's god of protection, whose charge is to march in front of the people leading and confronting all threats to the community. Like Ezeulu, the writer has to be able to find ways of maintaining balance in the community. However, Achebe, the artist emphasizes the Igbo art tradition more than the religion. This does not mean that Igbo religion is absent in his works; rather, he uses descriptions of aspects of the people's religion to delineate the role and significance of traditional religious objects as art objects. His explanation of Igbo world view emphasizes the need for those familiar with the background, setting and characters to begin to see the utility and application of traditional wisdom and its possibilities in the reassessment of current experiences and problems. As with the priest/artist's religious objects, Achebe's works demonstrate the artist/priest's commitment to the wellbeing of the society.

Works Cited

Primary Source

Achebe, Chinua. *Arrow of God*. New York: Doubleday and Company, 1969. Subsequent references to this text are from this edition.

Secondary Sources

Achara, D.N. *Elelea Na Iha O Mere*. London: Longmans, 1953.

Achebe, Chinua. *Morning Yet On Creation Day*. New York: Anchor/ Press Doubleday, 1975.

———. "The Uses of African Literature." In *Okike*. No. 15. August, 1979: 8–17.

Bell-Gam, Leopold. *Ije Odumodu Jere*. Lagos: Longman, 1963.

Fischer, Ernst. *The Necessity of Art*. Trans. Anna Bostock. New York: Penguin, 1963.

Isichei, Elizabeth. *Igbo Worlds*. Philadelphia: Institute for the Study of Human Issues, 1978.

Lindfors, Bernth. "The Palm Oil with which Achebe's words are Eaten." In *Critical Perspectives On Chinua Achebe*. Ed. C.L. Innes and Bernth Lindfors. Washington D.C.: Three Continents Press, 1978.

Nwanna, Pita. *Omenuko*. London: Longman, 1933.

Nwoga Donatus I. "The Igbo World of Achebe's *Arrow of God*" In *Research in African Literatures*. Vol. 12, No. 1. Spring, 1981.

Nzeako, J.U.T. *Okuko Agbassa Okpesi*. London: Thomas Nelson and Sons Ltd, 1964.

Olisa, M.S.O. "Political Culture and Stability in Igbo Society". In *Couch*. Vol. III, No. 2. September, 1971.

Soyinka, Wole. *Myth, Literature and the African World*. Cambridge: Cambridge University Press, 1976.

Chapter 16

The Man Behind the Priest in *Arrow of God*

Umelo Ojinmah

MANY CRITICS RECOGNIZE THE colonial intervention as a critical factor in Ezeulu's downfall in Achebe's *Arrow of God,* even as they acknowledge Ezeulu's inherent tendency to mix his personal wishes with that of his deity. It is my contention, however that Achebe views the colonial intervention as merely catalytic not causal: "It looked as though the gods and the powers of event finding Winterbottom handy had used him and left him again in order as they found him" (Achebe 230). As will be evident in the course of this analysis, Achebe believes Ezeulu was guilty of gross abuse of power and sees the fundamental reasons for his downfall as woven into the resolution and answer to the opening analysis in *Arrow of God* where Ezeulu was, himself, ruminating on the scope and nature of his power. The colonial factor, therefore, only accelerated the resolution of the issues which Ezeulu's analysis highlights.

Arrow of God is thematically consistent with Achebe's famous book, *Things Fall Apart;* but even more than in that book, Achebe examines the issue of abuse of power, While in *Things Fall Apart* this theme was subordinated to that of "putting in a word for (one's) history,... tradition,... religion, and so on" (Lindfors et al 7), in *Arrow of God* Achebe culls it out for in-depth analysis and," chooses for his central character someone who embodies this dilemma in its most acute form – the chief priest of Ulu" (Carroll 91). More than in any other of his writings, it is in this novel that Achebe delineates the relation between the society and its gods, and significantly, what emerges is an illustration of the reciprocity of this relationship. Achebe writes that Ulu was created in response to a special need of the clan:

> In the very distant past… the six villages … lived as different peoples, each worshipped its own deity, Then the hired soldiers of Abam used to strike in the dead of night, set fire to the houses and carry men, women and children into slavery. Things were so bad for the six villages that their leaders came together to save themselves. They hired a strong team of medicine men to install a common deity for them. This deity which the fathers of the six villages made was called Ulu …. The six villages then took the name of Umuaro, and the priest of Ulu became their chief priest. From that day they were never again beaten by an enemy (Achebe 14–5).

Therefore, Ulu's primary purpose and function is the protection of the clan, and as if to underline this utilitarianism Nwaka recounts the experience of a deity in Aninta which failed it's society and states that, "we have all heard how the people of Aninta dealt with their deity when he failed them. Did they not carry him to the boundary between them and their neighbours and set fire on him?" (Achebe 28) Carpool writes that "Ezeulu's role is to interpret to Umuaro the will of the god and to perform the two most important rituals in the life of the village – the festival of the Pumpkin Leaves and that of the New Yam. The first of these ceremonies cleanses the six villages of their sins before the planting season…. The second … sanctifies the harvest and so marks the end of the old year and the beginning of the new" (Carroll 88–90).

Achebe's exploration exposes not only the dilemma and stresses of a man poised between two worlds, an intermediary between the human world and the spirit world, but those of a man nonetheless who is prone to human foibles. On this, Achebe, talking to Lewis Nkosi, stated that:" I'm interested in this old question of who decides what shall be the wish of the gods" (Killam 60). Achebe's characterisation of Ezeulu assumes importance in the overall quest, particularly because, as I intend to show, Achebe believes that Ezeulu's abuse of the powers vested in him, as is the case with many contemporary African leaders, stems from arrogance and total disregard for the ultimate source of his power – the people.

Achebe establishes Ezeulu's arrogance and pride early in the narrative. His philosophical speculations on the nature and scope of his power and relationship to his god and the people only underscore this arrogance, pride and ambition:

> Whenever Ezeulu considered the immensity of his power over the year and crops, therefore, over the people he wondered if it were real. It was true he named the day for the feast of the Pumpkin Leaves; but he did not choose the day. He was merely a watchman. His power was no more than the power of a child over a goat that was said to be his. As long as the goat was alive it was his; he would find it food and take care of it. But the day it was slaughtered he would know who the real owner was. No! the Chief Priest of Ulu was more than that, must be more than that, *If he should* refuse to *name the day there would* be no *festival – no*

> *planting and no reaping.* But could he refuse? No Chief Priest had ever refused. So it could not be done. He would not dare (Achebe 3–4).

It needs be mentioned at this point that Achebe's characterisation of Ezeulu in an intellectual mould ensures that the issue of ignorance becomes untenable, for Ezeulu in his ruminatings would have realised that Ulu, and consequently himself, remain strong and powerful because they are faithful to the original motive and justification for the creation of the god which is the protection of the clan; and the clan reciprocates. Achebe in his discussion with Serumaga says of Ezeulu: "He is an intellectual. He thinks about why things happen – of course as a priest; you see, his office requires this – so he goes into things, to the root of things" (Achebe 16).

In Achebe's view, being the priest of the most powerful deity in a confederation of six villages, and in a society that traditionally abhors the concentration of too many powers in an individual hand, should have sufficiently alerted Ezeulu to the dangers of even the slightest excesses. Achebe outlines some manifestations of Ezeulu's vanity and pride as prelude to the subsequent happenings when he states that, "Ezeulu did not like to think that his sight was no longer as good as it used to be and that some day he would have to rely on someone else's eyes as his father had done when his sight failed,... But for the present he was as good as any young man, or better because young men were no longer what they used to be (Achebe 1). Achebe goes on to show the sort of pranks that he plays on unsuspecting young men: "There was one game Ezeulu never tired of playing on them. Whenever they shook hands with him he tensed his arm and put all his power into his grip, and being unprepared for it, they winced and recoiled with pain" (Achebe 1).

Achebe sees some elements of irresponsibility bordering on juvenility in Ezeulu's act, but more than this, it highlights Ezeulu's human side which he seems to acknowledge only when it suits him.

Achebe seems to sustain Nwaka's accusations that Ezeulu was ambitious and wanted to arrogate more powers to himself, for he told Serumaga (Duerden and Pieterse 9) that "What (Nwaka) was saying in reality was that Ezeulu was getting too powerful.... The word 'king' was used here to describe someone who was trying to become too powerful, and this runs against the Ibo belief in the complete integration of life, against their concept of an individual versus society". The concept which Achebe mentions relates to the republican nature of Igbo traditional society, and their recognition of the all too frequent human tendency towards unfettered abuse of power. Continuing, Achebe tells Serumaga that Ezeulu "had enough priestly arrogance to attempt to assume too much power. This shows from time to time, [as] when he is confusing his thinking with the thinking of the god" (Duerden and Pieterse 9). Carroll further observes that, "by means of these two festivals Ezeulu controls both planting and harvesting and the village year which is dependent upon them", and consequently the people's lives (Carroll 91).

The central question which plagues Ezeulu is the extent to which the power he wields is discretionary and Carroll illustrates that this emanates from the fact that: "As his ceremonial appearance indicates, Ezeulu is half man, half spirit; in the world of man he is very powerful, in the world of spirits he is a servant, Ezeulu's dilemma is to find the appropriate locus of the individual (himself) in the scheme of things. This also raises two fundamental questions whose resolutions are linked to Ezeulu's final tragedy: "What is the true relationship between the two roles? Where does his primary duty lie, with the god or the tribe?" (Carroll 91) Continuing, Carroll states that Ezeulu, "like Okonkwo, ... is convinced that he must obey to the letter the commands of the god; [but] unlike Okonkwo, he alone is equipped to translate these commands to the tribe. In this situation, Ezeulu is constantly tempted to mingle his own wishes with those of the god and then assert his authority over the six villages by means of Ulu's oracular power" (Carroll 91–2). This implies that Ezeulu was aiming at absolute powers which, as stated earlier, is alien to lgbo traditional world view, In an essay on *Chi,* Achebe says that:

> At the root of it all lies that belief ... in the fundamental worth and dependence of every man and his right to speak on matters of concern to him and flowing from it, a rejection of any form of absolutism which endangers those values. It is not surprising that Igbo held discussion and consensus as the highest ideals of political process. This made them 'argumentative' and difficult to rule. But how could they suspend for the convenience of a ruler limitations which they impose even on their gods (Achebe 103).

Against this view of *chi,* Ezeulu's rhetorical question to his friend, Akugbue: "Who tells the clan what to say? What does the clan know?" assumes significance implying, as it does, that since he knows better than the clan what is best for it, the clan should take his advice. In Achebe's view, Ezeulu's two roles – as the powerful intermediary for the people and servant of the god – need not be at variance if he adequately recognises his responsiblilities and the ultimate source of his power – for the simple reason that Ulu belongs to, and functions for the benefit of the society. Ezeulu is, therefore, both the servant of the god and of the people. The inclination of individuals in positions of power to forget this derivative source of their power thus constitutes a main focus of Achebe's enquiry.

To Achebe, the harmonious integration of the traditional society, and the individual's place in that society are reflected in the relationship that exist between the society, in its entirety, and the deity or deities to which that society subscribes. In the Igbo worldview, propitiatory rites become essential rituals in the maintenance of this cosmic balance. As Onenyi Nnanyelugo, one of the ten most titled elders and leaders of Umuaro says: "We have asked Ezeulu what was Ulu's grievance and he has told us.

Our concern now should be how to appease him: Let us ask Ezeulu to go back and tell the deity that we have heard his grievance and we are prepared to make amends, *Every offence has its sacrifice from a few cowries to a cow or human being*" (Achebe 208). Ezeulu's response highlights his reluctance to acquiesce to their request: "If you ask me to go back to Ulu I shall do so. But I must warn you that a god who demands the sacrifice of a chick might raise it to a goat if you went to ask a second time" (Achebe 209). Such a quibbling response from a priest who should be concerned about the welfare of the people makes his subsequent pronouncements suspect. It is pertinent to recall the argument of Onenyi Nnanyelugo, representing the voice of Umuaro, that the deity would not want Umuaro to perish: "Although I am not the priest of Ulu I can say that the deity does not want Umuaro to perish. We call him the saver." He goes further to spell out to Ezeulu his duty and responsibility to the society, saying;" Therefore you must find a way out, Ezeulu,... It is for you, Ezeulu, to save our harvest" (Achebe 207).

The most important point in this argument is the fact that consistent with the cultural norm, the elders and leaders as representatives of Umuaro have the inherent right to absolve Ezeulu of any repercussions that may result from his obeying their collective wishes:

> Yes, we are Umuaro. Therefore listen to what I am going to say. Umuaro is now asking you to go and eat those remaining yams today and name the day of the next harvest, Do you hear me well? I said go and eat those remaining yams today, not tomorrow; and if Ulu says we have committed an abomination let it be on the heads of the ten of us here. You will be free because we have set you to it, and the person who sets a child to catch a shrew should also find him water to wash the odour from his hand. We shall find you the water (Achebe 208).

Achebe deftly structures the complex issue of motive in such a way that, given the society's world-view and sequence of events, Ezeulu stands convicted of abuse of power, of arrogating the powers of his deity to himself. Carroll remarks that the complexity of [the] opening situation is controlled by the author's narrative focus", but by the time the different points of views in the argument have been considered, *"Ezeulu the man begins to appear from behind the priest"* (Carroll 94). As has already been mentioned, Achebe uses foreshadowing as a structural device. In considering the Umuaro versus Okperi land dispute which is the root of the acrimony in Umuaro (if one excludes the jealousy of the gods and their priests for the moment), the situational ambiguity from which Ezeulu advises the clan has to be put into proper perspective. Of note is that throughout Ezeulu's advice and warnings to the clan, Achebe was careful in his diction; Ezeulu never told the clan that Ulu has categorically forbidden Umuaro from going to war because it was a war of blame: "Who would have thought that they would disregard *the warning of the Priest of Ulu* who originally brought the six villages together and made them what they were" (Achebe 14).

As Ezeulu himself suggests: "One half of him was man and the other half *mmo* – the half that was painted over with white chalk at important religious moments. And half of the things he ever did were done by this spirit side" (Achebe 192). If half of what Ezeulu ever did was ascribed to his *mmo* or spirit side, conversely, the other half of whatever he did were done by his human side. This duality, therefore, creates interpretative ambiguity, for later, when Ezeulu warns: "Is there any man or woman in Umuaro who does not know Ulu, the deity that destroys a man when his life is sweetest to him?.... Do [they] think Ulu [will] fight in blame?" (Achebe 27). It is difficult to know which of his dualities is giving the warning because, again, he does not state that Ulu says it will not fight a war of blame, This point is further compounded when Nwaka makes a snide but true remark that Ezeulu's mother hails from Okperi. Furthermore, the comment that "One man said that Ezeulu had forgotten whether it was his father or his mother who told him about the farmland", emphasises the fact that this was a normal village palaver at which every one was entitled to contribute opinions as of right, including Ezeulu (Achebe 17). Achebe underlines Ezeulu's later reluctance to accede to the wishes of the clan: "Leaders of Umuaro, do not say that I am treating your words with contempt; it is not my wish to do so, But you cannot say: *do what is not done and we shall take the blame.* I am the Chief Priest of Ulu and what I have told you is his will not mine.... The gods sometimes use us as a whip" (Achebe 208). To Ezeulu's argument that they cannot ask him to "do what is not done"; a statement which Achebe highlights by italicizing, the elders of the clan replied by giving "numerous examples of customs that had been altered in the past when they began to work hardship on the people" (Achebe 209). This shows that irrespective of what the problem is, its resolution must of priority take into account the welfare of the clan. Ezeulu's unyielding stance also creates the impression that his human side was overshadowing his spirit side. Achebe does not only unequivocally denote Ezulu's unwillingness to undertake the task of presenting the clan's request to their deity, but underscores the fact that when he eventually does, he is distracted, thus casting doubt on the final pronouncement: "As Ezeulu cast his string of cowries the bell of Oduche's people began to ring. For one brief moment he was distracted by its sad, measured monotone and he thought how strange it was that it should sound so near – much nearer than it did in his compound" (Achebe 210).

If one agrees with such critics as Killam (1973) and Eldred Jones (1973), among others, that the narrative structure of *Arrow of God* is carefully and competently organised, the final resolution of the narrative becomes anticlimatic in that it raises the question of Ezeulu's credibility as a priest. Is he telling the truth when he tells the elders of the clan that the message he has is from Ulu? Carroll, Awoonor, Killam, and even Achebe, all agree that Ezeulu had a tendency to ascribe his wishes to his god, but there is more. This issue assumes importance if one recalls that chapter sixteen of the novel ends with the deity, Ulu, mortifying his preist, Ezeulu, for arrogating to himself the powers that rightly belong to his deity, and for plotting revenge, and even scheduling the revenge to suit his convenience: "Ta! Nwanu!" barked Ulu in his ear, as a spirit would in the ear of an impertinent child. "Who told you that this was your own fight?" .... "I **say** who told you that this was your own fight to arrange the way it suits you:... Beware you do not come between me and my victim or you may receive blows not meant for you!" (Achebe 191–2).

But most significant is that the deity's chastisement comes immediately after Ezeulu decided what time he plans to have his revenge on Umuaro: "Behind his thinking was of course the knowledge that the fight would not begin until the time of harvest, after three moons more. So there was plenty of time (Achebe 91). So one would naturally assume that after such a rebuke, Ezeulu would shelve his plans and allow the deity to decide how he wants to conduct the fight, particularly as Ezeulu himself had already acknowledged that: "It was a fight of the gods, He was no more than an arrow in the bow of his god (Achebe 192). But again Achebe foreshadows Ezeulu's later action by adding that: "This thought intoxicated Ezeulu like palm wine" (Achebe 192); an expression which connotes relish. If one were to believe, for a moment, that Ezeulu was carrying out the wishes of Ulu, and that he had interpreted Ulu's words as assent for him to punish Umuaro, the above comment dispels that belief. One would think that, in recognition of his role as an intermediary between the people and their deity, and considering the portentous implications of the punishment to the clan, *the thought* would not intoxicate Ezeulu like palm wine.

The opening statement of chapter eighteen plainly demonstrates that Ezeulu's subsequent pronouncements and arguments are suspect. Achebe writes that "after a long period of silent preparation Ezeulu finally revealed [what he had been planning all along] that he intended to hit Umuaro at its most vulnerable point – the feast of the New Yam". There is no indication that this was Ulu's decision because Ezeulu's actions are calculated to mortally wound, if not destroy, the clan, for as Ezeulu remarks, "the punishment was not for now alone but for all time. It would afflict Umuaro like an *ogulu-aro* disease which counts a year and returns to its victim", Such a situation would have made the deity impotent, thus destroying the people's dependence on it. Therefore, no other resolution of the conflict would have sufficed except *unmasking the man behind the priest* and making him irrelevant in the lives of the clan. Achebe again repeats the remarks that: "so in the end only Umuaro and its leaders saw the final outcome, to them the issue was simple. Their god had taken sides with them against his headstrong and ambitious priest and thus upheld the wisdom of their ancestors – that no man however great was greater than his people; that no one ever won judgment against his clan (Achebe 230).

The concluding paragraph is remarkable for its introvertive irony: "If this was so then Ulu had chosen a dangerous time to uphold that truth for in destroying his priest he had also brought disaster on himself" (Achebe 230). This was precisely the point. It is my contention that Ulu's decision to self-destruct by destroying his priest was consistent with the original purpose of its creation, which is to protect the clan. In a world in which it was progressively becoming redundant, being likened to a dead god, it was proper that in its death throes the deity should in the face of such unimaginable recurrent calamity as faced Umuaro, raise its demise "to the stature of a ritual of passage". Obika's death thus becomes an appropriate propitiation in this ritual of pasage in conformity with the people's world-view, recalling Onenyi Nnanyelugo's comments about sacrifice of appeasement: "Every offence has its sacrifice, from a few cowries to a cow or a human being" (Achebe 209). Moreover, it would be recalled that at Ulu's creation the clan had sacrified one of themselves as appropriate to the potency of the "medicine" that became the deity. The god, in reciprocation, efficaciously carried out its functions, for as Achebe writes, "from that day they were never beaten by an enemy" (Achebe 15).

Therefore, faced once more by a threat of similar magnitude, an impending calamity that had the potential of wiping out the clan, it is fitting that the god should rise to the challenge. But this time the resolution of the foreboding disaster requires the death of the deity itself. Hence, this, as in the creation of the deity, requires a propitiatory sacrifice that is commensurate with the "task" the deity has to perform, of saving the clan. To "cushion" its demise, as in its creation, in accordance with Igbo worldview, requires an appropriate sacrifice. Obika's death fulfils this function, but more than this, it represents the most proportional resolution that conclusively incorporates Ezeulu without leaving any loose ends. As happened in Okonkwo's case in Achebe's *Things Fall Apart,* the final resolution has to leave the existence of the society itself uncompromised, Ulu has to vindicate the society's original belief and trust in it, even at the risk of its own destruction, or the downfall of its priest:

> It was not simply the blow of Obika's death, great though it was. Men had taken greater blows: that was what made a man a man. For did they not say that a man is like a funeral ram which must take whatever beating comes to it without opening its mouth; that the silent tremor of pain down its body alone must tell of its suffering?
>
> At any other time Ezeulu would have been a match to his grief. He would have been equal to any pain not compounded with humiliation. But why, he

> asked himself again and again, why had Ulu chosen to deal thus with him, to strike him down and then cover him with mud? (Achebe 229).

In conclusion, therefore, the resolution of Achebe's repetitive proverb; "that no man however great was greater than his people; that no one ever won a judgment against his clan" becomes symbolic. For it evokes and underlines the derivative basis of power which its holders would not forget. And in a rhetoric manner the proverb becomes the answer to Ezeulu's earlier questioning of the scope and nature of the power and authority which he holds.

Works Cited

Achebe, Chinua. (1987) *Anthills of the Savannah*. London: Heinemann.

———. (1983) *The Trouble with Nigeria*. London: Heinemann.

———. (1975) *Morning Yet On Creation Day*. London: Heinemann.

———. (1964) *Arrow of God*. London: Heinemann.

———. (1958) *Things Fall Apart*. London: Heinemann.

Carroll, David. (1980) *Chinua Achebe*. New York: St. Martin's Press.

Cook, David. (1977) *African Literature: A Critical View*. London: Longman.

Duerden, D. and Pieterse, C. Ed. (1972) *African Writers Talking*. London: Heinemann.

Echeruo, M.J.C. (1973) *Joyce Cary and the Novel of Africa*. London; Longman.

Jones, D.E. (1973) "Chinua Achebe" *Beware, Soul Brother* In *African Literature Today*. No. 6. Ed. Eldred Jones. Oxford: James Currey Publishers: 181-182.

Killam, G.D. Ed. (1973) *African Writers on African Writing*. Evanston: Northwestern University Press.

———. (1969) *The Novels of Chinua Achebe*. London: Heinemann.

Lindfors, Bernth and Others. (1972) *Palaver: Interviews with Five African Writers in Texas*. Texas: African and Afro-American Research Institute.

McEwan, N. (1983) *Africa and the Novel*. London: Mcmillan.

Ohaeto, E. (1977) *Chinua Achebe: A Biography*. Oxford: James Currey Ltd.

Ojinmah, U. (1991) *Chinua Achebe: New Perspectives*. Ibadan: Spectrum Books Ltd.

Chapter 17

The Tragic Muse and the Cultural Hero: Achebe's Art in *Arrow of God*

Virginia U. Ola

MY RECENT AND TOTALLY casual re-reading of George Bernard Shaw's *St. Joan* and a re-thinking of Joan's travails recalled for me Ezeulu's fate in all its dimensions: historical, psychological and philosophical. The pattern of their lives somehow typifies that of most geniuses, at all times, and in all places. It is easy to isolate some similarities in the psychological and intellectual dispositions of such personalities. Otherwise it should appear totally preposterous to embark on any form or degree of comparison between an English village girl of sixteen, wielding authority over sheep and pigs, goats and chickens, and a powerful African chief priest, the arbitrator between his people and their gods. That Judith Gleason had earlier made such a comparison was reassuring, for many reasons both literary and personal. Gleason sees their exceptional and fanatical tendencies as posing fundamental psychological and moral questions, which different cultures must handle differently (36). But Joan and Ezeulu are similar in more ways than these. They are both independent thinkers with a tendency towards willful self-exertion; they possess great natural capacity, push, courage, devotion, originality and oddity, qualities which are bound to provoke crisis and confrontation with constituted authority as defenders of the beliefs and norms of any society. Both of them, like Socrates, Luther, Blake, were seers of visions and hearers of revelations.

They are both geniuses; and what is a genius?

> A genius is a person who, seeing farther and probing deeper than other people, has a different set of ethical valuations from theirs, and has energy enough to give effect to this extra vision and its valuations in whatever manner best suits his or her specific talents (Shaw 10).

There is therefore always in the genius an element of the exceptional and the fanatical, a determination to test out a belief or a personalized command; an act which often ends in tragedy. The doubt of the skeptical, the adoration of followers and the threat to established norms of behavior are responses to be accommodated; but the genius is doomed to be misunderstood by his society, and to be judged according to the degree of tolerance attainable at that historical moment by the society. And so fifteenth century England burnt Joan at the stake and early twentieth century Umuaro drove Ezeulu into insanity. Here ends the comparison.

This paper on *Arrow of God* and therefore on Ezeulu its hero is based on a string of literary and subjective assumptions most of them verifiable through the normal critical processes. The dominant assumption is that *Arrow of God* is Achebe's most successful novel, a claim supported by Abiola Irele (1967), Margaret Lawrence (1968), John Povey (1971) and Michael Echeruo (1975). The second assumption is that Ezeulu is his best realized hero within the context of his early village novels, where character and history are inseparable. Echeruo summarizes its merits in these words:

> *Arrow of God*, a much denser and more technically sophisticated novel than the two earlier novels, tells three stories in one integrated style: the trials of Ezeulu, the disintegration of the indigenous political and religious order in Umuofia, and the establishment of British rule and the Christian religion (157).

The critic who concentrates on the destruction of Ezeulu to the exclusion of Umuaro, its gods and its traditions misses the central imperative of the novel, which is that *Arrow of God* is about the death throes of an age, and signals the turning-point in the history of a people (Echeruo 155). Such a critic would have made the mistake of the Umuaro people in not recognizing the sanctity and precariousness of Ezeulu's office, which the title of the novel underscores.

Abiola Irele claims that the best criticism implies an affective and intense participation in the creative act:

> The most worthy and enduring appreciation of the writer's work is that which partakes in the imaginative process in which the senses are alive to the verbal signposts which the writer has planted along the path to his profound intentions ... whatever form of analysis he employs cannot suffice unless he brings to his task the full measure of his own sensibilities (14).

This is perhaps one of the best opportunities to re-examine the dense content, the complex ironic network and the fated machinery from which Ezeulu was meant not to escape; for as Irele states:

> The work of art is an invitation to a dialogue of sensibilities and nothing can replace the immediate response to this invitation if one is to arrive at a satisfac-

> tory apprehension of the essential coherence of the work, at an intuitive and real awareness of its profound truth (15).

A slightly different approach to the profound truth of this work is to presuppose that the tragedy of Ezeulu is far from being about the punishment of an arrogant and "impressive looking fetish priest" to borrow Winterbottom's words, crushed by a stronger communal and supernatural force for daring to stand against his community; and to assert that it is rather an elaborate fictional cum dramatic dirge on the fall of the classic prophet unrecognized and ultimately rejected by a blind and arrogant people. *Arrow of God* is Achebe's masterpiece; Ezeulu is his most successfully delineated hero and the most impressive. The work shows Achebe's genius at its most ironic, most challenging and most rebellious. This paper can be regarded as an exercise in literary metaphysics which intends to violate the sentimental and communalistic theory of Obiechina and Larson, and to situate in its place the thesis that the tragedy before us is that of the inability of a people, albeit a great people, to understand its own savior, and not that of an angry god joining forces with its devotees to destroy a head-strong chief priest. Ezeulu is a man of extraordinary strength of mind; everything he did was thoroughly calculated, based on policy rather than on blind impulse. These are some of the special features of his mental constitution, which made him so unmanageable. He dared to posit his individual will and personal yearnings against the long cherished social dictates laid down by Umuaro to suppress such yearnings. So he is also the lonely rebel, the injured ruler and arrogant autocrat in one. The complexity of the ironic network, which gave birth to this almost ambivalent and enigmatic hero, will be analyzed as we share once more with Achebe the artistic experience of creating him.

Arrow of God has been called "an insightful study of power, leadership and their joint interplay with history and community" (Jabbi 147). Ezeulu is at the pivot of that history; he represents the best in a people and in an age, but he is a man under siege, psychologically and intellectually. Commenting on the central conflict of this novel. Bu-Buakei Jabbi asserts:

> Major dramatic conflict and action in this novel are consistently informed by two related basic concerns. The first, which is essentially philosophic relates to the general quality of Ezeulu's personal apprehension of the highest purposes of the Ulu priesthood. And the second, ultimately of a more dramatic and political upshot, concerns the depth and consistency of his practical adherence to the fundamental principles and circumstantial dictates of an Eze-Ulu historic destiny (142).

The issue of the withheld harvest and the balance of blame and liability have tended to dominate comments on this text. As insistent as this point is a total conception of the priesthood of Ulu and an appreciation of Ezeulu's personal exertions in respect of it throughout the narrative are imperative, for on them hinge the tragic center of the work which is built on a delicate moral balance. At the end Ezeulu emerges as a victim rather than an ambitions or stubborn chief priest who deserted the relevant dictates and implications of his office, and betrayed the sacred charge of the public office reposed on him by his people.

This episode and Ezeulu's response underscore his essential humanity, which must also be understood, and has been an essential ingredient of most classical tragedies. At the height of his disagreement with his people the hero saw the harvest and the eating of the new yams, which precedes it as a precious opportunity to punish them for not trying to obtain his release when he was imprisoned by the white man. By refusing to consume the ritual yams faster than is allowed he was indeed upholding a tradition with very complex ramifications. Without consuming the five yams the harvest festival, which is also Ulu's most prized ceremony and the period of his highest glory and appreciation by the community cannot take place. The destiny of the community, the harvesting of their crops and the celebration of the deity's care and protection over his people are all tragically interwoven. Unknown to the chief priest therefore he was punishing Ulu through the people of Umuaro. He was, in his search for revenge, stepping on the toes of his god who in his less than divine aspect enjoyed the annual tribute of a grateful people.

Ezeulu was only being human, yet this episode remains the one instance in his leadership when he allowed himself to be swayed by personal rather than rigorous objective considerations. He was not in his high historic office permitted to exact punishment by depriving a capricious deity of his special annual feast. It almost required him to be more than human. He gave in to his hubris and failed the ultimate test by succumbing to the human.

In presenting Ezeulu Achebe was not only giving us "a truly memorable creation, an impressive figure, cast in a mould that is at once forceful and noble, and whose external stature reposes upon the firm foundations of a stable coherent mental structure" (*Irele* 16); he was consciously experimenting and improving on the tragic form which he had tried in his first two novels. The choice of the tragic medium gives him the opportunity to work out in Ezeulu's life that rigorous fatality under which great men like Oedipus, King Lear or Othello have been destroyed through a well-ordered and inevitable course of events. In his search for the meaning of tragedy through the destiny of Ezeulu Achebe traversed the Aristotelian requirements for the greatness of a hero, his transition from happiness to disaster; character domination by hamartia, the Elizabethan celebration of revenge, murder, intrigue and carnage, to find the ultimate meaning of tragedy in the more modern definition by Soren Kierkegaard and Northrop Frye. The former writes:

> The true tragic sorrow consequently requires an element of guilt, the true tragic pain an element of innocence; the true tragic sorrow requires an element of transparency, the true tragic pain an element of obscurity (Kierkegaard 551).

In his discussion of the "Theory of Modes" Frye holds the basic outline of liability in tragic fiction to be a much more ironic one, which rather then lay emphasis on hamartia or clear guilt depends on the scapegoat motif which singles out the hero as a victim or "institutional scapegoat".

The "pharmakos" is neither innocent nor guilty. He is innocent in the sense that what happens to him is far greater than anything he has done provokes, like the mountaineer whose shout brings down an avalanche. He is guilty in the sense that, he is a member of a guilty society, or living in a world where such injustices are an inescapable part of existence (Frye 41).

Within this framework Ezeulu's predicament crystallizes into that of his vicarious role as a carrier, a sacrifice for the sins of a community. Irele was commenting on the same tragic pattern when he said, "Achebe has woven the two movements of the individual and social drama into such unity that it would be artificial to separate them" (Beier 174). Even more emphatically Irele claims: "For indeed Ezeulu has been all along an instrument of fate – the blind accessory of a monumental process that culminates not only in his own undoing, but in the fall of the gods of the land" (Beier 177).

Ezeulu comes to the reader in the magnificence and full splendor of an Ulu high priest, singled out in his awesome loneliness as he with consuming concentration and curiosity performs his priestly responsibility of welcoming the new moon, this time a very ominous one, "as thin as an orphan fed grudgingly by a cruel foster-mother" (*Arrow of God* 1). The main literary relevance of the rite, apart from the sheer drama of it, accordingly springs from its being the most heightened evocation of the scapegoat psychology in the novel. He is thus summarily situated as the spiritual guardian and initial vicarious bearer of his people's communal consciousness, experiencing with them in all its intensity the passage of time and flow of history. But *Arrow of God* is also about "power, leadership and their joint interplay with history and community" (Jabbi 147). But Achebe like his hero was fascinated by the philosophic perception and reality of Ezeulu's power and responsibilities; or why would the artist endow him with a restless searching mind, a meditative habit of intellectual curiosity which posed a temptation to him in his ambivalent office held in trust for his people and their gods? Says Achebe, "His mind never content with shallow satisfactions crept again to the brinks of knowing (4). The knowledge stored for him within that realm was irritating as it was frustrating. It was a challenge:

> Whenever Ezeulu considered the immensity of his power over the year and the crops, and therefore over the people he wondered if it was real. It was true that

> he named the day for the Feast of the Pumpkin Leaves and for the New Yam feasts but he did not choose it. He was merely a watchman. His power was no more than the power of a child over a goat that was said to be his. As long as the goat was alive it could be his; he would find it food and take care of it. But the day it was slaughtered he would know soon enough who the real owner was. No: the chief priest of Ulu was more than that, must be more than that. If he should refuse to name the day there would be no festival – no planting and no reaping. But could he refuse? No chief priest had ever refused. So it could not be done. He would not dare. Ezeulu was stung to anger by this as though his enemy had spoken it (3).

It is not surprising that no chief priest had ever dared; for the two we know, the first chief priest of Ulu was a member of the weakest village. The other Ezeulu, his all – powerful father held the offices of chief priest and great medicine man. Ezeulu inherited the former and lost the latter to his brother. Such anxieties, agony and resentment had festered in the buffeted mind of the hero. To crown it all he lived in the perpetual fear of going mad like his mother, in the manner of Bessie Head's Elizabeth. In both cases the fear partly came true. He was also the chief priest of a man-made god with questionable legitimacy and still looked at with jealousy by the stronger ones.

Coming to family problems, what about the abomination committed by Oduche whom he had sent to be his "eyes" at the white man's church? Oduche was sent to the white man's church to acquire his knowledge and learn his secrets for his father's benefit. In other words he was expected to be a worthy representative, but in his nascent fanaticism he imprisoned the python of Idemili in a box, to the shock of the whole community and badly dented the already battered reputation of his father. The next son, Obika, Ezeulu's most handsome and favorite son, was energetic, quick-tempered and noted for his youthful excesses; and despite his good intentions he only worsened his father's predicament and problems. Ironically Obika was like him in more ways than one. The thought of his third son, Edogo, a recalcitrant artist, exacerbates his fear that the dignity of the Ulu priesthood could not but he dragged into the mud by a string of such unworthy successors. In his artistic temperament Edogo was withdrawn, lonely, rebellious and spent his time carving masks that were prohibited by tradition.

Ezeulu's lonely rebuke of his invisible opponents on the question of the limitations of his ceremonial rather than real power is therefore understandable in this context of fundamental dissatisfaction, insecurity, powerlessness of himself and his god and the threat of an ever possible insanity. Surely, this is an ambiguous destiny. Like Okonkwo of *Things Fall Apart* Ezeulu's dignity, courage and commitment to his god and people were tainted by a very personal fear, which gnawed at the edges of his greatness.

Such an austere sense of tragic irony of history and character is rare in African literature. It belies a sober philosophic vision, a mature psychological sophistication which was itching for release; hence Achebe's decision to revisit the theme and the people of *Things Fall Apart*. His greatest tool was irony, personal, situational and cosmic. Echeruo's words, "It is a novel of great fear and great tenderness" (155) contain some of the most sublime ever uttered in appreciation of the philosophical grandeur of the work. That early episode of daring speculative willfulness on the hero's part heralds the major dramatic encounters of the work, all held by a taut ironic thread. The ultimate irony of his position is that he who stands as the strongest exponent of tradition should turn out to be the major instrument of its disintegration.

One of the major dramatic episodes is that of his testifying against his people in the land case of Okperi. Characteristically in the explosive land case between Ezeulu's village and the people of Okperi the chief priest truthfully and courageously testified that the land in question rightfully belonged to the village of Okperi and not to his own people. Umuaro considered that position a betrayal and openly denounced the chief priest. Critical opinion does not seem to find it incongruous that Umuaro should ostracize its chief priest for standing up for the truth, for acclaiming that Ulu would not fight a war of blame. Emphasis has rather been laid on the much-quoted Ibo saying that no man however great ever won judgment against his people. Even John Povey believes that Ezeulu, like Okonkwo is so uncompromisingly harsh in the definition of his belief that he must of necessity be crushed by circumstances which require adjustment rather than firmness" (106). The tight ironic structure of *Arrow of God* does not admit such a simplified interpretation. In fact, events of the novel call up the very morality of such a saying for scrutiny.

It is Umuaro, which emerges as an uncompromising society bent on disciplining what it considers an ambitious and treacherous chief priest. It has misunderstood the foresight and political flexibility of its own leader in adjusting to the imperatives of a new age, and has proved ungrateful to a god that protected it from the incessant attacks of its neighbors; an additional source of concern for Ezeulu. In all their splendor, authority and influence the only observable preoccupation of Nwaka and Idemili the two most powerful antagonists of Ezeulu are scheming and struggling for power and wealth.

Indeed Nwaka's moral obtuseness is a direct foil to the strength of Ezeulu's moral frame. He towers above them in his superior intelligence. This force of personality which set him apart in noble solitude ironically attracts him to Winterbottom whose miscalculation in offering Ezeulu the "honor" of a warrant chief set in motion the final tragic movement of the novel. These characters are all symbolic vehicles in this movement, for despite intervening circumstances Ezeulu's declaration for truth ultimately precipitates his own ruin and threatens the very survival of Umuaro and its central priesthood. His refusal to eat the new Yam is the climax of the encounter. Here too Achebe suspends judgment on Ezeulu's moral liability: for when the chief priest says to his kinsmen in the heat of the crisis:

> You have spoken well. But what you ask me to do is not done. Those yams are not food and a man does not eat them because he is hungry. You are asking me to eat death (260).

The reader has no reason to doubt the speaker's sincerity. Achebe does not in language or action dispute the claim, nor can the examples proffered by one of his opponents prove it, since such cited violations of customs have concentrated on areas of human not divine interests. There is also no guarantee that Ulu in his capriciousness would take out its anger on the ten chiefs in case of an abomination, rather than on his mouthpiece. Despite the recognizable tinge of revenge in the episode of the new Yams the total outcome assumes in its resolution the working out in the lives of these men, especially the hero, of a rigorous fatality that transcends their ability to comprehend or to arrest its pre-ordained course. They are all cogs in the historical wheel of fortune. All in all the picture of Umuaro is an unflattering one and their squabbles only serve to hasten the historical trauma of the moment. Ezeulu's battle was mainly internal, within himself and from his own people, the initial blunder of Clark notwithstanding. Umuaro tried to discipline Ezeulu and failed. It was inevitable since he heard songs and danced dances none of them could hear nor dance. It was as if the colonial administration set the tragedy in motion and left Umaro to destroy its own god in destroying Ezeulu.

The gods constitute the final group in any consideration of his fight with his equally beleaguered clansmen. In handling Ezeulu's predicament, Achebe widened the tragic canvass of his novel into a bicosmic affair involving each god and his mentor, Ulu, Eru and Idemili for Ezeulu, Nwaka and Ezidemili respectively. But these are strange gods whose power hardly transcends the jealousy and pettiness of their earthly representatives. Their anger and interest in no way upset the tragic movement whose outcome is easily attributable to sheer coincidence or irony.

In this state of cosmic irony Ezeulu's relationship with Ulu is the most ironic. The former's troubled and fated destiny begins in the first page of the book as he indulges in metaphysical analysis of his non-existent power; for despite his physical, and intellectual endowments he remains essentially an agent, an arrow in the bow of Ulu. The dramatic fulcrum of this position is the annual ritual of the Pumpkin Leaves where Ezeulu performs the purification rite as thousands of Umuaro women symbolically hurl at him the evils and misfortunes of their households in the form of bunches of pumpkin leaves for burial at Ulu's shrine. It is at once the most glorious moment in the ceremonial aspect of the Ulu priesthood and at the same time signifies the heaviest spiritual responsibility of that office. It emphasizes

Ezeulu's role as victim and scapegoat. Despite this joint experience of man and god Ulu apparently abandons his priest during the struggle with Umuaro and suddenly re-appears to chide him to keep away when he contemplates reconciliation with Umuaro. This final impetus propels the tragedy to its pre-ordained end. The cynic would claim that the lonely Ezeulu translated his half-hearted will to reconciliation into Ulu's warning for by the time he goes into his shrine for his final divination Ulu, the god of Umuaro was long dead and had been displaced by Oduche's Christian God whose bells were now being heard in place of Ulu's voice. Even if one should adopt Palmer's extreme view that what Ezeulu heard as Ulu's warning "is probably the figment of a fever-crazed imagination which has been subject to hallucinations, nightmares, dreams and visions during his long captivity" (94) the ironic truth of the work lies in Akuebue's in-law's remark that "a priest like Ezeulu leads a god to ruin himself and in Akuebue's remark that "a god like Ulu leads a priest to ruin himself" (213). Their destinies are inseparably woven together and one cannot fall without dragging the other with him. Whether Ezeulu "appears to be spiteful, ill-tempered, contemptuous, overbearing, tactless, proud, haughty, uncompromising and even vindictive," to use Palmer's string of inglorious epithets, Akuebue, his best friend understands that the stubborn chief priest agonized in his loneliness over Umuaro's fate; and that the god-ridden old man was being obedient to Ulu rather than self-willed against his clan. That the chief priest is not even permitted a change of mind in his error of judgment and contemplation of revenge is part of the fatal mechanics of the work. The death of Obika, if Ulu was indeed responsible, would have restored Ulu's good name as a living and breathing god. But Ulu's performance remains consistently unimpressive, unlike the gods of Elechi Amadi's novels who strike their victims even on the spot of the offence. Indeed Idemili, Ulu's rival could not punish Oduche for imprisoning his totem. Ulu features as a dull, selfish, and confused god; render his priest totally ineffectual.

The end of the book is as ironic as the beginning. The fighting hero falls after the death of his favorite son Obika, in a perfect conjunction of natural logic, coincidence and superstition accusing Ulu of standing by and watching him destroyed. But Ulu died symbolically long before Ezeulu's son did, and had been replaced by the Christian God. In keeping with his last days in the haughty splendor of a demented high priest, it remains a heavily ironic yet sympathetic conclusion. Umuaro people emerge from the encounter believing they and Ulu have won the battle, but Achebe makes their claim conditional, "If this was so" says the author, Ulu had chosen the wrong time for his punishment.

Achebe offers no simple explanation for Ezeulu's fate. He leaves us with the terrible truth of his hero and his ambiguous fate, allows this priest that heart-rending soliloquy on his disaster and concludes in his authorial voice with a rather ominous reservation (Echeruo 156).

The author is as awe-struck as we are. His concluding remarks on the Preface to the Second Edition of the book are vital:

> For had he been spared Ezeulu might have come to see his fate as perfectly consistent with his high historic destiny as victim, consecrating by his agony – thus raising to the stature of a ritual passage – the defection of his people. And he would gladly have forgiven them.

Arrow of God is an ambitious work, sublime in conception, powerful in impact. It marks the highest point in Achebe's artistic endeavor. This paper, with all its imperfections, is therefore a celebration of Achebe's art at its best.

Works Cited

Primary Source

Achebe, Chinua. *Arrow of God.* London: Heinemann, 1964. Subsequent references are from this edition.

Secondary Sources

Beier, Ulli. (Ed). *Introduction to African Literature.* Ibadan: Longman, 1964.

Echeruo, Michael's Article in *A Celebration of Black and African Writing.* Ed. Bruce King and Kolawole Ogungbesan. Zaria: ABU Press and Oxford University Press, 1975.

Frye, Northrop. *Anatomy of Criticism.* Princeton, New Jersey: Princeton University Press.

Gleason Judith. "Out of the Irony of Words." In *Transition* 18.

Head, Bessie. *A Question of Power.* London: Heinemann, 1974.

Irele, Abiola's Article in *Perspectives on African Literature.* Ed. Christopher Heywood. London: Heinemann, 1968.

Jabbi, Bu-Buakei. "Myth and Ritual in *Arrow of God.*" In *African Literature Today.* No. 11. Ed. Eldred D. Jones. London: Heinemann, 1980.

Kierkeguard, Soren. "The Ancient Tragical Motive as Reflected in the Modern." In *Dramatic Theory and Criticism: Greeks to Grotowski.* Ed. Bernard F. Dukore. New York: Holt, Rinehart and Winston Inc. 1974.

Palmer, Eustace. *The Growth of the African Novel.* London: Heinemann, 1979.

Povey, John. "The Novels of Chinua Achebe". In *Introduction to Nigerian Literature.* Ed. Bruce King. Lagos: University of Lagos Press and Evans Brothers Ltd. 1971.

Shaw, Bernard. *St Joan Definitive Text.* Ed. Dan H. Lawrence. England: Penguin, 1946.

Chapter 18

The Stylistic Significance and Lexical Collocabilities in Nigerian Proverbs in English: A Study of Proverbs in Chinua Achebe's *Arrow of God*

Macpherson Nkem-Azuike

IN THIS ARTICLE WE shall present the stylistic significance of proverbs in an African socio-cultural milieu. The collocational pattern of the internal structures of the proverbs will also be examined. Proverbs in Achebe's *Arrow of God* will constitute our corpora.

The use of proverbs is not only an essential feature of the spoken form of the Nigerian variety of English but also an integral part of the Nigerian Literary works. This can be seen in the writings of Achebe, the distinguished Nigerian novelist. The profuse use of proverbs in Achebe's novels is a testimony to his firm belief in the use of proverbs as a pedagogic strategy in literature. In his novel *Things Fall Apart*, for instance, Achebe (1978) writes:

> Among the Ibo the art of conversation is regarded very highly, and proverbs are the palm-oil with which words are eaten.

Although, here, he refers specifically to the *Ibo*, because this novel is set in an Igbo socio-cultural milieu, it is also true of and applicable to the other Nigerian ethnic groups.

The Stylistic Significance of Proverbs

Proverbs are stylistically significant and they are regarded very highly in the Nigerian society. For instance, they are used to enliven conversations, speech and literary works. Social control in traditional Nigerian society has been effectively maintained over the years with the use of proverbs. They are not only an acceptable and normal gauge for judging behaviour according to tacitly directing societal norms but also a reflection of the people's spiritual and material culture. Many of Nigeria's cultural practices are evident in the content of the proverbs her citizens have recourse to in daily conversations.

On account of the incisive, witty and sententious nature of proverbs, they become convenient vehicles for dealing with explosive issues involving both friends and foes. Proverbs imbue their users with tact and dexterity in situations which would normally cause embarrassment or even social disaster for those who lack such oratorical treasures; because that is what proverbs are. Fully aware of the immense part proverbs play in African societies Dundee (1965: 295) observed that proverbs are used to express social approval and disapproval; praise for those who conform to accepted social conventions and criticism or ridicule of those who deviate; warning, defiance or derision of a rival or enemy and advice, counsel, or warning to a friend when either contemplates action which may lead to friction, open hostilities or direct punishment by society.

This is the Nigerian experience *in to to*. Proverbs also confer respectability on the user. The ability to use interminable strings of proverbs during a speech smacks of cultural erudition; and the more proverbs a man has at his command, the better he knows how and when to "release" them, the more enhanced is his image during private and public performances. In consonance with this feeling of prestige Arora (1977: 2ff) remarks that:

> The individual's skill as a verbal stylist resides, then first of all in his ability to store up for retrieval when required [a large repertoire of conventional modifiers,] and secondly, in the appropriateness with which he is able to apply them to suit his purpose.

Messenger, J.C. in his article "The Role of Proverbs in a Nigerian Judicial System" which appears in Dundee, A. (1965: 302) is also aware of this attribute of proverbs. He comments that "listeners are especially appreciative of an original or little known proverb that captures their imagination and is cleverly introduced at a crucial moment".

The permeating influence or control which proverbs exert on society derives from the authority conferred upon them by the traditions of the people who use them. Such traditions reinforce the attitude or advice conveyed in the proverbs. Some proverbs compare in opacity with idioms; i.e. they possess something similar to homonymous literal counterparts which make them deceptively simplistic. McMordie and Seidl (1979: 241) observe that:

> The proverbs which have a metaphorical quality whose meaning must be transferred from the literal plane to the metaphorical plane, are not so easy to the foreign ear. On the other hand, many proverbial sayings say directly what they mean in straight forward language.

They present the following examples:

a) Metaphorical Plane

"A burnt child dreads fire" (241).

They argue that while this is literally, a true experience, it "has a much wider application". It is not only used in situations in which someone has been hurt it is also used when someone has been disappointed or deceived. One thus avoids the repetition of a painful experience.

b) Literal Plane

i) "the more you have, the more you want" (242).
ii) "If you want a thing well done, do it yourself" (242).

These two proverbs are self-explanatory as they mean what they say.
Our Examples:

a) Metaphorical Plane

"Do we not say that the flute player must sometimes stop to wipe his nose" (*Arrow of God* 120).

The meaning of this rhetorical type of proverb can easily be literally interpreted. But there is much more to it than one taking time off to wipe perspiration. In addition, it is a reference to the necessity to reward a labourer for a job well done. One carrying out a function equally deserves to eat.

Literal Plane

i) "A disease that has never been seen before can not be cured with everyda herbs" (133).
ii) "The unexpected beats even the man of valour" (142).

Here also, the implications of the two proverbs are to a large extent overt.

Proverbs provide individuals with a compensatory escape, as it were, a leeway, from the hardships, the inequalities, the injustices of their daily life. Thus proverbs can be consolatory and a refuge for the helpless and more often than not problems which can not be easily resolved are explained away with an appropriate proverb. In the Nigerian cultural setting, the authenticity and truth-value of proverbs are never questioned. To conclude a comment or a point made in writing with a proverb is like appealing to the highest court in a nation. However, a counter proverb can be cited to justify opposition.

Even when some Nigerian undergraduates write essays, they use proverbs to shore up or conclude points. Such proverbs, when employed in this circumstance are believed to give their speech or essay weight, some force or sanctity and truth-value. By appealing to the traditional and cultural wisdom borne in the proverbs, the teacher, reader or listener is invited to see the points made as irrefutable because they are grounded in age-old practices. For Achebe to have strategically employed the numerous proverbs which we find in *Arrow of God* as well as in *Things Fall Apart, No Longer at Ease* and *A Man of the People* means that he benefitted from that treasurable age-old wisdom which could only be acquired by young men of his time who kept close company with the elders. The use of proverbs is often the preserve of elders; a time-tested preserve which is grounded in and given sanctity by age, experience and hindsight. A man may have knowledge but lack primordial wisdom borne by proverbs. Achebe has both.

Lexical Collocabilities in the Proverbs

Having discussed the significance of proverbs we shall here turn attention to their internal patterning. The collocational behaviour of the words that make up the proverbs will now be examined. By collocation we mean the "habitual co-occurrence of individual lexical items," Crystal (1980: 68). Words, like gregarious animals, keep company. Particular words combine with a select set for particular meanings. In a proverbial environment certain words combine with some others to achieve the desired sensibilities. It is this pattern of lexical association that will be examined in this section of our paper.

Some of the studies on proverbs so far have been carried out under the general heading of folklore (see *Dundee*, 1965; *Arora*, 1977). However, an attempt is made here to "dissect" Nigerian proverbs in English linguistically. They will be examined with a view to verifying their essential form and function. This approach is designed to illuminate the collocational characteristics of words in Nigerian proverbs in English. And we begin to ask: do words arbitrarily join to compose proverbs or should they possess any special *desiderata* – entry qualifications – before appearing in a proverbial environment?

We have attempted a breakdown of the proverbs drawn from our corpora according to the *Headword*, usually the operative nominal in the proverb; the lexical item(s) it collocates with, its implication and category. We want to point out, at this juncture, that what is considered the *implication* is either obviously antonymous from the association of the Head and its "collocator" or entirely contextual. For example:

Head: Little bird Nza
Collocator: god
Implication: Folly

Category: E

A close look at this example will show that the matching of a 'little bird' and a 'god', to say the least, does not readily yield or reveal an implication. This has accordingly been labelled E, under 'category' to indicate that the implication of folly is more cultural than linguistic. *Folly*, as implication is inherent in the meaning of the proverb which derides anyone who in a thoughtlessly and ephemerally self-aggrandizing revelry forgets, ignores or challenges the basis of his existence.

> But Umuaro had grown wise and strong in its own conceit and had become like the little bird, Nza, who ate and drank and challenged his personal god to a single combat (*Arrow of God* 14).

Here the action of Umuaro, like that of the little bird, *Nza*, tantamounts folly. This ever-ready use of proverbs in Nigerian literature in English and especially in Achebe's novels is a palpably distinguishing stylistic feature which is at present wanting in British English. Proverbial usage is almost extinct in the latter variety. In many English literary works like Shakespeare's plays, e.g. *King Lear*, we see the character who plays the fool. This character often exhibits oratorical flourishes which include a rich knowledge of proverbs. It could be said that Shakespeare's 'fools' speak in proverbs. The point being made here is that while such 'fools' exhibit a great depth of wisdom, they are treated basically as 'fools'. The Nigerian experience is a diametric opposite of this Shakespearean attitude. Why? Those who show a rich knowledge of proverbs in speech and writing in Nigeria, are not regarded as 'fools' but revered and applauded. Consequently, while the stylistic significance of proverbs is on the wane in British literature, it is waxing stronger in the Nigerian literature.

The categories used in the analysis that follow are:

1) A = Attributive: eg; Man :Valour : Strength.
2) P = Predicative: eg; Head : Carry : Function.
3) O = Opposition: eg; Rain : Dry : Incompatibility.
4) C = Co-hyponymic: eg; Head : Toe : Body.
5) I = Identical: eg; Bitter : Sour : Similarity.
6) E = Exophoric: eg; Little Bird Nza : Folly.
7) L = Location: eg; Lizard : House : Habitat.

The examples under 'Category' E, in this analysis are typical of exophoric reference. That is, when *implication* is sought extra-textually – beyond the constituents of the proverb.

Lexical Analysis of Proverbs

The proverbs analysed here are provided in the appendix. They are presented in the order they appear in Chinua Achebe's *Arrow of God* (1977) edition. They have therefore been numbered according to the pages on which they appear. Where there are several possibilities of lexical collocabilities in a single proverb we have represented such with the letters of the alphabet. To fully appreciate the analysis we present below the reader is urged to refer to the individual proverbs in the appendix.

Lexical Analysis of Proverbs (*Arrow of God*)

PAGES		HEAD	COLLOCATOR	IMPLICATION	CATEGORY
2.		Moon	bad	certainty	A
9.		Vulture	carcass	eat/food	P
12.		Wisdom	foolishness	incompatibility/ humility	O
13.		Hand	shake	greeting	P
14.		Nza	god	folly	E
16.	a.	Wisdom	bag	content	I
	b.	Bag	carry	personal possession	P
	c.	Goatskin	bag	handcraft	P
17.	a.	Lizard	house	habitat	A/L
	b.	Lizard	field	habitat	A/L
18	a.	She-goat	parturition	labour	E
	b.	Thief	break	audacity	P/O
	c.	Boy	father	consent/support	P
20.	a.	Man	cunning	dishonesty/ cleverness	A
	b.	Death	burial	sadness/sorrow	P
21.	a.	Toad	run	slow	O
	b.	Toad	daylight	danger	E
26.		Hair	chew	anger	P
27.	a.	Live coal	palm	pain	O
	b.	Corpse	fly	decay	A
	c.	Corpse	grave	burial	A
	d.	Slave	grave	torture	A
	e.	Man	deity	authority	A
	f.	King	deity	authority	O
28.		Man	guardian	spirit agreement	A
40.	a.	Bird	bush	habitat	A
	b.	Drummer	dance	music	C
	c.	Bird	Middle of pathway	audacity/risk	O
42.		Handshake	embrace	friendship	P
44.		Monkey	bullet	hunting/risk	P
45.	a.	Men	shoot	hunting	P
	b.	Fly	perch	characteristic	P
49.	a.	Sympathizers	weep	sorrow	P
	b.	Mourners	corpse	death	A

PAGES	HEAD	COLLOCATOR	IMPLICATION	CATEGORY
50. a.	Coward	word	strength	A
b.	Coward	run	fear	P
c.	Coward	fight	incompatibility	O
59. a.	Wind	blow	rough	A
b.	Fowl	rump	exposure	A
60. a.	Man	home	domicile	A
b.	Ant	lizard	food	A
62.	Wife	marry bride	price	P
63. a.	Man	orator	speech	A
b.	Man	kinsman	speech	P
64.	Woman	beard	unlikelihood	O
69.	Old woman	dance	familiarity	P
70. a.	Anus	small	caution	E
b.	Child	man	consent/support	E
c.	Shrew	wash	odour	A
d.	Hand	wash	odour	P
76.	Labourer	hire	reward	E
84. a.	Seat	stool	co-hyponymic	C
b.	Suffering	worry	discomfort	A
85.	Visitor	host	hospitality	A
89.	Death	appetite	similarity	I
94.	King	kolanut	personal possession	E
96.	Yam	knife	control/discretion	A
99.	Cat (fox)	hen	danger	O
100a.	Woman	cook	expertise	P
b.	Utensil	break	fragility	P
111. a.	Morning	wake	time	A
b.	Ear-pick	eye	incompatibility	O
113.	Visitor	craftsman	busy host	A
120.	Flutist	nose	reward	E
126 a.	Water	ankle	control/height	P
b.	Maize	ripe	certainty/patience	P
128.	Hawk	chicken	incompatibility	O
130.	Fly	dung	decay	A
131.	Man	clan	size	E
133 a.	Disease	cure	medicine	P
b.	Herb	cure	medicine	P
134.	Hand	knee	refuge/support	C
136 a.	Spirit	death	cause/agency	A
b.	Spirit	god	support/consent	P
137.	Snake	stick	exaggeration	A
141.	Animal	trap	danger/humiliation	E
142 a.	Man	valour	strength	A
b.	Penis	bearded meat	hope	P
c.	Grass-cutter	backyard	habitat	A/L
146.	Evil medicine	rain	incompatibility	O

PAGES	HEAD	COLLOCATOR	IMPLICATION	CATEGORY
149.	Bell	sound	function	A
153 a.	Adolescent	destruction	exuberance	A
b.	Adult	conciliation	caution/wisdom	A
154 a.	Spirit	mask	secrecy	A
b.	Spirit	appease	sacrifice	P
155 a.	Priest	soup	incompatibility	O
b.	Soup	lick	food	P
157.	Fowl	goat	independence	A/E
160 a.	Man	wrestle	intruders	P
b.	Homestead	path	intrusion	A
165 a.	Offence	fear	cowardice	A
b.	Poison	swallow	intimidation	A
168 a.	Woman	husband	marriage	P/A
b.	He-goat	upper lip	sex	E
c.	Traveller	enemies	incompatibility	O
169.	Rat	tortoise	competition	E
171 a.	Stone	eye	incompatibility	O
b.	Lizard	belly	posture/seat	A
c.	Belly	ache	illness	P
173 a.	Cow	grass	food	P
b.	Mother-cow	calves	offspring	A
181 a.	Tortoise	excrement	punishment	P
b.	Excrement	stench	decay	A
c.	Market	day	date	E
185 a.	Badness	hat	concealment	A
b.	Pregnancy	baby	contradiction	A/E
c.	Baby	nurse	care	P
d.	Toad	tail	incompatibility	O
187 a.	Finger	oil	spread	A
b.	Oil	mess	melt	A
189.	Man	dance	conformity	E
192 a.	Noise	loud	event	A
b.	Market	week	date	E
213.	House	fire	destruction	P
220 a.	Brother	stranger	incompatibility	O
b.	Fight	death	loss	A
c.	Father	estate	inheritance	A
224.	Bull	catch	risk/danger	P
225 a.	Darkness	great	fear	A
b.	Dog	horn	incompatibility	O
226 a.	Man	walk	characteristic	A
b.	Man	spirit	incompatibility	O
c.	Bat	ugliness	characteristic	A
d.	Bat	fly	characteristic	P
e.	Bat	night	nocturnal/time	A

PAGES	HEAD	COLLOCATOR	IMPLICATION	CATEGORY
f.	Ugliness	night	similarity	I
g. i.	Air	foul	odour	A
ii.	Man	tree	climb	P
iii.	Fly	tree	incompatibility	O
h. i.	Water	teeth	mouth	E
ii.	Man	drink	liquid	P
iii.	Water	drink	liquid	A
i. i.	People	talk	characteristic	P
ii.	Rat	bite	wild	P
iii.	Lizard	money	incompatibility	O
iv.	teeth	file	sharpness/ preparation	P
j.	Sleep	death	similarity	I
k. i.	Man	meat	food	P
ii.	Ram	meat	food	P
iii.	Funeral	ram	sacrifice	P
iv.	Sickness	recovery	health	A
l.	Tree	fall	refuge	P
m. i.	Bird	hop	characteristic	P
ii.	Ground	ant-hill	sand	I
n. i.	Sickness	suffering	health	A
ii.	Nurse	sick	care	P
iii.	Sick	fire	warmth	A
o. i.	Death	dog	prevention	E
ii.	Dog	excrement	food	P
iii.	Excrement	smell	odour	A
227 a.	Boy	utensils	errand	E
b.	Goat	leaves	food	P
c.	Palm	leaves	plant	A

From the above analysis we can establish:

1. a Collocational Preponderance Result (C.P.R.)
2. a Functional Preponderance Result (F.P.R.)

A = Collocational Preponderance Result (C.P.R.)
B = Functional Preponderance Result (F.P.R.)

Nominals = 96 Verbs = 45
Adjectives = 11 Adverbs = 2

A = Attributive 52 C = Co-hyponymic 4
E = Exophoric 18 I = Identical 4
O = Opposition 20 P = Predicative 48

In order to establish the preponderant output of the lexical collocates in the proverbs analysed above, we have adopted a simple taxonomy and statistical quantification of the lexical items under the heading *Collocator*. While giving the *Head*, the benefit of a *Constant*, the Collocators have served as our variables.

From the Collocational Preponderance Result (C.P.R.) it is observed that there are 96 nominals, 45 verbs, 11 adjectives and 2 adverbs which collocated variously with the operative nominals under *Head*. From these figures, we can see that more nominals than verbs, adjectives or adverbs tend to co-occur in the same structural environment with other nominals. This gives the impression that the structure of the Nigerian proverbs is essentially nominal in character. And this could be the case because other events in the proverbs revolve around the nominal, which serves as the "centre-pin" on which the occurrence of verbs, adjectives and adverbs depends. It would also seem that the nominal stands for the main participant – the subject in the proverb.

Again, we see that the occurrence of verbs is appreciably high. This picture reflects the amount of action or activity the Nigerian proverbs explain or rationalise. The number of adjectival occurrences comes a poor third. And this can be an indication that there are more proverbs expressing one type of action or the other, than those that merely describe. In content, the nominal and the verb form the heart of the proverb and the figures above reflect this. Adjectives in the proverbs have been used for exaggerative or extenuatory effects. 'Tree' has been described as 'great' and the 'moon' as 'thin'. The adverbials analysed here are those of place, eg, 'backyard' and 'middle of pathway' and they are insignificant in quantity.

However, from the Functional Preponderance Result (F.P.R.) we notice a high occurrence of Collocators which have been used attributively (52). Although there is a comparatively low occurrence of pure adjectives (11) in (C.P.R.), the high frequency of Attributes in (F.P.R.) may have occurred because what constitutes Attributes is not necessarily only adjectives. Again, this pattern may be explained by the correspondingly high occurrence of nominals in (C.P.R.). Such nominals have been qualified, limited, distinguished or simply described. Of note also is the predicative function of "collocators" here which is high in (F.P.R.), 48, and comparable to the fairly high incidence of verbs in (C.P.R.).

Furthermore, we have 20 instances of "collocators" whose co-occurrences with the Head are inherently antonymous. In such instances, the opposition not only contrasts but also clearly underlines the wit in the affected proverbs; eg.

> The offspring of a *hawk* can not fail to devour chicks (*Arrow of God* 128).

By bringing *hawk* and *chicks* under the same proverbial umbrella, we can not help but appreciate their incompatibility. The cultural appeal here lies in the fact that it is still a common sight in Nigerian villages for a hawk to swoop down on chickens even when there are human beings at close quarters. This experience may not be very evident in for instance, the British society where fowls are not often seen wandering about in search of food.

As stated earlier in this article, the exophoric references are extra-textual; eg, their *implication* and *category* are not derived from a matching of the Head and its "collocator". The exophoric references are cultural and/or a largely contextual classification – beyond the constituents of the proverbs. We have 18 exophoric references in all. The co-hyponymic category merely expresses the co-occurrence of two or more collocates which are parts of a larger entity, eg, the *hand* and *knee*, which are parts of the human body. Collocates which exhibit varying degrees of resemblances are entered as identical.

There are instances of collocates which have been assigned combined categories whenever deemed probable, eg, A/E, P/O or A/L. Such instances are not represented in CPR and FPR because our main concern here is to reflect the collocations which are significant and carry considerable functional weight in the proverbs analysed. These combinations have therefore been ignored.

From our analysis, it is clear that individual proverbs manifest a capacity for diverse lexical collocabilities. A similar capacity in idioms is described by Makkai, A. as "Multiple Reinvestability Principle" (MPR), in J.H. Greenberg ed. (1978: 401). In such examples a single proverb yields more than one set of collocates. It has also been seen that words do not arbitrarily join to compose proverbs. Rather, special words are chosen for effect. Words are selected for comparison and contrast, to predicate ideas; to qualify nouns thereby providing emotive heightening in the truth value of affected proverbs. So, the words which usually occur in a proverbial environment are those that best realise the relationship being underlined. Their selection is institutionalised through cultural and social experience. The values they emphasize are common beliefs or knowledge in the society in general; for example, the temerity with which a hawk swoops down on chickens.

Over the years Nigerian proverbs have remained resilient to radical changes because the sense or effect in a proverb may be lost or misunderstood if the proverb's internal structure is radically reconstituted. A major alteration to an Igbo proverb for example will not only sound awkward to an Igbo ear but will also seem to shake the proverbs validity; it will seem as if the proverb has lost its cultural sanctity. But this is not to say that there are no lexical variations at all (however minor) in the constituent structure of Igbo proverbs. Such variations arise where one Igbo dialect has a different word for one of the regular constituents of a proverb. The variation notwithstanding, the underlying concepts in the affected proverbs will be recognized by a majority of Igbo speakers. Finally, we observe that there is economy in proverbial expressions because they condense in a single clause what in deep structure grammar demands more than a clause.

Conclusion

In this article we explored the immense stylistic significance of proverbs in speech and writing in the Nigerian cultural environment. Proverbs enjoy an appreciable degree of catholicity and institutionalisation within the various Nigerian communities. The Igbo society which Achebe describes in *Arrow of God* from which our proverbs are drawn, is a good example of a cultural milieu which encourages the generation and dispersal of proverbs as effective verbal and literary strategy. As a faithful product of that culture, Achebe has fully employed the services of proverbs in his novels to great stylistic advantage.

As we suggested, concluding a speech or essay with an appropriate proverb is comparable to successfully appealing to the highest court in a nation. The number of proverbs found in *Arrow of God*, (see appendix), is an indication that Achebe drank from the same cultural wisdom stream which sets the Elders apart from the boys and other literary neophytes.

We also suggested that there is a strong structural tie between lexical items which collocate in Nigerian proverbs. And the reason for this is the cultural sanctity and traditional wisdom which seem to be shaken when one juggles with the make-up of a proverb. The structure of Nigerian proverbs we also discovered is essentially nominal and this we suggested is the case because other events in the proverb revolve around the nominal which serves as the "centre-pin" of the proverb. The prominence given proverbs in speech and literary endeavours in Nigeria is a function of the oral literary heritage which has been jealously preserved in the Nigerian and African cultures.

Work Cited

Achebe, C. (1977) *Arrow of God*, London: Heinemann.
———. (1978) *A Man of the People*, London: Heinemann.
———. (1978) *No Longer at Ease*, London: Heinemann.
———. (1978) *Things Fall Apart*, London: Heinemann.
Arora, S.L. (1977) *Folklore Studies* No. 29, Los Angeles: California University Press.
Crystal, D. (1980) *A First Dictionary of Linguistics and Phonetics*, London: Andre Deutsch.
Dundee, A. (1965) *The Study of Folklore*, N. Jersey, Prentice Hall, Inc.
Greenberg, J.H. (ed) (1978) *Universals of Human Language* Vol. 3. Stanford: Stanford University Press. 401–418.
Seidl, J. and McMordie, W. (1979) *English Idioms and How to Use Them*. Oxford: Oxford University Press.

Appendix

Proverbs Analysed in the Article. Source: *Arrow of God*

Pages

2. A bad moon does not leave anyone in doubt.
9. Do you blame a vulture for perching over a carcass?
12. We have not come with wisdom but with foolishness because a man does not go to his in-law with wisdom.
13. When a handshake goes beyond the elbow we know it has turned to another thing.
14. But Umuaro had grown wise and strong in its own conceit and had become like the Little bird Nza, who ate and drank and challenged his personal god to single combat.
16. Wisdom is like a goatskin bag; everyone carries his own.
17. If the lizard of the homestead should neglect to do the things for which its kind is known, it will be mistaken for the lizard of the farmland.

18a. When an adult is in the house the she-goat is not left to suffer the pains of parturition on its tether.

b. Have we not heard that a boy sent by his father to steal does not go stealthily but breaks the door with his feet?

20. So leave them to me because when a man of cunning dies a man of cunning buries him.
21. We have a saying that a toad does not run in the day unless something is after it.

26a. But there were others who, as the saying goes, pulled out their hair and chewed it.

b. I told him that he should have spoken up against what we were planning, instead of which he put up a piece of live coal into the child's palm and ask him to carry it with care.

27a. The fly that has no one to advise it follows the corpse into the grave.

b. But let the slave who sees another cast into a shallow grave know that he will be buried in the same way when his day comes.

c. The man who carries a deity is not a king.

28. If a man says yes his chi also says yes.
40. For when we see a little bird dancing in the middle of the pathway we must know that its drummer is in the near-by bush.
42. Allow him a handshake and he wants to embrace.

44. The inquisitive monkey gets a bullet in the face.
45. Men of today have learnt to shoot without missing and so I have learnt to fly without perching.
49. So I want to tell you now that I will not be led astray by outsiders who choose to weep louder than the owner of the corpse.
50. A coward may cover the ground with his words but when the time comes to fight he runs away.
59. Unless the wind blows we do not see the fowls rump.
60. You must be telling me in your mind that a man who brings home ant-infested faggots should not complain if he is visited by lizards.
62. You know that a man's debt to his father-in-law can never be fully discharged. When we buy a goat or cow we pay for it and it becomes our own. But when we marry a wife we must go on paying until we die.
63. I have not said anything because the man who has no gift for speaking says his kinsmen have said all there is to say.
64. It is this lick, lick, lick which prevents woman from growing a beard.
69. An old woman is never old when it comes to a dance she knows.
70a. A man who knows that his anus is small does not swallow an udala seed.
b. Fear not. The man who sends a child to catch a shrew will also give him water to wash his hand.
76. The natives can not be an exception to the aphorism that the labourer is worthy of his hire.
84. When suffering knocks at your door and you say there is no seat left for him, he tells you not to worry because he has brought his own stool.
85. The stranger will not kill his host with his visit, when he goes may he not go with a swollen back.
89. The death that will kill a man begins as an appetite.
94. The king's kolanut returns to his hand.
96. You have the yam and you have the knife.
99. But let us first chase away the wild cat, afterwards we blame the hen.
100. You forgot that a woman who began cooking before another must have more broken utensils.
111a. The time a man wakes up is his morning.
b. We do not apply an ear-pick to the eye.
113. And they also say that a man who visits a craftsman at work finds a sullen host.
120. Do we not say that the flute player must sometimes stop to wipe his nose?
126a. What you say is very true and I do not blame you for wanting to bale the water before it rises above the ankle.
b. A ripe maize can be told by merely looking at it.
128. The offspring of a hawk can not fail to devour chicks.
130. The fly that perches on a mound of dung may strut around as it likes, it can not move the mound.
131. No man however great can win judgement against a clan.
133. A disease that has never been seen before can not be cured with everyday herbs.
134. '... a man who has nowhere else to put his hand for support puts it on his own knee.'

136. '... no matter how many spirits plotted a man's death it would come to nothing unless his personal god took a hand in the deliberation.'
137. A snake is never as long as the stick to which we liken its length.
141. When as the saying was an animal more powerful than *nte* was caught by *nte's* trap.
142a. The unexpected beats even the man of valour.
b. Unless the penis dies young it will surely eat bearded meat.
c. When hunting day comes we shall hunt in the backyard of the grass-cutter.
146. Only those who carry evil medicine on their body should fear the rain.
149. No, all I need is a change of air and you'll see me back as sound as a bell.
153. As you know, the language of young men is always pull down and destroy; but an old man speaks of conciliation.
154. When a masked spirit visits you, you have to appease its footprints with presents.
155. I told them that the chief priest of Umuaro is not a soup you can lick in a hurry.
157. A fowl does not eat into the belly of a goat.
160. For until a man wrestles with one of those who make a path across his homestead the other will not stop.
165. My father used to say that it is the fear of causing offence that makes men swallow poison.
168a. A woman can not place more than the length of her leg on her husband.
b. The young He-goat said that but for his sojourn in his mother's clan he would not have learnt to stick up his upper lip.
c. Our wise men have said that a traveller to distant places should make no enemies.
169. If the rat could not run fast enough it must make way for the tortoise.
171a. The stone rarely succeeds like the eye in hitting the mark.
b. Every lizard lies on its belly, so we can not tell which has a bellyache.
173. When mother-cow is cropping giant grass her calves watch her mouth.
181. I am the tortoise who was trapped in a pit of excrement for two whole markets but when helpers came to haul him out on the eight day he cried! Quick, quick: I can not stand the stench.
185a. Their badness wears a hat.
b. It is pregnant and nursing a baby at the same time.
c. I kept saying: Tomorrow, I shall go, tomorrow, I shall go, like the toad which lost the chance of growing a tail because of I am coming, I am coming.
187. He knew he could say with justice that if one finger brought oil it messed up the others.
189. A man must dance the dance prevalent in his time.
192. The noise even of the loudest events must begin to die down by the second market week.
213. The house he has been planning to pull down has caught fire and saved him the labour.
220. When brothers fight to death a stranger inherits their father's estate.
224. But he whose name is called again and again by those trying in vain to catch a wild bull has something he alone can do to bulls.
225. Darkness is so great it gives a horn to a day.

226a. The man who walks ahead of his fellows spots spirits on the way.
b. Bat said he knew his ugliness and chose to fly by night.
g. When the air is fouled by a man on top of a palm tree the fly is confused.
h. An ill-fated man drinks water and it catches in his teeth.
i. Even while people are still talking about the man Rat bit to death Lizard takes money to have his teeth filed.
j. The sleep that lasts from one market day to another has become death.
k. The man who likes the meat of the funeral ram, why does he recover when sickness visits him?
l. The mighty tree falls and the little birds scatter in the bush.
m. The little bird which hops off the ground and lands on an ant-hill may not know it but it is still on the ground.
n. The man who belittles the sickness which Monkey has suffered should ask to see the eyes which his nurse got from blowing the sick fire.
o. When death wants to take a little dog it prevents it from smelling even excrement.

227a. Give me a sharp boy even though he breaks utensils in his haste.
b. Goat has eaten palm leaves from off my head.

Chapter 19

Technique and Meaning in Achebe's *Arrow of God*

Charles E. Nnolim

> All things have their season, and in their times all things pass under heaven: a time to be born and a time to die. A time to plant and a time to pluck up that which is planted. A time to destroy, and a time to build. A time to weep, and a time to laugh. A time to mourn, and a time to dance (Ecclesiastes 3: 1–4, Douay Version).

There is indeed a paucity of critical exegesis on structure and technique in Achebe's *Arrow of God*, structure and technique which total up to "mean." Critical analysis of the form and meaning of this novel seems to have eluded the same critics who have written so perceptively on *Things Fall Apart*. The reason seems to stem from the fact that much of the sociological background of the novel seems to have blurred its artistic and aesthetic merits by the sheer weight of its intrusive presence. This study, therefore, is an attempt to examine the technique through which meaning is achieved, by turning away from examination of the anthropological or sociological background.

Achebe seems to be obsessed with the concept of mutability from one important novel to another. Heroes who in every way are created free and given a free hand to pursue what ends they will, seem to have their ends determined by the general and external force of mutability. The statement Achebe seems to make from one novel to another is that no one can successfully resist the forces of change because the forces of change are by far stronger than the stubborn individuals. If one interprets him correctly, Achebe seems to be saying that the prudent man must go along, even if grudgingly, and change with the times. Here, then, is the ambivalence in Achebe's concept of tragedy, for it is hard to escape the generalisation that in his novels all men and nations must submit to what is ordained. The more we read Achebe the harder it is not to come to the conclusion that the forces of change are the modern Fates, the Nemesis that must forcefully tame the stubborn individual. Yet, the individual – an Okonkwo, an Ezeulu – never seems to have his hands tied by events, never seems to be rushed by forces greater than he which give him no option of choices.

So, the theme of mutability looms large in *Arrow of God.* "All things have their season," says Ecclesiastes – a reference point that John Nwodika seems to have in mind in *Arrow of God* when he reports what Ekemezie told him. He says:

> Everything was good in its season, dancing in the season of dancing. A man of senses does not go hunting for little bush rodents when his agemates are after big game... If the rat could not run fist **enough,** it must make way for the tortoise (190–191).

With this theme in mind, Moses Unachukwu advises the Otakagu age grade who were deliberating whether to kick against the forced labour imposed upon them by the white man:

> I have travelled in Olu and I have travelled in Igbo, and I can tell you there is no escape from the white man. He has come. When suffering knocks at your door and you say there is no seat left for him,' he tells you not to worry because he has brought his own stool. The white man is like that ... As daylight chases away darkness, so will the white man drive away all our customs. I know that as I say it now it passes by your ears, but it will happen (96–97).

Furthermore, after the elders had failed to persuade Ezeulu to eat the two sacred yams in one month in order to enable Umuaro harvest their yams and escape starvation:

> Nnanyelugo deftly steered the conversation to the subject of change. He gave numerous examples of customs that had been changed in the past when they began to work hardship on the people Nnanyelugo reminded them that even in the matter of taking titles there had been a change. Long, long ago there had been a fifth title in Umuaro – the title of king. But the conditions for its attainment had been so severe that no man had ever taken it, one of the conditions being that the man aspiring to be king must first pay the debts of every man and every woman in Umuaro. Ezeulu said nothing throughout this discussion (239).

To press further the major theme of the inevitability of change, Achebe makes Ezeulu try to justify his radical decision to send his son Oduche to the white man's school (an action that made Ezeulu's detractors conclude that he was at once chasing with the hounds and running with the deer) with the following proverb:

> The world is like a Mask dancing. If you want to see it well you do not stand in one place. My spirit tells me that those who do not befriend the white man today will be saying *had we known* tomorrow (51).

And throughout the narrative *of Arrow of God*, the author keeps hammering at the theme of change by an almost rhythmic repetition of one proverb which seems to act as a thematic refrain. As Ezeulu sends Oduche to school he adds, in addition to the proverb just quoted above:

> If anyone asks you why you should be sent to learn these new things, tell him that a man must dance the dance prevalent in his time (213).

And as the crisis finally began to engulf Ezeulu because of his stubborn resistance to pleas that he eat the two sacred yams to save Umuaro from mass starvation, Ogbuefi Ofoka tells Akuebue that he, Ogbuefi, had recently reminded Ezeulu of the latter's own saying:

> that a man must dance the dance prevailing in his time and told him that we had come – too late – to accept its wisdom. But today he would rather see the six villages ruined than eat two yams (232).

In his rejoinder Akuebue said that he knew Ezeulu more than most people and thus knew that Ezeulu "is a proud man and the most stubborn person is only his messenger" (242–232).

Now, we must confront the ambivalence in Achebe's vision of tragedy in *Arrow of God*. While Ezeulu is not a mere toy at the hands of destiny or the gods, and while there is neither a primordial curse on Ezeulu's head nor a preordained tragic end, Ezeulu still faces the Sophoclean dilemma: that a man must take full consequences for his actions and pay full price for his frailties; in addition, a man must one day confront what he is most afraid of and has most feared to face. What Achebe did with the Sophoclean dilemma in *Arrow of God* is to keep the tragic outcome while befuzzing the path which leads to the tragic end. It was not inevitable that Ezeulu had to end the way he did, for Ezeulu had all along shown himself through his words and actions as a man with foresight and quite ready to change with the times. However, Achebe insists that no one who resists change shall survive the inevitable force of mutability. So, he first of all makes Ezeulu a very stubborn man. Then, he forces him to have the highest regard for his god, Ulu, whose voice and directives Ezeulu must obey, even if they were against his better judgment. Next, he lays very highly charged explosives on Ezeulu's path: Ezeulu must confront both the white man and his fellow elders on matters of principle against which his own very stubborn nature will pitch itself. In his stubbornness, therefore, Ezeulu inevitably detonates the explosives those sensitive mines laid on his path, and the end engulfs him in the conflagration. So, a man like Ezeulu who combines nobility of character with nobility of intention devoid of hypocrisy, goes down to defeat, nobility and all, because he insists all along on steering a highly harassed and dangerous course that leads to nothing but disaster.

Why, then, we wonder, is a pragmatic man like Ezeulu who has consistently acted according to the highest dictates of reason and has adhered to the highest principles of truth, as he sees it, made to suffer such a *humiliating* defeat for obeying his god? Why does Achebe portray an enigmatic relationship between Ezeulu and an inscrutable god who leads him to ruin, and then proceed to saddle Ezeulu with the fatality of his own actions? The answer seems to lie in Achebe's attempt to give a classical twist to the character of Ezeulu: Ezeulu, as well as Oedipus, bears a fate that rightly belongs to the unjust and the malicious – but neither of the two is unjust or malicious. Ezeulu, it seems, is as blind as Oedipus, and this gives cosmic dimensions to the character of the former. Ezeulu's blindness to the realities of the brittle quality of his position in Umuaro as Priest-King is the source of his own gragedy. The ambivalence surrounding the fragile nature of the source of his power over Umuaro was revealed to him right from the beginning, but in his blindness, he failed to take a long, critical look at the true position of things out of his own exaggerated opinion of himself. From the very beginning, he has deliberately refused to face the truth that though:

> it was true that he named the day for the feast of the Pumpkin Leaves and for the New Yam Feast, but he did not choose the day. He was merely the watchman. His. power was no more than the power of a child over a goat that was said to be his .. What kind of power was it if everybody knew that it would never be used? Better to say. that it was not there, that it was no more than the power in the anus of the proud dog who tried to put out a furnace with his puny fart (3–4).

Thus, Ezeulu fails himself and Umuaro because he chooses to be blind to the limitations of his powers: The very fact that he bristles on realizing the *true* nature of the fragility of his powers ("Take away that word *date*... Yes I say take it away. No man in Umuaro can stand up and say that I dare not. The woman who will bear the man who will say it has not yet been born") (4) helps to trigger his own final tragedy and reveals to us that he is not a very adroit politician. The delegation of ten elders sent to Ezeulu to persuade him to roast and eat the two yams realized more than Ezeulu himself that Ulu was not a nature-god (like the Earth-goddess or Amadiora-god of lighting) but god over Umuaro by convention and *compromise*, and could only retain its power over. Umuaro by "dancing the dance prevalent in their life-time." Ezidemili had once reminded the audience that:

> Every boy in Umuaro knows that Ulu was made by our fathers long ago. But Idemili [Pillar of Water] was there at the beginning of things (46).

On another occasion, Nwaka's words (the implications of which seem to have been lost on Ezeulu) were that unless Ezeulu trod very carefully, what happened at Aninta might happen at Umuaro, because when the deity of Aninta failed the people they repudiated him:

> And we have all heard how the people of Aninta dealt with their deity when he failed them. Did they not carry him to the boundary between them and their neighbours and set him on fire? (31).

He later pressed his point to the logical conclusion by reminding Umuaro (as Ezeulu saw in his dream) that Ulu is a god who boa outlived his own usefulness who, thought he:

> saved our fathers from the warriors of Abam but he cannot save us from the white man. Let us drive him away as our neighbours of Aninta who drove out and burnt Ogba when he left what he was called to do and did other things, when he turned round to kill the people of Aninta instead of their enemies (180).

In sum, then, blindness to reality and a false sense of grandeur coupled with stubbornness unrelieved by a proper sense of history constitute Ezeulu's tragic flaw. The anlage of tragedy for Ezeulu as well as for Ulu is the apparent blindness to the limitations of their authority, their failure to appreciate that from the very beginning Ulu was a god of concensus, that the war it was established to fight had long been won when the warriors of Abams were beaten off for good, and that in the light of the present challenges they must, to continue to be relevant, dance the dance prevalent in their life time. The theme of mutability is once again evident: The old order changeth/Yielding place to new.

Now, the issue of technique should engage our attention. According to Mark Schorer ("Technique as Discovery" in *Hudson Review*, Vol. I, Spring 1948), the "achieved content" of the work – its art – is accomplished through technique. Technique is the means by which an author organises his material, the rhythm or form he imposes on his work in order to achieve his meaning and in order to convey that meaning to his audience. How then does Achebe organise his art in *Arrow of God* to achieve his meaning, to expatiate on the idea of mutability, to impress upon us that the forces of change are by far stronger than the stubborn individual? First of all, he arranges a bi-partite device which he repeats in other novels. This bi-partite device is me that corresponds to the folkloric formula of "exile and return" which. we encounter in myth criticism. In *Things Fall Apart*. This bi-partite formula hinges on (a) Okonkwo before exile when his fortunes rise and crest at their zenith during which time he occupies the second highest position among the masked Egwugwu that delivered judgment in Umuofia, and (b) after exile when his fortunes sink to their nadir,ending in an ignominious suicide by hanging. On his return from exile, Okonkwo became the rat that cold not rum fast enough and had to make way for the tortoise!

In *No Longer at Ease*, the formula is (a) Obi Okonwo before "exile" overseas, when he was "at ease" with the traditions and customs of Umuofia at the same time when village lore and custom were still the guiding light for proper behaviour, mad (b) after hiss return from temporary exile Prom overseas when he was "no longer at ease" amidst his people in the cities created by the colonial masters. His inability to learn the tricks of the game of survival in "bribe-eating" Nigeria landed him in tragedy.

Now, in *Arrow of God,* the formula is repeated by Achebe. It appears thus: (a) Ezeulu before imprisonment or "exile" at Okperi, when he was master of his household and in control of all the refractory forces in Umuaro, and (b) after imprisonment or "exile" when, owing to his exaggerated interpretation of his powers over Umuaro, coupled with the capricious behaviour of his god, he acts irresponsibly and with dubious motives and thus loses grips both on his sanity and over Umuaro as a whole. On this note, one must mention that Achebe's use of the "exile and return" theme ia an inver-sion of the classical formula where the hero normally returns on an enhanced status after journeying to the underworld. But Achebe deliberately inverts the *formula* in order to drive home his message which is a pessimistic one: that in the general theme of mutability those who do not change with the Lima will be swept aside, or in the words of John Nwodika: "if the rat could not run fast enough, it must make way for the tortoise."

Examing Achebe's technique in *Arrow of God,* we must note that there are two dramatic centres-in the novel: a) the arrest and detention of Ezeulu during which the dramatic confrontation between him and the full forces of colonial administration fonder the Assistant District commissioner Taw Clarke (who was carrying out the orders of his superior, Captain.Winterbottam) was beginning to cause him sans, inconvenience, even sorrow, and (b) his stubborn confrontation with and insistent refusal, on coming hams, to listen to a delegation of elders who urge him, for¯the sake of Umuaro and themselves, to roast two sacred yams in one month. Now, this basic bi-partite formula traced so far, tough whit Achebe achieves his meaning, underlines,internal dynamics of the structure of *Arrow of God.* on close examination of the novel, one can easily see that, the tensions in the novel are decipherable under two main, forces: (a) centripetal forces, or forces drawing Umuaro together, and (b) centrifugal forces, or forces pulling:Umuaro apart. We must remember that initially Umuaro came into existence through fear and throe the need for collective security in order to fight off external forces preying on the absence of unity and collective response to common threat from the Abam military forces from the outside. As we shall later on see in this study, by the irony – things, Umuaro fell apart by experiencing a new sort of security which a more superior but external colonial force could provide – a security which, this time, seriously undermines the need to stay together as agreed upon during the amalgamation.

So, first to the centripetal forces – forces which draw and keep Umuaro together. On the outermost fringes is the amalgamation and the principle which brought it into existence – the need for collective security. The ceremonies that crystallize the amalgamation are concretized and memorialized around two "shrines" – the stream into which one amalgamation-fetish was thrown, and the market place where the other was buried? (Mahood 181). The sustaining water of the stream gives and nourishes life for all the *villages* while the market square which is also the seat of the great Ikolo which calls the villages together during important occasions gathers the people every four days. The market square lends a *cyclic* and ritual importance to the spirit and intent of the amalgamation. In the stream and the market square, the ritual and cyclic-nature of the amalgamation is eternally renewed and kept alive. Then, life further secretes around the feasts and the ceremonies and the festivals, each with its own cyclic and ritual implications and according to its season.

First is the Feast of the Pumpkin Leaves, with its cleansing and sacrificial idea with the Priest-King acting as the scapegoat (for past sins of the last farming season) on whom the pumpkin leaves – symbol of coming life – spring – is flung. Then, follows the New Yam Feast – a thanksgiving offering with its implications of ritual comedy in its celebration of life. The two feasts complement life: the one, a sacrifice and a wish; the other, a celebration and a thanksgiving. The one, a wish prayer feast in which women are the chief actors: the other, a ritual *thanksgiving* in which men, the heads of each family, are the dramatic personae. And in each occasion, the object of cynosure, the centre of the drama, is the chief priest, the supreme symbol of Umuaro's unity. In the and, we shall see that *Arrow of God* is like ritual drama where Ezeulu is Priest King as sacrificial scape-goat who must be sacrificed in the end for ritual cleansing of the body-politic, to restore normalcy after an upheaval.

Then we have other centripetal forces – the shared local myths and legends, the *age-grade groups* each committed to working together as a team for the progress of Umuaro. And just as each family in Umuaro gravitates around the *Obi* and family shrine, under the acknowledged *hegemony* of the *eater-families,* so the entire Umuaro' gravitates around the shrine of Ulu under the acknowledged hegemony of the Chief Priest. Irony creeps in later because the gravitational pull (what I have identified as the centripetal forces) continues by sheer force of habit when it was no more than mere echoes. And when *things* did finally fall apart, the one rallying point of unity – the Chief Priest becomes the instrument of subversion and disintegration, as seen by his detractors.

As the centripetal forces began to weaken, and as cracks in the wall of unity began to show in Umuaro, the agents of *centrifugal* forces – forces pulling and tearing Umuaro apart began to rear up their *ugly* heads and wax strong. We must remember that even at the best of times, Allegiance by each village to its local deity plus other centrifugal local ceremonies and observances existed as minor centrifugal forces *pulling* apart each village a each tries to establish its own local identity. But under these circumstances, this made for variety and added to local colour in Umuaro. When, however, the centripetal forces were an efforts and centrifugal forces began to gain ascendancy, efforts at separate identities by the villages became major destabilising forces as could be seen in the fight-to-the-death struggle between Ezeulu and Ezidemili of Umunneora. And, "when two brothers, fight, a stranger reaps their harvest."

Centrifugal forces themselves come in a bi-partite form: from outside Umuaro, and from within Umuaro itself and even within Umuaro, two minor undercurrents of tensions operate: within Ezeulu's household and within Ezeulu's personality as well. From the periphery – from outside Umuaro – the strongest destabilising forces centre around the white man's *imperial* forces, the incursions of Christianity, and the rivalry with Opera, the neighbouring town. But first, to the white man and the colonial imperative:

One member had warned the *Otakagu age-group* which *began* the dangerous debate of stopping work on the new road unless the white man paid them for the labour, that it was useless to fight the white man for it would be a *fight* that would be lost before ever it was *begun:*

> The white man, the new religion, the soldiers, the new road – they are all part of the same thing. The white man has a gun, a matchet, and a bow and carries fire in his mouth. He does not fight with one weapon alone… I know that many of us want to fight the white man. But only a foolish man can go after a leopard with his bare hands (97).

Now, although the white man was so powerful, his conquest and dismemberment of Umuaro was helped by the march of history which had begun to erode the primacy of the protective role of Ulu and the cohesive influence It wielded among the six villages; for the Abam warriors against whom the amalgamation was effected were no longer a threat to collective security. And in the wake of the liberties which Nwaka and Ezidemili (both of Umunneora) began to take, the white man merely came to deliver the *coup de grace*… Everyone ten understood that ultimate power resided with the white man who, after disarming both Umuaro and Opera and destroying their capabilities to make war, quietly brought with him his own native court system which in itself ensured the complete subversion of traditional methods of settling disputes – methods he replaced with his corrupt court messengers and venal court interpreters.

Before Umuaro could catch its breath, Christianity had quietly established itself in the wake of the white man's imperial power, bringing in its own wake strange and heretical ideas – ideas which were to bring about culture change and undermine traditional social life and beliefs by unleashing and entrenching forces which work against established tradition (Obiechina 234). And with Christianity came the local school to further take away the children of Umuaro and teach them not only to despise the age-old customs and sacrosanct taboos but to actively try to desecrate them. And no less a person than Douche, the son of no less a person than Ezeulu, the Chief-Priest himself, was involved in this nefarious practice, thus frustrating the efforts of the community to *appeal* to the Chief-Priest to help eliminate such agents of a *disintegration.*

Opera, with its quarrelsome stance and its claim of portions of the land of Umuaro should, under normal circumstances, have united Umuaro to face a common enemy. But the white man had become involved in the dispute. Furthermore, Umuaro's own Chief-Priest, Ezeulu, played the execrable role of being on the side of the enemy by testifying. before the white man's court, against Umuaro. From here on, the position of Opera as a *destabilising* factor. within Umuaro begins to loom large. First, it helps make the enemies of Ezeulu within Umuaro more brazenly vocal than would have been possible. Secondly, those enemies were able to assumeble a larger opposition than would have been imaginable. Thirdly, the very fact that Government Hill was located in Okperi and the 'white man wielded his power from there and invited. his "friend" Ezeulu from there exacerbated the already explosive opposition against Ezeulu within Marc. The ultimate victors became Nwaka and Ezidemili of Umuaro – the traditional enemies of Ezeulu within Umuaro.

Rivalries and tensions from the outside are paralleled. It by rivalries and tensions within Ezeulu's household: between Adage, Ezeulu's eldest son and Nwafor, his youngest, over inheritance of the priestly mantle; between Matefi, the older wife and Ugoye, the younger over undefined jealousies; between Ezeulu the husband who saw the wisdom of sending Oduche to school and Ugoye, the wife who saw no wisdom in choosing her son as a guinea pig; between Ezeulu who inher ited the priestly mantle from his father and his elder brother, Okeke Onenyi who had been led to believe that the priestly mantle would fall to him. And even within the personality of Ezeulu, the bi-partite tension is not absent. Ezeulu himself boasts:

> I can see things where other men are blind. That is why I am Known and at the same time Unknowable.... You cannot know the thing which beats the drum to which Ezeulu dances (149).

Ezeulu's friend, Akuebue, tells him: "that does not mean I forget that one half of you is wan and the other half spirit." (150) In Ezeulu's performance of his priestly duties during the Festival of the First pumpkin Leaves, Achebe writes: "The left aide of his body – from forehead to toes – wad painted with white chalk!' (80). This was the spirit side of Ezeulu as contradistinguished from hid human side which wad not painted In the end, Ezeulu whose human side was on the side of compromise and accommodation with Umuaro over the problem of roasting: and eating the *two* sacred yams in one month in order to alleviate the human suffering among his people wax ruined because the spirit side of Mar (representing the voice of his god, Ulu) barked disagreement at his conciliatory thoughts;

> 'Taa Nwanu barked Ulu in his ear as a spirit would in the ear of an impertinent human child. "Who told you that this was your own fight?" Ezeulu trembled and said nothing "I say who told you that this was your own fight which you could arrange to suit you? You want to save your friends who brought you palm wine... Beware you do not come between me and my victim or you may receive blows not meant for you. Do you not know what happens when two elephants fight? Go home and sleep and leave me to settle my quarrel with Idemili, who wants to destroy me so that his python may come to power. Now tell me how it concerns you.... As for me and *Idemili* we shall fight to the finish; and whoever throws the other down will strip him of his anklet (219).

Thus, Ezeulu deferring to Ulu and discovering that "it wad a fight of the gods," and that "he was no more than an arrow in the bow of his god," left the fight to Ulu. The rest is prologue, "and when the damage was irreparably done, Ogbuefi Ofoka tells, Akuebue: "Let me tell you one thing. A Priest like Ezelu leads a god to ruin himself. It has happened before." But Akuebue qualifies that: "Or perhaps a god like Ulu leads a priest to ruin himself" (243). Thus, the ambivalence is kept alive till the end, and the general theme of mutability triumphs, finally.

Having so far traced the bold outlines through which Achebe has depicted the theme of mutability in *Arrow of God*, we would now turn to the subtle artistic devices through which he further highlights this theme and through which the bi-partite structure of his work is maintained. We have just examined certain tensions observable in the actions of the novel. These tensions are buttressed by certain parallel occurrences which the author maintains throughout his narrative. First and foremost, Ezelu's with the white men on Government Hill (an external force) parallels his other confrontation with a delegation of elders of Umuaro (an internal force). His unbending resistance to both forces lead to his own final undoing. Second, Akukalia's confrontation with Ebo, early in the novel, which leads to his breaking of the guns of the two towns by the white man – a situation that echoes a more cosmic confrontation between Umuaro and England through the latter's emissaries both as Christian missionaries and imperial agents on Government Hill.

Next, Ezeulu's frustration in trying to rule a volatile and fractious Umuaro parallels Winterbottom's frustrations over how to deal with Wright (who birches volunteer workers and sleeps with local women) and also his frustrations over how to deal with starry-eyed superiors at headquarters about the application of indirect rule in the hinterland. And again, Ezeulu's body painted half white half black on ceremonial occasions parallels his household now half traditional religion half Christian which by. extension parallels Umuaro at the end, half traditional religion half Christian parallelling even further the new government, half traditional half alien. The end-result of these parallels still touch on the theme of mutability: the society is no longer the same. Then, Nwaka's boasts with the Mask on, parallels Ezeulu's boasts while in ceremonial regalia. And Oduche's imprisonment of a royal python in a box (an abomination for which there is no prescribed sanction) parallels Akuenu Nwosisi's kinsmen's abomination of copulating with a she-goat (another aberrant, behaviour for which there is equally no prescribed sanction). Furthermore, Ezeulu who admires Captain Winterbottom but easily misreads his mind parallels Winterbottom himself who respects Ezeulu but easily, misinterprets his ambitions. Then, Ezeulu watching the new moon from his Obi parallels Winterbottom watching for the first signs of the first year's rain from the verandah of his house; and Ezeulu, the eon of a High Priest, who follows the dictates of *his* god against his own better judgement and lost his influence in Umuaro, parallels Winterbottom, the am of a Church of England clergyman, who follows his own better judgement against pressures from the "gods" at Headquarters and lost his promotion.

Contrast and counterpoint are used by Achebe in his artistic pursuit of the bi-partite structure of his narrative in *Arrow of God*. There. are two opposing gods: Ezeulu's god, Ulu, represents the old but dying order and Ezeulu Is the arrow in its bow; this contrasts Goodcountry's god who represents the new forces of Umuaro, and Goodcountry is the arrow in his bow. Then one easily observes the loneliness and isolation existing on Goverrment Hill where the major occupants have no children. This contrasts markedly with the teeming life replete with wives and children down in the villages. Stylistically, we have the language of colonial officials with its administrative jargon contrasting with the language of Igbo villagers, emphasizing the cultural barriers separating the colonizer from the colonized. So do both groups of people have two different and opposing concepts of time. Then, *Arrow of God* opens with Umuaro coming together for collective security under the protective umbrella of a single deity. This contrasts with the ending, for the book closes with Umuaro disintergrating *through* the winning and ring *influence* of a new religion. And following closely on the technique of contrasts is the use of juxtaposition, which further highlights the bi-partite structure of the novel. Ezeulu. who emerges from detention and loses a beloved son is juxtaposed with Winterbottom' who emerges from his illness and gains a beloved wife. Then, the promiscuity of Ogbanje Onenyi "whose husband was said to have sent to her parents for a matchet to cut the bush on either side of the highway *which* she carried between her thighs" (138), is juxtaposed with the "enormous goat" Which Obika sent to his mother-in-law the morning following his wedding because, his young bride, Okuata, was feted on the bridal night to be "at home" (138) and was an "unspoilt bride." Finally, Winterbottom's collapse into coma on the morning he ordered Ezeulu's arrest (a relapse that, thoroughly alarmed those on Government Hill) is juxtaposed with Ezeulu's incaceration at Okperi (a coincidence that enhanced the reputation of Ezeulu as a man with potent magic powers).

The crowning technique *which* enriches the structure of *Arrow of God* is Achebe's use of irony and ambiguity. In *Arrow* of *God* as in all literature of the highest order, ambiguity results from the fact that language artistically functions on other levels than those of mere communication, than those of the merely literal. Ambiguity is the expression of an idea in language of such a nature as to give more than one meaning and to leave an aura of uncertainty as to the true significance of the statement. And, of course, to speak of ambiguity is to speak of irony in its most refined form. Irony and ambiguity in *Arrow of God* stem from the double-edged nature of things and events in the novel. These help to structure the story and give it its bi-partite form. Achebe succeeds several times in conveying in one deft stroke a meaning which contains multi-levelled overtones of great richness and complexity. Was it, for example, sheer coincidence that when Winterbottom seemed to have got better he relapsed dangerously into a coma the very morning Clarke wrung from him an order to continue to detain Ezeulu: or was it, as John Nwodika claimed, through Ezeulu's much vaunted potent fetish:

> The first person to point the connection was John Nwodika...He said it was just as he feared; the priest hit him with a potent charm...Was it for nothing that I refused to follow the policeman? I told them that the Chief Priest of Umuaro is not a soup you can lick in a hurry....Our master thinks that because he is a white man our medicine cannot touch him (174).

And as "the story of Ezeulu's magical powers spread through Government Hill hand in hand with the story of Captain Winterbottom's collapse" (175) fear led the two police officers sent to arrest him (though they missed him) decide that "to be on the safe side they should go and see a local dibia straight away" (177). They did.

It is irony writ large that Ezeulu's unquestioning acceptance of Ulu's barked directive not to fight the fight as if it were his own (when Ezeulu's better judgment inclined him towards compromise) leads both priest and god to ruin so that in the eyes of discerning elders both became the proverbial lizard that ruined his own mother's funeral. As a corollary, it subsumes of the highest irony that the pragmatic

Ezeulu who had sent Oduche to school because "a man must dance the dance prevalent in his life time," refuses to do that dance when eating two sacred yams in one month became the wish of the elders because the situation called for it for the survival of the body politic. It subsumes of further irony that while Ezeulu was at Okperi, John Nwodika from Umunneora (Nwaka's village) whom Ezeulu and everyone else had reason to distrust – and Akuebue certainly distrusts – turns out in the end to be the best intentioned and most kindly disposed towards Ezeulu, while Captain Winterbottom, whom Ezeulu had reason to trust as a very good friend, is the one who actually ordered his arrest and who insisted on detaining him indefinitely. And the dramatic irony persista in Ezeulu's continued good opinion of Winterbottom, Clarke, and his chief messenger. There is further irony tinged with comedy at the incredulity of Clark at the "proud inattention" and scorn with which Ezeulu turns down the signal honour of being made a Paramount Chief ("a witch-doctor making a fool of the British Administration in public"), while Ezeulu thinks that any other chieftaincy that that of Chief Priest of Ulu is by the continuing irony when Ezeulu arrives back at Umuaro who could not believe that Ezeulu would "refuse the very thing he had been planning and scheming for all these years" that if Ezeulu did actually refuse the white man's offer, it "proves what I have always told people, that he inherited his mother's madness" (198).

It subsumes of continuing irony that as Ezeulu sat anguished over not roasting the two sacred yams in one month, others thought that he was gloating in victory over the people of Umuaro; for people did not appreciate as did Akuebue that Ezeulu was actually helpless, and that he sat anguished because "a greater thing than *nte* was caught in *nte*'s trap." But the true position of things is wrapped in irony and ambiguity: Ezeulu is actually smarting at his own powerlessness, the powerlessness he had rebelled against at the very beginning of the novel:

> Whenver Ezeulu considered the immensity of his power over the year and the crops and, therefore, over the people he wondered if it was real. It was true' he named the day for the feast of the pump do leaves and for the New Yam feast; but, hp did not choose the day. He was merely a watchman His power was no more than the power of a child over a goat that was said to be his. As long as the goat was alive it was his; he would find it food and take care of it. But the day it was slaughtered he would know who the, real owner was. No! the Chief Priest of Ulu was more than that, must be more than that: If he should refuse to name the day: there would be no festival – planting and no reaping – But could he refuse? No Chief Priest had ever refused. So it could not be donor. He would not dare (3).

That moment just arrived, and as Ezeulu looked on in the full realization of his own powerlessness, others – his enemies and detractors – concluded that he was gloating in victory over Umuaro. And other ironic situations are still evident: It is in the house of Ezeulu, the most zealous custodian of culture, 'that the royal python' was desecrated by no less a person than his own son. And it is supremely ironic that the triumph of Christianity over traditional religion in Umuaro is triggered off, not by the iconoclastic Oduches and the Goodcountries but by Ezeulu and his god, Ulu, the arch symbols of traditionalism and orthodoxy.

We must not assume that the tragedy of the novel is unrelieved by humour. Although this angle will not be pursued in detail, a few that touch on the bi-partite construct of the novel will be dealt with slightly: Achebe harps on the tragedy of the relationship (in the eyes of Ezeulu) between his son, Obika, and Ofoedu, his close friend. He tells us that as the pair who were notoriously heavy drinkers arrived very late to join their age group who were working on the new road, they appeared laughably "like a pair of Night Masks caught abroad by day" (91), and he concluded gratuitously for the reader that "today there was as little to choose between them as between rotten palm nuts and a broken mortar" (91). It is with the same subtle irony that he later refers to Obika's temporary restraint from excessive drinking after his recent marriage:

> His temporary restraint had been largely due to the knowledge that too much palm wine was harmful to a man copulating with his wife – it made him pant on top of her like a lizard fallen from an iroko tree (221).

And it is with a sort of leering irony that he contrasted the virginity of Obika's wife, Okuata, who was found "at home" on the night of her wedding (so that Obika sent a goat in gratitude to his mother-in-law for giving him an unspoilt bride), with the promiscuity of Ogbanje Omenyi "whose husband was said to have sent to her parents for a matchet to cut the bush on either side of the highway which she carried between her thighs" (138).

Finally, we must draw attention to the imagery of the lizard which acts as a thematic refrain in the novel and which, in the end points to the final tragedy. In Igbo folklore the lizard is constantly depicted as a braggart because of his vaunted prowess for jumping down the iroko tree and remaining unscathed, a feat that no other animal could boast of. Obika had given us this image of the lizard in self-cengratulation because he has had no sexual knowledge of his future bride until all the traditional rites were performed.

> He felt entitled to praise himself if nobody else did – like the lizard who fell down from the iroko tree without breaking any bone and said that if nobody else thought highly of the feat he himself did (130).

But in *Arrow of God* Achebe goes beyond this simple lore. The imagery of the lizard becomes one of the controlling metaphors of the entire novel in a way that inextricably ties it with the total meaning of the work. In the final analysis Ezeulu and his god, Ulu, had become the proverbial lizard that ruined his own mother's funeral. Earlier in the novel, after Ezeulu had sent Oduche to the white man' a school, people were asking:

> If the Chief. Priest of Ulu could send his son among people who kill and eat. the sacred python· and commit other evils, what did he expect ordinary men and women to do? The lizard who threw confusion into his mother's funeral rite did he expect outsiders to carry the burden of honouring his dead? (14).

Much later on, Ezeulu was to blame Oduche for the tragedy that was befalling him (Ezeulu) when he learns that Oduche had known all along without informing him that Umuaro were asked to bring their harvest yams to the church rather than' to Ulu. He dismissed Oduche in anger, saying;. "Go away and rejoice that your father cannot count on you. I say, go away from here, lizard that ruined his mother's funeral" (251).

At the mid-point in the novel, Moses Unachukwu had warned the overzealous Good country not to lead the converts into excesses, saying:

> Nobody here has complained to you that the python has ever blocked his way as he came to church.... but if you want to be the lizard that ruined his own mother's, funeral you may carry on as you are doing (55).

Once, in self-defence against accusations that he was consorting with the white man, Ezeulu had retorted using the imagery of the lizard:

> Who brought the white man here? Was it Ezeulu?....Who showed them the way to Abame? They were not born there; how then did they find their way? We showed them and are still showing them. So let nobody came to me and complain that the white man did this and did that. The man who brings ant-infested faggots into his hut should not grumble when lizards begin to pay him a visit (148).

Later on, when Ezeulu consults Umuaro to advise him on the proper action to take concerning Winterbottom's invitation to him to come to Okperi, his arch enemy tells him in derision:

> A man who brings ant-ridden faggots into his hut should expect the visit of lizards. But if Ezeulu is now telling us that he is tired of the white man's friendship our advice to him should he: You tied the knot, you should also know how to undo it. You passed the shit that is smelling; you should carry it away (162).

The final tragedy of the novel is enuciated with the imagery of the lizard. The triumph of Christianity over traditional religion is accomplished not by a vigorous and volatile white agent but by Ezeulu and his god, Ulu. The stable voice of the author informs us:

> So in the end only Umuaro and its leaders saw the final outcome. To them the issue was simple. Their god had taken sides with them against his headstrong ambitious priest and thus upheld the wisdom of their ancestors – that no man however great was greater than his people; that no man ever won judgment against his clan. If this was so then Ulu had chosen a dangerous time to uphold the wisdom. In destroying his priest he had also brought disaster on himself, like the Lizard in the fable who ruined his mother's funeral by his own hand (261) (emphasis mine).

Now, to round up, we should really end where we began. The tragedy of Ezeulu is really the tragedy of a man who tries very hard to come to terms with change but dies, swept away by the forces of change. His attempts to come to terms with change are seen both in his decision to send Oduche to school and in the arguments with which he surrounds his decision. First, he tells his son that "the world is like a Mask dancing. If you want to see it well you do not stand in one place." Then he keeps repeating that a man must dance the dance prevalent in his life time. Once he tells Oduche: "I am like the bird Eneke-nti-oba. Men of today have learnt to shoot without missing and so I have learnt to fly without perching." Much later he tells the elders why he sent Oduche to school, saying:

> A disease that has never been seen before cannot be cured with everyday herbs. When we want to make a charm we look: for the animal whose blood can match its. power; if a chicken cannot do it we look for a goat or a ram; if that is not sufficient we send for a bull. But sometimes even a bull does not suffice, then we must look for a human (150).

Now, this theme of change, of mutability, is touched upon in an interview by Achebe with Serumaga as he tried to explain what he attempted to do in *Arrow of God*. He says:

> Ezeulu, the chief character of *Arrow of God*, is a different kind of man from Okonkwo. He is an intellectual. He thinks about why things happen – he is a priest and his office requires this – so he goes into the roots of things and he's ready to accept change, intellectually. He sees the value of change and therefore his reaction to Europe is completely different from Okonkwo's. He is ready to come to terms with it – up to a point – except where his dignity is involved. This he could not accept; he is very proud. So you see it's really the other side of the coin, and the tragedy is that they come to the same sticky End. So there is no escape whether you accept change or whether you don't (iii–iv) (emphasis mine).

Finally, the theme of mutability which has occupied us so much in this study is really enthroned in the symbolism of the moon – the moon which Ezeulu was busy watching as the novel opens, the moon which, as the author says, "while it played its game the Chief Priest sat up every evening waiting" (1). The moon is the arch symbol of mutability, of inconstancy, of the double-edged sword wielded by the gods in dealing with us mortals. The novel opens with Ezeulu watching the moon which played pranks with him. It ends with Ezeulu as a lunatic. The symbolism of the moon depends the ambiguity of *Arrow of God* and points to the artistic depth and richness of the novel.

Works Cited

Achebe, Chinua. *Arrow of God.* New York: Doubleday and Co., 1969. Subsequent references are from this edition and enclosed in parentheses in the text.

Mahood, M.M. "Idols of the Den: Achebe's Arrow of God." In *Critical Perspectives on Chinua Achebe.* Ed. C.L. Innes and Bernth Lindfors. Washington, D.C.: Three Continents Press, 19778.

Obiechina, Emmanuel. *Culture, Tradition and the West African Novel.* London: Cambridge University Press, 1975.

Serumaga, Robert. Interview with Chinua Achebe. In *Cultural Events in Africa.* No. 28. March 1967.

Chapter 20

The Human Dimension of History in Chinua Achebe's *Arrow of God*

Emmanuel Obiechina

THE FORCES WORKING AGAINST tradition seem already entrenched in the Umuaro of *Arrow of God*. The local school and mission station, irreverent strangers like the catechist Goodcountry, and the inarticulate though palpable reality of the white man's administrative presence, all these have undermined traditional confidence and shaken the sense of common purpose and solidarity which in the past constituted the spirit of traditionalism. The natives of Umuaro bear witness to these changes in matter-of-fact remarks which show that they are realistic enough to recognize that these things are there to stay. A character, for example, sees Mr Wright's new road connecting Umuaro to the administrative town of Okperi as a part of the new forces that are transforming the old society. "Yes, we are talking about the white man's road," he reminds his audience. "But when the roof and walls of a house fall in, the ceiling is not left standing. The white man, the new religion, the soldiers, the new road-they are all part of the same thing. The white man has a gun, a matchet, a bow and carries fire in his mouth. He does not fight with one weapon alone" (105). The theme of contact and change is not carried by such overt statements but rather by the human drama, in which those deeply entrenched in the past attempt to adapt to the present.

The conflicts in *Arrow of God* develop around the person of the Chief Priest of Ulu, who is the ritual and religious leader of Umuaro. On the one hand, there is the conflict between the local British administration represented by the old-fashioned administrator, Winterbottom, and the native authority represented by the Chief

Priest. On the other hand, there are the internal politics of Umuaro and the conflict between the supporters of the Chief Priest and those of his rival, Idemili. On yet another level belongs the conflict taking place within the Chief Priest himself, a conflict between personal power, the temptation to constitute himself into an "arrow" of God, and the exigencies of public responsibility. All these are handled in the main plot. A subsidiary plot deals with the domestic tensions and crises in Ezeulu's own house, the tensions and stresses between the father and his grown-up sons and between the children of different mothers in his polygamous household.

Not all these conflicts are a result of culture-contact. Personality deficiencies and mistaken judgements have something to do with some of them. The intervention of fate and chance also plays a part. But the contact situation exacerbates the conflicts and radicalizes the incipient oppositions and contraditions within the native tradition. Where this shows most emphatically is in the breakdown of the sense of solidarity among the traditionalists. Ezeulu. the Chief Priest and a man whose role marks him out as keeper of collective security, is the person who feels most keenly this breakdown, and he never tires of attributing the change, deprecatingly, to "the new age". At a critical stage in the narrative, after he has seen his advice set aside by the community not once but twice in quick succession, Ezeulu reviews the situation, using the opportunity to reiterate the historical and ritual charter of his role as first among the leaders of the clan:

> In the very distant past, when lizards were still few and far between, the six villages-Umuachala, Umunneora. Umuagu. Umuezeani, Umuogwugwu and Umuisiuzo-lived as different people, and each worshipped its own deity. Then the hired soldiers of Abam used to strike in the dead of night, set fire to houses and carry men, women and children into slavery. Things were so bad for the six villages that their leaders came together to save themselves. They hired a strong team of medicine-men to install a common deity for them. This deity which the fathers of the six villages made was called Ulu. Half of the medicine was buried at a place which became the Nkwo market and the other half thrown into the stream which became Mili Ulu. The six villages then took the name of Umuaro, and the priest of Ulu became their Chief Priest. From that day they were never again beaten by an enemy (17–18).

But all that seems to have suddenly changed. When the story begins, the authority of the Chief Priest is under active attack from the Priest of Idemili who uses his kinsman, the wealthy, volatile and demagogic titled elder Nwaka of Umunneora. Idemili is one of the old gods relegated to subordinate status by the coming of Ulu. Its priest had never altogether forgotten this setback and had been in latent opposition to the priest of Ulu from time immemorial. Ezeulu himself is aware of this: "He knew that the priests of Idemili and Ogwugwu and Eru and Udo had never been happy with their secondary role since the villages got together and made Ulu and put him over the older deities" (49). But the resentment was played down as long as the threat to collective security continued, since group solidarity is necessary to meet external threat and since only a deity evolved in the spirit of collective solidarity could be an adequate unifying symbol to ensure this solidarity. The presence of the colonial administration has the effect of increasing the need for collective security, since the colonial authority has taken away from the traditional authority and peoples their right to exercise judicial or even non-legal violence. The exercise of judicial coercion and violence belongs solely to the colonial regime from now onwards, as the people of Umuaro are to learn when they wage war on the people of Okperi. But the worst forms of local insecurity such as those caused by the Abam slave-raiders are certainly over. It is not surprising that institutions evolved to ensure collective security begin to weaken when the threats which gave rise to them are no longer felt. And the effect of the superimposition of a higher authority with a greater power of coercive violence is to create a ferment in the structure of traditional authority itself. Specifically, the older gods of Umuaro accepted the dominance of Ulu as long as the old power structure remained. But now, with the imposition of a higher authority over Ulu, the minor gods see the situation as an opportunity to shake off an irksome hegemony. The resentment that lay dormant in pre-colonial days becomes active again. The speech in which Nwaka repudiates the right of Ulu to lead the clan expresses all this. The speech is made at a secret rally attended only by Nwaka's partisans:

> Nwaka began by telling the assembly that Umuaro must not allow itself to be led by the Chief Priest of Ulu. "My father did not tell me that before Umuaro went to war it took leave from the priest of Ulu," he said. "The man who carries a deity is not a king. He is there to perform its ritual and to carry sacrifice to it. But I have been watching this Ezeulu for many years. He is a man of ambition; he wants to be king, priest, diviner, all. His father, they said, was like that. But Umuaro showed Him that Igbo people knew no kings.
>
> "We have no quarrel with Ulu. He is still our protector, even though we no longer fear Abam warriors at night. But I will not see with these eyes of mine his priest making himself lord over us. My father told me many things, but he did not tell me that Ezeulu was king in Umuaro. Who is he, anyway? Does anybody here enter his compound through the man's gate? If Umuaro decided to have a king we know where he would come from. Since when did Umuachala become head of the six villages? We all know that it was jealousy among the big villages that made them give the priesthood to the weakest. We shall fight for our farmland and for the contempt Okperi has poured on us. Let us not listen to anyone trying to frighten us with the name of Ulu. If a man says yes to his chi also says yes. And we have all heard how the people of Aninta dealt with their deity when he failed them. Did they not carry him to the boundary between them and their neighbours and set fire on him?" (33).

This is a piece of dangerous demagogy, to be treated with reserve. For instance, it is difficult to credit the view that the Chief Priest whose deity leads the people to war and protects them from external and internal insecurities did not have a strong voice in determining war policy. After all, if he refused to perform the ritual functions of his priesthood, it is hard to **see** how his deity could be involved in action at all. The incitement against the authority of the Chief Priest is possible because the threat that made the founding of Ulu necessary has receded. Nwaka says as much. But traditional people are not so foolish as to base their institutions so narrowly. Indeed Ulu's power is not tied only to the provision of security. He is also the guardian of social well-being and keeper of the calendar. His priest keeps the agricultural calendar and calls the biggest feast of the year, the Feast of the New Yam which ushers in the harvest season. So his protection of security is not only religious, political, military and ethical, but also economic, and extends to such things as keeping the communal census. Nwaka's uncompromising attack is therefore a serious schismatic move indicative of the falling apart of the old collective ideology. His charge of ambition is exaggerated, though there is no doubt that Ezeulu's conception of his power is exorbitant. A peacetime Chief Priest has less scope for extending his power. Ezeulu is unaware of the limitation of his power and of the precise nature of his priesthood as the expression of corporate rather than personal will. This is shown in his own soliloquy:

> Whenever Ezeulu considered the immensity of his power over the year and the crops and, therefore, over the people he wondered if it was real. It was true he named the day for the feast of the Pumpkin Leaves and for the New Yam feast; but he did not choose the day. He was merely a watchman. His power was no more than the power of a child over a goat that was said to be his. As long as the goat was alive it was his; he would find it food and take care of it. But the day it was slaughtered he would know who the real owner was. No! the Chief Priest of Ulu was more than that, must be more than that. If he should refuse to name the day there would be no festival-no planting and no reaping. But could he refuse? No Chief Priest had ever refused. So it could not be done. He would not dare.
>
> Ezeulu was stung to anger by this as though his enemy had spoken it. "Take away that word dare," he replied to this enemy. "Yes I say take it away. No man in all Umuaro can stand up and say that I dare not. The woman who will bear the man who will say it has not yet been born" (3–4).

This is a dangerous speculation-as dangerous as Nwaka's demagogic incitement. Even though until he refuses to call the feast of the New Yam the Chief Priest acts within his ritual rights and authority, in his mind he has already begun to assume for himself vast illegal powers that justify Nwaka's accusation. His thought is to prove father to his subsequent act. Though no overt act of his justifies the accusation of ambition, he has within him undoubted authoritarian urges at odds with the republican outlook of the people. So Nwaka's accusation cannot be dismissed out of hand, but is borne in mind, and lights up the subsequent action. The authoritarian streak in the Chief Priest contributes to the final crisis when a greater flexibility and devotion to the common weal would have eased the situation. Nwaka's appeal to republican sentiment is an astute move, calculated to carry weight with an egalitarian people, as the people of Umuaro appear to be. But this egalitarianism is itself overplayed. "That Igbo people knew no kings" is only true as a figure of speech; some Igbo communities do have kings, and certainly they recognize certain specific roles which are defined in the social structure and they also recognize personal achievement (Jones 5).

In addition, there are prescribed roles pertaining to those successful members of different families who have taken titles (ozo and ndichie in the area of Igboland in which *Things Fall Apart* and *Arrow of God* are set) and who perform ritual functions in their family segments and have political and judicial roles in the clan. An elder who fails to take a title, like Unoka in *Things Fall Apart,* is an unfulfilled elder. It is fair to say that personal achievement is recognized in Igbo society within the framework of a hierarchy of titles, and a certain degree of ascription also obtains, since the process of title investiture takes place through elaborate ritual ceremonies which vest title-holders with semi-sacred attributes. Nwaka is aware of the mobile nature of the society, as well as its hierarchical features, but he chooses to emphasize the one and to ignore the other.

Nwaka and Ezeulu as types of character and temperament have always been a part of the traditional society. Since they differ so widely, they always repel each other and become a focus of intercommunal rivalry, factiousness and disagreement. But where the overall security of the community is paramount, personal rivalries and temperamental oppositions would not be allowed to undermine collective security. Nwaka would not be able to openly challenge the leadership of the Chief Priest in a matter of security in which his deity has a dominant influence. One finds confirming evidence for this in *Things Fall Apart* where we are told that Umuofia "never went to war unless its case was clear and just and was accepted as such by its Oracle-the Oracle of the Hills and the Caves. And there were indeed occasions when the Oracle had forbidden Umuofia to wage a war" (10). The oracle is the interpreter of the will of the earth goddess, the deity in charge of security. In *Arrow of God,* the god of security is Ulu, and his will is interpreted by the Chief Priest, who is thus in the position of the Oracle of the Hills and the Caves. The open attack on Ezeulu's authority, which would have been unthinkable in Okonkwo's Umuofia, becomes possible in Umuaro because under the combined pressure of the new colonial administration, the Christian church and the new economic forces, the oracles and the priests are beginning to lose their hold on the people. Nwaka's subversion of the Chief Priest's power succeeds because of the encroaching changes which are working towards a realignment of relationships and a readjustment of attitudes.

Ulu's dominance in the structure of a traditional power is itself a result of social change. It represents a certain centralizing trend somewhat at odds with the federalizing, segmentary political relationships of earlier times. The centralization has not been consolidated or it would have led to a priest-kingship such as that of Umunri in Igboland and probably like the obaship among the Yoruba. This lack of consolidation is exploited by Ezidemili. He is always harking back to the golden age of the people's history "in the days before Ulu" when "the true leaders of each village had been men of high title like Nwaka" (49). This near-enactment of the Cassius-Brutus-Caesar syndrome is interesting because it supports the point that a feeling of greater security is behind the attack on Ulu's authority; the "security" role of Ulu is completely left out of Ezidemili's tirade. His conspiracy could only work at a time of increased security. The presence of the colonial administration and the end of the trans-Atlantic slave trade explain this feeling. But it should not be forgotten that the colonial presence generated its own insecurities, since the "pacification" involved the use of force. But the new threat to security differs from the sudden, unpredictable predations of marauding slave raiders.

Achebe here departs from the narrative strategy of *Things Fall Apart*. In *Arrow of God*, he starts the narrative in medias res, dipping back from time to time into the past for the historical material with which he impregnates the narrative present. From these brief but significant flashes back into the past, we build up a picture of the pre-colonial society with which the colonial present is contrasted.

His treatment is full of ironies. For example, the Chief Priest who, as a symbolic head, should be the rallying point of resistance to the colonial authority is unwittingly an instrument for subversion of the traditional system. At Winterbottom's prompting, he sends his young son Oduche to join the Christian sect and attend the village school. Oduche is to become Ezeulu's "eye" in the new situation.

His reason is perfectly rational: one must change with the changing times. Several times this pragmatism finds outlet in a recurrent proverb: "A man must dance the dance prevalent in his time" and more poignantly in the extended metaphor of the elusive bird. "I am like the bird Eneke-nti-oba," he asserts. "When his friends asked him why he was always on the wing he replied: 'Men of today have learnt to shoot without missing and so I have learnt to fly without perching'" (55). In other words, the Chief Priest sees the strength of the new forces and is attempting in his own way to come to terms with them. With Oduche as a look-out in the enemy camp, the Chief Priest feels more secure. The rest of the story shows how this feeling proves illusory and the Chief Priest is smashed by the forces he had imagined to be under his control.

Oduche, the sacrificial offering to the new forces, precipitates the first of Ezeulu's crises. He becomes a Christian diehard, tries to suffocate a royal python, the totemic animal sacred to Idemili, and is found out. This heightens the ill-will between the priest of Idemili and Ezeulu, their families, villages and partisans in the clan. Ezeulu's enemies cite the incident as proof of his ambition to destroy every other source of authority in the clan in order to promote his own. It is argued also that his sending his son to school is part of his strategy for reinforcing his personal power by ingratiating himself with the British administration. Earlier, the good opinion of the white District Commissioner, won by testifying against the clan in the land dispute with Okperi, had been chalked up by his enemies as Ezeulu's first open act of betrayal, and proof of his ambition. His son's sacrilege five years later revives the memory and bitterness of that betrayal. Taken together, the two events look like an attempt by the Chief Priest to reach a personal accommodation with the forces threatening the old social order. And this renders his motives suspicious and dishonourable to his enemies and disturbing to his friends. Even his best friend and kinsman, Akuebue, finds it hard to reconcile the Chief Priest's traditional role as protector of communal tradition with his implied attack on this heritage by sending his son to join the Christians. He expresses his doubts:

> When you spoke against the war with Okperi you were not alone. I too was against it and so were many others. But if you send your son to join strangers in desecrating the land you will be alone. You may go and mark it on that wall to remind you that I said so (166).

But the shattering blow is yet to fall. Captain Winterbottom, having received a directive to introduce Indirect Rule in his area of authority, decides to make Ezeulu a warrant chief for the Umuaro district. But the choice could not have been made at a less auspicious time than when the Chief Priest is taunted by his enemies as the creature of the British administration. Ezeulu at first refuses to leave his home immediately to go to Okperi as ordered by the white man. Instead, he summons an assembly of the leaders for advice and support. Nwaka and his partisans see this as an opportunity to accuse the Chief Priest openly of his deals with the white man. Nwaka makes a long speech full of taunts and innuendoes implying that Ezeulu should be cast out to face the music alone. His gibes are skilfully reinforced with his usual rhetoric and proverbs:

> The white man is Ezeulu's friend and has sent for him. What is so strange about that? He did not send for me. He did not send for Udeozo; he did not send for the priest of Idemili; he did not send for the priest of Eru; he did not send for the priest of Udo nor did he ask the priest of Ogwugwu to come and see him. He has asked Ezeulu. Why? Because they are friends. Or does Ezeulu think that their friendship should stop short of entering each other's houses? Does he

> want the white man to be his friend only by word of mouth? Did not our elders tell us that as soon as we shake hands with a leper he will want an embrace? It seems to me that Ezeulu has shaken hands with a man of white body (177).

The pun on "white man" and "leper" is Nwaka's indirect indictment of the Chief Priest and is calculated to wound most deeply. Ezeulu abandons the effort to mobilize support within his clan and sallies out to face his fate single-handed. His isolation is complete at a time when collective solidarity is a man's greatest strength. Totally embittered, he is in an uncompromising mood which is made no better by his being detained for not answering the summons promptly enough. Tony Clarke has taken over from Winterbottom, who has been suddenly taken ill, and finds the priest intransigent and baffling. Where he expects gratitude for the imperial favour of being raised to a paramount chief, he is confronted with haughty rejection. After two months, Ezeulu is released from detention to go back, still embittered against those who cast him out. The rest is a quick plunge into the molten centre of disaster. His two month's detention upset the agricultural calendar because he could not eat his ritual yams while in detention. He refuses to call the Feast of the New Yam until he has eaten all the remaining yams. The delay in harvesting the yams begins to hurt the people and threaten famine. Desperate and confounded, the people turn to the Christian religion for salvation.

They send their sons with yam offerings to the Christian harvest festival and thereafter harvest their crops in the name of these sons. A tailpiece to the drama is provided by the sudden death of Obika, Ezeulu's favourite son. The Chief Priest goes mad and the people draw their own moral from his tragedy: "To them the issue was simple. Their god had taken sides with them against his headstrong and ambitious priest and thus upheld the wisdom of their ancestors-that no man however great was greater than his people; that no man ever won judgement against his clan" (287). But the people of Umuaro do not have the last word. This belongs to the novelist who sees the story in its total historical and cultural context:

> If this was so [he argues] then Ulu had chosen a dangerous time to uphold this wisdom. In destroying his priest he had also brought disaster on himself, like the lizard in the fable who ruined his mother's funeral by his own hand. For a deity who chose a time such as this to destroy his priest or abandon him to his enemies was inciting people to take liberties; and Umuaro was just ripe to do so (287).

The mass defection to the Christians which follows must be seen as the result of the failure of the old dispensation to provide security, and the availability of an alternative source of security.

The historical basis of the story is well known. It was one of the major setbacks to the British colonial administration in Nigeria. The attempt to set up warrant chiefs in the predominantly republican Igboland came to grief in the late 1920s, and led to widespread turmoil and rioting by women, since known as the Igbo Women's Riot (1927). The failure of the experiment in Indirect Rule is recorded by, Dr P.C. Lloyd in *Africa and Social Change.* He writes:

> In attempts to "find a chief", men were often selected whose traditional roles had little to do with political authority. They were ritual experts or merely presided over councils of elders with equal status, Indeed the introduction of Indirect Rule on the Northern Nigerian pattern to the Ibo peoples and their similarly organized neighbours of Eastern Nigeria proved impossible. From the beginning of the century, administrative officers had created "warrant chiefs"-men who often had no traditional authority but who seemed powerful enough to act as British agents in recruiting labour. Then when direct taxation was introduced in 1927, widespread rioting, led by Ibo women, disclosed the extent of hostility to these warrant chiefs. In the 1930s, therefore, councils were instituted which were based upon traditional political units and their representation (65–66).

A good deal of the historical outline survives in *Arrow of God,* but Achebe's handling of the subject exposes the human realities, the dilemmas facing men and women who are caught up in the historical drama. He draws out of history the human dimension; by concentrating on the Chief Priest, a fully realized individual character, he brings the action out of the area of public gestures and abstract formulations to that of the emotions and attitudes of living people.

In *Arrow of God,* the cracks which had tragically developed in the traditional system in *Things Fall Apart* grow into chasms. But a good deal of the action is concerned with the attempt by the chief character to build a bridge over the widening chasm. Ezeulu fails because his grasp of the situation is inadequate and so he is constantly surprised.

Works Cited

Achebe, Chinua. *Arrow of God*. London: Heinemann, 1964. Subsequent references are from this edition and included in the text.

———. *Things Fall Apart*. London: Heinemann, 1958.

Jones, G.I. *The Trading States of the Oil Rivers*. London: Oxford University Press for the International African Institute, 1963.

Lloyd, P.C. *Africa and Social Change*. Harmonsworth: Penguin, 1972.

Part Four:

Critical Perspectives on A Man of the People

Chapter 21

Achebe's African Parable

Bernth Lindfors

CHINUA ACHEBE'S NOVEL, *A Man of the People*, details the rise and demise of Chief the Honorable Dr. M.A. Nanga, M.P., LLD, a corrupt, wheeling-dealing, opportunistic semi-literate who elbows his way to a lucrative ministerial post in the Government of an unnamed independent African country, uses his power and newly-acquired wealth to ensure his re-election, and is shaken from his lofty, befouled perch only when a group of idealistic young military officers topples the "fatdripping gummy, eat-and-let-eat regime" by launching a sudden *coup d'etat.* The novel published just nine days after the first military coup in Nigeria, has been hailed by many reviewers as a "prophetic" work, one in which Achebe predicted with uncanny accuracy the end of his country's First Republic.

Certainly the accuracy of Achebe's vision cannot be disputed. It was a rather eerie experience to read the last chapter of this novel in the early months of 1966 when Achebe's descriptions of fictional events seemed to correspond so closely to newspaper accounts of what was happening in Nigeria. For example, the coup was said to have been touched off by post-election turmoil:

> What happened was simply that unruly mobs and primate armies having tasted blood and power during the election had got out of hand and ruined their masters and employers (162).

> The rampaging bands of election thugs had caused so much unrest dislocation that our young Army officers seized the opportunity to take over (165).

The aftermath of the fictional coup corresponded with reality too.

> ...the military regime had just abolished oil political parties in the country and announced they would remain abolished until the situation became stabilized once again. They had at the same time announced the impending trial of all public servants who had enriched themselves by defrauding the State. The figure involved was said to be in the order of fifteen million pounds (165–6). Overnight everyone began to shake their heads at the excesses of the lost regime, at its graft, oppression and corrupt government: newspapers, the radio, the hitherto silent intellectuals and civil servants – everybody said what a terrible lot; and it became public opinion the next morning (166).

It was passages such as these that made Achebe appear a seer.

Yet I would like to argue that despite these seemingly clairvoyant passages, *A Man of the People* is not and was not meant to be a prophetic novel. Indeed, given the circumstances in Nigeria during the time Achebe was writing, *A Man of the People* should be recognized as a devastating satire in which Achebe heaped scorn on independent Africa by picturing one part of it just as it was. I believe Achebe ended the novel with a military coup in order to enlarge the picture to include Nigeria's neighbors, many of which had experienced coups. By universalizing the story in this way, Achebe could suggest to his countrymen that what had happened in other unstable independent African countries might easily have happened in Nigeria too. The coup was meant as an African parable, not a Nigerian prophecy.

The manuscript of *A Man of the People* was submitted to Achebe's publisher in February, 1965 (Smith's Letter) and the book was published in London eleven months later on January 24, 1966. Achebe's third novel, *Arrow of God*, was submitted to his publisher in February, 1963 and had been published March 3, 1964. Since it is unlikely that Achebe began *A Man of the People* until he had completed *Arrow of God*, it is probably safe to assume that *A Man of the People* was written sometime between February, 1963 and February, 1965. There is good evidence that he was at work on the novel early in 1964 (The Role of the Writer 158). During this period he was also working as Director of External Broadcasting for the Nigerian Broadcasting Company, a job that would have kept him abreast of the latest news.

Politics dominated the news in Nigeria at this time. By February, 1963 the seven-month state of emergency in the Western Region had ended, and Chief Obafemi Awolowo and twenty-nine others had been arrested and charged with conspiring to overthrow the Federal Government by force. In September, 1963, Awolowo and nineteen others were convicted of treasonable felony and imprisoned. On October 1, 1963 Nigeria became a Federal Republic. Then, because of the doubtful accuracy of the official results of the 1962 census, which were never publicly released, a new census was taken in November, 1963. Since regional representation in the Federal Government was to be determined by the results of this census, politicians were eager that every one of their constituents be counted at least once. When the bloated preliminary results of the census were released in February, 1964, they were rejected by the Eastern and Midwestern Regions and protest demonstrations were held. On March 25, 1964, an editorial in the Lagos *Daily Times* warned that "The Federal Republic of Nigeria faces the grave danger of disintegration' because of the census crisis.

Worse times were yet to come. A Federal Election was due before the year was out, and political campaigning gradually grew more and more vicious. One observer reports "countless acts of political violence and thuggery occurred almost daily throughout the campaign, but notably increased durinq the last few weeks." (Harris 27). Electioneering irregularities were so frequent and widespread that one of the major political parties, the United Progressive Grand Alliance, announced that it would boycott the elections. This precipitated another crisis, for President Nnamdi Azikiwe, judging the election invalid, refused to call upon victorious Prime Minister Abubakar Tafawa Balewa to form a new government. For five days the country teetered on the brink of political chaos. On January 4, 1965, Azikiwe and Balewa finally reached a compromise and Azikiwe announced to the country that Balewa would form a broadly-based national government." By-elections were to be held in constituencies where elections bad been totally boycotted, and allegations of fraud and intimidation were to be reviewed by the courts.

It should be remembered that Achebe's publisher received the manuscript of *A Man of the People* one month after this period of crisis and compromise. Achebe must have been working on the last chapters of the novel, which dramatize the turbulence and violence of an election campaign, during the months just preceding the Nigerian election. He was obviously drawing much of his inspiration from daily news reports. The last pages of the novel, those which describe the coup, must have been written very close to the time of the five-day crisis following the election. What relevance this has to my argument I shall attempt to demonstrate in a moment.

First, however, let us look at the role of the Nigerian military forces before, during and immediately after the 1964 election campaign. Before the campaign, they were used to restore civil order both at home and abroad. In December, 1960 Nigerian troops had been sent to the newly-independent Republic of the Congo (Leopoldville) to help United Nations forces keep order, and in April, 1964 were dispatched to Tanganyika to relieve British troops who had put down a Tanganylka Army mutiny. In Nigeria, Army troops had quelled a Tiv riot in 1960 and had maintained order in the Western Region during the 1962 state of emergency. During the 1964 election campaign they were ordered to put down another Tiv riot and did so at the cost of 700 lives (Dudley 22). Throughout the campaign, large squads of riot police were deployed to battle the thugs and hooligans hired by political candidates to terrorize their opposition. During the post-election crisis, troops were called out to safeguard the residences of Azikiwe and Balewa in Lagos and the cell of Awolowo in Calabar. Thus, before, during and after the 1964 election campaign the Nigerian Army played a prominent role as a peace-keeping force in Nigeria and abroad.

During the same period, armies in many other African countries had acted as a disruptive force. In 1963 there were military coups in Togo, Congo-Brazzaville and Dahomey, and a military plot to assassinate President Tubman was uncovered in Liberia. In 1964 there were army mutinies in Tanganyika, Uganda and Kenya, a revolution in Zanzibar, attempted coups in Gabon and Niger, and continued confusion and disorder in Congo-Leopoldville. On February 21, 1964 an editorial in the Lagos *Daily Times* deplored the use of bullets instead of ballots in French West Africa, and four days later the same paper remarked that "The constant cataclysms which have recently disrupted peace and order in Africa have produced a dangerous trend towards replacing the growing pattern of parliamentary rule with military juntas." Notice that at this time the trend toward military coups was regarded as "dangerous."

By the end of the year the mood of the country had changed considerably. The electioneering abuses, the breakdown of law and order, the numerous crises and compromises had produced a general distrust of politicians and disillusionment with democratic processes of government. In a nationwide broadcast on December 10, 1964, President Azikiwe himself predicted the end of democracy in Nigeria:

> ... I have one advice to give to our politicians; if they have decided to destroy our notional unity, then they should summon a round-table conference to decide how our national assets should be divided, before they seal their doom by satisfying their lust for office... Should politicians fail to heed this warning, then I will venture a prediction that the experiences of the Democratic Republic of the Congo (Leopoldville) will be child's play if it ever comes to our turn to play such a tragic role (Speech of 1964 3).

After the elections Azikiwe lamented that

> People in this country now evince a mood of weariness and frustration that is a sad contrast to the elation and confidence with which we ushered in independence barely four years ago. Far from presenting a united front our country now shows a pattern of disintegration (Speech of 1965 4).

The people themselves expressed their discontent with politicians in no uncertain terms. During the election crisis, Lazarus Okeke wrote a letter to the Lagos *Daily Express* asserting that ...no well-wisher of Nigeria would recommend a blow-up of the country just because certain politicians cannot have their demand (sic) met. The welfare of the people as a nation definitely supercedes (sic) in importance the various vain and sectional claims of erring politicians (4).

An unsigned article in the Lagos Sunday Express of January 3, 1965, went a step further:

> Democracy has bred corruption in our society on a scale hitherto unknown in human history. Nigeria needs a strong man with a strong hand. By this I mean, that Nigeria needs to be disciplined. Nigeria needs to be drilled. The leadership we want is the leadership of a benevolent dictator who gets things done; not that of democratic administrators' who drag their feet.

It is clear that a number of Nigerians would have welcomed a military coup in January, 1965. Indeed, several days after Azikiwe and Balewa had worked out their compromise, one disgruntled Easterner writing in Enugu's *Nigerian Outlook* expressed regret that the compromise had not been forestalled by military intervention:

> If civil strife had broken out on December 30,the armed forces might have gone into action as a last resort, and the President and the Prime Minister might never have had an opportunity for negotiations (3).

If further evidence is required to prove that many Nigerians had entertained the notion of a military coup during the election crisis, one need only turn to the Lagos *Sunday Times* of February 28, 1965 and read the text of an interview with Major General Aguiyi-Ironsi who on February 15th of that year had been appointed the first Nigerian Commander of the Nigerian Army". It is perhaps significant and – considering what happened in January, 1960 – certainly ironic that during the election crisis Ironsi led the troops that guarded Prime Minister Balewa's home. The interviewer tried to draw out Ironsi's views on the desirability of military intervention in State affairs in times of political turmoil, but Ironsi carefully side-stepped the questions.

> Q: Had you been the Officer Commanding the Nigerian Army during the constitutional crisis resulting from the Federal elections last December, what would you have done?
>
> Ironsi: You mean, military or what?
>
> Q: Both military or otherwise.
>
> Ironsi: I think what we should get clear is that the crisis was a political crisis. It did not require military action. It was a political thing, solved in a political way.
>
> Q: Tell me, if there's war, would you fight out of conviction or would you carry out the orders of the government regardless as to which side is right or wrong?
>
> Ironsi: I think it is true to say that any Army goes to war for justification... The job of the Army is to defend the country, no questions asked.
>
> Q: Now, suppose it's on internal war...

Ironsi: I don't know what you are trying to get at. Whatever you might have in mind, The army supports the government that is!
Q: If you were General Mobutu, how would you effect a solution [to the Congo impasse]?
Ironsi: I'm not. I should wait till I'm, confronted with such a situation.

That such questions could be asked and such cautious answers given eight weeks after the crisis suggests that the idea of a military resolution to Nigeria's political problems had occurred to many Nigerians other than Achebe and that it was still quite a live issue.

Seen in this light, Achebe's "prophecy" appears much less prophetic. He had only foreseen what many others, including President Azikiwe, had foreseen or had hoped to see. A military coup was not necessarily inevitable" in 1964–5 but it was regarded by a number of intelligent observers (Dudley 33) as one of the few options left for a nation on the brink of anarchy. In a recent interview Achebe put it this way:

> ...things had got to such a point politically that there was no other answer, no way you could resolve this impasse politically. The political machine had been so abused that whichever way you pressed it, it produced the some results; and therefore another force had to come in. Now when I was writing *A Man of the People*, it wasn't clear to me that this was going to be necessarily military intervention It could easily have been civil war, which in fact It very nearly was. Nigeria (Interview on Cultural Events ii).

Achebe chose military coup as the most appropriate ending for his story, and eleven months later Nigeria happened to make the same choice to close one of the ugliest chapters in its history.

To interpret the military coup in *A Man of the People* as a prophecy is to suggest that Achebe meant the novel to relate only to Nigeria. This, 1 think, is a mistake, While it is evident that the novel owes much to what Achebe had observed in his own country many of the events described had happened and were happening in other independent African countries. By ending with a coup, an event anticipated yet still unknown in Nigeria but familiar elsewhere in Africa, Achebe added a dimension of universality to his stow. It was no longer merely a satire on Nigeria but a satire on the rest of independent Africa as well. If the coup had a special meaning for Nigeria in the mid-sixties, it also contained a relevant moral for other emerging African nations, wracked (embroiled in) by internal upheavals. The ending was meant to be true to Africa and not merely truthful about Nigeria. The coup was an African parable not a Nigerian prophecy.

One of the most remarkable features of Chinua Achebe's fiction is that it never fails to transcend the local and particular and enter realms of universal significance. Achebe once said:

> ...After all, the novelist's duty is not to beat this morning's headline in topicality, it s to exp/ore in depth the human condition. In Africa he cannot perform this task unless he has a proper sense of history (The Role of the Writer 157).

The ending of *A Man of the People* reveals that Achebe has a proper sense of contemporary African history.

Works Cited

Achebe, Chinua. *A Man of the People*. London: Heinemannn, 1966. All refernces are made from this edition.
———. "The Role of the Writer in a New Nation." In *Nigeria*. 81. June 1964.
———. Interview on Cultural Events. In *Africa*. 18. March 1967.
———. Speech in *Nigerian Outlook*. January 16, 1965.
Azikiwe, Nnamdi. Speeches in *Nigerian Outlook*. December 10, 1964, and January 4, 1965.
Dudley, Billy. "Violence in Nigerian Politics." In *Transtion* 5, 21. April 1965.
Harris, Richard. "Nigeria: Crisis and Compromise." In *Africa Report*. 10, 2. March 1965.
Letter from W. Roger Smith of William Heinemann Ltd. London.
Okeke, Lazurus' Letter in the Lagos *Daily Express*. January 1, 1965.

Chapter 22

Morality and the Folktale: Political Symbolism in Achebe's *A Man of the People*

Emma Ngumoha

The stomach seems to be
A powerful force
For joining political parties
Especially when the purse
In the trouser pocket
Carries only the coins
With holes in their middle,
And no purple notes
Have ever been folded in it. – Okot p'Bitek

LIVING AS WE DID, through the tumultuous days of the twentieth century, numerous forces affect our moral and religious existence as human beings. A serious reader of a work of art cannot but turn to a literary imaginative work conceived as a moral allegory which teaches a lesson, the quality of which must conform or derive from right ideals of human conduct. In this regard, one can say that a moral reflection was behind the beginning of thought, feeling or perception which shaped the fictional composition of Achebe's *A Man of the People*.

The conflict between good ethical standards of life, and evil conducts that debase man has always been a common theme found in all the great literatures of the world, from the Greeks to the twentieth century. That literature must deal with moral and philosophical ends is indubitable; it cannot afford to ignore the problem of good and evil; it must edify by elevating itself to moral functions; it must strive to make the world a better place if it can. In the smithy of serious literature we are forged, and the base metals in our lives are transmuted into finer ones. Out of the smithy do we emerge like gold, shining forth in moral rectitude, and thus do we become refined, poised and balanced beings. Hence, Horace's conception of the function of literature as 'to teach and delight' (*dulce et utile*), and 'to speak the truth laughing' (*Ridentem dicere verum*). To Samuel Johnson, the end of writing is to instruct, the end of poetry is to instruct by pleasing" 2109) and "the greatest graces of a play are to copy nature and instruct life" (2114).

The idea of literature as a criticism of life is not new. Just as Horace's main concern was with the usefulness as well as the entertaining function of art, Plato's pre-occupation was with the education and edification of the guardians. Plato's position hinges on the moral effect of the artist in his ideal Republic. The poets (especially Homer) show the gods as committing adultery, getting drunk, promoting their favorites and engaging in other frivolities. By creating such images of the gods they give the young ones the wrong impression because "the Athenian child took his notions of the gods chiefly from Homer and Hestod, who, as Xenophanes more than a century earlier had complained, attributed to them every sort of immorality" (67). Plato then banished the poets from his Republic because their portrayal of the gods in these morally frivolous stances was untenable. It tended to corrupt the youth. The kind of literature that we read affects our general outlook in life. Good literature uplifts the human soul and makes man rise above the sordid business of just living. That which man reads is what he thinks, and that which he thinks is what he is. If he reads and thinks about beauty, then beauty unfolds to him; if he thinks evil, then he is evil. The light of imagination acts in that place to which it is directed. A reading of an exalted imaginative composition born out of a desire for that which is good and beautiful raises man up, whereas a reading of a low imaginative written work caused by a desire for that which is low and vulgar drags him down and degrades him. T.S. Eliot draws our attention to this fact when he asserts that

> The author of a work of imagination
> is trying to affect us, wholly,
> as human beings, whether he knows it
> or not; and we are affected by it,
> as human beings, whether we tend
> to be or not (48).

That literature can be highly enchanting, captivating and affective is also recognised by P.B. Shelley. This stems from the fact that when a poet sings, "his auditors are as men entranced by the melody of unseen musicians who feel that they are moved and softened, yet know not whence or why" (749). This then calls for control in selection of what we read. The emphasis should be on works that elevate man's reason. Since he is prone to animalistic urges and egocentric tendencies, he must select those works of art that teach about life while they entertain.

In the treatment of its subject matter, a novel, a poem, or drama comments obliquely on a moral issue or expounds a philosophy of life. This silent comment of the ideal is what benefits the man of reason, andmakes him cultivate high ethical standards. He thus becomes an embodiment of order, restraint, and discipline. Nnolim's views below invite attention:

> Literature teaches us about life while it entertains. Every short story, every novel, every poem, every drama worth its salt as a work of art, has a thing or two to say about life, has a moral view of life that it enunciates, has a philosophy of life that it imparts. A study of various works of literature is, in fact a study of various philosophies of life, for every author implants a little stamp of his philosophy of life in his story, poem, novel, drama ("Literature and the Individual Welfare" 23).

The moral approach to literature is basically relevant to the African experience, especially in the post-independence era when embezzlement of Government funds and moral insensibility are rife in the body politic of Africans; it is an era when materialism dethrones spirituality, when mediocrity reigns as excellence, and politicians wallow in the miasma of rank corruption.

Any study of the African aesthetic in literature, therefore, must recognize the fact that the well-spring of African writers' creative force in literature arose from one inherent, though isolated premise: to expose the enemy the colonialist masters – from without (see Achebe's *Things Fall Apart*, Oyono's Un vie do Boy, Ngug's novels). This premise has since moved forward to subsume another unstated premise (a very healthy growth): to expose the enemy from within (see Achebe's *A Man of the People* and Armah's *The Beautyful Ones Are Not Yet Born*) (*Nnolim*, "Prolegomenon", 65). It is from this standpoint and position that we shall base our discussion of Achebe's *A Man of the People* – "to expose the enemy from within" and discuss the moral and philosophical issues involved in the enemy's actions.

The story centers around the political exploits of Chief the Honorable M.A. Nanga M.P. whose hypocritical motto "do the right and shame the devil" could best be read as "do the wrong and sugar the devil". Achebe corroborates this fact when he writes that "he had that rare gift of making people feel – even while he was saying harsh things to them – that there was not a drop of ill will in his entire frame" (73). In this novel, Achebe shows direct commitment and communicates contemporary mood. It is a good portrayal of the corruption, economic mismanagement, enthroned nepotism, sectional interests and electoral vices that were rife after the attainment of independence in most African states. Achebes *A Man of the People* takes root from the fertile socio-political soil which nurtured its creation. Here is a bitter satirical work which shows what Africans (especially Nigerians) make of their countries many years after the attainment of self government. It has as its butt the political hypocrisy of the new governing class as is exemplified in Chief Nanga. Nigerian politics after independence bred semi-literate mediocre ministers, the "ash-mouthed paupers" who later became millionaires, ministers, "bloated by the flatulence of ill – gotten wealth, living in big mansions built with public money" (85). Corruption at the level of individual politicians is an issue on which many African writers have dwelt. A significant trait of the Nigerian politician is greed for power – power which is ironic in its temporary and transient nature, Political power is used as an oppressive mechanism and the people are its victims. The powerful man controls the finances of the nation and stuffs himself with food and wine; the masses suffer starvation and wallow in abject penury. Wielding his power, Nanga steals Odili's mistress. Absolute corrupt political power makes Edna's father tell Odili:

> My in-law is like a bull and your challenge is like the challenge of a tick to a bull. The tick fills its belly with blood from the back of the bull, and the bull doesn't even know it's there. He carries it wherever he goes – to eat, to drink or pass ordure. Then one day the cattle egret comes, perches on the bull's back and picks out the tick... (119).

Odili's disillusionment centers on the corrupting power of privilege and affluence. He is an idealistic young university graduate whose idealism is born of a desire to create a good political awareness. The promotion of the common good becomes his prime motivation. In Killam's view, "Odili initially from motives of revenge, but principally because of political idealism which re-asserts itself, joins a new and rival political party founded by a barrister friend" (89). Odili's position is that of an idealistic and ardent patriot who joins the new party because "Max and some of his friends having watched with deepening disillusion the use to which our hard-won freedom was being put by corrupt, mediocre politicians had decided to come together and launch the Common People's Convention" (87).

Odili, who was once a guest at Chief Nanga's house in the capital city Bori, was exposed to the moral depravity of senior members of government. His affiliation with the C.P.C. brings him to direct confrontation with Nanga. The relationship is made the worse when Odili decided to contest the seat held by Nanga under the platform of the C.P.C.:

> He has little chance of beating Nanga even though the latter fears what Odili represents – the young educated Nigerian whose actions are disinterested in

> the political sense that he and his peers seek to restitute a constitution whose prerogatives and guarantees have become vestigial (*Killam* 90).

Nanga fears the intellectuals, distrusts "our young university people" – a typical inferiority complex of the *nouveau riche*. Odili is offered a bribe to make him drop from the race, but he is scrupulous in this respect and is firm in his convictions. The refusal of the bribe makes Nanga realize that he has a stout opponent in Odili. That is why Odili becomes greatly grieved when he learns that Max accepted a large sum of money as bribe from Chief Koko. Hear him:

> Max's action had jeopardized our moral position, our ability to inspire that kind of terror which I had seen so clearly in Nanga's eyes despite all his grandiloquent bluff, and which in the end was our society's only hope of salvation (144).

To Odili, it is disheartening to know that Max's unguarded idealism is shown the snares of the corrupter (Chief Koko), and taught to distrust his political convictions. Max refuses to step down for Chief Koko, and uses the bribe money to sponsor his own campaign. What follows then is the bizarre spectacle of electioneering campaigns, intolerance, thuggery, brutality, reckless carnage and all manners of election vices.

At the People's Organisation Party (P.O.P.) political rally, Odili is subjugated, battered and made an object of ridicule. His car is burnt, and he is hospitalized. Max is killed by Chief Koko's thugs. In the midst of this political bigotry and anarchy, the character of Odili's father stands out unique.

> The character of Odili's father is presented as a type and an individual, one who embodies suggestions so typical of the generality of Nigerians of his generation, yet capable of noble and independent action (*Killam* 90).

As chairman of the local P.O.P. in Urua village, one would think that he would object to the C.P.C. rally in his premises

> but, He took the view (without expressing it in so many words) that the mainspring of political action Was personal gain, a view which, I might say, was much more in line with the general feeling in the country than the high-minded thinking of fellows like Max and I (128).

To Chief Samalu, squabbles are unnecessary in politics; bitterness should be eschewed; it best is a matter of live – and let – live, Of the C.P.C. rally in his compound he says: "What has my being in the P.O.P. got to do with it? I believe that the hawk should perch and the eagle perch, whichever says to the other 'don't', may its own wing break" (138). Because he received Max and other members of the C.P.C. in his compound, he is stripped of his post as chairman of the Urua village P.O.P. When he hears the news, his calm retort is "Their own palaver is not mine". Chief Samalu's philosophy of life thus epitomizes balance, tolerance and sanity which should guide any political setting. Max recognizes this fact as he tells Odili: "Your old man is a wonderful fellow. I like him" (142). Furthermore, Chief Samalu's tax levy is re-assessed, and increased; he is arrested and beaten up. Yet he remains calm and bears all with stoic fortitude. As Hamlet tells Horatio in *Hamlet* Chief Samalu is:

> As one in suff'ring all suffers nothing
> A man that fortune's buffets and rewards
> Has ta'en with equal thanks...

Chief Samalu's nobility of character is further stressed when he refuses to sign a certain document:

> When I came back with my papers the next day I was told that Councillor "Couple" had come to see my father with a promise that if he signed a certain document his recent tax levy would be refunded him. The document merely sought to dissociate him from his son's lunatic activities; it also said that the so-called launching of C.P.C. in his premises was done without his knowledge and consent and concluded by affirming his implicit confidence in our great and God-fearing leader, Chief Nanga (152).
>
> On why he refused to sign the document, Chief Samalu tells his son that "a man of worth never gets up to unsay what he said yesterday. I received your friends in my house and I am not going to deny it" (152).

The politicians are "men of worth" who "unsay what they said yesterday". They are "men of worth" who encourage arson, vandalism, brutality, and reckless bloodshed and human carnage. Politics has been represented in its various facets with an eye only to some of its characteristic evils and the consequences of its defects. Thus we are not treated to any glorious or romantic vision of an integrated or stable situation, but one harangued with a vision of reality which consists of nothing but ugliness and distrust, in various shades of corruption, crisis and hatred (Egudu 83–84).

In the folktale of the hunter and the vultures (140), Achebe sums up the moral issues in *A Man of the People*. The hunter killed a big game at night and searched in vain for it. At dawn, he returned to the forest, and found, much to his chagrin, two vultures having a sumptuous meal of what remained of the big game. Great anger gnawed at his heart as he saw the cursed creatures in a "eat-and-let-eat" feast, tucking away into their hateful guts the "fat dripping gummy" carcass of the big game. Max in narrating this tale likens the two vultures to the two dominant political parties – the P.O.P. and the P.A.P. The big game is the wealth of the federal government – the "national cake" which belongs to the hunter – the people. Obviously the vultures "had taken away enough for the owner to notice... and the owner, is the will of the people". The hunter's gun which belched fire can be likened to the detonation of the people's collective will. We can also hear the echoes of two pistol shots fired by Eunice, and finally the thundering sounds of armored tanks as the soldiers roll in. The vultures lay dead; Chief Koko is gunned down by Eunice; the corrupt government is toppled, and the heartless wastrels are rounded up. Nanga is arrested while "trying to escape in a canoe dressed like a fisherman".

These unhappy experiences of the post-independence politics in Nigeria constitute a creative milieu on which Achebe comments. Nnolim also discusses the moral issues involved:

> Wanton destruction of life and property are moral issues; unfair election practices and bribery and corruption are moral issues dwelt on by our novelists. The Nigerian novelist, therefore, is not a helpless on-looker but a courageous fighter against the moral decadence in our society. Achebe and Soyinka tackle these problems by making satiric thrusts at the ills of our society ("Moral Values" 7).

Achebe in *A Man of the People* presents a pessimistic picture of the unenviable predicament of the Nigerian politicians of the first republic who fell from power to imprisonment and even death. That moral depravity and fraudulent political behavior do not pay is hinted in the novel. Achebe sets a moral value and teaches that man is responsible for his actions. Part of this value in *A Man of the People* is realized in the paradigmatic parable of the hunter and the big game.

In Achebe, judgment is not suspended. It is tempered and chastened according to the facts under which the crimes are committed. In life's journey, we must balance on the scales of judgment as we go. "And of all the art forms, the novel most of all demands the trembling and oscillating of the balance. The 'sweet' novel is more falsified, and therefore more immoral than the blood-and-thunder novel" (Lawrence 129).

Works Cited

Achebe, Chinua. *A Man of the People*. London: Heinemann, 1966.

Egudu, Romanus. *Modern African Poetry and The African Predicament*. London: Macmillan, 1978.

Eliot, T.S. "Religion and Literature". *Five Approaches to Literary Criticism*. Wilbur S. Scott. New York: Collier Books 1962.

Johnson, Samuel. "The Preface to Shakespeare". *The Oxford Anthology of English Literature*. Eds. Frank Kermode and John Hollander. 2 vols. New York: CUP, 1973, 2107–2114.

Killam, G.D. *The Writings of Chinua Achebe*. London: Heinemann, 1969.

Lawrence, D.H. "Morality and the Novel". *20th century Literary Criticism*. Ed. David Lodge. London: Longman, 1972.

Nnolim, Charles. African Literary Aesthetic: A Prolegomenon". Ba Shiru 7.2 (1976): 56–74.

———. 'Literature and the Individual Welfare". *The Thinker*. 1 (1983).

———. "Moral Values in the Nigerian Novel". Paper presented at the Conference of Professors' World Peace Academy. Lagos Nigeria. (1985).

Plato. *The Republic*. Trans. F.M. Cornford. London: OUP, 1975.

Shelley, P.B. "A Defence of Poetry". *The Oxford Anthology of English Literature*. Eds. Frank Kermode and Jobn Flollander 2 vols. New York: OUP, 1973, 746–762.

Chapter 23

A Man of the People: A Serious Indictment of Post-Independence Africa

Sunday Osim Etim

A *MAN OF THE PEOPLE* can best be understood in the light of Achebe's pronouncement in 1967 in an interview with Tony Hall that:

> *A Man of the People* wasn't a flash in the pan; this is the beginning of a phase for me in which I intend to take a hard look at what we in Africa are making of independence (23).

In this light therefore, *A Man of the People* is best described as a "serious indictment of post-independence Africa". Indeed, it superfluously reflects Achebe's intense disillusionment with the way things had gone and a general sense of despair at the mess that had been made of self-rule.

Thematically, Achebe is essentially concerned with corruption and greed in high pieces. The sub-themes include disillusionment, betrayal, twisted love, political violence, thuggery, intolerance of opposition, materialism, among others.

Greed in High Places

Greed is the unscrupulous, uncontrollable desire to accumulate more and more wealth. This trait can be seen not only in the politicians, but also in the intelligentsia and the mass of the people. Obviously, the main spring of political action is personal gain:

> You chop, meself I chop, palaver finish... (167).

To put it differently nothing is done if some gain or benefit cannot be derived from it. For example, when Chief Nanga becomes very concerned about the completion of the road between Giligili and Anata, it is not that he has the interest of his constituency at heart, but because the completion of the said road will enable him to ply his ten luxury buses (48).

Our narrator-protagonist Odili, may be described too as being very greedy. When he visits the Minister in the capital city, Bori, and is accommodated in one of the master bedrooms, having considered the exquisite furnishings he soliloquizes 'If I were made a minister that moment I will be more anxious to be one forever' (41–42).

Another curious character is Josiah, who not contented with monopolizing the business life Anata, has to resort to other foul means of making more money. This is manifested as he attempts to use a blind beggar's walking stick for a charm supposed to magically attract more wealth (96).

Corruption

> Corruption happens to be one of the corner stones of the society of *A Man of the People,* inspiring such language as "let them eat…, after all, when the Whiteman used to do all the eating, did we commit suicide?" (161–162).

Generally speaking, the society itself inadvertently approves of corruption as it encourages the politicians to selfishly enrich themselves with public funds. The society thus judges the worth of every man on the basis of how much he or she has corruptly stowed away, and how much of that ill-gotten wealth, he or she can lavishly donate when occasion demands and that is often. This therefore encourages public office-holders to get as corrupt as possible in order to live up to the society's expectation.

Power of Privilege

This is another central issue in the novel. People use their privileged positions to achieve personal objectives. Chief M.A. Nanga uses his position as a member of parliament (M.P.) and Minister of Culture to buy cars, build a four-storey building, own landed property in the city, (112) and snatch Odili's erstwhile girlfriend, Elsie (81).

Odili too uses his position as Eastern co-ordinator of the C.P.C. (Common People's Convention) to misappropriate party funds for non-party purposes (165).

Political Violence, Thuggery and Electoral Merchandizing

The game of politics in the society of *A Man of the People* is characterized by bitterness. Political opponents are considered as arch-rivals end enemies. It is a game of "winner-takes-it-all", so that the politicians go to all extremes to ensure their success at the polls.

Chief Nanga's thugs pummel Odili to a state of coma (157–158), Maxwell is crushed to death by one of Chief S.I. Koko's jeeps (160), while Chief Koko himself is shot point-blank in the chest by Eunice (160), in retaliation for her fiancé's death.

To ensure victory at the polls, financial inducements are handed out to the electorate. Even the wives of the politicians help their husbands to corrupt the political machinery. The wife of Chief S.I. Koko for example, uses the women's wing of the POP (People's Organization Party) to "breast-feeds the ballot boxes in order to ensure the husband's victory (160).

The Politicians, Intelligentsia and the Mass of the People

Achebe clearly categorizes the society of *A Man of the People* into three distinct groups – 'Politicians" "Intelligentsia" and the "Mass of the People."

Politicians

The politicians are represented in this novel by Chief M.A. Nanga, M.P., Minister of Culture, Chief S.I. Koko, Minister of Overseas Training among others.

They are portrayed as greedy, Machiavellian, vicious, amoral, tribalistic, unscrupulous, incorrigible, hopelessly corrupt, opportunistic, intolerant of opposition, unprepared for public service, visionless and essentially illiterate. They are all people who went into politics at a time people did not know its cash prize (42). They are also pictured as being very unprepared for public service, no vision, and so it is not surprising that they should make a mess of governance. They are very eccentric, concerned with themselves, their immediate families and friends while criminally neglecting the masses with whose mandate they get into the corridors of power.

Self-aggrandizement and ostentation are their watch-words. They misappropriate public funds, and loot the national treasury for their own selfish purposes. They buy landed property, very long American cars, train all their children in Kindergartens and other schools abroad. Contracts are not awarded except a certain percentage of the contract fee is promised. It is not uncommon to unusually inflate contract costs to enable them get more money. With the down-turn of the economy, pragmatic solutions are rejected in favor of short-term ill-advised solutions. A case in point is Dr. Makinde's (dismissed Minister of Finance) suggestion to cutdown the price paid to coffee planters as a way of dealing with the slum in the international coffee market. The Prime Minister rejects this plan, but rather instructs the National Bank to print fifteen million pounds, not considering the inflationary implications of such a plan on the economy (4).

The Intelligentsia

The intelligentsia is represented by Odili Samalu, Maxwell Kulamo, Eunice and the majority of those that formed the CPC (Common People's Convention). Most of them are graduates, professionals. In the novel, they presume or arrogate to themselves the role of Messiahs and Saviours who hold the key that will automatically unlock the socio-economic and political fortunes of the nation. They give the impression of being masses-oriented, preach idealisms that lead nowhere, self-righteous and sit in judgment over the politicians. But a critical look at their utterances and actions reveal that they are false and inherently as corrupt as the politicians. It can even be argued that given the same opportunities as the politicians, the intelligentsia will do worse.

After all, Maxwell collects a bribe of one thousand pounds from Chief S.I. Koko, but refuses to step down for him (141–142). Odili misappropriates party funds for non-party purposes. At best, they are all sneaky and very vindictive. Look at Odili who lost his one-time girlfriend, Elsie to Chief Nanga due to his irresponsibility (not man enough to own up his affair with the girl), now goes back and schemes to snatch Nanga's intended parlor wife – Edna, which he eventually does at the end of the novel. The intelligentsia too is unprepared for public office. Odili for instance, goes into politics for the wrong reasons. Having lost his girlfriend to Nanga, he feels he could slight Nanga by becoming his political opponent.

The Mass of the People

The mass of the people is portrayed essentially as illiterate, cynical, gullible, docile, sycophantic, fearful of change and repeat performance. They encourage corruption and cannot do anything to bring the politicians into judgment, rather, they are resigned:

> "Let them eat, after all, when the whiteman used to do all the eating, did we commit suicide...? (161–162).

For Achebe, it is this non-chalant attitude of the people that destroyed their society. Achebe considers them as "the real culprits" (166).

It may be asserted that Achebe's central argument in *A Man of the People* presumably is that the people's cynic acquiescence,docility, and notorious sycophancy were instrumental to the collapse of their society. It is obvious that the people aid and abet corruption, graft, and oppression by judging the worth of the individual by how much he/she has corruptly stowed away and how much of that fraudulent wealth can be lavishly donated to irrelevant causes. Here is how Achebe sums up the matter:

> Over-night everyone began to shake their heads at the excesses of the last regime, at its graft, oppression and corrupt government.., everybody said what a terrible

> lot... And these were the same people that only the other day had owned a thousand names of adulation... Chief Koko in particular became a thief and a murderer, while the people who had led him on, in my opinion, the real culprits, took the legendary bath of the hornbill and donned innocence (166).

Stylistically, *A Man of the People* draws its strength and significance from the suggestive power and interplay of a number of narrative devices particularly the modes of allegory, the proverbial, transliteration, flashback, irony and sarcasm.

Very significantly, the story is told in the first person narrative point of view which gives a further illusion of intimacy to the events being related. Secondly, this device also enables the author to fight shy of interpreting the events in an authorial voice which would have been regarded as intrusive since it would have amounted to a condemnation of both Odili and Nanga; and would thus, ultimately have left him without a moral center for his novel.

Max resorts to the analogical mode in order to powerfully tell his listeners how Machiavellian the POP and PAP have become. He likens them to a hunter who kills some big-game at night, but because he couldn't find his quarry, goes home to wait for the break of dawn. Coincidentally, by the time he gets to the scene the next morning, two vultures were already happily feasting on the carcass. In annoyance, he shot the vultures. The hunter here is the people, the two vultures – POP and PAP. Therefore, just like the hunter, the people should unanimously pass a vote of no confidence on the thieving POP and PAP and join the CPC (140).

Interestingly too, there is an ironic thrust in designating Chief Nanga as "a man of the people" because there were no people at least, not on the level of democratic nationhood. At another level, it may suggest that the society willfully denies itself heroes, idealists and revolutionaries preferring rather the slimy, hopelessly corrupt, incorrigible Chief Nangas and Kokos.

Very significantly too, Achebe displays his artistic sophistication in his handling of flashbacks. It is through this device that insights into Chief Nanga's pre-parliament days are pictured, and how he now rises from poverty and insignificance to opulence (14).

As is Achebe's practice, the proverbial is effectively employed. Odili's father tells his son, "the hawk should perch, and the eagle perch, whichever says to the other don't, may its own wing break' (138). This goes to emphasize the need for compromise and accommodation. In other words, there is the need to be aligned a "little to the left and a little to right" so that one can grab with either hand whatever trappings fall from either the POP and, or CPC.

On the contrary, Max advocates a fierce, rugged individualism and the dangerous ethnicization of the democratic process. He tells the Urua audience at the CPC campaign, "A goat does not eat into a hen's stomach no matter how friendly the two may be" (140). In other words, the Urua electorate should consider itself uniquely distinct from Anata. Therefore, it will be foolish to waste their vote on an Anata man (Chief Nanga), since Urua is Urua, and Anata is Anata.

Artistic Limitations

Despite the numerous encomiums showered on this novel, there are a number of artistic flaws that are totally unacceptable.

First, Achebe does not proffer any solution to the socio-economic and political malaise in society delineated in the novel. Neither the formation of new political parties such as the CPC, nor the military *coup de'tat* that ousted the corrupt political regime is the panacea. This crippling cynicism suggests no illuminating possibilities to the prevailing currents of our national disabilities. As Ebony (1986) observes, whereas the writer has been adept in criticizing and commenting on these vices, he has provided no solutions to them yet.

Second, Achebe may be heavily criticized for his effete depiction of the masses. All he does so far is to portray the weak, the exploited, the downtrodden masses as being incapable of will and action to effect a change of their destinies. This position is reinforced by Ngugi (1969) who indicts writers for their abysmally feeble depiction of the creative contribution of the masses to nation-building. As Eshiet (1989) puts it, the writer must not only question the entire gamut of socio-economic stasis in society; probe the forces of attrition and malaise that circumscribe life, but must also catapult the masses beyond the strangulating shackles of disillusionment to explore avenues of hope and renewal.

As Gakwandi (1982) observes, one of the major limitations of *A Man of the People* is that the audience is only allowed to see the events of the story through the eyes of the narrator. He notes further that Odili's comments never rise above naive speculations which are often loaded with clichés. Also, Odili's interpretation of events is too limited to satisfy the interest of the reader. A case in point is when Chief Nanga praises himself openly and declares that his guiding philosophy is, "Do the right and shame the devil", Odili adds this comment for the reader:

> Somehow I found myself admiring this man for his lack of modesty. For what is modesty but inverted pride? We all think we are first class people. Modesty forbids us from saying so ourselves though, presumably, not from wanting to hear it from others. Perhaps it was their impatience with this kind of hypocrisy that made men like Nanga successful politicians while starry-eyed idealists strove vaingloriously to bring into politics niceties and delicate refinements that belonged elsewhere (11).

This kind of comment blatantly reveals more about Odili's own immaturity than about the situation he is trying to describe. More often than not, the voice of the author is suspected though uncertainly. As noted earlier, there is the impression that the author hides behind the narrator to escape from having to make an evaluation himself.

The role of the female characters – Edna, Mrs. Nanga, Elsie, Maxwell's fiancee are preposterous and therefore, objectionable. However, Achebe presents female lawyers, nurses, diplomats – they do not occupy center stage. They are all the same portrayed as unscrupulous good-time girls, abused, exploited and dehumanized. This explains why Umeh (1972), generally indicts African male writers for their lack of empathy, sympathy and consciousness of the female psyche. As Acholonu (1994) points out, the female predicament in the Nigerian novel lies not only in the failure of the male writers to update the female status in the literatures, but equally, in the novelists' inability to achieve artistic realism in the delineation of their female characters.

Finally, the ending of *A Man of the People* is contrived and does not ring true. As Dathorne (1979) notes, Achebe seems to have sacrificed a convincing development of plot to the presentation of a theme. In pursuit of this theme – the corruption of politicians – Achebe introduces too many characters who appear and disappear without making much impact.

Works Cited

Achebe, Chinua. (1966) *A Man of the People*. London: Heinemann.

———. (1967) Interview with Tony Hall: "I had to write what I foresaw." In *Conversations with Chinua Achebe*. Ed. Bernth Lindfors. Jackson: University Press of Mississippi: 18–26.

Acholonu, R. (1994) "The Female Predicament in the Nigerian Novel" In *Feminism in African Literature*. Ed. Helen Chukwuma. Enugu: New Generation Books.

Darthorne, O.R. (1979) *African Literature in the Twentieth Century*. Ibadan: Heinemann.

Duerden, O. and Cosmo Pieterse eds. (1978) *African Writers Talking*. Ibadan: Heinemann.

Ebong, I.A. (1986) "Towards the Revolutionary Consciousness: The Writer in Contemporary Africa" In *Literature and Society: Selected Essays on African Literature*. Ed. Ernest Emenyonu. Oguta: Zim-Pan African Publishers.

Eshiet, I. (1987) "The Social Relevance of Femi Osofisan" A Paper Presented at the 7th Annual International Conference on African Literature and the English Language. May 5–9, 1987. University of Calabar, Nigeria.

Gakwandi, S.A. (1982) *The Novel and Contemporary Experience in Africa*. Ibadan: Heinemann.

wa Thiong'o, Ngugi (1969) "Satire in Nigeria." In *Protest and Conflict in African Literature*. Ed. Cosmo Pieterse and Donald Munro. London: Heinemann.

Umeh, M. (1972) "African Woman in Transition in the Novels of Buchi Emecheta. In *Presence Africaine*, No. 116.

Chapter 24

Igbo Leadership Ideals and Conflicts in Chinua Achebe's *A Man of the People*

Teresa U. Njoku

The Igbo traditional society had certain leadership ideals. These ideals expressed the possible perfect standards a leader was expected to embody or personify. These ideals ensured that the leader was acceptable to his people, and he on his own part, championed their values and promoted their welfare. However "the real problem with the Igbo since independence," according to Achebe, "is precisely the absence of the kind of central leadership which their competitors presume for them" (Achebe, 1983: 47). The negation of the ideals have led to the enthronement of "mediocrity and mass corruption in both social and political spheres. Achebe perceives the situation thus:

> The lack of real leaders in Igboland goes back of course, to the beginnings of colonial administration. Once the white man had crushed Igbo resistance it was relatively easy for him to locate upstarts and ruffians in the community who would uphold his regime at the expense of their own people. From those days the average Igbo leader's mentality has not been entirely free of the collaborating Warrant Chief syndrome (Achebe, 1983: 48).

Thus, Igbo leadership ideals have undergone change since the colonial and post independence era. Such a variance in ideals has resulted in conflicts, though Achebe published *The Trouble with Nigeria* in 1983, readers notice that, Achebe had explored Igbo *Leadership* ideals and their conflicts in the post-independence era in *A Man of the People*. In *A Man of the People* and *The Trouble with Nigeria*. Achebe hinges the problems of Igbo leadership on the irresponsibility of the leaders and their inability to accept "the challenge of personal example which are the hallmarks of true leadership" (Achebe, 1983: 1).

What a titled Igbo elder, Ogbuefi Odogwu, states in *No Longer at Ease* could be applied to the discussion of leadership ideals in Igbo ethos. While welcoming Obi as a returning hero, a modern successor of the great warriors Okonkwo, Ezeudu, and other "giants" and nostalgically recalling Iguedo's days of glory, Ogbuefi Odogwu says:

> Today greatness has changed its tune. Titles are no longer great, neither are barns nor large numbers of wives and children. Greatness is now in the things of the whiteman. And so we have changed our tune. We are the first in all the nine villages to send our son to the white man's land. You cannot plant greatness as you plant yams or maize.... The great tree chooses where to grow and we find it there, so it is with greatness in men (49).

Ogbuefi Odogwu's statement captures the spirit of what exists in the Igbo society which is reflected in *No longer at Ease*. For him, greatness involves extraordinary talent of some kind. For men to be admired for their achievement and noble qualities in the past, they had to become great warriors, farmers, titled men or priests. Through different avenues and occupations, these men displayed marked degrees of natural endowments and excellence which earned them the respect and worship of ordinary men. Significantly, the rules of conduct and forms of behavior of these great men were portrayed as worthy of emulation: their lives became worthy models for others.

Ogbuefi's statement, therefore, lists those tasks that put to the test the exceptional qualities of individual characters. The statement clearly reveals a change of attitude to these special tasks and forms of social behaviour that characterize greatness in the past. To Ogbuefi Odogwu, the lgbo society of old had produced men of godlike strength and courage like "Okolo, Nwosu and Ndu" (49) whom he had known in his youth. As far as he is concerned, greatness in the present age is stymied qualities defined and influenced by Western culture. For example, going overseas now equals the greatness in warfare. Consequently, emphasis has shifted from tasks requiring physical prowess to the training of the modern Obi Okonkwos (modern elite) who manifest such qualities as intellectual excellence, tact and resourcefulness – qualities which enable them to acquire the white man's wisdom. Thus, Obi Okonkwo and his ancestors exemplify different qualities demanded by their periods and environment.

Achebe as novelist here brings out the aspect of Igbo ethos which stresses unique achievements of individuals who could be regarded as the "expressions of the spirit of their times and the souls of their culture" (Hook, 1955: 61). They thereby exemplify those qualities which mark them off from others and raise them up as models in life or in leadership. In fact, Achebe tries to reflect this aspect of Igbo ethos on unique achievements when he shows that the Umuofia community commend Okonkwo who by his abilities makes such remarkable achievements that he is referred to as child who has washed his hands clean, and can deservedly eat with elders" (*Things Fall Apart* 6).

Special tasks and unique achievement apart, names reveal the leadership qualities of their bearers in Igbo ethos. Igbo names do not only point to the religious attitudes of the people, but more importantly reveal clearly lgbo cultural values and traditional wisdom from the point of view of ability for leadership. This idea about Igbo names is given abundant treatment in literatures about Igbo life in both the English and Igbo languages. Achebe, for example, highlights this significant aspect of Igbo ethos when he calls the Igbo titled elder whose statement was quoted earlier Ogbuefi Odogwu. Achebe uses this name to reveal the personality of his character. This is so because, "Ogbuefi" – killer of cow, and "Odogwu" – a man of strength, (when combined Oghuefi Odogwu means a man of great strength who has killed a cow) suggests stature, courage, and a great personality/leader whose fame rests solidly on bravery. The acts of bravery that have brought the honor might have been physical and risky confrontations with the enemy (man or animal) in warfare or in hunting. Through Ogbuefi's names, the ordinary people share the splendor and honor the names conjure up. The particular quality which the name calls up distinguishes Ogbuefi Odogwu from other men because he has revealed it in action. In this regard, Ogbuefi Odogwu's name is self-praising: "through it he rehearses his past experience and heroic feats, and vindicates his power" (Egudu and Nwoga, 1971: 15). In this way, his name accords him individual uniqueness and points to his potentialities for leadership roles.

But those leaders in the Igbo traditional society who have good names command great honor. The reason for this is that the Igbo associate good names with moral integrity. This ideal of moral integrity in Igbo ethos is illustrated by Iwundu when he says in his paper on Igbo Anthropnyms that in Igbo ethos, "a man's good name is his honour". Good names are based on moral integrity manifested in such qualities as purity, holiness, delicacy, honesty, and generosity. These strong moral virtues transform ordinary personalities into heroic ones and consequently identify them with the ancestors.

It is this moral integrity that is reflected in novels written in English and Igbo when some of the Igbo characters express their individualism and leadership qualities through the exercise of their moral integrity. For example, Ezeulu's moral integrity forces him to warn his community against fighting a war of blame, Again, he singly witnesses against his people in the land case between them and Okperi. One could also say that it is deep loyalty to his deity and tradition that makes him stick to the time – sanctioned rituals of loyalty to eating the sacred yams even when such rituals are exposed to attack from the community.

Yet, the impact any Igbo leader makes in his community depends on how much success he makes in his chosen career. But the excessive ambition to succeed is what I choose to call mania for success in the expression of Igbo leadership in this study. Risks and dangers often hinder success, but they do not deter the lgbo ambitious leader whose belief is: *Anaghi aso mgbagbu aga ogu*," – you don't run away from battle because people get killed. Personal ambitions are achieved despite obstacles; in fact, success is a quality reverred in Igbo ethos; it is associated with leadership qualities. This mania for success revealed in the ambition to achieve fame demands resourcefulness, intelligence and tenacity of purpose. Craftiness with its connotations of negativity and weakness often combines effectively with these other qualities. It is as a result of this mania that most Igbo struggle doggedly to make the best out of situations. The admiration for personal achievement in Igbo ethos is reflected in literature. Nnolim succintly puts it thus in his analysis of *Things Fall Apart*:

> It is now established that in the absence of hereditary kingship Igbo society was governed by a group of hand picked self achievers so that the ideal to which the Igbo tend was the individual whose position in society rests on solid personal achievements. To succeed, or not to succeed; that was the question confronting every Igbo man, the fear of failure is a hauntingly tangible fear (57).

Nnolim's statement highlights certain facts about the character of individuals in Igboland: the individual leader or person is assessed by his social achievements. When Nnolim goes on to state that "the Igbo in a figurative and literal sense is a wrestler all his life," he is pointing out the regard the Igbo society accords to self – made men who have achieved great success by their struggles and efforts – revealing sterling qualities that distinguish them in their society. And to do this, they make maximum use of the quality of resourcefulness.

"This quality is even revealed in the exploits of the trickster hero in Igbo folktale, a tortoise, a spider in some parts of West Africa and a mouse in the Congo" (Ruth Finnegan, 1977: 337). The trickster hero is weak when compared with other animals, but it encounters obstacles that are apparently formidable and uses his resourcefulness to circumvent them. In some folktales however, he meets with failures. The resourcefulness of the tortoise is pointed out in the education of the young so that while his greed and unscrupulousness are criticised, his ingenuity and wisdom which enable him to exploit every situation to his advantage are often encouraged.

But in real life, the Igbo leader is also distinguished by the qualities of leadership he displays. These qualities are exceptional. Uchendu observes that the qualities "emphasize transparent living" expected of Igbo leaders. According to him, the Igbo leader "should be accessible to all," and since his leadership role could be religious or political, he should "maintain the necessary condition of his high office." Those who provide this leadership are "self-achievers": elders, priests, chiefs, councilors and politicians. They gain the support of their people if only they do not govern too much." As long as they help others to achieve success they retain the support of their people. Helping others to achieve success reinforces the idea that the leader should also give good service to his people after achieving success.

This leadership ideal in Igbo ethos is also captured in literature. Ezeulu in *Arrow of God* commands both secular and divine authority and comes near to being a god when he sets the traditional calendar by announcing the seasonal events and ceremonies without which, it is believed, the seasons would fail to run their expected course. When Ezeulu, therefore, paints half his body white and the other half black during the feast of the Pumpkin Leaves, he manifests this duality in his being. Besides this religious role, he has a special concrete knowledge of his society; his tragedy occurs because he displays a dis-similar knowledge about the capricious god he serves. In the end, his god joins his people in passing judgment against him. Ikechi also emerges as a leader during the conflict over the Pond of Wagaba in Elechi Amadi's *The Great Ponds*. Even in works by non-Igbo, heroic characters emerge also in other African communities often during crises; Karega, Wanga and Munira emerge as leaders of their rural community in Ngugi wa Thiong'o's *Petals of Blood*. Such fictional personalities, who often exercise secular leadership roles, are rewarded with communal honor and glory for their courage, bravery, and skills during crisis situations,

Another point that needs to be noted is that the Igbo in Igbo ethos ensures that no one person lords it over others. If a man wants to become a dictator, he can do that in his household. It is as a result of this ideal that individualism is highly recognized in Igbo ethos; consequently, a leader is never imposed on a society. Thus, the Igbo accept that a person's leadership position results from the fact that he has been fundamentally set apart by his *chi* – personal god. Consequently, individual traits and different qualities are accepted and accommodated in Igbo ethos. This recognition of the guardian spirit in the life of every individual, ensures that people are allowed their freedom to pursue their individual goals in order to make their own individual achievements and to apply their own initiative in whatever occupation they engage in. Since everybody has his/her individual destiny, the Igbo recognize differences in character and leadership qualities. While a person engages in his concern, moderate ambitions are usually encouraged whereas excesses are frowned at and criticized.

Thus, the values that mark out a person as an individual or leader derive their force from group ideals: the type of leadership is "rooted in group solidarity;"

(Uchendu, 1965: 103) therefore often, the group puts pressure on the leader to conform and to co-operate in its demands for the communal good and to ensure communal achievements. Extreme individualism is not tolerated. But often in literature portraying the Igbo culture, one finds individuals who have achieved "separateness" and individual expression even in their communal traditional societies. When such characters exercise their individualism. the society reacts by expressing outrage if the individual is one who has achieved status in the society. These characters experience isolation because of their individualism. But while the Western society provides a fertile ground for a complete and unrestrained individualism, the Igbo traditional society strives to limit and often suppress such impulses. When Achebe makes the people of Umuaro say that "their god had taken sides with them against his head strong and ambitious priest, and thus upheld the wisdom of their ancestors – that no man however great was greater than his people; that no one ever won judgement against his clan, (*Arrow of God* 230) he is conforming to Obi Wali's statement that "rebels" are not usually allowed to thrive in traditional society.

A study of Igbo leadership ideals and conflicts in *A Man of the People* thus, demands a study of Chief Nanga as a politician for through politics, he reveals his mania for success, his fraudulent political achievements, and his lack of moral integrity. Some of Nanga's qualities reflect certain attributes of the Igbo leader while some link him to other post – independence politicians in Nigeria and those of other Anglophone countries in Africa.

Eventually, there are contradictions in the leadership ideals exposed in the novel. *A Man of the People* portrays the post – independence era in an unnamed country. Politics is a new type of venture and "the politician" is relatively new in African culture" (*G.C.M. Mutiso*, 1974: 40). Therefore, when Achebe presents Nanga in his novel he portrays him as "a type embodying the ideals common to the power elite in Nigeria during the years 1960–1966, the years immediately following Nigeria's attainment of independence. While doing so he ostensibly portrays Nanga as a clever politician...." Consequently, Nanga resembles Uncle Taiwo in Cyprian Ekwensi's *Jagua Nana*. But Nanga also shares some of his qualities and attributes with other politicians in Anglophone African literature like Koomson in Armah's *The Beautyful Ones are Not Yet Born* and Nderi in Ngugi wa Thiong'o's *Petals of Blood*.

Nanga enters his first profession with the ambition to make personal achievements. With his little education, youthful vigor, and the ambition to succeed, Nanga achieves popularity in his school and makes himself admired by the impeccable Scout-master's uniform he used to wear. As a scoutmaster, Nanga must have accepted through the Scout pledge to exemplify certain qualities. Since his Scout pledge would demand that he "does his best; does his duty to God and his country; keep the law, and do a good turn every day", Nanga would be efficient, dutiful, law-abiding and selfless in his service to others. One imagines that Nanga must have carried out the Scouts' pledge to the letter, as the picture of him on the wall of his former school depicts. The "memorable words" below the picture – "Not what I have but what I do is my kingdom" (*A Man of the People* 3) show Nanga's commitment to the ideals of service to mankind.

Nanga's qualities, therefore, earn him admiration and popularity in his school. Odili, his former pupil, worships him as his hero early in the novel. In this regard, he looks at Nanga as a model. But admiration and popularity do not satisfy Nanga's personal ambition to achieve distinction in his achievement – oriented society. Teaching as a special task tests Nanga's qualities and gives him the opportunity of becoming a leader – at least to his pupils and his fellow teachers; the artist who drew Nanga's picture in his former school had surrounded it with flowers as a sign of his admiration. That Nanga's picture is retained in the school long after he has left it, shows that his school looks up to him as a hero and a leader and that he could have achieved a leadership position there.

Here Nanga's ideals and those of his pupils differ. Whereas the pupils think that Nanga is in every way a model teacher and scoutmaster, Nanga manifests his mania for success in his yearning for a higher degree. The nick-name he assumes: "M.A. minus Opportunity" (12) points to the fact that while the teaching job offers him opportunity for action it does not give him an equal opportunity to satisfy his academic yearnings for a leadership role in his society.

Initially, however, the political arena does not offer him all the opportunities he wants – he is only an unknown back-bencher in the parliament. But a national crisis offers him the opportunity. A slump in the international market causes the economy of the newly independent nation to crumble. The Minsiter of Finance Dr. Makinde recommends strict economic measures to the government; he and his group have good ideas about dealing with the situation; but the Prime Minister rejects their proposals owing to a forthcoming election and his lack of understanding of the issues invoked, and above all, dismisses the Minister and his supporters.

At this critical moment in his country's development, Nanga plays such a significant role that misdirects the progress of the debate in parliament. Whereas the country needs intelligent leadership at this time, it unfortunately gets unsatisfactory people to misdirect her and assume authority. While it is obvious that the economic crisis is not originally caused by Nanga, we know that he enhances the effects by his role in removing Dr. Makinde and his team from office. Nanga perceives Dr. Makinde and his group as obstacles on his way to progress as well as that of his country. To achieve his plan for the exploitation of the crisis situation, he gives "primitive loyalty" (7) to the Prime Minister.

Thus, in his ambition to achieve political leadership, he sees the vacant seats of the dismissed ministers as worth fighting for, and therefore, enthrones himself as the leader or the enemies of the dismissed ministers. His verbal affront during the debate scheduled to humiliate the ministers is remarkable:

> They deserve to be hanged; shouted Mr. Nanga from the back benches. This interruption was so loud and clear that it appeared later under his own name in the Hansard. Throughout the session he led the pack of back-bench hounds straining their leash to get at their victims. If anyone had cared to sum up Mr. Nanga's interruptions they would have made a good hour's continuous yelp. Perspiration poured down his face as he sprang up to interrupt or sat back to share in the derisive laughter of the hungry hyena (5).

Nanga leads "the pack of back – bench hounds straining to get at their victims." The picture here is that of a hunter leading his dogs to attack game. Since Nanga appoints himself the leader of the "hounds" – dogs, it means he has "game" in sight – the vacant Cabinet seats. Therefore, he constitutes with his fellow "hounds" "killers" for the "victims" in the conflict, – here the dismissed ministers. One could say then that Achebe shows that Nanga and his gang become the predators while their "victims," the ministers become the prey. Intellectuals are rejected for mediocres in economic planning.

It is significant that Nanga's rude and loud remark "they deserve to be hanged" should appear in the Hansard. The period depicted in the novel is one in which traditional avenues and tasks for testing greatness have given way to the education of the elite. That Nanga's remark fails to reflect intellectual excellence in the Parliament shows how far he is below the intellectual excellence he should manifest in his new venture politics.

Again, Nanga's "continuous yelp" takes "a good hour." "Perspiration poured down his face as he sprang up to interrupt or sat back to share in the derisive laughter ...." The time element in Nanga's verbal attack and his sweat – covered face are remarkable, and contrast with the "tall, calm, sorrowful" and superior posture of Dr. Makinde. Dr. Makinde's sorrow is for his country "being started off down the slopes of inflation" (2), and his superior appearance depicts confidence and intellectual excellence. Thus, Nanga's attack on the patriotic ministers in his country's parliament parodies such other encounters in the battle fields where greatness is achieved.

Here too, he fails to display those qualities that had earned him popularity in the teaching field. To get at the Cabinet post, he relinquishes his earlier pledge to do his duty to God and his country. If he had loved his country, he would have like Odili – his idol in the novel, espoused the cause of the dismissed ministers; he would support the strict economic measures to arrest the inflation in his country. Further more, his pledge would make him stand for the truth. But we see that while Odili gets at the truth during the debate in parliament, Nanga helps to win the condemnation of the ministers.

In the same way, the parliament suggests a national body concerned with the making of the laws of the country. One imagines that only matters of great importance are discussed there. Thus, it becomes ridiculous that Nanga displays irresponsibility in his lack of respect to this great body, by his rude remarks and shouts. The fact that Nanga entertains the other parliamentarians by his shouts and remarks reveals that they too are as ignorant and unpatriotic as Nanga. That the dismissal of some ministers should attract such a national attention exposes the lack of seriousness of the parliament.

Again, Nanga has no previous training in politics. Therefore, his knowledge of the principles of good leadership in government is questionable. He looks at his political leadership as basically that of acquiring and retaining power. Since Nanga has no clear purpose of what he does as a politician, or any idea of the effects of his deeds on his country, he misrepresents by his lack of knowledge of good government his country whose Minister of Culture he is supposed to be. Thus, Achebe portrays him as a character whose pattern of behavior should not be emulated. When he exposes his lack of knowledge about his country's most important writer and his works, sends his children to expensive schools run by foreigners in his country, and defrauds his country with the help of foreign companies, Achebe points to Nanga's failure to espouse his country's culture, and his failure in his responsibility as a Minister of Culture. His leadership becomes destructive rather than redemptive to his nation and hastens the collapse of the system he and his colleagues lead.

Nanga's non-democratic approach to politics depicts him as a shallow-minded politician. Consequently, he becomes a threat to the democratic processes which his young country is learning to establish. By rigging elections and enforcing his will on the electorate, he opposes the nationalist ideals which Max and Odili embody. In this way, Achebe points out that Nanga influences the political history of his country negatively by his failure to espouse democratic processes. Nanga hires thugs who later prove uncontrollable, thereby helping to create a chaotic situation where law and order are trampled upon. The action of the thugs also promotes Nanga's fall in the end.

Nanga's political achievement as a Cabinet Minister and the economic status this confers on him, cause his people to accept him as their leader. Consequently, his achievement-oriented society holds a reception for him. In this manner, Nanga's society reflects the Igbo society that reveres achievements if such achievements are based on moral probity. The reception given to Nanga is ironically that type that is normally given to a hero of great moral integrity. The students of Odili's school mount a guard of honor for Nanga, the respected hunters' guild who demonstrate their skills in hunting only during outstanding events also accord Nanga honor; the women even compose praise songs for him. All levels of the society honor him as a hero: men, women, and children, and accept him as their leader.

Here, Achebe seems to suggest that Nanga's highly competitive society regards his political and economic leadership as their own because he is their kinsman. In this way, their own aspirations are gratified; by cheering Nanga as a hero they forget their own hard conditions and reinforce their individual ambitions. Besides, the economic crisis which causes great inflation in the country increases the interest of the people in Nanga. They hope that, at least, he would help them resolve the difficult economic situation they face. They, therefore, listen keenly to his words and are impatient when other characters delay Nanga from speaking to them. Again, the teachers are in "an ugly rebellious mood" (9), and would like solutions to their economic problems.

Furthermore, the people are proud that Nanga and his colleagues have replaced the white man over whom they had no control. Even though they prove defenceless in controlling the excesses of Nanga and his group, Nanga's political role gives them hope: they, therefore, pay him homage even when he does not merit it. When Nanga betrays their hope and fails to provide any solutions to the problems of the nation, Achebe suggests that Nanga is not worthy of the new nation.

The cause of the people's massive support early in the novel and during his election campaign can be attributed also to Nanga's political attitude to the people. This is so because he reflects the highly "socialized Igbo who is able to integrate with others, to speak out his mind freely even if it hurts to do so" (Uchendu, 1965: 14). For the people "good citizenship" "demands transparent living" and Nanga reflects this ideal by his being accessible to all, by his false humility and generosity, by his claims of service to his people and by his attractive personality. Odili, Nanga's political opponent and critic, concedes that Nanga "was the most approachable politician in the country. Whether you asked in the city or in his home village, Anata, they would tell you he was a man of the people" (1). Nanga recognizes Odili – his former pupil after fifteen years and makes himself friendly to all; Nanga's "transparent orientation" (Uchendu, 1965; 17), is also pointed out by Odili:

> Chief Nanga was a born politician; he could get away with almost anything he said or did. And, as long as men are swayed by their hearts and stomachs and not their heads the Chief Nangas of this world will continue to get away with anything. He had that rare gift of making people feel – even while he was saying harsh things to them that there was not a drop of illwill in his entire frame (65).

Even though the people are disarmed by what they see as Nanga's humility and generosity we know that Nanga is a hypocrite who claims qualities he lacks. When he calls the principal of Anata Secondary School "Sir," and refers to Odili's father as his political father, Nanga tries to create an image of himself that his people would accept even though he knows that he lacks such qualities he claims. That the people take Nanga on his word and fail to recognise his deceit is amply illustrated in Odili's father's statement:

> In spite of your behaviour Chief Nanga has continued to struggle for you and has now brought you the scholarship to your house. His kindness surprises me; I couldn't do it myself. On top of that he has brought you two hundred and fifty pounds if you will sign this paper…." (118)

Here Odili's father thinks that Nanga's interest is to pacify his son (Odili) and make him step down. Odili's father is taken in by Nanga's hypocrisy.

Nanga's claims of service to his people also make them accept him as their leader. The cause of Nanga's claim is that a leader is supposed to be of service to his people and community but, Nanga's claims make up for his deficiency. He claims that he is the servant of his people. This gives the ignorant people except the critical ones, a false sense of importance. Thus, when Nanga asks Odili to come to him for a job in the Civil Service, the people see Nanga as helping Odili to achieve success like Nanga. The villagers believe that Nanga helps others to get on in life; even though this is not effected, their unfulfilled aspirations seem to have been achieved.

The thugs whom Nanga employs and who the villagers consider Nanga as helping to succeed, promote his downfall. Josiah, the local trader and thief, Dogo – Nanga's one-eyed praise-singer, and the members of Nanga's Youth Vanguard are all thugs in Nanga's employment. Maduka analyses Nanga's action succinctly when he says:

> Nanga resorts to the use of the thugs because he feels obligated to consolidate his hold on the people. To him the thugs are the means of making his power impregnable. His illusion is strengthened by the fact that he successfully uses them to win the elections and to get reappointed as a minister. But at this point, there is the turning of the screw: after the elections the thugs run riot and plunge the country into a state of chaos forcing the army to move in and take over control of government (Maduka, 1976: 252).

It is also to give the image of rendering service to his people that Nanga makes financial donations to them. His gifts of money make the people accept him as a generous leader but as we see in another Anglophone novel reflecting urban and Igbo life, the money according to Uncle Taiwo in *Jagua Nana* "is party money. I give dem de money like dat, so them kin taste what we goin to do for them, if they vote us into power" (Jagua Nana 104). Uncle Taiwo's assertion differs from what Nangas one-eyed praise-singer would want us to believe, when he says:

> "You see how e de do as if to say money be san san," he was saying. "People wey de jealous the money gorment de pay minister no sabi say no be him one de chop am. No so so troway" (14).

Here the impression is that the money Nanga distributes is his personal money. But as Uncle Tawlo confidently tells Jagua Nana, it is party money. When Chief Nanga tells Odili later that he spends a lot of money on generosity and so "no de keep anini" (15) for himself, he is confirming his praise-singer's impression and by so doing reveals his hypocrisy because the money and gifts are bribes used to corrupt his people.

Furthermore, Nanga's use of gifts to corrupt his people is manifested in the issue of the Rural Water Scheme pipes. Nanga gains credibility among his people when he plans to give them pipe-borne water. As the police man who is Nanga's firm supporter puts it, "we know they are eating.... but we are eating too. They are bringing us water and electricity. We did not have those things before; that is why I say we are eating too" (124). To the villagers, the pipes for the water scheme show that Nanga is concerned about their welfare but the pipes are a strategy to make the villagers vote for him during the elections. When some of them assemble to listen to the members of Odili's party, Nanga takes that as an indication that he would lose their votes and carts away the pipes.

This action shows that Nanga's assertions about his selfless service to his people are widely opposed to his actions; in this regard, Nanga is a hypocrite who claims what he cannot execute. Again, Nanga's false claims confirm the truth of what Odili's father asserts and which is the general belief among the people: "the mainspring of political action was personal gain" (114). Andrew Kadibe, Odili's colleague from Nanga's village, who at other times gives Nanga "primitive loyalty" (7), has this to say of Nanga's political interest: "people like Chief Nanga don't care two hoots about the outside world, He is concerned with the inside world with how to retain his hold on his constituency and there he is adept" (23).

Nanga's concern is, therefore, centered on promoting his political interest. Through out his political career he nurses this ambition. Nanga's actions and attitudes suggest that he regards himself as indispensable in the political life of his people and that his downfall is the downfall of many even though it is clear at the end that he is not. Achebe seems to be saying that Nanga is convinced of his social right to exercise political leadership and does not expect anyone to contest it. Having gained political leadership and power, his quest is to retain it and to do this he employs blackmail and violence. He is ruthless even to the social class he claims to represent; adopts violence and blackmail as political weapons when he allows his thugs to beat up Odili, and when he ensures that Odili's nomination papers do not reach the electoral office.

While moral integrity is an important attribute of leaders in Igbo ethos, its deficiency in Nanga points to the fact that he does not reflect this important ideal. Nanga's lack of moral integrity is rooted in his "lack of moral conscience" as Andrew Kadibe aptly puts it. Nanga's lack of moral conscience makes him defraud his nation by colluding with a foreign company. He manifests his immorality by his seduction of young girls. Bribery is another aspect of his corruption and he employs it to gain his economic and political positions. With the wealth he acquires through bribery he builds expensive houses, buys expensive cars and clothes – the status symbols his society cherishes. In fact, Nanga's defect in moral integrity pushes him to give undue importance to money and possessions.

Odili's idealism,however, helps us to assess Nanga's moral integrity. Odili is guided by moral principles in his political struggles with Nanga. Odili rejects violence as a weapon of political struggle and also rejects Nanga's bribe. Odili's moral probity is a contrast to Nanga who employs violence, bribery and blackmail in politics.

Furthermore, Odili's love – hate relationship with Nanga enables us to gauge Nanga's moral decline. Early in the novel, Odili is proud of Nanga and worships him; at this time Nanga is a school teacher When Odili discovers in the parliament that Nanga is a corrupt and mean politician, his admiration turns to bitterness against Nanga and the group he represents.

But the people perceive Nanga differently. They know that Nanga is corrupt and that he exploits them. On the other hand, they are ignorant of the powers they – as the electorate – command. Consequently, they think they are defenceless in their political situation and adopt escapist attitudes by becoming cynical.

> They were not only ignorant but cynical. Tell them that this man had used his position to enrich himself and they would ask you as my father did if you thought that a sensible man would spit out the juicy morsel that good fortune placed in his mouth" (2).

The idea that Nanga's "good fortune" has placed him in his exalted leadership position where he can exploit the people as he likes points to one of the reasons for their cynicism. Uchendu's analysis of this attitude as a reflection of Igbo life shows that the people's belief about Nanga's good fortune is rooted in their belief in the *Chi* concept and in re-incarnation. According to Uchendu:

> The social importance of reincarnation is that it provides the "ideal system" that rationalizes, interprets, accommodates, or rejects changes and innovations as well as tolerates certain character traits" (Uchendu, 1965: 16).

Thus, the people accept Nanga rather than Odili because they reject radical changes; they also accommodate the extreme individualism of Nanga manifested in his acquisitiveness. On the purely physical level, the people are attracted by Nanga's easy charms, and his warm personality. Nanga is exceptional in his ability to make spontaneous speeches and his people extol him for it. This is so because the Igbo accept a leader who "has mouth", that is, the power of oratory and wisdom (Uchendu 6). Again, they are drawn to him by his handsomeness. Nanga's handsomeness makes the women singers liken him to the "perfect sculpted beauty of a carved eagle" (1). Throughout the novel, Nanga's handsomeness is pointed out; its significance is that Nanga's physical qualities reflect the heroic physical stature of Igbo leaders.

While we condemn the unpredictable masses for supporting Nanga, we must also realise that the people are ignorant of the intricacies of government. Again, Nanga helps to keep them in ignorance by speaking to them in English and by using abstract concepts they do not understand. For instance, they applaud when he uses the expression "national cake" to refer to the country's wealth. The fact that the expression itself portrays Nanga's ethnic politics is beyond the people. Therefore, as Achebe has fully demonstrated, there is no relationship between political leadership/responsibility and popularity. This is true of the Igboland reflected in *A Man of the People* as it is true of Kenya reflected in Ngugi wa Thiong'o's *A Grain of Wheat*. Mugo in the later novel is acclaimed a hero by his people until he reveals that he is a traitor. Similarly, Nanga is popular and regarded as a man of the people" despite his exploitation of his people.

Nanga as has been shown, shares many of his qualities with other Nigerian politicians. They enter politics when their countrymen are ignorant of it: they are opportunistic. Nanga, like them, is ignorant of political ideals and exercises incompetent leadership. Besides, Nanga shares his qualities with other politicians in many African novels written in English. For example, many of his traits: handsomeness, acquisitiveness and self centeredness are reflected in Koomson in Armah's *The Beautyful Ones are not Yet Born*. The leadership qualities of these politicians give significance to the type of literature written after the independence period in many Anglophone countries in Africa. This is the literature of disenchantment and disillusionment in which the people seem to have exchanged the white man with the black white man. Achebe's *A Man of the People* belongs to this literary tradition in English concerned with the post-independence period.

Finally, names promote the honor of their bearers in Igbo ethos. As a result, Nanga accumulates titles all in an effort to achieve honor, win acclaim and the love of his people. But his names seem hollow when examined in the light of his leadership traits. It is significant that the true man of the people is not Nanga but Max, because Max's patriotism enables him to plan a social change for his country. When at the end of the novel Nanga is caught fleeing from military justice dressed as a fisherman, he indicates the ordinary person and villain he is. His lack of moral principles and crimes are not atoned for before the end of the novel. Perhaps, his humiliation and fall are ways of making him suffer trials and become purged of his crimes against his people who had taken him as a leader.

Works Cited

Achebe, Chinua. *Things Fall Apart*. London: Heinemann, 1958.

———. *No Longer At Ease*. London: Heinemann, 1960.

———. *Arrow of God*. London: Heinemann, 1960.

———. *A Man of the People*. London: Heinemann, 1966.

———. *The Trouble With Nigeria*. Enugu: Fourth Dimension Publishing Co. Ltd., 1983.

Amadi, Elechi. *The Great Ponds*. London: Heinemann, 1969.

Armah, Ayi Kwei. *The Beautyful Ones Are Not Yet Born*. London: Heinemann, 1969.

Egudu, Romanus and Nwoga, Donatus. *Poetic Heritage – Igbo Traditional Verse*. Enugu: Nwankwo Ifejika & Co. Ltd., 1971.

Ekwensi, Cyprian. *Jagua Nana*. London: Granada Publishing Ltd., 1961.

Finnegan Ruth. *Oral Literature in Africa*. Nairobi: Oxford University Press, 1977.

Hook, Sidney. *The Hero in History*. Boston: Beacon Press, 1955.

Iwundu, Mataebere. "Igbo Anthroponyms: Linguistic Persectism in Omenuko". A Seminar Paper Presented at Colloquium on Linguistics and Nigerian Languages, University of Port Harcourt, Nigeria, March 22-23, 1979.

Maduka. Chidi T. *Politics and the Intellectual Hero: Achebe, Abrahams, Plaubert and Wright*. Ph.D Thesis: Graduate College, The University of Iowa, Iowa City, 1979: 159–260.

Nnolim, Charles. "*Things Fall Apart* as an Igbo National Epic: In *Modern Black Literature*. Ed. S. Okechukwu Mezu. Buffalo, New York: Stack Academy Press, 1971.

Uchendu, V.C. *The Igbo of South Eastern Nigeria*. New York: Holt, Rhinehart and Winston, 1965.

Part Five:

Critical Perspectives on *Anthills of the Savannah*

Chapter 25

The Trouble with Narrators: The Role of Chinua Achebe in *Anthills of the Savannah*

Jennifer Wenzel

Chinua Achebe's 1983 book, *The Trouble with Nigeria*, begins with a sentence that serves as a textbook-perfect thesis statement: "The trouble with Nigeria is simply and squarely a failure of leadership" (1). Achebe attends to various subtopics in the essay that might intimate more widespread social troubles within the nation, including corruption, patriotism, and tribalism. Yet the focus of Achebe's scathing, despairing critique remains simply and squarely the leadership of the state, even years after the publication of the essay. In a 1987 interview with Anna Rutherford, Achebe spoke about the "vicious circle" of societal and state corruption: "what I'm really interested in is how you could begin to solve this problem.... And it is at the level of the leadership that th[e] break must occur" (Rutherford 2).

Anthills of the Savannah, Achebe's long-awaited fifth novel published in 1987, was intended in part to propose fictional solutions to the problems outlined in *The Trouble with Nigeria*. Given Achebe's persistent interest in the failures of Nigerian leadership, a logical critical approach to *Anthills of the Savannah* would be to evaluate the literary solutions to the troubles with Nigeria represented in the novel through the fictional nation of Kangan. David A. Maughan Brown has examined the novel's treatment of leadership and concluded that Achebe's imprecision in the use of terms such as "society," "class," and even "leadership," compromises the novel's usefulness in ameliorating Nigeria's troubles. More damningly, Maughan Brown maintains that Achebe's ambivalence about the relationship between the leaders and the led in the novel raises questions about the desirability of the rather undemocratic solutions vaguely proposed in *Anthills*.

In evaluating Achebe's contribution to solving the problems of Nigeria, Maughan Brown draws not only upon *The Trouble with Nigeria*, but also upon Achebe's numerous extrafictional comments in interviews and shorter essays. In the body of criticism on Achebe, Maughan Brown's is, of course, not a unique interpretive method; to list examples of analyses of Achebe's novels based in part upon his non-fictional work would be to include most of the criticism published about Achebe's fiction. A brief glance at the titles of some of Achebe's essays – "The Novelist as Teacher," "The Writer and His Community," "The Truth of Fiction," "The Role of the Writer in a New Nation" and "The African Writer and the English Language" – suggests that the role of the writer who writes a kind of fictional truth in sometimes didactic English and whose community is an African nation has long been a topic of interest for Achebe.

If *Anthills* is partly intended as a novelistic appendix to the critique of leadership begun in *The Trouble with Nigeria*, the novel is also a dramatization of Achebe's continuing negotiation of the role of the writer in an African nation not unlike Nigeria. *Anthills* is on many levels a novel about writing: the novel contains two speeches by its characters about the role of the writer in a community defined by regional, national, or international boundaries. Omar Sougou notes that Ikem Osodi's replies to questions after his lecture at the university "combine to read like an essay on the theme of writers and politics" (44). Although Sougou is primarily interested in intertextuality in *Anthills*, he fails to comment on the irony or inevitability of the presence of such an "essay' within a novel by Chinua Achebe. The Abazon chieftain's privileging of the story-teller (who preserves the past) over the drum-beater and the warrior nicely complements Ikem's Marxist insistence upon the writer's function as an asker of questions about the present and the future: within these character's set pieces, we can find a rationale for the entire corpus of Achebe's previous novels.

My aim here is neither to measure how well Achebe has met in *Anthills* the standards for a writer that he has set in his essays, nor to reiterate Maughan Brown's treatment of the trouble with leadership in *Anthills*. Rather, I am interested in the convergence of leadership and writing within the novel: while presidents and generals serve as the leaders of nation-states, the imaginary communities created in novels are effectively "led" by their narrators. The complicated structure of *Anthills* represents a major landmark for Achebe in explicit experimentation with multiple narrators. Of equal interest is the novel's depiction of the ways in which the official story of the nation of Kangan is "narrated" through various state-controlled media. That Christopher Oriko and Ikem Osodi function both as narrators of the novel and official narrators of the nation demonstrates the important links between leadership, writing, and narration within *Anthills of the Savannah*.

Sougou argues that the narrative structure of *Anthills* represents a synthesis of the third-person narrative strategy of *Things Fall Apart*, *No Longer at Ease*, and *Arrow of God* and the first-person narration of *A Man of the People* (40–41). Indeed, Anthills is narrated by three first-person narrators, Christopher Oriko, Ikem Osodi, and Beatrice Nwanyibuife Okoh; third-person narration links each of these characters' sections. Chris's narration opens the novel; he also narrates a later chapter in which he, Beatrice, Ikem, and Elewa have cocktails with hospital administrator John Kent (a.k.a. Mad Medico) and his editor friend, Dick. Ikem also narrates a chapter near the beginning of the novel. In the chapter headings, both characters are introduced as "witnesses," although it is unclear who or what is on trial, who the judges are, and what their verdict might be. Since both characters are dead by the end of the novel, Chris' and Ikem's narratives cannot be read as post-coup testimony delivered in the aftermath of the story. Beatrice narrates two chapters immediately after Chris' and Ikem's "testimony". Each of these characters' narratives provides a multiplicity of perspectives on the characters, as well as the events within the novel.

Intervening among the first-person narratives of Beatrice, Ikem, and Chris are chapters, and sections within chapters, narrated by an unnamed third-person narrator. It would be inaccurate to say, however, that the narrative structure of the novel consists of only four discrete voices. The "third-person narrator" is not a coherent persona throughout the novel; the switch from third-person narration after Beatrice's chapter perhaps best illustrates the shifts within the third-person narrative voice. Achebe decidedly allots to Beatrice the most uninterrupted first-person narration space; the third-person narrator, however, is at his most omniscient immediately after her chapter.

The chapter after Beatrice's first-person narration is entitled "Daughters" and subtitled "Idemili". The chapter opens thus:

> That we are surrounded by deep mysteries is known to all but the inscrutably ignorant. But even they must concede the fact, indeed the inevitability, of the judiciously spaced, but nonetheless certain interruptions in the flow of their high art to interject the word of their sponsor, the divinity that controls remotely but diligently the transactions of the marketplace that is their world (93).

What follows is a telling of the myth of Idemili, the goddess who was sent to the world in a Pillar of Water in order to "bear witness to the moral nature of authority" and thus restrain and humanize masculine Power (93). Within the cultural space of the myth, Idemili's divine intervention into the profane marketplace of human power illustrates the necessity for brute (masculine) force to be tempered by moral feminine) restraint. The narrator's subsequent commentary about Beatrice, however, makes the telling of the myth within the novel seem like what the narrator calls "a word from [our] sponsor."

After telling the Idemili myth, the narrator examines Beatrice's relationship to such myths of her heritage. Beatrice grew up "barely knowing who she was" because she did not learn her people's legends (96). As the narrator's commentary continues, we discover that the narrator, unlike Beatrice herself, knows exactly who and what Beatrice is. "As we have seen" the narrator notes, Beatrice lived "into a world apart" from that of her ancestors (96). The use of the narrative "we" is a departure from the third person narrator's previously unobtrusive mediation of Chris and Ikem's testimonies. This new voice, however, is not merely the "we" of the narrator in sudden complicity with the reader. Shifting away from the realm of knowledge shared with the reader, the narrator continues: "Barely, we say though, because she did carry a vague sense more acute at certain critical moments than others of being two different people" (96). The collective voice, rather than establishing a link to the reader's perspective on Beatrice, foregrounds the narrators continual access to her psyche; it reads omnisciently as a royal or divine "we." The narrator further distances himself from the reader, and, indeed, the narrative itself, by evaluating Beatrice's father's, Chris', and Ikem's interpretations of Beatrice. Ikem wins this semiotic contest: he "alone came closest to sensing the village priestess," and "he knew it better than Beatrice herself" (96). Thus, the narrator not only tells us what the characters think about Beatrice, but he also steps out of the chronology of the narrative, almost like a telepathic literary critic, to tell us which assessment is "right."

The narrator's explication of Beatrice's character through the Idemili myth and through other characters' varying perceptions of her divine aspect thus reads as an analogue to Idemili's own appearance in the world. Both are folkloric, "judiciously spaced...interruptions" into the "marketplace... world" (Idemili) or "high art" of the novel (Idemili myth). Both are delivered by "[our] sponsor, the divinity that controls remotely but diligently the transactions" of the profane realm. In the case of the telling of the Idemili myth, the narrator serves as this divine sponsor, although the remote control of the fictional world suggests that Achebe himself is our godly adman. The return from this divine under/overworld of narration, accompanied by Beatrice's return from the farawayworid of Sam's remote palace, is signalled in the next chapter by a conventional third-person narration, almost a novelistic aubade, of Beatrices waking to an unfamiliar sunrise complete with birdsong (98).

One reading of this mediation of Beatrice's first-person narrative might consider the narrator's extraordinary commentary as a kind of reversal of the Idemili myth, a reversal that would imply the need for Beatrice's female narrative power to be constrained by divine (male) intervention. A similar kind of narrative interruption, however, occurs in other places throughout the novel. David Diop's poem "Africa" serves as an exegetical parallel to the narrator's treatment of the Idemili myth. The poem is presented as an epigraph to Chapter 10, "Impetuous Son" in which Ikem encounters the obsequious (yet scornful) taxi drivers during their visit to his home. A third person narrator relates the exchange, but in the subsequent meditation on the oppressed's desire for their oppressors to flaunt (not flout) their privilege, Ikem's thoughts merge with the structure of the novel. The meditation concludes thus:

> ...what is at issue in all this may not be systems after all but a basic human failing that may only be alleviated by a good spread of general political experience, slow of growth and obstinately patient like the young tree planted by David Diop on the edge of the primeval desert just before the year of wonders in which Africa broke out so spectacularly in a rash of independent nation states! (128).

This exclamation is rather far afield from the narrative event that inspired it, the visit of the taxi drivers; indeed, the climactic conclusion is reined back into the tenor of the novel by Elewa's concurrence with the taxi drivers that Ikem should drive a car more suited to a person of his class: "I no tell you that before say this kind car wey you get de make person shame" (128).

Whether the taxi drivers actually make Ikem think of the Diop poem or whether we are to read this exuberant explication as the narrator's voice is difficult to determine. Omar Sougou points out however, that Achebe had previously used the image of Diop's "young tree" in his essay "The Writer and His Community" in order to speculate with less ambivalence on the developing relationship between the artist and the community (47). Achebe's language in "The Writer and His Community" is remarkably similar to the passage in *Anthills*:

> We can see in the horizon the beginnings of a new relationship between artist and community which will not flourish like the mango-trick in the twinkling of an eye but will rather, in the hard and bitter manner of David Diop's young tree, grow patiently and obstinately to the ultimate victory of liberty and fruition (61).

The development of general political experience, perhaps fostered by increasing interaction between the artist and the community, will occur "obstinately," "patiently." While the 1984 essay implies hope for "the ultimate victory of liberty and fruition," it is not Diop's tree in the 1987 novel that bears fruit but rather the body of Africa that breaks out "spectacularly in a rash of independent nation states." Despite the shift in tone, the narrator's rift on the Diop tree, which is supposed to be a representation of Ikem's thoughts, closely resembles Achebe's voice in the essay. The visit of the taxi drivers thus provides another opportunity for a "word from our sponsor," this time not Achebe-as-narrator-as-god, but instead Achebe-as-narrator-as-literary-critical-figure.

As a poet-journalist, Ikem would probably be familiar with the work of someone like Diop, assuming that the literary distribution networks of Ikem's Kangan were similar to those of Achebe's Nigeria. The Diop poem, then, merges the character of Ikem with the voice of the narrator as well as with the perspective of the author. Although the narrator penetrates Beatrice's consciousness during his discussion of the Idemili myth, his superior access to the heritage of "her people,' and his ability to evaluate other characters perceptions of her, distances her limited perspective from his omniscient one. The narrator validates Ikem's understanding of Beatrice as a half-divine being. The third-person narrative intrusions in the novel do not always, however, buttress the psychic links between Ikem, narrator, and Achebe.

David A. Maughan Brown has noted that Ikem's important speech at the University of Bassa on "the imperative of struggle" is not presented in the novel, thus sparing Achebe "the difficulty of providing, or even summarizing, the content of the speech" (*Anthills* 141, Maughan Brown 14). What Achebe does provide is an account of the Q&A after Ikem's majestic "epic prose-poem" has been delivered (*Anthills* 142). Although we do not have access to the transcript of the speech, its presentation and the consequent discussion are narrated in a seemingly straightforward, "unedited" chronology. At the beginning of the following chapter, however, the narrator switches from this reportage style to an anecdotal one by focusing on one section of the speech not previously narrated: Ikem's purported call for "regicide."

"One of the ifs of recent Kangan history," the narrator muses, "is what the fate of Ikem might have been had he backed out of that speaking engagement at the university (150). While this "if does not put the narrator in a divine or literary-critical realm, nor into ambivalent throes of nationalist euphoria, it does position the narrator at some point beyond the chronology of the novel. This narrator not only has his thumb on the pulse of his characters' thoughts; he also is conversant with the controversies that surround "recent Kangan history" after the events of the novel have been concluded. Furthermore, the narrator's retrospective characterization of the role of the speech both emphasizes Ikem's role in the history of the nation and increases the distance between Ikem's purportedly rash decision and the narrator's all-seeing hindsight.

These shifts in the voice of the third-person narrator – from the mythopoetic analysis of Beatrice/Idemili, to the cultural study of African society through Diop's "Africa," and finally to the armchair speculations of the Kangan history buff-raise questions both about who is in control of the novel and about who is, or should be, in control of the society portrayed within it. The opening lines of the first narrative shift can be read as an attempt to forestall criticism of this narrative strategy: even the "inscrutably ignorant...must concede the fact, indeed the inevitability, of... judiciously spaced, but nonetheless certain, interruptions" (93). Only those readers even worse off than the "inscrutably ignorant" would dare to question the efficacy or the implications of Achebe's manipulation of narration. Sougou takes the plunge and traces the confusing shifts between Chris' and Ikem's testimony and the third-person narration in the opening chapters of the novel. In these chapters, the modulations between an objective bystander and an omniscient voice lead Sougou to conclude: "In the end, this narrator's game...turns inconclusive and perhaps self-deceptive for he becomes the all-knowing and omnipresent witness' (38). The passages that I have examined reveal how the narrator's position of occasional omniscience moves from the divine to the literary to the historical realm. Is this sometime omniscient narrator to be read as unreliable, as self-deceived, or is it Achebe who has deceived himself?

In the interview with Anna Rutherford after the publication of *Anthills*, Achebe spoke of the lessons offered by the novel: "You have to broaden out so that when you are talking you are talking for the people, you are not only talking for a section or a group interest" (3). Perhaps Achebe has misguidedly taken his conviction to heart and created a narrator who selectively enjoys a perspective so broad that he does not speak "for" the people, he speaks at them. The first-person narratives do little to expand the aggregate voice of the novel beyond that of the elite initiate to British-schooled knowledge. Ikem concludes after the visit of the taxi drivers that the "prime failure of this government" – or the trouble with Kangan-is not corruption, foreign influence, capitalism, nor repression, but instead "the failure of our rulers to re-establish vital inner links with the poor and dispossessed of this country, with the bruised heart that throbs painfully at the core of the nation's being" (130–131). Yet the narrators, the "rulers" of the novel, maintain only the most tenuous of connections with the still silent masses who are purported to be the core of Kangan.

If Chris, Ikem, and Beatrice are not the nation's heart, they are perhaps, to varying degrees, its mouth. Chris is a former newspaper editor and Minister of Information, or "Honorable Commissioner for Words"; he keeps a journal of his tenure as a government official (6). While Ikem replaces Chris as editor of the National Gazette, he is also a speechmaker and a poet. Beatrice combines her official post as Senior Assistant Secretary in the Ministry of Finance with the composition of a chronicle/autobiography that attempts both to "bring[...] together as many broken pieces of this tragic history as I could lay my hands on" and to "expose my life.. .to see if perhaps there are aspects of me I had successfully concealed even from myself (75, 77). With the characters' endeavors in the national and literary realms of communication, *Anthills* reads almost as a novel-length dramatization of the tug-of-war between what Achebe calls "beneficent" and "malignant" fictions in his essay, "The Truth of Fiction." "What distinguishes beneficent fiction from such malignant cousins as racism," writes Achebe, "is that the first never forgets that it is fiction and the other never knows that it is" (148). Malignant fictions "demand and indeed impose...absolute and unconditional obedience" (141).

While Benedict Anderson has written influentially on the relationship between the proliferation of newspapers and novels and the rise of nationalism, his argument about the role of these media in imagining the community of the nation does not sufficiently account for the *statist* fictions purveyed through official media in repressive regimes such as the one fictionalized as Kangan. Beatrice's perusal of the obituaries, personal notices, and criminal reports in the Sunday *Gazette* leaves her "wondering why one must keep on buying and trying to read such trash. Except that if you didn't you couldn't avoid the feeling that you might be missing something important, few of us, alas having the strength of will to resist that false feeling' (101). Here we see Beatrice resisting "that false feeling" of the nation's citizens coherently living their synchronous lives, yet the photographs of the "newly disreputable" foreshadow the malignant official fiction of Ikem's abduction and death that is narrated in newspapers and radio and TV broadcasts, all of them, of course, state-owned (101).

Malignant fictions abound in the various media depicted in *Anthills*. Sam and Chris recruit the half-literate but well-received Professor Okong to be Commissioner for Home Affairs in the newly formed cabinet for "without having any clearer ideas than either of us [hel would be helpful in puffing whatever came into our heads into popular diction and currency" (12). This division of labor between Sam's decision-making and the public narration of people like Chris and Okong is remarkably parallel to Achebe's warning in "The Truth of Fiction" about the "desperate man" and his dangerous imagination:

> when...he wishes to believe something however bizarre or stupid, nobody can stop him. He will discover in his imagination a willing and enthusiastic accomplice. Together they will weave the necessary fiction which will then bind him securely to his cherished intention (153).

What is most dangerous about the malignant fictions of Kangan is that they aim to bind not only Sam, but the entire nation to "his cherished intention." In an attempt to control the story of Ikem's death, the State Research Council publicly associates him with "a plot by unpatriotic elements in Kangan working.. .to destabilize the lawful government of this country" (155). This plot provides a pretext for collecting information from other "elements" and ultimately leads to Chris' flight from the capital. The stakes of controlling the narration of the story of Kangan are high; in the consequent coup (not orchestrated by Ikem), Colonel Johnson Ossai, author of the announcement is missing and presumed to have been executed by Sam.

That an actual, unrelated coup follows the dissemination of fear about a trumped-up plot to overthrow the government reveals that malignant statist fiction is never completely successful in asserting its absolute truth. Sam's equation of a distorted representation of his countenance on the cover of *Time* with his "funeral" illustrates his awareness of his lack of control over versions of the story of Kangan in media that his government does not own (14). Indeed, the international media provide an alternative fiction to the "national anguish [dispensed] in carefully measured milligrammes" on state TV (139). Even Chris admits that "while the ministry over which I preside dishes out all that flim-flam to the nation on KBC I sneak away every morning when no one is watching to listen to the Voice of the Enemy [BBC radio]" (107). While the unfavorable portrait of Lou Cranford, the American UP reporter, undermines the reliability and sensitivity of the international media, Achebe shows how the Kangan official media are not inviolable. Readers learn that items that are designated "Not To Be Broadcast" end up circulating anyway; Ikem's unofficial editorials inadvertently influence votes in Abazon; strategically untrue stories of Chris' exile are planted to protect his safety (56, 116, 175). Even Sam's use of the term 'Kabisa,' much to his dismay, trickles down to the underclasses as it is disseminated through the low-tech grapevine, what Beatrice calls "VOR, the Voice of Rumor" (155).

All of the varieties of malignant fiction present themselves as absolute truth and cannot afford to recognize themselves as fictions: such fiction, according to Achebe, "breaks the bounds and ravages the real world" ("The Truth of Fiction" 149). Beneficent fiction, as a self-conscious construction, calls into full life our total range of imaginative faculties and gives us a heightened sense of our personal, social and human reality" ("The Truth of Fiction" 151). Considering his own position and his convictions about the role of the writer, it is not surprising that Achebe posits literary fiction as a beneficent exercise of the imagination; *Anthills of the Savannah* potentially heightens the reader's awareness of the very real consequences and weaknesses of malignant fiction. Within the novel are several examples of what Achebe might call beneficent fiction. Two of them, the Idemili myth and David Diop's "Africa," are central to the third-person narrator's assumption of an omniscient stance.

Other works of beneficent fiction in the novel, however, are created by the characters themselves. Ikem's prose poem, "Hymn to the Sun," is provided in full and later re-interpreted by Chris as he journeys into Abazon for the first time. The poem's significance is emblematized in Ikem's metaphor, which gives *Anthills* its title. What must certainly be a fragment of Beatrice's pseudo-autobiography serves as a portion of her first-person narration. Even Chris, the least literary and most institutionally powerful of the three first-person narrators, keeps a diary that could either expose the fictionality of the "information" released by his ministry or serve as source material for a novel very much like *Anthills*. Certainly the traditional stories valorized by the Abazon elder are to be considered beneficent for they "save[...] our progeny from blundering like blind beggars into the spikes of the cactus fence" (114).

The Abazon elder admits that he has not read the editorials by Ikem that have guided his community. Unlike Beatrice and Ikem, he is not only bereft of institutional authority; he does not even enjoy literate access to the state's official narration (112). Nonetheless, his oration on the role of the storyteller reveals the difficulties the first-person narrators face in attempting to negotiate their governmental, literary, and (within the novel) narrative roles. The elder speaks of the storyteller:

> So fully is he owned by the telling that sometimes – especially when he looks around him and finds no age-mate to challenge the claim-he will turn the marks left on him by the chicken-pox and yaws he suffered in childhood into bullet scars.
>
> But the lies of those possessed by Agwu are lies that do no harm to anyone. They float on the top of the story like the white bubbling at the pot-mouth of new palm-wine. The true juice of the tree lies coiled up inside, waiting to strike... (115).

This explanation of the truth and lies contained within stories reads as a folkloric parallel to Achebe's more scholarly definition of beneficent fiction in his essay. The thematic thrust of the novel, however, might seem to emphasize the potential harm done by unchallenged storytellers so engrossed in the telling that they misrepresent their own significance within the tale. Beatrice chastizes Chris, Sam, and Ikem for overestimating their own importance in the story of Kangan: "you fellows, all three of you, are incredibly conceited. The story of this country, as far as you are concerned, is the story of the three of you" (60).

Perhaps the three green bottles go wrong in thinking of Kangan as a story rather than as a society in need of sensitive leadership. Throughout the novel, the national project is conceived in literary terms. Chris initially keeps his position in Sam's regime because he wants "to see where it will all...well, end," as if he is engrossed in a mystery novel rather than responsible for (and to) a nation (2). Ikem insists that he is not repulsed by Sam's dictatorial style of leadership because "He is basically an actor and half the things we are inclined to hold against him are no more than scenes from his repertory to which he may have no moral commitment whatsoever (45). Ikem suggests, quite unconvincingly, that malignant fiction clothed in the beneficent garb of dramatic literature ceases to be malignant. Even Beatrice, who warns Chris of the green bottles' dangerous show-stealing, alienates Sam by sharing with him her resentment at being involved in a Desdemona story whose Othello is "the symbol of her nation's pride" (74). All of the novels first person narrators view the trajectory of the nation as a storyline in which they enjoy a starring role; as the novel is narrated through them, *Anthills of the Savannah*, the story of Kangan, is indeed the story of the four of them.

In some sense, *Anthills* is also the story of Achebe's own career. Achebe probably experienced the tension between official and literary fictions during his tenure at the Nigerian Broadcasting Corporation. While *Things Fall Apart* and *No Longer at Ease* took their titles and, to varying degrees, their themes from staples of the Western literary canon, *Anthills* finds itself in a different world, a world in which, as the British publisher Dick sneers, "the best English these days is written either by Africans or Indian" (57). Yet *Anthills* as trendy postcolonial literature foregrounds its roots in the world of the early novels. Beatrice recognizes, in thinking of the tales her mother used to tell, that "two generations before the likes of me...there were already barely literate carpenters ...subverting the very sounds and legends of daybreak to make straight my way" on the path to her first-rate English literature degree. Ikem's "Hymn to the Sun" represents, like *Things Fall Apart*, a modern retelling of the kinds of stories the Abazon elder praises. Ikem's speech at the university may have sounded a bit like "The Trouble with Kangan," and his heretofore trouble with women begins to be addressed within the pages of the novel.

Anthills demonstrates that the relationship between Achebe and his reading community, symbolized as Diop's "young tree" in "The Writer and His Community," has indeed been growing patiently. Achebe has spun a web of proverbial and folkloric knowledge throughout his succession of novels; while he relies upon this cultural context in *Anthills*, he also mocks his own characteristic style. Sam tells Okong at the beginning of the novel, "Please cut out the proverbs, if you don't mind" (18). Less self-mocking, however, and more self-indulgent is his inclusion not only of the cultural content of the earlier novels, but the novels themselves in *Anthills*. Beatrice admits to Chris, "I do sometimes feel like Chielo in the novel, the priestess and prophetess of the Hills and Caves" (105). Achebe's inclusion of *Things Fall Apart* within Kangan's literary canon emblematizes the conflict over narration within *Anthills*: out of twenty million stories, it is Beatrice's reading of Achebe's first novel that helps her to understand herself.

In 1967, not long after the publication of *A Man of the People* and two decades before the publication of *Anthills of the Savannah*, Wole Soyinka expressed concern over the fascination with the past held by many African writers:

> Isolated by his very position in society, he mistook his own personal and temporary cultural predicament for the predicament of his entire society and turned attention from what was really happening to that society. He even tried to give society something that the society had never lost – its identity (qtd. in Agovi 45).

Achebe's body of work has helped to connect the Nigerian past with the real predicament of its present and his exploration of contemporary Africa in *Anthills* includes a warning that those in power not mistake their own predicaments for that of the society as a whole. Yet the novel is very much about Achebe's predicament as the English language novelist who put African fiction on the literary map before Nigeria was even an independent nation-state.

Chris defends his focus on his "one tiny synoptic account" of the story of Kangan by admitting, "that's the only one I know' (60–61). By now, Achebe's stories are the ones that many readers across the globe know. Chris' defense is undermined by Achebe's insistence, in interviews and through Beatrice, that the other twenty million stories be heard. The narrative structure of the novel reflects Achebe's concerns about leadership, but the voices of Chris, Ikem Beatrice, and the privileged third-person narrator ensure that the people of the nation will continue to be spoken for. Those who are to be led remain effectively silent, their stories untold. Still, the novel insists that the stories at hand are not the ones that matter, as if leadership is irrelevant without substantial input perhaps even guidance, from the masses. Within this tension between personal knowledge and the stories of the masses, the supposedly harmless "lies" of a storyteller who misrepresents his participation in the tale of his people take on an ominous, perhaps even "malignant," aspect. While these "lies" are but bubbles in fresh palm wine, "the true juice of the tree lies coiled up inside, waiting to strike" (115). Even within beneficient literary fiction, the untold stories of the masses lie in wait like a venomous snake. Chris, Ikem, and Beatrice make small gestures toward reestablishing those supposedly vital links with the nation's heart; within the narrative structure of the novel, however, poems, speeches, and news broadcasts speak louder than heartbeats.

Works Cited

Achebe, Chinua. "The Truth of Fiction." *Hopes and Impediments.* New York: Anchor, 1989, 138–153

———. "The Writer and His Community." *Hopes and Impediments.* New York: Anchor, 1989, 47–61.

———. *Anthills of the Savannah.* New York: Anchor, 1987.

Agovi, K.E. "The African Writer and the Phenomenon of the Nation State in Africa." *Ufahamu* 18.1 (1990): 41–62.

Maughan Brown, David A. "*Anthills of the Savannah*: Achebe's Solutions to the 'Trouble with Nigeria.'" *Matatu* 8 (1991): 3–22.

Rutherford, Anna. "Interview with Achebe." *Kunapipi* 9.2 (1987): 1–7.

Sougou, Omar. "Language, Foregrounding and Inertextuality in *Anthills of the Savannah.*" *Matatu* 8 (1991): 35–54.

Chapter 26

Male Politics and Female Power in Chinua Achebe's *Anthills of the Savannah*

Teresa U. Njoku

POWER AND POLITICS DOMINATE the issues in Chinua Achebe's *Anthills of the Savannah*. Politics, however, has many different levels of meaning in *Anthills*. Firstly it implies the scheming of those seeking personal power, position, or status. 'His Excellency", the president, and the commissioners are included in this meaning of politics. For all the characters, however, politics deals with "power, influence, and authority" (Bell, 1975). This is so because politics is a way of interaction with others in order to influence and charge their behaviors, attitudes, and ideas. Thus, "in the widest sense", politics is "concerned" in the text "with how people affect each other" (Bell, 1997: 10). The interaction and influence occur among people with similar interests and also across the class divide. Although masculine control and domination in politics is directly tackled in the novel, Achebe credits the female with greater power than in his other novels. Though this power according to Berenice Carroll, means "control, dominance, and influence", in recent times, the primary meaning that is attached to power as late as 1933 is "ability, energy and strength" (*Berenice Carroll*, 1972). Ability is manifested in achievement and competence. The two central female characters, Beatrice and Elewa, have power as well as the background from which power accrues to the individual: education, employment, patriotism, self definition, and self-control in the case of Beatrice, and for Elewa the ability to relate with the elite and with the ordinary people, ability to express her beliefs, and the transcendence of motherhood. Beatrice interacts with the three main male characters in the text. The interaction does not diminish her power, but promotes its growth and permanence. Thus, the power divisions between men and women get a jolt by what Achebe portrays as happening in the seat of government in Kangan. While seeming at the beginning of the novel to adopt the usual exclusion of females from the politics and government of Kangan, the dynamics of female power provides the subterranean force that upset all the power structures erected by men. By the time the novel ends however, women are ascribed greater powers in political and social affairs and female power is entrenched in both politics and government.

The beginning of *Anthills* is a session in the cabinet of the military administration in the independent African state of Kangan. The President, Sam, occupies the highest seat of government without any preparation for political leadership. The eleven commissioners he has appointed are supposed to play participatory roles in the affairs of government. That is why Chris, the first narrator of the events in Kangan, describes the group as the hope of the black race". In traditional power relations, the ruler chooses advisers who are his equals to guide him in his actions and policies; in this way, adult males participate in decision-making.

The picture Achebe presents however, about the national executive council is that it has transformed under a military dictator to become "a theatre of the absurd", where the president is merely "acting" and "directing", while his members of cabinet engage in the "game" and the "theatricals". Consequently, the affairs of government lose their meaning, because there are no rules and programmes guiding the actions of the "decision makers". The affairs of government now become centered on the Presidents mood; this determines whether success or failure is recorded for each day. The cabinet celebrates its happiness when the president is in a happy mood and gossips about him and fellow commissioners when their backs are turned. In this way, the appearance of government replaces its activities: "Appearing is important to him. Not appearing is, of course, the worst kind of disgrace" (*Anthills* 147). Sam's stand for appearance means that he goes for what society approves as right rather than face the reality of doing the right thing, which is the true expression of the society. Beatrice, on the other hand, does not accept what society considers alright for woman; she determines her own standards and actions based on the principle of truth.

Sycophancy takes the place of debates in the government of Kangan. The educated elite in government reduces itself to an obsequious group, which the President treats with disdain. Consequently, he does not have any qualms detaining them for the failure to inform him about the delegation from Abazon. Ikem Osodi calls this cabinet a "circus show" and echoes Chris' statement that there is no national cabinet because the President has an inner caucus of cronies. When Chris in his narration calls Professor Okong "a buffoon" because he lacks morality in politics, we know that the appellation fits the other commissioners particularly the Attorney General. The ineffective cabinet breeds the monster of dictatorship in Sam, while Chris as the former editor of the *National Gazette* nurtures the "freak baby" that is Professor Okong himself. Misfits are thus produced at different stages of national life and the welfare of the ordinary man is forgotten.

Among the ordinary people in the novel contests of nerves occur. Such a contest occurs between Ikem and the taxi driver; and the taxi driver concedes to him only after a struggle. Ikem's own personal contests occur during his speech to the students after his dismissal as the editor of the *National Gazette*. It also reveals itself in the, "crusading editorials" despite Chris' warnings that he should desist from writing them. These contests are like these of the tortoise before he is overpowered. The wise old leader from Abazon who points out the symbolism of the tortoise and contests shows that contests/struggles should be part of living. The cabinet in the government of Kangan does not give room for contests. The commissioners capitulate and apologise to the President without opposing anything he decides. Though contests imply struggles the actors in government do not provide models for such. The cabinet thus represents men who have "died"; they are dead because they keep silent when they should speak. This is a political lack because "politics is talk." (Bell, 1975: 10). On the other hand, the populace keeps silent during its oppression under a dictator. It however breaks the silence at the end of the novel when it takes a political action that destroys the President.

Women are excluded from direct involvement in the affairs of the government of Kangan and the power hierarchy this implies. Though the government is masculinized, most social and domestic responsibilities fall on them. In opposition to the undemocratic cabinet at the beginning of the novel is the democratic gathering at the end. Such a gathering of the ordinary people constitutes a force and possesses grassroot power. Beatrice is in control in this cultural/political gathering. The cultural dimension is the naming of a child which ushers it into humanity and gives it identity. Beatrice names kern's baby girl and thereby assumes a prerogative which is entirely male. By this very act, Achebe ascribes to Beatrice the status and role of a father. In lgbo onomastics, "Amechira" is an entirely male name and a principle of promogeniture. Beatrice deliberately subverts this. Patriarchal tradition also determines that the father names since Ikem is dead, the Elewa's s uncle comes late so the responsibility would have fallen on the uncle. Since ceremony, Beatrice and the members of the group claim a fatherhood that is symbolic for the child. Child ownership which the traditional system emphasizes is here dismissed because the child belongs to all; afterall, it arrives into the world fatherless. Achebe here legitimizes woman's role as both the one who procreates and the one who names the child. Patriarchal convention is also jettisoned by the fact that the events in the novel had 'thrown her (Beatrice) into a defensive pact with a small band of near strangers that was to prove stronger than kindred or friendship. Like old kinships this one was pledged also on blood. It was not, however, blood flowing safe and inviolate in its veins but blood causally split and profaned" (218). Both Ikem and

Elewa leave for the future: something Ikem sows the seeds of ideas in Emmanuel and Elewa brings forth a child. Elewa's uncle is surprised that the bride – price was not paid before he is invited to name the offspring of the relationship. Though the bride price is an essential element in the establishment of the legality of a traditional union, Elewa's uncle is in agreement with the change that seems to overtake traditional custom

Unlike the leadership during the cabinet meeting at the beginning of the novel, Beatrice is a leader who is sensitive to the peculiar needs of her company. The political idea that is generated by the group attributes power to the ordinary people living in solidarity, "not to any little caucus, no matter how talented" (232). The youth, Emmanuel, is emboldened by the lives of kern and Chris. Ikem imbues him with ideas and Chris shows him how to die like a man. On the other hap, the members of cabinet in the government of Kangan have no idea of their responsibilities and the expectations of the public from them.

The religious fraternization that occurs among the members of the group at the naming ceremony must be noted. The spirit of ecumenism is also promoted by the group. Similarly, the power resources that are deployed by Beatrice in the exercise of power become obvious. According to Agatha, Beatrice is "too strong" and "To strong too much no de good for woman" (230). In her native wisdom however, Elewa recognizes that to become "too strong" is not good for man or woman: "E good make person cry small (230). Beatrice's strength of character is considered masculine. Elewa shows that the division of people's emotions along gender lines should not be accepted. Earlier, Ikem and Chris had recognized Beatrice's writing as masculine while kern and Chris are described as sensitive, a quality associated with women. In this way, each of the three characters embodies qualities that could be regarded as both masculine and feminine. Beatrice's father calls her a "female soldier". Achebe makes the reader identify equally with both the male central characters and the female ones, Beatrice and Elewa. In accepting these characters other standards rather than gender show the androgynous ideal towards which *Anthills* seems to tend. Androgyny involves the effacement of gender differentiation in art, the men embody feminine qualities while the women have male traits. Thus, in *Anthills,* Achebe enunciates some feminist ideas through Beatrice while writing an androgynous novel. *Anthills* is androgynous because Achebe exposes in it, "a sense of waste of lost spiritual and sexual power, of equality of worth between the sexes.... (Heilbrun, Carolyn 1982: 59). The degeneration of male political actors shows the absence of the spiritual ideal. Equally, there is a national loss since the female population is not given a political role. Achebe goes to a great extent to show the potentiality in the complementarity of the sexes. In a feminist novel a reader identifies only with the female protagonist. Coleridge was right: "great minds do tend to be androgynous" (Heilbrun, Carolyn, 1982: 77). Achebe has created both male and female characters that are likeable. The society of the novel is not andrgynous but the author prescribes androgyny for the society.

Unlike the cabinet under Sam the President, Beatrice exudes the spirit of nationalism. The strategy she uses for this is to expose all the situations in the novel during which her country is brought into disrepute. By the simple way she asks inconvenient questions she outrages both John Kent ("Mad Medico"), and His Excellency (Sam), through what may be regarded as "impudence" of speech. She attacks John Kent for his criticism of the President and at the President's party she deliberately flirts with His Excellency in order to get him away from the American female journalist who has got the main actors in government under her thumb. She sacrifices her life and respect in order to rescue the "endangered" President, Her act of sacrifice is recreated in mythic terms because she relinquishes her own power of self-control in order to save the sacred hierarchy of power and authority of her country from contamination and scandal. In the past, men who quested for power and authority depended on the mystical female; their lives and death depended on the quest whose futures depended on female approval or rejection. *Idemili*, the traditional female deity symbolizes the moral nature of authority. As *Idemili* mediates between man and his ambition for power and authority, so does Beatrice mediate by bringing sanity and modesty to the "embattled" President. In both cases cited above, male false claim to all knowledge and pomposity is exploded. Similarly, the hypocrisy of government is exposed. When the new Head of State invites Beatrice to the state funeral organized for Chris, Beatrice rejects the invitation because General tango was the former Chief of Staff of President Sam whose dictatorship and mismanagement had caused the crisis which took kern and Chris. General Lango had himself been one of the perpetrators of the crimes committed in the country under Sam. Beatrice depicts thus, more awareness of the nature of the Presidency than Sam, and her political consciousness outweighs his and that of his cronies.

Beatrice's social and political effectiveness earn her criticisms – the barbs of male chauvinism. This results in Beatrice's autobiography, a genre often associated with males and not females. The autobiography summarizes her background, beliefs, and feelings. It seems a manifesto for female liberation in Africa. She dismisses the idea of influencing people through her "bottom power". She recreates the world to which she belongs: she is in control of this world and refuses to engage in anything that "would require her to call on others" (87) or embark on anything that is "beyond her own puny powers" (87). Her ideas about herself as a woman originate from the conditions under which she had grown. The autobiography becomes a means of dismantling false ideas about marriage and male female relationship. Her intellect is brought into judgments, decisions relating to herself, and to external authorities whether patriarchal, military dictator or social relations. She resolves the conflict between the conditioned expectation that a woman has to depend on others and the equally strong urge to do things in her own way. The later choice leads to her attainment of autonomy. Her autonomy finds expression in her actions and speech (aspects of politics) which exhibit her exemption from rules or conditions of female limitation in her country.

Achebe uses the duality in the female personality to indicate power. The two parts/ essence in Beatrice are complementary: "In a way felt like two people living inside one skin, not two hostile tenants but two rather friendly people, two different enough to be interesting to each other without being incompatible" (89). In this regard, Beatrice resembles Chielo in *Things Fall Apart*. Unlike the wrangling men, she perceives the danger that will overtake the three central characters: Chris, kern, and Sam. Her prophecy that kern will go before Chris and Sam, is fulfilled before the novel ends. The crisis, according to her, connects everyone: We are all in it, Ikem, you, me, even Him" (115). The spiritual and mystic role she plays heightens the political action and also gives it depth.

Beatrice's dual essence makes her relationship with Chris be suffused with ethereality. She recognizes her mystic worth and Chris also perceives it. She perceives acutely when the relationship with Chris comes to a "crossroads" beyond which a new day would break, unpredictable, without precedent (196). The perceptions influence the characters concerned and are sources of knowledge and power. The relationship on the last night with Chris is captured in ritualistic terms. Achebe describes Beatrice as carrying "a strong aura of that other Beatrice who Chris refers to "in fearful jest" as "goddess". The fear" in Chris' perception heightens the significance of the ritual because as a goddess, her ritual is one of enactment. The spirit essence makes Chris liken her movement to that of "the maiden spirit Mask, coming in to the arena, erect, disdainful, high coiffured, unravished yet by her dance" (199). Thus, Beatrice becomes a spiritual core of love and strength from which Chris draws before his fateful journey of escape. The nocturnal encounter is desired by her and she controls and dictates the tune of the relationship. Here, male domination in sexual matters gives way to female desire and dictation and the sexual act is shown as a union that is deeply mysterious and which removes "separateness" (113). Earlier in the novel, and after attending the President's party, Beatrice also controls and commands sexual act and directs what happens. The authority she commands enforces obedience and influences action. In sexuality Beatrice thus holds absolute power and Chris is like a child cradled in her arms and breasts her eyes watching anxiously over him" (114). In these instances sexuality is ritualized and assumes mythic proportions.

At first Kern is a chauvinistic male who regards a female as a "comforter" only to hate her and her body on waking up in the morning. Unable himself to cope with his sexuality at first, he transfers his loathing to the female body and claims that it is hard work that makes him dismiss his girl friends to their homes in the night. It is Elewa's understanding of this aspect of male chauvinism that makes her lament her woman's lot and the abuse to which female sexuality is put: "... If I no kuku bring my stupid nyarsh come dump for your bedroom you for kick me about like I be football.... (34). Elewa perceives Ikem's love/hate attitude to her sexuality. Kern states that he conceives of women as people without brains. Initially, he fails to see them as complex beings; when he is no longer working, his imagination finds escape in the nature and oppression of women. The attitude to female sexuality also shapes Chris' suggestion to Beatrice that she should keep all the options open during the private party with the president. By his statement Chris gives consent for Beatrice to sleep with Sam, his boss, if need be, to harmonize the relationship among the "troika" in control of the government of Kangan. Female sexuality is readily sacrificed for the reconciliation of erstwhile friends. Beatrice shatters this stereotype of the easily, available female sexuality by exposing her sound mental and psychological personality.

Chris and Kern's political power and actions are "built of and around words" (Bell 1975: 12). They are in control of the organs of information in Kangan: Chris as the commissioner of information, and Kern, as the editor of the National Gazette. Their positions enable them to use the weapons of information for political action. Kern's crusading editorials and public speeches and Chris, use of "radio rumour" and telephone calls to subvert the dictatorship of Sam make them be regarded as enemies of the government. The editorials speak for the masses who are politically silent. At the end of the novel, the masses break the silence caused by their victimization by eliminating the dictator through violent means. Violence would be unnecessary as a form of political action if the President had listened to Chris and kern. Each commands political power because each affects other characters and moulds ideas which remain even when they die. Ikem seems to understand the extent of power they command and does not underestimate it:

> ...I am sure Sam can still be saved if we put our minds to it. His problem is that with so many petty interests salaaming around him air day, like that shyster of an Attorney – General, he has no chance at knowing what is right. And that's what Chris and I ought to be doing rotting him glimpse a little light now and again through the chinks in his solid wall of court jesters... (46).

Sam remains blind to the "light" and his political action of withdrawal from the people he claims he can rule for life lead to his doom. As a Commissioner for information, on the other hand, Chris is involved in the politics of communication for the government. When he is in hiding he reverts to the use of "radio rumour" the language strategy of the silent majority. In the social stereotype women are associated with gossip. "Radio rumour" has its basis on gossip; therefore, Chris resorts to a verbal strategy used mostly by women.

However, Ikem's political consciousness about the nature of female oppression undergoes change. The catalyst for this change is Beatrice. His "annunciation" about his understanding of the female question occurs after his suspension from the National Gazette. His insight on the women question does not however, materialize in suggesting new roles for modern women. His assertion that women will determine and tell themselves what their new roles should be shows that at this stage he equates femaleness with brains and intellect which he had earlier denied the group. Knowledge of the nature of oppression is necessary for meaningful political action. However, contradictions occur in the individual and in the society. Beatrice does not identify with Ikem's perspective on the woman question which Ikem seems to have presented as universal ideas. The way to liberation that kern enunciates is reform" because it will promote real freedom by reforming society around what it is" (100).

Chris is a character readers also identify with. As the Commissioner for Information who helps Sam (His Excellency) select his commissioners, he believes he is sufficiently in control of the political situation in his country. But Sam's love of foreign models, lack of initiative, selfishness, etc. thwart his efforts. At first he sees himself as the watchdog of society and later he is the only man who protests the police officer's rape of Adanma. He fights for Sam and Kern at different times and for different reasons but has no opportunity to defend himself when he confronts death. With kern's death, he gains new perception of the political and social life and realities in Kangan. His death at the hands of the police officer ushers in a moment of truth because he discovers the truth of being oneself. It is at that moment that he understands man's limited power and is freed from his earlier knowledge of being more powerful than he is. He recognizes at the point of death that life and power resemble the green bottle standing perilously on the wall. Similarly, Ikem understands himself more as he comes to the end of his life. A prominent feature of the past of human beings and his own is the oppression of women which underlies the oppression of the sexes. His life is terminated at that point when he comes to a full recognition about the complementarity of gender so that he does not take action to promote his new idea in his public speeches. The truth he and Chris discover is that Beatrice's roles go beyond that of a female and through them Achebe challenges the discrimination against women in politics.

In Conrad's *Heart of Darkness* Kurtz's fiancée is not told the truth about her lover's death. In *Anthills*, Emmanuel tells Beatrice of Chris' death. In the social stereotype, women are never associated with the truth. The last statement Beatrice makes however, is that "truth is... unbearably beautiful (233). Both Chris (male) and

Beatrice (female) recognize and discover this beauty of truth which can transform the world because truth belongs to both genders.

Achebe's *Anthills* uses myth, humor, and feminization of literary vision to achieve greatness. Humor is used to criticize the military dictatorship in the novel by making the system seem ludicrous. In the end, humor becomes an expression of the triumph of the superior characters over the inferior ones. Laughing at oneself seems feminine and Chris dies laughing at himself. Therefore, he is a male but embodies some feminine qualities. In addition, Achebe recreates the myth of the quest for survival in the myth of *Idemili* the guarantor of authority and power. The myth of the ceremony of birth and identification shown in the naming ceremony enables Achebe to enthrone the female characters in the work and to teach his readers in a male dominated society. Females have the last say in the novel.

Works Cited

Achebe, Chinua. *Things Fall Apart*. London: Heinemann, 1958.
———. *Anthill of the Savannah*. New York: Anchor, 1987.
Carroll, Berenice. Ed. *Liberating Women's History*. Illinois: University of Illinois Press.
Conrad, Joseph. *Heart of Darkness*. New York: Penguin, 1982.
Heilbrun, Carolyn G. *Toward a Recognition of Andrology*. New York: W.W. Norton & Co., 1982.

Chapter 27

"A Woman is Always Something": A Re-Reading of Achebe's *Anthills of the Savannah*

Chinyere Nwagbara

PERHAPS IN NO OTHER work of the master story – teller have women been portrayed in a more positive light than in *Anthills of the Savannah*. Achebe's portrayal of women in his fictional works, especially in the very early ones, shows serious macho heroism. He makes no pretensions about women playing serious roles in his earliest works. In Achebe's masterpiece, *Things Fall Apart,* and even in *Arrow of God*, both situated in rural communities, male heroism and patriarchy take center stage, while women have a liminal defined role. Okonkwo is an embodiment of his society's collective ethos on success and achievement. But his lack of flexibility and tolerance which border on pride is in conflict with the society's. His patriarchal society keeps women on the periphery of social contact. It is even more so in *Arrow of God*, where there are many titled men and voiceless women. Women in these earliest works are essentially objects and causative agents as evident in the war between Mbaino and Umuofia. The death of one of the women is the cause for the inter-communal conflict. These "dumb" women are often mere symbols, executing traditional female roles of wife, mother and domesticity, serving the needs of their chauvinistic men. More often than not, a life of servitude and obedience has been imbibed in these women that they acquiesce to their situations. For instance, Achebe in *Things Fall Apart* depicts Anasi, first wife of Nwakibie, as accepting her "subordinate" role to her husband.

> Anasi was the first wife and the others could not drink before her, so they stood waiting ... She walked up to her husband and accepted the horn from him. She went down on one knee, drank a little and handed back the horn. She rose, called him by his name and went back to her hut. The other wives drank in the same way, in the proper order, and went away ... (TFA 21).

The thematic emphasis on patriarchy, manliness, bravery and survival, puts the African woman in the background. She is to be seen and not heard in traditional society, though in practical terms, a minimal percentage of women are seen as well as heard. There is, however, a remarkable shift from Achebe's rigid, stereotypic mould of women in his novels set in traditional life to a more positive portrayal of women in novels that have rural and urban influences like *No Longer at Ease* and *A Man of the People*. In these later novels, no matter how one wants to look at the depiction of the female sex, it is apparent that "a woman is also something". But in *Anthills of the Savannah*, Achebe creates Beatrice, a female character, who particularly defies gender conventions to be first and foremast a human being with all the rights and privileges so bestowed, while to be a woman comes second if at all. Achebe's portrayal of Beatrice in *Anthills* shows clearly that "a woman is always something".

Women in Achebe's Early Fiction

The literature reveals a deep reverence for men which borders on fear by their women. Women are terrified by such men with a heart of steel like Okonkwo, who rules his household with iron hands. Okonkwo's handling of his wives is not only ruthless, but reflective of masculine invincibility and bravery. He almost kills his wife Ekwefi for cutting banana leaves. He dares to violate the week of peace as he threatens Ojiugo, his wife. Wives drink only after men have drunk and they do so on bended knees. Often, their only reverence is being just wives and mothers. There is, however, dignity in motherhood as it is celebrated. Mothers, especially those with male children, are respected. This is apparent in the philosophy of NNEKA (mother is supreme). But a man's wealth is counted in terms of the number of wives he can marry and keep-in his premises as can be seen from Nwakibie's household. Priestesses are however respected and even feared as exemplified by Chielo, the priestess of Agbala. When Okonkwo gets into serious trouble, he seeks protection in his motherland, Mbanta. Masculinity is revered to such a ridiculous extent that becoming a missionary is gendered and men who become missionaries are no longer considered masculine, but feminine. Okonkwo warns his other sons against it as he says, "if any one of you prefers to be a woman, let him follow Nwoye now while I am alive so that I can curse him" (122). Such is the low esteem in which women are held.

Arrow of God constitutes another celebration of patriarchy and chauvinism. Achebe crafts the story in such a manner that leaves no room for any serious role for the women. They are only there to highlight their men's heroic ethos. They are often voices, eyes and eyes: "voices of women returning from the stream broke into Ezeulu's thoughts". So Matefi, Ojiugo and other women are mere embellishments of the story. They are intangible as far as the men are concerned. They do not have any place in a patriarchal society that is preoccupied with notions of wealth, bravery and power, which are all associated with the masculine power.

Chinua Achebe's portrayal of the female sex takes a consciously different angle in *No Longer at Ease*. The story shows an increasing preoccupation with women as Achebe positions women more centrally than in earlier works. Clara is not placed peripherally as her story is delicately interwoven with Obi Okonkwo's and some strength of character is revealed in her. Clara, Obi Okonkwo's girl though defined as an untouchable by the customs and traditions of their people, refuses to be a pitiable appendage to Obi. She declares her status as that of an untouchable and she remains undaunted as she upholds her self-esteem. She is a self-confident professional. There are clear manifestations of self-pride and integrity in her comportment. Clara does not like condescension or patronizing attitude from her friends. She proves her good nature and consideration of the feelings of others when she decidedly refuses to blackmail Obi into marrying her, even as she is carrying his baby.

Obi's mother is another female whom Achebe depicts with a mind of her own in the story. She is firm and convinced that her son should not marry an outcast. She threatens him with suicide if he dares, and this threat reaches the inner recesses of Obi's heart. So, Clara and Obi's mother play fairly significant roles as they both stand their grounds on issues that concern them. Mary Kolawole affirms that:

> In Clara and Obi's mother, we have women who have moved from the initial social space and traditional conditioning created by Achebe.... His representation of Clara and Obi's mother is closer to a slice of reality (114).

Besides these two women, the others in the book remain on the periphery as the emphasis is still on women's domestic roles.

In *A Man of the People*, there is a shift from domesticity to a more broad-based activation of events in the life of the protagonists. Women are introduced into politics. They are used as political campaigners. Although Mrs. John raises important questions about Chief Nanga, she remains more of a physically loud person as "her massive royal beads were worth hundreds of pounds according to the whisper circulating in the room while she talked" (15). Though she is said to be a wealthy princess, she plays a minimal role. She is truly a bundle of good looks and strong determination, but has no formal school education. This, however, does not justify the "ludicrous" role assigned to her. She tells Chief Nanga some home – truths about the society as she alleges that women are only recognized as having equality with men only during elections so as to cart away their votes.

Mrs. Nanga, on her part, acquiesces under the prototype image of the unambitious, complacent "angel in the house", accepting repression and subjugation with equanimity. She, however, stresses that being a minister's wife is not the best thing that can happen to a woman like her who is old and old fashioned. Her feeling of rejection and loneliness worsens as her husband, Chief Nanga, decides to take a younger wife to fill the social role she is too old to play.

While the story of *A Man of the People* focuses on men, there are still some women characters that cannot be ignored. Though Mrs. Agnes Akilo is not put centrally in the book, she cannot but be noticed. Her physical outlook is compelling. Her beauty and sophisticated outlooks are enabling. She is a successful lawyer, owns a private firm of solicitors with her husband. Chief Nanga admits that she is "*She*, who must be obeyed". Achebe does not give Mrs. Akilo any serious role to play in the socio-political arena, rather, "Achebe's apologia seems to be aimed at proving his condescension to women from time to time" (*Kolawole* 116). Odili confirms it as he confesses:

> ... Chief Nanga and I having swooped many tales of conquest, I felt somehow compelled to speak in derogatory terms about women in general (59).

Generally, female characters like Jean, Edna and Elsie are treated with condescension as they are seen to be of little importance. Odili sees female characters as tools of revenge to massage his wounded ego. He is ready to use them as pawns, and he derives joy from exploiting them. He is instrumental to arousing Edna's political consciousness, which is not fully utilized. His relationship with Edna is motivated by selfish reasons. Achebe's women in these first four novels have specified roles, some bordering purely on domesticity, obedience, subordination and suppression, while others attempt to give freedom and independent thinking though liminal. It shows recognition of the female sex and their possibility of participating in the socio-political roles of nation building. That Clara and Eunice are well educated reflects positive thinking on the part of Achebe. But in his latest novel, *Anthill of the Savannah*, Achebe makes spirited efforts to give women clearly defined roes, placing them centrally in the tests as they play indispensable roles in society.

Achebe Re-inscribes the African Woman

In Achebe's earliest fiction, his portrayal of the female sex represents the original view of women in the Old Testament. This view buttresses that of the New Testament's and differs only in refinement and strategy, whereby:

> The idea came to Man to turn his spouse into the very Mother of God, to pick her up from right under his foot where she'd been since creation and carry her reverently to a nice corner pedestal. Up there her feet completely off the ground

> she will be just as irrelevant to the practical decisions of running the world as she was in her bad old ways (*Anthills* 98).

Our ancestors, however, worsened the situation working out a parallel subterfuge of their own, seeing mother as one whom they can consult only belatedly though, after a crisis, when "the waist is broken and hung over the fire and the palm bears its fruit at the tail of its leaf" (*Anthills* 98). This unrealistic position of the woman being tucked away and, therefore, made redundant or consulted after the milk is spilt and the impossible is not expected to happen cannot be considered a genuine portrayal of the African woman because sometimes the unexpected usually happens. Some African male writers have found it convenient to place women peripherally in their works and not give them credit. Achebe is guilty of this in his earlier works. Mary Kolawole's affirmation is remarkable:

> Whereas a re-reading of Achebe's earlier works reveals some efforts to focus on the female, he does not give women a definitive meaningful role until *Anthills*. His attitude remains ambiguous, sometimes ambivalent and ironic before this novel (118).

Due to Achebe's positive portrayal of women in *Anthills*, Ben Okri adjudges the novel to be Achebe's "most complex and his wisest book to date". This is probably because Achebe in this text is more attuned to gender in response to the global attention given to it. Achebe recognizes that it is time for African societies to be more liberal and accept women as their partners in nation building. So writers should invoke the female principle not necessarily in its original form of keeping them "in reserve until the ultimate crisis arrives and the waist is broken and hung over the fire..." But in recognizing and involving them from the outset in what Umelo Ojinmah refers to as:

> A system of government whose foundation would be laid on a deep appreciation of the ethnic and diversities of the new nations of Africa (104).

whereby women are key partners in progress seen as full-fledged human beings and not as the second sex or a societal construct. It appears that with this mind, Achebe's Anthills gives positive roles to women, and he does not find it pleasant anymore to create women with limited and negative roles. Mary Kolawole is of the view that the walls of the harem confining women have fallen apart and Achebe cannot hold on to the liminal role that he gives to some of the female characters. Moreover, this limited role is contrary to the reality of the lives of the African women in a changing modern society. Women have taken center-stage in the socio-political arena. So we see Beatrice, soaring high like an eagle, the king of birds. Her intellect proves a wonderful asset to society as she helps Ikem and Chris galvanize their thoughts for the upliftment of their community. She is both motivational and inspirational to her male partners in their efforts to conscientize the society. Achebe creates a remarkable character in Beatrice. Her strength of character, self confidence and superior intellect stand out even among men. Chris describes her as "beautiful without being glamorous. Peaceful but very strong". And I add, *Very, very independent, self actualizing and feminist* (my emphasis). All who are close to her recognize her worth.

The Kangan head of state affirms she is one of the most brilliant daughters of the country as he presents her thus:

> Beatrice Okoh ... a Senior Assistant Secretary in the Ministry of Finance – the only person in the service, male or female, with a first class honours in English. And not from a local University but from Queen Mary College, University of London. Our Beatrice beat the English to their game. We are proud of her (*Anthills* 75).

With such impeccable credentials, Achebe successfully rewrites the African woman. Beatrice refuses to take cognizance of certain gender conventions as she works uninhibited in the company of men. In fact Beatrice has no close female friends, until she finds herself saddled with Elewa, Ikem's girlfriend. She feels morally obliged to Elewa and her baby in memory of Ikem, her very good friend.

In rewriting the African woman, Achebe does not confine himself to the educated or the elite alone. He cuts across class barriers. Elewa, a virtual-illiterate is Ikem's (erudite scholar, social critic and journalist) girlfriend and she bears a child for him posthumously. Elewa, like Beatrice, has remarkable strength of character. She bonds with Beatrice to continue from where Chris and Ikem stopped. They both hold out until Ikem's baby is born. Beatrice's support of Elewa and her baby reinforces Elewa's position. Beatrice reforms tradition as she organizes a traditional naming ceremony for the baby and gives her a male name. Here, Beatrice defies convention as she sees herself as a human being and not as a societal construct. She is not particular about sex as is obvious from the baby's name. For her, a name is a mark of identity and is sexless. Thus, it does not matter to her what the sex of a child is, what matters is the significance of a name given a child. Beatrice's self-effacement and love for others is a step to self-definition. She is clearly at the vanguard of social transformation and not on the periphery as she continues to work hand in hand with the student leader, Emmanuel Obete, Captain Abdul, Buraimoh, the taxi-drivers union leader and Agatha her house girl. Even after the death of her friend and lover, Ikem and Chris respectively, Beatrice helps and associates with the down trodden and less privileged men and women in society. This is however, traditionally "men's role". But Achebe, conscious of the new role of women in nation building no longer discriminates as he re-writes the African woman through Beatrice.

"A Woman is Always Something"

> ... giving women today the same role which traditional society gave them of intervening only when everything else has failed is not enough, you know, like the women in the Sembene film who pick up spears abandoned by their defeated menfolk ... (*Anthills* 91).

A re-appraisal of the role of women in traditional society seen in the perspective of men reverting to them as a last resort, ironically puts them in a position of power. Historically, African women have been known to intervene in conflicts when all else fail. For instance, the Women's War of 1929, which stopped the British administration short on its tracks and the Egba women's uprising led by the activist Funmilayo Ransome-Kuti, speak for themselves. It is not always that coming to women as a last resort "is a damn sight too far and too late!" In fact, conscientization of women yeilds positive results as women act with a collective will. In traditional society, it is apparent that women wield more power in groups than individually. The Association of Umuadas and wives serve as examples. We read of only few powerful individual women in traditional society. A few writers like Wole Soyinka and Tess Onwueme have made efforts to represent powerful women with collective will in their respective plays: *Death and the King's Horseman* and *The Reign of Wazobia*.

Though Achebe does not create powerful women who have a collective will to protect the society from oppression by the government, he has given the duo, Beatrice and Elewa a formidable role in mobilizing opposition to the corrupt Kangan government. This traditional role of using women as a last resort has been passed on to Beatrice and Elewa representing modern day women, and more. Beatrice in particular is fully prepared to take on the challenges for the responsibility of social regeneration. From birth, Beatrice has been recognized as a human being, by acknowledging that she is also somebody, in spite of the fact that her mother expected a baby boy instead of her. Beatrice is quick to note thus:

> I didn't realize until much later that my mother bore me a huge grudge because I was a girl – her fifth in a row.... But I must mention that in addition to Beatrice they had given me another name at my baptism. Nwanyibuife – A female is also something (81).

This patronizing notion of the female sex ironically triggers Beatrice on to a life of achievements. She learns to be on her own and never asked to be noticed by anyone. Being a girl of "somewhat average looks, a good education and a good job", gives her courage and confidence to see herself as an equal partner with men and she proves this adequately. Her childhood experiences full of sexual discrimination and consequently her determination for achievement and self-actualization make her regard male chauvinism as "bullshit". She is a feminist, outspoken and fiery, a very self-actualizing woman. She knows what she wants, she dictates the pace in her relationship with Chris, her lover. She has a lot of insight and foresight. The analogy of Chielo the priestess and prophetess of the Hills and Caves is quite apt. Beatrice asserts that she does sometimes feel like Chielo in the novel. She says:

> It comes and goes. Imagine Yes. It's on now. And I see trouble building up for us. It will get to Ikem first. No joking, Chris. He will be the precursor to make straight the way. But after him it will be you (*Anthills* 114).

And indeed, it goes to Ikem first and then to Chris later. Beatrice is, however, not only full of insight and foresight, she is also full of action. Her opinions are reckoned with, by Ikem and Chris before their demise, and thereafter by Elewa and the rest of the group fighting against their oppressive government.

That a woman is always something in Igbo world view is not in dispute, as evident from the Association of Umuadas (daughters) an wives who have been very powerful in settling disputes in families and the wider society in Igboland. Husbands and brothers lay down their weapons of destruction at their interventions, pay them their due respects and acknowledge that "Nneka" (Mother is Supreme). This deep respect for women is traceable to a female principle, in their belief system. Idemili, the daughter of God, is central to Igbo cosmology, and according to Achebe in *Anthills*, the myth goes thus:

> In the beginning Power rampaged through our world, naked. So the Almighty, looking at his creation through the round undying eye of the sun, saw and pondered and finally decided to send his daughter, Idemili, to bear witness to the moral nature of authority by wrapping around Power's rude waist a loincloth of peace and modesty (102).

So Idemili brings peace to earth. She is also the goddess of wealth. All wealthy men who wish to pin the eagle's feather by buying admission into the powerful hierarchy of ozo must present themselves at her shrine to inform the "Daughter of the Almighty" of their ambitions. Because of the high regard for female deity in traditional society, these wealthy men seeking recognition by the deity, must be accompanied by *daughters* and not sons if they want to be granted hearing. So these daughters act as the arbiters between the ozo title seekers and the goddess of peace and wealth, Idemili. Achebe notes with regard to an ozo title seeker:

> His first visit is no more than to inform the Daughter of the Almighty of his ambition. He is accompanied by his daughter, or if he has only sons, by the daughter of a kinsman. *but a daughter it must be.* This young woman must stand between him and the daughter of the Almighty before he can be granted a hearing (*Anthills* 103–104) (emphasis mine).

Such is the respect and power imbued in the female in traditional society. A woman has always been and is still something and not just "also something" as Achebe affirms and Kolawole confirms, through decoding "Nwanyibuife", Beatrice's second name. Achebe has, in fact, confirmed that "a woman is always something" through his depiction of Beatrice, a modern woman, and the other woman in the book.

Though Beatrice does not know the traditions and legends of her people, she proves to be as powerful as Idemili in her own way. She defies traditional practice even as a child and she is regarded as a "soldier-girl". Ikem came close to sensing the "village priestess" who will prophesy when her divinity rides her abandoning if need be, her soup pot on the fire ..." resulting in great insights and foresight. With these traditional attributes, Beatrice forms "a formidable duo with Elewa in particular and the other male members of the society to conscientize the rest of the people on the evils of anarchy. Women in Anthills refuse to be scapegoats of social change. They have broken loose and relocated themselves firmly in the center of action in their society.

Conclusion

In *Anthills*, Achebe rejects limited and negative images of women prevalent in African literature especially by male writers. The women have broken the silence and are speaking out, defying the shackles of convention in male dominated societies. Beatrice, an example of the modern African woman, moves away from those processes that condemn women to oppression, suppression and non-existence. That African women are voiceless is sometimes more of a myth than reality, because it is apparent that there are some classes of African women whose voices are heard, though they are not in the majority. Molara Ogundipe-Leslie confirms this as she notes:

> Indigenous, structures of political participation equivalent or parallel to those for me, existed for women, whereby women's voices were heard, their opinions consulted ... (78–79).

That a woman is always something is as old as creation itself. Achebe has successfully redefined and rewritten the African Woman in *Anthills of the Savannah*.

Works Cited

Achebe, Chinua. *Things Fall Apart*. London: Heinemann, 1963.

———. *A Man of the People*. London: Heinemann, 1966.

———. *No Longer at Ease*. London: Heinemann, 1969.

———. *Arrow of God*. London: Heinemann, 1980.

———. *Anthills of the Savannah*. London: Heinemann, 1987.

Kolawole, Mary. *Womanism and the African Consciousness*. Trenton: Africa World Press, 1997.

Kriesten, P.H. and Anna Rutherford. *Chinua Achebe: A Celebration*. London: Heinemann, 1990.

Ogundipe-Leslie, Molara. *Re-Creating Ourselves: African Women and Critical Transformations*. New Jersey: Africa World Press, 1994.

Ojinmah, Umelo. Chinua Achebe: *New Perspectives*. Ibadan: Spectrum Books Ltd., 1991.

Chapter 28

Achebe and the African Womanhood: *Anthills of the Savannah* in Focus

E.L. Agukwe

IN THE EARLY NOVELS of Chinua Achebe, the image of women was that of people who depended on their husbands for most of their daily needs. For example, Ekwefi in *Things Fall Apart* and Matefi in *Arrow of God* were shown as typical African women who were always at the service of their husbands. However, recent African writings, especially the ones by female writers, have reacted strongly against this stereotyped view of the African woman and have gone a great length in their writings to show that the African woman is capable of independent existence. According to Chukwuma (1989) the earlier characterization of the African woman as "rural back-house, timid, subservient, lack-lustre, woman has been replaced by her modern counterpart, a full rounded human being, rational, individualistic and assertive, fighting for and claiming her own." Such positive characterizaton of the African woman is amply seen in the novels of Flora Nwapa, *Efuru* (1966), *Idu* (1970): Buchi Emechata *The Bride Pride* (1976); and Zaynab Alkali *The Still Born* (1984). It is against this background that one appreciates the new image of the African woman as portrayed in *Anthills of the Savannah.*

A New Vision of the African Woman

In *Anthills of the Savannah* Achebe deviates from his earlier characterization of the African woman and now elevates her to a position where she almost becomes god-like, a priestess and politician whose activities and advice ought to be taken seriously both in times of joy and in times of danger. Achebe uses the character of Beatrice to highlight this new image of the African woman, Chris, the Commissioner for Information, observed the priestly quality of Beatrice early in the novel.

> Sensing the village priestess who will prophesy when her divinity rides her, abandoning if need be her soup-pot on the fire but returning again when the god departs to the domesticity of her kitchen... (95).

Ikem, the editor of the *National Gazette* observes that Beatrice has style and face worthy of respect and even His Excellency the president of Kangan State recognises her as "one of the most brilliant daughters of this country". These qualities sharply contrast with the characters of Ekwefi or Ugoye in Achebe's early novels.

Though three classes of women are discernible in *Anthills of the Savannah*, namely, the educated and politically enlightened woman represented by Beatrice, the semi-literate woman represented by Elewa and her mother and the less privileged woman represented by Agatha, yet there are indications that these different classes of women have to achieve a measure of cohesion and understanding in order to be able to play a more effective role in the emergent political scenes in Africa.

Achebe believes that the solution to the endemic problem of political instability in Africa could be resolved through the application of what Ojinmah (1991) refers to as "the female principle". In the new political order, the African woman should assume a centre stage if progress has to be made. The involvement of women in the new political dispensation would be based on the modification of the existing traditional roles for women and not necessarily in its original form of being "the court of the last resort":

> But the way I see it is that giving women today the same role which traditional society gave them of intervening only when everything else has failed is not enough you know, like the women in the Sembene film who pick up the spears abandoned by their menfolk. It is not enough that women should be the court of the last resort because the last resort is a damn sight too far and too late (91).

Disillusionment with political systems and governance in Africa has been the dominant concern of Achebe's novels. The efforts of Odili in *A Man of the People*, to challenge the status quo fails and the intervention of the military does not help matters as seen in *Anthills of the Savannah*. What then is the solution to the problem of political instability in Africa? Achebe advocates the invocation of the female principle and de-emphasizing of male dominance in the political affairs of African states as a necessary step towards a stable polity. It is in this light that one appreciates the significance of the Almighty sending down his daughter, Idemili, "to bear witness to the moral nature of authority by wrapping around power's rude waist a loin cloth of peace and modesty". It was Idemili Her daughter (not the son) that came in a resplendent pillar of water, and those wishing to succeed must present themselves in purity to her. Idemili's contempt for man's unquenchable thirst to sit in authority on his fellows is "symbolic of woman modesty and sincerity in her approach to politics and governance. Achebe believes that the African woman would no longer be in reserve waiting for the world to crash around man's ears before the woman in her supremacy will descend and sweep the shards together" (98).

Achebe believes that for a rapid transformation of the society, a reform is necessary and this reform though should start with the individual, yet should be all embracing to include all categories of people, including the women who are regarded as "the biggest single group of oppressed people in the world". Achebe believes that women have an important role to play in this reformation of the society, which should be centered "around the core of reality and not around an intellectual abstraction". He uses the character of Beatrice to show the role which women could play in the transformation of the society. Thus, it is through interaction with Beatrice that Ikem, gets his first insight into the world of women that enables him to become aware of the nature of the injustices that women suffer. It is also this awareness, this consciousness, that enable him to appreciate the new role which women would play in the "days ahead". Ikem's resolve to marry Elewa – an ordinary semi-literate rural girl, is symbolic of the need to accord women more recognition, the need to redress the injustices being suffered by women and more importantly, the need to create a society where emphasis is not placed on class distinction. The marriage thus elevates the half-literate rural girl and transforms her into "an object of veneration".

Beatrice is made to be a source of inspiration to people around her, thus, raising her own level of consciousness and the consciousness of people around her to a level that is necessary for the reformation to succeed. It is this new awareness, that enabled Beatrice to begin to realize the need for understanding and cohesion among the women folk, if they must succeed in the struggle for a just society. Her house thus becomes the rallying point for the struggle. She rallies round all the women who now show "brutal courage" in the face of the overwhelming presence of military dictatorship. Unlike the male politicians who retreat "like frightened animals backwards into their holes", Beatrice rises to the challenges of her time. She now takes it upon herself not only to ensure the safety of Elewa, but also of the expected child – the last speck of him (Ikem) which must be nurtured and kept alive as a symbol of the struggle for which Ikem fights and dies. Her question "what must a people do to appease an embittered history?" though reveals an inner bitterness of mind that is not shown in the profanity of the open air, yet the narrator's voice which tells her: "It is now up to you woman to tell us what has to be done and Agatha is one of you."

This re-affirms Achebe's belief in the application of the female principle and the need for reconciliation and understanding among all classes of women as a step towards achieving stability in the political affairs of African States. It is in this light that one appreciates the reconciliation between Beatrice and Agatha.

Achebe condemns certain traditional practices that tend to relegate women to the position of irrelevance. Why, for example, should a man perform the ritual of a naming ceremony?

> I think our tradition faulty there, it is safest to ask the mother what her child is or means or should be called (223).

Beatrice opposes this age-long practice by proceeding to perform the rituals and the men can only shudder at the audacity of the modern African woman: "In you young people, our world has met its match" (227). Elewa's uncle, who was to perform the rituals, sees the futility of confrontation with the women folk and rather proceeds to preach tolerance and understanding with the women folk as the basis for peace and stability:

> A wise man agrees with his wife and eats lumps of fish in his soup but a fool contradicts his wife and eats lumps of cocoyam (225).

Achebe criticizes the Africa system of family life, which exalts the male child and relegates the girl-child. A female child is as important as the male child and can perform roles traditionally assigned males. By the end of the novel, Beatrice was almost the only visible character in the novel playing both male and female roles. Achebe condemns male chauvinism and advocates a relationship that is based on mutual respect and inter-dependence:

> That every woman wants a man to complete her is a piece of male chauvinistic bullshit (88).

Achebe believes that the woman holds the key to successful relationship and Beatrice is seen exercising that authority even in love-making as she pulled Chris up and back with such power and absolute authority (114).

Though the African woman as seen in *Anthills of the Savannah* has made much progress in the areas of education and politics, and contributes to the development of the society, yet such successes are not made without obstacles, frustrations and sometimes outright oppression. Thus, Beatrice is accused of using "bottom power" or being "The later day Madame Pompadour who manipulated Generals and patronizes writers." Her house is subjected to humiliating searches "executed with a vengeance". Inspite of all these problems, Beatrice remains steadfast and Chris' statement that the misunderstanding among "the troika who think they own Kangan State" could only be settled "under her management" shows the extent of the expectations placed on the modern African woman.

Conclusion

In *Anthills of the Savannah* Achebe shows through the character of Beatrice and others that the African woman is capable of independent existence and can withstand both social and political pressures even under extreme military dictatorship. Achebe advocates the application of the female principle in the political affairs of African States as a necessary step to a stable society. The women might provide the alternative political corruption, and sycophancy of the present political class dominated by men. In Achebe's view women should no longer occupy the back seat but should be in the forefront in the new political dispensation.

Achebe believes that for women to play effective role in the emergent African states, there is need for cohesion and understanding among the different classes of women, Hence the reconciliation between Beatrice and Agatha is symbolic of this understanding.

Finally, the fact that Elewa's expected child turns out to be a girl re-emphasizes Achebe's belief in the application of the female principle as a necessary factor in the political affairs of Africa. Amaechina – the new baby – thus, symbolizes the continuity of the struggle for a just society for which Chris and Ikem fought and died. The birth of Amaechina, which could be likened to the sending down of Idemili, the daughter of the Almighty, therefore heightens the expectation that the Anthills might still survive the scorching heat of the savannah sun.

Works Cited

Achebe (1987). *Anthills of the Savannah* Ibadan: Heineman Education Books Ltd.

Chukwuma (1989). "Positivism and the Female Crisis in the Novels of Emecheta" In Otokunefor and Nwodo (ed) *The Nigerian Female Writers* Lagos: Malthouse Press Ltd.

Koroye (1989).The Ascetic Feminist Vision of Zaynab Alkali" In Otokunefor and Nwodo (ed) *The Nigerian Female Writers*. Lagos: Malthouse Press Ltd.

Njola (1989). The Works of Flora Nwapa" In Otokunefor and Nwodo (ed) *The Nigerian Female Writers* Lagos: Malthouse Press Ltd.

Ojinmah (1991). *Chinua Achebe: New Perspectives*. Ibadan: Spectrum Books Ltd.

Chapter 29

Feminist Assertion in Achebe's Novels: A Study of *Things Fall Apart* and *Anthills of the Savannah*

Julie Agbasiere

THE FUROR THAT CHINUA Achebe's earlier novels caused in feminist circles is far from subsiding. *Ogunyemi* describes Achebe as a phallic writer whose writings denigrate women (60–61). By pointing at the societal imperatives that inform Achebe's novels, Palmer (38–39) justifies the formers delineation of the female characters. His creative genius has attracted reactions that pave the way for a new trend in literary pursuits with a bounteous harvest. Achebe might have been sensitive to these criticisms for there is a marked change in the portraiture of female characters in his later works. As the characters move from rural to urban setting, they tend to become bolder and more assertive. Ironically, traditional society contains germs of feminism which mature and blossom in an urban environment. This paper examines female assertion in *Things Fall Apart* (1958) and *Anthills of the Savannah* (1987).

Things Fall Apart is set in Umuofia, a patriarchal society whose value system favors men to the detriment of women. In this society that operates on the polarity of good and bad, male and female, manliness and effeminacy, a man who does not measure up to societal expectations is derisively called a woman. Woman symbolizes failure and inferiority. She is maltreated, serves as a "punch-ball" (Aidoo 2) for her husband; she is excluded from most gatherings and has no voice in public discussions. As Ojo-Ade remarks, she is "Dominated, Disadvantaged, Exploited and Excluded" (158–159). In this novel she is an episodic character.

Traditional society does not, however, always denigrate woman. It shows a certain level of ambivalence towards her. The very society that has little regard for the woman is poised to go to war because of a woman. The war-like and manly Umuofia is so incensed by the murder of its daughter and wife of Ogbuefi Udo in Mbaino that it hands down an ultimatum to the people: a boy and a girl as compensation or war! Although wife battering goes on from time to time, society does not consider it the norm. When Mgbafo is brutalized by her husband, Uzowulu, her brothers intervene, beat him up and take their sister and her children to the their father's house as a protective measure. When the case is being tried, the eldest of the seven spirits, in his ruling, emphasizes that "It is not bravery when a man fights with a woman" (66).

Traditional society is elastic and has room for people with different shades of behavior that are at times contradictory. Despite the strong chauvinistic tendencies, there is room for feminist assertion. Thus, Ekwefi, Okonkwo's second wife, runs away from her husband, Anene, two years after their marriage, to join Okonkwo, the man she has always loved. To some extent, she keeps this independent spirit in her husband's house. She alone makes unsavory remarks about Okonkwo to his hearing, a conduct for which Okonkwo shoots at her and nearly kills her. When Ezinma is sick, she bangs on Okonkwo's door and the latter knows immediately that it is Ekwefi because "Of his three wives Ekwefi was the only one who would have the audacity to bang on his door" (53).

There is also room for love in Achebe's *Things Fall Apart*. Ndulue and his wife Ozoemena are the quintessence of love, peace, harmony and companionship. They love themselves even unto death. This, contrary to Okonkwo's expectations, does not make Ndulue effeminate. He is a first class warrior having led Umuofia to war in the past.

Okonkwo, the protagonist, is the epitome of male chauvinism in Umuofia. By making him pursue exclusively male concerns and interests, Achebe discreetly unveils a strong female force in the community. Underneath the socially acclaimed male superiority and chauvinism lies a latent under-current of a female power that holds the male hubris in check. Thus Okonkwo constantly meets and has to reckon with "unmanly" situations. In a society that values boys more than girls, Okonkwo finds that contrary to his heart's desire, he is "very lucky with his daughters" (122) but not so with his sons. Nwoye, his first son, is "degenerate and effeminate" (108) whereas Ezinma has the qualities he wants in a son. He therefore spends his life "regretting that Ezinma was a girl" (122). Life contradicts him. Unoka, his father, dies poor and effeminate. After the killing of Ikemefuna and under the spell of despondency, Okonkwo finds himself, by his standards, effeminate, "When did you become a shivering old woman, Okonkwo asked himself. Okonkwo, you have become a woman indeed" (45). When calamity strikes, he commits a "female ochu" and when he goes on exile, it is to a less manly clan, Mbanta, where he is to stay with his mother's brother and relatives for seven years. By beating his wife during the Week of Peace, by killing Ikemefuna, by committing a female *ochu* and eventually by hanging himself, Okonkwo persistently offends *Ani*, the Earth goddess who reigns supreme in Umuofia, and meets appropriate punishment on people. Okonkwo is checkmated by, as Killam puts it, "a powerful" female principle "(that) pervades the whole society of Umuofia and sits in judgment of events in the community" (19–20). His reverses to some extent arise from his inflexible will which does not permit his masculinity to be tempered by some feminine touch – tenderness, tolerance, peace, love and harmony.

In *Anthills of the Savannah*, Achebe treats the denigration of woman as a topic for polemics between two major characters: Beatrice Oko representing feminist critics, and Achebe's Ikem Osodi, mouthpiece. Beatrice harps on a topical issue by accusing Ikem of having "no clear role for women in his political thinking" (91). When she remarks that in Ikem's writing "women don't feature too much in his schemes except as, well, comforters" (65), she is echoing past criticisms leveled against Achebe's writings in almost the very words of the critics. For instance, Eustace Palmer says that woman "has had to take second place to numerous other concerns" (38). Nnolim finds an "appalling image of the Nigerian woman (helpless, dependent, brutalized, disparaged, who are either prostitutes or concubines or good time girls) in the works of Achebe, Cyprian Ekwensi, and Elechi Amadi" (59).

For his defense, Ikem digs into traditional and biblical myths. He refers to the myths of Earth and Sky with the biblical counterpart of Adam and Eve, and Nneka – Mother is supreme – with its biblical counterpart of the Virgin Mary, to show that the denigration of woman has indeed been universal and long standing. Indeed Marie Umeh has pointed at the role of myths in the subjugation of the woman. Citing Nwoga, she asserts that male hegemony is sustained "through myths, legends, folk-tales and scripture which equate women with inferiority" (*The Poetics* 203). Achebe tries to prove that his portrayal of female characters is realistic because traditional society sees them as such. There is, however, a need for a review of the image of the woman and Achebe subscribes to "mythic revisionism" (Umeh, *The Poetics* 203). As the myths cited prove to be inadequate, Achebe replaces them with the myth of Idemili which assigns an active role to women in politics. This role devolves on BB.

Beatrice Oko, fondly called BB, is the principal female character and the fourth major character, the first three being male. Making a woman a major character, is clearly a departure from the *Things Fall Apart* model. Beatrice symbolizes the element of restraint checking the excesses of the three key figures in the governance of Kagan: Sam the president and Head of State, Chris the Commissioner for Information and Ikem, the Editor of the *National Gazette*. She advises Chris and Ikem to resolve their differences and avert a show down with the President, a situation that is bound to end their friendship and lead to their untimely death.

The role of moderator and adviser which Beatrice plays is sanctioned by tradition in the myth of Idemili. She becomes a mythic figure with attributes that liken her to a goddess. Her comportment and demeanor are "goddessy" (199). She embodies some attributes of the goddess Idemili who looks down disdainfully on men as they struggle for power. Hence she appears austere, imposing, awe-inspiring and majestic. She is like "the Maiden Spirit Mask coming into the arena, erect, disdainful, high coiffure, unravished yet by her dance" (199). Moreover, Beatrice feels herself a reincarnation of Chielo, the priestess of the Oracle of the Hills and the Caves, a character in Achebe's first novel, *Things Fall Apart*. She consequently becomes a prophetess. It is in this capacity that Beatrice predicts trouble for the four major characters and her predictions come true – Ikem goes first, assassinated: the President is killed in an abortive coup: Chris is shot dead by a police sergeant: and Beatrice is traumatized by their death. Through her insight and power of prediction, she tries to "dismantle, however briefly, the male world of unilateral power" (Caroll 177).

Although Beatrice is not a member of the President's cabinet, she nevertheless is interested in the political situation and feels committed to upholding the honor of her nation at all costs. She is by Achebe's definition a "patriot" (*The Trouble* 15). While Chris and Ikem keep quiet in a party, Beatrice calls John Kent, alias MM, to order for speaking disparagingly of the President, his cabinet and his government. She takes the risk of chiding the President himself for allowing a visiting American lady journalist, Lou, to treat him, his Chief of Army Staff and Director of State Research Council with levity and arrogance. For manifesting such guts, Beatrice is disgraced by the President but she remains undaunted.

Achebe has already dismissed the role of the woman in the Nneka myth as being not good enough for the modern woman (*Anthills* 91–92). He therefore creates his own myth by projecting Beatrice as a new leader in a society where men have failed. In Ezenwa Ohaeto's terminology, he is "replacing myth with myth" (215). As Caroll puts it, Beatrice survives as the crucial figure in imposing pattern and meaning ... upon the final flurry of events in which all members of the triumvirate are killed (180).

In presenting Beatrice as a leader, Achebe stresses the great importance of formal education as it instills confidence in the woman, and a sense of achievement and fulfillment, which in turn elicits admiration and respect from her male counterparts. The President is proud of Beatrice and shows her off as "the only person in the service, male or female, with a first class honors in English" (75) obtained not from a local university but from Queen Mary's College, University of London. Chris, Ikem and even Kent, a British man, all recognize her intellectual ability and educational achievements. In addition, Beatrice manifests a high level of courage, perspicacity, composure and selflessness. Her role is not to "descend and sweep the shards together" (98), but rather to remold the shards of Kangan into a new entity.

Beatrice has no problem in gaining acceptance. Unlike the Kangan dictatorship, she does not thrust herself on her followers. She becomes the center of the world of old friends, acquaintances and survivors of Chris and Ikem, the new community she is called upon to direct and lead. They have "kept together around her like stragglers from a massacred army" (217). She looks after the pregnant Elewa and keeps the new community going. Her authority is not in doubt, rather everybody takes her into confidence including Captain Audu who confesses to her that he has been assigned to keep an eye on the group. Everybody feels free to give his opinion and participate in discussions. Beatrice reverses the trend in governance by men which entails power belonging to a caucus and rulers are out of touch with the generality of the populace.

The path that Beatrice charts is revolutionary. She believes that old customs should give way to the new. So, she further reverses roles. When Elewa's baby is due to be named, it is not a man who performs the ceremony but a woman, Beatrice. The baby girl is given a boy's name, Amaechina. Elewa's uncle who should have performed the ceremony arrives late but does not hesitate to uphold the action of naming already done by Beatrice. Tradition is giving way to modernism. However, Elewa's uncle prays over and breaks the kola, signifying that this rite cannot be compromised. It is still a man's preserve.

In the novel, Beatrice forges a new solidarity among the female characters for if women are to rule, there should be no divisive tendencies in their fold. Therefore there is a new understanding and comradeship among the females: Agatha purges herself of her initial resentment and disdain for Elewa, Beatrice for the first time apologizes to her maid, Agatha for being harsh to her although Agatha deserves the scorn, and all three live peacefully and work together for the solidarity of the group and the success of the naming ceremony of Amaechina.

A look into her private life shows Beatrice as having gone beyond the feminist call for socio-economic cum political emancipation of the woman. Having been brought up in a chauvinistic family, she has had her reactions and is then seasoned enough to know what she wants and make her choices. She remarks, "There was enough chauvinism in my father's house to last me seven reincarnations" (88). Feminism to her is not a foreign concept and she did not acquire her feminist streaks from overseas. Consequently, she is economically well off, socially well adjusted, morally upright and feels fulfilled. To her, marriage is not the ultimate in a woman's life although it is not to be discarded. A career, on the contrary, is of the utmost importance to every woman. From the beginning to the end, she remains dignified, devoid of complexes. Chris loves her for it and in their love life, Beatrice dictates the pace and Chris does not complain.

Beatrice is unique as she combines feminist, mythic and certain traditional traits and roles. Her father sees in her "the soldier girl who fell out of trees;" for Chris she is "the quiet demure damsel whose still waters nonetheless could conceal deep overpowering eddies of passion"; Ikem senses "the village priestess" who after prophesying returns to the "domesticity of kitchen or the bargaining market stool behind her little display of peppers and dry fish and green vegetables" (105). Nadine Gordimer is right in describing her as "one of the most extraordinary, attractive and moving women characters in any contemporary novel" (Nwabueze 8–9).

In *Anthills of the Savannah,* Achebe paints the picture of dignified womanhood. The woman acquires her dignity partly through her personal endowments and achievements and partly through divesting herself of subjugating practices. Elewa is presented without a family name. She is just herself, Elewa. She is friendly with Ikem but does not formally get married to him before having his baby. Beatrice is friendly with Chris but their relationship does not result in motherhood. This is intriguing to Emenyonu and he asks, "Is Achebe excluding education, dynamism and leadership from motherhood or vice versa?" (111). It appears that motherhood is for the common woman but not for the elite. Elewa symbolizes the masses and her daughter Amaechina, "the new generation of the African humanity – a mixture of intellectual but revolutionary ideals, and ordinary but dignified personality" (Nwabueze 9). These are the attributes that the new generation inherits from Ikem and Elewa. The woman intellectual that Beatrice symbolizes will midwife, nurture and lead the new generation.

It can therefore be seen that society has room for female assertion for women who have the guts. Although *Things Fall Apart* portrays a chauvinist patriarchal society, there are manifestations of female power pervading the community. Some females rise above the level of mere stereotypes. In *Anthills of the Savannah*, the woman is dignified and free to live her life the way she wants. Traditional constraints are out of the way and the more educated she is, the more her prestige rises, and the more she is a good candidate for the governance of the community. Beatrice is so far the most balanced and successful feminist character to appear in the African letters. She is Achebe's olive branch to his feminist critics.

Works Cited

Achebe, Chinua. *Things Fall Apart.* London: Heinemann, 1965

Achebe, Chinua. *Anthills of the Savannah.* Ibadan: Heinemann, 1988

Achebe, Chinua. *The Trouble with Nigeria.* Enugu: Fourth Dimension, 1983

Aidoo, Ama Ata. "Unwelcome Pals and Decorative Slaves or Glimpses of Women as Writers and Characters in Contemporary African Literature". *Literature and Society: Selected Essays on African Literature.* Ed. Ernest Emenyonu. Oguta: Zim, 1986. 1–19.

Caroll, David. *Chinua Achebe: Novelist, Poet, Critic.* London: Macmillan, 1980.

Emenyonu, Ernest N. *Studies on the Nigerian Novel.* Ibadan: Heinemann, 1991.

Ezenwa-Ohaeto. "Replacing Myth with Myth: Feminist Streak in Buchi Emecheta's *Double Yoke". Critical Theory and African Literature.* Ed. Ernest N. Emenyonu. Ibadan: Heinemann, 1987. 214–224.

Killam, G.D. *The Writings of Chinua Achebe.* London: Heinemann, 1969.

Nnolim, Charles. "Trends in the Nigerian Novel". *Literature and National Consciousness.* Ed. Ernest N. Emenyonu. Ibadan: Heinemann, 1989. 53–65.

Nwabueze, P.E. "Characterization in Chinua Achebe's *Anthills of the Savannah:* A study in Transactional Analysis". *Language, Literature and Social Change* (Acts of the 7th Annual Conference of Modern Languages Association of Nigeria held at the University of Nigeria, Nsukka, 8–11 February 1989). Ed. A.U. Ohaegbu. 1–10.

Ogunyemi, Chikwenye O. "Women and Nigerian Literature". *Perspectives on Nigerian Literature: 1700 to the Present.* Vol. 1. Ed. Yemi Ogunbiyi. Lagos: Guardian Books Nigeria Limited, 1988. 60–67.

Ojo-Ade, Femi. "Female Writers, Male Critics", *African Literature Today.* 13 Ed. Eldred D. Jones. London: Heinemann, 1983: 158–179.

Palmer, Eustace. "The Feminine Point of View: Buchi Emecheta's *The Joys of Motherhood". African Literature Today.* 13 Ed. Eldred D. Jones. London: Heinemann, 1983: 38–55.

Umeh, Marie. "The Poetics of Thwarted Sensitivity". *Critical Theory and African Literature.* Ed. Ernest N. Emenyonu. Ibadan: Heinemann, 1987, 194–206.

"Children's Literature in Nigeria: Revolutionary Omission". *MATATU: Zeitchrift fur Afrikanische Kultur und Gesselschaft.* (Forthcoming).

Chapter 30

Chinua Achebe and Military Dictatorship in Nigeria: a Study of *Anthills of the Savannah*

Chidi T. Maduka

CHINUA ACHEBE HAS CONSISTENTLY used his works to fight for the restoration of Africa's place in world history. He firmly believes that a writer should be sensitive to the "burning issues" that ravage the economic, political and cultural life of the continent; if not, the writer will be socially irrelevant, just like the person he reminds us in the proverb who, on seeing his house on fire, prefers to run after the rats escaping from the flames rather than try to put out the fire.

He perceives his works as products of historical forces, although Amuta (51) accuses him of being blind to the driving power of economics in shaping those forces. In *Things Fall Apart* and *Arrow of God* Achebe focuses on colonialism and points out that African civilization has redeeming features in spite of the colonialists' self-indulgent claim that it is barbarous. In *No Longer at Ease* he grapples with the social predicament of creating new values in a society riddled with corruption and contradictions. The next novel *A Man of the People* rigorously questions the destiny of an African state (Nigeria) by x-raying the ineptitude of the ruling class which took over leadership from the white colonialists portrayed in *Things Fall Apart* and *Arrow of God*. The novel suggests that the misguided leadership of the corrupt, greedy and self-centered rulers will inevitably lead to a military intervention, a portrayal which has been deemed prophetic, because the military eventually toppled the civilian regime in Nigeria about the same time as the novel's first publication in 1966.

The advent of the military in government brought about new problems which led to the civil war that ravaged Nigeria for three years. Achebe had therefore shifted his attention to the civil war experiences of Nigerians. In *Beware Soul Brother* (a volume of poetry that won a Commonwealth award) and some of the stories in *Girls at War and Other Stories* he generally captures the spirit of the quest for survival characteristic of the lives of individuals spiritually paralysed by war, and obliquely points to the deficiencies of political leadership is Nigeria.

The blunders of the civilian government that succeeded the military regime in Nigeria between 1979 and 1983 became the inspiration for his polemical booklet *The Trouble With Nigeria* in which Achebe speaks directly in his own voice. Chagrined by the misadventures of the politicians of Nigeria's Second Republic, Achebe forcefully asserts in a tone of magisterial self-confidence that:

> The trouble with Nigeria is simply and squarely a failure of leadership. There is nothing basically wrong with the Nigerian land or climate or water or air or anything else. The Nigerian problem is the unwillingness and inability of its leaders to rise to the responsibility, to the challenges of personal example which are the hallmarks of true leadership (1).

Achebe yearns for a country where competence will replace mediocrity; hard work, indolence; national spirit, nauseating parochialism; excellence, federal character; and tolerance, ruthlessness. To him, there is nothing about the Nigerian society that cannot be changed through an exemplary, dynamic and public-spirited leadership.

With the consolidation of military dictatorships in Africa the problem of the ideal form of leadership for African nations becomes acute and haunts the imagination of well-meaning thinkers. Achebe grapples with this subject in his latest novel *Anthills of the Savannah* which casts a look at the role of the military in Nigerian politics and provides an insight which has a resonance for the whole of Africa. He feels disturbed that the soldiers who have routinely organized coups and taken over governments in various parts of Africa have become worse than the civilians they have replaced. After years of being in power, they have *out – Nangaed Nanga* in greed, avarice, selfishness, corruption, purposeless leadership and insensitivity to people's needs.

In the novel a group of army officers overthrows the civilian government of the West African State, Kanga, and hands over power to their senior officer Sam who is deferentially referred to as "His Excellency" by the generality of Kangans. The new Head of State is unprepared for his new role, so he depends heavily on his friend Chris Oriko and the political scientist, Professor Okong, for political advice. He soon becomes an adept at manipulating the apparatus of power which he ferociously uses to defend his self-interests. Accordingly, his cabinet is intimidated into operating as a mere rubber-stamp; the urban poor and the rural peasants are cowed into a position of docility; the student leaders are harassed and persecuted; and his political opponents and Leaders of pressure groups are detained and even eliminated. His mismanagement of the nation's affairs plunges the country into a deep crisis, resulting in his eventual overthrow and assassination.

As Head of State, Sam firmly believes that Kanga is his private estate over which he exercises limitless authority. This portrayal comes out clearly in his dealings with his cabinet, the people and dissidents. The opening of the novel is illuminating as it sets the stage for the struggle for power which is fully developed in the novel. It is, therefore, necessary to quote the first four paragraphs in full for its immediate topical significance:

> I am sorry, Your Excellency. But I have no difficulty swallowing *and* digesting your rulings, You're wasting everybody's time, Mr. Commissioner for Information. I will not go to Abason. Finish: *Kabisa*: Any other business? As your Excellency wishes. But...But me no bats, Mr Oriko The matter is closed I said. How many times, for God's sake, am I expected to repeat it? Why do *you* find it so difficult to swallow any ruling on anything?

The novel thus begins in *medias res* by intimating us with a controversy surrounding the Head of State's projected visit to Abazon. Obviously, His Excellency (who is in fact chairing a cabinet meeting) disagrees with Christopher Oriko (generally called "Chris" throughout the novel), the Commissioner for Information, over the issue. Sam's tone of disagreement is authoritarian, arrogant and even insulting. The first sentence – "You're wasting everybody's time" – sets up the mood for Sam's contemptuous treatment of Chris's position. As far as he is concerned, Chris has taken a frivolous stand on the issue because, as the second sentence shows, he (Chris) is not intelligent enough to perceive that the matter does not call for a debate, since by a presidential *fiat* a decision has already been taken on it. Hence the forceful assertion; "I will not go to Abazon". The choice of the auxiliary "will" is significant because it does not indicate a colourless auxillary normally associated with "shall" when used with the first person singular or plural; rather, it indicates volition or intentionality – Sam has made up his mind not to go to Abazon. Then come two words which give a tone of finality to the decisions "Finish! Kabisa!'" The chief executive is angry, firm and definitive, as the use of exclamation marks and the Kiswahill word *Kabisa* ("absolutely") suggests. The addition of the question "Any other business?" shows that Sam is the unchallengeable wielder of power which he does not intend to share with anybody. He therefore asserts it by closing the meeting.

The confrontation intensifies in the second and third paragraphs. Chris pretends to concede victory to Sam while, in fact, refusing to be psychologically cowed, hence he boldly uses the coordinating conjunction "but" which limits the effectiveness of the concession. This infuriates Sam who shouts at him in order to stop him from playing the dissident, a role he has gained some reputation for. Then comes Chris's response which has ironic overtones; on the one hand, he apologizes to His Excellency for having portrayed himself as a disloyal subordinate, but on the other hand he makes the reader perceive that he is laughing at Sam for believing that the members of his cabinet should "swallow and digest all his rulings". Sam assesses the situation differently by seeing himself as the unchallengeable boss who has the prerogative of forcing such pills down the throats of his subordinates.

Accordingly, he uses para-linguistic language to drive home this point and, make him realize that he is a mere commissioner. "For a full minute or so the fury of his eyes lay on me. Briefly our eyes had been locked in combat" (1).

Chris gratifies his ego by tactfully yielding grounds:

> Then I had lowered mine to the shiny table-top in ceremonial capitulation. Long silence. But he was not appeased. Rather he was making the silence itself grow rapidly into its own kind of contest, like the eyewink duel of children. I conceded victory there as well. Without raising my eyes I said again: "I am very sorry, Your Excellency" (1).

The battle is lost and won: Sam strongly feels that he is the victor who is in total control of the situation.

Thus Achebe deftly opens the novel with an apt dramatization of the power game which is a major concern of the work. Sam is a power seeker who ruthlessly silences opposition in order to show that he constitutes a formidable power base capable of resisting the assault of political opponents. He even views himself as a force that can shape the character of events and determine the mode of people's behaviour. It is therefore not surprising that he is incapable of realizing that Chris is playing up to his (Sam's) self-delusion by pretending to be a powerless subordinate, ready to carry out the instructions of an omnipotent boss, while in fact he is a bold, proud, astute, self-assured and highly critical individual who cannot play the sycophant. Achebe seems concerned here to use this scene to foreshadow the conflicting worlds of illusion and reality that characterize Sam's quest for absolute power as a military dictator.

The illusory dimension of this world hinges on Sam's manipulation of three strategies. The first centres on the mastery of his fear of becoming a Head of State. As we are told in the novel:

> His Excellency came to power without any preparation for political leadership – a fact which he being a very intelligent person knew perfectly well and which, furthermore should not have surprised anyone. Sandhurst after all did not set about training officers to take over Her Majesty's throne but rather in the high tradition of proud aloofness from politics and public affairs (2).

He is completely incompetent to take up the mantle of leadership because, as the narrative reveals, when:

> The young Army Commander was invited by the even younger coup-makers to become His Excellency the Head of State he had pretty few ideas about what to do. And so, like an intelligent man, he called his friends together and said 'What shall I do?' (12).

His ignorance and psychological unpreparedness to assume the new role gradually fade with Chris helping him to select his members of cabinet; and Prof. Okong, who is adept at using words, shouldering the responsibility of propagating the ideas of the new government to the public.

Although he holds the intellectuals in awe, he soon overcomes his fear of them by covering up his inferiority complex and outsmarting them in the power game. The scene in which he tries to humiliate the Attorney-general is revealing. Being an expert at histrionics he deliberately speaks in a low voice so as to subject the commissioner to a psychological pressure and pull him down from his intellectual heights thereby making him look inconsequential.

He seems to achieve his aim:

> As he watched his victim straining to catch the vital message he felt again that glow of quiet jubilation that had become a frequent companion especially when as now he was disposing with consummate ease of some of those troublesome people he had thought so formidable in his apprentice days in power. It takes a lion to tame a leopard, say our people. How right they are (22).

He feels elated at the debasement of the stature of the intellectuals who, in fact, look mean, petty and seem to be carried away by the glamour of the paraphernalia of power tossed before them by His Excellency. And here lies the effectiveness of the second strategy he uses to consolidate his authority.

Sam maintains a luxurious life-style. The Presidential Palace is gorgeously built and lavishly furnished. The surroundings are a veritable feast for the eyes. And the Presidential Retreat, a guest house built at Abichi, is fabulous. As the narrator tells us:

> The rumoured twenty million spent on its refurbishment by the present administration since the overthrow of the civilians who had built it at a cost of forty-five million may still be considered irresponsibly extravagant in our circumstances… (73).

The place is used as venue for extravagant parties for people carefully selected by His Excellency. The food and drinks served are unique. For instance, in one of such parties in which Beatrice is invited, we are told that:

> The food was simple and tasty. Shrimp cocktail; jollof rice with plantain and fried chicken; and fresh fruit salad of cheese and English crackers for dessert. The wines were excellent but totally wasted on the company, only His Excellency, the American girl and myself showing the slightest interest. The Bassa men stuck

> as usual to the beer they had been drinking all day; one of the ladies had double gins and lime and the other two a shandy of stout and Seven-Up (77).

The opulence is all the more resplendent when viewed in the context of the general misery of the people. Ikem, the indefatigable social critic, feels outraged at this:

> Retreat from what? From whom? ... From the people and their basic needs of water which is free from Guinea worm, of simple shelter and food. That's what you are retreating from. You retreat up the hill and commune with your cronies and forget the very people who legitimize your authority (73).

Sam views the situation differently. To him, the monument is indispensable for the upkeep of the Presidency which he cherishes as a pearl and runs as a private property.

In fact, the consciousness that informs his actions as a ruler is virtually rooted in the belief that the whole country is a family estate constituting a huge financial empire from which he derives immense profits. Elewa's uncle cogently observes towards the end of the novel that "... Those who make plans make for themselves only and their families" (228). And we are made to see that Sam has close associations with top businessmen who often front for him in his scandalous business deals. The case of Alhaji Mahmoud is typical. Mahmoud is portrayed as the Chairman of Kangan/American Chamber of Commerce, who owns:

> Eight ocean liners, ...two or three private jets; a private jetty ... No customs officials go near his jetty and so, say rumour-mongers, he is the prince of smugglers. What else? Fifty odd companies, including a bank. Monopoly of government fertilizer imports (117).

This concentration of wealth in a few hands and its flamboyant display tantamounts to the "President shitting on the heads of the people" (183).

His Excellency is even portrayed as an armed robber, and this is through the parallelism used in describing his dress and that of an armed robber. Specifically, we are told that "He is in mufti as he now tends to be more and more within the precincts of the Presidential Palace; a white *danshiki* tastefully embroidered in gold, and its matching trousers" (4). Later in the novel, one of the four armed robbers killed during a public execution is described as "a prince among criminals" who "had eluded them (the police) for two years, had three murders to his name and a fourth pointed to his direction". Then comes the description of his physiognomy:

> He wore a spotless white lace *danshiki* embroidered with gold thread, and natty blue terylene trousers. His appearance, his erect, disdainful walk hurled defiance at the vast mockery and abuse of the crowd and incensed it to greater vehemence (41).

Essentially, both of them wear "white", gorgeous "*danshiki*" which is "embroidered in gold", as well as "trousers" of a rich texture, although Sam's is white while the armed robber's is blue, In spite of this minor difference, the description develops a parallelism strongly suggesting that His Excellency is no less a criminal than the armed robber he has ordered to be executed in public. Even the demeanour of the armed robber parallels that of His Excellency in terms of his contempt for the people. This depiction is underscored by Ikem's rumination on the fate of armed robbers whom he believes should not be condemned to death, since political leaders who behave like they are not subjected to the same fate. As he puts it,

> Was he (armed robber) not standing right then, full grown, in other stolen lace and tereylene, in every corner of that disoriented crowd? And he and all his innumerable doubles. were they not mere emulators of others who daily stole more from us than mere lace and terylene? Leaders who openly looted our treasury, whose effrontery soiled our national soul (42).

Thus Achebe's observations capture the spirit of the attacks leveled by various social critics on African military leaders who parade wealth that their earnings can hardly justify. Emeka Odumegwu-Ojukwu's (1989) statement on the Nigerian situation is typical: "It is easy to notice these days that generals who are penniless are mostly those who served under Ironsi. The era of millionaire-generals has become the rule rather than the exception" (190).

The third strategy focuses on Sam's use of Machiavellian tactics in enforcing loyalty or dealing with forces of opposition. We are told, for instance, that after replacing all the military officers in his cabinet with civilians and adding "President to all his titles" (4), he so ruthlessly deals with the officers challenging these measures that "There were unconfirmed rumours of unrest, secret trials and executions in the barracks" (14). The machinery of repression is effectively run by "the young, brilliant and aggressive Director of the State Research Council" (14). Major Johnson Ossai is so vicious in manipulating the secret police and in masterminding murders, as in the case of Ikem, that he is catapaulted to the rank of a colonel. He, however, gets murdered himself:

> Colonel Ossai was last seen going in to see the Head of State and has not been sighted ever since. You remember Idi Amin? Well, according to unconfirmed reports he used to strangle and behead his rivals for women and put their head in the fridge as a kind of trophy. So perhaps Colonel Ossai is in the cooler, somewhere (221).

The present cabinet, the workers, students and peasants are all victims of the forces of coercion. Except for Chris, all the members of the cabinet are virtually intellectually moribund. Mean, petty and hypocritical, they have grown to be nauseating sycophants who are in the cabinet to advance their personal interests at the expense of their honour, integrity and the welfare of the people. The eleven intellectuals among them, who constitute the "cream of our society and the hope of the black race" (2), have become so greedy, timid, cowardly and psychologically insecure that they have disgracefully settled for a life of mediocrity. It is, for instance, undignifying to see the Commissioner for Justice and Attorney General feel so frightened of His Excellency that he confuses "flout" with 'flaunt" in talking to him (5); and Professor Okong (who tells His Excellency that the commissioners are his children) "undeserved" with unreserved" (16). Ikem is right in calling the cabinet a circus show" (188) and the commissioners, "court-jesters" (46) or "mesmerized toadies in daily attendance" (46).

With regard to the suppression of the voices of dissent, the narrator condemns the "... damnable shooting of striking railway-workers and demonstrating students and the destruction and banning thereafter of independent unions and cooperatives..." (141). The treatment of the peasants of Abazon province is equally "damnable". The people have voted "no" in the referendum organized by Sam to decide on his bid for life-presidency. In retaliation for their action, the President orders the removal of the pipes sent to the drought-stricken province for the installation of a water supply scheme. In desperation, the people send a goodwill delegation "of elders to the government who hold the yam today and hold the knife" (33) in order to appease His Excellency and woo him into providing amenities for them. His Excellency uses deceit to make them believe that they are welcome in the Palace but later in the novel, we are told that the "six leaders from Abazon who were involved in a recent illegal march on the Presidential Palace without police permit as required by decree had been arrested (150–151) and put into prison.

These actions portray Sam as politically immature, intellectually barren and psychologically insecure. To compensate for these weaknesses, he becomes extremely intolerant and arrogant. Mediocre to the core, he confuses sycophancy with loyalty and political wisdom, and criticism with indiscipline and irresponsibility. As is to be expected, the state apparatus becomes very dangerous in his hands, for he uses it to institutionalize mediocrity. He thereby equates personal interests with those of the state by tenaciously defending the former in the name of the latter. Corruption, favouritism and plofligacy become highly prized virtues for the regime.

His successes in taming his cabinet, banning trade union and students' movements, as well as arresting and imprisoning dissidents make him believe that he is Omnipotent. It is not surprising that his growth from a "baby monster" (10) to a hideous criminal is phenomenal, although in his grandiose conceit he perceives his various tyrannical acts as a legitimate exercise in maintaining law and order. He soon becomes the greatest enemy of his people, having constituted himself into the very source of their misery and destruction. In fact, Achebe subtly depicts him as the Fiery Sun that scorches the Kangas:

> The Sun in April is an enemy though the weathermen on television reciting mechanically the words of his foreign mentors tells you it will be fine all over the country. Fine! We have been slowly steamed into well-done mutton since February and all the oafs on our public payroll tell us we are doing just fine! No, my dear countrymen (27).

And in the highly lyrical and evocative poem "Hymn to the Sun" (written by Ikem), Achebe obliquely refers to his Excellency as the "Great Carrier of Sacrifice to the Almighty:

> Single Eye of God (30) who constitutes a plague to the people:
>
> Why have you brought this on us? What hideous abomination forbidden and forbidden and forbidden again seven times have we committed or else condoned, what error that no reparation can hope to erase? look, our forlorn prayers, our offerings of conciliation lie scattered about your floor where you cast them disdainfully away; and every dawn you pile up your long basket of day with the tools and emblems of death (30).

The lyric plays on the metaphorical significance of the sun in the novel, by equating Sam with the drought that has ravaged the Abazon province and, by extension, the whole state of Kanga.

Sam however sees himself as the "Single Eye of God" who, as the potential Life-President of Kanga, deserves the honour of having his effigy installed "on the nation's currency' (162). The more he perpetrates acts of horror against the population of the state the more he perceives himself as the omnipotent redeemer of the people. He lives in a world of illusion.

Chris and Ikem (as well as Beatrice, to some extent) serve as the counterpoint to this world. Both are patriots who doggedly defend the integrity of the republic. As we have already seen, the novel opens with the confrontation between Sam and Chris over the sanctity of the power exercised by His Excellency. Sam insists on seeing Chris as a conformist who must model his behaviour on the ethics of the prevailing power structure but Chris refuses to play this role, although his status as the Commissioner for Information compromises his position. Chris is basically a non-conformist who feels alienated from the government he serves. He is in government as a dispassionate observer of events, a chronicler who wants to record the follies of the government for humanity. We are even given an insight into his predicament as a player of this enigmatic role:

> But the real question which I have often asked myself is why then do I go on with it now that I can see. I don't know. Simple inertia, maybe. Or perhaps sheer curiosity: to see where it will all ...well, end. I am not thinking so much about him as about my colleagues, eleven intelligent, educated men who let this happen to them, who actually went out of their way to invite it, and who even at this hour have seen and learnt nothing, the cream of our society and the hope of the

> black race. I suppose it is for them that I am still at this silly observation post making farcical entries in the crazy log-book of this our ship of state (2).

Although he is in a dilemma he has no selfish motives for sticking to his job. There is no doubt that he espouses values opposed to those of the government.

As non-conformist, he goes all out to challenge the dictatorial tendencies of the government. Accordingly, he disassociates himself from Sam's plans to muzzle and destroy Ikem as the editor of the National Gazette and even openly defies Sam's authority. Out of fear for his life, he abandons his job and runs away from the capital since he has been declared a wanted person. In the ensuing confusion that engulfs the country, Sam is assassinated and Chris eventually loses the life in the hands of a policeman who gets infuriated at Chris's attempt to prevent him from abducting a young girl. Chris's gallant and patriotic defence of the rights of the people is construed by His Excellency as an act of sabotage. There is a touch of martyrdom to his death.

Ikem's image is similar. He is a single-minded, strongwilled, successful poet who, as editor of the national newspaper, sees journalism as an instrument for social change. Unlike his friend Chris who is more discreet and diplomatic in handling issues, Ikem is militant and very outspoken. He feels for the poor and enthusiastically champions their cause. His confrontation with the regime eventually leads to his death, an event that arouses public outrage and contributes to the overthrow of the government and the eventual assassination of the Head of State. In general, he incarnates the spirit of social justice in Kanga.

The resistance of Chris and Ikem to Sam's dictatorship serves a very important function in the novel. It helps to expose the hollowness of Sam's self-perception as an omnipotent ruler whose personal interests are inseparable from those of the State and also punctures his belief that he can use the apparatus of power to perpetuate evil. Sam's illusion that he is immune from the vagaries of political fortune falls to pieces; he associates Chris and Ikem with the failure of his projected plan to become a Life President and strongly feels that he can easily eliminate them but the task eludes him since in the process he loses his life in a *coup d'etat* that topples his government. Thus, the role of Chris and Ikem as "dissidents" swerves Sam's illusion to the plane of reality and reveals him as a victim of delusion of grandeur.

The rhythm of the movement of the plot captures the spirit of this interpretation. The plot moves on an even keel from the beginning of the novel to the middle when Sam feels relatively secure in the exercise of his power. The tempo increases as the scenes move in quack succession to reflect the world of Sam's feverish efforts to fight off his enemies and consolidate his power; then it momentarily jostles to an abrupt stop with the announcement of the *coup d'etat* that brings down his government; it again builds up momentum and gently grinds to a halt at the end of the novel where Beatrice organizes a naming ceremony for Ikem's child. The more Chris and his associates (who are on the run) succeed in slipping through the net of security cast by Sam to ensure their capture, the more Sam feels entrapped in the world of illusion he has created for himself. His eventual assassination suggests that he has been destroyed in his world of illusion. The message is clear! it is virtually impossible for a tyrannical Head of State to perpetually impose his authority on an unwilling population.

Achebe successfully dramatizes the allegory of power which is encapsulated in the story of *Power* and Idemili (102). The story emphasizes the necessity for a leader to cultivate the virtues of humility and sense of justice; and warns against the consequences of his abuse of his authority. Just as Nwakibie inevitably loses his life in the story for violating the injunctions of Idemili, Sam loses his for not bearing "witness to the moral nature of authority by wrapping around (his) rude waist a loincloth of peace and modesty" (102). Achebe suggests here that military dictatorships in Nigeria will inevitably crumble thus bringing about an era of justice and fair play for the people.

This point is clearly revealed by the name given to Ikem's child – *Amaechina: May-the-path-never-close* (222). Ikem's struggle for the rights of the people will continue until victory is won. The story of the Tortoise and the Leopard told by the Abazon elder and retold by Ikem during his lecture at the University of Kanga underscores the spirit of the imperative of struggle which will usher in the new era of the people's sovereignty. After all, as Beatrice positively affirms, "This world belongs to the people of the world not to any little caucus, no matter how talented" (232).

Thus Achebe takes a revolutionary stance on the question of political leadership of the military in Nigeria. He seems to be saying that the military is ill-prepared for political leadership. They are corrupt, incompetent and vindictive. They use their power to impose their will on the people and tenaciously cling to the belief that this state of affairs will continue for ever. They are mistaken, for they will finally lose the power. It is, therefore, wise for them to leave the political arena by handing over power to the people.

Achebe makes his points obliquely by using language and techniques that are loaded with meaning. The metaphorical density of his devices makes the work a great political novel.

Notes

1. See, for example, "The Novelist as Teacher" and "Colonialist Criticism" in *Morning Yet on Creation Day*. See also Madubike's "Achebe's Ideas on Literature" and Ogungbesan's "Politics and the Africa Writer: The Example of Chinua Achebe".

2. See, for instance, Chidi Amuta, *Towards the Sociology of African Literature*: although *Arrow of God* is a flawless artistic statement on the cultural of the colonial conquest, we look in vain for any suggestion of the economics axis of the colonial encounter. If we explore the reasons for this omission, we may be tempted to see them in Achebe's privileged education and his liberal individualist ideology" (51) Ngugi wa Thiong'o, although a Marxist like Amuta, holds a contrary view for he believes that Achebe's characters are quintessentially products of African history. *Homecoming*, 43–44).

3. See also his contemptuous remarks on university Professors: "But come to think of it, whatever put it into our head when we arrived on this seat that we needed these half-baked professors to tell us anything. What do they know? Give me good military training any day" (21).

4. See also Ikem's rumination on the issue: "Public affairs: They are nothing but the closed transactions of soldiers-turned-politicians, with their cohorts in business and the bureaucracy" (141).

Works Cited

Achebe. Chinua. *Things Fall Apart*. London: Heinemana, 1958
———. *No Longer at Ease*. London: Heinemana, 1960
———. *Arrow of God*. London: Heinemana, 1964
———. *A Man of the People*. London: Heinemana, 1966
———. *Beware Soul Brother and Other Poems*. London: Heinemana, 1972
———. *Girls at War and Other Stories*. London: Heinemana, 1972
———. *Morning Yet on Creation Day*. London: Heinemana, 1975
———. *The Trouble with Nigeria*. Enugu: Fourth Dimension, 1983
———. *Anthills of the Savannah*. London: Heinemana, 1987
Amuta Chidi *Towards a Sociology of African Literature*. Oguta: Zim, 1986
Madubuike, Ihechukwu. "Achebe's Ideas on Literature", *Presence Africaine*, 93 1975, 140–52
Ngugi, wa Thiong'o. *Homecoming*. London: Heinemana, 1972
Odumegwu-Ojukwu, Emeka. *Because I am involved*. Ibadan: Spectrum. 1989
Ogungbesan, Kolawole "Politics and the African Writer: The Example of Chinua Achebe, "*African Studies Review*, 17 1974. 43–54.

Part Six:

Critical Perspectives on *Beware, Soul Brother*

Chapter 31

Chinua Achebe's Critical Realism: *Girls at War* and *Beware, Soul Brother*

Craig W. McLuckie

> Belonging, then, is a school of love where we learn to open up to others and to the world around us, where each person, creature and thing in our world is important and respected (Jean Vanier Becoming Human).

THE CONTEXT FOR ACHEBE'S *Beware, Soul Brother* and the last three stories in *Girls at War and Other Stories* ("Civil Peace," "Sugar Baby," and "Girls at War") is the brief period following independence for Nigeria (October 1960), the war years (1966–1970), and a few years following the war. But the war is central. In the ensuing discussion of Achebe's realism I intend to concentrate on these works which relate directly to the Nigerian Civil War. My reasons for doing so are two fold: to examine the way(s) in which Achebe responds artistically to experienced historical events; and, to illuminate the ideology that is behind his art.

What I see as Achebe's critical morality in this is a realism aimed at envisioning his people and their place. His love and compassion for both are evident in the works under study here. According I.D. Lukacs, the aesthetic is "great literature … that which manages to penetrate beyond the surface appearances, to perceive and expose social totality, with all its contradictions" (Wolff 6). Emmanuel Ngara expands on this concept to show what is at work:

> The impact poets make depends on the significance of what they say about social reality and how effectively they communicate their vision to their readers. What they say about social reality depends largely on their social vision (authorial

> ideology) and how successfully they communicate that vision is largely a matter of the effectiveness of their stylistic stance or aesthetic ideology (Ngara xi).

Reflection on this point suggests that authorial ideology is authorial intent, that which the writer wishes to convey before the creative work of fiction (the employ of the imagination) has begun. Aesthetic ideology is that which is produced by the imaginative act, the style or execution of the intent. An examination of Achebe's non-fictional prose works will allow the development of a sense of what his authorial ideology is, while an examination of the workings of the poems and short stories will show how far the creative process has taken him.

Authorial Ideology/Social Vision

> True art, by specific technical means now commonly forgotten, clarifies life, establishes models of human action, casts nets toward the future, carefully judges our right and wrong directions, celebrates and mourns. It does not rant. It does not sneer or giggle in the face of death, it invents prayers and weapons. It designs visions worth trying to make fact (Gardner 100).

Achebe's first collection of essays, *Morning Yet on Creation Day*, gives some sense of his authorial ideology, its range and limitations the essays will be examined in chronological order, thus giving a sense of development and change in position.

The first essay of note is "The African Writer and the English Language" (1964). Here, Achebe emphasizes the adaptability of the English language. His purpose is to stress the international nature of the language, and so the African writer's ability to contribute to its growth, not the ability of the language to colonize: the African writer "should aim at fashioning out an English which is at once universal and also able to carry his peculiar experience" (Achebe, 1975: 61).

"The Novelist as Teacher" (1965) is Achebe's most oft-quoted essay. It is a clear and precise statement of the social role of the artist and his/her art. For himself, Achebe narrows the role as follows: "Here then is an adequate revolution for me to espouse – tot [sic] help my society regain belief in itself and put away the complexes of the years of denigration and self-abasement. And it is essentially a question of education, in the best sense of the word" (Achebe, 1975: 44). From these two essays, the reader is quickly stuck by the nature of Achebe's authorial ideology – what he wants the aesthetic to be – a movement from the individual's felt experience and knowledge out to the community. That movement indicates "what happened to [the community], what [it] lost" (Achebe, 1973: 8) or is losing if the work, as is the case with those under review here, is a recreation of the present.

Central to this paper is the way in which the Biafran experience affected Achebe's vision. In "The African Writer and the Biafran Cause" (1968), the argument is grounded in the experience of African writers as a whole: "the involvement of the Biafran writer today in the cause [of] his people ... is not different from the involvement of many African writers – past and present – in the big issues of Africa. The fact of war merely puts the issue in sharper focus" (Achebe, 1975: 78). So sharp is the new focus that the writer becomes an agent for change – lecturing to garner support for Biafra, and a more clear-sighted perspective from outsiders (Achebe, 1972b: 6). Rather than take his decision to support Biafra and turn it into an entrenched tribally-oriented position, Achebe seeks a larger more responsible correlative: humanity and human issues in Africa. This becomes most apparent when he calls on the artist to use his "heightened sensitivities" to make himself "aware of the faintest nuances of injustice" (Achebe, 1975: 79). From these broad issues, Achebe narrows in on his own choice – Biafra – where he will fight for "justice and true independence" (Achebe, 1975: 84). Obviously principles that Nigeria no longer held. The diction is appealing, but one soon begins to quibble with the lack of rigor in the analysis and the lack of definitions. What is "true independence"? Is it individual rights? Group rights? The context provides the answer – true independence is that which was not attained by all tribespeople in Nigeria following independence. The meaning of the rhetoric comes about through oppositions: Biafra/Nigeria; just and right! unjust and evil; revolutionary and egalitarian/conservative and hierarchical. Achebe's next essay "Chi in Igbo Cosmology" (1972), explains this sense of opposition or duality. Wherever something stands, something else will stand beside it. Nothing is absolute" (Achebe, 1975: 94). There is a relativism about this position, some would call it a pragmatic approach to life and events. In a writer of lesser intelligence than Achebe, it would be a cause of concern, dangerous, because of the simplicity and ease of naming one side in opposition to another rather than one side in addition to another with elements of each discarded as they are seen and felt and experienced to be of less use. The latter position is the one that Achebe espouses in later essays. Undoubtedly, there was more to Achebe's decision to act with and for Biafra – given the atrocities, and his obvious horror at them, one can speculate that an emotional psychic insularity was a large part of his response. Simon Gikandi handles the issue as follows: "If Achebe's commitment to Nigeria can be transferred-with ease and integrity – to Biafra, this should not be seen as an indication of the novelist's wavering allegiances, but of the shifting nature of African problematic, and of the writer's need to shape his own thinking to come to terms with the Afrkan problematic (Gikandi 8). That his major essay of the war "The Biafran Writer ... offers more rhetoric than earlier or subsequent pieces would seem to underscore this fact. In the *Palaver* interview, Achebe is less rhetorical. He spells out the writer's role vis-a-vis history: "I think our most meaningful job today should be to determine what kind of society we want, how we are going to get there, what values we can take from the past if we can, as we move along" (Achebe, 1972b: 12). Obviously, the view of history is not static, received; it is critical, evolutionary. During the war,

Achebe worked at the University of Biafra until it closed, ran the Citadel Press with Christopher Okigbo, and gave lectures in support of and aiming at increasing relief and supplies for Biafra. Without question, while Biafra existed, Achebe was actively engaged. "Africa and Her Writers" (1972) moves back to a more thorough analysis, re-emphasizing the communal ethic Achebe wants in art – "art is, and was always, in the service of man" (Achebe, 1975: 19). But, again, the individualized experience and locale are brought back into focus, as Achebe warns that "Ease and carelessness in our [i.e., the African writers'] circumstance will only cause a total breakdown of communications" (Achebe, 1975: 27). So, the writer stays rooted in the local, while his muse may take him and his community, by extension, elsewhere. Otherwise, the communal relationship is lost, and as Achebe would assert, so is the writer. Thus in "Language and the Destiny of Man" (1972) "a community where man 'doomed to be free' ... is yet able to challenge that peculiar and perilious destiny with an even chance of wresting from it a purposeful, creative existence" (Achebe, 1975: 30).

"Thoughts on the African Novel" (1973) further reinforces Achebe's prescription for a localized art, but opens the position up in a meaningful way to give a sense of "creative existence".

> The African novel has to be about Africa. A pretty severe restriction, I am told. But Africa is not only a geographic expression; it is also a metaphysical landscape – it is in fact a view of the world and of the whole cosmos perceived from a particular position (Achebe, 1975, 50).

More than any other point, this one brings home Achebe's authorial ideology most fully and clearly. Caution, however, is needed, for the nub of the argument in "Colonialist Criticism" (1974) is Achebe's assertion that he has "problems with universality and other concepts of that scope..." (Achebe, 1975: 3). The writer "cannot make history go away (Achebe, 1975: 11), must struggle "to alter things... to find for [himself] a little more room than has been allowed him in the world" (Achebe, 1975: 14), but within his society. Localized again, the term, from the foregoing, has to be seen in the sense of the individual's concerns growing out to a minimal society (perhaps one other person) for testing, and then to progressively larger communities (like the village, the Igbo) until the nation has been reached (Biafra, Nigeria).

Following the military resolution of the Nigerian Civil War, and following the return to civilian rule, Achebe made his most direct move away from the writer's product-as-teacher in the community and assumed the role of politician – Deputy National President of the People's Redemption Party. *The Trouble with Nigeria* is a product of that role, where Achebe utilizes a lower level of vocabulary, argumentation and stylistic finesse to address the nation's populace. The book is a useful, if somewhat surface-level description of Nigeria's woes. Obviously it is an election-oriented pamphlet, but does this mean that only the source of the problems and some of the types of problems can be shown? Blame for the past is placed on the nation's leadership and its people. There is little in the way of information or vision about the difficulties of change, or the ways of achieving it. Achebe has, in fact, fallen prey to the communal problem he identifies as a lack of intellectual rigor because he too is taking the easy road – stopping half-way. A poor example is thus set for others. The force of this criticism may be reduced if we take into account the proximity of national elections to the publication date and Achebe's role in one of the parties. On the other hand, though, it seems that too much politicking takes place in the world and not enough idealism and position-taking for the resolution of problems. The purpose of examining this text is not solely to task Achebe's approach to electioneering, but rather to examine his ninth chapter, "The Igbo Problem," to ascertain how, if at all, his position on Nigeria/Biafra has changed. Pragmatism and survival are the answers that two partially oblique statements attest to:

> Modern Nigerian history has been marked by sporadic eruptions of anti-Igbo feeling of more or less serious import; but it was not until 1966–7 when it swept through Northern Nigeria like "a flood of deadly hate" that the Igbo first questioned the concept of Nigeria which they had embraced with much greater fervor than the Yoruba or the Hausa/Fulani (Achebe, 1983: 45).
>
> ...pan-Igbo solidarity is a figment of the Nigerian imagination. It has never existed except briefly, and for a unique reason, during the civil war (Achebe, 1983: 47).

Biafra seceded from Nigeria to ensure that the Igbo people would survive. Once that end had been achieved, and even in defeat it was, then the next larger pan-tribal grouping (Nigeria) could be returned to.

Achebe's recent selected essays, *Hopes and Impediments*, bring his authorial ideology up to date. An analysis of them is beneficial because, though written some time after the war, like *The Trouble with Nigeria*, they illuminate Achebe's evolving authorial ideology, though the fact that five of the essays from *Morning Yet on Creation Day* are reprinted here emphasizes Achebe's core perspective.

"An Image of Africa: Racism in Conrad's *Heart of Darkness*" (1977) places style at the service of content:

> When a writer while pretending to record scenes, incidents, and their impact, is in reality engaged in inducing hypnotic stupor in his readers through a bombardment of emotive words and other forms of trickery, *much more has to be at stake than stylistic felicity* (Achebe, 1990: 5) (my emphasis).

Truth, or at least a conscious attempt to achieve an adequate representation is at stake here. Achebe does not find it in Conrad, but is saying that this is a goal of any writer – fictive or otherwise. This point is taken up again and reinforced in Achebe's discussion of Tutuola – "Work and Play in Amos Tutuola's *The Palm-Wine*

Drinkard" (1977). The interpretation Achebe provides is moral: the ethic of work and social responsibility dominate his sense of Tutuola's achievement in the novel.

In "The Truth of Fiction" (1978) Achebe concisely summarizes his sense of art's role in life; it is a perspective parallel to John Gardner's position in *On Moral Fiction*, which was published in the same year. Both writers see a central role for fiction in life. Achebe writes that:

> ...art is man's constant effort to create for himself a different order of reality from that which is given to him; an aspiration to provide himself with a second handle on existence through his imagination ... [it] ... helps us locate again the line between the heroic and the cowardly when it seems most shadowy and elusive, and it does this by forcing us to encounter the heroic and the cowardly in our own psyche... The fiction which imaginative literature offers us liberates the mind of the man. Its truth ... begins as an adventure in self-discovery and ends in wisdom and humane consciousness (Achebe, 1990: 153).

Note the proximity of this line of argument to Gardner's, in the epigraph above, which stresses a universality in art (or an internationalism among artists, in approach, at least).

"The Writer and His Community" (1984) continues this preoccupation and re-asserts points made in "The Novelist as Teacher" about the artist's strengths arising from ties to his community. Achebe's ties, as discussed earlier, are with himself first, his fellow Igbo second – his immediate social and cultural locale – and then with the Nigerian Nation. Thus, in "The Igbo World and Its Art" (1984), we find Achebe returning to his most specific communal roots, identifying the Igbo world view as "an arena for the interplay of forces a dynamic world of movement and of flux" (Achebe, 1990: 62), wherein the art "is never tranquil but mobile and active, even aggressive" (Achebe, 1990: 62). Art and society are inter-related, feeding the growth and direction of one another. Man finds himself in the world, observes, analyses, comments, debates and modifies, then hopefully his world follows; or, in some instances, he follows its offerings.

"What Has Literature Got to Do with It?" (1986) extends "The Truth of Fiction" through a reconsideration of what has occurred in the Nigerian society. It is an intertwining of the social and the artistic, a call for all citizens to their "cardinal duty of active participation in the political process" (Achebe, 1990: 166), and a reminder, in language that echoes earlier essays, that

> Literature ... gives us a second handle on reality; enabling us to encounter in the safe, manageable dimensions of make-believe the very same threats to integrity that may assail the psyche in real life; and at the same time providing through the self-discovery which it imparts a veritable weapon for coping with these threats whether they are found within problematic and incoherent selves or in the world around us (Achebe, 1990: 170).

In the more standard literary critical essays on Kofi Awoonor, Amos Tutuola, Joseph Conrad, and Christopher Okigbo, Achebe maintains a consistent view, focusing on the man, the work, the evocation of place and its morality, reinforcing the pedagogical value of good literature to the individual's and thus to society's development, "invoking reason and humanity to arbitrate" (Achebe, 1990: 176) the cause of the oppressed. Achebe's authorial ideology is that of a critical realist.

On several occasions since he made the remark that "Art for art's sake is just another piece of deodorized dog shit" (Achebe, 1974: 19), Achebe has tried to modify, if not soften the force of the statement, though not retract it. In spite of these occasions, the original phrase retains a resonance and impact. It is, I would argue, the most succinct expression of the authorial ideology that Achebe has made.

The question, though, in *Girls at War* and *Beware, Soul Brother* is what moves these collections away from an enclosed, self-referential artificially scented and ultimately untouchable aesthetic to a more dynamic aesthetic that corresponds with Achebe's authorial ideology?

Aesthetic Ideology/Stylistic Stance in *Beware, Soul Brother* Poems

> It seems to me that poems were spoken through it was their gift to be a voice of voices, a vehicle must have felt some primeval oracle forcing sound from their throats as they whispered of their people in their place
>
> place: when it used to be a place the gods of place seeking out voice incarnation of a people in its place
>
> lives caught in a time: a privilege maybe the lack of it of wounds and the great humble arching grin of any thought alive in any field celebrated: *locus* (Lent 103).

G. Douglas Killam offers a fine perspective on the world-view that dominates Achebe's poetry, where the poems: "... exploit the intuitive Igbo sense of duality which informs all things. Whatever the thematic content of the poems, they are manifestations in various moods and tones of this "world-view" (Killam 115). The fullest critical account of the first collection of poetry is given by Philip Rogers, who writes that they "are centrally concerned with the regeneration of belief after the blight of war" (Rogers 284), wherein "Achebe mounts a revolution of spirit to clear a space for "the dance of the future" (Rogers 284).

Of the individual sections, 'Prologue' opens with "1966", an ironic poem that "is rich in inference and reflects the duality of the poet's vision of Christianity" (Bruchac 23). A duality that has come about because of the "absent-minded," "thoughtless" and "indolent" nature of man's actions, which lead to "His first/ disappointment in Eden" (Achebe, 1972a: 3). So too with "Benin Road", where three assertions about violence are contrasted with the fragility of a butterfly, before it "pops open/in a bright yellow/smear in the silicon/hardness of" his vision (Achebe, 1972a: 4). "Mango Seedling" is dedicated to Christopher Okigbo, who died in the war and thus the withering seedling is meant to stand as an image of both Okigbo and Biafra. It is allegorical, particularly the last line, where Okigbo/the mango seedling become a "headstone on tiny debris of passionate courage" (Achebe, 1972a: 6). A death of idealism. Achebe's persona, "1," is a detached, slightly distanced observer, not an active participant. The final poem in the prologue, "The Explorer" renders the persona's "Explorer-Self" encountering "a body I didn't even know/I lost" (Achebe, 1972a: 8), most likely that of his youth, as represented in the crippled angelic vision before him and the associated curiosity, energy and innocence. In its return to the mature persona, it is reminiscent of Edwin Muir's "Horses" and the adult's discovery that he "must pine/Again for that dread country crystalline ..." (Muir 20). Achebe's persona, too, has "lost" one part of the self.

What the 'Prologue' offers as a group is an introduction to the poet's sense of what he is being caught up in. Each poem offers a sense that full engagement has not yet occurred, as the detached sense of the result of human actions on God, the windscreen of the car separating the persona from the butterfly, the view from the office block of the seedling, and the vision of loss through the medium of another attest. Violence, too, is a common threat that unifies this opening group, foreshadowing the more direct aspects of it that will be visited upon the Biafran people.

'Poems about war' opens with "The First Shot", a mark of the revolution's beginning.

> The poem sharply contrasts the human time of historical "first shots" with the mechanical time of real bullets. The contrast of historical and mechanical forces announces a central concern of these poems, exploring the kinship of things human and inhuman (Rogers 285).

Rogers goes on to discuss "Refugee Mother and Child" and "Christmas in Biafra"; these are "longer, more ambitious poems that attempt to evoke pathos through direct description of civilian casualties" (Rogers 285). "Christmas ..." is heavily ironic, as the inversion of seasonal traditions illustrates; it is a season for "distilling pure transcendental hate (Achebe, 1972a: 13). The repetition of "distance" further emphasizes "the gap between the people and the religion which has both harbinger and tool of the colonial era which led inexorably to the Biafran conflict" (Bruchac 26).

John Povey has written that the war was more fully felt on the Biafran side, "not only because they lost ... but because the optimism of the longing for independence suffocated under the greed and corruption" (Povey 355) within Biafra. And so, the lost ideal, the returned cycle of history provides an ironic and bitter undercurrent to the "apparently casual and detached" (Povey 356) poem, "Air Raid". Rogers, on the same poem, comments that it "further defines the contrasting modes of time seen in "The First Shot." The poem's juxtapositions are immediately and simply effective ..."

(Rogers 285). Bruchac takes up Killam's point on the Igbo world-view and shows Achebe's association of the MIG jets with places of ill omen to the Igbo, "the 'Evil Forests' where malicious spirits dwell ..." (Bruchac 26). The poem is weak because of its straightforward statement of events, enumerated as they happen. The last image of one man cut in half having other worries now "than a friendly handshake/at noon" (15) doesn't work because of the lack of emotional investment – the reader is left with a pathetic image rather than one that evokes pathos.

"An 'If' of History" and "Remembrance Day" shift responsibility away from the armaments dealers in the United Kingdom and Russia and place a portion of the blame on the Biafrans themselves. As Killam asserts, this poem:

> ...is worked out by identifying a series of paradoxes wherein the judgments of recent history in assigning right and wrong, guilt and innocence, in making moral judgments about the conduct of war are seen to be wholly relative to current judgments (Killam 117).

"Remembrance Day" works in a similar fashion, with the persona directly addressing the living and comparing their lives returning to normalcy, their forgetting the recent travails, and then undercutting these pronouncements with a query about the dead: "But when,/how soon, will they [forget] their death?" (Achebe, 1972a: 19). The question is rhetorical; the living are told to flee from their homes and cities to avoid visitations from the angered dead until "a season of atonement and rescue/from fingers calloused by heavy deeds" allows "the tender rites to reconciliation" to work. In the explanatory note to this poem, Achebe describes how the "dead [Igbo] hero hears the living a grudge. Life is the 'natural' state; death is tolerable only when it leads to life – reincarnation" (Achebe, 1972a, 64). Time and psychic resources become the healers as the dead remain enjoined to us in time and in memory.

"After a War" is an accomplished poem in its pacing. It begins tentatively, there is almost a disbelief that the war has ended, as the use of enjambment here demonstrates:

> After a war life catches Desperately at passing Hints of normalcy like Vines entwining a hollow Twig ... (Achebe, 1972a, 20).

The poem continues in this hesitant manner, until the last stanza, where the poem is stronger, more assured:

> After yearsof pressing deathand dizzy last hour reprieves we're glad to dump our fears and our perilous gains together in one shallow grave and flee the same rueful way we came straight home to haunted revelry (Achebe, 1972a, 21).

That "haunted revelry" conjures up the loss of the past – a particular mood and way of living life, not almost forgotten – as well as the presence of past actions in the future, and of the poet/narrator's guilt at celebrating and enjoying himself so soon after the horror.

Killam argues that the war poems "say and show that war is horrible and that its effects are always seen and experienced most powerfully by the innocent" (Killam 117). It is only in poems like "Remembrance Day" however that these experiences are fully transferred to the reader, for that poem is one of the few in this section about which the reader feels the emotional commitment and controlled outrage of the poet's persona; the others, largely, remain detached, ineffective through the clinical approach they offer.

'Poems not about war' opens with "Love Song (for Anna)." Rogers sees Achebe's recovery in this poem and 'Answer'. The first poem is "is personal in tone … and looks to the future. A sense of quiescent hopefulness is conveyed in metaphors of concealment and preparation …" (Rogers 287). The second poem "dramatizes…" the rooting of a new conception of the persona's self… his regeneration … a … bursting out of confinement" (Rogers 287, 288). Bruchac sees "Love Song" and "Answer" offering a movement from tentativeness to strong assertion in the persona's "duty to instruct and criticize" (Bruchac 27).

"Love Cycle" and "Question" have received scant critical attention. The first poem of this pair is a fairly simple metaphor for loving relationships. Here, there is a love song between the Sun and the Earth, where the dawn brings about a change in male-female relations, the Sun (male) becomes aggressive and turns its attention away from the woman. While "another night will/restore his mellowness/ and her power/over him" (Achebe, 1972a: 26). Nothing new has been said about the natural world, nor about human relationships. There is a sense of chauvinism in the image of woman's power existing only at night in an embrace. The latter poem is weak, posing the question of man's relationship with his environment, but not in particularly unique poetic language, not through the use of a complex of metaphors. The question asked, the reader is left dissatisfied. "Answer", the corresponding poem, works more fully in its testament to the individual's ability to overcome angst and rediscover self in a sense of home, "on whose trysting floor waited/my proud vibrant life" (Achebe, 1972a: 28). A sense of self comes through a reorientation to place.

In "*Beware, Soul Brother*" Achebe's persona "admonishes the reader to beware" (Rogers 284), but shows him/her the path to social regeneration. "*Beware, Soul Brother*" warns that "a man's/foot must return…" to the ground "lest [he] become/a dancer disinherited in mid-dance" (Achebe, 1972a: 30). Killam's perspective on this poem is that it is:

> …a meditation … on the duality of life and death as this is made manifest in the Igbo sensibility, made visible in the masks and the dance; as these beliefs

> are threatened by "the Cross", the "lures of ascension day' the "day of soporific levitation"; as these are expounded by the "leaden-footed, tone-deaf passionate only for the entrails of our soil." The mixture of Christian and non-Christian attitudes suggested in these opposing lines points a way to the need to find one's own way, to find a joy unique to one's own soul (Killam 125).

But, it remains a warning too that one's roots are in home. "NON-Commitment" and "We Laughed at Him," the volume's closing poem, are constructed from "contrasting images of defense and penetration" (Rogers 290). The uncommitted, not surprisingly, are represented as sterile, "like a diaphragm across/womb's beckoning doorway" (Achebe, 1972a: 31), caught in stasis, inactive except as agents of non-change, and thus to be vilified as traitors, like Pontius Pilate and Judas. While the poem has a certain effect, the lack of balance, present in earlier poems, works against it." "We Laughed at Him" is ... a defense of poetry and the poet's role in a society blinded by conventionality and contemptuous of the arts" (Rogers 290–91). The poem stresses the Igbo notion of a "free choice" (Achebe, 1972a: 68) in life as well as in art.

"Generation Gap", "Misunderstanding", and "Bull and Egret" have received minimal attention, perhaps because they offer statements without any attempt to embellish them into artifacts. The first says that the sense of a man comes from the birth of his grandson to his son; the second that the male cannot comprehend a lesson passed on from his father – "Wherever something stands, he'd say, there also something else will stand" (Achebe: 1972a, 33); the third is a straightforward series of statements on the nature of the bull and the egret's relationship, with man and machine briefly intervening and learning. "Vultures" and "Lazarus", in contrast:

> reveal the nadir of the poet's spirits. Both explore the idea that good and evil are inextricably linked; the very germ from which new growth may come is tainted with evil. In "Vultures" Achebe reexamines the theme of love's persisting in spite of the external evils that threaten it... "Lazarus" further dramatizes the inseparability of good and evil... now the blighting force can no longer be dismissed as external (Rogers 287).

"Public Execution in Pictures" closes the 'Poems not about war' section with a meditation on the nature of violence within a society at peace, emphasizing the attitudes people adopt and the effect an execution can have on one's children – even from a distance. Achebe is seeking the reader's interrogation of the subject presumably so that children may enjoy life and not be exposed too early to callous debates about why, in the newspaper pictures, the heads of the executed "always slump forwards/or sideways" (41).

Many of the poems in this section are meditations on the way Achebe sees the world, There is a sense of stasis in what the reader is offered; but there is also a location of what is wrong, of what needs adjustment. It is only when the persona's voice is direct and engaged with the reader that something worthwhile and of note is said, as in "*Beware, Soul Brother*," or hinted at, as in "Public Execution in Pictures."

'Gods, men and others' opens with "Penalty of Godhead," a poem which, when combined with "Lament of the Sacred Python", and "Dereliction" (from the 'Epilogue' section) reveal Achebe looking:

> ...back to the world of his ancestors ... only to express the pain he feels in abandoning them ... At the same time, however, Achebe takes no pleasure in escaping the past. If his need to put down new roots is paramount the uprooting of past ties is still painful. ... They remind us that a new birth entails the death of the old (Rogers 289–90).

"Those Gods are Children" and "Their Idiot Song" are reflections respectively on the persona's sense of the gods and on people's reactions to death. What unites the two is the sense that "they are footed/as easily as children those deities/their simple omnipotence drowsed by praise" (48); and, the "massing odours" at the undertaker's, "mocking [the people's] pitiful makeshift defences" (51) against death. In both poems, Achebe's critical realism comes to the fore, through irony, as in "These Gods" or sarcasm, as in "Their Idiot Song". No subject goes untouched, uncommented upon, all are subject to Achebe's scrutiny. Implicitly rather than explicitly, the poems in this section demand our attention be engaged in all areas of life.

The 'Epilogue' opens with an absurdity, "He Loves Me: He Loves Me Not" in which Achebe skewers Britain's then Labour Prime Minister Harold Wilson for selling armaments to both sides in the conflict. "Dereliction" attacks those who fail their culture, presumably because of a character defect ("oily palms"), or who would sell it. Simple, straighiforward, and prosaic, this piece exiles them to "the land/where the sea retreats" (56). Achebe's note stresses the poem's three part structure – enquirer, meditating diviner, and Oracle (67). "We Laughed at Him" presents a sense of skepticism going awry, as prophets within our midst may go unnoticed, their sayings unheard, unless we attend to them. Here, Achebe warns about the dangers of taking criticism too far, of disallowing the fantastic of today which could be the reality of tomorrow.

Killam concisely summarizes the aesthetic ideology of the poetry thus:

> The volume possesses an overall unity achieved by the relationship a poem bears to an examination of the speculation on the nature of individual human and extra-human existence as this is determined, directed, described by the relationship of the individual to the consequences of political action and the pressure of religious belief. These latter are determined within an African world-view which is in fact ... an Igbo-African world-view (Killam 125).

Aesthetic Ideology/Stylistic Stance in Girls at War and Other Stories

> I think you will know what I mean if I tell you love is worth nothing until it has been tested by its own defeat. I was being asked to try to love enough not be afraid of the consequences. I realized that love, even if it ends in defeat gives you a kind of honor; but without love, you have no honor at all... Love is to enable you to transcend defeat (Creina Alcock in Malan 409).

Although not about the civil war, the collection's first story. "The Madman" (1971) through the harshness of its "savage parable" forces the reader to determine what s/he believes sanity to be (Ngwube 6). In this respect, it is open-ended, the authorial ideology is submerged. The same cannot be said of the three stories set in the war. Yet, Achebe's social conscience remains clear: "What we say, what we write or what we paint is as human beings who live in society and are accountable to that society" (Achebe, qtd. in Lindfors, 1997: 35).

"Civil Peace" (1971) is the story of Jonathon lwegbu and his family, who have returned home after the Civil War to rebuild their lives on the conversion of Jonathon's Biafran pounds – earned by taxiing people around on his bicycle, running a palm-wine bar, and from the work of his wife – into twenty Nigerian pounds. In the evening of the same day that he exchanges the money, lwegbu and his family are visited by a band of thieves:

> He loses the 'ex-gratia' rewards of peace just as he had lost things in the war, the things he seeks now to re-achieve. And though he says that he can accept his losses in peacetime as he has accepted those in war, that he has survived and that 'Nothing puzzles God!', there is really faint consolation for him and little to distinguish 'civil peace' from civil war (Killam 109).

Although Killam does not describe the story as a parable of post war events, one is struck by the similarity between its outline and the fact that following the Nigerian Civil War, at the direction of the Federal Commissioner of Finance, Chief Obafemi Awolowo, "a banking policy was evolved which nullified any bank account which had been operated during the Civil War. This had the immediate result of pauperizing the Igbo middle class" (Achebe, 1983: 45–6) and providing the government with a four million pounds profit. Pre-war and post war, the Igbo suffered economically; as "Civil Peace" stresses, little had changed in theft lot.

The story is third person narrative that sticks close to Jonathon. It is gentle, fairly passive, with some comic touches, It is designed more to show the hardiness of the people after their sufferings in the war than it is a carefully developed character study revealing individual psychic and emotive responses. The story is therefore less aligned with Achebe's authorial ideology and more in tune with Faulkner's sense of enduring. The second half of Faulkner's prescription that we shall not *only endure* but prevail does not fall within the compass of the story. If the reader is affected by the family's stoic acceptance of their lot and perhaps angered to invoke legislative change or more specific social change, then the aesthetic ideology will reach out to and meet the authorial ideology.

"Sugar Baby" (1972) is about Cletus' problems, caused by an addiction to sugar during the war. It is narrated by a friend of Cletus', Mike, thus, like "Civil Peace" the narrative is at one remove from the character. Nevertheless, Mike does introduce a more personalized outlook, a stake in what occurs:

> I caught the fierce expression on his face in the brief impulsive moment of that strange act; and I understood. I don't mean the symbolism such as it was; that, to me, was pretty superficial and obvious. No. It was rather his deadly earnestness (Achebe, 1977: 90).

The strange act and superficial symbolism is Cletus' throwing a handful of sugar out of the window of his home to prove that he has overcome his addiction. At this early juncture, Achebe is removing one possible reading of the story and setting up another – the "deadly earnestness" – as a more complete reading of Cletus' character. Mike provides this reading by refusing to tell Cletus' other visitors the whole sordid story of his addiction, preferring to save both Cletus and himself the agony of it (Achebe, 1977: 91).

The story can move beyond the purely literal level of sugar as addiction – it would be easy to substitute a narcotic, particularly for those Westerners who have not experienced the deprivation that rationing or a blockade can cause. So, sugar can be read symbolically; "for Cletus sugar is ... what makes life bearable" (Achebe, 1977: 92). The story works well without such machinations though.

Achebe describes the disintegration of Cletus' nerves as he discovers that a wartime substitute for sugar cannot provide him with a 'fix'. The effect is a humorous description of Cletus jumping up and running "outside to give way to a rasping paroxysm of vomiting" (Achebe, 1977: 94), followed by "near nervous collapse" (94), and a two day stay in bed. Mike makes inquiries about sugar supplies, and eventually he and Cletus arrive at Father Doherw's mission, where relief supplies are kept. Tension is built as Mike seeks the fulfillment of a request for antihistamine tablets, until Cletus makes his request for sugar. Mike "... has been worrying since [they] got here how [Cletus] was going to put that request across, what form of words he would use. Now it came out so pure and so simple like naked truth from the soul" (97). Mike's admiration of Cletus' performance is shortlived, for Father Doherty chases them out of the mission in a rage, angered that the needs of others are not considered before individuals make requests for luxury items.

The story is spun out beyond this simple moral to show how Mike, chosen by the Foreign Affairs office to go abroad, will use that opportunity to aid his friend.

There is also irony in the fact that Mike is more concerned with the prestige of the trip and how it will affect his standing with friends than with any potential effects on Biafra and her people. Colleagues, too, use the trip as a means of garnering promises of some supplies-individual survival and needs make a backdrop of the communal goal: a Biafran revolution to change such self-serving habits.

Without belaboring the point, two packets of sugar are acquired in Sao Tome. One is stolen at the airport on Mike's return, and the other is passed on to Cletus. He becomes authoritarian about the dispensing of sugar; he "pounced" on his girlfriend Mercy, who had helped herself to a handful. His behavior is quite despicable. A later discussion of the incident leads to a moral summary by Mike: "I realized how foolish it was and how easy, even now, to slip back into those sudden irrational acrimonies of our recent desperate days when an angry word dropping in unannounced would start a fierce war like the passage of Esun between two peace-loving friends" (Achebe, 1977: 101). The lesson is, of course, that Biafra must remain internally unified and that its citizens must guard against any easy slippage into further civil strife. Cletus' desire for verbal flagellation of himself for his addiction, crying out for all of his ill acts to be made public (Achebe, 1977, 101), extends the point that individual self-criticism as well as a consciousness of the other is needed.

The story concludes on this note, but Achebe playfully brings in Cletus' other addiction – tea ("Tate and Lyle") – to suggest that a symptom rather than the problem has been dealt with. On the one hand, the story is a simple tale of wartime deprivation anti lack of psychological control in the individual. On the other, it speaks directly from Achebe's authorial ideology in its message which aims to keep the reader vigilant anti critical for the betterment of society.

The collection's last story, "*Girls at War*" (1972), illustrates most fully the detrimental effects of the war on civilians. Achebe creates this effect through the presentation of two main characters, whose perspectives and activities are oppositional. These two are observed on their three meetings, which cover the idealistic and "heady days of warlike preparation" (Achebe, 1977: 103), the competent, if overly pragmatic middle phase, economically conveyed through the check-point and the disillusioned corrupt final phase of the war.

"*Girls at War*" opens with a fairly straightfroward statement which raises our expectations about what will happen between the characters – Nwanko and Gladys – "The first time their paths crossed nothing happened" (103). Our expectations are increased by the incremental repetition – "The second time they met was at the check-point at Awka" (103). Reginald Nwanko, Minister of Justice has conflicting feelings about wartime measures. That his title "almost always did it" (103) emphasizes that he will try to use his authority to evade the inspections the State deems necessary. Rule of law is fine, for some. In this simple manner, the hierarchical problems of State are brought to the fore. The fact that Gladys, who Nwankwo vaguely remembers, is thorough in her search of his car reminds Nwankwo of the idealism of the biafran revolution, which has been replaced by complacency in him: "… he simply could not sneer at the girls again, nor at the talk of revolution, for he had seen it in action in that young woman whose devotion had simply and without self-righteousness convicted him of gross levity" (105). At their third meeting, things had deteriorated in Biafra. This system of enumerating the meetings draws attention to the fact that a story is being told and is a rather mechanical framework. Nonetheless it provides an efficiency that permits Achebe to summarize phases of the war in the early meetings, through brief descriptions of people's conditions, and move on to the period of principle concern. For example, the trip to Nkwerri to get food for his children, to stave off kwashiorkor, is brought to a head by the "independent accusation of [the] wasted bodies" (107) of the adults and children who cannot get food. Nwankwo's response is tribal in the microscopic sense of family and of being "some use to one's immediate neighbors" (108). This belief raises serious moral and ethical issues but Nwankwo is not prepared to reflect further on them. Achebe's purpose is to have the audience gauge its response to Nwankwo's (in) action. However Achebe loads the response fairly directly when he intervenes to comment that the remaining heroism "happened most times far, far below the eye-level of the people in this story…" (106).

Nwanko's reasonable suspicion that Gladys now lives with a war profiteer brings suspicion back on him, for he has access to supplies that are denied the people. Nwankwo is profiting from his own position, so the moral tone of his sense of Gladys is suspect because he will not apply it equally. That Nwankwo hopes Gladys is not kept by anyone in Owerri so that she will stay with him merely underscores his loss of values (110). The reader, then, reviews his/her assessment of earlier judgments on Nwankwo's character. Achebe, himself, intrudes through his narrator, to ensure that the point and the process have not been missed when he writes that Nwankwo's visit to the office, while Gladys:

> waits at his apartment, "must have been literally a look-in.., for he was back within half an hour…" (111).

It is not only the individual, but the group that Nwankwo serves as an example, who receives Achebe and the reader's condemnation, as Nwankwo's acknowledgment that wives and children stay out of town because of the nightilfe, not the war (110), and as the general reaction to lights off for an air raid – dancing in the dark, unseen (117) – illustrates. The idealism, as in "Sugar Baby", has diminished and the egalitarian communal agenda has been lost in the search for personal advancement and fulfillment

A story of the order described above would be heavily ironic and somewhat propagandist, proffering cardboard characters in place of more developed and complex ones. Achebe is too much of an artist not to cause the reader some thought, his characters some sustaining power. Nwankwo, for example, though he has ethical problems, is conscience stricken about the nightlife and parties (111) that seem to be planned and attended more fully than areas of the war effort. Similarly his criticism of Gladys' friends' trip to Libreville to go shopping, mid-war, reveals a degree of sarcasm, irony and enlightened consciousness (114). Achebe invokes the Igbo sense of duality to deflect some of the criticism, as he has Gladys retort that women go on such trips because it (or the fashionable clothing and cosmetics) is what the men want (114). Nwankwo's desire for Gladys explicitly supports this point. Where one perspective is available, another stands by its side. In this context John Povey has honed in on the core of the story:

> It is the overall disintegration of propriety and morality that enforces Achebe's despair, not because he has a naive belief that these things don't usually happen in war, but because this time it ought to have been different...The immoral women were only a part of a deeper disintegration (Povey 356).

Nwankwo, remembering the officious Gladys that he met at the check-point, becomes evangelical in his mission to save her from corrupting influences, to return her and the Biafran ideal to their respective origins. It does not require effort to understand the brutalization that their bodies and selves undergo, as Achebe's focus on the new phraseology for sex indicates: "shelling" and "pouring in the troops."

"In the end," as G.D. Killam writes:

> ...all of the moral speculation is made irrelevant by war. Nwanko and Gladys have collected a badly maimed solider on the road and driven him with them to Owerri. A sudden air attack takes place; Nwankwo is wounded and Gladys, seeking to release the car door to free the wounded soldier, loses her life (Killam 111). That is what war is about – blood and sweat and tears and maiming and useless death. And ideologies are lost in the wake of its destruction. The story says nothing new about war; there is nothing new to say about war. But [it] adds to the literature of war in an important way. It will move men to pause (Killam 112).

"Girls at War" is a complex story that does not 'fudge' over difficult issues. A variety of moral positions that appear sound are undermined or expanded by the addition of further events. Ultimately the decency of the 'girl', which Nwankwo made us question, is greater than his. Gladys has retained an altruistic essence at the end. In saving himself, Nwankwo's position is seriously undermined.

The aesthetic ideology is less controlled in "Girls at War" than in the two previous stories by the authorial ideology, but similarities in vision remain, especially given that the manner of the telling invites the reader's participation and thus an author/reader building of community.

Conclusion

For Achebe, creation was possible in war by limiting the size of his canvas, speaking largely in a plain, fairly unornamented style, and pushing across a program of questioning. "The Truth of Fiction" suggests that fiction can offer a "second handle on existence". In his critical realist approach, the 'handle' Achebe provides, in greater or lesser works of art, is a review of life wit a sense of what must change for social improvement – and survival – to occur. And improvement begins from one's critical sense of self and its relation to others and to place – geographic and cosmic.

As Albert Camus so poignantly puts it:

> ...if we listen attentively, we shall hear, amid the uproar of empires and nations, a faint flutter of wings, the gentle stirring of life and hope. Some will say that this hope lies in a nation; others in a man. I believe rather that it is awakened, revived, nourished by millions of solitary individuals whose deeds and works every day negate frontiers and the crudest implications of history. As a result, there shines forth fleetingly the ever threatened truth that each and every man, on the foundation of his own sufferings and joys, builds for all (Camus 272).

This is certainly the case with Achebe, an artist who utilizes the particular, the regional, the personal, but who speaks to the concerns of the universal.

Works Cited

Achebe, Chinua. (1972a) *Beware, Soul Brother*. London: Heinemann.

Achebe, Chinua. (1972b) "Interview with Chinua Achebe," In *Palaver: Interciews with Five African Writers in Texas*. Ed. Bernth Lindfors, et al. Austin, TX: African and AfroAmerican Research Institute, The University of Texas at Austin.

Achebe, Chinua (1973) "The Role of the Writer in a New Nation," *In African Writers on African Writing*. Ed. G.D. Killam. Evanston, IL: Northwestern University Press.

Achebe, Chinua. (1975) *Morning Yet on Creation Day*: Essays. London: Heinemann.

Achebe, Chinua. (1977) *Girls at War* and Other Stories. 2ud ed. London: Heinemann

Achebe, Chinua. (1983) *The Trouble with Nigeria*. Enugu: Fourth Dimension.

Achebe, Chinua. (1990) *Hopes and Impediments: Selected Essays*. New York: Anchor Books.

Bruchac, Joseph. (1973) "Achebe as Poet" New Letters, 40, 1 (October 1973).

Camus, Albert. (1974) "Create Dangerously," In *Resistance, Rebellion, and Death*. Trans. Justin O'Brien. New York: Vintage, 1974.

Gardner, John. (1978) *On Moral Fiction*. New York: Basic Books, 1978.

Gikandi, Simon. (1991) *Reading Chinua Achebe: Language and ideology in Fiction*. London: James Currey.

Graf William D. (1998) *The Nigerian State: Political Economy, Slate Class and Political System in the Post-Colonial Era*. London: James Currey; Porstmouth, N.H.: Heineinann.

Killam, G.D. (1969) *The Writings of Chinua Achebe* Rev. ed. London: Heinemann, 1969.

Lent, John. (1984) "Mid-Winter Suite, After David Mime" *Frieze*. Saskatoon: Thistledown.

Lindfors, Bernth. (1997) Ed. *Conversations with Chinua Achebe*. Jackson: University of Mississippi Press.

Malan, Riam. (1991) *My Traitor's Heart*. New York: Vintage.

Mctuckie, Craig W. (1990) *Nigerian Civil War Literature: Seeking an 'Imagined Community'*. (*Studies in Aftican Literature* Vol. 3. Lewiston; Queenston; Lampeter: Mellen Press).

Muir, Edwin. (1984) "Horses," In *Collected Poems 1921–58*. London: Faber.

Ngara, Emmanuel. (1990) "Preface," In *Ideology and Form in African Poetry*. London: James Currey.

Ngwube, Anerobi. (1974) "Nigerian War Literature" *Indigo* 2 January.

Ojukwu, Odumegwu C. *Principles of the Biafran Revolution*. Cambridge, Mass.: The Biafra Review, 1969.

Povey, John F. (1974) "The Nigerian War: The Writer's Eye" *In Journal of African* Studies I Fall.

Rogers, Philip. (1978) "Chinua Achebe's Poems of Regeneration," *In Critical Perspectives on Chinua Achebe* Eds. C.L. Innes and Bernth Lindfors. Washington, D.C.: Three Continents Press: 284–92.

Wolff, Janet. (1983) "Aesthetics," In *A Dictionary of Marxist Thought*. Ed. By Torn Bottomore. Cambridge, Mass.: Harvard University Press, 1983.

Chapter 32

Chinua Achebe as a War Poet

Innocent C.K. Enyinnaya

After a war
we clutch at watery
Scum pulsating on listless
eddies of our spent deluge...
Chinua Achebe (20).

ACHEBE, THE FIRST AFRICAN novelist of note, has four novels which were published before the Nigerian civil crisis in 1966. The fourth novel, *A Man of the People* (1966), a satirical novel which deals with corrupt leadership that ends in a military coup, coincided with the January 15, 1966 *coup d'etat*, a situation that made some people suspect that Achebe had foreknowledge of the coup.

Chinua Achebe's world-acclaim as an accomplished novelist has tended to eclipse his achievement as a poet. This paper focuses on this "pioneer of modern African Literature" as a war poet.

Beware, Soul Brother, which in 1972 won the Commonwealth Poetry Prize jointly with George McWhirter's Catalan Poems, is Achebe's first and only poetry collection. It contains thirty poems grouped into five sections. Of these only the "Prologue" and "Poems about War" are relevant here as they "speak directly about war ... (and) bear the mark of "its distress and tragedy". The eleven poems in these two sections were written between 1966 when the Nigerian crisis erupted and 1971, a year after the end of the physical hostilities.

The poems bear a vivid imprint of the troubled times and show Chinua Achebe as a sensitive and committed artist deeply concerned about the events around him. The first poem in the Prologue, entitled "1966", deals with the beginning of the crisis when men, as though absent-minded, allowed their thoughtless actions to take control, puncturing "residual chaos" which led to "rare artesian hatred". Written later in 1971 the poet in retrospect marks 1966 as the year when Nigerians re-enacted the fratricidal hatred of Cain for Abel. God's disappointment with Adam and Eve after their fall is confirmed by Cain's action. Achebe injects into this poem the type of pungent imagery that informs most of his other poems. The image of the artesian well symbolises the force with which the hatred, "residual chaos", was pushed up by recent catastrophic events in the environment. As if they were acting outside of themselves, Nigerians plunged themselves into a gory war. There is the image of a thoughtless being who through a subterranean remote control, unearthed a latent feud (... residual chaos to/rare artesian hatred) that erupted into the war.

Achebe delves into his commentary on the devastating war with "The First Shot" (11), a poem of seven lines. According to the poem the lone rifle-shot that triggered off the war is heavier and reverberates more than all the other greater noises that followed it:

> ...will lodge more firmly than the greater noises ahead in the forehead of memory.

This first shot is anonymous because the soldier who fired it cannot be identified; yet it was the greatest because it started off the carnage. It heralded the "season of thunders". 'Thunders' here re-echoes Christopher Okigbo's "Path of Thunder". The anonymity of the source of that first shot is brought into focus in the first line where the poet allows the noun "rifle-shot" precede the word "anonymous" (an adjective) that modifies it. All the other adjectives in the poem (dark, nervous, greater) take their normal position before the noun they modify. "The First Shot" seems to regret forever whatever led the country to that season of thunders.

"Refugee Mother and Child" (12) paints the pathetic picture of kwashiorkor-ridden children, of dirt, poverty, and uncertainty in Biafra. Through the use of imagery the reader is made to perceive the repulsive stench that fills the camp and see the lamentable sight of starving children:

> ...The air was heavy with odours of diarrhoea, of unwashed children with washed-out ribs and dried-up bottoms struggling in laboured steps behind blown empty bellies.

The first two lines give an assaulting appeal to the sense of smell. The squalid condition of life then in Biafra especially in Refugee Camps is very vividly portrayed. The picture of the unwashed children with dried-up bottoms struggling behind empty distended bellies is very pitiful. The movement of this poem is as choking as the languid "laboured steps" of the kwashiorkor-ridden children. This is achieved through the cumulative use of adjectives (some compound), which slow down the movement of the poem: "... heavy with odours/of diarrhoea of unwashed children/with washed-out ribs and dried-up/bottoms...." The cluster of the alliterative sound of /b/ in "behind blown empty bellies" also helps to slow down the pace. Through visual representation, Achebe in "Refugee Mother and Child" shows the pain of a mother who helplessly watches her child die by instalments. The "rust-coloured hair" of the famished child which the mother painfully combs in full realization that the child has little life in him is contrasted with that of a healthy child. What could have been the joy of motherhood is now to her "like pretty flowers on a tiny grave."

The poem operates on contrasts. There are the contrasting images of a healthy child and the sorry sight of a mother who tenders "a son she soon would have to forget". The contrasting image of a refugee mother and child on the one hand and the "Madonna and child" on the other brings out the painful lot of Biafran mothers who helplessly watched their children shrivel to death. To show the contrast between the peaceful past and the present war time, the poem indicates that combing the child's hair would have been a pleasurable chore for the mother getting the child ready for school "in another life". Nobody this war time ever thought of children going to School. This highlights the complete paralysis of developmental activities during the war.

The contrast in times is further handled in "Christmas in Biafra (1969)" (13), which highlights the contrast in this period of tension when the worldwide peace of Christmas brought from the waves from far-away lands seemed to mock the disquiet in Biafra. The "sounds of other men's carols floating" into the "death-cells" in Biafra seemed to compound the emotional stress of the Biafrans who did not know whether to regret the war, hope for a return to peace, or long for an end to hostilities or despair completely. The image of the "Child Jesus plump wise-looking and rose-cheeked" is contrasted with the "infant son flat like a dead lizard" on his mother's shoulder. The picture of the poor woman who pays her homage, offers her widow's mite with her famished child, shows the misery that was the people's in Biafra as well as re-inforces that deep sense of devotion which distinguishes the people.

Achebe's acuity in depicting with visual accuracy the plight of the war victims can be seen in this and many other poems:

> ...Her infant son flat like a dead lizard on her shoulder his arms and legs cauterized by famine was a miracle of its own kind (14).

This again is a poem that achieves great effect through contrasts. The peace of the Holy Family is in contrast with the tension of those war victims who, entrapped in death-cells, have neither hope nor despair. The serenity and peace of Christmas depicted in the mini-manger of palms set up by the nuns is also in contrast with the emotional disquiet of the poor worshippers. The sumptuous robes of the figures of men contrasts with the poverty of the woman and her shriveled child already "cauterized by famine". Her poverty, which symbolizes that of Biafrans then is shown in the worthless "new aluminium coins that few traders would take", which the poor worshippers drop as offerings. There is no doubt that the "new aluminium coins" alludes to the Biafran coins that could not, like cheap medals, resist strong medicated soap. Achebe again pitches the figure of the "plump wise-looking" child against the figure of the famished child with sunken eyes. Through this juxtaposition of contrasting images the poet impresses vividly the evils of war on the minds of his readers.

In "Air Raid" (15) Achebe pictures how swiftly the jet fighter – "the bird of death" – descends on unsuspecting victims and takes its toil. The poet depicts the uncertainty of life in Biafra by the possibility of a man being cut into two by a fighter-bomber as he crosses the road to exchange greetings with a friend. The murderous role of the Soviet Union in arming one side in this war of annihilation is shown by the death mission of "the bird of death from/evil forests of Soviet technology". The poem is short but mirrors vividly the devastating action of Russian-made war-planes that would in a flash slice a friend into halves before the full gaze of his companion. The words "his friend cut in halves" show the ease with which lives were being destroyed.

One of the touching accidents of military adventurism into politics is the fate of soldiers in the event of a failure in their bid to change a government. Coup-making is an act off treason if it fails. An eminent Nigerian scholar of International Law puts it thus: "Although prima facie a *coup d'etat* is unconstitutional and illegal vis-a-vis the constitution off the country, but once it succeeds, its illegality evaporates. The leader of any unsuccessful coup attempt becomes a villain. If on the other hand he succeeds all the history verdicts against him would be different. In "An 'IF' of History" (16) Achebe raises this issue of the "if" of history which after a war can make a saint of a villain and vice versa. He uses the much-maligned Adolf Hitler as an example and sets the reader conjecturing:

> ...Just think if Hitler had gambled and won what chaos the world would have known...

The poet observes that victory pushes people to actions that become questionable years after. The Americans who perpetuate war crimes in Vietnam now had, after World War II, punished people for war crimes.

> ...The Americans flushed by verdict of history hanged a Japanese commander for war crimes.

The poem maintains that history would have been different if World War II had ended in favor of Nazi Germany. Hitler's "implacable foe across the Channel/would surely have died for/war crimes". Harry Truman, "the Hiroshima villain (the United States President then), Charles de Gaulle of France and the Norwegian Prime Minister, Vidkun Quisling, would all have been killed "Simply by Hitler winning." The poem emphasizes the fact that victory re-writes history and makes heroes of villains and villains of the vanquished. It is the same point that Kole Omotoso makes in one issue of "A Writer's Diary" where he says among other things:

> The civil war has produced only unknown soldiers as heroes, the same set of unknown soldiers who are blamed for destruction of property, for rape, rampage and a general turning of their guns against the people from whom they originate. Can such unknown soldiers be heroes? (4).

The "heroism" of these unknown soldiers is celebrated on Remembrance Days and in his poem entitled "Remembrance Days" (18), Achebe highlights the futility of remembrance days when march-pasts are organised to mourn the death of those who died in active service. Achebe is of the view that the solemn faces, the march, and the glorious words for the dead will not appease their spirit. He says that if the dead had a choice they would have chosen to live and do the same "honour" to those now living. He observes that the living also passed through the same nervous and mental torture and suffered hunger and deprivation as the dead but because they are now alive they have "the choice of a dozen ways to rehabilitate" themselves. Achebe advises the living to choose one of the options of rehabilitation.

> Pick any one of them and soon you will forget the fear and hardship, the peril on the edge of the chasm.

The survivors doing this have the chance to "regain lost mirth/and girth and forget". Achebe maintains that the dead, on the other hand, will never regain anything. The poem confirms that the living should be grateful and happy that they are living as the dead are forever insensitive to the yearly ritual of parades and ceremonies held to honour the unknown soldier.

> Your glorious words are not for them nor your proliferation in a dozen cities of the bronze heroes of Idumota.

Achebe here reiterates Thomas Gray's contention as he contemplates with profound and sympathetic understanding the lives of the poor in his famous elegy:

> The cock's shrill clarion or the echoing horn
> No more shall rouse them from their lowly bed.
> For them no more the blazing hearth shall burn.

But more importantly the poem reinforces Achebe's conviction that it is better to have suffered the pangs of the war and live to tell the story of the war than to die and be remembered. Achebe captures the emotional turmoil of the Biafrans and the sufferings they underwent through such lines as these:

> ...You lived wretchedly on all manner of gross fare; you were tethered to the nervous precipice day and night; your groomed hair lost gloss, your smooth body roundedness. Truly you suffered much.

These can only be said to the living.

Achebe is noted for his very strong criticism of and repugnance to some orthodox practices. In "Remembrance Day", he condemns the cosmetic remembrance days set aside by the military to honour their dead colleagues. The poet instead calls on the living to remembar that they wronged the dead in death and should make amends for their bad deeds. Ossie Enekwe in reviewing Achebe's poetry put it succinctly thus: In "'Remembrance Day' ... the poet draws attention to the criminal deeds of those who led their people to perdition in wars, stressing that such leaders should atone for their evil deeds instead of indulging in empty and dishonest rituals" (6). The poet, in advising the survivor to seek ways of rehabilitating himself, observes that life-sustaining necessities have come back to life:

> The shops stock again a variety of hair-dyes, the lace and the gold are coming back.

These things, the poet seems to say, have easily returned to their stands. People who survive will, with the same speed, regain weight and happiness but the dead will never regain anything. Long after the living have forgotten, the dead will still be faced with the "hazards and rigors of reincarnation". All these emphasize the futility of the rituals of the remembrance days and the anger of the dead soldiers, the "fallen kindred wronged in death". The poet warns the living soldiers to avoid the wrath of their betrayed dead soldier colleagues.

Achebe's last poem in this section is "After a War" in which he wonders how life returns to normalcy after a war. It is a poem in which he piles up images through the use of simile and metaphor.

> ...life catches desperately at passing hints of normalcy like vines entwining a hollow twig.

Life is a tree whose roots get famished during a war and virtually starts from the scratch after a war. Above all, Achebe likens the survivors after the war to the convalescent dancers rising too soon to join their "circle dance" but are no longer adept as before but "contrive only half-remembered eccentric steps". According to Achebe, war is an illness which ravages the society and those who are lucky to survive, like the sick, spend a long time convalescing. He expresses gladness that after a period of this uncertainty and starting life anew the survivors really bury the ugly past and struggle arduously to fall in tune with normal life.

Achebe's central thesis here is that war dislocates a people's life and their attempts to gather themselves together again after the war are like learning to use the left hand at old age.

One peculiarity of Achebe's poems is the deliberate omission of periods (full stops) and commas. This is to achieve tension and sustain the pungency of the emotions through breathlessness and does not make for easy understanding in some of the poems. Naturally the lines run on one another. "The First Shot", for example, is a one-stanza poem of seven lines with forty words and has only one capital letter, the "I" that begins it, and the full stop that ends it. In some poems Achebe makes very effective use of the caesura. One notices this in "An 'IF' of History" where the middle pauses can be seen in lines one, three, six, fifteen, seventeen, etc.

L.1:	"Just think, had Hitler won ..."
L.3:	"books would be today. The Americans ..."
L.6:	"War crimes. A generation later ..."
L.15:	"load of manifest guilt. For even in lynching a judge is needed –"
L.17:	"a winner. Just think if Hitler..."

He uses this effectively to foreground the word that comes immediately after. This style is also adopted in "Remembrance Day" in lines six, seven, thirteen, fourteen, etc. In "Remembrance Day", Achebe piles up words and images without break and this device creates a vivid and lasting impression through the tension created by the build-up:

> Your proclaimed mourning your flag at half-mast your solemn face your smart backward step and salute at the flowered foot of empty graves your glorious words – none, nothing will their spirit appease (18).

The pile-up of the possessive adjective "your" and the abrupt appearance of the definite pronoun, 'none', preceded by a hyphen and followed by the word 'nothing', all have a climactic effect on the poet's contention.

The abrupt opening of some of the poems is very striking as "Just think, had Hitler won his war..." in "An 'IF' of History" and "It comes so quickly/the bird of death" in "Air Raid." As Ossie Enekwe points out: "When run-on lines (enjambement) combine with an unusually compact synthesis of metaphor, sharp images, adjectives and adverbs, the effect is bewildering".

Achebe's poetic diction is simple and the use of action words and modifiers gives his war poems a very sustaining effect. Arthur Ravenscroft's assessement quoted by Ossie Enekwe in *The Guardian* essay quoted above is very true. "Achebe's poems reveal a mind deeply scarred by the iniquities, derelictions, and betrayals that war induces in men and women".

Chinue Achebe in his poetry writes of the indelible scar of war and the dislocation of life occasioned by war. The experience of his people are to him a scar that never heals and in this regard his poems reveal an engaging passion for the plight of his people during the war and the hollowness that followed it as the survivors contrived "only half-remembered eccentric steps.'

Works Cited

Achebe, Chinua. *Beware, Soul Brother*. Enugu: Nwamife, 1972. (Futher references to this text will be indicated by page reference within the text).

Enekwe, Ossie "Achebe as a Poet" In "The Guardian Literary Series 49th Week", In *The Guardian* (Saturday), April 5, 1986

Gray, Thomas "Elegy written in a Country Churchyard" In *Seven Centuries of Verse* (English and American). Ed. A.J.N. Smith. New York: Charles Scribner's Sons, 1951.

Omotoso, Kole "The Future of Our Past" In "A Writer's Diary", *West African* 23 January, 1984.

Tjalaye, D.A. "Nigeria and International Law Today and Tomorrow", Inaugural Lecture Series 29. Ife: University of Ife Press, 1978.

Part Seven:

Critical Perspectives on "Short Stories"

Chapter 33

The Short Story as a Genre, with Notes on Achebe's *"The Madman"*

Charles E. Nnolim

In an earlier study, I had remarked that another challenge facing critics of African literature in the 80's is facing the neglected frontiers of our literary and critical endeavors. We all have, up to now, neglected the short story as a genre worthy of critical attention, even though there is already a respectable body of short stories written by our most celebrated writers. Whatever the case may be, our critics must be reminded that the short story as a genre is still stillborn on the African literary scene. To deliver this baby, to ensure the healthy birth of the short story (through vigorous critical response) into the mainstream of the African literary scene is a major challenge facing critics of African literature (*Nnolim* 51–56).

The present study is not really an answer to my own challenge but an attempt to focus attention on Achebe's "*The Madman*" which, by the near-perfection of its construction, advances the tradition by moving away from the traditional folk tale. The terms: the tale, the fairy tale, the folk tale, the short story, *et cetera*, are bandied about without critical distinction for the young African student. Is there not a difference, for example, between "the short story" and a story that happens to be short? Do we not have in the short story proper, certain formal properties that champion its genre and separate it from stories that just happen to be short? To begin with, the folk tale is important to the African student because that is the most documented of all the genres of short fiction in our literature. Among Igbo writers, the familiar titles: *Tales of Land and Death*: *Igbo Folk Tales*, by Uche Okeke, *A Calabash of Wisdom*, by Romanus Egudu, *The Way We Lived*, by Rems

Umeasiegbu, and Achebe's (with John Iroaganachi) *How the Leopard Got Its Claws*, are collections of the folk tale.

The Folk Tale is a popular tale handed down by oral tradition from a remote antiquity and usually told either by animals or the common folk to draw attention to their plight and to teach a lesson. Achebe usually weaves the folk tale into the narrative fabric of his novels to arouse interest and underline thematic meaning. In *Things Fall Apart*, the tale of tortoise and the birds who went to a feast in the sky is a case in point, embedded in the novel for its narrative interest and to draw attention to Okonkwo as the *All of You* of the Igbo hero, greedy of things Umuofia, and falling from power (as tortoise did in the story) when collective support was withdrawn from him by his people. Another important folktale by Achebe is embedded in *Arrow of God* to draw attention to the conflicts and jealousies, which mar the fortunes of the chief characters in the novel. It is the story of Ugoye to her children about the two jealous wives. Also, the fantastic tales by Tutuola in, *The Palm-Wine Drinkard* and *My Life in the Bush of Ghosts* are expansions of the folktale – here the folktale dips its toe into the realm of myth. The folktale is part of folklore and its basic requirement is that it be traditional and transmitted primarily through memory and practice rather than by the printed page, but forming part of the folk literature of a people. In any case, the folk tale is not a modern short story, as the modern interest of ethnology and anthropology in its collection can attest.

The fable and the fairy tale are aspects of the protean genre of the folktale. The fairy tale and fable are what the French call *le merveilleux traditionel* in which witches, dragons and ogres feature very prominently. They are stories of strange and adventurous happenings in which we have elements of magic and the supernatural. The enchanted princess (the story of Cinderella is the fairy tale *par excellence*) and the prince charming feature very prominently. These lead to the development of the modern short story because they have definite affinities to the *Tale*, which is nearer the modern short story. Now, what fairy tales share with the *tale* are the narrator's habits of speech and the manner in which these habits contribute importantly to the effect of what the narrator tells. In each of these, the author carries on a personal conversation with his readers and the tale (especially) is normally a narrative piece in which authorial intrusion is taken for granted. The personality of the narrator is obviously intruded and the characters of the tale are written simply to amuse the audience, the one distinguishing mark of the fable is its proclivity to point a moral. La Fontaine claimed pointedly that he used the stories of animals to instruct men. All subsume a narrative method with roots in oral delivery in which elements of fantasy, the supernatural and magic are blended. While the folktale, the fable, the fairy tale and the tale are not short stories in the modern sense, they are relevant in any study of the short story since they are undisputed antecedents of the more modern genre. To the German word *marchen* belong these stories of various kinds of marvels: the adventures of Cinderella, Jack and the Beanstalk, the Adventures of Snow White.

The one distinguishing factor which separates them from the modern short story is that they are not representational, not taken from the common idiom of our everyday life, since they 'catapult' us into another world which thwarts the normal order of events through the intervention of magic and fantasy and the supernatural which take over as the chief agents of aesthetic realization of the goals of the stories: in them, the outcome of events does not follow the explicable human and logical order of life's experiences.

The short story proper has suffered many disabilities created by the above-named antecedents. The French fabliau, the tricks of the magazine, short story or morning Sunday columns-all make it difficult to untangle the serious from the bogus hocus-pocus, the artistic from the sleight-of-hand of the quick-money grabber. One thing is thus established: the short story, as we know it today has no undiluted purity: it is a protean genre that thrives on its infinite variety.

One of the earliest definitions of the modern short story was made by one of its originators and early theorists, Edgar Allan Poe (although one must hasten to add that Poe and Nathaniel Hawthorne wrote largely what we nowadays identify as moral fables in which the essential feature of the story is its moral discovery) who defines the short story (in his review of Hawthorne's *Twice Told Tales*, 1842) as a narrative which can be read at one sitting of from one-half hour to two hours, and is limited to a "certain unique or single effect" to which every detail is subordinated. But whether or not we accept Poe's definition must be predicated (in the modern sense) on whether or not the subject matter is drawn from real life's experiences, or whether or not the story adheres to what we call "realism" in fiction: the ability of the writer to convince us of the validity of the world he has created, and to make us believe in and even associate with the characters as they exist in real life. In a modern short story proper, the incidents are true to life, the characters are those the reader can identify with, the dialogue is convincing, the setting is earth-bound and recognizable – a village, a city, a school compound, business premises. All these would separate the modern short story from the tale, the fable, and the fairy tale which are usually set in the vague past ("once upon a time") where, according to Hawthorne, the action takes place between the twilight of actuality and the midnight of dream.

Ian Reid asserts that the uniqueness of the short story genre lies in three related areas:

(a) It makes a single impression on the reader
(b) It does so by concentrating on a single crisis
(c) It makes that crisis pivotal in a controlled plot (54).

But Reid's list is by no means exhaustive. One might add the following:

(a) the style is compressed, tending through the use of highly symbolic language to register at first a microscopic effect that enfolds with full understanding into a larger significance; in other words, the meaning is so much larger than the facts themselves that the effect is a sudden illumination. This is what James Joyce calls an "epiphany": a sudden spiritual revelation in a moment that is luminous with meaning.
(b) There is no time for character development. Rather, in one dramatic moment, character is revealed under stress or that character's own view of events is epiphanized.
(c) a good short story does not *teach*, it *reveals*; it does not *preach*: it *interprets*.

Finally, one must observe with Reid that the modern short story invariably focuses on one or two individuals who are seen as separated from their fellow men in some way – individualistic, romantic, intransigent, at odds with the social norms. The short story, in fact, all fiction, pays more attention to wanderers, lonely dreamers, outcasts, scapegoat figures than to the ordinary folk. The modern short story is a romantic prose form that deals with a fragment of extracted experience with life in limited scope, zeroing in at those moments when the individual is most alert or most alone. And Achebe's "*The Madman*" is such a story.

Chinua Achebe's delicate short story, "*The Madman*," is one of those timeless gems that instantly assume the dimensions of a classic. Achebe, the great Nigerian writer, wrote this piece immediately after the Nigeria-Biafra war. Some people see Achebe in that story making satiric thrusts at the combatants on both sides, each claiming to have absolute moral justification for fighting the war, each accusing the other of sheer madness in its uncompromising justification for the fratricidal blood-letting. The Biafrans, for their part, felt they had been too deeply hurt by unrepentant and unremorseful Nigeria, and this had given them moral justification to defend themselves "to the last man".

The Nigerians on the other hand, believed strongly that whatever hurt the Biafrans felt, the unity of the country was too sacred an issue to be compromised. The outsider, of course, looked on both sides as totally insane, considering the amount of bloodshed involved in the internecine warfare. Those who see merit in ascribing "*The Madman*" to Achebe's satiric reaction to the war, point to a proliferation of fictional stories about madness that emerged from Nigeria immediately after the conflict: E.N. Obiechina's "Song of a Madman" and Chukwuma Azuonye's "The Lost Path" being cases in point, where the imagery suggests a world gone mad, a world peopled by lunatics.

But what makes the story a classic has nothing to do with this imagined background. It has a lot to do with Achebe's art. The charm of "*The Madman*" centers on that trembling equipoise between appearance and reality which irony subsumes, the discrimination between *what is* and *what merely seems*; hence the double-barreled vantage points from which the story is told. There are two worlds and two visions in the story, each vision and each world clearly etched: between the world of the madman and that of the sane people, the story is told through the interplay and quite often the melting together of these worlds and visions.

As I have just hinted, because there are two worlds in the story, it is divided into two parts. At the beginning, in the first part, we are solidly in the world of sane people looking into the topsy-turvy mind of the madman, and we see that world through his eyes. At once, the language is skewed, and Achebe's lighthearted irony comes to the fore:

> One market day was Afo, the other Eke. The two days between them suited him very well: before setting out for Eke, he had ample time to wind up his business properly at Afo. He passed the night there, putting right again his hut after a day of defilement by two fat-bottomed market women who said it was their stall.

First, in the Igbo four-market-day week, the madman already claims two, leaving two – Nkwo and Oye for sane people. In any case, in the passage quoted above, irony with a touch of ambiguity is already evident. Sane people cannot but laugh at the sort of "business" which the madman sees it fit to "wind up properly." And the word "defilement" which is appropriated by the madman is what the sane fat-bottomed market women are expected to apply against the unwarranted intrusion of the madman into their stalls. Again, the epithets, "hefty beasts of the bush" and vagabonds" which the madman has appropriated and applied against sane people properly belong to the madman himself, from the sane people's point of view.

In the second part of the story, we are solidly situated in a world of sanity and level-headedness by the introduction of Okafo Nwibe, "a man of wealth and integrity" – a man so sane and level-headed that the normal caution required by the titled men from aspirants to the *Ozo* title (for which Nwibe had recently applied) was, in Nwibe's case, "no more than a formality for Nwibe was such *a sensible man* that no one could think of him beginning something he was not sure to finish."

Here, already, the battle line is drawn between the two chief characters. Nwibe is drawn to provide a sharply realized contrast to the madman and the name Nwibe is significant and symbolic. Nwibe means "a child of the community" for he is completely integrated within his society in contrast to the madman who is integrated to no one, a loner who is completely alienated from his kith and kin. But that Nwibe should so suddenly surprise us in this second movement and join the ranks of the madman is one of the charms of Achebe's narrative technique. Although we are surprised, we don't feel his action is unmotivated or wholly incredible. It is part of the technique of opening sequences and spiraling action which we watch soaring to a conflict that unstoppably rushes to a climax, then to a puzzling, even ambitious denouement. A sane man, we know can, at certain moments of provocation act insanely. Nwibe's problem was not knowing when to retreat and following the instinct of blind anger to its logical conclusion. Hence, in the second movement of the story, the rush and precipitate action of Nwibe causes quite some confusion among onlookers. The madman, now appropriately attired in the sane man's "borrowed" (or shall we plainly say *snatched*) garment passes for a sane man, while Nwibe following unreflecting, the push of blind instinct now both appears and behaves like a madman.

The irony deepens as we proceed. In the first movement, sane people laughed at the madman's nakedness. In the second, the madman first laughed at Nwibe's nakedness – his parted buttocks – and later, after he had clothed himself in Nwibe's attire, laughed at his own clothed self and, I am sure, the strange feeling and elation which this new appearance confers on himself.

The symbolism of clothing becomes evident in the story. Madness is easily equated by society with lack of outer covering of clothes. So, when the madman strode into the market place draped in Nwibe's loin cloth, few people took notice, for he now appears quite normal and sane. And when relatives caught up with Nwibe in the full glare of the market place, the first thing they did was to drape him in a borrowed cloth donated by a sympathetic village woman – to make him appear sane to those who had not witnessed. So, what is in a cloth, in an outer covering? Is it, Achebe seems to ask, the mask with which individuals and society cover their inadequacies in the guise of normalcy, of sanity? Another symbolic object in the story "is the stubborn goat on a leash" whose owner Nwibe bumped against (Nwibe "laid flat a frail old man struggling with a stubborn goat on a leash"). For us in Igboland, the goat is the arch symbol, the epitome of insane, stubborn stupidity into which Nwibe in his uncontrolled anger has temporarily metamorphosed.

The bipartite structure of the story is further underlined in the characters of the two medicine-men to whom Nwibe was taken for cure. They deepen the ambiguity and irony inherent in the story. The first, the very famous "mad-doctor" to whom Nwibe was taken fails to see the difference between excessive anger pushed to the periphery of madness from real madness "deep and tongue-tied," and declares himself incapable of curing this brand of madness which, in addition, has set foot "irrevocably within the occult territory of the powers of the market." But the second "mad-doctor," humble and unsung, takes Nwibe in, if not with enthusiasm, at least stoically (and for practical purposes: he has to feed his family!), winning fame in the process for "curing" what to all intents and purposes is now a sane and sobered Nwibe.

In sum, "*The Madman*" is structured on a skein of ironies and ambiguities and belongs among those rare literary gems that are shaped like an hourglass. A change of place between the two chief characters takes place at the end. Nwibe who at the beginning *was* genuinely sane, now near the end *seems* incurably mad, thus changing places with the madman who at the beginning *was* genuinely mad but at the end, passed for a sane man and thus *seems* genuinely sane in the market place. This is counterpointed against the change of place that takes place at the end between the famous "mad-doctor" and his not-so-famous doctor who wins fame for "curing" (for all intents and purposes) a sane and sobered Nwibe whose anger had subsided, while his famous counterpart sank into oblivion. And just as the madman laughs at himself at the strange elation which draping himself with Nwibe's cloth had elicited, Nwibe weeps openly on recognizing his shame at the poor figure he had cut in the market place, in his nakedness.

The turn of events thus underlines for Nwibe, the central theme of the story, which is that "Anger is a temporary madness." A second, ancillary theme could be that "appearances are deceptive" or that "things are not what they seem," as Achebe seems to satirize the *blindness* of people to reality, especially their blindness to what constitutes real madness. He further satirizes the blindness of the so-called experts on what really constitutes madness – in the inability of the two "mad-doctors" to distinguish between a genuinely mad man and a man who seems to have temporarily lost his cool. And to the populace, the surfaces of things – having no clothes on and "setting foot irrevocably within the occult territory of the market"– are more significant than the hard facts. Of course, one could, with conviction, argue that Okafo Nwibe has exceeded the bounds of what constitutes sane behavior, and this is madness:

> For how could a man be the same again of whom
> witnesses from all the lands of Olu and Igbo
> have once reported that they saw today a fine,
> hefty man in his prime, stark naked, tearing
> through the crowds to answer the call of the
> market place.

Those who see "*The Madman*" as an expansion of a proverb will never fail to note the Kafkaesque parable embedded in the story – "a parable of paranoia, of man's vulnerability, of the infectious spread of frenzy, be it in war or peace; or...an individual case of mental disarray symbolizing the collective madness of a country in crisis" (*Reid* 54). Professor W.F. Feuser further sees this story as "an abstract conundrum of human irrationality" as he identifies the setting and dramatis personae with concrete historical figures:

1. the primary madman: Nigeria
2. the secondary madman: Biafra
3. the market place: the UNO as the consensus of those that deny Biafra nationhood (27–28).

One can only follow Feuser up to a point. One would rather identify the market place as the civilized world at large, watching with varying reactions to the fratricidal bloodletting, some lending a helping hand (the woman who donated her cloth), some making concrete suggestions as to how best to settle this "quarrel between brothers," some preoccupied with idle gossip and thoughtless comments. Under this line of argument, the first and second "mad doctors" who handled Nwibe's case naturally come in. The first famous "mad doctor" metamorphoses into professionally recognized peace-making bodies – the United Nations and its agencies, and the OAU and its agencies who threw their hands up in despair with the specious argument that this was "an African affair" that must be settled in a uniquely "African way." The second, unsung "mad doctor" who, in a situation where everyone has given up, worked wonders becomes identifiable as the various charitable organizations who risked everything to bring a helpless situation to manageable proportions – Caritas international and the World Health Organization. Just as in the case of Nwibe, they may not have completely rehabilitated Biafra but may have helped her assume a reasonable dignity, in spite of the ravages and devastations and degradations of war – among the community of fellow Nigerians.

The charm of Achebe lies both in his versatility and in his unique ability to convey meaning and symbol in a deceptively simple language within a watertight compass. This is his legacy, and "*The Madman*" is the perfection of a narrative style that he began in *Things Fall Apart*.

Works Cited

Achebe, Chinua, "The Madman," in *The Insider: Stories of War and Peace from Nigeria*, ed. Arthur Nwankwo and Samuel Ifejika Enugu, 1971.

Feuser, W.F. "Nigerian's Civil War in Fiction". *New Literature Review*, No 11, 1982.

Nnolim, Charles E. "The Critic of African Literature: The Challenge of the 80s." *Afa: Journal of Creative Writing*, No. 1, 1982.

Reid, Ian. *The Short Story*. Methuen, 1977.

Part Eight:

Critical Perspectives on "Children's Stories"

Chapter 34

Selection and Validation of Oral Materials for Children's Literature: Artistic Resources in Chinua Achebe's Fiction for Children

Ernest N. Emenyonu

> I enjoy writing for children, it's very important for me. It's a challenge which I like to take on now and again because it requires a different kind of mind from me when I'm doing it – I have to get into the mind of a child totally, and I find that very rewarding. I think everybody should do that not necessarily through writing a story, but we should return to childhood again and again. And when you write for children it's not just a matter of putting yourself in the shoes of a child – I think you have to be a child for the duration. –Chinua Achebe

FOLKTALES ARE RICH AND authentic sources of raw African values in traditional African societies. They were used for purposes of acculturation and were therefore, necessarily didactic and morality-laden. Children generally grew up under the tutelage of their mothers who at chosen times during the formative years, told them folktales in which enshrined community values were explicitly extolled. Such occasions served as pastimes, and to sustain the interest and curiosity of the children, the raconteur must make the story real and entertaining and the experience worthwhile. She would embellish the tales, sing interesting songs or refrains, mimic voices of animals, birds and ghosts, perform acts, improvise lavishly, add humor, induce audience participation, and vary her narrative devices and methods constantly for maximum effects.

Some of the values espoused were direct, blunt and uncoated, the narrator often using a particular story to reinforce a moral issue of the moment. Some stories advocated instant justice through a revenge or retaliation of an evil act, or the deployment of a *deus-ex-machina* who kills off miscreants and hardened criminals. Good must invariably prevail over evil, and right over wrong. Wit and cunning (the sharp use of common sense) must excel over brute force and abusive might. Hardwork must yield good results and be rewarded. Honesty always paid off. Falsehood and fraud were anti-social behaviors and must never escape severe punishments. Corruption in any form or manner was strictly frowned upon and the "soul that sinned" died instantly to serve as deterrent to others.

In the Igbo culture, a popular folktale, "Ebeleako" allowed the death of a grandmother at the hands of her grandson because she had earlier quite unnaturally, viciously schemed and plotted the death of the grandson. In another popular folktale, the tortoise out-tricked the elephant and got his eyes plucked, to teach a necessary harsh lesson against stupid gullibility and sheepish credulity. In yet another folktale, a wicked stepmother perished in flames as due punishment for her heartless wickedness and cruelty to a helpless little orphan. The message was always clear – "the wages of sin is death". In contrast, an individual who lived a life of loyalty to his parents and elders, and showed constant and unshakable dedication to the community was rewarded with honors and titles. Extreme individualism or non-conformity was taboo. Community was paramount. So clear were the intended prescriptive morals that at the end of each story, the children had little difficulty responding to the raconteur's question, "What lesson, children, do we learn from this story?"

Today, the telling of folktales in the traditional mode and format has all but disappeared in the face of rapid urbanization and modernization. The television, radio, movies, film strips, videos etc. have become popular entertainment organs in the home. It is becoming rare even in remote villages to find the traditional moon-lit settings or the around-the-fire, after-the-evening-meal formations where folktales were told by fathers, mothers, uncles, aunts, elder brothers or elder sisters, and through which esteemed cultural values were transmitted by word of mouth from one generation to the other. Where folktales are told at all, they are staged sessions for the benefit of curious researchers or collectors of tales. In such situations it will not be unheard of to listen to folktales told in the English Language in rural village settings! Village settings or habitats are, in themselves, becoming anachronistic as the push for more modern environments grow charmingly day by day. Among some contemporary African groups, it has become a sign of progress to wipe out the past and all its anchors. The ancestral homesteads are becoming a thing of the past, as economic hardships have driven village home-owners to lease part of their houses to total strangers who commute from nearby villages to work in the newly emergent urban and semi-urban locations. Thus what used to be a homogeneous community with its own mores and values – a tightly knit homestead in which everyone related to, and was related to everyone; a compound in which everyone knew everyone and the business of one was the business of all – is now a thing of the past. In its place is a new era which has brought with it new ideas and new relationships, some tantamounting to a breakdown of the old cherished moral order and codes. Some analysts attribute the present excessive incidence of juvenile delinquency in the emerging urban centers in Africa, to the loss of the moral values which traditionally had kept all social actions and human behavior in check. The proverbial notorious masquerade had broken loose from his chains and gone on a wild rampage leaving every onlooker and passerby at his mercy!

Blood relationships are being redefined, and are no longer simply determined by the proximity of habitation, resulting in conscious and unconscious incest which in the traditional society never failed to earn the offender capital punishment, and his or her family, humiliation of the worst order. Disobedience to parents, the flouting of communal authority and voluntary self-isolation from the group, are not unknown in the new dispensation. Loyalty to a communal cause can no longer be assumed or taken for granted. Folktales have ceased to be important and significant sources of social values for the younger generation. Children now imbibe values from peer groups and television programs among others.

Some established African writers, notably Chinua Achebe and Ngugi wa 'Thiong'o see a challenge for the committed artist in the moral crisis and value disorientation which have engulfed the younger generation in Africa. For them, it is a challenge for the artist to re-assert his creative imagination and cultural re-affirmation through the rediscovery of the folktale tradition as a valid form of instruction and entertainment which can even form a part of the modern school curriculum. Chinua Achebe has declared in an interview with Kalu Ogbaa (1981), that the committed African literary artist must dramatize for the new African, "his predicament so that he can see the choices and choose right." And he suggests that this can be done by putting "something solid and permanent into his consciousness, something in the form of what he reads, what he believes, and what he loves." Achebe who describes himself as "a conscious artist," has approached this vision in various manners in his fiction. In the stories he has written for young readers, he has reached into the past and selected some oral materials and folktales and adapted them to present conditions by modifying their thematic emphasis, re-shaping their structures, and refining the embedded values to suit contemporary standards and ideas. It is not an easy process and the African folktale of the future may well be evaluated and validated on the basis of the artist's aptness in discriminating and choosing wisely. Achebe however, insists that first and foremost, the folktales must be collected in their raw forms, and quickly too, before they disappear totally. The modern artist must then, in a conscious manner, use his intellect and judgment to refashion the stories without destroying their essence as oral materials designed for specific purposes. A modern writer who chooses traditional oral performance as his source, must be able to decide wisely what to retain, what to drop, and what to modify when transforming original folktales into modern forms and frameworks. This paper will now focus on Chinua Achebe's new and exciting literary techniques in the four volumes of stories he has written for children, three of them, recreations of popular traditional folktales.

Chinua Achebe has universally been acclaimed for pioneering the art of modern African literary tradition with the publication of his first novel, *Things Fall Apart* (1958). Although not as publicized as his adult fiction, Achebe's stories for children have been no less spectacular in their pioneer visionary trails and stylistic impacts. The mission is no less defined and pungent as in his adult socially –oriented writings. These stories for children have attracted little attention from critics, readers, publishers and teachers because of two major factors. The first is the abysmal neglect of children's literature in Africa where often it is mistaken as childish literature undeserving of serious attention even by publishers. Writers of children's stories are, therefore, seen as the lesser gods in the realms of creativity. Children account for 45% of Nigeria's 1995 estimated population of 1001, 232, 251 (0–14 years: 45, 493, 348). By any standards, this gurantees a ready market for children's literature. Yet today, nowhere in Africa is children's literature more neglected than perhaps, Nigeria, where the value of children's literature as a major catalyst for the development of a permanent reading culture seems easily over-looked in national priorities.

The second factor is the enormous impact which Achebe's adult novels have made on the art of the novel not only in Africa but in all locations throughout the world where creative writing is done in English by non-native speakers. And added to this is the fact that Chinua Achebe himself, hardly talks about his stories for young readers whether in interviews with researchers and the media, or in his countless public lectures all over the globe. Yet a careful study of his children's fiction soon reveals that Achebe has blazed another trail in modern African Literature, for through these stories, he has opened a new vista of experimentation for writers in cultures with rich oral traditions to draw from. As in his adult fiction Achebe uses the Nigerian setting and his Igbo cultural background to introduce his new mission of cultural re-orientation and rejuvenation for children and young adults who are secondary sufferers of the legacies of colonialism and neo-colonialism.

Achebe has published to date four children's books namely, *Chike and the River* (1966), *How the Leopard Got His Claws* (1972), *The Flute* (1977), and *The Drum* (1977). All but *Chike and the River* are animal stories recreated from popular folktales which from time immemorial have circulated in many versions throughout the Igboland. Some of the versions are also well known among other African cultural groups. By virtue of their nature, animal stories deal with issues in the animal world. Achebe's versions retain the major story-lines and in some cases, the major characters and the plot. But within these familiar features Achebe has added some significant structural retouches and redirected the focus of the central moral messages. He has simplified and up-dated the language and introduced meaningful dialogues, but most of all, he has infused new meaning into the imagery and symbolisms embedded in the stories. This is a conscious development, different from the human story, *Chike and the River*.

Achebe wrote *Chike and the River* to fulfill a personal family need. He discovered to his consternation while living with his family in Lagos in 1965, that their three-year old daughter "was developing very strange notions about race and colour" something unusual and absurd for her age and cultural environment. Achebe as a concerned parent, was very worried about how this might affect his daughter's social and mental development and determined to find out where she was getting the ideas from.

> She couldn't have picked up any of that from home, so my wife and I tracked it down to the racially mixed school that she attended, and I immediately wrote in protest to the headmistress, a white lady. Most of the teachers were white. And we found that it wasn't just that, but the entire educational system, including the books they read. So even if the teachers did nothing at all the books would have done it ... I never read those books myself when I was growing up so I didn't know what was in them. This was in Nigeria not in Europe and America. (Ezenwa Ohaeto: *Chinua Achebe: A Biography*, 105).

Achebe did not stop with the protest. He set out immediately to write a children's book which would be culturally relevant, linguistically appropriate, and thematically proper for children growing up in the Nigerian background. Predictably, he dedicated the 64 page book to "my daughter, Chinelo, and for all my nephews and nieces." Under the circumstances, the materials selected for the story had to be carefully thought out and had to be socio-culturally and politically correct. It had to be so designed as to be able to reverse the misconceptions which Achebe's daughter and others like her may have imbibed about themselves, the land and people of their birth.

Chike and the River is a simple adventure story centered around the life of an eleven year old child, Chike, who had lived all of his life with his mother in a village setting, Umuofia, but was haunted by the curiosities and fantasies of an emerging urban metropolis, Onitsha, not too far from the village.

> Chike was now eleven years old, and he had never left his village. Then one day his mother sent him in the new year to live with his uncle who was a clerk in one of the firms there. At first Chike was full of joy. He was tired of living in a bush village and wanted to see a big city. He had heard many wonderful stories about Onitsha. His uncle's servant, Michael, had told him that there was a water-tap in the very compound where they lived. Chike said this was impossible

> but Michael had sworn to its truth by wetting his first finger on his tongue and pointing it to the sky. Chike was too thrilled for words. So he would no longer wake up early in the morning to go to the stream. The trouble with the village stream was that the way to it was very rough and stony, and sometimes children fell and broke their water-pots. In Onitsha Chike would be free from all those worries. Also he would live in a house with an iron roof instead of his mother's poor hut of mud and thatch. It all sounded so wonderful (5–6).

With such great expectations, Chike embarks on his adventure into the city where he soon finds out that the city may indeed glitter, but it is not all gold. Within the context of this story, Achebe incorporates all the right elements of childhood acculturation and socialization. Although Achebe's family lived in the city, the setting of the story had to begin with the village to emphasize the essence of one's roots. The child-hero is exposed to the values of the village before embracing the city and all its unknowns. The younger reader can see the contrasting pictures of the rural and urban environments. The former lacks modern amenities, good water supply, electricity and modern infrastructures, but it is safe, serene and has human touch and a human face. The urban centers, on the other hand, have physical structures and amenities but life in them is relatively unsafe; there are frequent robberies, gambling, drug abuse, and fraud. But Achebe is careful to show through the experiences and actions of the child-hero in the book that if a child holds on to his or her good upbringing he can survive in any environment. He or she has to be selective and discriminating in the values he or she pursues, does not have to succumb to fancies and fantasies, and does not have to fall into temptations by peer groups to get into bad ways in the bid to achieve instant wealth. But Achebe does also allow Chike to often learn by trial and error, and burn his fingers occasionally. He learns through his various encounters with good and bad people that the best form of education in life is self-education. Chike is able to appreciate even while in the city that "a big town was not always better than a village. But there were things he liked in Onitsha" (13). Thus there are good and bad sides of life. A child has to learn to pick the good while discarding the bad. When Chike and his friend play into the hands of a fraudulent money-doubler, "Professor Chandus", Achebe allows them to learn the hard way from experience, and in the end, Chike is able to realize that he should not put any trust in illusions and self-delusions.

What makes *Chike and the River* a very successful children's book is that it serves as a kind of laboratory of life for the young readers. The hero of the book moves from naivette and ignorance to self knowledge and self discovery. Life for the young child is like a jig-saw puzzle, indeed a maze. He succeeds through determination and constant hard work. In spite of temptations to go astray. Chike stuck to the lessons he learnt from home and from his mother. He is honest, truthful, courageous and polite and these are qualities which earn him success at the end of the story. It is significant also that although Chike was attracted by the good life, by wealth and material acquisitions, the ultimate success that Achebe allows him to achieve in the end which gives him great pride and self confidence, is the scholarship he won to go to school and receive a good education, as a reward for exposing and turning in some criminals. That then was the path of life that Achebe wanted his "daughter, Chinelo, and all his nephews and nieces" to follow and if they became firmly grounded in it, no racist illusions or ideologies can divert them then or later in life.

Achebe's literary techniques in the book make it worthwhile for children. There are familiar folksongs, "native" idioms, and code mixing, humorous anecdotes, games that children play for entertainment and amusement, children's pranks and slangs, children's fantasies and day-dreaming, children's nicknames for each other, and children's perceptions of the adult world which they discuss among themselves in their peculiar types of dialogue. All these reinforce the authenticity of the story, the reality of the children's world created in the book and the author's artistic integrity. Because Nigerian children who would read the story are already familiar with the folktales and the folktale tradition, Achebe kept quite close to the folktale narrative structure, and the values and morals espoused in folktales. And in the pattern of the traditional narrator, he ends the story with an explicit moral:

> So Chike's adventure on the River Niger brought him close to danger and then rewarded him with good fortune. It also exposed Mr Peter Nwana, the rich but miserly trader. For it was he who had led the other thieves (60).

This ending, however, has an unfortunate flaw which would perplex some children too. At the time Achebe published this story, there was in existence a very popular novel in the Igbo Language which every child who went to school in Igboland would have read. This novel, *Omenuko*, published in 1933 was a best seller for decades, and is today a classic. The author was Mr. Peter Nwana, a legendary figure in Igbo history and culture. By a printer's devil, the criminal at the end of *Chike and the River*, "Mr Peter Nwala" was rendered as Mr Peter Nwana and in spite of Achebe pointing out the error to the publishers, it was not corrected to this day.

Chike and the River is a father's gift to his daughter and her cousins. It is a story consciously designed to instruct and entertain. It was not meant to strain or stretch the imagination of the young reader. Its simplicity of language and clarity of plot would recommend it to teachers, parents and young readers. However, the other children's stories that followed it were not as personally motivated. They had more "universal" and out-reach goals. At least one of them was shrouded in the symbolism of a historical catastrophic national event recreated to permit comprehension by the young.

How the Leopard Got His Claws is Achebe's best manifestation of the skillful adaptation of a traditional oral tale to a modern written form. I had documented elsewhere (Emenyonu 1998), the chequered story of the origin and publication of *How the Leopard Got His Claws*. First, the original title was *How the Dog Became a Domestic Animal* and it was written by a veteran Nigerian writer of children's stories, John Iroaganachi who appears on the cover page of *How the Leopard Got His Claws* as Achebe's co-author. Secondly, the original story was submitted to Chinua Achebe for possible publication in his short-lived Citadel Press. Achebe found it publishable and proceeded to edit it. When he finished editing it, the title, the story-line and the structure of the story had all been transformed. And perhaps, most significantly, the new story was steeped in heavy imagery and symbolism of the political upheavals which rocked the Nigerian nation six years after its independence in 1960, culminating in a civil war, July 1967 to January 1970. The new story was no longer John Iroaganachi's but because of its basic origin Achebe had it published in 1972 as co-authored with Iroaganachi.

Achebe's explanation of the transformation of the original story as he edited it is quite interesting:

> It just seized on my imagination and it went on changing and changing. It was almost like an obsession, and by the end of my involvement with it, it was a totally different story... The story was actually a folktale about the dog, a 'charming, traditional – type story', in which the dog is the nice guy, a wonderful fellow who became a slave. But I don't like slaves, so this is why I turned the plot around 180 degrees (*Ezenwa Ohaeto* 125).

The myth of "How the Dog Became a Domestic Animal", abounds in various versions in many African cultures. Achebe's dexterous transformation achieved three major things. With the change of the title to "How the Leopard Got His Claws", the focus shifted from the dog to the leopard. Secondly, the character of the dog changed from that of victim to villain. Then the story acquired a new symbolic thrust, from a simple myth of why the dog is a domestic animal (pet), to how the dog caused disunity in the animal kingdom, drawing in the process, various lights on the roles of different animals in the conspiracy and crisis. Some were blackmailers, some traitors, some sycophants, while there were some who could not take a stand on issues choosing like the chameleon to change colors and switch allegiances as often as necessary, to be on the winning team. This new dimension acquired a political meaning when Achebe used the symbolism to connote in allegorical manner the calamity that befell a whole race of people, notably the Igbo, in the Nigerian civil war. "The transformation of the story possesses obvious symbolic implications: it reflects the divisive deeds that led to the civil war, while the lament of the deer reiterates the violence and dispossession associated with these deeds. The development of the war confirmed the injustice of the deer's lament..." (*Ohaeto* 126). The "Deer's Lament" was an ingenious literary device which further illustrates Achebe's strategies in the transformation of the original story. He sought and obtained the collaboration of the late great Nigerian poet, Christopher Okigbo, in the insertion within the story of a poem, a kind of dirge, which articulates the history of the tragedy. Okigbo who was killed fighting for the Biafrans in the civil war was truly in his element when he composed "The Lament of the Deer":

> O Leopard our noble king, where are you? Spotted king of the forest, where are you? Even if you are far away come, hurry home: The worst has happened to us, the worst has happened to us... The house the animals built the cruel dog keeps us from it. The common shelter we built the cruel dog keeps us from it. The worst has happened to us, the worst has happened to us... (21).

The process of transformation involved three authors – John Iroaganachi who provided the original framework, Achebe who re-configured the tale and Okigbo whose poem fulfilled the role of the *Chorus* in classic tragedies. "The transformation of the story was made to retain the essence of Igbo philosophy, while at the same time extending its wider implications. It was also shaped in terms of dialogues, narrative sinew, cultural notions and moral values in order to suit the envisaged readership – children – while maintaining an appeal to adults" (Ohaeto 125). To suit the tastes of children, the story was beautifully illustrated by Adrienne Kennaway. Children can follow the narration through the pictures and decipher at their level the content and meaning of the story, much as they would do a riddle, which was popular traditional pastime. To the adults the story is a parable. Unwrapping the mysterious symbols in the story will be an adult exercise. Interpreting "The Lament of the Deer" (the song of the deer at the point when he was thrown out by the dog from the house built by all the animals) will be an intellectual task for adult readers. Matching animal names, locations in the forest, and specific events and conflicts with their equivalents in the Nigerian civil war situation will remain a complex and controversial puzzle at all times. All these will keep the story and events of the Nigerian civil war alive from generation to generation. Chinua Achebe could not have achieved a greater artistic feat. In a small children's book of less than fifty pages, he has left for present Nigerians and posterity a visionary artist's impression of the most sordid tragedy in Nigerian history to date, and preserved it in a form which is accessible to children as well as adults. The civil war may have ended on January 15, 1970, but Chinua Achebe has provided an enigmatic dialogue or debate on it which will transcend every age and time. Yet, in literary terms, *How the Leopard Got His Claws* will always be classified as an imaginary children's animal story, and any resemblance to actual events, places and people, will be presumed coincidental. This story, in thematic relevance and stylistic innovativeness, occupies in Chinua Achebe's children's fiction the status that *Things Fall Apart* occupies in his adult fiction – a timeless legacy, an immemorial presence.

Achebe's two other children's stories –*The Flute* and *The Drum* were designed exclusively for children. They are moral tales meant to convey specific messages to children. Both are animal stories recreated by Achebe through the extension of the original plot and the infusion of more pragmatic meanings in the contemporary setting. Achebe, in much the same way that he explained his artistic process in *Arrow of God* (1964), has analyzed his artistic purpose in the re-creation of *The Flute* a simple folktale well known in many African cultures, so that it could produce desirable results in the behavior patterns and socialization process for children.

> Now this is the story of a child who forgets his flute in the farm. It is a fairly common story in Africa. When the child and his family reach home at dusk, he remembers his flute and wants to go back for it. But that is not permissible. You see, the world is divided. Spirits have their own time. We have our own time. You go to the farm in the day time, in the night it is the turn of the spirits. So if you go there at night, you are breaking the law of jurisdictions and you can expect all kinds of problems. So when this boy wants to go to the distant farm at night, his parents beg him not to go. But still he goes. And so in one sense this is a story about disobedience. And true enough, the boy meets the spirits. All of this is in the tradition. What is not there is the king of the spirits saying to the boy: "Why did you disobey your parents?" Being a spirit, you see, he has seen far away into the boy's home, before he came. So he says, "what about your mother? Didn't she promise to buy you another flute on the next market? Why did you disobey your mother?" The boy looks down, he knows he is beaten, you see, he knows about disobedience. He rallies and says, "That flute, I made it myself; it is the only thing that I could call my own". Now I put that in, quite shamelessly, you see, because I think you require that kind of justification for disobedience. Children may not ask you, but it will be bothering them, you know, if you tell them, "You should obey your parents." Why is it that this boy didn't, and yet he is rewarded in the end? Now I insist the question should be asked. So the boy gives a good answer and the spirit says indulgently: "Well that is not good enough. But I like your spirits, I like your guts." So the point is made that obedience is still the rule, but courage is also important. And we make the point that the song which the boy makes about his flute lying out there all alone, in the cold, is another saving grace. And so, making things – a flute or a song – adds to build up the story, I think. And that way, the idea of making things, which I feel very strongly about, is injected into the story without destroying it. That is what Senghor was talking about, incidentally, that we have become a society of consumers. We don't make things. Making things is very important. Any chance one has to sneak it in, to smuggle in something about making, would be justified art in terms of what our traditional culture intended to do. Art was intended to be useful, to be entertaining, yes, but also to be doing something useful in the society (Bernth Lindfors 125–126).

It is necessary to quote Achebe's words in full not only to show their practical ramifications, but also to show the theoretical basis of his creative experimentation. The elaborate and explicit narration of his artistic process, is like the laying of a blue-print for other writers, showing them in practical terms how a traditional folktale could be transformed for specific goals in a modern context.

The second part of *The Flute* retains the story-line as in the traditional folktale until the very end when Achebe adds purposefully another interesting twist. The boy in the second half of the story was brought in as a contrast to the good manners of the first boy, the hero of the story. He is everything the first boy is not – rude, irresponsible, thoughtless and disrespectful to elders. His mother, the senior wife too, was brought in as a contrast to the well-meaning and open-minded disposition of the junior wife. The senior wife is greedy, insatiable and vicious. Although she has many children as against the junior wife's only son, she is still full of malice and envy towards the less privileged wife. When her humble son because of his good manners comes back with the charmed pot that the spirits had given him, filled with "gold and silver and bronze, cloths and velvets, foods of all kinds, sheep and goats and cows and many other things of value," she characteristically "fills two baskets with gifts and offers them to the senior wife." But true to her nature, the senior wife "was so jealous that she rejected the gift." (16). Predictably she forces her first son at the crack of dawn (having passed a sleepless night), to bring his flute and follow her to an unplanned day at the farm, at the end of which she compels him to forget the flute and go back at dusk for it.

> When they got to the farm there was no work for them to do because all the work had been done on the previous day. But they hung around until sunset then she said, "Let us go home." They picked up their baskets and the boy picked up his flute. "Foolish boy," said the woman boxing his ears, "don't you know how to forget your flute?" So the boy dropped his flute and they set out for home. As soon as they entered their hut the woman said to her son, "Now, go back for your flute," He cried and protested but she pushed him out of the hut and told him not to come back without his flute and a pot of presents (18).

The boy naturally reflected in words and actions the mood and attitudes of his mother when he encountered the spirits; and instead of a pot of presents, he brought home a pot of woes.

> Without stopping to thank the spirits, the boy lifted the pot on his head and walked away. He reached home at last, having crossed the seven rivers and seven forests. His mother who had been waiting outside the compound gate all evening was happy to see him carrying such a big pot. "They said I should break it before my father and yourself," said the boy. "What does your father know about it?" she snapped back and steered him to her hut. She shut the doors and then filled every crack in the wall so that nothing might escape to the other huts in

> the compound. When everything was ready, she broke the pot. Immediately leprosy, small pox, yaws and worse diseases without names and every evil and abomination filled the hut and killed the woman and all her children (24).

The narration is characterized by its lucidity and clarity. Achebe effectively dramatized the predicament of the polygynous family in the story, so that today's children and wives caught in similar circumstances can make informed choices. The moral embedded in the tale is so explicit that children would not forget it. It warns children about the dangers of the sins of greed, inordinate ambition, jealousy, envy, treachery, disobedience, haughtiness and self-centeredness. On the other hand, it extols the virtues of innocence, humility, courage, truth, honesty, hardwork, kindness and self confidence. As part of the transformation, Achebe, added features of the contemporary times. Thus, the gifts of the first boy included "gold and silver and bronze, cloths and velvets" which are modern symbols of wealth. He also extended the folktale from where it ended in the tradition. The tragic death of the senior wife and all her children was reported by the husband who discovered it through "a peep in the door". In some other versions of the story, the husband perished with them. But Achebe had to separate the good from the bad, for there seemed no just reason to have an innocent husband die because of the sins of his notoriously vicious and inhuman wife who brought an end to her life through a suicidal act. And whereas the traditional tale ended with a short list (which any narrator could expand) of terrible diseases which killed the woman and her children, Achebe expanded it with, "He struggled with the hideous things fighting to come out and luckily managed to shut and secure the door again. But a few of the diseases and abominations had escaped and spread through the world. But luckily the worst of them – those without a name remained in that hut" (24). The unnamed diseases and abominations which escaped and spread through the world, would cover any new diseases and maladies known to mankind. Thus, elasticity which is a familiar feature of the traditional folktale, is preserved in its modern context.

The Drum published in the same year as *The Flute* shares many of its features and was tailored to a specific moral goal. It centers around one of the many exploits of tortoise, the most popular character in the Igbo folktale tradition. The name "tortoise" serves now as a frame of reference for anyone notorious for any of the tortoise's wily ways – cunning, crafty, self-centered, ingenious for evil purposes and incurably egotistic. The story is about tortoise's ingenuity to find food during a period of acute famine in the animal world. "He goes in search of food, he's just wandering, miserably, and then he stumbles, by sheer accident, into the world of spirits, and he is rewarded with a drum that produces food. So the tortoise takes this home and beats it and feeds the animals" (Lindfors 126–7). The traditional version of the tale shows the animals suffering because of an irresponsible use of the drum which leads it to break and the replacement spills disasters and punishments on the animals instead of sumptuous dishes. Achebe in his transformation of the tale, introduces a political twist by making tortoise use his food-power to impose himself as a king of the animals. Achebe explains:

> He (tortoise) sets up a committee for the coronation, and makes the biggest animal his drum major! The elephant beats the drum too heavily and breaks it. It is a very desperate situation. The tortoise tries to patch it up but it won't work. So he says to the animals: "Well, don't worry; after the coronation, I'll go back and get a new one." But the animals reply, "No drum, no coronation." So the tortoise is compelled to go on a second journey which is faked, and this is the whole point of the traditional story. Adventure, fine. Faked adventure, no. Because in faking it, all the things that happened by chance before are now contrived and false (Lindfors 127).

What is mainly condemned in the story (as in *The Flute*) is the vice of fake appearance and hypocrisy. But the added political twist is intended to serve as a serious commentary on the purpose of individuals in any community seeking the position of leadership and their use or abuse of the power when acquired legitimately or illegitimately. In both *The Flute* and *The Drum*, the first adventure is involuntary and results in good fortune, while the second adventure is contrived and fake, and ends in tragic consequences.

The stories which Chinua Achebe as recreated from the oral tradition are models both in their message and artistic devices. They help to restore dignity and authenticity to a fast-fading tradition. They provide young African writers, impressive and credible ways of articulating the traditional and the modern in African literary tradition. The African folktale can be kept alive by a skillful and harmonious integration of valuable ingredients such as timeless wisdom and faith from the old, with the best elements in the new order. Achebe has through his experimentations opened a new vista of creativity for African writers. He has shown how myths, legends, and folktales can be preserved in exciting forms. He has provided a challenge for African writers especially of the younger generation, to expand the frontiers of African oral heritage to accommodate new insights and new creativities. It is a veritable legacy and one hopes that Achebe has not stopped doing for African children, what he knows best how to do.

Works Cited

Achebe Chinua, *Things Fall Apart*, London, Heinemann, 1958

———. *Chike and the River*, Cambridge University Press, 1966

———. *How the Leopard Got His Claws*, London, Heinemann, 1972

———. *The Flute*, Enugu (Nigeria), Fourth Dimension, 1977

———. *The Drum*, Enugu, Fourth Dimension, 1977.

Emenyonu, Ernest, "(Re) inventing the Past for the Present: Symbolism in Chinua Achebe's *How The Leopard Got His Claws*, in Meena Khorana (Ed.)

———. *Bookbird World of Children's Books*, Vol. 36, no 1, 1998.

Lindfors, Bernth, *Conversations with Chinua Achebe*, Jackson, University Press of Mississippi, 1997.

Nwana, Pita, *Omenuko*, London, Longman, 1933.

Ohaeto, Ezenwa, *Chinua Achebe: A Biography*, Indiana University Press, 1997

Chapter 35

The Writer as Teacher: Chinua Achebe's Children's Books

James S. Etim

> ... you don't go and write fiction just for people to enjoy themselves. You write with a message (*Emecheta*, 1990: 6).
>
> It is the story that saves our progeny from blundering like blind beggars into the spikes of the cactus fence. The story is our escort; without it, we are blind (*Achebe, Anthills of the Savannah*, 1987).

Among other things, many children's and young adult novels emanating from Africa are didactic in nature. The concept of didactism in literature has been an age-old one. Beginning with Aristotle's *Poetics*, there has been the idea that literature should have a moral and an aesthetic base. Although there has been some shift in the canon to the idea of "art for art's sake", still many hold tenaciously to the idea that the artist, no matter the period and culture, should impart the mores and values of that society. In post-colonial Africa, given the enormous tasks of nation building and the revision of history and literature, there have been constant calls by educators and critics for a reevaluation of children's literature and that children's and young adult novels used in Africa "should have an African background and reflect the realities of the African environment" (*Agbasiere* 1996; *Anozie* 1992; *Etim* 1992–93). Writing on the didactism of Nigerian novels, Osa (1986) indicated that "a significant aspect of Nigerian junior novels, however, is didactism, which is part of Nigerian culture. The adult has always felt and still feels duty bound to teach the young" (253).

Some of the themes covered in many of these novels have been explored by Agbasiere (1996), Etim (1993–94), Fatunde (1996), Odejide (1987) and Osa (1986, 1995) to mention a few. In her analysis of the works of Emecheta, Agbasiere, reflecting on *The Moonlight Bride*, points out that "Emecheta postulates that a child brought up in traditional society imbibes the virtues of bravery, loyalty, obedience to and respect for elders, humility, communalism and good neighborliness. The child's behaviors are most of the time rooted in the traditions of the people" (4, 15). I have elsewhere discussed the findings of a study on the themes covered by Nigerian female novelists (*Etim* 1992/3). The themes include love, friendship and unfaithfulness in marriage evident in Helen Oviagele's *You Never Know*; teenage pregnancy and hardships associated with war as in Rosina Umelo's *Felicia*, and teenage love, jealousy and anger as in *Sisi* by Sikuade just to mention a few. Fatunde analyzes the works of Emecheta and points out that *Niara Power* reflects the corruption and mismanagement of resources prevalent in the Nigerian society.

Writing in *Morning Yet on Creation Day*, Achebe rejects the often held European idea that "art should be accountable to no one and needs to justify itself to nobody." Rather, following the African oral tradition, he believes that "art is, and always was, at the service of man. Our ancestors created myths and told their stories for a human purpose." In viewing his writings, therefore, we begin with the idea that any good story should have a purpose, should have a message. In this paper, I will consider three thematic areas, which are part of his children's literature. These are greed, character building (as a result of positive parental influence on the young) and the nature of power and nation building. For a discussion of these three broad thematic areas, four of Achebe's children's novels will be used. These are *Chike and the River*, *The Drum*, *The Flute* and *How the Leopard Got His Claws.*

At one level, *Chike and the River* is an adventure story. A little boy from the village of Umuofia gets into the town and desires to cross the River Niger from Onitsha to Asaba. He needs some money to fulfill this desire and the novel explores this process. In exploring this process, Achebe also presents the concepts of greed, the need for hard work and perseverance, and the importance of parental influence in child rearing. Many of the adults are greedy and corrupt. We see that in the Money Doubler, Professor Chandus. He is a type, representing those adults who do not want to work but earn a living by misleading others. He knows that he cannot double money but he wants to be rich anyway. So he lives a life of deception, promising to fools and children what he knows he cannot do. Throughout Nigeria especially in the 1960s–1980s, there was a preponderance of these "magic-Professors" and today, they operate through the popular or notorious 419 fraudsters. Chike falls a victim and when he goes back with SMOG to confront him (the Money Doubler) and ask for his money to be returned, he shouts at them warning:

> Make una com ot from here one time or I go learn you lesson you no fit forget. Imagine? Why small boys of nowadays no de fear. You get bold face to come my house and begin talk rubbish. Na your father steal threepence no be me. Stand there when I come back and you go see. He rushed into an Inner room and scraped a matchet on the hard floor (36).

With this kind of behavior, Chike and SMOG are forced to run away with Chike leaving without his money.

Mr. Nwana is not different. He is described as a man well known in the town who went to church regularly "Every Sunday morning he put on his gorgeous *agbada,* went with his family to the nearby church, and every Friday he went to Bible class" (42). However he is living a life of deception. His hypocrisy is made immediately apparent to us for the author makes Chike to wonder "how such a cruel man could pay so much attention to religion" (42). His life is also troubling – he lived miserably in a one-room apartment with his wife and five children and he hardly ate well and his children wore threadbare clothes. Moreover, he was not generous with his money. It is not surprising that at the end of the story, we find that Nwana lived on ill-gotten wealth. He was a thief, the ring leader of the thieves involved in stealing bales of velvet from a store in Asaba. He is caught and disgraced. Even though he was stern and had imbibed religion, he did not allow that religious faith to change his morality and make him a law abiding citizen and a better man.

Greed is so pervasive that we have a dishonest trader selling pills to innocent children who hope that these pills will help their memory and that this will result in enhanced performance in examination. This was not to be the case and the children almost went insane.

Achebe shows that children are not immune to greed. Of course, if the adults act so disreputably, it is not surprising that many of the young children will follow. Ezekiel is a good example. He develops a scheme to steal money from boys his age in Britain:

> He wrote to them asking one to send him money, another to send him a camera and a third to send him a pair of shoes.... He promised each of the boys a leopard skin in return. Of course he had no intention of fulfilling his promise. For one thing he had never seen a leopard skin in his life (16).

He also helps his friends to write letters to young boys in Britain asking for money. Of course, Ezekiel is found out by his headmaster and he and his friends are punished accordingly. After warning all the students, "Ezekiel was given twelve strokes of the cane... Samuel was given six strokes, and the others nine strokes each" (18).

In *The Flute*, we have a story of two little boys – one, an only son, who is humble and makes his mother rich and proud and the other, a son from a mother with many children whose haughty behavior, lack of respect and greed cause death to his mother and himself. Reflected in this story is Shakespeare's line in *The Merchant of Venice* that "All that glitters is not gold/Often have you heard that told" (II. Sc. 7). The only son forgets his flute in the farm. This is the only toy he has and although it is getting to nightfall and his mother admonishes him not to go back to the farm he persists. In the farm, he meets some spirits and when they give him a "miserable-looking bamboo flute", he jumps up and down declaring, "That's my flute" (17) As he is getting ready to depart from the spirits, one of them gives him two pots, one small and the other large. He is asked to choose one and "...The boy took the smaller pot. The spirits nodded one to another in satisfaction" (22). He is not greedy neither does he allow appearances to fool him. He further obeys the instructions of the spirits who tell him how to behave on the road home and at home. On getting home, he "called his parents together as the spirits had told him and broke the pot in front of them. Immediately the compound was filled with every good thing: gold and silver and bronze, cloths and velvets, food of all kinds ... and many other things of value" (26). In not being greedy and acting in obedience and with respect to the spirits, he receives a great reward for himself and his family. His mother could have been greedy by hoarding these "gifts". Rather, she extends her hand of love and community to her co-wife when she "filled two baskets with gifts and offered them" (26) to her. The senior wife acting in hate and greed tries to replicate the journey for her son in hopes of being wealthy. However lacking character (more of this later on), he disobeys all the instructions of the spirits to his peril and that of his mother. Their sad ending is recorded this way: "Immediately leprosy, small pox, yaws and worse diseases without names and every evil and abomination filled the hut and killed the woman and all her children" (38). In these two texts, Achebe shows the consequences of greed, disobedience and lack of respect to constituted authority.

The behavior and actions of children in these two novels are in large part determined by the moral upbringing they received from their parents and other significant individuals around them. Achebe is echoing the point made in the Bible that sparing the rod means spoiling the child and that parents and significant others in the child's life are totally responsible for the morals and values of the child and when they are derelict in their duty, the child grows up to be wayward, immoral and antisocial. When we first meet Chike, we find that he grew up in an environment where his mother "worked very hard to feed and clothe her three children and send them to school" (5). As he is leaving Umuofia, the mother advises him to "Listen to whatever your uncle says and obey him. Onitsha is a big city, full of dangerous people and kidnappers. Therefore do not wander about the city" (6). His uncle is also described as a very strict man who did not like him playing and wasting time with other children. We see therefore inculcated in Chike the concepts of hard work, honesty and integrity. Indeed when he asks for money from his uncle, the uncle questions what he needs the money for and his attitude to him impresses on him that if he needs money, he would have to work for it. This is strengthened further when he loses his money to Chandus and when he sees what happened to Ezekiel and Samuel, it is not surprising that he works hard (by washing cars) to obtain the money he needs to cross the Niger and he does not involve himself in any criminal act. Instead, he solves the crime at the end of the story.

On the other hand, Ezekiel has a loose moral upbringing and he behaves accordingly. His mother was a well-to-do trader who made a lot of profit from her trade:

> But she was not a wise mother. She allowed Ezekiel to do whatever he liked. So, he became a spoilt child... – His mother said housework was only for servants and girls. So Ezekiel was developing into a lawless little imp. He would sneak quietly to the soup pot at night and search with his fingers for pieces of fish and meat. By morning, the soup would go sour and his mother would punish the servants. One day one of his sisters caught him red handed... But Ezekiel denied it all; and his mother believed him (15).

This description gives us the family environment that Ezekiel grew up in. We find that he is lawless, lazy, a thief, a liar and one who bore false witness against others. These character traits are not attractive for anyone. We see, therefore, that when he goes to school he develops the scheme to steal money from his pen-pals. His mother still does not help him to be a decent law-abiding citizen for when he is corrected by the school, the school acting as *loco parentis*, she "...went to the headmaster's house that evening and rained abuses on him" (18).

In *The Flute*, we find the idea that motherly influence has a lot to do with the child's character, reinforced. We have two women who treated their children differently. The senior wife had many children and was very lax with one of the sons. So, when he is pushed to go back to the forest in order that he may come back to make his mother rich, we find that he is disrespectful and abusive to the spirits and does not follow any of their directions on his way home or at home. On the other hand, the boy from the younger wife was very respectful to the spirits and did exactly as he was told. Therefore, both of them ended differently, one in death and the other living to enjoy the riches from these spirits.

The Flute, *The Drum* and *How The Leopard Got His Claws* are either animal tales or folktales. According to Jesse Goodman and Kate Melcher, "folktales were often used to teach children about their own heritage, values and customs. ... Children are often faced with complex situations and ethical dilemmas, and folktales provide concrete, rather than an abstract reason for living an ethical life" (200). Some of the thematic concerns in *The Flute* have been explored. As in *The Flute*, the world of *The Drum* is that of spirits, forests and rivers. Achebe uses this setting peopled with animals to explore the concepts of greed, power and leadership. There is famine in the land and the Tortoise goes out in search of food. He climbs several palm trees before he finds one that satisfies his hunger. In this introductory scene, we find that the tortoise has very good qualities – frugal in not allowing any of the fruits to waste away, he shows perseverance in going about to obtain food and he is good-natured when he decides to share the food given by the spirits with all the animals. Everything went well until he tried to use the gift from the spirits for his advancement to become king. He became ambitious forgetting that service to the community was more important. Earlier in the novel, we see the genesis of his ambition when he declares, "If I feed the animals at this time when they are all about to perish from hunger, they will honor my name and perhaps even make me their king. That would be really nice" (12). In his long speech to the animals to show that he had taken a sacrificial journey in order to save all the animals, he declares that the king of the spirits had given him a chieftaincy title. "He called me Chief Tortoise Who Never Stops a Fight Half-way" (15). Of course the reason for such a speech was to ingratiate himself to all the animals and position himself to being made king. Indeed, he refers to the land of the animals as kingdom, a way of ensuring that he could one day be king. It is not surprising that when one day one of the drunken singers called him King Tortoise, he does not object but jumps at the idea and the day was set for his coronation. However, as in most tragedies, there is a flaw or an error in judgment. Tortoise miscalculates and delegates his responsibility to someone else – he allows Elephant to beat the Drum. In his new task, Elephant beats the Drum to destruction. Although Tortoise calls this a temporary setback, he is not able to recover for since there is no more food, the animals refuse to go along with him and make him king. "The drum first and then the coronation. What's the good of a king without a food drum?" (22). In continuation of his desire to be king, he replicates his earlier journey to the kingdom of the spirits in order to get a new drum. This time however, he acts in disrespect to the spirits and he is greedy when presented with several drums:

> 'The choice is yours, sir,' said the spirit with a wave of the arm towards the drums. Tortoise was overjoyed at the way things were turning out. The last time he was given a miserable little drum with a delicate skin. Now he had the chance to pick a drum befitting a king. So he marched up to the end of the hanging row of drums, looking at each as he passed, and finally pointing at the largest one of all (26).

His greed causes problems for himself and the other animals for he is severely beaten by the spirits when he beats the drum. For the other animals, "Suffice it to say that they dragged themselves out of Tortoise's compound howling and bleeding. They scattered in every direction of the world and have never stopped running" (28).

Agbasiere points out that "Achebe's *How the Leopard Got His Claws* reflects the Nigerian civil war of 1967–1970" (412). While agreeing with her, I go further by maintaining that Achebe uses *How the Leopard Got His Claws* to explore the nature of leadership and nation building. For purposes of discussion, it would be useful to divide this story into five sections:

1. Introduction. Building with one vision under the leadership of the leopard
2. Dog reappears, fights and defeats the leopard. Coronation and rulership of Dog
3. Leopard departs, hurt and disgraced. Arms himself with the help of Blacksmith
4. Reappears and becomes king. Dismantles the common vision
5. Disarray in the kingdom, everyone for himself/herself

In the introductory section, we see the leopard as an honorable and noble king who ruled a kingdom in harmony. The animals all had one vision and whenever there was a problem, King Leopard helped them to solve the problem together. The building of a village hail for the meeting of the animals is the best example of this comradeship and vision:

> As they built the house, they sang many happy songs. They also told many jokes. Although they worked very hard everyone was merry.
>
> After many weeks they finished the building. It was a fine building. The animals were pleased with it. They agreed to open it with a special meeting (13–14).

However, the dog does not share this vision. He refuses to help build but when the rains come, he is able to drive all the animals away from the hall and take over the building because he had sharp teeth. When King Leopard returns from his journey and implores the animals to go with him to "drive out the enemy", the others refuse since "He is too strong for us" (21). This is the beginning of the demise of the kingdom. Leopard faces the dog alone and loses. He leaves battered, hurt and in disgrace. The other animals quickly rally around the dog, proclaim him king and sing his praises. This is the beginning of sycophancy. They declare in praise:

> The dog is great
> The dog is good
> The dog gives us our daily food
> We love his head,
> We love his feet and all his claws (23).

These animals are so concerned about food and safety that they will do anything including throwing away their good king, Leopard. That is why leopard looks at them with contempt. Those who do not act with any principle or have no principle but only concerned about their belly will be destroyed. Leopard goes on to the blacksmith, obtains "terrible teeth and claws," and then receives a loud voice from Thunder. At this point, he is well armed to take up dog and the other animals. When he returns, he calls the other animals shameless cowards, asks them to dismantle the village hail they all built together and he takes over. The dog runs away battered and becomes a slave to the hunter in order not to be destroyed by the leopard.

The lessons that are being taught to children and young adults in this story are that friendship, cooperation and consensus building lead to the building of a community. Where individuals come in with a different agenda, they slowly cause the disintegration of the nation. Such individuals need to be subdued quickly or else the nation will be completely destroyed. There is also the question of power. Who should have power? How do individuals react to those with power? What leadership style seems to be most appropriate in nation building? At the beginning, we see leopard being a democratic leader – although king, he reasons with the animals and gets them to discuss issues before a final decision is reached. At the end, when he becomes autocratic, there is no more kingdom to rule but everyone is for himself. We may, therefore, safely assume that the author is subscribing to a leadership style that seeks to bring people together instead of a dictatorial autocratic style. The author is also subscribing to the idea that individuals need to have a principle and fight if necessary to maintain such instead of being more interested in food and safety alone. Thus the fickleness of followers is regarded as foolish and cowardly. There is also the idea that might is not always right since it can cause the destruction of the nation and lead to everyone being for himself/herself.

There is a certain level of irony in this story. The dog wanted power, refused to listen to the leopard and be part of the community. At the end, the individual who wanted to rule becomes a slave to others. He thought he could be alone and still survive. But the elements proved him wrong. Moreover, at the end, he (the dog) seeks to be part of something in order to survive. This is a true lesson for the young – that one's survival may be assured if one is part of the community instead of trying to be alone, of course, in western societies, individualism is more important than the community. Achebe is showing the young that in the African context, communalism, friendship and good neighborliness are more important than tyrannical individuality.

The four children's books analyzed were written from 1966 to 1977, a very trying period in Nigerian polity. *Chike* was published in 1966 but shares the same historical framework as the other three published in the 1970's. Right before 1970 and right after, the question of national development – direction, role of leaders how to build a unified nation, the problems of greed and corruption in destabilizing the nation etc were areas of concern and constantly reflected in national papers in Nigeria. The children's stories to some extent deal with these issues and suggest some direction that will help children begin to develop positive character traits so that these attributes will be used in building a better nation. This supports the notion opined by Elizabeth Ashimole that thematically, there has been quite a strenuous attempt to reflect the contemporary realities in many of the books written for young children in Nigeria (78).

According to Karen Winkler, Achebe believes that art has a social function and artists contribute to social development (1994 A9) In this analysis of four of his children's stories, we have seen that his concern for the use of children's literature for social development has been reflected in his treatment of three broad thematic areas – greed, parental influence in the upbringing of the child and the nature of power and leadership. We have seen that many of the characters who are greedy come to a sad end, whether it is Mr Nwana or Tortoise. We see that characters like Ezekiel and his friends who do not have strong parental influences turn out badly, giving credence to the saying that 'sparing the rod spoils the child.' Achebe also demonstrates that the community will survive if those in that community have a shared vision and work together towards the achievement of such goals.

Works Cited

Achebe, Chinua. *Chike and the River.* London: Cambridge UP, 1966
———. *The Drum.* Enugu, Nigeria: Fourth Dimension, 1977
———. *The Flute* Enugu, Nigeria: Fourth Dimension, 1977
———. "The Novelist as Teacher" *Morning Yet on Creation Day.* London: Heinemann, 1975.
———. Morning Yet on Creation Day. London: Heinemann, 1975.
———. and John Iroaganachi. *How The Leopard Got His Claws.* Enugu, Nigeria: Nwamife, 1972
Agbasiere, Julie. "Towards a Cultural Symbiosis: A Study of Buchi Emecheta's Children's Books *Emerging Perspectives on Buchi Emecheta.* Ed. Marie Umeh. Trenton, N.J. Africa World Press, 1996.
Anozie, Sunday O. "The Drum and The Flute, Reconstruction in Children's Literature". *Children and Literature in Africa.* Eds Chidi Ikonne et al Ibadan, Nigeria: Heinemann Educational Books, 1992
Ashimole, Elizabeth O. "Nigerian Children's Literature and the Challenges of Social Change". *Children and Literature in Africa.* Eds Chidi Ikonne et al, Ibadan, Nigeria: Heinemann Educational Books, 1992.
Etim, James. "Themes in Female-authored YA novels preferred by Nigerian Secondary School Students. *Journal of Reading.* 36.4 (Dec. 1992–Jan. 1993): 270–275
Fatudne, Tunde "Conflicting Social Values in Buchi Emecheta's *Niara Power* and *A Kind Of Marriage*" *Emerging Perspectives on Buchi Emecheta.* Ed. Marie Umeh. Trenton, N.J.: Africa World Press, 1996.
Goodman, Jesse and Kate Meicher. "Culture at a distance: An anthroliteraty approach to Cross-cultural education" *Journal of Reading* 28.3 (Dec. 1984).
Odejide, Abiola. "Children's biographies of Nigerian figures: A Critical and Cultural Assessment" *Reading Teacher.* 40.7 (March 1987): 640–645.
Osa, Osayimwnse. "The New Nigerian Youth Literature". *Journal of Reading.* 30.2. (Nov. 1986).
———. *African Children and Youth Literature.* New York: Twayne, 1995.
Shakespeare, William. *Merchant of Venice.* In *The Complete Works of Shakespeare.* Ed. David Bevington. 3rd ed. Glenview, Il: Scott, Foresman, 1980.
Winkler, Karen J. "An African Writer at the Crossroads" *The Chronicle of Higher Education* 2. Jan 1994: A9.

Chapter 36

Chinua Achebe's *The Flute* and the Apache Folktale, *The Flute Player* by Michael Lacapa: A Cross-Cultural Rhythm

Don Burness

At first glance it might seem that cultural connections linking Africa and Amerindian worlds is tenuous at best. But recent scholarship has shown there are very direct connections. William Loren Katz' *Black Indians – A Hidden Heritage* (1986) explores the centuries old story of slaves finding refuge among native Americans, particularly among the Seminoles. And we now know that black Seminole Indian scouts in the 1850s crossed into Mexico to find a dar-es-salaam, a haven in a hispanic land where slavery was prohibited. Of course Mexico has its own geography of slavery and the spirit of Yanga still echoes from San Lorenzo de Sarralvo in the state of Veracruz.

Apart from such direct contacts, Africa and meso-American civilization share cultural patterns. I am not an anthropologist and make no claim as such, but surely a traveler to Nigeria and Ghana and a traveler to Arizona or Oaxaca cannot fail to see distinct parallels. Color, the color of the tropics, dances everywhere. Navajo blankets – kente cloth. And dance itself links the living to the ancestors in these ancient civilizations.

The flute too is found throughout West Africa and throughout meso-America. In *Rabinal Achi*, the only extant written Mayan drama (from the early 1500s in Guatemala), the captured chief of the Cavek Queche brags about the superiority of the flutes and drums of his people.

> A esas flautas, esos tambores! Les seria posible sonar ahora como mi flauta, como mi tambor?
>
> These alien flutes, these drums! Will it be possible to make music of the same quality as with my flute, my drum?

The flute must have played a central part in the lives of the early settlers in the Americas. There is in the Rufino Tamayo Museum in Caxaca a statue of the flute player from the 2nd Century B.C. in the state of Colima.

In Africa too, the flute player brought his art to the arena of a people's life. Like the more celebrated drummer the flute player was ubiquitous. In *Things Fall Apart* Chinua Achebe, in the second paragraph, describes the victory of Okonkwo over Amalinze the Cat in that fierce and memorable wrestling match. "The drums beat and the flutes sang and the spectators held their breath." And Unoka, Okonkwo's father, has a touch of the poet in him. Two things bring him joy – the dazzling beauty of bird and sun and landscape as well as his flute. Unoka is an artist, a musician invited to other villages because of his art. Achebe tells us "he was very good on his flute and his happiest moments were the two or three moons after the harvest when the village musicians brought down their instruments.... Unoka would play with them, his face beaming with blessedness and peace." Surely Chinua Achebe the artist who entertains and moves his readers shares much more with Unoka than he does with the hard working but insensitive Okonkwo.

In fact, Achebe himself pays tribute to the serious and capable musicians in his children's fables – *The Drum* and *The Flute* both published in 1977. Among various Native American people there are tales of the flute player. In 1990 Michael Lacapa brought forth his children's story *The Flute Player – An Apache Folktale*. Both Achebe and Lacapa bring to their tales the influence of oral tradition. As children these two men from different worlds heard the melodies of oral tradition and as adults carry on that tradition in written form. Oral tradition is as old as a people and by returning to a source, Chinua Achebe and Michael Lacapa honor their ancestors, especially the story-teller who has kept alive the soul as well as the history of a people.

It is interesting that Achebe's *The Flute* and Lacapa's *The Flute Player* are vastly different, probably because their worlds are different. So are the flutes – the Apache flute is made of wood and in Achebe's tale there are flutes of bamboo and gold and even a flute "shining like the kernels of the water of heaven." Achebe is always the teacher and his story aims to elevate the human behavior of his reader-listener.

The Flute teaches that good taste, personal humility, purity of soul and respect for the world of the spirits matter and that jealousy, greed, and disrespect for the spirits can only bring pollution or disease to the social and moral fiber of man and community. Obierika would hear Achebe's noble flute player at his door and would laugh and say *nno* (welcome).

Achebe's allegory can be summed up as follows. Two wives of a farmer are at odds – the senior wife who has many children resents the good fortune of the younger wife who has an only son. This only son's greatest joy is playing the bamboo flute, which he himself made. When tempted by the spirits to accept a golden flute or the flute "shining like the kernel of the water of heaven" the boy stubbornly refuses. He loves his flute and he plays with feeling. He charms the spirits with his music and when they offer him a choice of two pots to take home, he chooses the smaller pot. Upon his return home across the seven rivers and seven forests, he presents the magical pot to his mother. The pot is broken and gold and silver and clothes and velvets and food and animals and other things of value appear.

Seeing the good fortune of her rival the senior wife calls her eldest son sending him to the land of the spirits. Given the same choice this boy selects a gold flute and the large pot and when he plays, instead of praise songs for the spirits, there are insults. When he returns home across the seven rivers and the seven forests, he presents his pot to his mother. When this pot is broken disease and pestilence – abominations fill the hut, kill the woman and all her children, and some evils even spread throughout the world! Achebe is ever the prophet and these abominations continue to plague Nigeria today where the greedy and oily generals have failed to honor the ways of the past, the ways of the spirits, the ways of the ancestors. *The Flute* is a children's story with serious implications.

Lacapa too honors tradition. He remembers when he was a boy when the White Mountain Apache story teller taught him and entertained him. Lacapa has never been far from his people of the canyon. And like other Native American writers such as the Kiowa N. Scott Momaday, his journey to American universities has not destroyed his bond with the world of his childhood and in *The Flute Player* he seeks to keep alive words of the elders.

The Flute Player is a tragic love story. It begins:

> Listen! Did you hear that sound? Some say it's the wind blowing through the trees, but we know it isn't.

The sound that echoes through the canyon is the soul of the flute of the flute player of long ago. During a hoop dance, where young people get together a boy and a girl fell in love. When the girl heard that the boy played the flute she encouraged him to play in the canyon where they lived. If she approved of his playing she would place a leaf in the river that runs through the canyon. When the boy saw the leaf, he would know she approved of his song.

We know the girl approved of the song. The boy played and in the canyon a leaf floating down the river announced that love applauded. But after several days of the music of young love, the boy was told he had to go hunting. The girl listened for the melody; there was no sound. She became sad; she became very ill. Medicine and prayer did not work. She died.

The young boy, returning to the canyon after his hunting experience, played his flute and waited for a leaf that was never to float down the river. Everyone who heard him play remarked on how beautifully he played – like the wind blowing through the trees.

Upon hearing of the death of his girlfriend, the boy played a song for her on his flute – the saddest song he ever played. Then he left the cornfields and the river and the canyon. He left his people. He was never seen again.

This romantic legend still echoes in the canyons of the Southwest. It is important to note that Michael Lacapa is an artist as well as a story teller and he did the illustrations for *The Flute Player*. It is obvious that the illustrations in Achebe's story and the Apache story have a different impact. In *The Flute* the illustrator Tayo Adenaike seeks to offer a visual accompaniment to the story. The spirits, those supernatural forces, look otherwordly indeed and the pot of pestilence looks like a ghost unleashed. Adenaike does what most illustrators of children's books do – he paints scenes from the story.

This is not quite true for Michael Lacapa. His drawings have a life of their own – independent of the story. They express an Apache worldview, so to speak. The landscapes of the Southwest are presented – red rocks, butterflies, mesas, huge boulders, cottonwood trees, horses, and the moon over the canyon. These images of nature at the beginning of the story are dominated by greens, but towards the end yellow dominates. Perhaps there is symbolism here that is beyond the scope of my knowledge.

Also the geometric patterns of Apache clothing are present in the natural word as presented by the story-teller artist. It reminds me somewhat of the *Uli* art school of Igbo painters like Obiora Udechukwu, Uche Okeke and the Achebe artist himself Tayo Adenaike. (In *The Flute* the Nigerian artist does use one noticeable *Uli* pattern in the drawing of the hair of the spirits.) In *The Flute Player* design dominates the pictoral world. Through form and color, Lacapa unites man and moon, flute and forest, canyon and clouds. The music of the flute player is the music of the wind – eternal, beyond the understanding of science or reason – a force of undying beauty in the world of the flute player.

Both tales tell of a time long long ago. Both of them depict farming communities. In both of these tales, stories for children, children are at center stage. And in both these of tales the flute players from different worlds, belong to the same clan, the clan of the artist, whose music is still heard in an Igbo village and an Apache canyon.

Chapter 37

The Dynamics of Cultures on the Child's Personality in Chinua Achebe's *Chike and the River*

Iniobong I. Uko

THE CHILD IN THE African society is influenced by several cultural factors to which he is exposed from infancy. These factors constitute the values of the people. The child is not taught these values as he would a creed, but he naturally grows to imbibe them and makes efforts to uphold them as he knows that a violation of any of them brings to him unpleasant consequences.

Chinua Achebe captures these processes in the personality of Chike in *Chike and the River* (1966). Achebe demonstrates the child's ability to internalize the cultural values and how these values have direct impact on the child's reasoning and attitude as he grows into a young school boy in an urban milieu.

This paper explores the fundamental relevance of the cultural values of the Igbo people of Umuofia and Ontisha in Achebe's *Chike and the River* and how these make dominant positive contributions to the personality of the young boy. It also highlights the essence of inculcating African cultural values into the African child. At first Chinua Achebe's *Chike and the River* may seem to trace the life of a young boy, Chike, in his rural Umuofia village, but later revelations indicate that though the story is meant for children, it makes important comments on the efficacy and vivacity of the Igbo cultural norms in the average Igbo child. Both in Umuofia village and in Onitsha, there are issues which Achebe subtly highlights as constituting the cultural value systems of the people and which inform Chike's personality as he grows. This story begins with a portrayal of Chike in Umuofia:

> Chike lived with his mother and two sisters in the village.... His father had died many years ago. His mother worked very hard to feed and clothe her three children and to send them to school. She grew most of the food they ate – yams, cassava, maize, beans, plantains and many green vegetables. She also traded in dry fish, palm-oil, kerosene and matches (1).

Achebe's female portrait here is realistic because as Chike's mother is conscious of her status as a widow, she knows that it is needless to be helpless. In her determination to provide for her three children, she is hardworking, powerful, and caring.

Achebe's depiction of Chike's mother with an enormous strength of character sharply contrasts with Okonkwo's wives in Achebe's *Things Fall Apart*:

> ...the tree was very much alive. Okonkwo's second wife had merely cut a few leaves off it to wrap some food, and she said so. Without further argument Okonkwo gave her a sound beating and left her and her only daughter weeping. Neither of the other wives dared to interfere beyond the occasional and tentative 'it is enough, Okonkwo', pleaded from a reasonable distance (27).

Indeed, the helplessness displayed by Achebe's women in *Things Fall Apart* reveals Chike's mother as a typical "New Woman". According to Stegeman:

> The New Woman represents a theory of personhood where the individual exists as an independent entity rather than her kinship relations, where she has a responsibility to realize her potential to happiness rather than to accept her role, where... she must reason about her own values rather than fit into a stereotype tradition (82).

Chike's mother, as a New Woman, debunks female stereotypes and strives to succeed under the circumstance she finds herself. She determines not to be mute, "lack-lustre" and complacent, but to have an aim and pursue that aim.

As Chike is about to leave with his uncle for Onitsha, his mother gives him many words of advice, and as Chike cries on his departure, his mother cautions him:

> Stop crying.... Remember you are now a big boy, and big boys don't cry (6).

Evidently, the image of Chike's mother pervades Chike's personality while in Onitsha. He does not forget the advice she gave him at his departure from Umuofia:

> Go well, my son. Listen to whatever your uncle says and obey him. Onitsha is a big city, full of dangerous people and kidnappers. Therefore do not wander about the city. In particular do not go near the River Niger; many people get drowned there every year... (6).

These words continue to reverberate in Chike's mind while in Onitsha. The close affinity between Chike and his mother is explained by Emenyonu as follows:

> The bond of affection between mother and child in the Igbo Culture is a very strong one, especialy when the child happens to be a son (3).

Achebe subtly contrasts between the peaceful communal life in Umuofia and the unhealthy conditions, which characterize urban life in Onitsha:

> Chike did not like sleeping on the floor and he longed for the bamboo bed in his mother's hut.... There were other things he did not like. For example there were bedbugs on their mat. Sometimes Michael sprinkled kerosene on the mat to kill them off. But after a few days they were there again. Another thing Chike did not like was the large crowd of other tenants livinq in the same house and more than fifty men, women and children living in them. Many families lived in one room. Because there were so many strangers living together they were always quarrelling about firewood and about sweeping the yard or scrubbing the bathroom and the latrines.
>
> There were only two latrines in the yard for the fifty people. One was for adults and the other for children. Both were filthy but the children's was worse. It swarmed with flies bigger than any Chike had ever seen at Umuofia. They revolted him. And so he learnt that a big town was not always better than a village... (42–43).

This comparison is significant to Chike's life, for although he finds some attractions in the city, he does not get carried away, but actually protests against the way of life in the city. The things he is exposed to in Onitsha are strange to him and it is obvious that he will grow nurturing, the ideals his mother inculcated into him in Umuofia.

Throughout the story, Chike seems to be guided by the virtues he learnt from his mother. Achabe contrasts Chike's mother and Ezekiel's mother. Ezekiel is Chike's friend in Onitsha:

> Like Chike, Ezekiel was his mother's only son. He had four sisters. Ezekiel's mother was a well-to-do trader who sold cloths in the Onitsha market and made much profit. But she was not a wise mother. She allowed Ezekiel to do whatever he liked. So he became a spoilt child... he never did any work.... He would sneak quietly to the soup-pot at night and search with his fingers for pieces of fish and meat. By morning the soup would go sour and Ezekiel's mother would punish the servants.... When Ezekiel grew bigger he began to steal sums of money from his mother... (15).

These tendencies develop in Ezekiel to the stage that he is courageous enough to write deceitful letters to three boys in England who want Nigerian pen-pals. He asks for money, camera and a pair of shoes and promises each of the boys leopard-skin in return. A month later, he receives a ten-shilling postal order

from one of the boys and his mother helps him cash the postal order. She commends him as a "Clever Boy". This achievement fascinates Chike and other friends of theirs in school. The others immediately write to pen-pals in England, but Chike is unable because he has no money to buy postage stamps.

Consequently, Chike is troubled because he is unlikely to have this money except he steals or someone gives him. Unfortunately, he can hardly afford any of those two options: he knows that he should not steal and he knows it is nearly impossible for any reasonable person to part with money for no just cause. Understanding these, Chike determines to work to earn the money he needs. This resolve drives him to go into car-washing from which he earns a shilling with which he eventually crosses the River Niger to Asaba:

> Chike's dream had come true. At last he could go to Asaba. He jumped up and down several times and sang 'One more river to cross'...
>
> He joined the queue of other passengers.
>
> When his turn came he gave the shilling to the cashier who gave him a ticket and sixpence change. His heart was aglow with happiness. After today he would be able to say to his friends 'I too have been to Asaba. There only remains Lagos' (45).

As a young boy, Chike is very curious to explore and as he boards the ferry, he is fascinated by a lot of things:

> The ferry's engine started. The siren sounded above, then a bell rang in the engine room. It sounded like a giant bicycle bell...
>
> It was all like a dream. Chike wondered whether it was actually happening 'So this is me,' he thought Chike Anene, alias Chiks the Boy of Umuofia, Mbaino District, Onitsha Province, Eastern Nigerian, Nigerian, West Africa, Africa, World, Universe.' This was how he wrote his name in his new reader. It was one of the things he had learnt from his friend Samuel, alias S.M.O.G.

During the journey Chike felt as proud as Mungo Park when he finally reached the Niger. Here at last was the great River Niger. Chike stuck out his chest as though he owned the river, and drew a deep breath. The air smelt clean and fresh. He remembered another song he had learnt at Umuofia and began to whistle:

> Row, row, row your boat
> Gently down the stream
> Merrily, merrily, merrily, merrily
> Life is but a dream (47).

As the ferry-boat arrives Asaba, Chike goes into the town, and although it does not carry the beauty and charm be expects, Chike still goes on to explore Asaba until evening sets in. By the time he returns to board the ferry and return to Onitsha, he finds that the ferry had just left and he faces the problem of having to spend the night in a town he knows nobody and no place.

Chike wanders and finds a parked lorry and as night falls, he enters the back of the lorry and lies under the benches. His sleep is not peaceful as he is disturbed by mosquitoes, and the voices of a gang of thieves. In his fright, he listens to them until he finds it safe to escape into the nearby bush. In the morning, Chike is amazed at the sight of a man tied to a mango tree and his mouth covered with black cloth. As two policemen arrive and untie the man, he tells the crowd of how some armed robbers attacked him tied him to the tree and stole from the shop. Thereafter:

> The policemen were about to go and
> look at the shop when a small boy
> suddenly shouted from the crowd.
> 'The man is telling lies', cried the
> boy; 'I saw them'... I saw the
> thieves', said Chike. 'This man
> helped them. I heard him talking with them' (58).

Chike here becomes a very important help to the police and assists in uncovering the role of the night-watchman in the shop-robbery incident of the previous night:

> As Chike told his story the night-watchman began to shake, he covered his face with his hands to hide his tears. Chike became a hero. One big man in the crowd lifted him up and placed him on his shoulders. The others applauded. They said they had never seen such bravery from such a little boy. The police arrested the three thieves that same day. They also recovered the bales of velvet they had stolen (58).

Essentially, the basis of Chike's heroism may easily be traced to his background, his upbringing under his mother's tutelage in Umuofia. Fortunately, as he leaves Umuofia for Onitsha, his uncle whom he stays with is yet another strict and hard-working person who does not engage in frivolous activities:

> Chike's uncle was a very strict man. He rarely spoke and never laughed except when he drank beer or palm-wine with his neighbour, Mr. Nwana, or with one of his new friends. He did not like to see Chike playing with other children. He called it a waste of time. In his opinion children should spend their time reading and doing sums (11).

It is really the dynamics of his culture which informs Chike's bravery and strange revelation of what he witnessed at night. This dynamics which constitutes the very fabric of Chike's life makes him different from his contemporaries with the city orientation which does not make one's problem the other person's.

Evidently, in African communal set-up, problems as well as joys are usually shared. This characteristic sense of brotherhood marks the rural life from urban life. Chike has already imbibed from his mother and uncle the essence of life that is captured in such virtues as honesty, hard-work and respect. This fact explains why

Chike does not take to stealing to fulfill his dream of crossing the River Niger, but strives to work and earn the money he needs. Chike is duly rewarded eventually:

> Everywhere people spoke of Chike's adventure. His photograph appeared in the local newspaper and his name was mentioned on the radio. Then after the three thieves and the night-watchman had been tried and imprisoned, Chike got a letter from the manager of the shop. He announced that the company which owned the shop had decided to award a scholarship to Chike which would take him right through secondary school.
>
> So Chike's adventure on the River Niger brought him close to danger and then rewarded him with good fortune (60).

Chike's heroism in this story is really dueto his approaching life with courage and honesty and making concerted effort to get through life, as Killam notes, with honour and reward (11).

Chinua Achebe achieves the skill he displays in *Chike and the River* particularly through his appropriate mode of language. He has been able to adjust his language to suit the reasoning faculty of a young boy. Generally, the use of language in this story is consistent with each character. Achebe has been careful to ensure that the language his characters use adequately carries "the peculiar burden or conveying his sensibilities and (he) owes no one any apologies for this" (*Morning Yet On Creation Day* 55–56). And Chukwuma (x) notes that Achebe makes the successful effort of adapting the language relating it to a home audience. The cultural elements he handles are also familiar and sharpen characterization and lay emphasis. Achebe himself asserts in "The Role of the writer..." that:

> African peoples did not hear of culture for the first time from Europeans; that their societies were not mindless, but frequently had 'a philosophy of great depth and value and beauty, that they had poetry and above all, they had dignity (157).

This conviction is responsible for Lindfors' observation that Achebe is:

> ...a careful and fastidious in full control of his art, a serious craftsman who disciplines himself not only to write regularly but to write well. He has that sense of decorum, proportion and design lacked by too many contemporary novelists African and non-African alike. He is also a committed writer, one who believes that it is his duty to serve his society. He feels that the fundamental theme with which African writers should concern themselves is African culture (47).

This may account in part for Achebe's concern in *Chike and the River* with a society at an early stage of economic development with people living the simple unsophisticated life, "but with political organization, moral consciousness and a code of behaviour handed down by the elders and supported by tradition and custom. Into this social framework everyone tries to fit himself..." (*Taiwo* 29). These are clearly revealed in Onitsha (and Asaba) of Chike's time where there are money-doublers, fraudsters, dishonest traders who sell harmful brain pills to school boys, petty thieves, and robbers whose activities are aided by the very people meant to provide security. These are indices of a society in transition into which Chike and his contemporaries have to fit. These children can either be carried away by the dynamics of the society as does Ezekiel, or be guided and disciplined by the dynamics of the culture they were exposed to.

Works Cited

Achebe, Chinua. *Chike and the River*. Cambridge: Cambridge University Press, 1966.

———. *Morning Yet on Creation Day*. London: Heinemann, 1975.

———. "The Role of the Writer in a New Nation". *Nigeria Magazine*. No. 81, June 1964: 157–160.

———. *Things Fall Apart*. London: Heinemann, 1958.

Chukwuma, Helen. *Accents in the African Novel*. Enugu: New Generation Books, 1991.

Emenyonu, Ernest. *The Rise of the Igbo Novel*. London: Oxford Univ. Press, 1978.

Killam, G.D. *The Writings of Chinua Achebe*. London: Heinemann, 1975.

Lindfors, Bernth. "The Palm-Oil with Which Achebe's Words are Eaten". *Critical Perspectives on Chinua Achebe*. Eds. C.L. Innes and Bernth Lindfors. Washington: Three continents press, 1978: 47–66.

Stegeman, Beatrice. "The Divorce Dilemma: The New Woman in Contemporary African Novels". *Critique*. 15, 1974: 81–90.

Taiwo, Oladele. *Culture and the Nigerian Novel*. London: Macmillan, 1982.

Notes on Contributors

Julie Agbasiere teaches in the English Department at the Nnamdi Azikiwe University, Awka, Nigeria.

E. L. Agukwe teaches in the Department of English at the Federal College of Education, Yola, Nigeria.

Chiji Akoma teaches in the English Department at Villanova University, Pennsylvania.

Ada Uzoamaka Azodo teaches African Literature and French at the Indiana University, Northwest.

Macpherson Nkem Azuike teaches in the English Department at the University of Jos, Nigeria.

Don Burness teaches in the English Department at Franklin Pierce College, Rindge, New Hampshire.

Blessing Diala teaches in the Department of Humanities and Media, Coppin State College, Baltimore, Maryland.

Innocent C. K. Enyinnaya teaches in the English Department at the Alvan Ikoku College of Education, Owerri, Nigeria.

James S. Etim was formerly of the Department of English and Foreign Languages at the Mississippi Valley State University, Itta Bena, Mississippi.

Sunday Osim Etim teaches in the Department of English at the College of Education, Akamkpa, Cross River State, Nigeria.

Anthonia C. Kalu teaches African Literature at the Northern Colorado State University, Greeley.

Bernth Lindfors is a renowned scholar and authority on African Literature and author of several books. He teaches at the University of Texas at Austin.

Chidi T. Maduka teaches in the Comparative Literature Program at the University of Port Harcourt, Nigeria.

Craig W. Mcluckie teaches in the Department of English at Okanagan University College, Kalamalka Campus, Vernon, British Columbia, Canada. He has published in several international journals of African Literature.

Francis Ibe Mogu teaches in the English Department at the University of Calabar, Nigeria.

Emma Ngumoha teaches in the Department of English at Abia State University, Uturu, Abia State, Nigeria.

Francis Ngaboh-Smart teaches in the Department of English at the University of Wisconsin, Oshkosh.

Teresa Njoku teaches in the Department of English at the Alvan Ikoku College of Education, Owerri, Nigeria.

Charles E. Nnolim is a Professor and former Dean, School of Humanities at the University of Port Harcourt, Nigeria. He is a renowned critic of African Literature and has published extensively in leading literary journals in Africa, Europe and the United States.

Chinyere Nwagbara is a Deputy Director at the Nigerian Education Research Council (NERC), Lagos, Nigeria.

Joseph Obi is an Associate Professor of Sociology and International Studies at the University of Richmond, Virginia.

Emmanuel Obiechina is a veteran scholar and a distinguished literary critic whose works on African Literature have continued to serve as models for critics of African Literature. He was recently the *Langston Hughes Professor of African American Studies* at Kansas State University, Lawrence, Kansas, and more recently with the Institute of African and African American Studies, Harvard University.

Umelo Ojinmah teaches English and African Literature in the General Studies Division of the Federal University of Technology, Owerri, Nigeria.

Clement Okafor teaches at the University of Maryland, Eastern Shore. He was formerly Professor and Chair of English at the University of Nigeria, Nsukka, Nigeria.

Augustine C. Okere is a Reader (Associate Professor) of English at the Alvan Ikoku College of Education, Owerri, Nigeria. He has published in international literary journals in Africa, Europe, Canada, and the United States.

Virginia U. Ola was until recently with the Department of English at Kuwait University. She has published in leading literary journals in Africa, Europe, and the United States. She now lives and teaches in Canada.

Ifeoma Okoye is the author of four award-winning novels, and the 1999 Joint regional winner (Africa) of the Commonwealth Short Story Competition, with her story, "Waiting for a Son". She was formerly with the Department of English at the Nnamdi Azikiwe University, Awka, Nigeria.

Ifeoma Onyemelukwe teaches in the Department of Languages at the Institute of Education, Ahmadu Bello University, Zaria, Nigeria.

Joseph R. Slaughter teaches in the English Department at Columbia University, New York.

Iniobong I. Uko teaches African, African American and Caribbean Literatures at the University of Michigan-Flint where she is currently a Visiting Assistant Professor. She is also a Senior Lecturer in the department of English at the University of Uyo, Nigeria.

Chris Walsh currently teaches at the Writing Center at Boston University. Boston, Massachusetts.

Jennifer Wenzel was until recently in the English Department at the University of Montana, Missoula.

Index

O

P

U